GUNI SERIES ON THE SOCIAL COMMITMENT OF UNIVERSITIES

Higher Education in the World 4

Higher Education's Commitment to Sustainability: from Understanding to Action

GU GLOBAL UNIVERSITY
NI NETWORK FOR INNOVATION

palgrave
macmillan

First published 2012 by
PALGRAVE MACMILLAN

Palgrave Macmillan in the UK is an imprint of Macmillan Publishers Limited,
registered in England, company number 785998, of Houndmills, Basingstoke,
Hampshire RG21 6XS.

Palgrave Macmillan in the US is a division of St Martin's Press LLC,
175 Fifth Avenue, New York, NY 10010.

Palgrave Macmillan is the global academic imprint of the above companies
and has companies and representatives throughout the world.

Palgrave® and Macmillan® are registered trademarks in the United States,
the United Kingdom, Europe and other countries.

ISBN: 978–0–230–53555–8

This book is printed on paper suitable for recycling and made from fully
managed and sustained forest sources. Logging, pulping and manufacturing
processes are expected to conform to the environmental regulations of the
country of origin.

A catalogue record for this book is available from the British Library.

A catalog record for this book is available from the Library of Congress.

10 9 8 7 6 5 4 3 2 1
21 20 19 18 17 16 15 14 13 12

Printed and bound in Great Britain by
CPI William Clowes Ltd, Beccles, Suffolk

TEAM INVOLVED IN THE PREPARATION OF THIS PUBLICATION[1]

PRINCIPAL EDITOR
GUNi

EDITORIAL TEAM
Miquel Barceló (Guest Editor)
Yazmín Cruz
Cristina Escrigas
Dídac Ferrer
Jesús Granados
Francisco López-Segrera
Jeymi Sivoli

BIBLIOGRAPHY
Sonia Fernández-Lauro

MAPS AND GRAPHICS
Clara Guixà Solé
Martí Rosas

AUTHORS
Osamu Abe, Japan
Maik Adomssent, Germany
Eduardo Aponte, Puerto Rico
Irena Ateljevic, Netherlands
Sonia Bahri, Tunisia
Aristides Baloi, Mozambique
Javier Benayas, Spain
Sjur Bergan, Norway
Alícia Betts, Spain
Cristina Bolívar, Spain
Lester R. Brown, USA
Miguel Chacón, Guatemala
Kiran Banga Chhokar, India
Yazmín Cruz, Mexico
Carole Després, Canada
Gulelate Desse, Ethiopia
Jana Dlouhá, Czech Republic
Lorna Down, Jamaica
Heather Elliott, Canada
Zinaida Fadeeva, Japan
Jo Anne Ferreira, Australia
Dídac Ferrer, Spain
Andrée Fortin, Canada
David Francis, Sierra Leona
Moacir Gadotti, Brazil
Laima Galkute, Lithuania
Gilberto Gallopín, Argentina
Nadja Gmelch, Spain

Edgar González-Gaudiano, Mexico
John Holmberg, Sweden
Jesús Granados Sánchez, Spain
Barbara Ibrahim, Egypt
Mireya Imaz, Mexico
Peter Kanyandago, Uganda
Steve Larkin, Australia
Walter Leal-Filho, Germany
Claudia Lenz, Norway
Heila Lotz-Sisitka, South Africa
Rodrigo Lozano, UK
Clemens Mader, Austria
Marlene Mader, Austria
Evangelos Manolas, Greece
Daniel Mato, Argentina
Gerd Michelsen, Germany
Goolam Mohamedbhai, Mauritius
Bedřich Moldan, Czech Republic
Ingrid Mulà, Spain
Karel Mulder, Netherlands
Claudio Naranjo, Chile
Ko Nomura, Japan
Stefan Nortier, Netherlands
María Novo, Spain
Akpezi Ogbuigwe, South Africa
Is-Haq Oloyede, Nigeria
M. Laura Ortiz, Mexico
Agustí Pérez-Foguet, Spain
Ana Perona–Fjeldstad, Norway
Scott Peters, USA
Paul Raskin, USA
Dzulkifli Abdul Razak, Malaysia
Negussie Retta, Ethiopia
Jos Rikers, Netherlands
Debra Rowe, USA
Paul Rowland, USA
Orlando Sáenz, Colombia
Ramzi Salamé, Lebanon
Roger Schank, USA
Lisa Schwarzin, Netherlands
Michael Scoullos, Greece
Rajib Shaw, Japan
Geert de Snoo, Netherlands
Magdalena Svanström, Sweden
Aurea C. Tanaka, Japan

Daniella Tilbury, UK
Geneviève Vachon, Canada
Rietje van Dam-Mieras, Netherlands
Hilligje van't Land, France
Josep M. Vilalta, Spain
Tom Waas, Belgium
Arjen E.J. Wals, Netherlands
Aurora Winslade, USA
Tarah S. Wright, Canada
Masaru Yarime, Japan
Zióle Zanotto Malhadas, Brazil
Friederich Zimmermann, Austria

GUNi SECRETARIAT

Staff
Miquel Cano
Melba Claudio
Àngels Cortina
Yazmín Cruz
Cristina Escrigas
Jesús Granados
Sònia Mascarell
Mariví Ordóñez
Jeymi Sivoli

Interns
Gerardo Arriaga
Adriana Cortes
Jonathan Fredi

External Collaborators
Francisco López-Segrera
Natalia Orellana

GUNi EXECUTIVE COMMITTEE

Founding Institutions

UNESCO
Stamenka Uvalić-Trumbić (Section of Higher Education, Director)

UNU
Konrad Osterwalder (Rector)

1   Posts at the time of closing the edition, September 2011

TEAM INVOLVED IN THE PREPARATION OF THIS PUBLICATION

CONTENTS

LIST OF FIGURES, BOXES, TABLES AND MAPS

FIGURES

BOXES

TABLES

MAPS

AAAS	American Association for the Advancement of Science	AIBS	American Institute of Biological Sciences
AACC	American Association of Community Colleges	AIDESEP	Interethnic Association for Development of the Peruvian Rainforest
AAC&U	Association of American Colleges and Universities	AIDS	Acquired Immune Deficiency Syndrome
AAPT	American Association of Physics Teachers	AIM	Academic-industry-media
AASHE	Association for the Advancement of Sustainability in Higher Education	AISHE	Assessment Instrument for Sustainability in Higher Education
AAU	Association of African Universities	AIT	Asian Institute of Technology
		ALTC	Australian Learning and Teaching Council
ABS	Australian Bureau of Statistics	AMCEN	African Ministerial Conference on the Environment
ACA	Academic Cooperation Association	ANPED	National Association for Postgraduate Studies and Research in Education
ACEGES	Agent-based Computational Economics of the Global Energy System	ANUIES	National Association of Universities and Higher Education Institutions
ACP	African Caribbean Pacific		
ACPA	American College Personnel Association	APA	American Psychological Association
ACS	American Chemical Society	APA	Academic Performance Audit
ACTE	Association for Career and Technical Education	APEID	Asia-Pacific Programme of Educational Innovation for Development
ACTS	Action Research for Curriculum Transformation Towards Sustainability	API	Asia-Pacific Initiative
ACTS	Australasian Campuses towards Sustainability	ARIES	Australian Research Institute for Environment and Sustainability
ACUDES	Continental Association of Universities for Sustainable Development	ARQM	African Quality Rating Mechanism
ACUP	Catalan Association of Public Universities	ARIUSA	Alliance of Ibero-American Networks of Universities for Sustainability and the Environment
ACUPCC	American College and University Presidents Climate Change Commitment	ARWU	Academic Rankings of World Universities
ADB	Asian Development Bank	ASEAN	Association of South-East Asian Nations
ADEA	Association for the Development of Education in Africa	ASEE	American Society for Engineering Education
AECID	Spanish Agency for International Development Corporation	ASC	Academic Staff Colleges
		ASOE	African School of Open Education
AFRITEIS	UNESCO-led ESD Teacher Education network	ASU	Arizona State University
		AUB	American University of Beirut
AGS	Alliance for Global Sustainability	AUC	American University in Cairo

AUEDM	Asian University Network of Environment and Disaster Management	COBES	Community Based Experience and Service
AUGM	Association of Universities of the Montevideo Group	CoE	Centre of excellence
AUIP	Postgraduate University Association	COMSATS	Commission on Science and Technology for Sustainable Development in the South
AULP	Association of Portuguese Language Universities	COMPLEXUS	Mexican Consortium of University Environmental Programmes for Sustainable Development
AVA	African Volunteers Association	CONACyT	Mexican National Council of Science and Technology
AVCC	Australian Vice-Chancellors' Committee	CONAMA	Guatemala's National Environment Commission
BSc	Bachelor of Sciences	CONCORD	Confederation for Relief and Development
BA	Bachelor of Arts	COP	Communication on Progress
BP	British Petroleum	COP17	United Nations Conference on Climate Change
BRESCE	Regional Bureau for Science and Culture in Europe	CPLP	Portuguese Speaking Community Countries
BUP	Baltic University Programme	CRC	Carbon Reduction Commitment Energy Efficiency Scheme
CA	Copernicus Alliance	CRE	Confederation of EU Rectors
CACP	Clean Air Cool Planet	CRLE	Center for Respect of Life and Environment
CADEP	Sectoral Committee on Environmental Quality, Sustainable Development and Risk Prevention	CRUE	Conference of Rectors of Spanish Universities
CAREC	Regional Environmental Centre for Central Asia	CRWS	Centre for Research on Work and Society
CBR	Community-based research	CSAF	Campus Sustainability Assessment Framework
CCA	Climate Change Adaptation	CSBR	Center for Sustainable Building Research
CCSDR	Canadian Consortium for Sustainable Development Research	CSD	Centre for Sustainable Develooopment
CDU	Charles Darwin University	CSR	Corporate Social Responsibility
CEA	Certified Evaluation and Accreditation	CTIE-AMB	Network for Research on Science, Technology, Innovation and Environmental Education in Ibero-America
CECADESU	Centre for Education and Training for Sustainable Development		
CEE	Centre for Environment Education	CURC	College and University Recycling Council
CEE	Central and Eastern Europe		
CEI	Chalmers Environmental Initiative	CYTED	Ibero-American Programme for Science, Technology and Development
CERMES	Centre for Resource Management and Environmental Studies		
CIESM	Commission Internationale pour l'Exploration Scientifique de la Mer Mediterranee	DANS	Disciplinary Associations Network for Sustainability
		DEEWPR	Research Quality Framework
CIFCA	International Centre for Training in Environmental Sciences	DFID	Department for International Development (UK)
CIGEA	Centre for Environmental Management, Information and Education	DG	Directorate-General
		DIT	Dublin Institute of Technology
CINARA	Institute for Environmental Sanitation and Water Conservation	DRR	Disaster Risk Reduction
CIPAST	Citizen Participation in Science and Technology'	EAUC	Environmental Association for Universities and Colleges
CIS	Commonwealth of Independent States		
CLLN	Campus Living Laboratory Network		
CMEC	Council of Ministers of Education (Canada)		
CNI	Confederaçao Nacional da Industria		

ECLAC	(UN) Economic Commission for Latin America and the Caribbean		GIS	Geographic Information System_*Geospatial Information Systems
ECTS	European Credit Transfer System		GIZ	Deutschen Gesellschaft für Internationale Zusammenarbeit
EE	Environmental Education			
EEAC	European Environment and Sustainable Development Advisory Councils		GLUK	Great Lakes University of Kisumu
			GMES	Global Monitoring Environment and Security
EECCA	Eastern Europe, the Caucasus and Central Asia		GMS	Greater Mekong Subregion
EFA	Education for all		GMV	Gothenburg Centre for Environment and Sustainability
EFQM	European Foundation for Quality Management			
			GP	Good Practice
EfS	Education for Sustainability		GUNi	Global University Network for Innovation
EFS West	Education for Sustainability Western Network			
			GUNi HEiOBS	GUNi's Higher Education Institutes Observatory
EHEA	European Higher Education Area			
EIT	European Institute of Technology		GUPES	Global Universities Partnership for Sustainability
EMAS	Environment and Management System			
			HDI	Human Development Index
EMSU	Environmental Management for Sustainable Universities		HEASC	Higher Education Association Sustainability Consortium
ENQA	European Association for Quality Assurance in Higher Education		HEFCE	Research Excellence Frameworks
			HEI	Higher Education Institution
EP	Environmental Plan		HES	Higher education for sustainability
ERA 21	Education Reaffirmation campaign for the 21st century		HESA	Higher Education Sustainability Act
			HESD	Higher Education for Sustainable Development
ESD	Education for Sustainable Development			
			HIV	Human Immuno-Deficiency Virus
ESDRC	Education for Sustainable Development Research Centre		IAF	Industrial Areas Foundation
			IAU	International Association of Universities
ESG	European Standards and Guidelines for Quality Assurance in Higher Education			
			IBCHE	International Barcelona Conference on Higher Education
ESRI	Enviromental Systems Research Institute		ICARDA	International Center for Agricultural Research in the Dry Areas – Aleppo, Syria
ESS	Environment, Sustainability and Society			
			ICP	Innovation in Civic Participation
ETSAV	UPC's School of Architecture of Valles		ICSS	International Conference on Sustainability Science
EU	European Union		ICSU	International Council of Scientific Unions
EUA	Europe University Association			
EVS	European Virtual Seminar		ICT	Information and Communication Technologies
EWC	European Wergeland Centre			
FAO	Food and Agriculture Organisation		IDEA	Institute for Environmental studies (Colombia)
FLASCO	Latin American Faculty of Social Sciences (Ecuador)			
			IDPs	Internally displaced persons
FNMA	Brazil's National Environment Fund		IDRC	International Development Research Centre
GCLF	Green Campus Loan Fund			
GDP	Gross Domestic Product		IESALC	International Institute for Higher Education in Latin America and the Caribbean
GE	General Education			
GER	Gross Enrolment Ratio			
GIOS	Global Institute of Sustainability		IESD	Institute for Environment and Sustainable Development
GIRBa	Interdisciplinary Research Group on Suburbs			

IETC-AMB	Network for Research on Science, Technology, Innovation and Environmental Education in Ibero-America	MEdIES	Mediterranean Education Initiative for Environment and Sustainability
IHEI	Intercultural Higher Education Institution	MEDUNSA	Medical University of Southern Africa
IIK	Institute of Indigenous Knowledge	MESA	Mainstreaming Environment and Sustainability in Africa
IIT	Indian Institute of Technology	MESCA	Mainstreaming Environment and Sustainability in Caribbean universities
ILPEC	Latin-American Institute of Communication Pedagogy	MESE	Mainstreaming Environment and Sustainability in Ethiopia
IMF	International Monetary Fund	MEXT	Ministry of Education, Culture, Sports, Science and Technology of Japan
INDERENA	Colombia's National Institute for Natural Resources and the Environment	MFU	Mae Fah Luang University
IPCC	United Nations Intergovernmental Panel on Climate Change	MHE	Ministry of Higher Education
		MIO-ECSDE	Mediterranean Information Office for Environment, Culture and Sustainable Development
IR3S	Integrated Research System for Sustainability Science	MMA	Colombian Ministry of the Environment
ISCN	International Sustainable Campus Network	MQA	Malaysia Qualification Framework
ISO	International Organization for Standardization	MSc	Master of Science
IS.UPC	Institute for Research in Science and Technology for Sustainability (UPC)	MUST	Mbara University of Science and Technology
ITSE	Initiative for Transformative Sustainability Education	HE	higher Education
IUCN	International Union for Conservation of Nature	NABT	National Association of Biology Teachers
JBTE	Joint Board of Teacher Education	NAGT	National Association of Geoscience Teachers
JFDHOP	Jeunes et Femmes pour les droits de l'homme et la paix	NEP	National Education Policy
K-12	kindergarten through 12th grade schools	NEPAD	New Partnership for Africa's Development
KAUST	King Abdullah University of Science and Technology	NGO	Nongovernmental Organization
KIST	Kigali Institute of Science and Technology	NIAD – UE	National Institution for Academic Degrees and University Evaluation
LAC	Latin America and the Caribbean	NIU	Network of Island Universities
LECH-e	Lived Experience of Climate Change e-learning	NNN	National Numeracy Network
		NSF	National Science Foundation
LEED	Leadership in Energy and Environmental Design	NUCE	National University Corporation Evaluation
LENSUS	Lifelong Learning Network for a Sustainable Europe	NWF	National Wildlife Federation (USA)
LLB	Bachelor of Laws	ODL	Open and Distance Learning
LSF	Learning for a Sustainable Future	OEI	Organisation of Ibero-American States
M&E	Monitoring and evaluation	OER	Open Educational Resources
MAA	Mathematical Association of America	OIUDSMA	International Organization of Universities for Sustainable Development and the Environment
MBA	Master of Business Administration		
MDGs	Millennium Development Goals	OPEDUCA	Dutch acronym for Open Educational Environment and Region
MEC	Conselho de Ministros (Mozambique)	OUI-IOHE	Inter-American Organisation for Higher Education
MECIT	Middle East College of Information Technology	PACE-SD	Pacific Centre for Environment and Sustainable Development

PCE	Parliamentary Commissioner for the Environment	RUPEA	University Network of Environmental Education Programmes
PEER	Programme for Education for Emergencies and Reconstruction	SACEP	South Asia Cooperative Environment Programme
PERL	Partnership for Education and Research about Responsible Living	SADC	Southern African Development Community
PhD	Doctor of Philosophy	SAP	Structural Adjustment Programmes
PIF	Pacific Island Forum	SARUA	Southern African Regional Universities Association
PIMA	Programme for Academic Exchange and Mobility	SAT	Seekers After Truth
PIRG	Public Interest Research Groups	SCUP	Society for College and University Planning
PISA	Programme for International Student Assessment	SD	Sustainable Development
ProNEA	Brazil's National Environmental Education Programme	SEAC	Student Environmental Action Coalition
ProSPER.Net	Promotion of Sustainability in Postgraduate Education and Research Network	SEDUE	Mexican Ministry of Urban Development and Ecology
		SEED	Sustainability Education and Economic Development
PRSPs	Poverty Reduction Strategy Papers	SEK	Swedish Kroner
PV	Photovoltaic	SEMARNAT	Mexico's Secretariat of the Environment and Natural Resources
QA	Quality Assurance		
R&D	Research and Development	SEP	Mexican Ministry of Public Education
RAUSA	Argentine Network of Universities for Sustainability and the Envrionment	SES	Socio-Ecological System
		SESI-SENAI	Federation of Industries of Paraná
RC–GAU	Cuban Network for Environmental Management in Universities	SFA	Sustainable Futures Academy
		SHE	Sustainability in Higher Education
RCE	Regional Centres of Expertise	SIDA	Swedish International Development Agency
RCFA	Colombian Network for Environmental Training	SIGCSE	Special Interest Group on Computer Science Education
REASul	Southern Brazilian Network for Environmental Education	SPREP	Pacific Regional Environmental Programme
REBEA	Brazilian Network for Environmental Education	SQU	Sultan Qaboos University
REDFIA	National Network for Environmental Research and Training	SSC	sustainability and social commitment
REEP	Regional Environmental Education Programme	SSHRC	Social Sciences and Humanities Research Council of Canada
REMEPPAS	Mexican Network of Multidisciplinary Postgraduate Courses on the Environment and Sustainability	STARS	Sustainability Tracking, Assessment & Rating System
		STAUNCH	Sustainability Tool for Assessing Universities Curricula Holistica
REPEA	Paulista Environmental Education Network	STEM	(from Mobilizing STEM for SD) science, technology, engineering, and mathematics
RFA-LAC	Environmental Training Network for Latin America and the Caribbean		
RMIT	Royal Melbourne Institute of Technology (Viet Nam)	S&T	Science and Technology
		STS	Science & Technology Studies
ROLAC	Regional Office for Latin America and the Caribbean	SYC	Sierra Youth coalition
		TA	Technology Assessment
RSA	South Africa's Department of Science and Technology	TEC	Performance Based Research
		TEEN	Tripartite Environmental Education Network
RUC	Regional University Consortium		
RUCAS	Reorient University Curricula to Address Sustainability	TEMM	Tripartite Environment Ministers Meeting

TEMPUS	Trans-European Mobility Programme for University Studies	UNECE	United Nations Economic Commission for Europe
TERI	The Energy and Resources Institute	UNEP	United Nations Environment Program
TISS	Tata Institute of Social Studies	UNEP-ROAP	UNEP's Regional Office for Asia and the Pacific
TTSSA	Teacher Training in Sub Saharan Africa	UNESCO	United Nations Educational, Scientific and Cultural Organisation
UAE	United Arab Emirates		
UAEM	Universidad Autónoma del Estado de Morelos	UNILAB	University of International Integration of Brazil-Africa Lusophony
UASB	Simón Bolívar Andean University in Ecuador	UNISA	University of South Africa
		UNISWA	University of Swaziland
UASLP	Autonomous University of San Luis Potosí	UNITWIN	University Twinning and Networking Programme
UBC	University of British Columbia	UNU	United Nations University
UCGL	United Cities and Local Governments	UNU-IAS	United Nations University Institute of Advanced Studies
UCORED	ROLAC Coordinating Unit		
UDCA	University of Applied and Environmental Sciences (Colombia)	UNU-IIST	United Nations University's International Institute for Software Technology
UDS	University for Development Studies		
UDUAL	Union of Universities of Latin America and the Caribbean	UPC	Polytechnic University of Catalonia
		USM	Universiti Sains Malaysia
UGC	University Grants Commission	USP	University of São Paulo
UIS	UNESCO Institute of Statistics	USP	University of the South Pacific
UK	United Kingdom	USPESD	United States Partnership for Education for Sustainable Development
UK-DFID	Department for International Development of the United Kingdom		
ULA	University of the Andes (Venezuela)	USSR	Union of Soviet Socialist Republics
ULSF	University Leaders for a Sustainable Future	UTC	Universities that Count
		UWI	University of West Indies
UMAP	University Mobility in Asia and the Pacific	UWS	University of Western Sydney
		VCT	Voluntary Counselling and Testing
UMU	Uganda Martyrs' University	VET	Vocational Education and Training
UNAIDS	United Nations Programme on HIV/AIDS	WCED	World Commission on Environment and Development
UNAM	Universidad Nacional Autónoma México	WCHE	World Conference on Higher Education
UNBC	University of Northern British Columbia	WG	Working Group
		WSSD	World Summit on Sustainable Development
UNCED	UN Conference on Environment and Development	WUSC	World University Service of Canada
UNDESD	United Nations Decade of Education for Sustainable Development	WWF	World Wildlife Fund
UNDP	United Nations Development Programme		

GU GLOBAL UNIVERSITY
NA NETWORK FOR INNOVATION

GUNi IS

GUNi is a network created in 1999 by UNESCO, the United Nations University (UNU) and the Universitat Politècnica de Catalunya (UPC). It was founded after the 1998 World Conference on Higher Education to give continuity to and facilitate the implementation of its main decisions. Ten years later, in 2009 GUNi played a significant role in the second WCHE, following its mandate to further reflection and action frameworks to facilitate the exchange of value between higher education and society globally.

The Network comprises UNESCO chairs, higher education institutions, research centres and networks involved in innovation and the social commitment of higher education. It has 214 members in 79 countries and is represented across the world by five regional offices (sub-Saharan Africa, the Arab States, Asia and the Pacific, Latin America and the Caribbean, and Europe and North America). The UPC, in Barcelona, Spain, hosts its presidency and the International Secretariat.

GUNi AIMS TO

GUNi's mission is to strengthen the role of higher education in society contributing to the renewal of the visions, missions and policies of higher education across the world under a vision of public service, relevance and social responsibility.

In the beginning of this century there is a strong need to establish new bases for a sustainable global society that, taking into account environmental limits, re-examine the dynamics of global economic, political, human, social and cultural models, as well as their local manifestations. We are currently experiencing a crisis of civilization, in which we must facilitate the transition towards a paradigm shift aimed at rebuilding society, with the collective desire and responsibility of attaining a better world for future generations. There is a requirement to reconsider what the social contribution of higher education should be.

GUNi encourages higher education institutions to redefine their role, embrace this process of transformation and strengthen their critical stance within society.

Therefore, GUNi's goals are to:

- Encourage higher education institutions to reorient their role to broaden its social value, embrace this process of transformation and strengthen their critical stance within society.
- Promote the exchange of resources, innovative ideas and experiences to facilitate higher education's role for supporting social evolution.
- Foster networking among higher education institutions and cooperation between them and society.
- Help bridge the gap between developed and developing countries in the field of higher education and foster the cooperation North–South and South–South.
- Allow the collective and cooperative reflection, exchange and production of knowledge regarding what social responsibility and relevance in the emerging Planetary era should mean.

GUNi DOES

HIGHER EDUCATION IN THE WORLD REPORT

The Report is a collective work published as part of the GUNi series on the social commitment of universities. It is the result of a global and regional analysis of higher education in the world, with a specific subject chosen for each annual edition. The Report reflects on the key issues and challenges facing higher education and its institutions in the 21st century. It is currently published in English, Spanish, Chinese, Portuguese and Arabic.

INTERNATIONAL BARCELONA CONFERENCE ON HIGHER EDUCATION

The GUNi Conference is an international forum for debate on the challenges that face higher education. Each edition of the Conference deals with a hot topic that is chosen as a key working-subject for a period. Held every two years in Barcelona, and attended by renowned experts, university leaders, academics, policymakers and practitioners from all over the world, the Conference addresses innovative proposals and ideas, as well as the results of the latest research on each subject.

NETWORKING

GUNi reinforces and expands its network by encouraging the dynamic involvement of a wide range of actors in higher education in its activities. It fosters cooperation between them and promotes debate and the creation and exchange of knowledge on higher education worldwide through both on-site and online activities. The website and the monthly Newsletter are cornerstones of the accomplishment of this objective.

KNOWLEDGE COMMUNITY

GUNi.KC is created as a virtual meeting point with the objective to support the creation, transfer and application of knowledge. Through a variety of specific topics focused on the transformation of higher education and its role in responding to global challenges, GUNi.KC will offer tools to stimulate the direct participation of the affiliates in order to facilitate the exchange of expertise, resources and good practices that returned as a knowledge gain to community members.

RESEARCH PROJECTS

GUNi undertakes research projects on higher education by its own initiative, alone or in collaboration with other institutions. So far three Delphi surveys have been conducted – one for each of the three first reports issued by GUNi – addressing research on Financing Higher Education, Accreditation and Social Commitment and Higher Education for Human and Social Development.

In addition GUNi undertakes research projects on higher education for public and private not-for-profit institutions.

www.guninetwork.org

Regional representatives

	0
	<= 0 and > 2
	<= 3 and > 6
	<= 7 and > 10
	<= 11 and > 16

Notes:
Members approved until November 2010
Classification method: natural breaks (Jenks optimization)
Vector layer source: ESRI Data; Projection: Robinson

MAP 1 **Number of GUNi members per country**

MAP 1   xix

ABOUT THE AUTHORS

CONTEXT AND REGIONAL PERSPECTIVES AUTHORS

Osamu Abe is based at the College of Sociology and Graduate School of Intercultural Communication, Rikkyo University, Japan. He is also the Director of Rikkyo University's ESD Research Centre; the President of the Japanese Society of Environmental Education; the Chair of the Board of the Japan Council on the UN Decade of ESD (ESD-J); a board member of the Japan Environmental Education Forum and a member of the Commission on Education and Communication, the World Conservation Union (IUCN).

Javier Benayas is a Professor of Ecology at the Autonomous University of Madrid, where he was Vice-President of Campus and Environmental Quality from 2003 to 2009. In 2003, he promoted the creation of the Sectoral Commission on Environmental Quality and Sustainable Development and Risk Prevention (CADEP) at the Conference of Rectors of Spanish Universities (CRUE). He is currently its Executive Secretary. Since 2000, he has been the coordinator of the Interuniversity PhD programme 'Environmental Education' which is being taught by nine Spanish universities.

Lester R. Brown started his career as a farmer, growing tomatoes with his younger brother during high school and college. Shortly after earning a degree in agricultural science in 1955, he spent six months living in rural India where he became intimately familiar with the food/population issue. From 1964 to 1969, he worked for the Secretary of Agricuture's department. Afterwards, he left government to help establish the Overseas Development Council.

In 1974, he founded the Worldwatch Institute, the first research institute devoted to the analysis of global environmental issues. In 2001, he founded the Earth Policy Institute to provide a vision and a road map for achieving an environmentally sustainable economy.

He is the recipient of many prizes and awards. More recently, he was awarded the Borgström Prize by the Royal Swedish Academy of Agriculture and Forestry, and was selected one of Foreign Policy's Top Global Thinkers of 2010.

Heather Elliott is a Master of Environmental Studies Candidate at Dalhousie University, Canada. Her thesis research focused on investigating the conceptualizations of student leaders concerning sustainability and sustainable universities. She is now designing the first module of a new Sustainability Certificate programme for university employees.

Heila Lotz-Sisitka holds the Murray & Roberts Chair of Environmental Education and Sustainability at Rhodes University. She has actively contributed to the inclusion of environment and human rights concerns in South Africa's National Curriculum Statement. She serves on UNESCO's International Reference Group of the UN DESD and is editor of the *Southern African Journal of Environmental Education*. She coordinates the Environmental Education programme at Rhodes University and served as the Scientific Chair of the World Environmental Education Congress in 2007.

Ko Nomura is an Associate Professor at the Graduate School of Environmental Studies, Nagoya University, Japan. His research interests have been in the fields of environmental politics and environmental education in East Asia, particularly the role of environmental non-governmental organizations. Previously, he held research positions at Rikkyo University's ESD Research Centre and the Institute for Global Environmental Strategies. He has also worked on development assistance activities in Southeast Asia, particularly Indonesia.

Jos H.A.N. Rikers is a Senior Policy Adviser International Relations at the Open University in the Netherlands. He started his academic career as a researcher at Twente University's School of Education. In 1990, he began to work at the Open University of the Netherlands, where he has held several positions. Since 2001, he has been a senior policy adviser to the university's Executive Board on both sustainable development and international relations. In 2004, he helped found the Rhine-Meuse RCE, a regional centre of expertise on learning for sustainable development. He is a member of the city of Kerkrade's Climate Advisory Council.

Orlando Sáenz is a PhD of Education and Society Candidate at the UAB. He is a researcher at the University of Applied and Environmental Sciences (UDCA) and coordinator of the Alliance of Ibero-American Networks of Universities for Sustainability and the Environment as the Colombian Network of Environmental Training (RCFA) representative. He also coordinates the Network of Research on Science, Technology, Innovation and Environmental Education for Ibero-America (CTIE-AMB).

Ramzi Salamé is Delegate of the Rector of Saint-Joseph University (Beirut) for Quality Assurance, his professional life started as a teacher in Lebanon. Between 1994 and 2008, he worked as senior specialist of HE and acting director for the UNESCO Regional Bureau for Education in the Arab States. He has served as principal consultant for the reorganization of the Ministry of Education and Higher Education in Lebanon and principal consultant to the UN Group regarding the reform of the education and higher education systems in Iraq. He also contributed to the First Arab Knowledge Report published in 2009 by UNDP and the Mohammed bin Rashid Al Maktoum Foundation.

Geert de Snoo is director of the Institute of Environmental Sciences of Leiden University and full professor in Conservation Biology. His main fields of research are related to the impact of human activities on biodiversity and environmental quality and the sustainable development of rural areas. He is an endowed professor at Wageningen University in the field of Nature Conservation on Farmland. He is also a member of the Dutch Board for Authorization of Plant Protection Products and Biocides in Wageningen.

Daniella Tilbury is a Research Chair in the area of leadership, change management and education for sustainability in higher education. She has been the recipient of several awards including the Macquarie Innovation Award for Research (2007) and a Marie Curie International Research Fellowship (2009) as well as a Green Gown Award (2010) for Institutional

Change. She was the Founding Director of the Australian Research Institute in Education for Sustainability, which pioneered learning based change across government, education and business. She serves as Chair of the UN's Global Monitoring and Evaluation Expert's Group, which advises on the assessment of progress during the UN Decade in ESD, and is a member of the UNECE Expert Group on ESD competences. She is also Co-Chair of the Sustainable Futures Academy (Austria) and a Fellow of the Leadership Trust (UK). Professor Tilbury resides in the United Kingdom, where she is Director of Sustainability at the University of Gloucestershire, responsible for the university's sustainability strategy and performance.

Rietje van Dam-Mieras is Vice-Rector Magnificus at Leiden University, where she holds the chair 'Sustainable Development and Innovation of Education'. She also holds the UNESCO chair 'Knowledge Transfer for Sustainable Development Supported by ICTs' at the Open University of the Netherlands. She has worked at Maastricht University and the Open University of the Netherlands where she became professor in 'Natural sciences, especially biochemistry and biotechnology' in 1993. She is actively involved in the RCE initiative of United Nations University as a member of the Ubuntu Committee of Peers for RCEs. In 2010 she became a member of the Dutch national UNESCO Committee.

Tarah Wright is an associate professor at Dalhousie University, Canada, where she has played a pivotal role in the successful creation of the Environmental Science Program and co-creation of the university's new and innovative College of Sustainability. She serves on the editorial boards of the *International Journal of Sustainability in Higher Education*, and the *Encyclopaedia of Quality of Life Research*, is a Member of the Scientific Advisory Board for Environmental Management for Sustainable Universities (EMSU), and is a co-organizer for World Sustainable Development Teach-In Day.

OTHER AUTHORS OF THIS REPORT

Maik Adomssent, Research Fellow, Institute for Environmental and Sustainability Communication, University of Luneburg.

Eduardo Aponte, Professor and researcher, Higher Education Research Centre and UNESCO Chair in Higher Education, University of Puerto Rico.

Irena Ateljevic, Assistant Professor, Social-spatial Analysis Department, Wageningen University.

Sonia Bahri, Chief for Science, Technology and Innovations Policies and Reforms Science Sector, UNESCO.

Aristides Baloi, Department of Geography, Universidade Eduardo Mondlane.

Sjur Bergan, Head of the Department of Higher Education and History Teaching, Council of Europe.

Alícia Betts, Project manager, Catalan Association of Public Universities.

Cristina Bolívar, Manager, Cris Bolívar Consulting.

Miguel Ángel Chacón, Associate professor at the Universidad de San Carlos de Guatemala.

Kiran B. Chhokar, Programme Director, Higher Education, Centre for Environment Education and Co-Editor of the *Journal of Education for Sustainable Development.*

Yazmín Cruz, Project Manager, GUNi's Secretariat, UPC.

Gulelat Desse, Director of the Food Science and Nutrition Program, Addis Ababa University.

Carole Desprès, Professor of Architecture and Coordinator of the Interdisciplinary research group on suburbs, Laval University.

Jana Dlouhá, Environment Centre, Charles University.

Lorna Down, Lecturer, Institute of Education, University of the West Indies.

Cristina Escrigas, Executive Director, GUNi's Secretariat, UPC.

Zinaida Fadeeva, Associate fellow, Education for Sustainable Development Programme, Institute of Advanced Studies, United Nations University.

Sonia Fernández-Lauro, Poet and former Chief Documentalist of UNESCO.

Jo-Anne Ferreira, Director of the EcoCentre and Convenor of the Master of Environment (Education for Sustainability) program, Griffith University.

Dídac Ferrer, Coordinator of Campus Sustainability Plans, Organization Area, UPC.

Andreé Fortin, Professor at the Sociology Department, Laval University.

David Francis, Professor of African Peace and Conflict Studies, University of Bradford.

Moacir Gadotti, Associate Professor at the University of Sao Paulo and Director of the Paulo Freire Insitute.

Laima Galkute, Research and Higher Education Monitoring and Analysis Centre, Lithuanian Ministry of Education and Science.

Gilberto Gallopín, Independent scholar and former Regional Adviser on Environmental Policies, United Nations Economic Commission for Latin America and the Caribbean (ECLAC).

Nadja Gmelch, Project Manager, Catalan Association of Public Universities.

Edgar González Gaudiano, Tenured researcher, Veracruzana University, coordinator of the UNESCO Chair of Citizenship, Education and Environmental Sustainability of Development and member of UNESCO's Reference Group for the UN DESD.

Jesús Granados Sánchez, Research and Content Coordinator, GUNi's Secretariat, UPC.

John Holmberg, Professor and vice-president at Chalmers University of Technology. UNESCO chair in Education in Sustainable Development and member of UNESCO expert panel for the UN DESD.

Barbara Ibrahim, Founding director of the John D. Gerhart Center for Philanthropy and Civic Engagement, American University in Cairo.

Mireya Imaz, Director, Environmental Programme, Universidad Nacional Autónoma de México.

Peter Kanyandago, Director of the School of Postgraduate Studies, Uganda Martyrs University.

Steve Larkin, Pro-Vice-Chancellor of Charles Darwin University and Chair of Indigenous Higher Education Advisory Council, Australia.

Walter Leal-Filho, Senior Professor, London Metropolitan University; Head of the Research and Transfer Centre 'Applications of Life Sciences', Hamburg University of Applied Sciences, and Founding editor of the *International Journal of Sustainability in Higher Education.*

Claudia Lenz, Research and Development coordinator, European Wergeland Centre.

Rodrigo Lozano, Managing director, Organisational Sustainability Ltd and Lecturer, Sustainability Research Institute School of Earth and Environment, University of Leeds.

Clemens Mader, Director, RCE for Sustainable

Development, University of Graz, and member of the management team, COPERNICUS Alliance.

Marlene Mader (formerly Trummler), Research associate, RCE for Sustainable Development, and Department of Geography and Regional Sciences, University of Graz.

Evangelos Manolas, Associated Professor, Democritus University of Thrace.

Daniel Mato, Project coordinator, Tres de Febrero National University and International Institute for Higher Education in Latin America and the Caribbean.

Gerd Michelsen, Vice-Chair, COPERNICUS Alliance and head of the Institute for Environmental and Sustainability Communication, University of Luneburg.

Goolam Mohamedbhai, former President, International Association of Universities.

Bedřich Moldan, Head of the Environment Centre, Charles University.

Ingrid Mulà, Researcher, International Research Institute in Sustainability, University of Gloucestershire.

Karel Mulder, Head of the unit of Technology Dynamics & Sustainable Development, Delft University of Technology.

Claudio Naranjo, Philosoper and Director of SAT Educa Programme.

Stefan Nortier, Trainer, Education and Competence Studies Group, Wageningen University.

María Novo, UNESCO Chair in Environmental Education and Sustainable Development at the National Distance Education University.

Akpezi Obuigwe, Head of Environmental Education and Training, Division of Environmental Policy Implementation, UNEP-Nairobi.

Is-Haq Oloyede, Professor of Islamic jurisprudence and Vice-Chancellor, University of Ilorin.

M. Laura Ortiz, Leader of the Environmental Research Lab, Universidad Autónoma del Estado de Morelos and General Secretary of the Mexican Consortium of University Environmental Programmes for Sustainable Development.

Agustí Pérez-Foguet, Commissioner of sustainability, cooperation and development, Universitat Politècnica de Catalunya.

Ana Perona-Fjeldstad, Executive director, European Wergeland Centre.

Scott Peters, Associate Professor of Education, Cornell University.

Paul Raskin, President and founder, Tellus Institute.

Dzulfiki Abdul Razak, Vice-chancellor, University Sains Malaysia.

Negussie Retta, Dean of the Science Faculty and director of the Food, Science and Nutrition Program, Addis Ababa University.

Debra Rowe, President, US Partnership for Education for Sustainable Development and US Designee, World Federation of Colleges and Polytechnics' international sustainability group.

Paul Rowland, Executive Director, Association for the Advancement of Sustainability in Higher Education.

Roger Schank, Professor Emeritus, Northwestern University and CEO of Socratic Arts and Engines for Education.

Lisa Schwarzin, Coordinator, Initiative for Transformative Sustainability Education, Wageningen University.

Michael Scoullos, Coordinator, Mediterranean Education Initiative for Environment and Sustainability (MEdIES), University of Athens.

Rajib Shaw, Associate Professor, Graduate School of Global Environmental Studies, University of Tokyo.

Jeymi Sivoli, Project Officer, GUNi's Secretariat, UPC.

Magdalena Svanström, Director, Learning Center, Chalmers University.

Aurea C. Tanaka, Research Associate, Institute of Advanced Studies, United Nations University, Yokohama.

Geneviève Vachon, Professor, Architecture School, Laval University.

Hilligje Van't Land, Director Membership and Programme Development, International Association of Universities.

Josep M. Vilalta, Executive secretary, Catalan Association of Public Universities.

Tom Waas, Research Fellow, Human Ecology Department, Vrije Universiteit Brussels.

Arjen E.J. Wals, Professor of Social Learning and Sustainable Development and UNESCO Chair in Social Learning and Sustainable Development, Wageningen University.

Aurora Winslade, Director of Sustainability, University of California.

Masaru Yarime, Associate Professor, Graduate programme in Sustainability Science, University of Tokyo.

Zióle Zanotto Malhadas, Senior Professor, Universidade Federal do Paraná.

Friedrich Zimmermann, Chair, Department of Geography and Regional Science, University of Graz, and President, COPERNICUS Alliance.

FOREWORD

SUSTAINABILITY
AND KNOWLEDGE
IN CONTEMPORARY
SOCIETY

Cristina Escrigas

In terms of social value, higher education's greatest challenge in the coming years is to materialize the contribution made by knowledge to building a sustainable future for humanity and for the planet.

Sustainability involves the development of a new culture. This should encompass an analysis of knowledge itself, including a review of the assumptions that sustain our understanding of the world and the human dynamics within it.

Two levers of change are needed to bring about a substantial shift in systems. The first is to question thoroughly concepts that we think are obvious (which have been classed as truths and have therefore become immovable). The second is to be able to imagine what we want to bring into being. This second lever is the greater challenge, as it is limited by the collectively accepted beliefs on which we constructed the previous system.

The current education system is created within and is framed by a model of civilization that includes values, a development model and an understanding of contemporary society, and it responds to this model's needs.

What is at issue today is the need for a new conception of human progress. This changes the context for education, which has been too focused, in recent decades, on short-term instrumental performance, within a socioeconomic system that is growing exponentially. We are on the verge of a change in the model of civilization, which cannot be built from the old paradigm of a system that has reached its limits.

Inherent to the way in which we educate is a given understanding of reality. Therefore we need to review, in current education systems, the often non-explicit assumptions on which this understanding of reality is based.

We know that we cannot solve problems using the same level of awareness and understanding with which they were created. We need to create a new consciousness of being in the world, based on a new understanding of the dynamics of this relationship.

We are witnessing the end of a cycle, though with a certain amount of resistance and even greater uncertainty. We know that we must change the bases of economic, political and social systems to channel the harmonic coexistence of all life on the planet. We are already aware of the multifactorial interrelation that underlies all reality, all dynamics and all activities.

In this context, an ever-widening gap could arise between the space and the value we give in our systems to knowledge that facilitates *human and social welfare* and instrumental knowledge for intermediate human operations.

- What knowledge do we prioritize as the most useful and what purpose does it serve?
- What ethics and values do we transmit in the existing education process?
- Can we maintain current quality standards in higher education without shifting towards complex thought in the creation and transmission of knowledge?
- Are we ready to investigate the concept of knowledge in depth in order to progress towards interdependence and uncertainty?

Nowhere is it prescribed that the knowledge that should be gained in the higher education (HE) process should be that which leads to a deep understanding of humans and their relationship with the Earth. However, it would certainly be reasonable to expect that knowledge to be incorporated into HE, given the mission of HE to prepare people to be professionally competent and to consciously co-create the reality in which they live.

We must explore how to tackle ethical issues and values, recognize their inherent existence and question the idea of an absolute truth. We must also review our monocultural perspective and promote dialogue between different types and sources of knowledge.

The academic community and society need to reconsider the supremacy of the scientific-rational paradigm and the accepted knowledge of experts as the only kind of knowledge that is valid.

This is linked to a second issue: the capacity to put knowledge at the service of society. On the whole, educational institutions are not at the centre of the debate on the global crises that are affecting our world, nor are they partici- pating actively in the critical renewal of ideas for change. Consequently, it is even more necessary to establish new ways of transferring knowledge to society. Universities have progressed in devising strategies, processes and activities for businesses, and they should now focus on transferring knowledge to society as a whole.

At least three sources of tension influence the role of institutions in social dynamics:

● The ability of institutions to anticipate change and be proactive rather than reactive.
● The departmental organization of knowledge vs. the organization of knowledge around topics of social interest.

The United Nations University (UNU) is a leading example of an institution that has clearly adopted this latter approach. There is no need for all universities to move towards this model, but we should adopt some of its principles.

Higher education institutions (HEIs) can contribute to the renewal of thought in our society through the proactive, systematic criticism of ideas, particularly established beliefs about the way we organize our community and how these beliefs are reflected in our education systems. Universities can also help to distin- guish between knowledge, information and ideology, to facilitate a diversity of positions, based on available knowledge.

In addition, HEIs can generate the knowledge required to support political decisions that affect the entire world population or large parts of it. In the future, this will be an increasingly pressing need (and hopefully a demand).

Therefore, we need to reduce the time it takes to transfer new knowledge to society and we also need to open up access to knowledge to ensure that it is as useful as possible. This can be done by establishing relation- ships with institutions, civil society organizations, inter- national organizations, governments and the citizenry, and providing them with plural and expert advice. In addition, HEIs need to become cosmopolitan centres by building bridges between different cultures, and to participate openly in the debate on their social relevance.

We have already explored several assumptions. When we consider all of them together, emerging issues related to **managing knowledge in our educa- tion systems and institutions** are brought to the fore.

1. We work with a fragmented, linear and cumulative model in knowledge management. However, in its growth and interconnectedness, knowledge is begin- ning to behave as a living organism.

2. The interrelationship between disciplines, a holistic approach and the topic-based organization of knowl- edge is necessary, but our structures are centred on disciplines.
3. Knowledge multiplies, at the same time as part of it becomes obsolete, increasingly rapidly, in all fields. In addition, there is a long delay between the generation of knowledge and its inclusion in curricula.
4. All the knowledge that is generated is not enough to reduce the level of uncertainty about social, environmental and human circumstances. In fact, we increasingly feel that we have less control over what happens.
5. We cannot cover all available knowledge in the design of degree courses. The difficulty of selecting relevant knowledge is a well-known, controversial debate in intradisciplinary terms and an emerging one in cross-disciplinary terms. The tendency to cover more under the same concept of education, including lifelong learning, is unlikely to succeed if the above premises are true.
6. Paradigm shifts are essential in the development model, energy sources, the economic system, politi- cal and representational models, in the forms of human relationships with respect to diversity and coexistence, and in our relationship with nature. Education itself requires a paradigm shift on which to base learning and teaching.

One option is to strike a balance between the impor- tance we give to transmission, that is, 'the accumulation of knowledge', and the importance we give to the trans- formational process of 'training the one who knows'. That is, we should develop the potential for knowing using the least energy and as effectively as possible.

We should prepare people to handle complex realities in a simple way and we should integrate emotional abilities with instrumental and knowledge abilities. We need to train people to learn to learn; to fully understand and tolerate uncertainty and change; to handle a vast and complex universe of information from many sources and of many different natures; and to discriminate between information, knowledge and wisdom. We must train people to understand what we are, what we are like and how to be, both as individuals and as a group, and to manage their own education and development throughout life.

We should recover the notion of an education based on the development of the individual, and ensure that there is a balance between transcendental and lasting aspects and practical and temporary ones, so that the purpose of knowing also becomes collective harmony, peace and prosperity. We should move from a model in which the main focus is on the content, to one that also emphasizes the container – a model centred on **being**.

If we move in this direction, we will have a wealth of new horizons to explore in relation to the function of HE. This should bring us closer to the transcendent meaning of life and to the transmission of wisdom, which will probably makes us feel happier and more in tune with life, while we remain in a rigorous academic context that is focused on the search for and dissemination of what we call truth.

ABOUT THIS REPORT

The aim of the fourth GUNi Report *Higher Education in the World* is to explore HE's commitment to sustainability. In this task, the first step is to present the current context and its impact on HE, and then to share experiences of what is already being done in the different world regions, to identify barriers in HEIs and possible solutions, and finally, to propose different visions for higher education and sustainability to make the transition from understanding to action.

We start by analysing the context because it still seems strange to talk of a Planetary era, which is simply humanity's awareness of what has always existed. However, this reality changes everything, as we now know the opportunities, the limitations and their impact; we know what works and what does not. An awareness of the state of the world is what justifies the need to transform the purpose of education and the systems in which it is carried out.

The second part of the Report, 'Regional perspectives: What has been achieved at this stage', aims to illustrate how Africa, the Arab states, Asia and the Pacific, Europe, Latin-America and the Caribbean, and USA and Canada have introduced sustainability in HE, complemented with subregional or national analysis and a selection of trending topics related to the different aspects of sustainability and the role of HE. This section also includes examples of networks on HE and sustainability working in each region as well as experiences and good practices on how some HEIs in the different regions are introducing sustainability into the curricula, research, social and community engagement and institutional management.

In Part III, the reader will also find a study 'Moving from understanding to action: Breaking barriers for transformation' intended to establish which barriers prevent HEIs from achieving sustainable development (SD) in their performance and to seek ways of trying to overcome them and propose some solutions. For this study, participative channels have been created to involve all those experts interested in the transformation of HE towards sustainability, such as:

- the GUNi 1st Round Poll: Breaking barriers for transformation
- the work done during the Parallel Workshops: Moving from Understanding to Action: Breaking Barriers for Transformation, held at the 5th International Barcelona Conference on Higher Education, 'Higher Education's Commitment to Sustainability: from Understanding to Action'
- the GUNi 2nd Round Poll: Breaking barriers for transformation, based on the results of the first poll and the workshops
- the creation of a working group within the GUNi Knowledge Community for discussing the results and preparing the final piece in which ten international experts have participated.

The fourth section of the Report, 'Visions for transformation', aims to shed new light on the current paradigm and to propose a different perspective on it, where alternative ideas can be raised. Within this section of the Report we would like to make a breakthrough on the established paradigms; renovating and adjusting them into the current realities in which we live. We have encouraged authors to move away from the normal and conventional way of thinking and suggest innovative ideas that can offer new future perspectives and give new horizons for academia and policymakers working in the field of HE. We expect readers to find different proposals for acting in alternative and creative pathways.

We are very pleased to bring together 85 experts from the worldwide academic community who are working on the transformation of HE systems and institutions towards sustainability. In their works they present an exciting series of ideas, options, visions and specific challenges for the commitment of HE towards sustainability.

The final goal of this Report is to stimulate debate among all those whose different links with the world of HE could contribute to enriching the discussion. We aim to stimulate serious and profound thought, which will open opportunities that should be jointly analysed, discussed and hopefully used by academics, university leaders, policymakers and members of civil society and the business community. Thus, we invite everyone to follow the discussion in the GUNi *Knowledge Community*, a new collaborative network initiative by GUNi.

HIGHER EDUCATION'S COMMITMENT TO SUSTAINABILITY: FROM UNDERSTANDING TO ACTION – UNESCO'S POINT OF VIEW

Stamenka Uvalić-Trumbić

As one of the co-founders of the Global University Network for Innovation, UNESCO commends GUNi on the dedication of its fourth issue of *Higher Education in the World* to 'Higher Education's Commitment to Sustainability: from Understanding to Action', as it is most timely and appropriate.

We at UNESCO place a strong emphasis on sustainable development and particularly on the contributions which higher education(HE) can offer. This has been demonstrated by two major international UNESCO Conferences, both organized in 2009, that I would like to evoke.

First, UNESCO, as responsible for implementing the UN Decade of Education for Sustainable Development (DESD), organized the UNESCO World Conference on Education for Sustainable Development (Bonn, Germany, March/April 2009).

Second, to mark a shift of emphasis towards post-basic education, particularly on higher education, UNESCO organized its Second World Conference on Higher Education entitled 'New Dynamics of Higher Education and Research for Societal Change and Development' (UNESCO, Paris, July 2009).

The Bonn Conference Declaration underscores that the world faces substantial and complex challenges arising from values that have created unsustainable societies. The Declaration places a focus on the role of higher education institutions (HEIs) and research networks in Education for Sustainable Development (ESD) by encouraging and enhancing scientific excellence, research and new knowledge development for ESD. It also calls for identifying universities and other HE and research institutions that could serve as centres of expertise and innovation to develop and share knowledge and create resources for ESD.[1]

However, as stated by one of the authors[2] in this report, Sonia Bahri, the commitment of HE to sustainable development should be perceived in the broader context of social responsibility, a theme underpinning GUNi's mission but also highlighted at the 2009 WCHE.

Indeed, the 2009 WCHE addressed the new dynamics of a changing HE landscape, underlining its intrinsic connections with development. The Conference reaffirmed the social responsibility of HE and the fundamental role of HE and research in responding to the global challenges encapsulated in the Millennium Development Goals, and in particular underlined its crucial role in building inclusive, vibrant and diverse knowledge societies through the achievement of Education for All.

The participants of the Conference all agreed that 'at no time in history has it been more important to invest in higher education as a major force in building an inclusive and diverse knowledge society and to advance research, innovation and creativity' (WCHE Communiqué, Preamble).[3]

However, with the impact of the economic crisis, HE is experiencing austerity in all countries, developing and developed alike. Higher education must do more with less.

The two principal trends in contemporary HE are the rising demand for it and its massification. Nearly one-third of the world's population (29.3%) is under 15 and today there are 158 million people enrolled in tertiary education.[4] Projections suggest that participation will peak at 263 million in 2025. Accommodating the additional 105 million students would require more than four major universities (30,000 students) to open every week for the next fifteen years.[5]

I don't think we have yet come to terms with the expansion of HE that is going to take place in the next decade.

To assure the sustainability of HE, especially in the developing world, new dynamics are at play and must be embraced enthusiastically in order to respond to this significant challenge. However, widening access to quality HE through a diversification of providers, and identifying and promoting innovative and multiple sources of funding will not be sufficient to assure its sustainability.

A session at the WCHE addressed, specifically, the issue of HE and sustainable development, concluding that sustainable development must be understood today as a process in which human beings are actors of change and called for a move from expectation to action, which the GUNi Report captures. The role of HE is to continue educating citizens to be the agents and facilitators of sustainable development and be in close contact with its community and include academics, community members, civil society and government.

In addition to widening access to quality HE and interacting closely with the wider community, a shared challenge of HE worldwide is a common need to increase the relevance of programmes and to enhance the employability of graduates.

Trends show that the number of unemployed graduates is continually rising due to different imbalances in the economy as well as imbalances in the relevance of HE programmes, curricula and content. The phenomena of unemployed and *under*employed graduates are very common in many countries of the world and are of priority concern for many regions, including Africa, as outlined at the 2009 WCHE. While the economy and labour market shift and develop according to various actors and factors, employability lies within the province of HE.

Indeed, employability reinforces cooperation between HEIs and the labour market by connecting the areas of curriculum development and degree reform, institutional culture of quality, relevance, and social responsibility while it also relies on the academic knowledge base which is the backbone of traditional HE.

With employability as a goal and academic freedom as the framework, HEIs will retain and strengthen their status as integral elements of the Lifelong Learning knowledge society. This, in turn will hopefully contribute to the sustainability of HE systems, especially in more fragile states, and constitute a significant part of HE's commitment to sustainability.

NOTES

1   Bonn declaration, www.esd-world-conference-2009.org
2   Sonia Bahri (2010) Social Responsibility of Higher Education in Addressing Major Global Issues. Paper present at the 5th International Barcelona Conference on Higher Education.
3   2009 WCHE Communique, www.unesco.org/en/wche2009/
4   1SCED levels 5 & 6 UNESCO Institute of Statistics figures.
5   British Council and IDP Australia projections.

HIGHER EDUCATION AND SUSTAINABILITY: UNU'S VISION

Konrad Osterwalder

Higher education is one of the major determinants in the well-being of a society and of the whole world. What it is aiming for, what it is asked to deliver, what it achieves, what it needs, these are the most important factors to be considered.

One of the most burning problems of today and tomorrow is the question of whether we are able to move sufficiently fast towards the sustainable development of our society, whether we succeed in securing for coming generations a decent life in peace, in freedom and in good health, and whether we manage to pass on to them a world that offers them similar or even better conditions as the well-off part of today's world population enjoys.

If we aim at sustainable development, then two fundamental goals have to be formulated and must be achieved. In the first place, we must do research that tells us how to proceed to bring the menacing risks and shortages under control, and we have to take the necessary steps in the right direction. But second, we have to make sure that all our knowledge and all our insight is transmitted to the next generation. Our generation will not be able to solve most of the basic problems. We know now that many of the Millennium Development Goals cannot be reached by 2015, in spite of the enormous efforts and the good progress that is evident. It is up to the next generation, to the young people, to take a fresh look at the problems, with optimism and without prejudice. But for this to be successful we must offer the next generation a good education, we must hand over to them all the tools and insights that we and earlier generations have developed – that is the easy part of teaching and education. But we also must make sure that they know how to address a new problem, one that has never before been solved, maybe has not even been identified and formulated; a problem that requires openness and a new and critical assessment and that will force them to come up with original, innovative ideas and solutions. They have to rethink not only *what* has to be done, but also *how* it has to be done. Maybe our present power structures, the present balance (or missing balance) between the three circles of society – political, economic and cultural – have to be revised and redefined so as to make the necessary societal adjustments possible. To help and support students to develop these abilities is the difficult part of education. This is of course true at all levels of education, but it is of particular importance at the tertiary level.

Envisaging sustainable development as a strategic goal, the United Nations University sees it as one of its main tasks to engage in research and capacity building in selected areas of problems that are crucial for sustainable development. With this in mind it develops strong partnerships between researchers, teachers and students from the developing and the developed world, thus strengthening the flow of ideas and knowledge from one part of the world to another and contributing to the building of greatly needed new capacities. One of the crucial steps will be the establishment of Twin Institutes, that is, institutes that have two campuses, one in a developed country and one in a developing country. Eventually, all institutes of UNU will have this twin structure. Another important step will be to establish UNU as a true graduate school, offering master's and doctoral programmes and degrees. The students will be taught in classes that truly bring together young people from all parts of the globe, and they will take place in at least two different parts of the world. They will be educated in the art of finding science-based solutions to the world's most burning problems. This means among other things that the programmes will not be structured according to scientific disciplines but rather following a particular complex of problems, thus reflecting the structure of UNU as a whole. In that context it is clear the focus has to be on genuine interdisciplinarity. Interdisciplinarity is best achieved by integrating relevant methods, theories of knowledge and the ontology of natural, social and human sciences. One of the most effective ways of being interdisciplinary in our academic pursuits is to follow a systems approach. Systems thinking means that textual analysis, modelling, theory building, data analysis, interpretation, and so on, are woven together seamlessly without being constrained by disciplinary strictures and boundaries.

Higher education is the ideal carrier for the dissemination of the idea and the concepts as well as the practical sides of sustainable development. But our traditional institutions of higher learning have to rethink the way they are structured, the way they put together their curricula, the way they choose their students and, their faculty, the way they interact and collaborate with other parts of the world and last but not least, the way they are financed. The place and the role they play in the modern society calls for a thorough overhaul and many redefinitions. And society has to be convinced that the new ways of doing things are ultimately in its own interest.

HIGHER EDUCATION'S COMMITMENT TO SUSTAINABILITY: THE UPC'S POINT OF VIEW

Antoni Giró

We live in an international context of changes and global crises in which universities must find their place.

The overall effects of the energy, economic and financial crises, climate change and the loss of biological and cultural diversity, food insecurity and huge social inequities, as well as armed conflicts, are just some of the major challenges that humanity must face this century.

A range of global problems, with very different local manifestations in an overpopulated world with overexploited resources, reflect the imbalance between human society and natural ecosystems.

We are now able to document the relationship between these crises. It is also possible to prove that there is a link between them, and that the expansive economic growth model linked to the concept of development must be reviewed.

The ecological footprint that modern societies have left on the planet is one of the main indicators of the inappropriate use of ecosystems. It is also a sign that we have exceeded our limits and that we need to restore the balance by reducing the impact of our lifestyles and by reconsidering the relationship between nature and culture.

A global map of the world's problems makes it clear that when it comes to introducing a sustainable way of life, we are talking about creating a new culture.

The word **sustainability** refers to a paradigm from which to articulate new ways of living and of understanding our place in the world. Sustainability implies changing the way we relate to ecosystems and the possibility of moving towards a culture based on harmonious coexistence and equality. To do so, a new area of knowledge must be created so that actions can be taken to tackle one of the greatest challenges of our times.

The paradigm of sustainability takes in the economic, social, human, environmental and cultural dimensions through a holistic and interconnected vision of the world, which must have its roots in education.

The international meetings held to move in this direction have resulted in several statements that constitute the nucleus of many educational institutions. The UN Decade of Education for Sustainable Development and, more recently, the Bonn Declaration, as well as the final communiqué of the World Conference on Higher Education held in Paris in 2009, are examples of a process that is contributing to a greater understanding of the implications of sustainability for education and the realization that it must become one of education's primary objectives.

Principles such as interdisciplinarity, the contextualization of knowledge, systemic thinking, an intergenerational perspective and social commitment are part of an increasingly widespread language among professionals from the fields of education and sustainability. This language should percolate educational curricula at every stage.

In recent years, many educational institutions have included sustainability in their curricula and have dedicated resources to research in order to recover a healthy ecosystem, while others have moved forward by establishing participatory networks for the purposes of providing socially relevant knowledge.

However, the perspective of sustainability must become part of the learning and teaching processes in educational projects. We need to educate people so that they can *understand* and *act* in an interconnected, complex and global world. To do so, we need to know how to integrate all areas of knowledge and how to apply the right methodologies to put words into action. We must be able to educate from a holistic vision of reality and learn how to work transversally by identifying which competences are necessary for future citizens and which priorities should be established in research.

All these issues are part of the challenge inherent to the cultural paradigm of sustainability, and they must be clarified so that we can set the path we must follow as a global society.

Therefore, innovation in higher education now means acknowledging the need for a paradigm shift and the interdisciplinary restructuring of knowledge, so that the urgent problems of our times can be addressed, researched and understood through a complex and plural prism.

The Universitat Politècnica de Catalunya (UPC) made inroads in this field almost 13 years ago. The work done then survives in the framework of the university's Institute for Research in Science and Technology for Sustainability (IS.UPC), whose aim is to generate technical and conceptual tools to create a more sustainable production model, and to collaborate in the UPC's endeavour to provide scientific and technical support for social, cultural and economic progress.

The path travelled so far is a small step in a major project that requires the collaboration of other universities and social stakeholders from different countries.

This GUNi report highlights the crucial role that higher education plays in building a sustainable world. It has opened up a toolbox to reveal the numerous initiatives that have arisen since this approach was taken and to bring about new courses of action that will enable us to make advances in this direction.

It would not have been possible to elaborate this publication without the help of the Banco Santander and its president, Emilio Botín, to whom I am greatly indebted for providing the financial support required for GUNi to fulfil its mission. I would also like to express my sincere gratitude to the Directorate of Universities and the Directorate of International Promotion of the Government of Catalonia for the support they gave to the publication and to the project as a whole. I am also deeply grateful to UNESCO, not only for their faith in the project and the expert advice they have provided, but also for contributing articles and financial support to the publication. Thanks also to UNESCO International Institute for Higher Education in Latin America and the Caribbean (IESALC) for their financial support to this project. GUNi and the UPC would like to repay their invaluable help with gratitude and, most importantly, tangible results.

I would like to express my belief in the value of a diverse publication such as this, in which stakeholders from every region in the world come together to contribute their experience and thoughts on an issue as critical as the commitment of higher education to sustainability.

On behalf of the UPC and GUNi, I would like to thank all the authors from all over the world who have made their personal views known and whose knowledge and efforts have enriched this initiative, which we hope readers will find equally rewarding.

This project needs and greatly benefits from the convergence of such diverse perspectives. The meeting between the people from different cultures and with different beliefs who have contributed to this publication is the ideal template for promoting a different way of working. Dialogue is essential to reaching a consensus throughout academia on how to foster and sustain learning processes for a sustainable world.

I hope that all those who read this work will find in it an honest debate that will lead to multiple initiatives for identifying and generating new ways of moving from understanding to action.

Human Development Ranking
- 0 - 30
- 31 - 71
- 72 - 109
- 110 - 146
- 147 - 182

Gross Enrolment Ratio
- 0 - 13
- 14 - 36
- 37 - 55
- 56 - 75
- 76 - 118

Notes:
This map shows a correlation: in general, countries with high GER have a better place in the ranking of HDI.

Sources: UNESCO Institute for Statistics, *Global Education Digest 2010*. Comparing Education Statistics Across the World. Available at: http://www.uis.unesco.org/Library/Documents/GED_2010_EN.pdf

MAP 2 Higher education enrolment ratio (GER) by country and human development index (HDI), 2010

UNDP, *Human Development Report 2010*. The Real Wealth of Nations: Pathways to Human Development.
Available at: http://hdrstats.undp.org/en/tables/default.html

Vector layer source: ESRI Data; Projection: Robinson

MAP 2   XXXV

DATA EXPLORATION

Martí Rosas Casals

GUNi has published higher education statistical data since its first report: *Higher Education in the World 2006*. In each report a selection of statistical information about education, higher education, expenditure, research and development, and economic and social indicators are included.

Institutions and societies, though, are not static. Education, culture and global issues evolve and change over time, as do statistical data and indicators. In this sense, and for this year's issue of the report, we have used Google Public Data Explorer (http://www.google.com/publicdata/home) in order to dynamically add the time dimension.

This exercise is based on the information about the gross enrolment ratio (GER) in tertiary education and the human development index (HDI) that GUNi has published in two different formats, a map and a statistical table, since 2006. This information shows a relation between GER and HDI rank. In general, countries with a higher GER have a better place in the ranking of HDI.

For those countries that report these data to the UNESCO Institute for Statistics (UIS), Google Public Data Explorer allows us to correlate HDI rank and GER in tertiary education and witnesses its evolution in time. The dataset, which can also be accessed at the GUNi website (www.guninetwork.org), covers the period from 2006 to 2010 and includes the following features:

● Correlation variability over time

● World map location
● Countries HDI and/or GER classification by line and bar chart
● An option to sort by world regions
● Evolution trails for selected countries
● Bubble size as a function of countries' population
● … and many others, depending on the user's will and disposition!

Four graphics showing the evolution of the GER and HDI rank during the past few years are included to give readers a snapshot on how this tool can be used.

There are some points that have to be taken into account when analysing the information. For some years, countries' positions remain unchanged in relation to the previous year. One reason for this behaviour is that GER data are sometimes reported every two years to the UIS. Another reason is the invariant character of some of the data, which can remain constant through the years (for example Lithuania). In some cases HDI rank evolution does not imply variation in GER (for example Norway) or the other way around (for example Colombia, Uruguay or Ukraine). Sometimes it is unclear how the data have been reported by the country and processed by the UIS (for example Cuba). In any case, though, the data reported have been thoroughly checked with the UIS database and represent the best officially published statistical data on tertiary education.

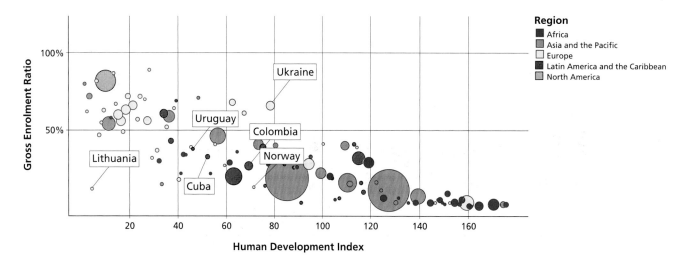

FIGURE 1 GER and HDI rank in 2007

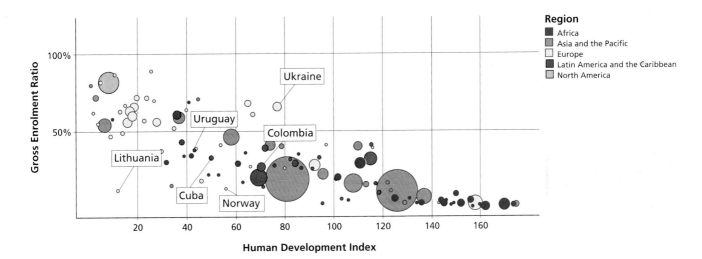

FIGURE 2 GER and HDI rank in 2008

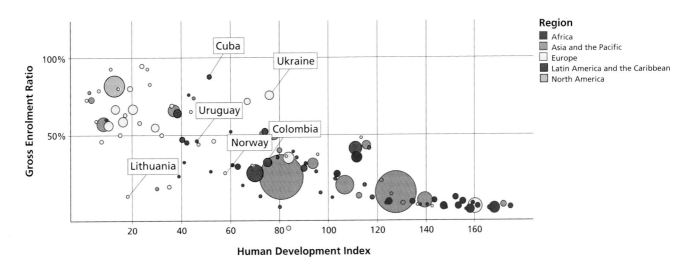

FIGURE 3 GER and HDI rank in 2009

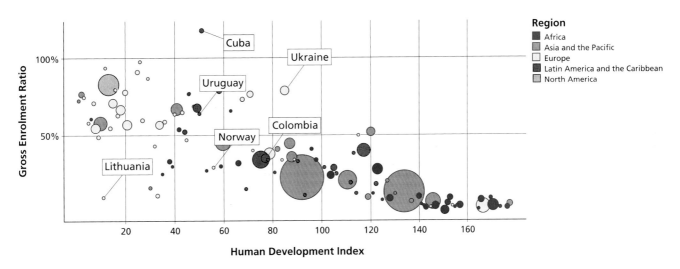

FIGURE 4 GER and HDI rank in 2010

PART I
THE CONTEXT

ON THE EDGE

In the summer of 2010, record-high temperatures hit Moscow. Twice during the heat wave, the Moscow temperature exceeded 100 degrees Fahrenheit, a level Muscovites had never before experienced. Fires were starting every day, Moscow was bathed in seemingly endless smoke, forest burned and crops withered.[2]

The most intense heat in Russia's 130 years of recordkeeping was taking a heavy economic toll. Thousands of farmers faced bankruptcy.[3] The world's number three wheat exporter, Russia banned grain exports in a desperate move to rein in soaring domestic food prices. Between mid-June and mid-August, the world price of wheat climbed 60%.

But there was some good news coming out of Moscow. On 30 July, Russian President Dmitry Medvedev announced that in large parts of Western Russia 'practically everything is burning.' While sweating, he went on to say, 'What's happening with the planet's climate right now needs to be a wake up call to all of us.' In something akin to a deathbed conversion, Russia's president was abandoning his country's position as a climate change denier and an opponent of carbon reduction initiatives.[4]

Even before the Russian heat wave ended, there were reports in late July of torrential rains in the mountains of northern Pakistan. The destruction was everywhere. Some 2 million homes were damaged or destroyed. More than 20 million people were affected by the flooding. Nearly 2000 Pakistanis died. Some 6 million acres of crops were damaged or destroyed. Over a million livestock drowned. Roads and bridges were washed away. Although the flooding was blamed on the heavy rainfall, there were actually several trends converging to produce what was described as the largest natural disaster in Pakistan's history.[5]

On 26 May 2010, the official temperature in Mohenjo-daro in south-central Pakistan reached 128 degrees Fahrenheit, a record for Asia. Snow and glaciers in the Western Himalayas were melting fast. As Pakistani glaciologist M. Iqbal Khan noted, the glacial melt was already swelling the flow of the Indus River even before the rains came.[6] The pressure of population on natural resources is intense. Pakistan's 185 million people are squeezed into an area 8% that of the United States. So far, 90% of the original forests in the Indus Basin are gone.

Twenty or more years ago, Pakistan chose to define security largely in military terms. When it should have been investing in reforestation, soil conservation, education, and family planning, it was short-changing these activities to bolster its military capacity. In 1990, the military budget was 15 times that of education and a staggering 44 times that of health and family planning. As a result, Pakistan is now a poor, overpopulated, environmentally devastated nuclear power where 60% of women cannot read and write.[7]

What happened to Russia and to Pakistan in the summer of 2010 are examples of what lies ahead for all of us if we continue with business as usual. The media described the heat wave in Russia and the flooding in Pakistan as natural disasters. But were they? Climate scientists have been saying for some time that rising temperatures would bring more extreme climate events.

The signs that our civilization is in trouble are multiplying. During most of the 6000 years since civilization began we lived on the sustainable yield of the Earth's natural systems. But in recent decades humanity has overshot the level that those systems can sustain.[8]

We are liquidating the Earth's natural assets to fuel our consumption. Half of us live in countries where water tables are falling and wells are going dry. Soil erosion exceeds soil formation on one third of the world's cropland, draining the land of its fertility.

Meanwhile, with our massive burning of fossil fuels, we are overloading the atmosphere with carbon dioxide (CO_2), pushing the Earth's temperature ever higher. This in turn generates more frequent and more extreme climatic events, including crop-withering heat waves, more intense droughts, more severe floods, and more destructive storms.[9]

1.1
THE WORLD ON THE EDGE[1]

Lester R. Brown

The Earth's rising temperature is also melting polar ice sheets and mountain glaciers. It is the ice melt from the mountain glaciers in the Himalayas and on the Tibetan Plateau that helps sustain the dry-season flow of the major rivers in India and China – the Ganges, Yangtze, and Yellow Rivers – and the irrigation systems that depend on them.[10]

At some point, what had been excessive local demands on environmental systems when the economy was small became global in scope. A 2002 study by a team of scientists led by Mathis Wackernagel aggregates the use of the Earth's natural assets, including CO_2 overload in the atmosphere, into a single indicator – the ecological footprint. The authors concluded that humanity's collective demands first surpassed the Earth's regenerative capacity around 1980. By 1999, global demands on the Earth's natural systems exceeded sustainable yields by 20%. Ongoing calculations show it at 50% in 2007. Stated otherwise, it would take 1.5 Earths to sustain our current consumption. Environmentally, the world is in overshoot mode. If we use environmental indicators to evaluate our situation, then the global decline of the economy's natural support systems – the environmental decline that will lead to economic decline and social collapse – is well under way.[11]

No previous civilization has survived the ongoing destruction of its natural supports. Nor will ours. Yet economists look at the future through a different lens. Relying heavily on economic data to measure progress, they see the near tenfold growth in the world economy since 1950 and the associated gains in living standards as the crowning achievement of our modern civilization. During this period, income per person worldwide climbed nearly fourfold, boosting living standards to previously unimaginable levels. In the eyes of mainstream economists, the world has not only an illustrious economic past but also a promising future.[12]

Mainstream economists see the 2008–9 global economic recession and near-collapse of the international financial system as a bump in the road, albeit an unusually big one, before a return to growth as usual. Projections of economic growth, whether by the World Bank, Goldman Sachs, or Deutsche Bank, typically show the global economy expanding by roughly 3% a year. At this rate the 2010 economy would easily double in size by 2035. With these projections, economic growth in the decades ahead is more or less an extrapolation of the growth of recent decades.[13]

How did we get into this mess? Our market-based global economy as currently managed is in trouble. The market does many things well. It allocates resources with an efficiency that no central planner

could even imagine, much less achieve. But as the world economy expanded some 20-fold over the last century it has revealed a flaw – a flaw so serious that, if it is not corrected, will spell the end of civilization as we know it.[14]

The market, which sets prices, is not telling us the truth. It is omitting indirect costs that in some cases now dwarf direct costs. We delude ourselves with our accounting system. Leaving such huge costs off the books is a formula for bankruptcy. Environmental trends are the lead indicators telling us what lies ahead for the economy and ultimately for society itself. Falling water tables today signal rising food prices tomorrow. Shrinking polar ice sheets are a prelude to falling coastal real estate values.

Modern economic thinking and policymaking have created an economy that is so out of sync with the ecosystem on which it depends that it is approaching collapse. How can we assume that the growth of an economic system that is shrinking the Earth's forests, eroding its soils, depleting its aquifers, collapsing its fisheries, elevating its temperature, and melting its ice sheets can simply be projected into the long-term future? What is the intellectual process underpinning these extrapolations?

We are facing a situation in economics today similar to that in astronomy when Copernicus arrived on the scene, a time when it was believed that the sun revolved around the Earth. Just as Copernicus had to formulate a new astronomical worldview after several decades of celestial observations and mathematical calculations, so too must we formulate a new economic worldview based on several decades of environmental observations and analyses.[15]

The archaeological record indicates that civilizational collapse does not come suddenly out of the blue. Archaeologists analyzing earlier civilizations talk about a decline and collapse scenario. Economic and social collapse was almost always preceded by a period of environmental decline.[16]

For past civilizations it was sometimes a single environmental trend that was primarily responsible for their decline. Sometimes it was multiple trends. For Sumer, it was rising salt concentrations in the soil as a result of an environmental flaw in the design of their otherwise extraordinary irrigation system. For the Mayans, it was deforestation and soil erosion. As more and more land was cleared for farming to support the expanding empire, soil erosion undermined the productivity of their tropical soils.

Although we live in a highly urbanized, technologically advanced society, we are as dependent on the Earth's natural support systems as the Sumerians and

Mayans were. If we continue with business as usual, civilizational collapse is no longer a matter of whether but when. We now have an economy that is destroying its natural support systems, one that has put us on a decline and collapse path. We are dangerously close to the edge. Peter Goldmark, former Rockefeller Foundation president, puts it well: 'The death of our civilization is no longer a theory or an academic possibility; it is the road we're on.'[17]

Judging by the archaeological records of earlier civilizations, more often than not food shortages appear to have precipitated their decline and collapse. Given the advances of modern agriculture, I had long rejected the idea that food could be the weak link in our 21st-century civilization. Today I think not only that it could be the weak link but that it is the weak link.[18]

The reality of our situation may soon become clearer for mainstream economists as we begin to see some of the early economic effects of overconsuming the Earth's resources, such as rising world food prices. We got a preview when, as world grain demand raced ahead and as supplies tightened in early 2007, the prices of wheat, rice, corn, and soybeans began to climb, tripling historical levels by the spring of 2008. Only the worst global economic downturn since the Great Depression, combined with a record world grain harvest in 2008, managed to check the rise in grain prices, at least for the time being. Since 2008, world market prices have receded somewhat, but as of October 2010, following the disastrous Russian grain harvest; they were still nearly double historical levels and rising.[19]

On the social front, the most disturbing trend is spreading hunger. For the last century's closing decades, the number of chronically hungry and malnourished people worldwide was shrinking, dropping to a low of 788 million by 1996. Then it began to rise – slowly at first, and then more rapidly – as the massive diversion of grain to produce fuel for cars doubled the annual growth in grain consumption. In 2008, it passed 900 million. By 2009, there were more than a billion hungry and malnourished people. The UN Food and Agriculture Organization anticipated a decline in the number of hungry people in 2010, but the Russian heat wave and the subsequent climb in grain prices may have ended that hope.[20]

This expansion in the ranks of the hungry is disturbing not only in humanitarian terms but also because spreading hunger preceded collapse for so many of the earlier civilizations whose archaeological sites we now study. If we use spreading hunger as an indicator of the decline that precedes social collapse for our global civilization, then it began more than a decade ago.[21]

As environmental degradation and economic and social stresses mount, the more fragile governments are having difficulty managing them. And as rapid population growth continues, cropland becomes scarce, wells go dry, forests disappear, soils erode, unemployment rises, and hunger spreads. In this situation, weaker governments become failing states – countries whose governments can no longer provide personal security, food security, or basic social services, such as education and healthcare. The term 'failing state' has only recently become part of our working vocabulary. As the list of failing states grows longer each year, it raises a disturbing question: How many states must fail before our global civilization begins to unravel?[22]

How much longer can we remain in the decline phase, whether measured in natural asset liquidation, spreading hunger, or failing states, before our global civilization begins to break down? Even as we wrestle with the issues of resource scarcity, world population is continuing to grow. Tonight there will be 219,000 people at the dinner table who were not there last night, many of them with empty plates.[23]

If we continue with business as usual, how much time do we have before we see serious breakdowns in the global economy? The answer is, we do not know, because we have not been here before. But if we stay with business as usual, the time is more likely measured in years than in decades. We are now so close to the edge that it could come at any time.

Food price stability now depends on a record or near-record world grain harvest every year. And climate change is not the only threat to food security. Spreading water shortages are also a huge, and perhaps even more imminent, threat to food security and political stability. Water-based 'food bubbles' that artificially inflate grain production by depleting aquifers are starting to burst, and as they do, irrigation-based harvests are shrinking. The first food bubble to burst is in Saudi Arabia, where the depletion of its fossil aquifer is virtually eliminating its 3-million-ton wheat harvest. And there are at least another 17 countries with food bubbles based on overpumping.[24]

If world irrigation water use has peaked, or is about to, we are entering an era of intense competition for water resources. Expanding world food production fast enough to avoid future price rises will be much more difficult. A global civilization that adds 80 million people each year, even as its irrigation water supply is shrinking, could be in trouble.[25]

Further complicating our future, the world may be reaching peak water at more or less the same time that it hits peak oil. Fatih Birol, chief economist with the

International Energy Agency, has said, 'We should leave oil before it leaves us.' I agree. If we can phase out the use of oil quickly enough to stabilize climate, it will also facilitate an orderly, managed transition to a carbon-free renewable energy economy. Otherwise we face intensifying competition among countries for dwindling oil supplies and continued vulnerability to soaring oil prices. And with our recently developed capacity to convert grain into oil (that is, ethanol), the price of grain is now tied to that of oil. Rising oil prices mean rising food prices.[26]

Once the world reaches peak oil and peak water, continuing population growth would mean a rapid drop in the per capita supply of both. And since both are central to food production, the effects on the food supply could leave many countries with potentially unmanageable stresses. And these are in addition to the threats posed by increasing climate volatility. As William Hague, Britain's current Foreign Secretary and a former leader of the Conservative party, says, 'You cannot have food, water, or energy security without climate security.'[27]

Among other things, the situation in which we find ourselves pushes us to redefine security in 21st-century terms. The time when military forces were the prime threat to security has faded into the past. We are facing issues of near-overwhelming complexity and unprecedented urgency. Can we think systemically and fashion policies accordingly? Can we move fast enough to avoid economic decline and collapse? Can we change direction before we go over the edge?

We are in a race between natural and political tipping points, but we do not know exactly where nature's tipping points are. Nature determines these. Nature is the timekeeper, but we cannot see the clock.

The notion that our civilization is approaching its demise if we continue with business as usual is not an easy concept to grasp or accept. It is difficult to imagine something we have not previously experienced. We hardly have even the vocabulary, much less the experience, to discuss this prospect.

Since it is the destruction of the economy's natural supports and disruption of the climate system that are driving the world toward the edge, these are the trends that must be reversed. To do so requires extraordinarily demanding measures, a fast shift away from business as usual to what we at the Earth Policy Institute call Plan B (see Table I.1.1).

With a scale and urgency similar to the US mobilization for the Second World War, Plan B has four components: a massive cut in global carbon emissions of 80% by 2020; the stabilization of world population at no more than 8 billion by 2040; the eradication of poverty; and the restoration of forests, soils, aquifers, and fisheries.

Carbon emissions can be cut by systematically raising world energy efficiency, by restructuring transport systems, and by shifting from burning fossil fuels to tapping the Earth's wealth of wind, solar, and geothermal energy. The transition from fossil fuels to renewable sources of energy can be driven primarily by tax restructuring – steadily lowering income taxes and offsetting this reduction with a rise in the tax on carbon.

Two of the components of Plan B – stabilizing population and eradicating poverty – go hand in hand, reinforcing each other. This involves ensuring at least a primary school education for all children – girls as well as boys. It also means providing at least rudimentary village-level healthcare so that parents can be more confident that their children will survive to adulthood. And women everywhere need access to reproductive healthcare and family planning services.

The fourth component, restoring the Earth's natural systems and resources, involves, for example, a worldwide initiative to arrest the fall in water tables by raising water productivity. That implies shifting both to more-efficient irrigation systems and to more water-efficient crops. And for industries and cities, it implies doing worldwide what some are already doing – namely, continuously recycling water.

The situation the world faces now is even more urgent than the economic crisis of 2008 and 2009. Instead of a housing bubble, it is food bubbles based on overpumping and overploughing that cloud our future. Such food uncertainties are amplified by climate volatility and by more extreme weather events. Our challenge is not just to implement Plan B, but to do it quickly so we can move off the environmental decline path before the clock runs out.

One thing is certain – we are facing greater change than any generation in history. What is not clear is the source of this change. Will we stay with business as usual and enter a period of economic decline and spreading chaos? Or will we quickly reorder priorities, acting at wartime speed to move the world onto an economic path that can sustain civilization?

SAVING CIVILIZATION

We need an economy for the 21st century, one that is in sync with the Earth and its natural support systems, not one that is destroying them. The key to restructuring the economy is to get the market to tell the truth through full-cost pricing. If the world is to move onto a sustainable path, we need economists who will calculate indirect costs and work with political leaders to incorporate them into market prices by restructuring taxes. This will require help from other disciplines, including ecology, meteorology, agronomy, hydrology, and demography. Full-cost pricing that will create an honest market is essential to building an economy that can sustain civilization and progress.

If we can get the market to tell the truth, to have market prices that reflect the full cost of burning gasoline or coal, of deforestation, of overpumping aquifers, and of overfishing, then we can begin to create a rational economy. If we can create an honest market, then market forces will rapidly restructure the world energy economy. Phasing in full-cost pricing will quickly reduce oil and coal use. Suddenly wind, solar, and geothermal power will become much cheaper than climate-disrupting fossil fuels.

We are economic decision makers, whether as corporate planners, government policymakers, investment bankers, or consumers. And we rely on the market for price signals to guide our behaviour. But if the market gives us bad information, we make bad decisions, and that is exactly what has been happening.

We are being blindsided by a faulty accounting system, one that will lead to bankruptcy. As Øystein Dahle, former Vice President of Exxon for Norway and the North Sea, has observed: 'Socialism collapsed because it did not allow the market to tell the economic truth. Capitalism may collapse because it does not allow the market to tell the ecological truth.'[28]

If we leave costs off the books, we risk bankruptcy. Another major flaw in our market economy is that it neither recognizes nor respects sustainable yield limits of natural systems. Not only do we distort reality when we omit costs associated with burning fossil fuels from their prices, but governments actually subsidize their use, distorting reality even further. Worldwide, subsidies that encourage the production and use of fossil fuels add up to roughly $500 billion per year, compared with less than $50 billion for renewable energy, including wind, solar, and biofuels. In 2009, fossil fuel consumption subsidies included $147 billion for oil, $134 billion for natural gas, and $31 billion for coal. Governments are shelling out nearly $1.4 billion per day to further destabilize the Earth's climate.[29]

Carbon emissions could be cut in scores of countries by simply eliminating fossil fuel subsidies. Some countries are already doing this. Belgium, France, and Japan have phased out all subsidies for coal. Countries in the European Union may phase out coal subsidies entirely by 2014. President Obama has announced plans to start phasing out fossil fuel subsidies in 2011. As oil prices have climbed, a number of countries that held fuel prices well below world market prices have greatly reduced or eliminated their motor fuel subsidies because of the heavy fiscal cost. Among those reducing subsidies are China, Indonesia, and Nigeria.[30]

A world facing economically disruptive climate change can no longer justify subsidies to expand the burning of coal and oil. Shifting subsidies to the development of climate-benign energy sources such as wind, solar, and geothermal power will help stabilize the Earth's climate. Moving subsidies from road construction to high-speed intercity rail construction could increase mobility, reduce travel costs, and lower carbon emissions.

Closely related to the need to restructure the economy is the need to redefine security. One of our legacies from the last century, which was dominated by two world wars and the cold war, is a sense of security that is defined almost exclusively in military terms. Douglas Alexander, former UK Secretary of State for International Development, put it well in 2007: 'In the 20th century a country's might was too often measured in what they could destroy. In the 21st century strength should be measured by what we can build together.'[31]

Although security is starting to be redefined in a conceptual sense, we have not redefined it in fiscal terms. The United States still has a huge military budget, committed to developing and manufacturing technologically sophisticated and costly weapon systems.

Given the enormity of the antiquated military budget, no one can argue that we do not have the resources to rescue civilization. The far-flung US military establishment, including hundreds of military bases scattered around the world, will not save civilization. It belongs to another era. We can most effectively achieve our security goals by helping to expand food production, by filling the family planning gap, by building wind farms and solar power plants, and by building schools and clinics.[32]

The restructuring of the energy economy will not only dramatically drop carbon emissions, helping to stabilize climate, it will also eliminate much of the air pollution that we know today. The idea of a pollution-free environment is difficult for us even to imagine, simply because none of us has ever known an energy economy that was not highly polluting. Working in coal mines will be history. Black lung disease will eventually disappear. So too will 'code red' alerts warning us to avoid strenuous exercise because of dangerous levels of air pollution.

The new energy sources are inexhaustible. While

wind turbines, solar cells, and solar thermal systems will all need repair and occasional replacement, investing in these new energy sources means investing in energy systems that can last forever. These wells will not go dry. Although some of the prospects look good for moving away, timing is key.

Similarly, can we eradicate poverty and fill the family planning gap fast enough to help countries escape the demographic trap? Can we halt the growth in the number of failing states before our global civilization begins to unravel?

The overarching question is: Can we change fast enough? When thinking about the enormous need for social change as we attempt to move the world economy onto a sustainable path, I find it useful to look at three models of social change. One is the Pearl Harbor model, where a dramatic event fundamentally changed how Americans thought and behaved. The second model is one where a society reaches a tipping point on a particular issue, often after an extended period of gradual change in thinking and attitudes. This I call the Berlin Wall model. The third is the sandwich model of social change, where there is a dedicated grassroots movement pushing for change that is strongly supported by political leadership.

When scientists are asked to identify a possible 'Pearl Harbor' scenario on the climate front, they frequently point to the possible breakup of the West Antarctic ice sheet. Sizable blocks of it have been breaking off for more than a decade already, but far larger blocks could break off, sliding into the ocean. Sea level could rise a frightening two or three feet within a matter of years. Unfortunately, if we reach this point it may be too late to cut carbon emissions fast enough to save the remainder of the West Antarctic ice sheet. By then we might be over the edge.[33]

The Berlin Wall model is of interest because the wall's dismantling in November 1989 was a visual manifestation of a much more fundamental social change. At some point, Eastern Europeans, buoyed by changes in Moscow, had rejected the great 'socialist experiment' with its one-party political system and centrally planned economy. Although it was not anticipated, Eastern Europe had an essentially bloodless revolution, one that changed the form of government in every country in the region. It had reached a tipping point. Many social changes occur when societies reach tipping points or cross key thresholds. Once that happens, change comes rapidly and often unpredictably.

The sandwich model of social change is in many ways the most attractive, largely because of its potential for rapid change. For example, strong steps by the US Envi-

ronmental Protection Agency to enforce existing laws that limit toxic pollutants from coal-fired power plants, for instance, are making coal much less attractive. So too do the regulations on managing coal ash storage and rulings against mountaintop removal. This, combined with the powerful grassroots campaign forcing utilities to seek the least cost option, is spelling the end of coal.[34]

Of the three models of social change, relying on the Pearl Harbor model for change is by far the riskiest, because by the time a society-changing catastrophic event occurs for climate change, it may be too late. The Berlin Wall model works, despite the lack of government support, but it does take time. The ideal situation for rapid, historic progress occurs when mounting grassroots pressure for change merges with a national leadership that is similarly committed.

Whenever I begin to feel overwhelmed by the scale and urgency of the changes we need to make, I reread the economic history of US involvement in the Second World War because it is such an inspiring study in rapid mobilization. In his State of the Union address on 6 January 1942, one month after the bombing of Pearl Harbor, President Franklin D. Roosevelt announced the country's arms production goals. The United States, he said, was planning to produce 45,000 tanks, 60,000 planes, and several thousand ships. He added, 'Let no man say it cannot be done.'[35]

No one had ever seen such huge arms production numbers. Public scepticism abounded. But Roosevelt and his colleagues realized that the world's largest concentration of industrial power was in the US automobile industry. Even during the Depression, the United States was producing three million or more cars a year.[36]

After his State of the Union address, Roosevelt met with auto industry leaders, indicating that the country would rely heavily on them to reach these arms production goals. Initially they expected to continue making cars and simply add on the production of armaments. What they did not yet know was that the sale of new cars would soon be banned. From early February 1942 through the end of 1944, nearly three years, essentially no cars were produced in the United States.[37]

In addition to a ban on the sale of new cars, residential and highway construction was halted, and driving for pleasure was banned. Suddenly people were recycling and planting victory gardens. Strategic goods – including tyres, gasoline, fuel oil, and sugar – were rationed beginning in 1942. Yet 1942 witnessed the greatest expansion of industrial output in the nation's history – all for military use. In retrospect, the speed of this conversion from a peacetime to a wartime economy is stunning.

The point is that it did not take decades to restructure the US industrial economy. It did not take years. It was done in a matter of months. If we could restructure the US industrial economy in months, then we can restructure the world energy economy during this decade.

With numerous US automobile assembly lines currently idle, it would be a relatively simple matter to retool some of them to produce wind turbines (as the Ford Motor Company did in the Second World War with B-24 bombers), helping the world to quickly harness its vast wind energy resources. This would help the world see that the economy can be restructured quickly, profitably, and in a way that enhances global security.[38]

The world now has the technologies and financial resources to stabilize climate, eradicate poverty, stabilize population, restore the economy's natural support systems, and, above all, restore hope.

We can calculate roughly the costs of the changes needed to move our 21st-century civilization off the decline and collapse path and onto a path that will sustain civilization. What we cannot calculate is the cost of not adopting Plan B. How do you put a price tag on social collapse and the massive die-off that it invariably brings?

The external funding needed to eradicate poverty and stabilize population requires an additional expenditure of $75 billion per year. A poverty eradication effort that is not accompanied by an Earth restoration effort is doomed to fail. Protecting topsoil, reforesting the Earth, restoring oceanic fisheries, and other needed measures will cost an estimated $110 billion in additional expenditures per year. Combining both social goals and Earth restoration goals into a Plan B budget yields an additional annual expenditure of $185 billion (see Table I.1.1).

Unfortunately, some countries continue to focus their fiscal resources on building an ever-stronger military, largely ignoring the threats posed by continuing environmental deterioration, poverty, and population growth. US 2009 military expenditures accounted for 43% of the global total of $1,522 billion. Other leading spenders included China ($100 billion), France ($64 billion), the United Kingdom ($58 billion), and Russia ($53 billion).[39]

For less than $200 billion of additional funding per year worldwide, we can get rid of hunger, illiteracy, disease, and poverty, and we can restore the Earth's soils, forests, and fisheries. We can build a global community where the basic needs of all people are satisfied – a world that will allow us to think of ourselves as civilized.

As a general matter, the benchmark of political leadership will be whether leaders succeed in shifting taxes from work to environmentally destructive activities. It is tax shifting, not additional appropriations, that

is the key to restructuring the energy economy in order to stabilize climate.

TABLE I.1.1 Plan B budget: additional annual expenditures needed to meet social goals and restore the Earth	
Goal	Funding (billion dollars)
Basic Social Goals	
Universal primary education	10
Eradication of adult illiteracy	4
School lunch programmes	3
Aid to women, infants, and preschool children	4
Reproductive health and family planning	21
Universal basic healthcare	33
Total	75
Earth Restoration Goals	
Planting trees	23
Protecting topsoil on cropland	24
Restoring rangelands	9
Restoring fisheries	13
Stabilizing water tables	10
Protecting biological diversity	31
Total	110
Grand Total	**185**
US Military Budget	**661**
Plan B budget as share of this	28%
World Military Budget	**1,522**
Plan B budget as share of this	12%
Source: Military from SIPRI; other data at www.earth-policy.org.	

One of the questions I hear most frequently is: What can I do? People often expect me to suggest lifestyle changes, such as recycling newspapers or changing light bulbs. These are essential, but they are not nearly enough. Restructuring the global economy means becoming politically active, working for the needed changes, as the grassroots campaign against coal-fired power plants is doing. Saving civilization is not a spectator sport.

Inform yourself. Read about the issues. Share this information with friends. Pick an issue that's meaningful to you, such as tax restructuring to create an honest market, phasing out coal-fired power plants, or developing a world-class recycling system in your community. Or join a group that is working to provide family planning services to the 215 million women who want to plan their families but lack the means to do so. You might want to organize a small group of like-minded individuals to work on an issue that is of mutual concern. You can begin by talking with others to help select an issue to work on.[40]

Once your group is informed and has a clearly defined goal, ask to meet with your elected representatives on the city council or the state or national legislature. Write or email your elected representatives about the need to restructure taxes and eliminate fossil fuel subsidies. Remind them that leaving environmental costs off the books may offer a sense of prosperity in the short run, but it leads to collapse in the long run.

During the Second World War, the military draft asked millions of young men to risk the ultimate sacrifice. But we are called on only to be politically active and to make lifestyle changes, working together for a common goal. What contributions can we each make today, in time, money, or reduced consumption, to help save civilization?

The choice is ours – yours and mine. We can stay with business as usual and preside over an economy that continues to destroy its natural support systems until it destroys itself, or we can be the generation that changes direction, moving the world onto a path of sustained progress. The choice will be made by our generation, but it will affect life on Earth for all generations to come.

NOTES

1   This article is a synthesis of two chapters from the book *World on the Edge: How to Prevent Environmental and Economic Collapse* written by Lester R. Brown. The book is available at Earth Policy's Website (http://www.earth-policy.org) were readers can find data, end notes and additional resources on the topic.

2   Moscow Temperatures Reach Record Highs," *RIA Novosti* (Moscow), 26 June 2010; Jeff Masters, "Over 15,000 Likely Dead in Russian Heat Wave; Asian Monsoon Floods Kill Hundreds More," *Dr. Jeff Masters' WunderBlog, Weather Underground* HYPERLINK "http://" , at www.wunderground.com/blog/JeffMasters, 9 August 2010; Alexei Anishchuk, "Deadly Russian Heatwave Declared Over," *Reuters*, 18 August 2010; Jeff Masters, "Colin Takes Aim at Bermuda; the Great Russian Heat Wave of 2010: 102°F in Moscow," *Dr. Jeff Masters' WunderBlog, Weather Underground*, at www.wunderground.com/blog/JeffMasters, 6 August 2010; Terence Roth and William Mauldin, "Heat Wave and Drought Shrivel Harvests Across Europe," *Wall Street Journal*, 4 August 2010; "Wildfires Rage on Shrouding Moscow in Blanket of Smog," *The Voice of Russia*, 10 August 2010.

3   Jeff Masters, "Over 15,000 Likely Dead in Russian Heat Wave; Asian Monsoon Floods Kill Hundreds More," *Dr. Jeff Masters' WunderBlog, Weather Underground* HYPERLINK "http://", at www.wunderground.com/blog/JeffMasters, 9 August 2010; Lucian Kim and Maria Levitov, 'Russia Heat Wave May Kill 15,000, Shave $15 Billion of GDP,' *Bloomberg*, 10 August 2010; Anna Smolchenko, 'Fires Cost Russia "300 Billion Dollars" in Deforestation,' *Agence France-Presse*, 26 August 2010; Alfred Kueppers, 'Wildfires Sweeping Russia Kill at Least 25,' *Reuters*, 30 July 2010.

4   Simon Shuster, 'Will Russia's Heat Wave End Its Global-Warming Doubts?' *Time*, 2 August 2010.

5   Humanitarian Communication Group, 'Floods in Pakistan,' fact sheet (Islamabad: United Nations Pakistan, 24 September 2010); Government of Pakistan, National Disaster Management Authority, 'Pakistan Floods,' at www.pakistanfloods.pk, updated 9 October 2010; FAO, *Executive Brief: Pakistan Flooding* (Rome: 5 October 2010); Karin Brulliard, "Livestock Losses Compound Pakistan's Misery," *Washington Post*, 30 August 2010; 'Pakistan Floods "Hit 14m People"' *BBC News*, 6 August 2010.

6   Jeff Masters, 'Asia Records Its Hottest Temperature in History; Category 4 Phet Threatens Oman,' *Dr. Jeff Masters' WunderBlog, Weather Underground*, at www.wunderground.com/blog/JeffMasters, 2 June 2010; Government of Pakistan, Pakistan Meteorological Department, 'Record Breaking Heat in Pakistan,' press release (Islamabad: 26 May 2010); Mason Inman, "Pakistan Flooding Because of Farms?" *National Geographic Daily News*, 16 August 2010; U.N. Food and Agriculture Organization (FAO), *Executive Brief: Pakistan Flooding* (Rome: 10 September 2010); 'Melting Glaciers Main Cause of Floods,' *Associated Press of Pakistan*, 3 August 2010.

7   World Bank, *World Development Report 1992: Development and the Environment* (Washington DC: May 1992), p. 238; U.N. Population Division, *World Population Prospects: The 2008 Revision Population Database*, at esa.un.org/unpp, updated 11 March 2009; UNESCO, *Education for All Global Monitoring Report 2010: Reaching the Marginalized* (Paris: 2010), p. 312.

8   Mathis Wackernagel et al., 'Tracking the Ecological Overshoot of the Human Economy,' *Proceedings of the National Academy of Sciences*, vol. 99, no. 14 (9 July 2002), pp. 9,266–71; Global Footprint Network, WWF, and Zoological Society of London, *Living Planet Report 2010* (Gland, Switzerland: WWF, October 2010).

9   "Summary for Policymakers," in Intergovernmental Panel on Climate Change (IPCC), *Climate Change 2007: The Physical Science Basis. Contribution of Working Group I to the Fourth Assessment Report of the Intergovernmental Panel on Climate Change* (Cambridge, U.K.: Cambridge University Press, 2007), pp. 1–18; Gerald A. Meehl and Claudia Tebaldi, "More Intense, More Frequent, and Longer Lasting Heat Waves in the 21st Century," *Science*, vol. 305 (13 August 2004), pp. 994–97; James B. Elsner, James P. Kossin, and Thomas H. Jagger, "The Increasing Intensity of the Strongest Tropical Cyclones," *Nature*, vol. 455 (4 September 2008) pp. 92–95.

10 I. Velicogna, 'Increasing Rates of Ice Mass Loss from the Greenland and Antarctic Ice Sheets Revealed by GRACE,' *Geophysical Research Letters*, vol. 36 (13 October 2009); U.N. Environment Programme (UNEP), *Global Outlook for Ice and Snow* (Nairobi: 2007), p. 131; Upali A. Amarasinghe et al., *Spatial Variation in Water Supply and Demand Across River Basins of India* (Colombo, Sri Lanka: International Water Management Institute (IWMI), 2005), p. 8; Upali A. Amarasinghe et al., *Water Supply, Water Demand and Agricultural Water Scarcity in China: A Basin Approach* (Colombo, Sri Lanka: IWMI, 2005), p. 10; Lester R. Brown, 'Melting Mountain Glaciers Will Shrink Grain Harvests in China and India,' *Plan B Update* (Washington, DC: Earth Policy Institute, 20 March 2008). See Chapter 4 for a detailed discussion of ice melting and food security.

11 Mathis Wackernagel et al., "Tracking the Ecological

Overshoot of the Human Economy," *Proceedings of the National Academy of Sciences*, vol. 99, no. 14 (9 July 2002), pp. 9,266–71; Global Footprint Network, WWF, and Zoological Society of London, *Living Planet Report 2010* (Gland, Switzerland: WWF, October 2010).

12 Angus Maddison, 'Statistics on World Population, GDP and Per Capita GDP, 1–2008 AD,' at www.ggdc.net/maddison, updated March 2010; Herman E. Daly, 'Economics in a Full World,' *Scientific American*, vol. 293, no. 3 (September 2005), pp. 100–07; Robert Nadeau, 'The Economist Has No Clothes,' *Scientific American*, vol. 298, no. 4 (April 2008), p. 42.

13 World Bank, *Global Economic Prospects: Fiscal Headwinds and Recovery* (Washington, DC: 2010), pp. 1–3; Simon Kennedy, 'Wall Street Sees World Economy Decoupling from U.S.,' *Bloomberg*, 4 October 2010; Deutsche Bank AG, *Outlook 3rd Quarter 2010: Orientation Needed* (Frankfurt: June 2010).

14 Angus Maddison, "Statistics on World Population, GDP and Per Capita GDP, 1–2008 AD," at www.ggdc.net/maddison, updated March 2010.

15 Nicolaus Copernicus, *De Revolutionibus Orbium Coelestium, Libri VI (Six Books on the Revolutions of the Celestial Spheres)* (1543).

16 Sandra Postel, *Pillar of Sand* (New York: W. W. Norton & Company, 1999), pp. 13–21; Guy Gugliotta, 'The Maya: Glory and Ruin,' *National Geographic*, August 2007; Jared Diamond, *Collapse: How Societies Choose to Fail or Succeed* (New York: Penguin Group, 2005); Joseph Tainter, *The Collapse of Complex Societies* (Cambridge, UK: Cambridge University Press, 1988).

17 Peter Goldmark, Environmental Defense Fund, e-mail to author, 28 June 2009.

18 Sandra Postel, *Pillar of Sand* (New York: W. W. Norton & Company, 1999), pp. 13–21; Guy Gugliotta, "The Maya: Glory and Ruin," *National Geographic*, August 2007; Diamond, op. cit. note 16; Joseph Tainter, *The Collapse of Complex Societies* (Cambridge, U.K.: Cambridge University Press, 1988).

19 USDA, *Production, Supply and Distribution*, electronic database, at www.fas.usda.gov/psdonline, updated 10 September 2010; Chicago Board of Trade futures data from TFC Commodity Charts, 'Grain & Oilseed Commodities Futures,' at futures.tradingcharts.com/grains_oilseeds.html, viewed 11 October 2010.

20 FAO, *The State of Food Insecurity in the World 2010* (Rome: 2010), pp. 8–11; FAO, 'Number of Undernourished Persons,' at www.fao.org/economic/ess/food-security-statistics, updated 13 September 2010; USDA, *Production, Supply and Distribution*, op. cit. note 19; USDA, *Feed Grains Database*, electronic database, at www.ers.usda.gov/Data/FeedGrains, updated 1 October 2010.

21 FAO, *The State of Food Insecurity in the World 2010* (Rome: 2010), pp. 8–11.

22 Elizabeth Dickinson, 'Anthropology of an Idea: Dangerous Weakness,' *Foreign Policy*, July/August 2010, p. 21; Fund for Peace and Foreign Policy, "The Failed States Index," *Foreign Policy*, July/August 2010, pp. 74–105.

23 U.N. Population Division, *World Population Prospects: The 2008 Revision Population Database*, at esa.un.org/unpp, updated 11 March 2009.

24 USDA, *Production, Supply and Distribution*, op. cit. note 19; Andrew England, 'Saudis to Phase Out Wheat Production,' *Financial Times*, 10 April 2008. Countries with food bubbles from Table 3–1 in Lester R. Brown, *Plan B*

2.0: Rescuing a Planet Under Stress and a Civilization in Trouble (New York: W. W. Norton & Company, 2006), p. 43; Isam E. Amin et al., 'Major Problems Affecting the Principal Aquifers in Lebanon,' Paper 301-25 in Geological Society of America, *Abstracts with Programs*, vol. 40, no. 6 (2008), p. 471; Dale Lightfoot, *Survey of Infiltration Karez in Northern Iraq: History and Current Status of Underground Aqueducts* (Paris: UNESCO, September 2009); and from 'Afghanistan: Groundwater Overuse Could Cause Severe Water Shortage,' *Integrated Regional Information Networks (IRIN) News*, 14 September 2008.

25 U.N. Population Division, op. cit. note 23.

26 Fatih Birol, 'Outside View: We Can't Cling to Crude: We Should Leave Oil before It Leaves Us,' *Independent* (London), 2 March 2008.

27 Danielle Murray, 'Oil and Food: A Rising Security Challenge,' *Eco-Economy Update* (Washington, DC: Earth Policy Institute, 9 May 2005); 'Energy Use in Agriculture,' in USDA, *U.S. Agriculture and Forestry Greenhouse Gas Inventory: 1990–2001*, Technical Bulletin No. 1907 (Washington, DC: Global Change Program Office, Office of the Chief Economist, 2004), pp. 94–100; William Hague, 'The Diplomacy of Climate Change,' speech to the Council on Foreign Relations, New York City, 27 September 2010.

28 Øystein Dahle, discussion with author, State of the World Conference, Aspen, CO, 22 July 2001.

29 Total fossil fuel subsidies from Global Subsidies Initiative, *Achieving the G-20 Call to Phase Out Subsidies to Fossil Fuels* (Geneva: October 2009), p. 2; renewable energy subsidies from Bloomberg New Energy Finance, 'Subsidies for Renewables, Biofuels Dwarfed by Supports for Fossil Fuels,' press release (London: 29 July 2010); 2009 consumption subsidies from Amos Bromhead, International Energy Agency (IEA), e-mails to and discussion with Alexandra Giese, Earth Policy Institute, 15 and 26 October 2010; IEA, *World Energy Outlook 2010* (Paris: 9 November 2010).

30 Belgium, France, and Japan from Seth Dunn, 'King Coal's Weakening Grip on Power,' *World Watch*, September/October 1999, pp. 10–19; 'EU Seeks to End Coal Subsidies by 2014,' *EUbusiness*, 20 July 2010; Tom Doggett, 'Obama Budget Seeks to End Oil, Gas Subsidies,' *Reuters*, 1 February 2010; US Office of Management and Budget, 'Budget of the U.S. Government, Fiscal Year 2011,' at www.whitehouse.gov/sites/default/files/omb/budget/fy2011/assets/budget.pdf, viewed 4 October 2010; China, Indonesia, and Nigeria subsidy cuts from Gerhard P. Metschies, *International Fuel Prices 2007* (Eschborn, Germany: GTZ Transport Policy Advisory Services, April 2007), p. 3; IEA, *World Energy Outlook 2010* (Paris: 9 November 2010); Philip Sanders, 'Nigeria to End Fuel Subsidies by End of 2011 at the Latest, Aganga Says,' *Bloomberg* (3 September 2010).

31 Patrick Wintour and Julian Borger, 'Brown Message to U.S.: It's Time to Build, Not Destroy,' *Guardian* (London), 13 July 2007.

32 DOD, *Base Structure Report, Fiscal Year 2009 Baseline* (Washington, DC: 2009), pp. 77–94.

33 National Snow and Ice Data Center, 'State of the Cryosphere: Is the Cryosphere Sending Signals about Climate Change?' at nsidc.org/sotc/iceshelves.html, updated 25 February 2010.

34 EPA, 'Civil Enforcement: Coal-Fired Power Plant Enforcement Initiative,' at www.epa.gov/compliance/

resources/cases/civil/caa/coal/index.html, updated 23 July
2010; EPA, *"EPA Announces Plans to Regulate Coal Ash/
Agency Proposals would Address Risks of Unsafe Coal
Ash Disposal, while Supporting Safe Forms of Beneficial
Use,"* press release (Washington, DC: 4 May 2010);
John M. Broder, 'Departments to Toughen Standards for
Mining,' *New York Times*, 11 June 2009; EPA, 'EPA
Issues Comprehensive Guidance to Protect Appalachian
Communities From Harmful Environmental Impacts of
Mountain Top Mining,' press release (Washington, DC:
1 April 2010); Ted Nace, 'Stopping Coal in its Tracks,'
Orion Magazine, January/February 2008; Western
Resource Advocates, 'Clean Energy Accomplishments,' at
www.westernresourceadvocates.org/energy/coal/cleanen-
ergyaccomplishments.php, viewed 15 October 2010.

35 Franklin Roosevelt, "State of the Union Address," 6 January 1942, at www.ibiblio.org/pha/7-2-188/188-35.html.

36 Harold G. Vatter, *The US Economy in World War II*
(New York: Columbia University Press, 1985), p. 13;
Alan L. Gropman, *Mobilizing U.S. Industry in World War
II* (Washington, DC: National Defense University Press,
August 1996).

37 Harold G. Vatter, *The US Economy in World War II*
(New York: Columbia University Press, 1985), p. 13;
Alan L. Gropman, *Mobilizing U.S. Industry in World War
II* (Washington, DC: National Defense University Press,
August 1996).

38 'Despite Dreams, Idle Auto Plants Stay that Way,' *msnbc.
com*, 11 January 2010; David L. Lewis, 'They May Save
Our Honor, Our Hopes – and Our Necks,' *Michigan
History*, September/October 1993; Harry Braun, *The
Phoenix Project: Shifting from Oil to Hydrogen with
Wartime Speed*, prepared for the Renewable Hydrogen
Roundtable, World Resources Institute, Washington, DC,
10–11 April 2003, pp. 3–4.

39 Military spending from Stockholm International Peace
Research Institute (SIPRI), *Military Expenditure Database*, electronic database at www.sipri.org, updated 2010;
foreign assistance and diplomatic spending (including
State Department operations, global health, obligation
to the United Nations, disaster response, agricultural
productivity, democracy promotion, and education) is
from Office of the Director of U.S. Foreign Assistance,
"International Affairs FY 2009 Budget," fact sheet
(Washington, DC: 4 February 2008).

40 Susheela Singh et al., *Adding it Up: The Costs and
Benefits of Investing in Family Planning and Maternal
and Newborn Health* (Guttmacher Institute and UNFPA:
New York, 2009), p. 4.

Further Insights I.1
Higher education in an unsettled century: handmaiden or pathmaker?

Paul D. Raskin

THE PLANETARY PHASE

If we lived in a 'business-as-usual' world of stable social structures and incremental change, limning the long-range outlook for higher education (HE) would be a relatively tractable exercise. It would be enough to identify the driving factors now influencing the evolution of HE institutions, assess the ways such institutions respond, and project these trends over the time horizon of interest. The analysis would yield a rather narrow envelope of future scenarios, all bearing a strong family resemblance to the present.

Instead, we confront a world moving through a period of great turbulence and uncertainty, where unprecedented challenges and intertwined perils leave the fundamental shape of the future open and contested. In these singular times, circuits of almost everything – goods, currency, people, ideas, conflict, pathogens, effluvia – spiral around the planet faster and thicker in a blur of economic, technological, cultural, and environmental change. In binding an increasingly integrated global system, these multiple entanglements

announce a new historical epoch: the Planetary Phase of Civilization (Raskin et al., 2002).

In this emerging reality, pathways for global-scale macrodynamics to impinge on sub-global components proliferate. Climate change alters local hydrology, ecosystems and weather. The worldwide web plugs individuals into an intercontinental pulse, and, penetrating remote villages and outposts, unsettles traditional values and cultures. Supranational mechanisms of governance challenge the prerogatives of sovereign states. Economic globalization drives, and sometimes disrupts, national and regional markets. The global poor, inundated with images of affluence, demand justice and seek access to wealthy countries, while despair and anger feed the globalization of terrorism. Most profoundly, the awareness of being part of an interdependent world system gradually spreads in human consciousness.

The global system and its components shape one another in a complex and reciprocal dance that changes the whole, which in turn changes the parts. This is the dynamic

of transition. Until now, the world could be reasonably approximated as a set of separate, interacting entities – independent states, autonomous ecosystems and distinct cultures. Such partitioning has become inaccurate and misleading. The bromide 'the whole is more than the sum of its parts' takes on fresh and literal meaning: something is fundamentally new on the face of the Earth.

As a planetary socio-ecological system crystallizes, the world-as-a-whole becomes a primary domain of social evolution and environmental transformation, and arena for contending forms of consciousness. The erosion of geographic and cultural boundaries brings people and places into a transboundary space of interaction that engenders new forms of affiliation and conflict. This larger enmeshment does not abolish communities and nations, which endure as vital loci of political and cultural identity. Rather, it forms as an outer encircling, a de facto global place (if not yet a de jure political community), the site of great cultural and political struggles to come.

BRANCHING FUTURES

The civilization we race toward could be very different from the one we leave behind. The road taken will depend in good measure on the way two key unknowns play out in the coming years: the form and intensity assumed by social and environmental crises now germinating, and the collective human choices made along the way in responding to the threats and opportunities of the Planetary Phase (Raskin, 2008). With so much uncertainty, any robust consideration of the outlook for HE institutions must first envision the range of 21st-century worlds they might plausibly inhabit.

Taking a wide panorama on the possibilities, we must transcend gradual evolutionary scenarios to include, as well, transformative development trajectories that track possible ruptures in structural continuity. Trend projections are useful for identifying critical uncertainties and unsustainable trends, but occlude vision and truncate awareness. Dystopian visions face the dire risks of inaction or unwelcome surprise, but foster only a self-fulfilling Zeitgeist of despair and fatalism. Hopeful scenarios of fundamental shifts toward a just and sustainability civilization, though they may seem improbable, in fact serve to expand the terrain of the possible by stimulating the imagination and social discourse.

Picture, then, three broad channels radiating into the imagined future: worlds of incremental adjustment, worlds of catastrophic discontinuity, and worlds of progressive transformation. We refer to this archetypal triad – evolution, decline, and progression – as *Conventional Worlds*, *Barbarization*, and *Great Transitions*.[1]

In *Conventional Worlds*, the prevailing dynamics of globalization persist in the forthcoming decades. Episodic setbacks notwithstanding, economic interdependence deepens as developing countries converge toward rich-country cultural norms and patterns of production and consumption. In the *Market Forces* variant, powerful global actors advance the priority of free markets, relying heavily on price signals and spontaneous innovation to reconcile economic growth with ecological limits. In the *Policy Reform* variant, governments are able to establish a globally coordinated portfolio of sustainability initiatives to reverse environmental degradation and dampen social friction.

Barbarization scenarios explore the real risk of the market and policy adjustments assumed in *Conventional Worlds* being overwhelmed by deepening environmental and social stress. As a general crisis mounts and civilized norms erode, world development takes a venal turn. In the *Fortress Worlds* variant, a powerful international coalition acts to impose an authoritarian world order: elites retreat to protected enclaves with an impoverished majority outside. In *Breakdown* versions, chaos spirals out of control and institutions collapse.

Great Transition scenarios, the central focus of this inquiry, also assume the inadequacy of *Conventional Worlds* solutions, but envision instead the eventual emergence of a development paradigm rooted in revised values and restructured institutions consonant with the opportunities of the Planetary Phase. In these narratives, deepening planetary interdependence fosters a corresponding enlargement of consciousness – global citizenship, humanity's place in the wider community of life, and the well-being of future generations. The ascendant sensibility of cosmopolitanism, quality of life, and respect for nature displace the modernist value triad of individualism, materialism, and domination. Effective and democratic global governance structures balance pluralism and unity in a cooperative search for a sustainable and humanistic civilization.

The world today, an admixture of all these contradictory tendencies, faces a branching web of possibilities. All our scenarios are problematic. Muddling forward in *Market Forces* mode, we risk crossing critical thresholds of socio-ecological instability. The predicate of *Policy Reform* – sustained, globally coordinated political will for sustainability and poverty alleviation – is nowhere in sight, undermined by myopic national agendas and public attitudes. Establishing the authoritarian world order of a *Fortress World* would require a coherent response of elite institutions in the face of chaos and resistance, while *Breakdown* would enact on a global stage the wholesale collapse visited upon regional civilizations of the past. The alternative to all these scenarios, the deep transformation of *Great Transitions*, would take a vast cultural

and political rising of global citizens, a development far from guaranteed.

HE PROGNOSIS DUBIOUS

Each tale of the global future weaves corresponding subplots for places and groups. The unfolding Planetary Phase moulds all within its realm, as people and institutions, in turn, influence the overarching story. As a significant protagonist in this unscripted drama, HE will influence the outcome, either passively, by adapting to and reinforcing its dominant themes, or actively, by moving to centre stage with vision and commitment to help shape the narrative arc (Escrigas and Lobera, 2009).

The previous 'great transformation' from the feudal to the modern era offers an instructive antecedent (Polanyi, 1944). Modernity churned all the old social institutions and reconstituted them in a form coherent with the imperatives of the ascendant order. The university, of course, was no exception, though its hierarchical and rigid medieval structures long resisted change. By the 19th century, though, more flexible institutions were established, attuned to the democratic and entrepreneurial impulses of the time. Educational purpose shifted from training the few in the received arts of law, theology, and medicine to a mission more consonant with the rising industrial order: training the many for a rapidly changing economy, conducting basic research, and promoting innovation (Altbach, 2008).

Suitably transformed, HE institutions became essential for the continued spread and deepening of the project of modernity over the past two centuries. In the *Market Forces* scenario, this role would persist (so long as the scenario itself remained viable), as HE would continue to struggle to accommodate its practices to the exigencies of deregulation, privatization and corporate-driven globalization (Slaughter and Rhoades, 2004; Nayyar, 2008). In this context, emphasis would further shift from the classical liberal arts education to applied science, business and economics. General research funding would face more stringent cost-effectiveness tests, while applied research would centre on commercially viable technological innovation and market-based social policies. Persistent budget gaps, as increasing student enrolment demand outpaces stagnant public funding, would reinforce trends toward entrepreneurial research and career-oriented curricula. Many conventional HE institutions with untenable business models would perish, while the market share of a new breed of for-profit training companies would expand.

The intensive governmental sustainability efforts in *Policy Reform* alter this picture in significant ways. Basic research would tilt toward ascendant pursuits matched to the complexity and uncertainty of the challenge, such as integrated modelling, ecological economics, and global change science. Applied research would highlight appropriate technology, ecosystem restoration, poverty alleviation, industrial ecology, and negotiations, diplomacy, and institutions for governing an interdependent world. As career opportunities proliferated, universities would respond with new curricula to prepare a growing cadre of sustainability professionals. In this scenario, the impact on HE of the 'sustainability race' could well rival that of the Space Race a half century ago.

By contrast, were a systemic global crisis to usher in an age of *Barbarization*, darkness would descend across HE, as well. In a *Fortress World*, elite universities would no doubt endure, reinventing themselves as citadels of privilege, not socially remote medieval ivory towers, but relevant agents of a repressive order. The logic of survival would dictate harsh suppression of surviving pockets of resistance from within these institutions. In many ways, the heart of the humanistic tradition and democratic mission of HE would be sacrificed on the altar of expediency. If this polarized world were swept toward the chaos of *Breakdown*, remnants of desiccated HE might survive, refugia where the long march back to civilization might begin anew.

In all these contrasting stories, HE serves as a dependent variable in the calculus of the future. Carried along by tides of change, it adapts to altered conditions – good, bad, and ugly – assuming the coloration of the dominant social formation and adjusting its internal logic to prevailing rationality. By contrast, the very plausibility of *Great Transitions* depends to a significant degree on whether HE assumes a forceful and proactive role in advancing the necessary shift in culture and knowledge.

TRANSITION POSSIBLE

Visualizing a culture of expanded solidarity emerging from our world, racked by conflict and blinded by denial, stretches the critical imagination. Still, as the Planetary Phase interconnects people and biosphere in a single community of fate, it nurtures worldviews more cosmopolitan and ecological, at least in a growing subculture. The age-old dream of an organic planetary civilization has become, for the first time, anchored in the objective conditions of history. The globalizing human project becomes the locus of common dangers and nascent dreams. Indeed, the integral Earth grounds the imagined global community more firmly than the arbitrary boundaries of imagined national communities.

Supranational awareness and commitment promise to rise further in the times ahead, but at what pace and to what degree? Can planetary consciousness and a global polity develop fast and broad enough to deflect a world system now rumbling with great momentum down a dangerous path? Social observers have long noted that changes in the hard culture of the techno-economy tend to outpace adjustments in the soft culture of values and behaviours (Ogburn, 1922). Old ways of thinking and acting have always clung like 'a nightmare on the brains of the living', to borrow Marx's memorable phrase.

The disjuncture of hard and soft culture today has widened to an unstable chasm between 21st-century conditions and 21st-century mindsets. As old ideas lose their efficacy and sway, the opportunity opens for rapid and fundamental change in ways of thinking and organizing society. Yet, the major actors now dominating the world stage – intergovernmental bodies, transnational corporations, and global civil society – are problematic for the task of aligning cultures and institutions with the desiderata of global sustainability and justice. State-centric geopolitics enfeebles the United Nations system. Myopic corporate and financial institutions advance interests at odds with the long-term common good. Civil society activism, enfeebled by fragmented politics and lack of a shared vision, can at best moderate the worst trepidations of the *Market Forces* juggernaut.

A vast, coherent movement of engaged global citizens, the only social force argu-

ably matched to the scale and complexity of a *Great Transition*, remains latent in the global field (Raskin, 2009). Global citizenship carries affective, as well as institutional meanings. People become global citizens to the degree their concerns and identity extend to the human family and the biosphere. This enlarged sense of moral and political community is spreading among a growing band of 'citizen pilgrims' (Falk, 1992). Ultimately, however, the full manifestation of global citizenship awaits the formation of effective institutions of democratic global governance.

Still, the precursors of a historically consequential 'global citizens movement' are ubiquitous: in the ongoing actions of countless civic groups working for sustainability, justice, and peace; in the transnational communities fostered by information technology; in the deepening scientific understanding of the dynamics of the Earth system; and in the awareness of interdependence that spreads with each new crisis that ripples across the globe. If the global citizens movement may be ready to be born, then seeking to give it life stands as both opportunity and responsibility for all concerned with the quality of the future.

In this quest, HE has a leading role in the domains of *education, understanding,* and *action*. The educational mission embraced by a university attuned to the needs of transition would centre on the cultivation of informed and thoughtful global citizens. Its core undergraduate curricula doubtless would include transdisciplinary study of interacting and co-evolving social and ecological systems, placing unfolding planetary challenges and visions in a holistic, historical context. New graduate programmes would prepare a new generation of sustainability professionals for understanding and managing complex socio-ecological systems.

Correspondingly, research and scholarship would highlight building the knowledge foundations for the transition, in particular, integrated assessment of global dynamics, cultural change, and institutional design. The transition to modernity brought a powerful scientific revolution rooted in reductionist epistemology and mechanistic models, and with it compartmental disciplines and an approach to knowledge based on analysis and deconstruction of complex systems. *Great Transitions* promises an equally significant intellectual adventure toward more integrative modes of understanding, of complex, nested systems that display emergent characteristics irreducible to the properties of subsystems (Schellnhuber et al., 2004). In these scenarios, emphasis shifts to the *systemic* (considering whole structures, reciprocal interactions, and cross-scale influences), *synthetic* (integrating biophysical, sociocultural, and ideational dimensions), *prospective* (taking a long view to capture delayed processes, deep uncertainties, and emerging developments), and *dynamic* (highlighting transformational shifts, co-evolution, and novel structures).

In addition to revising the way it pursues the core purposes of education and research, HE can advance the transition through its interactions with society. One channel is through a commitment to raise public awareness and debate on a new development paradigm that highlights interdependence, the quality of life, and respect for the environment. Another is to advise governments on policies that flow from an integrated and long-range perspective. More indirect, but no less important, would be making universities centres of cosmopolitan ferment, both cultural and political, for a just and sustainable future. Such a unified agenda of education, research, and action would go a long way toward resolving the debate about the purpose of education between advocates of 'excellence' and 'relevance' that first raged in the 1960s (Toulmin, 1990). The soaring intellectual challenge of creating knowledge, pedagogy, and engagement for the transition would align the twin desiderata of advancing cutting-edge scholarship and human good.

With the winds of historical change blowing hard at our backs, the time of choice has arrived. HE can be borne compliantly to its dubious fate or act with foresight to renew itself and society for the planetary age. On the journey into a portentous future, the mere passenger's passive question – Where we are going? – lacks substance and purpose, for no pilot or navigator stands ready to answer. Rather, with urgency and determination, let us pose the traveller's questions of vision and engagement: Where do we want to go? How do we get there? The very meaning of the humanistic university in this unsettled century hangs on the answers.

REFERENCES

Altbach, P. (2008) The complex roles of universities in the period of globalization. In: GUNi (ed.) *Higher Education in the World 3*. New York: Palgrave Macmillan.

Escrigas, C. and Lobera, J. (2009) New dynamics for social responsibility. In: GUNi (ed.) *Higher Education at a Time of Transformation*. New York: Palgrave Macmillan.

Falk, R. (1992) *Explorations at the Edge of Time: The Prospects for World Order*. Philadelphia, PA: Temple University Press.

Nayyar, D. (2008) Globalization and markets: Challenges for higher education. In: GUNi (ed.) *Higher Education in the World 3*. New York: Palgrave Macmillan.

Ogburn, W. (1922) *Social Change*. New York: Viking.

Polanyi, K. (1944) *The Great Transformation: The Political and Economic Origins of our Time*. Boston, MA: Beacon Press.

Raskin, P. (2009) Planetary praxis: On rhyming hope and history. In: Kellert, S. and Speth, J. (eds) *The Coming Transformation*. New Haven, CT: Yale School of Forestry and Environmental Studies. Available on line at http://www.tellus.org/publications/files/Planetary_Praxis.pdf

Raskin, P. (2008) World lines: A framework for exploring global pathways. *Ecological Economics*, **65**: 451–70.

Raskin, P., Banuri, T., Gallopín, G., Gutman, P., Hammond, A., Kates, R. and Swart, R. (2002) *Great Transition: The Promise and the Lure of the Times Ahead*. Boston, MA: Tellus Institute. Available on line at http://www.gtinitiative.org/documents/Great_Transitions.pdf

Schellnhuber, H.J., Crutzen, P.J., Clark, W.C., Claussen, M. and Held, H. (eds) (2004) *Earth System Analysis for Sustainability*. Cambridge, MA: MIT Press.

Slaughter, S. and Rhoades, G. (2004) *Academic Capitalism and the New Economy: Markets, State, and Higher Education*. Baltimore, DE: Johns Hopkins University Press.

Toulmin, S. (1990) *Cosmopolis. The Hidden Agenda of Modernity*. Chicago, IL: University of Chicago Press.

NOTE

1 For details, see the literature gathered at www.GTInitiative.org, the website of the Great Transition Initiative, an international network of scholars and activists.

Human Development Rank
- 0 - 30
- 31 - 71
- 72 - 109
- 110 - 146
- 147 - 182

CO2 Emissions
- 0% - 0.3%
- 0.3% - 0.8%
- 0.8% - 1.6%
- 1.6% - 3.2%
- 3.2% - 5.3%

Notes:
This map shows the relation between the HDI rank and the CO_2 emission per country. Classification method: natural breaks (Jenks optimization)

Sources: UNDP, *Human Development Report 2010*. The Real Wealth of Nations: Pathways to Human Development.
Available at: http://hdrstats.undp.org/en/tables/default.html

MAP 3 HDI and CO_2 emissions

IEA Statistics (2010) Co 2 Emissions from Fuel Combustion. Highlights.
OECD: Paris
Vector layer source: ESRI Data; Projection: Robinson

I.2
HIGHER EDUCATION FOR SUSTAINABILITY: A GLOBAL OVERVIEW OF COMMITMENT AND PROGRESS

Daniella Tilbury

PREAMBLE

Higher education (HE) is uniquely placed to play a leading role in the attainment of sustainable development (SD). This catalyst potential needs grounding, however, in a context where universities and colleges are currently seen as contributing to the sustainability crisis.

Sustainability challenges the current paradigms and structures as well as predominant practices in HE. This is a consistent message found throughout the literature. Universities and colleges are facing this reality as they seek to meaningfully contribute to sustainability. The paper argues that this requires going beyond the integration of key ideas in existing curricula, the commissioning of a new sustainable building or supporting the sustainability action projects which often occur at the fringes of the institution. Instead, the sustainability journey engages universities and colleges in a quest for interdisciplinarity, participatory pedagogies, 'real world' research and the opening of institutional boundaries so that the notion of sustainable communities is extended beyond university and college walls. The paper proposes that a systemic or connected view of sustainability across institutions is required to transform the educational experience of students and lead social change for sustainability.

Through mapping the international declarations and frameworks for HE, this paper confirms the, in principle, commitment of universities and colleges to transform the HE experience towards sustainability. The paper then contrasts these public intentions with a review of global and regional progress in the areas of leadership and strategy; modelling practice; education and learning; partnerships and outreach for sustainability in HE. It suggests that achievements have been random and mostly disconnected from the core business of HE. The paper concludes that if the HE sector is to be transformative, it needs to transform itself. This will be a lengthy and ambitious process, which will require strong leadership but also time.

INTRODUCTION

A history of HE reveals that universities and colleges have been at the forefront of creating as well as deconstructing paradigms. They have led social change through scientific breakthroughs but also through the education of intellectuals, leaders and future-makers (Cortese, 2003; Elton, 2003; Lozano, 2006; Tilbury et al., 2005b). Professor Lord Stern of Brentford, an opinion leader in climate change, connects these important roles to addressing sustainability challenges of our day. Higher education, he argues, can change the world through training and expanding young minds; researching answers to challenges and informing public policy; showing its own understanding and commitment through careful campus management; and by being a responsible employer and active member of the business and local communities (Stern, 2010). In an era of globalization, universities and colleges also have an impact through their global procurement and offshore partnerships as well as through the education of national and international students. Their potential influence not only on economic development and poverty alleviation but also on health and community building should not be overlooked (Boks and Diehl, 2006; Galang, 2010; Lotz-Sisitka, 2011).

This catalyst potential needs grounding, however, in a context where universities and colleges are currently seen as contributing to the sustainability crisis and reproducing the paradigms that underpin our exploitative relationships with people and environment (Huisingh and Mebratu, 2000; Barab and Luehmann, 2003; Mochizuki and Fadeeva, 2008; Sanusi and Khelgat-Doost, 2008).

The literature argues that sustainability challenges the current paradigms, structures as well as predominant practices, across social sectors including HE (Sterling, 1996; Calder and Clugston, 2003; Lozano, 2007). It is therefore not surprising to discover that universities and colleges that have committed to sustainability are struggling to meaningfully contribute to it (Lozano et al., 2010; Su and Chang, 2010; Huisingh and Mebratu, 2000).

In practice, it is relatively simple to initiate projects that address key sustainability issues but these tend to engage minority groups, failing to reach the core of staff, students and stakeholders or indeed influence the culture of the institutions. Equally the commissioning of a new sustainable building or development of a specialist course in the area is providing some opportunity to shape minds and practices but attempts to mainstream this agenda across HE have so far failed to have impact. To make sense of this challenge, one needs to appreciate that sustainability is more a journey than a checklist as worldviews pervading thinking and practice need to be questioned. It engages universities and colleges in a quest for interdisciplinarity, participatory pedagogies and 'real world' research as well as the opening of institutional boundaries so that the notion of sustainable communities is extended beyond university and college walls. The difficulty is that these need to occur in a connected way. The systemic complexity of this agenda challenges university silos, corridors of power as well as the criteria and processes of decision-making. Furthermore, sustainability is underpinned by democratic and participatory processes of change and by cross-departmental (and faculty) teaching and research, as well as by a redefinition of teacher–student, leader–employee and academia–community relationships. In other words, the transformation of a university towards SD requires a realignment of all its activities with a critically reflective paradigm that also supports the construction of more sustainable futures.

SUSTAINABILITY MOVEMENTS AND MILESTONES IN HIGHER EDUCATION

A review of the sustainability movements and milestones in HE is needed to understand the current expectations on, and challenges to, HE. The journey began in the early 1970s with the Stockholm Conference on the Human Environment (1972) being the first to formally identify the role of HE in progressing sustainable development at the international level. This was followed by the Belgrade Charter (1975), the Tbilisi Declaration (1977) and the United Nations Conference on Environment and Development (1992) all acknowledging the importance of education and higher education in progressing this agenda. More significant, however, were the signing of international declarations by university leaders, higher education associations and government ministers committing to

a step change towards sustainability. These documents call for universities and colleges to operate ethically and be more accountable to their stakeholders. They argue for better environmental and carbon management on campuses; the training of employees; the reorientation of the curriculum towards education for sustainable development (ESD); and a greater contribution to social agendas through research and public engagement. The details and significance of these declarations are mapped in Table I.2.1.

While these international declarations provide visible commitment to encourage progress, they are not sufficient to change institutional and disciplinary practices in HE (Bekessy et al., 2007). The review below indicates that it is government support combined with the reach of international partnerships (such as the International Association of Universities, the Global Higher Education for Sustainability Partnerships, the Pacific Network of Island Universities, the Copernicus Alliance and Global University Network for Innovation) that are playing a critical role in promoting the innovation needed to reorient HE towards sustainability.

STEPS FORWARD

It has been twenty years since the HE sector first committed to innovating for sustainability. The key question now becomes: what progress has there been and how can is it evidenced? This section of the paper reviews international and regional progress in the areas of leadership and strategy; modelling practice; education and learning; partnerships and outreach for sustainability in HE in an attempt to begin to address this question.

MODELLING PRACTICE ACROSS CAMPUSES

The majority of the universities engaged with sustainability are preoccupied with the greening of the campus. The evidence for this can be found within research papers published in HE journals but also across institutional webpages which document extensive sustainability efforts to minimize waste and energy consumption; develop low carbon buildings; protect biodiversity and natural space; source sustainable goods and services; and model sustainability to influence behaviours of staff, students and local communities.

The *Greening the Campus* movement can be traced back to North America where HE has taken green strides in demonstrating sustainability in practice within the management and administration of university sites (see Wright and Elliott, 2011). US and

TABLE I.2.1
Key international declarations

Year	Declaration/Charter	Partners(s) Involved	Scope	Key Words
1990	Talloires Declaration	University Leaders for a Sustainable Future	Global	Unprecedented scale and speed of pollution and degradation Major roles: education, research, policy, information exchange Reverse the trends
1991	Halifax Declaration	Consortium of Canadian Institutions; IAU; UNU	Global	Responsibility to shape their present and future development; Ethical obligation; Overcome root causes
1993	Kyoto Declaration on Sustainable Development	IAU	Global	Better communication of the what and why of SD; Teaching and research capacity; Operations to reflect best SD practice
1993	Swansea Declaration	Association of Australian Government Universities	Global	Educational, research and public service roles; Major attitudinal and policy changes
1994	COPERNICUS University Charter for Sustainable Development	Association of European Universities	Regional (Europe)	Institutional commitment; Environmental ethics and attitudes; Education of university employees; Programmes in environmental education; Interdisciplinarity; Dissemination of knowledge; Networking; Partnerships; Continuing education programmes; Technology transfer
2001	Lüneburg Declaration	Global Higher Education for Sustainability Partnership	Global	Indispensable role; Catalyst for SD building a learning society; Generate new knowledge to train leaders and teachers of tomorrow; Disseminate SD knowledge; State of the art knowledge; Continually review and update curricula; Serve teachers; Lifelong learners
2002	Unbuntu Declaration	UNU, UNESCO, IAU, Third World Academy of Science, African Academy of Sciences and the Science Council of Asia, COPERNICUS-CAMPUS, Global Higher Education for Sustainability Partnership and University Leaders for Sustainable Future	Global	Called for the creation of a global learning environment for education in SD; To produce an action-oriented tool kit for universities designed to move from commitment to action; To indicate strategies for taking SD; To suggest strategies for reform, particularly in such areas as teaching, research, operations and outreach; To make an inventory of best practice and case studies
2005	Graz Declaration on Committing Universities to Sustainable Development, Austria	COPERNICUS CAMPUS, Karl-Franzens University Graz, Technical University Graz, Oikos International, UNESCO	Global	Called on Universities to give status to SD in their strategies and activities. It also called for Universities to use SD as a framework for the enhancement of the social dimension of European higher education
2005	Bergen	European education ministers, European Commission and other consultative members	Regional (Europe)	For the first time since 1999, made a strong reference that the Bologna Process for establishing a European Higher Education Area by 2010 and promoting the European system of higher education worldwide should be based on the principle of sustainable development
2006	American College and University Presidents' Climate Commitment	AASHE	National (USA)	Called for an Emissions inventory; Within two years, universities are to set a date for becoming 'climate neutral'; Integrating sustainability into the curriculum and make it part of the educational experience; make action plan, inventory and progress reports publicly available
2008	Declaration of the Regional Conference on Higher Education in Latin America and the Caribbean – CRES 2008	UNESCO	Regional (Caribbean and Latin American)	Emphasis on SD for social progress; Cultural identities; Social cohesion; Poverty; Climate Change; Energy Crisis; Culture of Peace; Need contributes to democratic relations and tolerance; Solidarity and cooperation; Critical and rigorous intellectual ability
2008	Sapporo Sustainability Declaration	G8 University Network	Global	Universities should work closely with policymakers; Universities' leadership role is becoming increasingly critical; Educating; Disseminating information; Training leaders; Interdisciplinary perspective
2009	World Conference on Higher Education	UNESCO	Global	Advance understanding of multifaceted issues and our ability to respond; Increase interdisciplinary focus; Promote critical thinking; Active citizenship; Peace, well-being, human rights; Contribute to education of committed ethical citizens
2009	Turin Declaration on Education and Research for Sustainable and Responsible Development, Italy	G8 University Network	Global	It called for new models of social and economic development consistent with sustainability principles; Ethical approaches to SD; New approaches to energy policy; Focus on sustainable ecosystems

Canadian university networks have played a key role in catalysing efforts across the globe. Leaps forward in this area can be partly attributed to the 2008 US Higher Education Sustainability Act (HESA), which legislated for the 'University Sustainability Grants Program'. In 2010 the programme had a budget of $50 million to support the implementation of major sustainability initiatives on campus. The US is the only country in the world to offer this type of incentive and support. More recently in the UK, the Salix loan grant has supported institutional initiatives mostly associated with estate refurbishment or development.

Examples of good practice in campus management for sustainability have been documented in Europe and the US but also in Africa, Asia and particularly Latin America. The ISCN Sustainable Campus Excellence Awards capture and celebrate the diversity of responses to challenges in this field. Interesting examples often not celebrated through high-profile awards include: the University of Hong Kong's systematic efforts to reduce environmental impact and conserve natural environments; the University Autónoma of Madrid eco-campus which creates innovative and effective opportunities for engaging staff and students in sustainability activities; Mabada Univerity in Lebanon which recycles its water and generates its own electricity (Salame, 2010). Equally, the Universidad Autónoma del Estado de Morelos (UAEM) in Mexico provides an exemplary case study of how to progress campus change for sustainability through internal and external partnerships.

Schemes such as the ISO 14001 or Eco-campus have played a role in catalysing efforts in this area. These activities, mostly driven by estates directors and their teams rarely make an impact on students' formal learning opportunities. The Mirvac School of Sustainable Development at Bond University, Australia provides an outstanding example of how sustainable buildings can contribute to minimizing ecological footprints but also become a source of inspiration for curriculum work. Examples of campus activities extending their influence on core university provision are rare.

The recent swell of interest in carbon may well reverse this trend in northern universities. In the UK, for example, the government's Carbon Reduction Commitment (CRC) Energy Efficiency Scheme introduced in April 2010 is a mandatory carbon emissions reporting and pricing scheme aimed at non-energy intensive sectors in the UK economy, including higher education. HE institutions affected by the legislation (that is, using more than 6000 MWh electricity per year) are required to measure and report their carbon emissions annually, using specific measurement rules. From 2012, they will be required to purchase allowances (at £12/tonne in the first year) to cover their emissions from the previous year. Parallel to this, the Higher Education Funding Council for England published its Carbon Strategy in 2010, committing the university sector to the achievement of the UK government's carbon reduction targets (set out in the Climate Change Act 2008). The Strategy also expects universities to promote carbon reduction through teaching, research and public communications. The increasing interest in curriculum activities from professional associations such as ASSHE (US), EAUC (UK), ACTS (Australia) and ISCN (which bring together HE practitioners with an interest in sustainability) signals a movement towards greater alignment between what is preached in classrooms and practised on campuses.

RESEARCH FOR SUSTAINABILITY IN HIGHER EDUCATION

It is widely acknowledged that sustainability requires forms of research activity that challenge boundaries at several interfaces, not least between academic disciplines and research paradigms, across professional roles and in relation to professional values (Marie Curie IIF, 2011). However, it has only been in the last ten years that movements towards these more complex forms of research activity are evident in sustainability research arenas. These are summarized in Table I.2.2.

TABLE I.2.2
Research for sustainability in higher education: key movements over the last 10 years

Shifts from	To be more inclusive of
Research that is discipline focused	Research that is inter- and multidisciplinary
Research that has academic impacts	Research that has social impact
Research that informs	Research that transforms
Research on technological and behaviour change	Research that focuses on social and structural change
Researcher as expert	Researcher as partner
Research on people	Research with people

INTERDISCIPLINARY RESEARCH

Research councils and funding agencies, such as the European Union, are increasingly recognizing the need to uncover new conceptual and practical spaces for research. In recent years, they have directed resources and attention to interdisciplinarity and recognize it as a new source of insight to advance human understandings of the sustainability challenge (Tilbury, 2011b). These funding sources are encouraging academics to go beyond their discipline boundaries and seek partnerships with colleagues who have similar interests but differing methodologies and/or perspectives. The result is an emergent research landscape with potential for alternative academic frameworks and new sustainability pathways in the areas such as sustainable consumption; wildlife and water conservation; reducing poverty; community development; transition towns; sustainable business development; ecological resilience; sustainable food and change management for sustainability. The regional papers featured in this publication provide examples of such initiatives and record a growth in research meetings and centres that take this interdisciplinary stance.

RESEARCH WITH IMPACT

There has also been a push towards research that has impact in a social as well as in an academic sense. The Research Excellence Frameworks (HEFCE), Research Quality Framework (DEEWPR) and Performance Based Research (TEC) and similar systems used for assessing the quality of research in higher education institutions (HEIs) are still key for academics seeking promotion, funding and/or external recognition for their research. Criteria that acknowledge the impact of the research on thinking and policy as well as communities of practice are slowly making their way into these high-profile assessment systems. This is beginning to influence the type of sustainability research to which institutions and researchers are turning their attention, with an emphasis on more practical and concrete projects that can create changes as well as make an academic contribution.

In the context of HE itself, and in this context of research impact, there has been a notable investment in research that can change strategies for sustainability in universities and colleges. In Australia, for example, the Australian Teaching and Learning Council has invested in research-informed resource development (ALTC, 2011). Similarly, in Africa, Mainstreaming Environment and Sustainability in African Universities (MESA) has received funding to support situated inquiry that seeks to influence institutional thinking and practice. In Asia, Japan's Education for Sustainable Development Research Centre and China's Tongi Institute of Environment and Sustainable Development are progressing, following similar lines of inquiry with government and UNEP funding.

FROM INFORMING TO TRANSFORMING

Although there is still significant investment in exploratory research, particularly in the areas of science and technology for sustainability, there has also been increasing attention attached to transforming research practice itself (El Zoghbi, 2011). This new wave of research seeks to go beyond problem-solving or technological developments and instead questions the role of research in reproducing exploitative relationships with people and environment. Underpinning this movement is an explicit challenge to dominant research paradigms and the professional practice of the researcher.

This trend is characterized by the phrase 'research as social change' (Schratz and Walker, 1995) and promotes forms of research that are conscious and explicit about the power, politics and participatory relations underpinning research practice. They challenge the dominant role of the researcher as an expert and encourage participatory inquiry techniques so that research is undertaken 'with people' rather than 'on people'. The movement is driven by a series of 'critical' questions captured in Table I.2.3.

TABLE I.2.3 Questioning research practice
Key questions driving changes in research practice:
Q. How can different disciplines combine to present new insights in the sustainability challenge?
Q. Who commissions the research?
Q. Whose interests does the research serve?
Q. What is the relationship between the researcher and the researched?
Q. Is the research 'on' or 'with' people?
Q. Who can access the research and how?
Q. How can the research transform and not just inform practice?
Q. How is complexity embraced within the research?
Q. How do researchers engage with, and recognize, systems within the research?
Q. Is there congruence between the 'what 'and the 'how' of research?

PARTNERSHIPS AND OUTREACH: SUSTAINABILITY BEYOND THE UNIVERSITY WALLS

Initial reports of sustainability in HE would suggest that the issues and solutions for progressing sustainability lie with universities and the sector itself. However, through experience and over time, the sector has learned that it must reach beyond the university walls to address sustainability within the communities of practice that they serve (Ryan et al., 2010; Mochizuki and Fadeeva, 2008; Lozano, 2007; Lotz-Sisitka, 2011). The past ten years have therefore seen a stepping up of activity relating to partnerships and outreach for sustainability.

The University of Western Sydney is an example where sustainability efforts have been constructed through an approach situated within their locality and with a focus on supporting the communities closely linked to the university. The partnership is particularly active in issues of watershed management. The journey of transforming the institution towards sustainability has been shared particularly with community and government stakeholders. In Saudi Arabia, the King Abdullah University of Science and Technology runs a community-wide recycling and compost scheme where problems and solutions to the waste issue are co-constructed with local stakeholders (Salame, 2011). In the Philippines, teacher education partnerships have redefined town and gown relationships (Galang, 2010). At the University of Gloucestershire in the UK, an edible garden had brought together local residents, students and staff as well as local government support and enforcement agencies in learning skills in permaculture design, food awareness and community building.

Worthy of attention are the United Nations University (UNU) accredited Regional Centres of Expertise (RCE) which focus on partnership learning and action for sustainability. Over the last six years the UNU has acknowledged 63 RCEs in Africa, Australia, the Asia-Pacific region, Europe, the Middle East, South America, the Caribbean, and North and Central America. RCEs seek to expand the span of local partnership work as well as link people and activities across wider regions in order to link urban and rural development issues, to understand dynamics that cut across local boundaries, and to connect local and national activities.

In the US, Partnership for Education for Sustainable Development, established in 2003, has brought together schools, science and research, faith organizations, NGOs, government agencies and youth advocacy groups to support implementation of sustainability initiatives.

Partnership platforms that bring together universities committed to this agenda continue to be important. For example, the Copernicus Alliance; Pacific Network of Island Universities; the Japanese Higher Education for Sustainable Development Network; the Australasian Campuses Towards Sustainability network; Association for the Advancement of Sustainability in Higher Education (US); the Mexican Consortium University for Sustainable Development (COMPLEXUS) and Mainstreaming Environment and Sustainability in African Universities (MESA) Partnership have all experienced significant increases in their membership numbers recently. Their annual meetings confirm that universities increasingly recognize the need to work together to share common issues but also learn from best practice and combining scarce resources to address the sustainability imperative.

Parallel to this key trend is a greater accountability of higher education to the communities that it serves, particularly in Western nations currently in economic decline. As national debt increases, governments are forced to rethink their investment strategies. They are asking questions regarding the value and impact of university activity on economic as well as social development. Universities are being held to account and, through various funding mechanisms, encouraged to establish stronger links with their local–regional communities to support the recovery. The result is a reorientation of university activity to provide this greater accountability in terms of outreach. It has led to an array of studies such as that undertaken by the New Economics Foundation which found that the social impact of universities in the UK is worth over £1.31 billion. It opens with the strapline 'benefits are felt by everyone, not just those who go to university'. The study undertaken by the New Economics Foundation (Shaheen, 2011) documents how UK universities add value to UK society in the form of health, well-being, citizenship and political engagement.

Lotz-Sisitka (2011) reports a parallel trend in Africa, where universities are seeing sustainability as an opportunity to redefine university–community relationships. She presents evidence that institutions are making tangible contributions to local communities through addressing issues of peace, security, conflict resolution and HIV/AIDS. She cites Uganda Martyrs University and its improving livelihoods initiative which has resulted in improved income, food security, water conservation and sustainable livelihoods as well as better relationships between the university and its neighbouring communities.

EDUCATION AND LEARNING FOR SUSTAINABILITY

Education has always been seen as key to improving quality of life, not just of individuals but also collectively for humankind (Galang, 2010). The higher education declarations on sustainability (see Table I.2.1) explicitly acknowledge this and confirm the importance of learning, communication and capacity building for sustainability.

Paradoxically, David Orr (2004) reminds us that the global issues facing us cannot be attributed to a lack of higher education when he asks why it is:

> that those who contribute to exploiting poor
> communities and the earth's ecosystems are those
> who have BAs, MBAs, MSCs and PhDs and not the
> 'ignorant' poor from the South?

The paradigms deeply embedded in our higher education knowledge systems and relationships are contributing to unsustainable development. The '*UN Decade in Education for Sustainable Development International Implementation Scheme*' echoes this perspective and calls for reorientation of education towards more sustainable forms of living (UNESCO, 2005). It acknowledges that it is not simply a matter of integrating new content into our education programmes or building sustainability literacy across all subject areas but that it requires the unpacking of social, economic, cultural and environmental assumptions which serve the status quo and which are reproduced by our education systems (UNESCO, 2002). As Galang (2010) remind us, centuries of teaching resource extraction need to be questioned and learning efforts redesigned so that professionals understand the responsibility and implications of sustainability for their area of influence.

There is evidence to suggest that HE does not understand the true nature of the challenge (Verbitskaya et al., 2002; Abdul-Wahab et al., 2003; Cortese, 2003; Thomas, 2004; Moore, 2005; Park, 2008; Cotton and Winter, 2010; Ferreira and Tilbury, 2011; Nomura and Abe, 2011). The focus has been on developing new specialist courses on SD (for example University of Phillippines; TERI India; Dalhousie University), which are improving the sustainability literacy and capabilities of those interested in pursuing careers in this area. However, teachers, architects, accountants, doctors and business managers are still being schooled into social assumptions and practices that serve to exploit people and planet. Curriculum and pedagogy, which are at the core of HE experiences, need to be transformed if universities and colleges are to make a meaningful contribution to sustainable development (UNECE, 2011).

Ryan et al. (2010) present evidence which suggests that the Asia Pacific region has played an important role in directing attention to pedagogy and learning for sustainability across education, including HE, and shows a stronger overall trajectory in this respect. The UN Decade in Education for Sustainable Development originated in the region with the proposal from the Japanese government and NGOs at the World Summit for Sustainable Development (Nomura and Abe, 2009). The Asia Pacific Regional Bureau of Education has provided much strategic guidance and practical tools in ESD (see for example UNESCO, 2005; Elias, 2006; Tilbury et al., 2007; Elias and Sachathep, 2009).

Arguably the most ambitions initiatives in these areas have been driven by the Australian Research Institute in Education for Sustainability and through its business education (see Mah et al., 2006; Martin and Steele, 2010; Thomas and Benn, 2009; Tilbury et al., 2005a) and teacher education (see Steele, 2010; Ferreira et al., 2009; Ferreira et al., 2007a and b) projects. The ARIES work has challenged dominant assumptions within existing programmes; developed inter and intra-university partnerships to support systemic change; built staffs' confidence and expertise in sustainability; addressed the professional capacities as well as responsibilities of the students; and also embraced the dual challenge of pedagogical and curriculum development for sustainability. This has been evidenced through independent evaluations commissioned by the Australian federal government, which funds this work.

A UK HEFCE funded project '*Leading Curriculum Change for Sustainability*' seeks to embed education for sustainability into university quality assurance and enhancement systems and is another example of ambitious curriculum change in HE being incentivized by a government agency (HEFCE, 2011). In a similar vein, Swedish, UK, Australian, Canadian, Japanese and Dutch aid agencies have played an important role in funding curriculum development for sustainability in Africa and Asia as well the Pacific Islands (for example SIDA, 2011; MedIES, 2010; AusAid, 2010). Case studies of HE change triggered or supported by such funding are documented across various journals such as *Journal of Education for Sustainable Development; Australian Journal of Environmental Education; South African Journal of Environmental Education* and *Environmental Education Research* journal which all evidence learning transitions towards education for sustainability.

There is also evidence from Latin America and parts of South East Asia that university education programmes are being challenged to reorient themselves towards sustainability by school and community education initiatives whose influences are slowly making their way in HE curricula (Galang, 2010).

When studied closely, the initiatives identified above reveal learning transitions towards ESD. These shifts are summarized in Table I.2.4.

TABLE I.2.4 Learning transitions towards ESD (Tilbury and Cooke, 2005)	
Shifting from:	**Moving Towards:**
Bolt-on additions to existing curricula	Innovation within existing curricula
Passing on knowledge and raising awareness of issues	Questioning and getting to the root of issues
Teaching about attitudes and values	Encouraging clarification of existing values
Seeing people as the problem	Seeing people as change agents
Sending messages about SD	Creating opportunities for reflection, negotiation and participation
Raising awareness and trying to change behaviour	Challenging the mental models that influence decisions and actions
More focus on the individual and personal change	More focus on professional and social change
Negative 'problem-solving' approaches	Constructive creation of alternative futures
Isolated changes/actions	Learning to change

LEADERSHIP AND STRATEGY FOR SUSTAINABILITY

The strategic implications of sustainability are that of innovation not integration of this agenda into mainstream institutional structures and practices (Bawden, 2004, p. 29; Corcoran and Wals, 2004, p. 4; Sterling, 2004; Tilbury et al., 2005a). In other words, translating signatures on international declarations into institutional responses requires adjustments to academic priorities, organizational structures, financial and audit systems (Bekessy et al., 2007; Sharp, 2002; Ryan et al., 2010). A recent project commissioned by the Australian Teaching and Learning Council recognises that these changes do not just happen they must be led (Scott et al., 2011). The *Turnaround Leadership for Sustainability in Higher Education Project* seeks to define the capabilities that make an educationally effective HE leader for sustainability and produce resources to develop and enhance these leadership capabilities. This international project involves researchers from Australia, UK and the US and seeks to make a step-change contribution to an area which has been deprived of attention and which forms an important piece of the transformation puzzle.

A review of journal articles accompanied by a web search reveals that there are several leadership for sustainability initiatives across the globe that essentially target senior managers from the corporate sector (see for example the *Cambridge Programme for Sustainability Leadership*). Universities do oper-

ate as businesses at one level but, at another level, academic change for sustainability requires a different model of leadership. This means that existing leadership programmes are of limited value to senior managers working within HE. The lack of leadership development opportunities for HE managers may go some way to explaining why progress towards sustainability in HE has been piecemeal (Lozano, 2007; Tilbury, 2011a).

Emerging practice may well change this scenario. For example, a recently established Sustainable Development Education Academy at York University is supporting Canadian teams engaged in teacher education to plan and implement academic and programme change for sustainability. At another level, the Salzburg Global Academy founded the Sustainable Futures Academy (SFA) in 2010 recognizing the criticality of leadership in the transition towards more sustainable universities and colleges. The SFA has the reorientation of academic offerings towards sustainability firmly in its sight and seeks to progress it through North–South partnerships that can embed sustainability into the core business of universities and colleges (Sharp, Scott and Tilbury, 2010).

FINAL REMARKS: INTEGRATING SUSTAINABILITY INTO THE CORE BUSINESS OF HIGHER EDUCATION

Sustainability is a multifaceted agenda for organizations, but when harnessed effectively, its integrative potential is substantial. Yet to achieve this level of engagement in academic institutions involves profound leadership challenges. Leading change for sustainability in universities requires more than knowledge of, or commitment to, the principles of sustainability. It requires a facility for bringing about change that deals with complexity, uncertainty and multiple stakeholders, as well as ambiguous terminology (Tilbury and Wortman, 2008). It is complex, confusing, time consuming and difficult to implement, which explains why, to date, only a handful of university leaders have taken on the challenge.

Evidence suggests, that despite this inertia, there are movements towards more sustainable planning and practice in HE. Government incentives, socioeconomic expectations, partnership platforms, student leadership and experimental practice, described in this paper, are all contributing to changes: although these may not be deep or systemic. University leaders now need to help join these dots of activity in ways that align mainstream practices to sustainability innovation in their institutions. Senior management teams, at this moment, hold the key to transforming HE so that it can play its part in transforming social practices and contribute to more sustainable futures.

REFERENCES

Abdul-Wahab, S.A., Abdulraheem, M.Y. and Hutchinson, M. (2003) The need for inclusion of environmental education in undergraduate engineering curricula. *International Journal of Sustainability in Higher Education*, **4**(2), pp. 126–37.

ALTC (2011) http://sustainability.edu.au/news [Accessed 13 June 2011].

American College and University Presidents' Climate Commitment (2011) *American College and University Presidents' Climate Commitment*. Available at: http://www.presidentsclimatecommitment.org [Accessed 18 May 2011].

Association of Australian Government Universities (1993) *Swansea Declaration*. Available at: http://www.iisd.org/educate/declarat/swansea.htm [Accessed 3 May 2011].

AusAid (2010) http://www.usp.ac.fj/index.php?id=9701 [Accessed 13 June 2011].

Baltic University Programme (2011) *Baltic University Programme – A regional University Network*. Available at: http://www.balticuniv.uu.se/ [Accessed 6 June 2011].

Barab, S.A. and Luehmann, A.L. (2003) Building Sustainable Science Curriculum: Acknowledging and Accommodating Local Adaptation. *Science Education*, **87**(4), pp. 454–67.

Bawden, R. (2004) Sustainability as emergence: the need for engaged discourse. In: Corcoran, P.B. and Wals, A.E.J. (ed.) *Higher Education and the Challenge of Sustainability: Problematics, Promise, and Practice*. Dordrecht, Netherlands: Kluwer Academic Publishers, pp. 21–32.

Bekessy, S.A., Samson, K. and Clarkson, R.E. (2007) The failure of non-binding declarations to achieve university sustainability: A need for accountability. *International Journal of Sustainability in Higher Education*, **8**(3), pp. 301–16.

Boks, C. and Diehl, J.C. (2006) Integration of sustainability in regular courses: experiences in industrial design engineering. *Journal of Cleaner Production*, **14**(9–11), pp. 932–9.

Calder, W. and Clugston, R.M. (2003) International efforts to promote higher education for sustainable development. *Planning for Higher Education*, **31**, pp. 30–44.

COPERNICUS (1994) *COPERNICUS University Charter for Sustainable Development*. Available at: http://www.iisd.org/educate/declarat/coper.htm [Accessed 3 May 2011].

Corcoran, P.B. and Wals, A.E.J. (eds) (2004) *Higher Education and the Challenge of Sustainability: Problematics, Promise, and Practice*. Dordrecht: Kluwer Academic Publishers.

Cortese, A.D. (2003) The critical role of higher education in creating a sustainable future. *Planning for Higher Education*, **31**(3), pp. 15–22.

Cotton, D.R.E. and Winter, J. (2010) It's not just bits of paper and light bulbs: A review of sustainability pedagogies and their potential for use in higher education. In: Jones, P., Selby, D. and Sterling, S. (ed.) *Sustainability Education:*

Perspectives and Practice Across Higher Education. London: Earthscan.

DEEWPR http://www.dest.gov.au/archive/sectors/research_sector/policies_issues_reviews/key_issues/research_quality_framework/ accesses 13 June 2011.

Elias, D. and Sachathep, K. (ed.) (2009) *ESD Currents: Changing Perspectives from the Asia-Pacific*. Bangkok, Thailand: UNESCO Bangkok.

Elias, D. (2006) UNESCO's approach to implementing the decade of education for sustainable development (DESD) in Asia and the Pacific. *Australian Journal of Environmental Education*, **22**(1), pp. 83–6.

Elton, L. (2003) Dissemination of innovations in higher education: A change theory approach. *Tertiary Education and Management* (9), pp. 199–214.

G8 University Network (2008) Available at: http://g8u-summit.jp/english/ssd/index.html [Accessed 4 May 2011].

Galang, A.P. (2010) Environmental education for sustainability in higher education institutions in the Philippines. *International Journal of Sustainability in Higher Education*, **4**(2), pp. 138–50.

Global Higher Education for Sustainability Partnership (2001) *The Lüneburg Declaration on Higher Education for Sustainable Development*. Available at: http://portal.unesco.org/education/en/files/37585/11038209883LunebuurgDeclaration.pdf/LuneburgDeclaration.pdf [Accessed 3 May 2011].

El Zoghbi, M. (2011) The Interdisciplinary Researcher: Paradigms, Practices and Possibilities for Sustainability. PRISM Conference Report. University of Gloucestershire, Cheltenham, 19–20 May 2011.

Ferreira, J. and Tilbury, D. (2011) Higher education and sustainability in Australia: transforming experiences. In: *Higher Education in the World 4, Higher Education's Commitment to Sustainability: from Understanding to Action*. Barcelona: GUNi.

Ferreira, J., Ryan, L. and Tilbury, D. (2007a) Mainstreaming education for sustainability in initial teacher education in Australia: A review of existing professional development models. *Journal of Education for Teaching* Routledge Publications, **33**(2), pp. 225–339 ISSN 0022-4871.

Ferreira, J., Ryan, L. and Tilbury, D. (2007b) Planning for success: factors influencing change in teacher education. *Australian Journal of Environmental Education*, 23, pp. 45–55.

Ferreira, J., Ryan, L., Davis, J., Cavanagh, M. and Thomas, J. (ed.) (2009) *Mainstreaming Sustainability into Pre-service Teacher Education in Australia*. Canberra: ARIES and Australian Government Department of the Environment and Heritage.

HEFCE (2011) http://www.hefce.ac.uk/research/ref/ [Accessed 13 June 2011].

Huisingh, G. and Mebratu, D. (2000) Educating the educators' as a strategy for enhancing education on cleaner production. *Journal of Cleaner Production*, 8, pp. 439–42.

International Association of Universities (1991) *The Halifax Declaration*. Available at: http://www.iisd.org/educate/declarat/halifax.htm [Accessed 3 May 2011].

International Association of Universities (1993) *Kyoto Declaration on Sustainable Development*. Available at: http://www.iau-aiu.net/sd/sd_dkyoto.html [Accessed 4 May 2011].

Lotz-Sisitka, H. (2011) The 'event' of modern sustainable development and universities in Africa. In: *Higher Education in the World 4, Higher Education's Commitment to Sustainability: From Understanding to Action.* Barcelona: GUNi.

Lozano, R. (2006) Incorporation and institutionalization of SD into universities: breaking through barriers to change. *Journal of Cleaner Production,* **14**(9–11), pp. 787–96.

Lozano, R. (2007) Collaboration as a pathway for sustainable development. *Sustainable Development,* **16**(6), pp. 370–81.

Lozano, R., Lukman, R., Lozano, F.J., Huisingh, D. and Zilahy, G. (2010) *Jumping Sustainability Meme. SD transfer from society to universities* Paper presented at the Environmental Management for Sustainable Universities, Delf, The Netherlands.

Mah, J., Hunting, S. and Tilbury, D. (2006) *Education about and for Sustainability in Australian Business Schools: Business Schools Project Stage 2.* Canberra: Australian Government Department of the Environment and Heritage and Australian Research Institute in Education for Sustainability. ISBN 10: 1 74138 199 1 ISBN 13: 978 1 74138 199 3*.

Marie Curie IIF (2011) Marie Curie Project Learning and Living Sustainably: Building Interdisciplinary Research Capacity and Expertise in Social and Professional Responses to Sustainability at the University of Gloucestershire. http://insight.glos.ac.uk/sustainability/Education/Pages/MarieCurieIIFProjectonSustainability.aspx (accessed 22 August 2011).

Martin, A. and Steele, F. (2010) *Sustainability in Key Professions: Accounting.* A report prepared by the Australian Research Institute in Education for Sustainability for the Australian Government Department of the Environment, Water, Heritage and the Arts.

MEdIES (2010) The MEdIES Network for ESD - Baltic University Programme www.balticuniv.uu.se/index.php/.../doc.../502-the-medies-network-for-esd

Mochizuki, Y. and Fadeeva, Z. (2008) Regional centres of expertise on education for sustainable development (RCEs): an overview. *International Journal of Sustainability in Higher Education,* **9**(4), pp. 371–9.

Moore, J. (2005) Barriers and pathways to creating sustainability education programs: policy rhetoric and reality. *Environmental Education and Research,* **11**(5), pp. 537–55.

Nomura, K. and Abe, O. (2011) Sustainability and Higher Education in Asia and the Pacific In: *Higher Education in the World 4, Higher Education's Commitment to Sustainability: From Understanding to Action.* Barcelona: GUNi.

Nomura, K. and Abe, O. (2009) The education for sustainable development movement in Japan: a political perspective. *Environmental Education Research,* **15**(4), pp. 483–96.

Orr, D.W. (2004) *Earth in Mind – On Education, Environment and the Human Prospect* (10th anniversary edn). Washington, DC: Island Press.

Park, T.Y. (2008) ESD of Korean Universities. *Presented at International Symposium 'Sustainability in Higher Education: Learning from Experiences in Asia and the World'.* Rikkyo University, Japan.

Ryan, A., Tilbury, D., Corcoran, P.B., Abe, O. and Nomura, K. (2010) Sustainability in higher education in the Asia-Pacific: developments, challenges and prospects. *International Journal of Sustainability in Higher Education,* **11**(3), pp. 106–19.

Salamé, R. (2010) Higher Education Commitment to Sustain-

ability in the Arab States. *Presented at the 5th GUNi International Barcelona Conference on Higher Education, 23–26 November 2010.* Barcelona, Spain.

Sanusi, Z.A. and Khelgat-Doost, H. (2008) Regional centre of expertise as a transformational platform for sustainability: a case study of Universiti Sains Malaysia, Penang. *International Journal of Sustainability in Higher Education,* **9**(4), pp. 487–97.

Schratz, M. and Walker, R. (1995) *Research as Social Change. New Opportunities for Qualitative Research.* London: Routledge.

Scott, G., Deane, L., Tilbury, D. and Sharp, L. (2011) *Turn-Around Leadership for Sustainability: An ALTC Project.* Sydney, Australia: University of Western Sydney.

Sharp, L. (2002) Green Campuses: the road from little victories to systemic transformation. *International Journal of Sustainability in Higher Education,* **3**(2), pp. 128–45.

SIDA (2011) https://itp.sida.se/itp/Programcatalog.nsf/0/D5EBEB0386E2EDF4C125772E002AED7E?opendocument

Sharp, L., Scott, G. and Tilbury, D. (2010) Executive Leadership Programme for Sustainability in Higher Education: The Sustainable Futures Academy Salzburg: Global Salzburg Academy

Shaheen, F. (2011) *Degrees of Value: How Universities Benefit Society.* London: New Economics Foundation.

Steele, F. (2010) *Mainstreaming Education for Sustainability in Pre-service teacher Education in Australia: Enablers and Constraints,* Sidney: ARIES.

Sterling, S. (1996) Education in change. In: Huckle, J. and Sterling, S. (eds) *Education for Sustainability. London: Earthscan,* pp. 18–39.

Sterling, S. (2004) An analysis of the development of sustainability education internationally: evolution, interpretation and transformative potential. In: Blewitt, J. and Cullingford, C. (eds), *Sustainable Development: A Challenge for Higher Education,* London: Earthscan.

Su, H.J. and Chang, T.C. (2010) Sustainability of higher education institutions in Taiwan. *International Journal of Sustainability in Higher Education,* **11**(2), pp. 163–72.

Stern, N. (2010) cited in http://www.insidegovernment.co.uk/environment/higher-education-sustainability/ accessed 1st June 2011.

Thomas, I. (2004) Tertiary or Terminal: A Snapshot of Sustainability Education in Australia's Universities, *Proceedings of Effective Sustainability Education Conference 18–20 February, 2004, University of New South Wales, Sydney.*

Thomas, J. and Benn, S. (2009) *Education* about *and for Sustainability in Australian Business Schools Stage 3.* A Report prepared by the Australian Research Institute in Education for Sustainability for the Government Department of the Environment, Water, Heritage and the Arts.

Tilbury, D. (2011a) Are we learning to change? Mapping global progress in education for sustainable development in the lead up to 'Rio Plus 20'. In: *Global Environmental Research, 14 No. 2, Education for Sustainable Development: Promises and Challenges.* 101–7.

Tilbury, D. (2011b) *Education for Sustainable Development: An Expert Review of Processes and Learning.* Paris: UNESCO. Available in Spanish, French and English. ED-2010/WS/46

Tilbury, D. (2010) Change for a better world: assessing the contribution of the DESD. In: *'Tomorrow Today'.* Paris: UNESCO: Tudor Rose. Publication released at the UN General Assembly in New York November 2010. (pp. 146–9).

Tilbury, D. and Wortman, D (2008) Education for sustainability in further and higher education: reflections along the journey. *Journal for Planning in Higher Education, Society for College and University Planning US*, **36**(4), pp. 5–16.

Tilbury, D., Janousek, S., Elias, D. and Bacha, J. (2007) *Monitoring and Assessing Progress during the UNDESD in Asia Pacific Region: A quick guide to developing indicators'* Bangkok: UNESCO Asia and Pacific Regional Bureau for Education IUCN. ISBN: 92-9223-115-4.

Tilbury, D. and Cooke, K. (2005) *A National Review of Environmental Education and its contribution to Sustainability in Australia: Frameworks for Sustainability.* Canberra: Australian Government Department of the Environment and Heritage and Australian Research Institute in Education for Sustainability.

Tilbury, D., Crawley, C. and Berry, F. (2005a) *Education about and for Sustainability in Australian Business Schools: Stage 1.* Canberra: Australian Government Department of the Environment and Heritage and Australian Research Institute in Education for Sustainability.

Tilbury, D., Keogh, A., Leighton, A. and Kent, J. (2005b) *A National Review of Environmental Education and its Contribution to Sustainability in Australia: Further and Higher Education.* Canberra: Australian Government Department of the Environment and Heritage and Australian Research Institute in Education for Sustainability (ARIES).

United Nations (2002a) *Press Conference on 'Ubuntu Declaration' on Education.* Available at: http://www.un.org/events/wssd/pressconf/020901conf1.htm [Accessed 3 May 2011].

United Nations (2002b) *Agenda 21.* Available at: http://www.un.org/esa/dsd/agenda21/ [Accessed 3 May 2011].

United Nations (1992) *The Rio Declaration on Environment and Development.* Geneva: Centre for Our Common Future.

UN Economic Commission for Europe (UNECE) UNECE Annotated Agenda for the Fifth Meeting, ECE/CEP/AC/.13/2010.1, Geneva: UN Economic and Social Council, 2010a.

UN Economic Commission for Europe (UNECE) UNECE ESD Competencies for Educators: First Draft for Consulttation. Unpublished. Geneva. UN Economic and Social Council, 2010b.

UNESCO (2009) *UNESCO World Conference on Education for Sustainable Development: Bonn Declaration.* Available at: http://www.esd-world-conference-2009.org/fileadmin/download/ESD2009_BonnDeclaration080409.pdf [Accessed 4 May 2011].

UNESCO (2008) *Declaration of the Regional Conference on Higher Education in Latin America and the Caribbean – CRES 2008.* Available at: http://www.iesalc.unesco.org.ve/docs/wrt/declarationcres_ingles.pdf [Accessed 3 May 2011].

UNESCO. (2005). *United Nations Decade of Education for Sustainable Development (2005–2014): International Implementation Scheme.* Paris: UNESCO.

UNESCO. (2002a). *Education for Sustainability, From Rio to Johannesburg: Lessons Learnt from a Decade of Commitment.* Paris: UNESCO.

University Leaders for a Sustainable Future (1990). *Talloires Declaration.* Available at: http://www.ulsf.org/programs_talloires.html [Accessed 3 May 2011].

Verbitskaya, L.A., Nosova, N.B. and Rodina, L.L. (2002) Sustainable development in higher education in Russia: the case of St Petersburg State University. *International Journal of Sustainability in Higher Education*, **3**(3), pp. 279–87.

Wright, T. and Elliott, H. (2011) Canada and USA Regional Report. In: *Higher Education in the World 4, Higher Education's Commitment to Sustainability: from Understanding to Action.* Barcelona: GUNi.

Further Insights I.2
Making sustainable development in higher education a reality: Lessons learned from leading institutions

Walter Leal Filho and Evangelos Manolas

INTRODUCTION

Sustainability is today one of the most widely used words in the scientific field as a whole and in the environmental sciences in particular. The analysis of the evolution of such a concept, as performed by Leal Filho (2010a) is a difficult exercise. This is because the records of the systematic use of such an expression, whose reference in the current vocabulary and political discourse is nowadays so popular, are scattered around. Until the late 1970s, the word 'sustainability' was only occasionally employed in most cases to refer to ways

through which forest resources should be used. It has, in other words, strong connections with the forestry sector from where, some believe, it is originated.

A key question one might ask at this stage – a question that is posed over and over again, every day, by millions of people all over the world – is *what does sustainable development really mean?* Depending on the ways it is looked at, it may have many meanings, such as (Leal Filho, 2010a):

- The systematic, long-term use of natural resources – as defined in the Brundtland

Report – so that these are available for future generations (here referring to country and local policies)

- The modality of development that enable countries to progress, economically and socially, without destroying their environmental resources (here referring to country policies)

- The type of development that is socially just, ethically acceptable, morally fair and economically sound (here referring to the social ramifications of development)

- The type of development where environmental indicators are as important as economic indicators (here referring to the close links it bears with economic growth)

Many other variants may be listed and are indeed used by different organizations, taking into account their political perspectives and institutional aims. IUCN, which in liaison with UNEP and WWF produced 'Caring for the Earth' (IUCN, WWW, UNEP, 1991), suggested at the time that the expression 'sustainable development' be replaced in some context by 'sustainable living', since although the suffix 'development' is associated with governments and refers to a government's responsibilities, the word 'living' is closer to an individual's life.

The authors defend the view that there is unlikely to be a consensus – at least a total one – on the *meaning* of sustainable development, although most people would agree on what it is all about. The reason for this is rather simple: one's own definition will be influenced by one's training, working experience and political and economic setting. There is nothing negative in that, but, equally, there is the need to establish some ground rules so that the search for a consensus on what it is and in what it means, may not be made hopelessly impossible due to individual differences in opinion and perspectives. Another way to overcome the problem is by looking at approaches to *sustainability* – this meaning the processes that may ultimately lead to sustainable development. This paper will thus refer to sustainability, as opposed to the broad spectrum of sustainable development, having universities as a focal point.

EXAMPLES FROM SOME LEADING UNIVERSITIES

The implementation of sustainable development in higher education (HE) is now a global trend and has been widely documented (for example Leal Filho, 2010b). Yet, the intensity and the depth with which higher education institutions (HEIs) are taking on the challenge of sustainability, significantly differs. Many HEIs across the world are including sustainability issues in different areas (for example teaching, research, outreach and institutional management).

The literature on sustainability contains a wealth of works that have been written on the subject of integration of sustainability in an HE context. Whether it is in respect of approaches and methods (Leal Filho 1999), communication (Leal Filho, 2000), teaching (Leal Filho, 2002) or research (Leal Filho, 2005), much ground has been covered. The same line of thinking applies to areas such as sustainability learning (Hansmann, Crott, Mieg, Scholz, 2009) or sectoral approaches to sustainability dealing, for example, with the academic profession (Hammond and Churchman, 2008) or in respect of campus operations (Conway, Dalton, Loo, Benakoun, 2008). The many efforts that have been made in trying to understand and promote sustainability at, within and around universities are the reason why it is so well developed today. Indeed, the introduction of sustainability approaches and the execution of sustainability-based projects is still a dynamic process and can be regarded as a growing trend. The rest of this section offers some examples of what universities across the world have been doing.

Starting with North America, perhaps a leading example of best practice in sustainability university campuses is offered by the University of British Columbia, which was the first university in Canada to have a sustainable development policy and a Campus Sustainability Office, which, for example, keeps a running score of the use on campus not only of paper but also of electricity and water. Futhermore, students are encouraged to sign a sustainability pledge requiring them to consider the social and environmental consequences of all their actions.

In addition, Michigan State University has produced a sustainability report describing social and economic as well as environmental indicators of performance. Yale University started a programme in 2007, which involves core courses from both the School of Engineering (water resources, industrial ecology, and sustainable design) and the School of Forestry and Environmental Studies (environmental science, social ecology, economics, and policy and law). The Engineering faculty at the University of Texas (Austin) have developed 'Signature Courses' such as the course titled 'Sustaining a Planet' which describes material

and energy cycles in the natural world, how natural systems interact with and are modified by engineered systems and how students' lives fit into these systems.

The University of California at Davis pursues research on strategies and technologies for sustainable management of urban forests. With regard to education, one may mention Harvard University's Center for the Environment, Brandeis University's master's degree programme in Sustainable International Development and Brown University's student projects on campus sustainability. On infrastructure, the green buildings of the University of California at Santa Barbara and of the University of Texas at Houston are well-known examples of sustainable construction. As far as outreach is concerned, Bates College has established responsible purchasing, composting, and recycling initiatives and at the University of South Carolina, students and campus recycling staff work with charitable organizations to donate food, clothes, building materials and furniture in order to reduce the university's disposal costs. Columbia University's Earth Institute, which was established in 1995, has a focus on sustainable development and the needs of the world's poor. The Earth Institute's activities are guided by the idea that existing science and technological tools could be applied to greatly improve conditions for the world's poor, while preserving the natural systems that support life on Earth.

In Europe, the University of Mid-Sweden was the first HEI to have an EMAS (Environment and Management System) accreditation, followed by Zittau-Görlitz University, which was the first one in Germany. Both are committed to sustainability as a matter of concern to the whole institution. The University of Malta offers a prime example of the impact of transformative pedagogies on pre-service teachers, preparing them to approach matters related to sustainable development among future generations of students. A further example of what is happening today comes from Hamburg, Germany where the Hamburg University of Applied Sciences set-up the 'World Sustainable Development Teach-In Day'. Organized to run every other year, it is directed towards disseminating information on the concept, aims and purposes of sustainable development so that it can be understood by a broad public, and will include elements relating to its environmental, social, economic and policy aspects. The University of Gloucestershire in the UK has an active Institute of Sustainable Development, whereas in Spain, UPC in Barcelona has been innovating in the areas of curriculum greening and extension. The Technical University of Delft in the Netherlands has been for many years active in respect of institutional sustainable development processes, while the University of Opole in Poland has specialized in economics and sustainable development.

In terms of Australasia, Hong Kong University in China is also committed to sustainability and this is evident from its curriculum structure and booklets promoting environmentally sustainable practices. In India, TERI University, which is devoted to environmental issues, provides a good example of an institutional focus on sustainable development. This is similar to the work done at the University of the Philippines at the Los Baños Campus, where matters related to sustainability are present in the curriculum of many courses. Deakin University, in Australia, has developed a suite of generic attributes graduates should have, which is called 'The Deakin Advantage', where attributes such as 'an understanding of the principles and applications of sustainable development' are meant to be applied to the graduates' own disciplinary fields and work situations. The Australian National University has also been for many years a driving force in the realization of sustainability goals in HE.

SOME LESSONS LEARNED
The overall positive trends should not hide the fact that there are many problems and barriers that prevent developments in respect of the integration of sustainability issues in HE. However, to the same measure, there are some concrete steps that may be undertaken in order to allow universities to integrate sustainable development in their activities. Indeed, the examples provided by the universities and listed in this paper indicate a number of features that successful universities have considered and dealt with:

- The need for political and institutional support for university initiatives

- The need for coordination between individual initiatives within a university
- The proper provision of suitable infrastructure for sustainability initiatives
- The existence of a team of well-motivated and competent staff

In addition, further reflection is needed in respect of ensuring sustainability is embedded into a university programme, as opposed to being a marginal part of it, as has largely been the case so far. Figure 1 outlines some elements that need to be considered in order to catalyse a greater integration of sustainability in university programmes.

This paper suggests a set of ten points that may help to foster the efforts of implementation of sustainability at HEIs:

1. Encourage and promote the development of initiatives and projects on sustainable development at universities, not only in respect of subjects (for example curriculum) and campus greening, but also in terms of research and extension (for example training events to an external audience).
2. Ensure universities take part in local, regional and national initiatives related to sustainable development, so as to put the principles of sustainability into practice and support initiatives in respect of sustainable consumption and production and the promotion of ecological, social and economic development.
3. Identify and use tools, toolkits, practical measures and monitoring mechanisms, which show how much progress can be achieved with the implementation of sustainability efforts.
4. Provide examples of approaches and methods that show how sustainability principles may lead to improvements in efficiency and in costs reduction, as well as in reducing environmental degradation, pollution and waste.
5. Mobilize sources for financial and technical assistance and capacity building for projects in both industrialized and developing countries.
6. Develop materials and instruments that show or illustrate environmental and health impacts, using, where possible and appropriate, case studies to implement them.
7. Run regular awareness-raising initiatives illustrating the importance of sustainable development and take part in information and dissemination schemes using the media.
8. Establish and seek peer support for sustainability programmes. If appropriate, by setting up centres around which university professors from different disciplines (faculty) may gather.
9. Collect and disseminate information on the activities taking place at the university and promote the exchange of best practices and know-how on sustainability methods and processes.

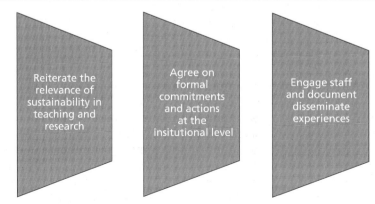

FIGURE 1 Some elements to catalyse a greater integration of sustainability in university programmes

10. Involve the university administration (for example Rector, Vice-Rector, Dean, and so on) in sustainability activities so that they can see it is worth it.

It may be the case that it is not possible to implement all ten measures at one go, but in trying to get them implemented, universities may realize they have a potential which has been dormant but which can be made concrete if they have the political will to do so.

CONCLUSIONS

As shown in this paper, HEIs worldwide are including sustainability issues in different areas such as in teaching, research, outreach and institutional management, but it has to be said that this is happening at different levels of depth and with different degrees of success.

Even though much progress has been made over the past years, there are still many problems and barriers that prevent developments in respect of the integration of sustainability issues in HE. These barriers and problems can be addressed if the necessary political will is available. When applied to various contexts such as water, energy, industry or transport, sustainable development has proved to be an important tool in fostering life quality and in reducing human impacts on the environment.

There are many universities that have excelled in putting the principles of sustainable development into practice, as this paper has outlined. For some of them, part their success is due to the fact that they have not only chosen innovative approaches and pursued innovative ideas, but they have also established partnerships and hence were able to provide added value to their own projects. Cooperation therefore may be one effective means by which universities may consolidate their own good work and at the same time open the door to new opportunities.

REFERENCES

Conway, T.M., Dalton, C., Loo, J. and Benakoun, L. (2008) Developing ecological footprint scenarios on university campuses: A case study of the University of Toronto at Mississauga. *International Journal of Sustainability in Higher Education*, **9**(1), pp. 4–20.

Hammond, C. and Churchman, D. (2008) Sustaining academic life: A case for applying principles of social sustainability to the academic profession. *International Journal of Sustainability in Higher Education*, **9**(3), pp. 235–45.

Hansmann, R., Crott, H.W., Mieg, H.A. and Scholz, R.W. (2009) Improving group processes in transdisciplinary case studies for sustainability learning. *International Journal of Sustainability in Higher Education*, **10**(1), pp. 33–42.

IUCN, WWW, UNEP (1991) *Caring for the Earth. A Strategy for Sustainable Living*. Gland, Switzerland: IUC.

Leal Filho, W. (ed.) (1999) *Sustainability and University Life*. Frankfurt: Peter Lang Scientific Publishers.

Leal Filho, W. (ed.) (2000) *Communicating Sustainability*. Frankfurt: Peter Lang Scientific Publishers.

Leal Filho, W. (ed.) (2002) *Teaching Sustainability – towards curriculum greening*. Frankfurt: Peter Lang Scientific Publishers.

Leal Filho, W. (ed.) (2005) *Handbook of Sustainability Research*. Frankfurt: Peter Lang Scientific Publishers.

Leal Filho, W. (ed.) (2010a) *Sustainability at Universities: Opportunities, Challenges and Trends*. Frankfurt: Peter Lang Scientific Publishers.

Leal Filho, W. (ed.) (2010b) Teaching sustainable development at university level: current trends and future needs. *Journal of Baltic Sea Education*, **9**(4), pp. 273–84.

Further Insights I.3
Towards a more effective and efficient SD incorporation into the universities

Rodrigo Lozano

INTRODUCTION

For centuries, universities have been at the forefront in creating and breaking paradigms, as well as educating the future leaders, decision makers, entrepreneurs, and intellectuals (Cortese, 2003; Elton, 2003; Lozano, 2006). However, universities have remained largely traditional (Elton, 2003), where far too much of modern education has continued to rely upon Newtonian and Cartesian mental models, which relegate learning and action to reductionist thinking and mechanistic interpretation (Lovelock, 2007; Nonaka and Takeuchi, 2001). Relying on these mental models and scientific positions has led to the conquest of nature through competition (Cortese, 2003), industrialization (Carley and Christie, 2000; Orr, 1992; Reid, 1995; WCED, 1987), overspecialization and disciplinary isolation (Cortese, 2003; Costanza, 1991), and testing by repetition (Burke, 2000; Lozano, 2010). Such reductionist education has fostered highly individualistic, greedy and self-interested behaviours (Lozano, 2007; Stead and Stead, 1994).

These paradigms present a daring challenge to higher education institutions (HEIs) and society in general, in order to achieve a sensible future for those not yet born generations, especially if the rate of change in universities is taken into consideration.

To overcome this an increasing number of HEIs have engaged in incorporating and institutionalizing sustainable development (SD) into their systems (Boks and Diehl, 2006; Calder and Clugston, 2003; Cortese, 2003; Lozano, 2006, 2010; Lozano-Ros, 2003; Wemmenhove and de Groot, 2001). It is commonly agreed that this system has the following principal elements (Cortese, 2003; Lozano, 2006):

(a) Education (referring to Curricula)[1]
(b) Research
(c) Campus operations
(d) Community outreach
(e) Assessment and reporting

These elements are not mutually excluding;

on the contrary, they are interlinked and interdependent.

The university system is also composed of different stakeholders such as academic directors (for example deans, rector, president, directors of department, directors of divisions), the professors (in the undergraduate and postgraduate courses), researchers, staff, and students, among others (Lozano, 2006).

Nonetheless, education for sustainable development (ESD) has not fully permeated all disciplines, scholars, and university leaders (Fien, 2002), or throughout the curricula (Matten and Moon, 2004). The number of universities engaged with SD is still small compared to the total number of universities in the world. For example, out of 14,000 universities in the world (IAU, 2011), only 15 have published sustainability reports (Lozano, 2011).

The burning questions for universities, as centres of excellence, and key players in the SD debate, are: (1) how can SD be effectively and efficiently incorporated into the university's system? And (2) how can universities better contribute to the four dynamic and interlinked dimensions of sustainability (economic, environmental, social, and time)?

This chapter aims to provide some answers to these questions with the help of the declarations, charters, and initiatives for SD in higher education, as well as through a brief overview of barriers to change and some strategies developed to overcome them.

DECLARATIONS AS MEANS TO FACILITATE EMBEDDING SUSTAINABILITY INTO THE UNIVERSITIES' SYSTEM

At the Stockholm Conference in 1972 (UNEP, 1972) education was formally recognized on an international level to play an important role in fostering environmental protection and conservation. Since then many academic declarations, charters and partnerships have been developed that were designed to foster environmental education (EE), SD, and ESD. From 1987 there has been a large increase in such initiatives. The declarations, charters and partnerships have been designed to provide guidelines or frameworks for HEIs to better embed sustainability into their systems.

The increasing importance of such decla-rations, charters and partnerships, to foster transformative SD is evidenced by the more than 1000 university leaders who ratified their commitment to work to advance SD education and research by signing the Talloires Declaration, the Kyoto Declaration, and the Copernicus University Charter by the end of 2003 (Calder and Clugston, 2003).

The declarations, charters and partnerships highlight the moral obligation of universities to work towards a sustainable future, as well as the following themes (Calder and Clugston, 2003; Lozano-Ros, 2003; Wright, 2004):

- Highlight the importance of education, especially higher education, as a multiplier of SD
- Focus on environmental degradation, threats to society, and unsustainable consumption
- Engage the institution to SD
- Create a culture of sustainable development within and outside the institution
- Include SD throughout the curricula in all disciplines, campus operations, courses, and research
- Encourage SD research
- Move towards more sustainability oriented university operations
- Engage with stakeholders, for example public, governments, non-governmental organizations (NGOs) and businesses, for collaboration, engagement and outreach
- Communicate SD efforts to the community
- Address intra- and inter-generational equity

From the above, and their recent analysis of 11 declarations, charters and partnerships Lozano et al. (2010) propose that five more elements that could be added to the university's system: (1) universities' collaboration, (2) transdisciplinarity, (3) implementing SD through campus experiences, by incorporating SD into the day-to-day activities in the university life experience, (4) 'educating-the-educators' on how to educate their students in SD and help foster multiplier effects, and (5) including SD in the institutional framework, where SD should evolve as the 'Golden Thread' integrating all of these.

RESISTANCE TO SD IN UNIVERSITIES
In spite of the calls from the declarations, there have been several other reasons that explain the resistance of universities to engage with SD, such as:

- Little or no motivation or realism (Boks and Diehl, 2006)
- Lack of SD awareness (Lozano, 2006)
- SD considered to be radical (Lozano, 2006)
- Changes in curricula translated into budget claims (Peet, Mulder and Bijma, 2004)
- Insecurity and threat to academic credibility from teachers and professors (Peet et al., 2004)
- Confusion about SD (Velazquez, Munguia and Sanchez, 2005)
- Broadness of SD (Chau, 2007)
- Lack of financial resources (Velazquez et al., 2005)
- Overcrowded curricula (Abdul-Wahab, Abdulraheem and Hutchinson, 2003; Chau, 2007)
- Lack of SD knowledge from administrators (Davis, Edmister, Sullivan and West, 2003) or support (Velazquez et al., 2005)
- Lack of mental and financial support, and discipline-restricted organizational structures (Lambrechts, Vanhoren, and Van den Haute, 2009; Velazquez et al., 2005)
- Some lecturers being unaware, or failing to see, the relevance of SD to their teaching (Lozano, 2006)
- Teachers who might prevent or fail to support the diffusion (Barab and Luehmann, 2003)
- SD considered to be radical (Lozano, 2006; Lozano-Ros, 2003)
- SD considered to have little or no relevance to the course or discipline
- Uncertainty of the efforts required to engage and incorporate SD (Lozano, 2010)
- Academic traditions that tie universities to old mechanistic mental models

Some of the proposals that have been made to help address and overcome the resistance to make universities more sustainability oriented, such as:

- Placing a higher priority on teaching SD concepts (Davis, et al., 2003)
- Including more realistic classroom experiences when teaching SD (Davis, et al., 2003)

- Using 'carrots and sticks' from financial, internal funds, staff promotion, or top-down managerialism (Elton, 2003)
- Intertwining SD as a concept in regular disciplinary courses, tailored to the nature of each specific course (Abdul-Wahab, et al., 2003; Kamp, 2006; Peet, et al., 2004; Shi, 2005; Thomas, 2004)
- Incremental implementation of SD (Lozano, 2006)
- Implementing SD through campus experiences, by incorporating SD into the day-to-day activities in the university experiences (Lourdel, Gondran, Laforest, and Brodhag, 2005)
- Making SD the 'Golden Thread' that permeates the university's educational, research, physical plant operations and societal outreach activities (Lozano Garcia, Kevany and Huisingh, 2006)
- Using leverage (Lozano, 2008)
- 'Educating-the-Educators' on the concepts, values, tools and procedures of SD (Huisingh and Mebratu, 2000)
- Utilizing multiplier effects (Elton, 2003; Rogers, 1995)
- Working to ensure the engagement of the institutional leaders in promoting SD (Ferrer et al., 2010)

MOVING TOWARDS MORE SUSTAINABILITY ORIENTED UNIVERSITIES

Even though SD came to prominence in 1987 with the publication of *Our common Future* (WCED, 1987), many higher education institutions in the world have not yet attempted to introduce it to their systems. The concept of SD contrasts with the existing Newtonian and Cartesian teaching methods in universities, mainly focused on resource depletion. Worldwide, university leaders must recognize that it is not possible to continue on such a path and that it is necessary to integrate the environmental and social aspects into the economic ones. This can be achieved by incorporating SD into their university's:

(a) Curricula
(b) Research
(c) Campus operations
(d) Community outreach
(e) Assessment and reporting

(f) Universities' collaboration
(g) Transdisciplinarity

and also through:

(h) Implementing SD through campus experiences, by incorporating SD into the day-to-day activities in the university life experience
(i) 'Educating-the-Educators' on how to educate their students in SD and help foster multiplier effects, and
(j) Including SD in the institutional framework, where SD should evolve as the 'Golden Thread' integrating all of these.

It should be noted that if any university in the world were looked at in detail, it would be discovered that it is already engaged with at least one SD issue. The questions that need to be asked are: to what extent and how can this be improved? How can SD be better incorporated into the system? And how can universities better contribute to SD?

To answer this, university leaders need to become more proactive, so that they can retake their forefront position in creating and breaking paradigms, and reintegrate sciences, arts, and the different disciplines to help societies become more sustainable. University leaders and SD champions must be aware of and understand individual needs; and also the change barriers and conflicts that could arise, in order to take the necessary steps to overcome the first and avoid and solve the last.

The declarations, charters, partnerships and conferences developed to foster SD can provide a framework or guidelines on how to better embed sustainability into universities' systems. The different initiatives emphasize that universities have a moral obligation to work towards sustainable societies, focusing on environmental degradation, threats to society, and sustainable production and consumption for this and future generations. The recognized university system needs to be complemented with the following elements: collaboration with other universities; making SD an integral part of the institutional framework; on-campus life experiences; and 'Educate-the-Educators' programmes. These key elements must be

integrated systemically into HEIs in order to provide learning and career value to those participating in the SD transition.

The evolution of HEIs' initiatives for SD suggests that universities are following society and the business world when it comes to integrating sustainability into their systems and better contributing to making societies more sustainable. Some HEIs tend to respond slowly to society's needs, although nowadays, through public policy or societal pressure, the HEIs with foresight and leadership are beginning to adopt and weave SD into their curricula, research, outreach, and campus operations.

In this perspective, university leaders need to review the SD declarations and charters and see how they could be used as means to: foster sustainability in the university and its relations to the community; introduce SD to the university's mission, policy and strategic planning; and select and empower an SD champion and help in the development and transformation of courses to be more transdisciplinary.

University leaders also need to recognize the many individual, group, organizational, and systemic barriers that are slowing down the incorporation and institutionalization of SD in universities (such as lack of awareness, funding, support, lack of relevance, and conservationism). They could, thus, better overcome these barriers by:

1. Recognizing that SD is a necessity in the current world.
2. Providing the necessary information and skills to all stakeholders.
3. Detecting and involving individuals interested in SD.
4. Educating and make champions of these individuals.
5. Providing the necessary institutional framework for the SD efforts to have continuity.
6. Embedding SD in the curricula.
7. Striving to incorporate SD into the entire system.

REFERENCES

Abdul-Wahab, S.A., Abdulraheem, M.Y. and Hutchinson, M. (2003) The need for inclusion of environmental education in undergraduate engineering curricula. *Internat-*

ional Journal of Sustainability in Higher Education, **4**(2), pp. 126–37.

Ball State University (2011) Greening of the campus conference. Retrieved 27 February, 2011, from http://cms.bsu.edu/Academics/CentersandInstitutes/GOC.aspx

Barab, S.A. and Luehmann, A.L. (2003) Building sustainable science curriculum: acknowledging and accommodating local adaptation. *Science Education*, **87**(4), pp. 454–67.

Boks, C. and Diehl, J.C. (2006) Integration of sustainability in regular courses: experiences in industrial design engineering. *Journal of Cleaner Production*, **14**(9–11), pp. 932–9.

Burke, J. (2000) *The Knowledge Web* (1st edn). New York: Touchstone.

Calder, W. and Clugston, R.M. (2003) International efforts to promote higher education for sustainable development. *Planning for Higher Education*, **31**, pp. 30–44.

Carley, M. and Christie, I. (2000) *Managing sustainable development* (2nd edn). London: Earthscan Publications Ltd.

Chau, K.W. (2007) Incorporation of sustainability concepts into a civil engineering curriculum. *Journal of Professional Issues in Engineering Education and Practice*, **133**(3), pp. 188–91.

Cortese, A.D. (2003) The critical role of higher education in creating a sustainable future. *Planning for Higher Education*, **31**(3), pp. 15–22.

Costanza, R. (1991) *Ecological Economics. The Science and Management of Sustainability*. New York: Columbia University Press.

Davis, S.A., Edmister, J.H., Sullivan, K. and West, C.K. (2003) Educating sustainable societies for the twenty-first century. *International Journal of Sustainability in Higher Education*, **4**(2), pp. 169–79.

Elton, L. (2003) Dissemination of innovations in higher education: A change theory approach. *Tertiary Education and Management*, (9), pp. 199–214.

Ferrer, D., Lozano, R., Huisingh, D., Buckland, H., Ysern, P. and Zilahy, G. (2010) Going beyond the rhetoric: system-wide changes in universities for sustainable societies. *Journal of Cleaner Production*, **18**, pp. 607–10.

Fien, J. (2002) Advancing sustainability in higher education: issues and opportunities for research. *Higher Education Policy*, **15**, pp. 143–52.

Huisingh, D. and Mebratu, D. (2000) 'Educating the educators' as a strategy for enhancing education on cleaner production. *Journal of Cleaner Production*, **8**(5), pp. 439–42.

IAU (2011) *World Higher Education Database*. Basingstoke: Palgrave Macmillan.

Kamp, L. (2006) Engineering education in sustainable development at Delft University of Technology. *Journal of Cleaner Production*, **14**(9–11), pp. 928–31.

Lambrechts, W., Vanhoren, I. and Van den Haute, H. (2009) Duurzaam hoger onderwijs. Appel voor verantwoord onderrichten, onderzoeken en ondernemen (Sustainable higher education. Appeal for responsible education, research and operations). Leuven: LannooCampus.

Lourdel, N., Gondran, N., Laforest, V. and Brodhag, C. (2005) Introduction of sustainable development in engineers' curricula. Problematic and evaluation methods. *International Journal of Sustainability in Higher Education*, **6**(3), pp. 254–64.

Lovelock, J. (2007) *The Revenge of Gaia*. London: Penguin Group.

Lozano Garcia, F.J., Kevany, K. and Huisingh, D. (2006) Sustainability in higher education: what is happening? *Journal of Cleaner Production*, **14**(9–11), pp. 757–60.

Lozano, R. (2006) Incorporation and institutionalization of SD into universities: breaking through barriers to change. *Journal of Cleaner Production*, **14**(9–11), pp. 787–96.

Lozano, R. (2007) Collaboration as a pathway for sustainability. *Sustainable Development*, **16**(6), pp. 370–81.

Lozano, R. (2008) Developing collaborative and sustainable organisations. *Journal of Cleaner Production*, **16**(14), pp. 499–509.

Lozano, R. (2010) Diffusion of sustainable development in universities' curricula: an empirical example from Cardiff University. *Journal of Cleaner Production*, **18**(7), pp. 637–44. doi: http://dx.doi.org/10.1016/j.jclepro.2009.07.005

Lozano, R. (2011) The state of sustainability reporting in universities. *International Journal of Sustainability in Higher Education*, **12**(1), pp. 67–78. doi: doi:doi:10.1016/j.jclepro.2007.01.002

Lozano, R., Lukman, R., Lozano, F.J., Huisingh, D. and Zilahy, G. (2010) *Jumping Sustainability Meme. SD transfer from society to universities* Paper presented at the Environmental Management for Sustainable Universities, Delf, The Netherlands.

Lozano-Ros, R. (2003) *Sustainable Development in Higher Education. Incorporation, assessment and reporting of sustainable development in higher education institutions*. Master thesis, Lund University, Lund.

Matten, D. and Moon, J. (2004) Corporate social responsibility education in Europe. *Journal of Business Ethics*, **54**, pp. 323–37.

Nonaka , I. and Takeuchi, H. (2001) Organizational knowledge creation. In: Henry, J. (ed.) *Creative Management* (2nd edn). London: Sage Publications Ltd.

Orr, D.W. (1992) *Ecological Literacy*. New York: State University of New York.

Peet, D.-J., Mulder, K.F. and Bijma, A. (2004) Integrating SD into engineering courses at the Delft University of Technology. The individual interaction method. *International Journal of Sustainability in Higher Education*, **5**(3), pp. 278–88.

Reid, D. (1995) *Sustainable Development. An Introductory Guide* (1st edn). London: Earthscan Publications Ltd.

Rogers, E.M. (1995) *Diffusion of Innovations* (4th edn). New York: Free Press.

Shi, C. (2005) Exploring effective approaches for 'education for sustainable development' in universities of China. In: Holmberg, J. and Samuelsson, B.E. (eds) *Drivers and Barriers for Implementing Sustainable Development in Higher Education*. Gothenburg: UNESCO.

Stead, W.E. and Stead, J.G. (1994) Can humankind change the economic myth? Paradigm shifts necessary for ecologicaly sustainable business. *Journal of Organizational Change Management*, **7**(4), pp. 15–31.

Thomas, I. (2004) Sustainability in tertiary curricula: what is stopping it happening? *International Journal of Sustainability in Higher Education*, **5**(1), pp. 33–47.

UNEP (1972) Declaration of the United Nations Conference on the Human Environment Retrieved 12 August 2010, United Nations Environment Programme, from http://www.unep.org/Documents.Multilingual/Default.asp?documentid=97&articleid=1503

Velazquez, L., Munguia, N. and Sanchez, M. (2005) Deterring sustainability in higher education institutions: An appraisal of the factors which influence sustainability in higher education institutions. *International Journal of Sustainability in Higher Education*, **6**(4), pp. 383–91.

WCED (1987) *Our Common Future* (1st edn). Oxford: Oxford University Press.

Wemmenhove, R. and de Groot, W.T. (2001) Principles for university curriculum greening. An empirical case study from Tanza-nia. *International Journal of Sustainability in Higher Education*, **2**(3), pp. 267–83.

Wright, T. (2004) The evolution of Sustainability declarations in higher education. In: Corcoran, P.B. and Wals, A.E.J. (eds) *Higher Education and the Challenge of Sustainability: Problematics, Promise, and Practice.* Dordrecht, The Netherlands: Kluwer Academic Publishers.

NOTE

1   The Sustainability Tool for Assessing UNiversities Curricula Holistically (STAUNCH®) 2010 can help to map how courses, programmes, faculties, and the entire university is contributing to sustainability. For details on STAUNCH, please visit http://www.org-sustainability.com/orgsust.php?str=staunch.

HIGHER EDUCATION FOR SUSTAINABILITY: A GLOBAL OVERVIEW OF COMMITMENT AND PROGRESS   **35**

This is a chronological selection of international events, declarations and agreements that refer to the concepts of environment, sustainable development and their relationship with education, more specifically with higher education.

For the sake of concision it was not possible to provide an exhaustive description of all of the information published to date. The content included here was therefore selected according to the following criteria: conference, events, documents, declarations or reports produced by international institutions such as the UN and UNESCO and endorsed by government representatives and university leaders, as well as some publications considered as landmarks on the topic.

	1948	The International Union for the Protection of Nature is founded
Rachel Carson publishes 'Silent Spring'.	1962	
	1963	International Biological Programme
	1964	
	1965	
	1966	
	1967	
Paul Ehrlich publishes 'Population Bomb'	1968	Intergovernmental Conference of Experts on the Scientific Basis for Rational Use and Conservation of the Resources of the Biosphere
		The Club of Rome is established
		UNESCO Intergovernmental Conference for Rational Use and Conservation of Biosphere
	1969	UNESCO conference 'Man and his Environment: A View Towards Survival'
	1970	First Earth Day held as a USA national teach-in on the environment
	1971	The Man and the Biosphere programme is founded by UNESCO
Founex Report is prepared by a panel of experts meeting in Switzerland		
Stockholm Declaration	1972	United Nations Conference on the Human Environment held in Stockholm
Meadows et al. publish 'The Limits to Growth'		
Barbara Ward and Rene Dubos publish 'Only One Earth'		
		Creation of the United Nations Environment Programme (UNEP)
	1973	
Bariloche Foundation publishes 'Limits to Poverty'.	1974	
Belgrade Charter	1975	International Workshop on Environmental Education held in Belgrade
	1976	
	1977	UN Conference on Desertification
Tbilisi Declaration		Intergovernmental Conference on Environmental Education held in Tbilisi
	1978	
	1979	
Independent Commission on International Development Issues publishes 'North:South – A Programme for Survival' (Brandt Report)	1980	
World Conservation Strategy released by IUCN.		
'Global 2000 Report' is released		
	1981	
United Nations World Charter for Nature	1982	The UN Convention on the Law of the Sea is adopted
		UN General Assembly adopts a World Charter for Nature prepared by IUCN
	1983	
Worldwatch Institute publishes its first 'State of the World Report'.	1984	OECD International Conference on Environment and Economics
		Third World Network is founded
	1985	
	1986	IUCN Conference on Environment and Development held in Ottawa, Canada
World Commission on Environment and Development issues its report 'Our Common Future' (Brundtland Report)	1987	
		Montreal Protocol on Substances that Deplete the Ozone Layer is adopted

	1988	Intergovernmental Panel on Climate Change is established
	1989	
	1990	UN Summit for Children
		International Conference of University's Leaders held in Talloires, France
Talloires Declaration	1991	Halifax Conference on University Action for Sustainable Development
Halifax Declarataion		
Rio Declaration and Agenda 21	1992	United Nations Conference on Environment and Development held in Rio de Janeiro, Brazil
		United Nations General Assembly sets up the Commission on Sustainable Development
		United Nations Framework Convention on Climate Change (UNFCCC) was adopted
The World Business Council for Sustainable Development publishes 'Changing Course'		
IAU Kyoto Declaration	1993	Ninth Round Table of the International Association of Universities
Swansea Declaration		Association of Commonwealth Universities Conference 'People and the Environment – Preserving the Balance'
COPERNICUS University Charter for Sustainable Development		Bi-annual Conference of European Rectors held in Barcelona
Barbados Declaration	1994	UN Global Conference on the Sustainable Development of Small Island Developing States
	1995	World Summit for Social Development held in Copenhagen, Denmark
Student Declaration for a Sustainable Future		Community Environmental Educational Development Conference
Learning: The Treasure Within. Report presented to UNESCO by the International Commission on Education for the Twenty-first Century	1996	
Thessaloniki Declaration	1997	UN General Assembly review of the Earth Summit (Rio+5)
		Thessaloniki International Conference on Environment and Society: Education and Public Awareness for Sustainability
		Kyoto Protocol
World Declaration on Higher Education in the 21st Century: Vision and Action	1998	UNESCO World Conference on Higher Education
	1999	
The Earth Charter	2000	United Nations Millennium Summit
Millennium Declaration		
Lüneburg Declaration on Higher Education for Sustainable Development	2001	International Copernicus Conference 'Higher Education for Sustainability – Towards the World Summit on Sustainable Development 2002'
Ubuntu Declaration on Education and Science and Technology for Sustainable Development	2002	World Summit on Sustainable Development held in Johannesburg
		Global Reporting Initiative
Cape Town Declaration on Research for Sustainable Development		
	2003	
	2004	
Millennium Ecosystem Assessment released	2005	United Nations Decade of Education for Sustainable Development (2005–2014)
Graz Declaration on Committing Universities to Sustainable Development		Conference on 'Committing Universities to Sustainable Development', held in Graz, Austria
		Alliance of Civilizations
Report of the High-level Group of the Alliance of Civilizations	2006	
Council of Europe Declaration on the Responsibility of Higher Education for a Democratic Culture – Citizenship, Human Rights and Sustainability		
		American College and University Presidents' Climate Commitment
	2007	
Sapporo Sustainability Declaration	2008	The G8 University Summit
Torino Declaration on Education and Research for Sustainable and Responsible Development		The G8 University Summit
Bonn Declaration	2009	UNESCO World Conference on Education for Sustainable Development
Communiqué of the World Conference on Higher Education		UNESCO World Conference on Higher Education
Abuja Declaration on 'Sustainable Development in Africa – The Role of Higher Education'		AAU 12th General Conference on 'Sustainable Development in Africa – The Role of Higher Education'
Tokyo Declaration of HOPE		
	2010	

PART II
REGIONAL PERSPECTIVES: WHAT HAS BEEN ACHIEVED AT THIS STAGE?

II.1 The 'Event' of Modern Sustainable Development and Universities in Africa

Heila Lotz-Sisitka

Abstract

This paper considers the actualization of sustainable development in modern African universities. It draws on Deleuze's (1995) concept of 'event' to develop analytical lenses for considering different ways in which sustainable development is interpreted in African universities; the problems that sustainable development is responding to; and the ways in which sustainable development is actualized in events, networks, practices and experiences of universities. This analysis is based on a review of a wide range of over 200 documents, policy statements and emerging university practices. It also draws on a recent survey involving a number of universities in Africa.

The analysis is located within a wider understanding of the short, yet complex history of African universities, and knowledge that foundational concepts of sustainable development are not new to Africa. The paper argues that actualization of sustainable development in African universities must be contextualized within history; and within contemporary constraints and influences on practice.

The paper closes by drawing attention to the *problématique* of narrowly or technically interpreting sustainable development in African universities. Reminded by Ferguson (2006) that our academic concepts are often inadequate for the times, the paper asks whether sustainable development is an *adequate concept or 'event'* guiding education in Africa.

INTRODUCTION

There are different starting points for thinking about sustainable development (SD) in African societies.

> Listen to things
> More often than beings
> Hear the voice of fire
> Hear the voice of water
> Listen to the wind to the sighs of the bush
> This is the ancestors breathing
>
> Birago Diop (1961, Senegal;
> in Larson, 2005: 31)[1]

Cosmological perspectives such as those reflected above show that interrelatedness of the natural and cultural order are not new to Africa. Foundational concepts of sustainable development are integral to cultural practices in a diversity of African societies, and elsewhere. Shiva (2006, p. 1) for example refers to a concept of *'vasudhaiva kutumbkam'* [the earth family] in India. She states that 'indigenous cultures worldwide have understood and experienced life as a continuum between human and nonhuman species and between present, past, and future generations'. Numerous livelihood practices in Africa *demonstrate* SD, for example the *Machobane*, *Chitemene* and *Fundkile* Farming Systems in Lesotho and Zambia respectively; and traditional agro-forestry practices in Tanzania (Stromgaard, 1989; Tembo et al., 2008). Most often these days, however, we find standard global commentaries on SD in Africa that typically read as follows:

> Global climate change reports indicate that Africa is highly vulnerable to the impacts of climate change … Other threats to the natural environment include deforestation, over-exploitation of resources, deterioration

of marine and coastal ecosystems and water quality issues … Problems of poverty, food insecurity, wars and violence, HIV/AIDS, environmentally related diseases, drought, water and sanitation are prevalent in the continent … Within the world economy, Africa holds a marginal position. Most African countries do not meet the human development index … and 19 countries with the lowest human development index are in sub-Saharan Africa … The challenge for Africa is to overcome these threats to development and utilise and manage its rich natural resources sustainably for the well-being of its people today and tomorrow … Africa needs to urgently increase human capacity and skills to improve development opportunities, and to respond and adapt to these risks. (extract from GUNi/IAU/AAU, 2011, p. 3)

This has implications for universities, which themselves have a complex history that is intertwined with modern development patterns. Popkewitz (2005, p. 23) notes that 'Science is a central marker to differentiate what is modern and what is not … In the 19th-century Europe and North America, scientific methods embodied what many intellectuals and social planners viewed as the most potent force shaping the world'. Scientific methods were exported, and became 'indigenous foreigners' that provide 'cultural theses about modes of living' (ibid., 2005, p. 31).[2] Before 1960 there were only a handful of universities on the African continent, all of them established in the colonial period following the 'university college' model (Africa Watch, 1991). These universities reproduced mainly the scientific and institutional patterns characteristic of British, French and Belgian universities and cultures[3] (ibid.). Universities in Africa, while having a long and ancient history,[4] are essentially a 'post-independence' phenomenon, established to service the independent nation state. Ironically, despite over 300 new universities and new forms of curriculum following independence; the history of science and the political economy of universities in Africa remain heavily shaped by the 'indigenous foreigner' phenomenon that Popkewitz (2005) alludes to.

Universities in Africa have also been affected by 'turbulent times', state control, economic decline, war and repression, and some loss of academic freedom. In particular, post-independent universities were hard hit by the impact of the global oil crisis in the 1970s and the subsequent recession and financial crisis in Africa. This influenced World Bank and International Monetary Fund (IMF) structural adjustment programmes, leading to cuts in education, health and social services spending in the 1980s. Higher education (HE) was categorized as *a secondary priority* in education systems. Universities in Africa still suffer from this today, notwithstanding recent attempts to 'revitalize' African universities by the African Union and others. Today there are increased calls for strengthening academic freedom and redefining the role of HE in Africa in terms that are important to the continent's realities. This involves promoting the public good; social transformation; democracy; human emancipation and giving greater attention to environmental issues (among others) (Africa Watch, 1991; Diouf and Mamdani, 1994; UNEP MESA, 2009; Singh, 2001; Zeleze and Olukoshi, 2004). However, all these objectives remain undermined by continued brain drain, financial difficulties, problems of purpose, conditions for scholarship, and epistemology in universities (Mamdani, 2011). They are also affected by high enrolment demands (enrolment numbers are increasing at rates of 10–14% annually, or doubling every 5–7 years) (Kellog and Hervey, 2010) and the broader, somewhat 'dismal' picture of the current status of HE in Africa. Enrolment rates for HE in sub-Saharan Africa are by far the lowest in the world. The region's enrolment ratio is in the same range as that of other developing regions 40 years ago (Bloom, Canning and Chan, 2006). UNESCO (2009) states that 'Despite the fact that the number of tertiary students in sub-Saharan Africa has dramatically increased since 1970, actual progress is muted by population growth. Over the same period, the "tertiary age group" population has grown by an average annual rate of 3%. Consequently, participation ratios (GER) only rose from 0.8% to 5.6% during this period [1970–2007]', with persisting gender inequalities. Added to this scenario, Africa's illiteracy rate of 176 million adults in sub-Saharan Africa (UNESCO, 2010) is a problem still staring the continent in the face.

Any reading of SD *actualization* in African universities must therefore be contextualized within history; and contemporary constraints and influences.

METHODOLOGICAL NOTE AND ANALYTICAL LENSES

Deleuze's (1995, p. 141) life work on the 'nature of events' provides a useful way of understanding the emergence and actualization of SD in African universities. He states that the notion of the 'event' is 'a philosophical concept, the only one capable of ousting the verb "to be" and its attributes', providing a *critical process framework* for analysis. His work suggests a process of coming to understand 'concepts invented' (such as the concept of sustainable development), and their articulation in social practices (in this case the social practices of universities in Africa). Concepts (such as sustainable development), he argues, need to be assessed not for their truth or falsity, but for *the degree to which they are 'Interesting, Remarkable, or Important'* (p. 82, my emphasis). Patton (2006, p. 109) explains further, 'Concepts are interesting, remarkable or important when they give expression to new problems or solutions to problems already posed'. The notion of 'event' produces the following *questions and analytical lenses* useful to this study:

- **Analytical lens 1:** Is sustainable development, in its contemporary form, an 'interesting, remarkable or important' concept in and for universities in Africa? And if so, how is SD being viewed on the African university landscape?
- **Analytical lens 2:** 'If the concept is a solution, the conditions of the philosophical problem are to be found on the plane of immanence presupposed by the concept' (Deleuze and Guattari, 1994, pp. 80–1). This requires interrogation of the problem to which sustainable development offers a solution on the African continent, and what the conditions of this problem are.
- **Analytical lens 3:** *Events are actualized in states of affairs* (for example national or university level policies); *bodies* (for example structures in universities), *and in the lived experiences of people* (for example the experiences of professors and students in universities) (Deleuze and Guatarri, 1994). This actualization is, in part, dependent on how the nature of the events is understood.
- **Analytical lens 4:** 'The event subsists in language, but happens to things' (Deleuze, 1990, p. 24). This indicates that incorporeal transformations occur that act upon the world and change social and institutional practices. Patton (2006) notes the need to differentiate between language and changed practices in these actualizations.[5]
- **Analytical lens 5:** Deleuze notes that it is important to differentiate between the problem-event (that is, why the event of sustainable development exists), and the possibility of other specifications and solutions (Deleuze, 1995, pp. 186, 203–4).

These analytical perspectives are used to focus the analysis of a wide range of over 200 documents, policy statements, and emerging university practices that were examined in and for the construction of this contribution to the Global Universities Network for Innovation (GUNi) publication on universities and sustainable development.[6]

SUSTAINABLE DEVELOPMENT AS AN 'INTERESTING CONCEPT' INFLUENCING PRACTICE IN UNIVERSITIES IN AFRICA (ANALYTICAL LENS 1)

Much has been written about the concept of SD, its origins and its contested contemporary appearances in policy discourses, appropriated privatization platforms and practices. Of significance to this paper is the widely recognized point that SD remains an *ambivalent concept*, best described by a South African environmental ethics scholar, Johan Hattingh (2002, p. 6) when he notes that:

> the highly contestable nature of sustainable development can be ascribed to its highly ambivalent ideological dimensions: it can either function as an ideology, or as a critique of ideology (which in itself can be interpreted as an ideology, in so far as it serves the interests of those engaged in ideology critique).

This ambivalence is present in the **five perspectives on sustainable development** that appear most prominent in the African university landscape at this time in history (apparent causal influences are indicated in italics below). Different perspectives sometimes live 'side-by-side' in one university context (Togo, 2009), or one perspective may dominate in an institution.

1. **Interpreting SD in terms of social development:** The emphasis is on the more dominant society-economy nexus, leaving out the environmental relation, reflecting what some would refer to as 'weak' notions of SD (Hattingh, 2004). *This appears to be linked to an inadequate analysis of the relationship between environment–economy–society in poverty contexts; particularly a political ecology analysis of social development.*
2. **'Back-grounding' the concept of SD while fore-grounding associated issues and risks such as climate change; water; land use and so on directly:** In such cases SD 'issues' or 'foci' tend to be dealt with in separate 'units' or disciplines, with little or no inter- or transdisciplinary engagement across issues or within complex issue contexts. *This appears to be linked to discipline or 'silo' thinking, and a lack of holistic engagement with complex issues. There also appears to be a strong link to global environmental research programmes.*
3. **Interpreting the concept of SD to mean 'community engaged university education':** Teaching and research is oriented towards local/national community-based and rural development problems, most

often associated with poverty, health, basic and adult education, environmental management, and food security. The focus is on making university education 'more relevant' in local context; and strategies such as fieldwork or service learning are typically used. *This appears to be linked to moral concerns with well-being and the role of the university in society.*

4. **Interpreting the concept of SD to mean participation in new science and technology trajectories:** These are most often oriented towards eco-efficiency, low carbon development, green economy, sustainability technology innovations and associated new market opportunities; and tend to reflect discourses of the 'knowledge economy'. This trend is heavily science and technology based. *This appears to be linked to technology transfer imperatives; ecological modernization and associated technology-centred developments. It is also most closely linked to new forms of global capital flow.*

5. **Critiquing SD discourse using political ecology arguments:** These critiques tend to reject global discourses of SD; particularly where evidence of neo-liberal appropriations of SD exist. Mainstream SD is viewed with suspicion. Other preferred discourses such as political ecology; environmental racism; social justice, and ecological economics are used to engage issues often associated with SD. *These arguments are premised on socially critical and social justice analyses focusing mainly on control of resource flows, and patterns of inclusion and exclusion. This work also deals critically with the manner in which certain appropriations of SD form part of a wider ongoing process of 'structuring under-development' on the African continent (Bond, 2006; Ferguson, 2006).*

From this, SD is potentially an 'interesting concept'; particularly if one begins to consider *how and why* different conceptions of SD are becoming visible; what *tensions and contradictions* exist between these the conceptions of SD and why this might be so. To understand these perspectives more fully, however, it is necessary to probe the 'problem' to which SD is responding.

TO WHAT PROBLEM IS THE CONCEPT OF SD RESPONDING? (ANALYTICAL LENS 2)

Diversity of perspective and problem conception is not surprising given the immense diversity and scope of the African continent and its complex histories. As Ferguson (2006, p. 1) so eloquently states:

Africa is a huge continent, covering one fifth of the world's land surface, where over 800 million people live an extraordinary variety of lives. Is there any meaningful sense in which we can speak of this [that is, Africa] as 'a place'? Looking at the range of empirical differences internal to the continent – different natural environments, historical experiences, religious traditions, forms of government, languages, livelihoods, and so on – the unity of a thing called 'Africa,' its status as a single 'place', however the continental descriptor may be qualified geographically or racially ('Sub-Saharan', 'black', 'tropical', or what have you) seems dubious … Indeed, it has often been suggested that the very category of 'Sub-Saharan Africa' with its conventional separation from a 'Middle East' that would include North Africa, is as much a product of modern race thinking as it is an obvious cultural or historical unity.

From this vantage point – of immense diversity – and historically constituted identity configurations that today hold purchase both internally on, and externally to the African continent, Ferguson goes on to state that most often:

When we hear about 'Africa' today, it is usually in urgent and troubled tones. It is never just Africa, but always the crisis in Africa, the problems of Africa, the failure of Africa, the moral challenge of Africa to 'the international community', even Africa as a 'scar on the conscience of the world' (Ferguson, citing the former British Prime Minister Tony Blair's phrase, 2006, p. 2).

Thus it is most often that SD is reported on, and mobilized within a framework of securing improved life chances and increased well-being via a strategy that first describes the 'problems' that SD is interconnected with – as noted in the introduction to this paper. There are many of these and they include:
- Poverty
- HIV/AIDS
- Loss of ecosystem services
- Deforestation
- Inadequate educational provisioning and quality
- War and famine, and so on

A wide array of United Nations (UN) programmes and reports (for example the UNDP Human Development Reports; the UN Millennium Development Goals reports and so on), define SD on the African continent in terms that most often focus on poverty; governance; agricultural modernization; health; education and environmental management. These reports tend to focus on identifying the 'lacks' and the 'problems' that need to be understood and responded to by various means. Such knowledge is produced through a particular form of science oriented towards monitoring the status quo, and providing policy-relevant resources, scenarios and guidelines. Peet and Watts (2004) however, are critical of this kind of policy-relevant research, and argue that it enrols the university in what they describe as an AIM (academic-industry-media) complex; which serves simply to promote continuities of the status quo. Achile Mbembe (2002) states that the types of analyses that focus on the 'lacks' and the 'problems' tend to focus on what Africa is not, and not on what Africa is. With such an argument at hand, it would be interesting to see equivalent research investment and emphasis on those sustainability practices that do exist in Africa (as briefly noted in the opening of this paper). This raises a question on how 'the problems' that SD may need to respond to are defined.

Ferguson (2006) describes 'the problem' in terms of transnational forms of power and globalization in a context where states (due to IMF policies that focused on 'rolling back the state') are 'in significant ways, no longer able to exercise the range of powers we usually associate with a sovereign nation state' (p. 93). He describes the emergence of new forms of governmentality (of which sustainable development may be one) emerging under the influences of globalization that 'bypass states altogether' (p. 100). Transnational topographies of power are establishing themselves in ways that 'hop' over whole sections of society, developing only those parts of the continent that are valuable for various reasons, a process that creates and sustains forms of structured underdevelopment. Transnational mining interests and conservation/ sustainable development programmes alike tend to create enclaves of power and control that fail to benefit the larger society, or even the nation states where the natural resource or mineral wealth lies. This transnational topography of power makes (sustainable) development of any kind exceedingly difficult. Consequently Ferguson argues for 'a heightened level of reflexive scrutiny of our categories of analysis' (2006, p. 89). Bond and Hallowes (2002) argue further that mainstream SD is an inadequate response to Africa's problems. They propose clear and explicit normative commitments to sufficiency, redistribution, equality and 'real' sustainability in development thinking. These complexities in problem definition provide the 'backdrop' to the emergent social practices of SD actualization in African universities.

HOW IS THE EVENT OF 'SUSTAINABLE DEVELOPMENT' ACTUALIZED IN AFRICAN UNIVERSITIES? (ANALYTICAL LENS 3)

While numerous examples of the actualization of sustainable development exist in African universities' social practices, there is little consolidated data on the exact nature of this actualization. Best available evidence (from over 200 documents), and data produced from a recent survey conducted by the Global Universities Network for Innovation (GUNi); the International Association of Universities (IAU), and the Association of African Universities (AAU) targeting 500 higher education institutions (HEIs) on the African continent shows that among the 73 universities that responded (14.6%); there is actualization of SD discourse in this percentage of universities. It states that:

> Results of the study show that higher education institutions in Africa are promoting sustainable development both on their campuses and in their communities. Commitment to sustainability is reflected in some of the universities' written statements. Some have integrated sustainability in their curricula; some are involved in sustainability research and outreach projects. African universities are also involved in sustainability partnerships at various levels and some are setting aside funds for sustainability projects. Involvement in sustainable development initiatives is however still significantly small in most universities. (GUNi/IAU/AAU, 2011, p. x)

As mentioned above, Deleuze (1995) notes that 'events' are actualized in *states of affairs*; in *bodies, structures* and *artefacts*; and in the *life experiences of people*. Actualization trends visible in the data[7] include:

1 ACTUALIZATION IN 'STATES OF AFFAIRS':
NEW PARTNERSHIPS FOR SD IN HIGHER EDUCATION

The formation of new partnerships is a significant 'actualization' process that influences other SD-oriented social practices in universities. These new partnerships operate at different scales, with some being international; and others being national and/or local. Some examples include:

- The Columbia University Earth Institute and the MacArthur Foundation established a partnership with universities in Africa and in other developing countries to develop and offer a Global Master's Degree in Development Practice (http://globalmdp. org). This is an interdisciplinary graduate degree programme, which prepares students to better identify and address the challenges of SD. The initial partnership was influential in charting out 'sustainable development competences' that are seen to be relevant to the African continent and other developing country contexts.

- The Mainstreaming Environment and Sustainability in African Universities Partnership (MESA) (www. unep.org/training) links the United Nations Environment Programme (UNEP) with key universities and partners that are actively engaged with environment and sustainability related social practices in universities. Partners include the AAU and UNESCO (among others). This network provides professional development support to academics to bring about curriculum innovations or SD social practices in their universities (UNEP, 2008).

- The United Nations University (UNU) linked Regional Centres of Expertise (RCE) Network on Education for Sustainable Development links universities with local community partners, but also with a continental and global RCE network. The focus of the RCEs is to strengthen transformative learning praxis in regional contexts. [www.ias.unu. edu/efsd/rce]

- The UNESCO-led Education for Sustainable Development (ESD) Teacher Education network (called AFRITEIS) links teacher education programmes to the UNESCO International ESD Teacher Education network; UNESCO's Education for All and other schools programmes, as well as to subregional networks, such as the Southern African Development Community (SADC) ESD Teacher Education network and wider Teacher Education networks such as the Teacher Training in sub-Saharan Africa (TTSSA) network [www.unesco.org/desd]

The examples show the 'mobilization power' of international organizations to bring a range of diverse actors together in SD actualization networks. Partnerships are, however, also a significant feature of ESD work *at university level*. The GUNi/IAU/AAU (2011) survey showed that over 60% of the responding institutions have established some form of partnerships. The partners include other universities and institutes, governmental agencies, national governments, international associations, research centres, corporations, foundations, and so on. They are either from other African nations or from outside the continent, especially Europe.

ESTABLISHMENT OF NEW/SPECIFIC INITIATIVES AND PROGRAMMES

Partnership formations tend to focus on the establish-

ment of new/specific initiatives such as development of new master's degrees; establishment of new local networks and/or professional development of academics. These all strengthen the capacity of universities to develop their ESD social practices; and to provide local and/or regional networked links. There are numerous such initiatives that are visible on the African universities' landscape, and again these can be international or national. For example:

- Sweden (SIDA) runs International Training Programmes on ESD in Higher Education; and Germany (GIZ) are developing International Training Programmes on ESD for Teacher Educators (there are many other similar international training programmes on offer for academics from African universities in all kinds of 'priority areas' related to SD)

- The African Caribbean Pacific (ACP)/European Union (EU) development programme formed a partnership with the African Union (AU), establishing specific 'research platforms and programmes' to strengthen SD research in universities. These link universities with each other (through mobility grants), and with the AU agenda for capacity building. Many other such examples exist.

In the GUNi/IAU/AAU (2011) survey sample, a total of 111 projects were listed by respondents as products of SD-oriented partnerships. These include education programmes; capability projects to develop leadership in SD; staff and student exchange; research projects; improvement of institutional facilities; library capacity building; resources management; waste management; strategies to support communities on topics of gender, peace, health and early childhood; issues of climate change; renewable energy projects; and cultural promotion, among others.

RESEARCH AND NEW KNOWLEDGE GENERATION

Another significant actualization process is research and new knowledge generation. For example, the Southern African Regional Universities Association (SARUA) recently commissioned a team of researchers to present papers on the 'status' of climate change and development knowledge in southern Africa, with the explicit purpose of influencing HE research and development capacity to respond to climate change in the region. This meeting led to an action plan for universities (SARUA, 2011).

There appear to be *more regional/subregional and international–African* partnership initiatives influencing SD research than locally constituted directions for SD research. This may be attributed to the funding situation for research in Africa. Examples here are research networks funded by the International Development Research Centre (IDRC) into eco-health development in West Africa; by the UK Department for International Development (DIFD) into ecosystem services and development; Deutschen Gesellschaft für Internationale Zusammenarbeit (GIZ) and EU-funded SD science and technology research; Sino–Africa research partnerships on water technologies and so on (there are many other examples). An example of a *national* level research plan guiding SD research is South Africa's Department of Science and Technology's (RSA, 2010) ten-year national research plan focusing on global change and energy research with associated national funding, but international partnerships form a core of this research plan.

The GUNi/IAU/AAU (2011) survey and the MESA review (UNEP, 2008) showed that *universities themselves were investing in SD research*, which indicates that research funding is not only coming from development partners, but also internally from national governments. This leads to mainly smaller scale research projects (funded locally with smaller scale funds) focused mainly on campus or in local community contexts. An example would be the Southern African Development Community (SADC) ESD Research Network support for small-scale case studies involving seed funds of $500 per local project (SADC REEP, 2011). The power and potential of the 'small scale research project' therefore remains poorly understood in/as sustainable development research on the African continent, as does its relevance to teaching and/or community engagement.

The GUNi/IAU/AAU (2011) survey indicated that student research projects tended to remain largely unpublished, and most publishing from African universities is 'co-authored' by international research partners. A substantive body of knowledge on SD in Africa may therefore be 'hidden' in student research outputs (theses) and in individual, small-scale research conducted by academics at a local level, reported in 'grey literature' and other forms of research reporting, and not in international ISI accredited journals.

Sustainable development research trends need to be read against the wider picture of research (or lack thereof) in African universities more widely. The recent 'Global Research Report: Africa' shows for example that Africa has extremely uneven distribution of research and innovative capacity (Adams, King and Hook, 2010). Research is concentrated in Egypt in the north, Nigeria in the west, and South Africa in the south. Africa produces only some 27,000 ISI accredited papers a year – about the same volume of published output as the Netherlands. As stated by Adams et al. (2010, p.1):

> A problem for Africa as a whole, as it has been for China and India, is the haemorrhage of talent. Many of its best students take their higher degrees at universities in Europe, Asia and North America. Too few return. The African diaspora provides powerful intellectual input to the research achievements of other countries but returns less benefit to the countries of birth. That is at least in part because of a chronic lack of investment in facilities for research and teaching, a deficit that must be remedied.

Participation in large-scale international research programmes is monopolized by larger universities with stronger international research profiles and capability; institutions that also dominate the formal academic publishing arena. There is a strong 'country bias' to research outputs. Formally accredited research outputs from the African continent also have a 'subject bias', with most research being linked to natural resources and their management and use. The Adams et al. (2010) report also correlates research output with GDP, indicating the important relationship that exists between research and development; which has implications for sustainable development of the continent. They state:

> The leading countries by [research] output are South Africa, Egypt, Nigeria, Tunisia, Algeria and Kenya. Four of these are also leading countries in terms of GDP (South Africa, Egypt, Nigeria and Algeria) while Kenya and Tunisia fall in the second GDP tier. (Adams et al., 2010, p. 5)

An important question may be how Africa's relative advantage in natural resources research can be mobilized for sustainable development of the continent; and also how the benefits of research can be strategically considered within development planning? This is particularly significant in the light of Kellog and Hervey's (2010, pg. 8) comment that 'Research in Africa has been a highly productive investment'. They (citing Alston et al., 2000) report that 'In one study by the International Food Policy Research Institute, it was found that the annual median returns from agricultural research were 34.3% for 188 R&D projects in Africa. The returns from 1800 agricultural research projects throughout the world were 44.3%.' They thus lament the fact that research investments in many African nations are stagnant or declining.

2 ACTUALIZATION IN 'BODIES, STRUCTURES AND ARTEFACTS'

Sustainable development actualization also occurs through existing bodies, structures and artefacts, and manifests in (new) bodies, structures and artefacts. This occurs at university level; at national and/or subregional levels; and at international level.

NEW AND/OR CHANGED UNIVERSITY ASSOCIATIONS AND SUBREGIONAL STRUCTURES

Little evidence was found of new university associations and/or subregional structures focusing directly on SD and African universities, beyond the networked partnership structures mentioned above. However, established university structures, such as the AAU; SARUA; UNESCO's Teacher Education Programme; and the Association for the Development of Education in Africa (ADEA) have engaged substantively with issues of SD on the African continent. They appear to be taking a leadership role in supporting African universities to give attention to issues associated with SD. For example, the Association of African Universities (involving a membership of some 225 universities) hosted its 12th Annual General Conference under the theme: 'Sustainable Development and Universities in Africa' (AAU, 2009. The AAU has actively supported the Mainstreaming of Environment and Sustainability in African Universities Programme Partnership. It also organized African Universities Day on the theme of Sustainable Development, and, as mentioned above, it has partnered with the IAU and GUNi to conduct a continent-wide survey on universities and SD. The ADEA are organizing a continental conference on Education and Sustainable Development in 2012 [www.adeanet.org]. Other examples of this kind of institutional leadership exist at subregional level (for example where SARUA are taking leadership in defining a climate change and development agenda for university development).

NEW POLICIES AND STRATEGIES

Another area where SD actualization occurs is at the level of policy and/or strategy development. Few/no examples of specific *national level university policy* on SD were found in the documents reviewed for this study. However, *indirect policy influences*, such as national commitment to Millennium Development Goals; poverty reduction strategies; national SD strategies; national environmental and/or social development policies and so on were found to be substantive influences on university research, teaching and community engagement practices. A typical example here would be the manner in which national environmental policy influences both teaching and research in environmental science departments; or the manner in which poverty reduction strategy priorities influence spending on education and training; as well as definition of national priorities. A further important finding is that there is an increasing trend towards defining SD policy statements or strategies (or associated policy statements and strategies) *at university level*. The GUNi/IAU/AAU (2011, p. 25) survey found for example, that: 'Among the responding institutions, 46.6% have stand-alone sustainable development strategies while 28% do not. The rest either did not respond or the respondents did not know if their institutions had such strategies.' The study also revealed that 'more stand-alone sustainable development strategies were available in smaller HEIs (with enrolment of up to 10,000) compared to the bigger ones. This finding negates the assumption … that the bigger the institution the more likely it will pursue sustainable development practices.'

The most widely practised approach to SD policy and strategy in universities seems to be the inclusion of 'sustainable development' in vision and mission statements, a good example here being the Vision and Mission Statement of Makarere University in Uganda (one of Africa's older universities) which states that the university seeks 'To be a centre of academic excellence, providing world-class teaching, research and service relevant to the sustainable development needs of society' (UNEP, 2006).

Some institutions were also beginning to define specific *Education for Sustainable Development Strategies*. This is different to including a statement on sustainable development in a vision and mission statement; or having a university SD policy that addresses integrated SD issues in the university and/or community. ESD strategies tend to be more oriented towards *changes in teaching, learning and research*. A good example is the ESD strategy of Jomo Kenyatta University in Kenya. It was noticeable that in countries with national ESD strategies (Lesotho, Swaziland, Kenya),[8] universities seemed to be more focused on the ESD practices as outlined above.

NEW STRUCTURES EMERGING AT UNIVERSITY LEVEL AND AT INTRA-UNIVERSITY LEVEL

The GUNi/IAU/AAU (2011, p. 27) survey reveals a diversity of new structures emerging at university and intra-university level. Of the 61 responses to the survey, it was found that:

Most institutions have an institutional research

agenda on sustainable development (60%). In descending order, this was followed by socially and environmentally responsible investment practices and policies (42.6%); Sustainable Development Coordinator (39.3%); Dean of Environmental Programmes or Director of Sustainability Programmes (39.3%); Environmental Council/Sustainable Development Task Force (37.7%); and orientation programmes on sustainability for faculty and staff (36%).

One of the most wide spread 'new' structures dealing with SD issues in universities are *Environmental Science Departments*, most often located in Science Faculties (although other configurations were also noted). There are, as yet, few departments titled 'Sustainable Development' – in fact no evidence of such a department was found. Most major universities in Africa today have Environmental Science departments or programmes. These have been variously supported by international donor organizations, or by national governments and universities themselves. This has led to an associated range of qualifications being offered in Environmental Sciences or Environmental Management related areas, which previously (around 20–30 years ago) did not exist in African universities (see below). Many of these programmes are including issues of sustainable development.

There are also specially dedicated *centres or institutes* that are established to deal with SD issues and risks. Most often these are closely associated with the environmental or water sciences, environmental health issues, sustainable agriculture, gender studies and increasingly with climate change. An example here is the Institute of Ecology and Environmental Studies, Obafemi Awolowo University, Ile-Ife, Nigeria. There are a few centres forming around the concept of sustainable development *per se*, although these are not widespread across the continent. Probably the most active and established of these would be the Sustainability Institute at the University of Stellenbosch in South Africa [www.sustainabilityinstitute.net]. Interesting too are the establishment of sustainable development 'sites' associated with university programmes, such as the Millennium Villages that are linked to the Global Masters Degree in Development Practice (http://globalmdp.org). These provide 'real-life' laboratories for SD practice, learning and research.

The GUNi/IAU/AAU (2011) survey also reports that interdisciplinarity is important in ESD as it enables a shift from scientific specialization to dialogue between the disciplines. From the survey, 44 institutions (60.3%) responded positively to having multi-

and interdisciplinary structures for research, education and policy development on sustainability issues.

NEW ARTEFACTS (CURRICULA, LEARNING MATERIALS, BUILDINGS)

There were very few examples of newly developed dedicated buildings for SD (although the University of Stellenbosch, South Africa has a dedicated Sustainability Institute; and Rhodes University, South Africa has a dedicated Sustainability Commons and Environmental Learning Research Centre, built with sustainability principles). This section will therefore focus more on curriculum as visible artefact of SD actualization. While it was not possible to undertake content analysis of all courses offered in all African countries, content analysis of all study material in one country context – South Africa – showed that environment and SD issues were being integrated into *most disciplines and programmes* in the country's 23 universities, although the levels of integration were uneven. The integration of SD content into programmes seems to be a 'bottom up' affair, with lecturers and professors driving the content changes; influenced primarily by international issues, links and networks, and national policies.

The GUNi/IAU/AAU (2011, p. 36) survey reflects this trend; and responses from the 69 institutions show that SD issues are woven into all the traditional disciplines; with greater emphasis in the social sciences; natural sciences and engineering disciplines (see Figure II.1.1). This same trend has been noted in smaller scale studies at university level (Togo, 2009), and even within single departments (Greyling, 2011). A key finding from these studies is that commerce and management disciplines and faculties appear to be *least engaged* with SD issues (ibid.). This is a cause for concern, given the need to engage the *nexus of economy–ecology–society* in SD thinking.

It would also seem that *integration into existing disciplines* is the primary manner in which SD is being actualized in curricula in African universities. The GUNi/IAU/AAU (2011, pp. 36–7) survey reports that 'Only 26% (out of 68 institutions which responded) offer specific sustainable development degree programmes; 72% do not'. Interdisciplinary teaching is also not widely practised, and the GUNi/IAU/AAU (2011, p. 38) study found that 'more than half of the institutions forming part of this study do not offer interdisciplinary courses on sustainable development. Considering the different types of institutions, such courses were mostly offered by public rather than private institutions. None of the private for-profit institutions had interdisciplinary courses on sustain-

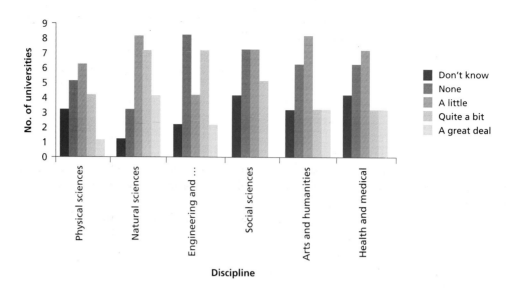

FIGURE II.1.1 **The extent to which sustainability is woven into traditional education disciplines**
Source: IAU/AAU/GUNi 2011, p. 36.

able development'. Where these courses were being offered, 'about 58% of the interdisciplinary courses on sustainability offered by the institutions were offered as compulsory courses' (ibid.).

The GUNi/IAU/AAU (2011) survey, and the MESA review (UNEP, 2008), showed that a number of factors can positively or negatively influence the introduction of new courses in SD. Positive factors are: implementation of national policy directions; new institutional policy development; new faculty leadership; new staff member; and introduction of reward system. Barriers hindering the introduction of SD-oriented courses are: lack of finance; lack of human resources or specialized staff; lack of awareness and information about SD; and inadequate leadership and/or structures. This makes professional development of staff and leadership development (that is, actualization through the experience of persons) an important factor.

There was also evidence of an *interest in mainstreaming* of environment and sustainability in African universities, particularly among those universities that have been participating in the MESA programme. Research conducted within the SADC Regional Environmental Education Programme context (where a MESA network has been operating for seven years); and the MESA first phase review both show that there are several factors influencing *mainstreaming*; most notably *capacity for whole institution mobilization*. The establishment of three 'MESA Chairs' in SADC with the specific mandate of mainstreaming

is proving to be a successful strategy to support mainstreaming of environment and sustainability. The University of Swaziland, which has one of the MESA Chairs, has a MESA Strategy, and a cross-faculty MESA implementation committee supported by the Vice Chancellor and university management, it has undertaken a university-wide MESA audit, and is planning cross-university interventions including student involvement, curriculum innovation, research development, and capacity development of staff (UNISWA, 2011). The MESA programme is showing that individual innovation, and establishment of communities of practice are also important strategies for mainstreaming, as are university-wide sustainability assessments. For this reason a Unit-based Sustainability Assessment (USAT) Tool was developed for MESA (Togo and Lotz-Sisitka, 2009; see www.unep.org/training), which is being used by an increasing number of universities, departments and/or faculties (although the practice is not widespread, nor is it a 'top down' initiative). The GUNi/IAU/AAU (2011, p. 61) survey shows further that mainstreaming is only taking place 'a little' (42 cases in total in the survey); and there are very few cases of a 'great deal' of mainstreaming. While this is the case, this information does not show a lack of awareness of the *need for mainstreaming*, and there is wide spread evidence that universities in Africa are either slowly beginning to engage with such processes, or are aware of what needs to be done. Universities were aware of what courses were needed to increase mainstreaming, and respondents noted the important role of policy and university leadership in mainstreaming (GUNi/IAU/AAU, 2011; UNEP, 2008).

The GUNi/IAU/AAU (2011, pp. 35–6) survey shows new management practices as another area of SD actualization in African universities. Even though institutional commitment to specific sustainability practices was rated to be low (see Figure II.1.2), institutions had plans to pursue some of these practices in future. In descending order, frequently identified practices for future action include energy conservation initiatives (identified in 54 institutions); developing new strategic plans with a strong sustainability component (48 institutions); developing compulsory courses in sustainability (32 institutions); and developing sustainable food programmes (20 institutions). In management operations, universities in Africa were found to be promoting initiatives like green building design, energy conservation, waste reduction, water conservation and sustainable landscaping among others. Promotion of these initiatives is however still very low, which might seem to suggest that physical operations are not a major focus for SD actualization in African universities. This can also be understood in the light of resource constraints. There is, however, an emerging relationship between scholarship focusing on these practices and the introduction and/or improvement of new management practices. Examples here include the Kigali Institute

of Science and Technology in Rwanda and Jomo Kenyatta University in Kenya which have, through their research, introduced biogas plants as innovations on their campuses, and these are also used as teaching resources. The Engineering Department at the University of Mauritius investigated 'green campus' technologies (UNEP, 2008), and through this, were able to reduce paper wastage. It would seem that sustainable campus management could be both a productive area of research and teaching, and a way of modelling and developing new practices.

3 ACTUALIZATION THROUGH THE LIVED EXPERIENCES OF PEOPLE

PROFESSIONAL INTEREST AND DEVELOPMENT OF UNIVERSITY STAFF

Theories of social change reveal that very little change can take place without the active engagement of people; that is, through the expression of individual and collective forms of agency (Archer, 2000). The actualization of SD in universities takes place through the agentive acts of university managers, teachers, researchers, students, administrative and support staff, and university community interactions. The significance of professional development of academic staff and university leaders emerged as one of the key elements that are enabling the actualization of SD (in all of the forms outlined above) in universities. This included participation in networks, professional development programmes, SD seminars and conferences, and in community of practice activities. Significant

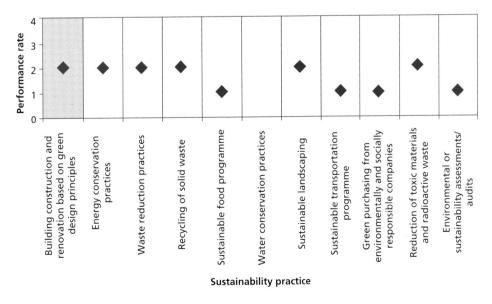

FIGURE II.1.2 Institutional commitment to specific sustainable development practices
Source: GUNi/IAU/AAU 2011, p. 35.

in the MESA programme review (UNEP, 2008) was substantive evidence of professional interest in sustainability issues among university staff participating in the MESA activities. In many cases, it is the professional interest and motivation of university staff members that was the *key driver* of SD innovation in universities, particularly where the SD interest was oriented towards community engagement, poverty reduction, environmental management and development. Other incentives, such as abilities to participate in international networks, and publishing opportunities were also revealed as being important to the development of interest and motivation among professionals in universities (Lotz-Sisitka and Lupele, 2006). The MESA review cites examples of the significance of professional development opportunities as follows:

'This (MESA Universities Partnership) has provided a broader context for our work and has opened up opportunities for collaboration more widely in Africa. This is **essential** if we are to find African solutions to Africa's environment and development challenges, especially new risks associated with climate change.' (MESA Professor, 2004, cited in UNEP 2008)

'I very much appreciate the opportunity given to me to participate in this MESA e-learning course and in the e-learning process. I think I would now find my way to register for it to learn it properly. It is a big way of learning how to develop our course content to address sustainable development issues in Africa … It is not only useful, but **needed** in my institution and in all African universities.' (MESA Professor, 2007, cited in UNEP, 2008)

Appropriate professional development opportunities are important for building internal capacity for actualizing SD (in any of its forms) in universities. The GUNi/IAU/AAU (2011, p. 62) survey indicated that while this is the case, few institutions were providing substantive opportunities for staff development in sustainability issues (only 49% of 65 responding institutions). This was also found to be the case in university wide studies (Togo, 2009); and at individual departmental level (Greyling, 2011).

STUDENT MOBILIZATION

The GUNi/IAU/AAU (2011, p. 62) survey revealed that 'involvement of student groups in sustainability was low, but universities had other ways of getting students engaged in sustainable development initiatives. Field work was the most common among universities with others being career counselling,

job fairs, role modelling etc.' Within the MESA network there are some examples of student groups getting involved in SD issues on campuses. For example, at Strathmore University in Kenya, and at Cairo University in Egypt, students are working with professors in a youth leadership programme; while at the University of Swaziland, the University's student-led 'Green Team' are actively engaging the student body in a range of sustainability initiatives. UNEP has also hosted a students' programme under the MESA initiative named the 'Sustainability Generation', and student organizations attending the MESA Conference in Nairobi in 2009 produced a 'Student Action Plan' which identifies three main action plans including 'theoretic learning', 'experiential learning', and 'sustainability leadership' (UNEP MESA, 2009). In South Africa student organizations are working together to host a 'Blue Buck Summit' (the Blue Buck was the first mammal to become extinct on the African continent) for student environmental organizations in preparation for the climate change negotiations at COP17.

NEW PEDAGOGICAL PRACTICES AND LECTURER–STUDENT RELATIONS

Another area of actualization lies in the creation of new pedagogical practices leading to new lecturer–student relations. Use of pedagogical strategies such as fieldwork, service learning and action research are noted as being popular among lecturers involved in SD issues. Students are therefore engaged in a wider range of experiential learning interactions. These are valued by students. As stated in the MESA Student Action Plan (UNEP MESA, 2009), there is a need to link sustainability field visits to credits, and to engage students in 'sustainability weeks' on campus that involve both symbolic and literal activities. Such practices among students appear to be on the rise in universities, and a number of case examples of student engagement in environment and sustainability issues were found on campuses (although these remain under-developed, and under-documented). Students were also interested in sustainability internships and volunteerism opportunities. Student mobilization remains a key area for increasing participation in SD actualization in Africa universities.

NEW UNIVERSITY–COMMUNITY RELATIONS

A further area of actualization at experiential level lies in the establishment of new university–community relations. There is firm evidence that universities in Africa are using SD as a key focus area for engaging in new forms of university–community relations. The GUNi/IAU/AAU (2011, pp. 51–4) survey showed that 41 out of 61 respondents (67.2%) stated that they were engaged in *rural development*. Among the 41, this involvement was in form of research (63.4%), staff and student outreach activities (48.8%) and internship (43.9%). Out of 61 respondents, 52.5% of institutions were engaged in *peace, security, conflict resolution/prevention training*. A total of 57 institutions responded to the question on promotion of *cultural diversity*. Of these, more than half (59.6%) indicated that they do promote cultural diversity, intercultural dialogue and understanding. More than 80% (out of 58 institutions) indicated that they are involved in *the prevention of HIV/AIDS*. The most common forms of initiatives that institutions were taking in engaging with HIV/AIDS prevention include staff/student outreach activities (32.5%), direct collaboration (27.7%) and research (22.9%). Fifty-five per cent (55%) of the 73 respondents indicated that they had some form of non-formal and informal SD programmes that they were involved in. High levels of participation in these kinds of issues are more significant when only half of the responding institutions did not receive support for SD projects or activities. This indicates that SD appears to be an important 'site' or focus for *new forms of voluntarism and/or community engagement*. Of significance too, was the finding from the document review that these kinds of activities often lead to *real, tangible benefits to communities at grassroots level*. Some good examples illustrate this point:

● The Kigali Institute of Science and Technology developed a research programme on biogas technology: 11 biogas plants were installed in prisons and 10 in schools, and to date 1500 domestic biogas plants have been installed in households of different districts of Rwanda and construction of other 1000 units is in process. Forty civilians and 350 prisoners have been trained in construction of biogas plants. This in turn has led to the establishment of new small and medium enterprises; as well as more sustainable energy production processes in public sector organizations (KIST, 2010).

● Uganda Martyrs University involved teaching staff and students in a community development programme aimed at improving the livelihoods of communities in a sub-county through sustainable agriculture interventions. The project established a small-scale farmers' association; supported improved planting materials; an input credit system; and new farming and marketing strategies. The results were improved income; improved varieties

and organic soil conditions; water conservation; and more sustainable livelihoods; as well as improved university–community relations and research and teaching practices (UMU, 2009).

LEADERSHIP SUPPORT AND FUNDING

The GUNi/IAU/AAU (2011) survey shows that institutions with leaders who were rated as having either 'quite a bit' or 'a great deal' of commitment to SD issues were the only ones that received support for SD activities. The assumption that larger institutions showed more commitment to SD issues was proved wrong in terms of funding as there was no relationship between size of institution and amount of funds allocated for sustainability activities. The GUNi/IAU/AAU (2011, p. 62) survey also reveals a positive relationship between the existence of multi- and interdisciplinary structures and management commitment to SD among university leaders. Institutions with higher levels of management commitment were found to have more multi- and interdisciplinary structures than those with lower levels. While this would need to be more carefully analysed, there appears to be a stronger correlation between leadership commitment and interest, funding generated and/or leveraged for SD activities, and structural changes in universities. Funding for sustainability initiatives in big and small institutions alike ranged from as low as less than $20,000 per year to over $200,000. Funding for SD activities in these institutions is received from various sources but mainly from development partners and foundations, governments, the private sector and the university's internally generated funds.

The MESA Conference Statement (UNEP MESA, 2009, p. 45) states that 'there is a need for systemic capacity building programmes for university leaders, government officials, civil society and other education sector stakeholders to ensure sustainability and climate change issues are integrated into the teaching, learning and research programmes of higher education institutions, including private universities'. As mentioned above, the actualization of SD in African universities seems to be constituted through a strange mix of 'bottom up' and 'international organization involvement'. Both levels are 'putting pressure' on university leadership to become more engaged. A positive signal in this regard is the involvement of university leaders organizations (such as SARUA and the AAU) in engaging university leaders at country level to deliberate SD issues, including climate change and development. As indicated above, SARUA's actions in this regard are exemplary, as a Deputy Vice Chancellor's committee has been established to develop a subregional university programme on climate change and development.

WHAT TRANSFORMATIONS ARE OCCURRING? (ANALYTICAL LENS 4)

It is possible to identify significant transformations that are occurring as a result of the actualization of the 'event' of SD in African universities. Careful analysis of the data shows three key types of transformations:

EPISTEMOLOGICAL RELATIONSHIPS ARE CHANGING

This is seen particularly in the manner in which SD questions and issues 'permeate' the disciplines. Oftentimes this is an 'invisible' process in the sense that disciplines remain unaware of the full range of integrations of SD taking place in other parts of the institution. Similarly, university leaders fail to see the full scope of this 'bottom up' form of integration as it occurs piecemeal, and 'bit by bit'; is not orchestrated from above or through university policy, but is rather a quiet revolution taking place in response to local needs; individual values and commitments; broader changes in the knowledge environment and external influences brought about by global and environmental changes. While it does not represent interdisciplinarity as such, it *lays a fertile foundation* for interdisciplinary approaches; which are beginning to emerge, particularly when located out of, or in association with specific centres that focus on key issues (for example water, poverty, climate change and so on) or with partnership-centred and applied research programmes.

PEDAGOGICAL PRACTICES ARE CHANGING

As shown above, there is also substantive evidence of changing pedagogical practices. These appear to involve shifts towards experiential learning and action centred pedagogies that are also community-engaged. Students are interested in these approaches to learning; and lecturers see new potential in such approaches, particularly for contributing towards solutions for societal change broadly. The MESA (UNEP, 2008) programme in particular, has supported *transformative, action-oriented approaches to learning*, but the need for these approaches was noted in *almost all of the 200 documents reviewed for this study*. Within these is a concern for critical thinking, engaging the potential of indigenous epistemologies, and development of new forms of agency (UNEP, 2008; SADC REEP, 2011). Interesting is that, while this is the case, actual changes in pedagogy are taking place in a 'piecemeal', bottom-up manner, and are not explicitly being proposed or supported at policy levels (particularly national policy levels).

SOCIAL CRITIQUE AND PARTICIPATORY ENGAGEMENT WITH THE MEANING(S) AND PRACTICES OF DEVELOPMENT ARE INCREASING

As shown above, the actualization of SD in African universities occurrs in a variety of 'shapes and forms'; and is underpinned by a variety of philosophical and/or material commitments. There is, however, little dialogue about these differing understandings of SD. Most often documents that refer to SD (particularly institutional documents produced by key institutions such as AAU, UNESCO or UNEP) fail to explicitly engage with the array of meanings that SD appears to hold in African university settings. The interest in SD (from the differing perspectives) is sharpening social critique and/or participatory engagement with the meaning(s) and practices of development. *Dialogical engagement* with the different emerging meanings of SD in African universities can potentially assist with the epistemological 'revitalization' of African universities; creating potentially new social epistemologies, particularly since SD appears to be of interest to a wide range of disciplines. As such, it could provide a 'common language' through which multiple disciplines can become engaged in the process of critically reviewing and revitalizing 'epistemology' and 'purpose' in African universities.

IS MODERN SUSTAINABLE DEVELOPMENT THE ONLY SPECIFICATION OR SOLUTION TO THE PROBLEM? (ANALYTICAL LENS 5)

As noted above, not everything that occurs under the 'banner' of sustainable development is named as such. This is sometimes purposeful (most often in resistance to), or not so purposeful (most often because the issue at hand has a more direct form or referent than the somewhat abstract/ambivalent terminology of sustainable development). The politics of naming university-based changes and activities within the framework of SD therefore warrants some discussion here, particularly since there seem to be many varied interpretations of, and diverse practices emerging in the name of sustainable development in African universities, while the development paradigm of the day remains under critique (sometimes including SD). Does everything that goes under the 'banner' of sustainable development need to be named as such?

Is it, for example feasible to accept that the SARUA initiative to focus on 'Climate Change, Adaptation and Higher Education'; the University of Cape Town's initiative appointing a DVC focusing on a university-wide strategy for 'Climate Change and Development'; or the International Development Research Centre (IDRC) Eco-Health programme are SD actualizations; even if these initiatives are not named as such? And is producing a 'Global Change' Grand Challenge National Research Plan for a country (RSA, 2010) an equally valid SD actualization? If this is the case, then one could interpret the 'event' of SD as a *'broad signifier' of changing nature-culture relations; and nature-culture interactions and practices*. While this may be so, SD actualizations also require differentiated and critical engagement at various levels; as discussed above – both at the level of problem definition, and at the level of response.

CONCLUSION

Akin-Aina (2010, p. 21) writes critically about the half-century of interventions and waves of 'reforms' affecting HE in Africa today. He states that they consist of 'institutions, systems, and practices that lack distinct values and goals, or a mission and vision connecting them to the major challenges of their local and global contexts'. He argues further that what is needed in African HE is 'true transformation, which will involve practical and epistemological ruptures with previous ways of doing things and a reconstruction of structures, relations, cultures, and institutions'. With this in mind, the GUNi/IAU/AAU (2011, pp. 68–70) survey makes a number of recommendations and suggestions to inform future sustainability practices in African universities. For example, it concludes that 'leaders should be targeted' to further SD actualization in universities. It also concludes that further investment in 'staff orientation, awareness, and exchange programmes in sustainable development can help equip university employees in sustainability issues'. Mainstreaming through policy development; support for ESD structures; sustainability assessments and information management; student engagement; pedagogical and curriculum reform and so on are also noted as 'ways forward'. Networking and conferences, establishment of Centres of Excellence and research investments are also key recommendations arising from this survey. Similar sets of recommendations are made in the MESA review (UNEP, 2008) all of which are useful for furthering SD actualization. While these recommendations are useful at a technical level, they can only really be meaningful if considered within wider transformation agendas.

In his analysis of Houtonji's work in philosophy, Ochieng (2010, p. 34) comments on some of the problems of later African philosophical works by Appiah, who he argues, conceptualizes the political as 'essentially consisting of technical problems, as a matter for suitable educated technocrats to puzzle over and solve'. Some perspectives on SD in African universities, as shown in the analysis above, may be making similar assumptions about SD and its relationship to and hence its practices in African universities. Ochieng (2010, p. 34) goes on to say that [in the case of Appiah's work on the political]: 'there is little engagement with the historical gravity within which particular problems [such as those described under the SD banner] are contested, little understanding of the fact that many of the deep conflicts in Africa [such as those concerning resource use associated with SD discourses] are powered by radically different *interests*, far more than by a lack of education or a simple matter of conceptual confusions.'

In closing this paper it is important therefore to draw attention to the *problématique*, and indeed the dangers of narrowly or technically interpreting SD in African universities, and to encourage a deeper probing of why SD, which is partially an 'indigenous foreigner' on the African continent, is manifesting in such a variety of ways? Reminded by Ferguson (2006) that our academic concepts are often inadequate for the times, we may continue to ask whether SD is or can become an *adequate concept* or *'event'* for education in Africa at this point in time when transnational topographies of power, as described by Ferguson (2006) and Bond (2002; 2006) sustain unequal global and local social policies and practices that continue to 'structure underdevelopment' in particular ways. Sustainable development actualization in African universities, while interesting and dynamic, is not simply a technical matter.

REFERENCES

AAU (Association of African Universities) (2009) *Sustainable Development and Universities in Africa*. Conference Proceedings. Dakar: Association of African Universities.

Adams, J., King, C. and Hook, D. (2010) *Global Research Report: Africa*. Leeds: Evidence, Thompson Reuters.

Africa Watch (1991) *Academic Freedom and Human Rights abuses in Africa. An Africa Watch Report*. USA: Human Rights Watch.

Akin Aina, T. (2010) Beyond reforms: the politics of higher

education transformation in Africa. *African Studies Review*, **53**(1), pp. 21–40.

Archer, M. (2000) *Being Human. The Problem of Agency*. Cambridge: Cambridge University Press.

Bloom, D., Canning, D. and Chan, K. (2006) *Higher Education and Economic Development in Africa*. World Bank: Africa Development Section. www.arp.harvard.edu/AfricaHigherEducation. Accessed July 2011.

Bond, P. (2006) *Looting Africa. The Economics of Exploitation*. Pietermaritzburg: University of KwaZulu Natal Press.

Bond, P. (2002) *Unsustainable South Africa. Environment, Development and Social Protest*. Pietermaritzburg: Univeristy of KwaZulu Natal Press.

Bond, P. and Hallowes, D. (2002) The environment of apartheid-capitalism: Discourses and issues. In: Bond, P. (ed.) *Unsustainable South Africa. Environment, Development and Social Protest*. Pietermaritzburg: Univeristy of KwaZulu Natal Press.

Deleuze, G. and Guattari, F. (1994) *What is Philosophy?*, trans. H. Tomlinson and G. Burchell. New York: Columbia University Press.

Deleuze, G. (1990) *The Logic of Sense*, trans. M. Lester and C. Stivale, with C. Boundas (ed.). New York: Columbia University Press.

Deleuze, G. (1995) *Negotiations 1972–1990*, trans. M. Joughin. Columbia: University of Columbia Press.

Diop, B. (2005) (first published in 1961), trans. Kennedy E. Sarzan. In: Larson, C.R. (ed.) (2007) *Under African Skies. Modern African Stories* (2nd edn). Edinburgh: Canongate Books Ltd.

Diouf, M. and Mamdani, M. (eds) (1994) *Academic Freedom in Africa*. Dakar, Senegal: CODESRIA.

Ferguson, J. (2006) *Global Shadows. Africa in the neo-liberal world order*. Durham and London: Duke University Press.

Greyling, L. (2011) Assessing Sustainability Integration of a Business School, through the Development and use of a Sustainability Assessment Tool: The case study of the MBA curriculum at Rhodes University's Business School. Unpublished MBA thesis, Rhodes University Business School, Grahamstown, South Africa.

GUNi/IAU/AAU. 2011. *The promotion of sustainable development in Higher Education Institutions in sub-Saharan Africa*. Survey Report. Accessed July 2011. http://147.83.97.154/repositori/Promotion_of_SD_by_HEIs_in_sub-Saharan_Africa.pdf.

Hattingh, J. (2002) On the imperative of sustainable development: A philosophical and ethical appraisal. In: Janse van Rensburg, E., Hattingh, J., Lotz-Sisitka, H. and O'Donoghue, R. (eds) (2002) *Environmental Education, Ethics and Action in Southern Africa*. EEASA Monograph. Cape Town: HSRC Publishers.

Hattingh, J. (2004) Speaking of Sustainable Development and Values … A Response to Alistair Chadwick's Viewpoint 'Responding to Destructive Interpersonal Interactions: A way forward for school-based environmental educators'. *Southern African Journal of Environmental Education*, **21**, pp. 157–65.

Kellogg, E. and Hervy, A. (2010) Contributions of Higher Education Investments to Development and Implications for African Higher Education. RUFORUM. http://ruforum.org/documents/contributions-higher-education-investments-development-and-implications-african-higher-edu?page=30. Accessed July 2011.

KIST (Kigali Institute of Science and Technology) (2010) Presentation made at the UNEP GUPES meeting, Nairobi, Kenya (November 2010).

Larson, C.R. (ed.) (2005) *Under African Skies. Modern African Stories* (2nd edn). Edinburgh: Canongate Books Ltd.

Lotz-Sisitka, H. and Lupele, J. (2006) Curriculum transformation in higher education institutions: Some perspectives from Africa. In: Holmberg, J. and Samuelsson, B.E. (eds) *Drivers and Barriers for Implementing Sustainable Development in Higher Education. Education for Sustainable Development in Action. Technical Paper No. 3*. Paris: UNESCO Education Sector.

Mamdani, M. (2011) The importance of research in a university. Makerere Institute of Social Research. 2011-04-21, Issue 526. http://pambazuka.org/en/category/features/72782. Accessed July 2011.

Mbembe, A. (2002) On the power of the false. *Public Culture*, **14**(3), pp. 629–41.

Ochieng, O. (2010) The African Intellectual: Houtondji and After. *Radical Philosophy. A journal of socialist and feminist philosophy*. November/December. 2010, 164, pp. 25–37.

Patton, P. (2006) The event of colonisation. In: Buchanan, I. and Parr, A. *Deleuze and the Contemporary World*. Edinburgh: Edinburgh University Press (pp. 108–24).

Peet, R. and Watts, M. (eds) (2004) *Liberation Ecologies: Environment, Development, Social Movements* (2nd edn). London: Routledge.

Popkewitz, T. (2005) *Inventing the Modern Self and John Dewey: Modernities and the Traveling of Pragmatism in Education*. New York: Palgrave Macmillan.

SADC REEP (2011) *Education for Sustainable Development and Educational Quality and Relevance. 2nd year Research Report*. Unpublished research report. SADC Regional Environmental Education Programme, Howick, South Africa.

RSA (Republic of South Africa) (2010) *Global Change Grand Challenge National Research Plan*. Pretoria: Department of Science and Technology.

SARUA (Southern African Regional Universities Association) (2011) *Climate Change, Adaptation and Higher Education: Securing our Future. SARUA Leadership Dialogue Series*, **2**(4). www.sarua.org. Accessed July 2011

Shiva, V. (2006) *Earth Democracy. Justice, Sustainability and Peace*. London: Zed Books.

Singh, M. (2001) Re-inserting the 'public good' into higher education transformation. *Kagisano (Council on Higher Education Discussion Series)*. 1(Summer 2001), pp. 7–21.

Slater, D. (2004) *Geopolitics and the Post-colonial. Rethinking North-South Relations*. Oxford: Blackwell Publishing.

Stromgaard, E. (1989) Adaptive strategies in the breakdown of shifting cultivation: the case of Mambwe, Lamba and Lala of northern Zambia. *Human Ecology*, **17**(4), pp. 427–44.

Tembo, A.B., Chamshama, S.A.O., Kung'u, J., Kaboggoza, J., Chikamai, B. and Kiwia, A. (eds) (2008) *New Perspectives in Forestry Education. Peer reviewed papers presented at the First Global Workshop on Forestry Education, September 2007*. ICRAF, Nairobi, Kenya.

Togo, M. (2009) A Systems Approach to Mainstreaming Environment and Sustainability in Universities: The case of Rhodes University, South Africa. Unpublished PhD thesis, Rhodes University, Grahamstown, South Africa.

Togo, M. and Lotz-Sisitka, H. (2009) *Unit-Based Sustain-*

ability Assessment Tool. A Resource Book to Complement the Mainstreaming Environment and Sustainability in African Universities Partnership. Nairobi: UNEP.

UMU (Uganda Martyrs University) (2009) MESA Award Application, UNEP. Nairobi: Kenya.

UNEP (2006) *Africa Environment Outlook. Our Environment, Our Wealth.* Nairobi: UNEP.

UNEP (2008) *Mainstreaming Environment and Sustainability in African Universities Partnership (2004–2008 report). Supporting universities to respond to Environment, Sustainable Development and Climate Change Challenges.* Nairobi: UNEP.

UNEP MESA (Mainstreaming Environment and Sustainability in African Universities). (2009). *The 1st Mainstreaming Environment and Sustainability in African Universities International Conference. 24–28 November 2008 Conference Report.* Nairobi: UNEP.

UNESCO (2009) *Global Education Digest 2009. Comparing Education Statistics Across the World.* Paris: UNESCO UIS. http://www.uis.unesco.org/Library/Documents/ged09-en.pdf. Accessed July 2011.

UNESCO (2010) UNESCO Institute For Statistics. Adult And Youth Literacy: Global Trends in Gender Parity. *UIS Fact Sheet*, September 2010, No. 3. Http://Www.Uis.Unesco.Org/Factsheets/Documents/Fact_Sheet_2010_Lit_EN.Pdf.

UNISWA (2011) *MESA Workshop Notes.* Swaziland: University of Swaziland.

Zelelza, P.T. and Olukoshi, A. (eds) (2004) *African Universities in the Twenty-First Century. Volume 1: Liberalisation and Internationalisation.* Senegal: Council for the Development of Social Science Research in Africa (CODESRIA).

Zeleza, P.T. and Olukoshi, A. (eds) (2004) *African Universities in the Twenty-First Century. Volume II: Knowledge and Society.* Senegal: Council for the Development of Social Science Research in Africa (CODESRIA).

NOTES

1   Cited in Larson (2005: 37) in a collection of short stories published with the title 'Under African Skies'. Interestingly, reflections of the cosmology of sustainability in Africa (while not called this) are most often found in African literature, and not as widely found in modern day sciences produced in Africa. This may be a result of the colonial roots of modern day science as practised in universities today. With the advent of sustainable development discourse however, more scientific practices are emerging that reflect more secular versions of this cosmology, as described later in the paper.

2   Popkewitz (1990), in his analysis of modern educational institutions, encourages us to produce what he calls 'social epistemologies' of our institutions, to trace the histories of the forms of reasoning that dominate.

3   These have post-colonial continuities.

4   For example the ancient universities of Timbuktu and Egypt.

5   Patton (2006: 112) comments that 'Stating, claiming or naming something is never sufficient to actualize a particular event [such as sustainable development], but … purely linguistic acts of declaration and attribution are often and sometimes necessary conditions of actualisation'. The politics of description in establishing modern sustainable development in African universities is therefore also of interest in this paper, and needs to be differentiated from 'its spatio-temporal realization in a state of affairs' (Deleuze, 1990, p. 53).

6   Over 200 documents were consulted for this review. These included macro-level policy and university assessment documents; international reports on the status of sustainable development in Africa; research papers addressing the topic/aspects of the topic; and available studies on universities and sustainable development in Africa. The two most substantive sources of data providing a consolidated perspective are from the UNEP Mainstreaming Environment and Sustainability in African Universities Network (2008 report, involving 77 universities); and from the recent GUNi/IAU/AAU (2011) survey involving 73 universities. This represents in the region of 10%–15% of universities on the African continent.

7   It should be noted here that it was not possible to establish comprehensive data sets across all countries in Africa, hence the trends are based on a reading of the existing data, documents and records pursued. Examples cited here are extracted from this available data, documents and records.

8   Only a few African countries have produced ESD Strategies, despite this being a key objective of the UN Decade on Education for Sustainable Development (www.unesco.org/desd).

Inside View II.1
Cartography of higher education and sustainability: the case of the lusophone community
Aristides Baloi

INTRODUCTION

This paper attempts to map issues of higher education (HE) and sustainability in lusophone countries. The African lusophone community consists of the following nations: Angola, Cape Verde, Guinea Bissau, São Tomé and Principe and Mozambique. Though spatially discontinuous in distribution over the continent, most of these countries share historical, economic, and cultural identity aspects, for example educational reforms, and reliance over agriculture as the backbone of economy. Education is regarded as a driving force for development, and as a key agent for economic, human and societal transformation. It must be sustainable, meaning that it must unfold human potentials in the countries and enable member states to achieve their development goals. The paper also proposes communication mechanisms that can reliably enhance and improve communication for education and sustainable development (SD) in these countries' higher education institutes (HEIs).

PATH TO HIGHER EDUCATION DEVELOPMENT IN LUSOPHONE COUNTRIES

African lusophone countries view education as the entry point for equilibrated development and cooperation towards meeting the Millennium Development Goals (MDGs). Member states have established their own development strategies, which are aligned with the MDGs, for example eradication of extreme poverty and access to quality education.

In the case of Mozambique, tertiary schooling is included in the Poverty Reduction Strategy Papers (PRSPs) (MEC, 2001, 2006, 2011). Mozambique PRSPs promote the development of large projects on HE that enhance its development. Likewise, other African lusophone countries place priority on HE for because of the need for people with relevant qualifications. The African lusophone countries, as developing countries, face a scarcity of resources (including financial) and multiple difficulties in the overall development fronts, including in HE. Therefore, universities, research centres, science and technology aim to support the development of an efficient and innovative network for global development, as strategy to overcome the limitations.

Thus the path to sustainable HE development in African lusophone countries is cooperation based on a set of priorities established by governments of the member states in the field of HE, through institutional networking. The overall objective of the cooperation is to promote capacity building and regional integration in the field of HE to support the quality of HE systems among member states. Through such a network, financial and human capacity needs could be better addressed by the member states, and local strengths and potentials across the countries better explored.

STRENGTHENING AFRICAN LUSOPHONE HIGHER EDUCATION PARTNERSHIP

The implementation of partnership in HE among African Lusophone countries is a recent initiative, and, as Scheider (2009) puts it, it is aimed at establishing a profound partnership amongst member states. Key aspects of the partnership include knowledge exchange, academic mobility, mutual recogni-

tion of knowledge, and open opportunities for the development of new research centres in the partner countries.

Several partnership initiatives have been undertaken so far. The following five examples show that existing initiatives either involve the lusophone countries as a whole or a part of it, namely the African countries only.

THE ASSOCIATION OF PORTUGUESE LANGUAGE UNIVERSITIES

In 1986, the Association of Portuguese Language Universities (AULP, Portuguese acronym) was launched with objective to promote scientific research and technology, considering subjects of members' interest as well as increasing members' participation on pedagogical, cultural and administrative activities in order to stimulate the knowledge base and development of each country.

THE FORTALEZA DECLARATION

The Fortaleza Declaration, which was launched in 2004, acknowledges the relevance of HE for sustainable development of the member states. The ambition is to stimulate a partnership in the context of HE that allows an education valorization within HEIs in Portuguese Speaking Community Countries (CPLP), to ensure its quality, and recognition of qualification in the CPLP and international arena. The CPLP includes African lusophone countries.

THE MINHO COMMITMENT

Another strategic positioning is expressed by the Minho commitment, which is a declaration on free access to scientific information on lusophone countries. Key objectives are to:

- Contribute to an increase in the global impact of scientific production developed in the countries
- Provide efforts of research and development in lusophone countries, and
- Sensitize institutions to finance free access of information

The Minho commitment also embraces the African lusophone countries.

THE MESA UNIVERSITIES PARTNERSHIP

The Mainstreaming Environment and Sustainability in Africa (MESA) Universities Partner-

ship aims to enhance the quality and policy relevance of university education in Africa through the implementation of sustainability as an underlying topic in diverse curricula and as practice in all other aspects of university life. The overarching goal is to create a scientific knowledge base on education for sustainable development (ESD) in Africa, for all students and staff, and to develop action competence and awareness, which will benefit the lives and careers of those who have directly participated in the programmes.

Mozambique falls within the MESA region and is part of the beneficiaries of capacity-building programmes in HE sustainability programmes. Together with Angola, the country is involved in the Regional Environmental Education Programme of the Southern African Development Community (SADC-REEP) network as well as in Regional Centres of Expertise on ESD.

All these provisions as presented above have been created as a platform to enhance and ensure the promotion of HE and stimulate networks among lusophone community members in Africa towards their roles that include education, training and research for development, poverty eradication and sustainability. It has, however, been observed that there is demand to expand the implementation of partnership across African lusophone countries, unlike partnerships between these countries and the other member states.

IMPLICATIONS OF STRATEGIES AND POLICIES FOR SUSTAINABILITY IN AFRICAN LUSOPHONE COUNTRIES

It is evident that HEIs in the lusophone countries have obligations to educate people, in order to meet development challenges. The tendency of HE has been to develop integrated and diversified academic degrees that are more comprehensive and of guarantied standard, and curricula that can easily be adopted for national development realities/needs. However, universities should have autonomy to incorporate issues of relevance based on local needs and realities on the ground.

Some HEIs have gained the necessary autonomy to influence their countries to use viable and useful competences required for sustainable education development. Angola is an example of this.

In the past few years, some lusophone countries have witnessed a significant shift in policies. Much effort has been placed on increasing the number of universities or expanding the enrolment rate, with a view to meeting rapidly growing demand. Policies are implemented that reproduce best practice in strategies for poverty alleviation, filling knowledge gaps (research), and attracting sustainability and development. In Mozambique, for example, expansion of HEIs doubled from 2005, reaching 38 HEIs in 2007 (MEC, 2007). Angola, Cape Verde, Guinea Bissau and São Tomé and Principe follow the same process and strategy and have seen a notable increase in HEIs. Table 1 shows the progress of lusophone countries among other communities following the level of enrolment growth rates in Africa.

Curriculum reform development is mentioned as a necessary strategy for improving and increasing competitiveness within the globalizing economy. The lusophone countries' universities have been making extensive efforts to reform their curricula in response to rapidly expanding scientific knowledge and changing economic opportunities.

In lusophone countries, the process of curriculum harmonization has been made following the Bologna process and regional harmonization, for example within the SADC (Southern Africa Development Community) curriculum. New courses at graduate and postgraduate levels are being implemented, based on the increasing demand of training needs.

The integration of SD in the curriculum follows the addition of an extra course to the curriculum, the incorporation of SD in several practical courses such as building design, or the addition of specific SD examples to theoretical courses and the redesign of a curriculum based on the need for SD.

This includes the development of abilities to:

- Operate and act responsibly, taking account of the need to progress environmental, social and economic outcomes simultaneously
- Use imagination, creativity and innovation to provide products and services that maintain and enhance the quality of the environment and community, and meet financial objectives
- Understand and encourage stakeholder involvement

Under curriculum reform, issues of sustainability are being considered so that new courses have been incorporated; modules are being developed to include the subjects of sustainability, climate change, and ecology among others.

Another important strategic issue in HE in African lusophone countries is the development of actions through information channels to introduce new educational technologies. Under this context, African lusophone countries view information and communication technology as alternative to achieve university sustainability and development of innovative learning processes.

DEVELOPING AN AFRICAN LUSOPHONE SCIENTIFIC NETWORK

CPLP universities created a platform for research and development with the purpose of collaborating with researchers of the Portuguese community and facilitating exchange of information and knowledge. However, there is a perceived need for a new approach that integrates the use of the internet to facilitate the access to and exchange of data and information among the participating institutions and members. There are outstanding examples, such as the Scientific Platform Digital Tropical Aquiver, Minho University. The Tropical Aquiver-Digital repository is a vision and strategy for the conception and development of innovating systems for the sharing and dissemination of Portuguese speakers' tropical knowledge.

Other relevant networks that could be mentioned include GMES Network and Africa: workshop for Southern Africa. GMES (Global Monitoring Environment and Security) is part of Europe Africa Strategy, which was developed as result of the Maputo Declaration.

BOX 1: EXAMPLES OF NEW COURSES UNDER CURRICULUM REFORM

ANGOLA

Agostinho Neto University

Graduate level
- Marine Biology
- Environmental engineering,
- Mineralogy and Environment

Postgraduate level
- Integrated Natural Resources and Environment

MOZAMBIQUE

Pedagogical University

Graduate level
- Education and Environmental Management
- Community development and Environmental management
- Environmental Education

Eduardo Mondlane University

Graduate level
- Environmental Engineering
- Environmental Education

Postgraduate level
- Agricultural Development
- Costal Geology and Environment

CONCLUSION

The tentative mapping of HE in the African lusophone community demonstrates that there is a great effort to develop this sector in all lusophone countries. This also includes the integration of sustainability issues in their different dimensions. The development of new HEIs such as universities, new partnerships, research centres and networks will actually lead to a new dynamic towards sustainability in HE.

TABLE 1 Average annual tertiary enrolment growth rates in Africa (percentages)				
Region	1985–90	1990–95	1995–98	1998–02
Francophone	8.2	6.2	7.9	11.0
Anglophone	12.3	4.4	1.8	18.2
Lusophone	6.2	2.9	13.4	37.6
sub-Saharan Africa	11.1	4.7	3.5	17.2
Source: Materu, 2006, cited in Davies, 2010				

BIBLIOGRAPHY

Chilundo, A. UNESCO Forum, Occasional Paper Series, Paper no. 12 Capacity building in HE in Mozambique and the role played by co-operating foreign agencies: The case of the World Bank Paper Commissioned by the Regional Scientific Committee for Africa June 2006.

Davies, B. (2010) Knowledge Acquisition for Sustainable Development in Africa. Paper presented at United Nations Economic Commission for Africa Seminar Series. August, 2010.

MEC (Conselho de Ministros) (2001) Plano de Acção para a Redução da Pobreza Absoluta, 2001-2005 (PARPA I). Versão Final Aprovada pelo Conselho de Ministros em Abril de 2001, Maputo.

MEC (2006) Plano de Acção para a Redução da Pobreza Absoluta 2006–2009 (PARPA II) Versão Final Aprovada pelo Conselho de Ministros aos 02 de Maio de 2006, Maputo.

MEC (2007) Estrategia Ambiental para o Desenvolvimento sustentavel, Aprovado na IX Sessão ordinaria do conselho de Ministro, 24 de Julho de 2007, Maputo.

MEC (2011) Plano de Acção para Redução da Pobreza (PARP) 2011-2014, Aprovado na 15a Sessão Ordinária do Conselho de Ministros 3 de Maio de 2011 Maputo.

Shneider, Alessandra (2009) Organizacao do Espaco Superior da Comunidade de Paises de Lingua official portuguesa-CPLP, 2009 Maio e 19; PUCRS/PortoAlegre.

World Bank (2000) Higher Education in Developing Countries: Peril and Promise. The International Bank for Reconstruction and Development U.S.A.

Spotlight Issues II.1
African universities responding to HIV/AIDS

Is-haq Olanrewaju Oloyede

BURDEN OF HIV/AIDS IN AFRICA

Current reports indicate that there are about 33.3 million people infected with HIV globally. Two-thirds of these live in sub-Saharan Africa, which conversely contains little more than 10% of the world's population (UNAIDS, 2010). It is estimated that since the beginning of the epidemic more than 15 million Africans have died from AIDS (UNAIDS, 2008). It was estimated that for the year 2009 alone there were an average of 22.5 million people living with HIV, 1.8 million adults and children newly infected with HIV, a 5% prevalence of HIV among adults aged 15–49 years and a total of 1.3 million adults' and children's deaths in sub-Sahara Africa alone (UNAIDS, 2010). The HIV/AIDS epidemic in Africa is growing increasingly dire by the year. Quinn and Serwadda (2011) projected that the number of people living with HIV/AIDS could reach 70 million by 2050 in Africa alone (see Figure 1). Although the most obvious effect of this crisis has been illness and death, the impact of the epidemic has certainly not been confined to the health sector. Households, schools, workplaces, life expectancy, productivity and economic growth and development have been negatively affected (AVERT, 2011).

GLOBAL RESPONSE TO HIV/AIDS

The United Nations General Assembly adopted the Declaration of Commitment on HIV/AIDS. The Declaration of Commitment reflects global consensus on a comprehensive framework for effective action to achieve the Millennium Development Goal of halting and beginning to reverse the epidemic by 2015 (UNAIDS, 2003).

AFRICAN UNIVERSITIES RESPONDING TO HIV/AIDS

The Association of African Universities (AAU) represents higher education institutions across the continent with over 200 members. Lotz-Sisitka (2010) has rightly observed that AAU has the richest compendium on African universities' responses to AIDS. The AAU's programme on HIV and AIDS has been in existence since 2002 and is focused on research, capacity building and the mobilization of higher education leaders in the response to the epidemic (AAU, 2009).

Africa's higher education sector's response to the pandemic so far has been divided into three categories by the AAU (2009) and its partners as follows:

1. **Sensitization:** The wake-up call in the early 2000s from external and internal pressures that generated a community of ideas to prevent and treat HIV/AIDS.
2. **Networking:** As the responses are growing, networks have flourished, which represent a community of interest.
3. **Adaptations and local initiatives:** At the institutional level, a community of practice has emerged that deserves recognition for its increasing sophistication, innovation and commitment.

The major response of African Universities to HIV/AIDS is the resolve of each University to have:

• A strong management and policy commitment on HIV/AIDS
• Effective and preventive educational programmes

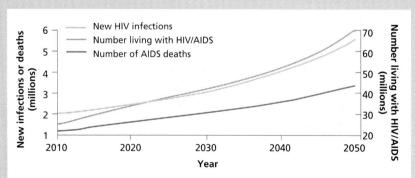

FIGURE 1 Projections of HIV/AIDS morbidity and mortality in Africa
Source: Institute of Medicine, Washington DC (http://www.iom.edu/reports.aspx)

- Care and support for the infected and the affected
- The integration of HIV/AIDS education into its curricula and strategic plan
- Utilization of teaching, research and community service for the prevention and mitigation of the scourge

The level of execution of the commitment varies from one university or subregion to another. The response got an impetus in July 2005 when the Swedish International Development Agency (SIDA) awarded a grant of 7.5 million Swedish kroner to the AAU to implement a three-year project dubbed 'African Universities Responding to HIV/AIDS'. The support, according to Inkoom (2007), was for the implementation of the HIV/AIDS components in the AAU's strategic plan (2003–2010) and Core Programme of Activities (2005–2009). The focus of the programme includes advocacy for integration of HIV/AIDS programmed within tertiary institutions; capacity development for care and support service, resource mobilization and networking on research and documentation of good practices in HIV/AIDS prevention and mitigation. The fund has gone a long way to accelerate the AAU's response to HIV/AIDS.

Findings of commissioned studies on the impact of the response were published and further disseminated at AAU statutory meetings and conferences.

An AAU's Toolkit on HIV/AIDS (AAU, 2004) is now available in English, French and Portuguese. The toolkit was the main instrument used in organizing four subregional, training workshops for universities on the epidemic as follows:

- East Africa (2006), coordinated by Kenyatta University, Kenya
- Central Africa (2006), coordinated by the National University of Rwanda, Rwanda
- West Africa (2008), coordinated by the University of Port Harcourt, Nigeria
- Southern Africa (2008), coordinated by the University of Limpopo, MEDUNSA Campus, South Africa

Each workshop led to the establishment of a subregional network of HEIs fighting the HIV pandemic with the aim of sharing best practices on HIV management in the subregions. While 22 African HEIs benefited from a UNDP HIV/AIDS mainstreaming training programme in 2003, 18 more HEIs were funded to train their academics to integrate HIV and AIDS into their curricula under the AAU Core Programme on HIV/AIDS (AAU, 2008). Furthermore, the AAU (2009) carried out a survey on 'The Response of Higher Education Institutions in Africa to the HIV and AIDS Epidemic' in 19 countries of sub-Saharan Africa. The study focused on higher institutional strategies to combat the epidemic, the inclusion of HIV and AIDS topics into the curricula of different disciplines; the behavioural modification based on the consciousness of existence of HIV/AIDS and the institutional mechanism for the mitigation and treatment of HIV. As expected, the survey shows a significant disparity among the subregions of Africa.

It established that funding from AAU sources greatly helped the universities in Eastern Africa and West Africa to develop their HIV/AIDS policies whereas the Southern African universities did not rely on such funding to develop their own policies. Most of the universities without policies were from West Africa.

The survey also indicated that universities in Western and Central Africa (with the exception of Gaston Berger University) had not included policies on HIV/AIDS in their institutional strategic plans, whereas 80% and 100% of the surveyed universities in Eastern and Southern Africa respectively had incorporated HIV/AIDS into their strategic plans.

The management of HIV/AIDS in universities in Western and Central Africa, according to the survey, was entrusted to low-level officers and ad hoc committees with no budgetary allocations whereas, except for universities of Burundi, Makerere and Kyambogo (whose HIV/AIDS project was, then, not funded by AAU), all surveyed universities in Eastern Africa had dedicated HIV/AIDS units headed by high-level officers with dedicated financial budgetary lines. The same applied to Southern African Universities except for the University of Zambia, National University of Science and Technology, Zimbabwe and University of Antsiranana (Madagascar).

On the whole, there are islands of good practices against HIV/AIDS in universities in sub-Saharan Africa. Some of the best practices are presented in Table I.

CASE STUDY OF UNIVERSITY OF ILORIN'S RESPONSE TO HIV/AIDS

The University of Ilorin, Ilorin, Nigeria (West Africa) models the expected response of African universities in addressing the HIV/AIDS epidemic. As a member of the AAU, the university participated in various AAU-led

TABLE 1
Best practices by some African universities in response to HIV/AIDS

University	Best Practice
University of Ghana, Ghana	Distance Education
University of Ibadan, Nigeria	Social Science Research on HIV and AIDS
Ahmadu Bello University, Nigeria	Prevention services
Kenyatta University, Kenya	Peer education
Maseno University, Kenya	Voluntary Counselling and Testing (VCT)
University of Dar es Salaam, Tanzania	Clinical care and support
Université de Cocody, Côte d'Ivoire	Student involvement
Copperbelt University, Zambia	Community outreach
National University of Rwanda, Rwanda	Access to treatment and care
University of the Western Cape, South Africa	Involvement of people living with HIV
Universidade Eduardo Mondlane, Mozambique	Policy development and advocacy
University of Namibia, Namibia	Curriculum reform
University of Ilorin, Nigeria	Integration into the Teaching Practice/ Community Based Service (COBES)

Source: Updated from version in AAU, 2007.

initiatives to combat the scourge. They include the following:

- **Development of the University of Ilorin's HIV/AIDS policy:** The university initiated the process for developing its institutional HIV/AIDS policy in 2002 with the establishment of its HIV/AIDS Technical Committee. A grant of 5,000 US dollars was received from the AAU and went a long way in facilitating a study and the eventual completion of the institution's HIV/AIDS policy. There is today a multidisciplinary committee charged with the implementation of the policy under the direct supervision of the vice-chancellor's office.
- **Curriculum integration:** The university has integrated HIV/AIDS education into the curricula for the B.Ed/BA(Ed)/B.Sc(Ed) programmes of its Faculty of Education. This is not taught as a standalone programme, but has been fully integrated to the various courses offered in the aforementioned programmes.
- **Integration into teaching practice:** This is showcased as an additional and unique initiative of the University of Ilorin. By integrating HIV/AIDS education into the teaching practice experience for undergraduate and graduate students in the Faculty of Education, the university has enhanced the proficiency of students and graduates in HIV/AIDS-related communication.
- **Research:** The university's academic staff continue to engage in research activities to promote further understanding of the behavioural, social and molecular factors related to HIV/AIDS management and control.
- **Community Service:** The university

established Community Based Experience and Services (COBES), initially for medical students and later extended to all Faculties. The programme requires the students to reside in a rural community for between three and four weeks in a year's study to educate the community on a particular issue. Since 2003, the COBES programme has substantially focused on HIV/AIDS prevention and control in rural communities in Nigeria.

CONCLUSIONS AND RECOMMENDATIONS

While many African universities have responded positively to the threat of HIV, in some cases, the response is more of an internal ad hoc occurrence than a coordinated activity. The AAU's effective platform for this coordination is being curtailed by lack of adequate financial resources. Furthermore, the rate of integration of HIV and AIDS into institutional strategic plans is slow or non-existent, particularly in francophone universities.

To move forward for a holistic HIV response, universities in sub-Saharan Africa need to mobilize substantial funds to strengthen the networks being created through AAU to combat the epidemic. The individual universities need to urgently create institutional HIV/AIDS policies, integrate the study of HIV/AIDS into their curricula, mainstream HIV/AIDS into their institutional strategic plana, establish dedicated unita and funds for HIV/AID programmes and publicize successful local initiatives on HIV/AIDS for the benefit of the entire university system in sub-Saharan Africa and beyond.

REFERENCES

AAU (Association of African Universities) (2004) *An HIV/AIDS Toolkit for Higher Education institutions in Africa.*

AAU (2007) *HIV and AIDS and Higher Education in Africa: A Review of Best Practice Models and Trends.* (http://www.aau.org/sites/default/files/AAUBP-report.pdf).

AAU (2008) *African Universities Responding to HIV/AIDS* (http:www.2.aau.org/aur-hiv-aids/index2.htm).

AAU (2009) *The Response of Higher Education Institutions in Africa to The HIV and AIDS Epidemic: A synthesis of four subregional surveys in sub-Saharan Africa.*

AVERT (2011) *Impact of HIV/AIDS in Africa.* http//www.avert.org/hiv-aids-africa.htm (accessed 14/04/2011).

Inkoom, D.K.B. (2007) *African Universities responding to HIV/AIDS; An independent Mid-Term Evaluation of the SIDA Funded Project.*

Lotz-Sisitka, Heila (2010) *African Universities responding to sustainable development challenges:* (http://blog.univ-provence.fr/blog/coordination-rgionale-paca/dveloppement-durable/2011/02/13/higher-education-s-commitment-to-sustainability).

Quinn, T.C. and Serwadda, D. (2011) The future of HIV/AIDS in Africa: a shared responsibility, *The Lancet*, 377, pp. 1133–4.

UNAIDS (2003) *Progress Report on the Global Response to the HIV/AIDS Epidemic.*

UNAIDS (2008) *Global Report: UNAIDS report on the global AIDS epidemic.*

UNAIDS/WHO (2009) *(Joint United Nations Programme on HIV/AIDS World Health Organisation) AIDS Epidemic Update.* Geneva, December 2009.

UNAIDS (2010) *The Joint United Nations Programme on HIV/AIDS: Report on the global AIDS epidemic.*

Spotlight Issues II.2
Role of higher education in reducing food insecurity in Africa

*Negussie Retta and
Gulelat Desse*

INTRODUCTION

According to the Food and Agriculture Organization (FAO, 2002), approximately 800 million people in the developing world are food insecure. In Africa, millions hover near starvation in a world of plenty. Since 1990, food availability per capita in sub-Saharan Africa has declined by 3%. This compares to per capita increases of more than 30% in Asia and 20% in Latin America. Almost 200 million Africans were undernourished at the dawn of the millennium compared to 133 million in 1980. Children undernourished in Africa now number 33 million, or more than one-third of pre-school children. Almost all of these children live in sub-Saharan Africa, the only region in the developing world where child undernourishment has been increasing.

Nutritional deficiencies, particularly deficiencies of iron, iodine, and vitamin A, have far-reaching consequences on growth, development and health, contributing to impaired immunity and cognitive function, growth failure, increased morbidity and mortality (Graham et al., 2001; Smith and Haddad, 2000; CGIAR, 2002).

Education plays a vital role in enhancing economic development, reduction of poverty and sustainable development. This can be accomplished through capacity building by offering proper training and research. Research assists in innovation of technology, increasing productivity and new food product development. As stipulated in the Millennium Development Goals, there is a focus on food security and poverty alleviation issues. In this regard, higher education has a critical role in strengthening innovative research, training and extension activities. This review assesses the role of tertiary level education to combat food insecurity in Africa.

MAJOR CHALLENGES TO FOOD SECURITY IN AFRICA

Part of the problem for not achieving food security in Africa is the very low levels of investment for agriculture. This has led to low incomes for farmers and rural residents, reduced competitiveness, and increasing food insecurity and child malnutrition. In addition, poor farming practices, limited access of farm products to the market, poor policies, diseases, demographics and climate have vastly contributed to African food insecurity. In some African countries food aid is regarded as insurance (Hoddinott, 2003).

FARMING

Africa's agriculture is generally primitive (Chema et al., 2003; Dixon et al., 2001). Low levels of external farm inputs, post- and pre-harvest crop losses, poor food storage and preservation, unfertile soil and degradation of the environment are a few of the factors contributing to poor farming practices in Africa. As the majority of food products' production is based on rain the production is affected by the adverse climatic conditions. The agricultural systems in general need to be sustainable (Brinkerhoff et al., 2002).

ACCESS TO MARKETS

Inadequate roads and transportation, and poor information technology and knowledge have hindered farmers in bringing their produce to the market. In addition, Africa's high export costs limit farmers' access to international markets.

POLICIES

Policies in Africa are not inclusive in their design, which brings about uneven development within countries. Polices that promote monopolistic competition for large-scale industries affect small industry.

DISEASE, DEMOGRAPHICS AND CLIMATE

Disease and infection have continued to be a serious challenge in Africa. These include, among others, malaria and HIV/AIDS. They vastly reduce the working manpower available to agriculture and household food security. The farming population in Africa is ageing, male workers are migrating to urban areas, and many rural areas are becoming urbanized.

ROLE OF HIGHER EDUCATION

Appropriate application of various technology options enhances crop and animal production and makes more effective, efficient use of land, labour and other resources. Universities need to create technologies having the potential to increase productivity of land, labour and farm inputs (Michelsen et al., 2003; Oehmke et al., 1996). This can be done through providing target-oriented, strong and holistic science-based training within a socio-economic background relevant to the needs of the continent, and conducting impact-oriented participatory research and also dissemination of knowledge and research outputs through extension services. One possible way of doing this is by aligning the research with that of the national development plans, which for most countries is likely to be poverty reduction strategy plan. This will ensure that it is both demand-driven action research and helps the country along the path of realizing its development goals and thereby addressing the issues of food insecurity. However, in many African countries this is not happening. Universities operate in silos and are not directly linked to national development plans.

Curricula in the African higher education

system need to be flexible and market driven, incorporating aspects of sensitivity to the environment and sustainability, natural and social science, information technology and entrepreneurship. They have to be able to produce scientists with commitment to lifelong learning and, furthermore, they should also reflect current issues and needs such as climate change and address them appropriately. This could be done by constant revision of the curriculum and linking it with the national development plan, which reflects the current needs and issues. They must be equipped with both problem-solving and critical thinking skills, and possess good communication and interpersonal skills. Among others, African higher education institutions should incorporate the following areas in their curricula:

- Create a community that integrates energy, climate, environment and social science researchers and educators to promote active and sustainable engagement to address food insecurity
- Implement a broad range of informal educational and outreach programmes to promote the study of achievement of food security through availability and affordability, poverty eradication strategies, and knowledge of productivity and competitiveness of farmers and agricultural business entrepreneurs
- Ways of establishment of sustainable domestic, intra- and inter-regional, and international agricultural markets
- Systems in achieving an equitable distribution of wealth
- Agricultural biodiversity management and development through the application of science and innovation and best practices that conserve and sustain the natural resources used in agriculture
- Develop interdisciplinary research, innovative courses at the interface of disciplines and new degree programmes that benefit all stakeholders including private industries and businesses
- Ways of developing micro, small and medium agricultural and agriculture-related enterprises, including in the 'informal' sector
- Innovation of technologies for the reduction of post-harvest losses
- Information and communication technologies

- Mainstreaming of environment and sustainability into agricultural activities

Impact-oriented participatory research is an area where science and technology can directly contribute to improved food security (Gemo et al., 2003). HEIs in Africa should focus on technologies that require less labour and minimum cost (pre- and post-harvest technologies, processing, packaging, marketing, traditional preservation methods and so on); research to improve seeds that can resist pests, diseases and drought; and the production of crops with both a high yield and nutrient content (bio-fortified crops) through breeding and molecular biology techniques. In addition, African universities need to look for technologies for food fortification and food safety, value addition for food staples, horticulture, and animal products through post-harvest research. As the role of women in ensuring household food security is high, technology options that are accessible to them are indispensible.

In Africa a number of establishments take part in planning, funding and conduct of agricultural research. These include national agricultural research centres, universities, international agricultural research centres and extension services. The institutions' research activity is dominated by the production of improved seeds and excludes pre- and post-harvest technologies, food fortification issues and extension services. Moreover, they work independently of each other and there is no coordination of efforts, which leads to duplication and thereby wastage of resources both human and financial.

Diffusion of technology is ended through extension (Hambly and Setshwaelo, 1997). It is believed that African scientists have shelved a high number of research outputs, thereby reducing their value towards achieving sustainable development of the nation states. Although, the scientists are determined to conduct impact-oriented research, limitations in budget and extension systems have hindered their activities. Investment in information and communication technologies, education and an extension system that involves smallholder farmers is indispensible. Therefore, the universities need more research pertaining to the future of extension systems in Africa.

CONCLUSION

Food insecurity in Africa can be challenged through the building of strong links among universities and all other stakeholders in order to increase agricultural productivity, improve pre- and post-harvest technologies and develop new food products. University curricula need to be flexible and reformed. In addition, curricula and research should be reorganized as a community approach in order to understand, identify and respond to scientific need and engage members of the government, business and the community concerning climate, environment and energy issues to address food security. It is essential to enhance and coordinate interdisciplinary interaction among universities, business, government and community that will lead to a better understanding of the links between the environment, socioeconomic relationships and interactions on both a local and a global scale.

To achieve impact-oriented participatory research universities need to mobilize sustainable funding and minimize support of external donors. Strong partnerships with government agencies, the private sector and universities in research, exchange of students, faculties and ideas to design innovative courses and research can address global concerns of food insecurity.

REFERENCES

Brinkerhoff, D.W., Gage, J.D. and Gavian, S. (2002) *Sustainable agricultural research systems: Findings and lessons from reforms in Cote d'Ivoire, Ghana, Senegal, Tanzania, and Uganda.* Bethesda, Maryland: Abt Associates.

CGIAR (Consultative Group on International Agricultural Research) (2002) Biofortified crops for human nutrition: A CGIAR challenge program proposal draft, June 25. Washington, DC.

Chema, S., Gilbert, E. and Roseboom, J. (2003) A critical review of key issues and recent experiences in reforming agricultural research in Africa. ISNAR research report no. 24. International Service for National Agricultural Research. The Hague, The Netherlands.

Dixon, J., Gulliver, A. and Gibbon, D. (2001) *Farming systems and poverty: Improving farmers' livelihoods in a changing world.* Washington, DC: FAO, Rome, and World Bank.

FAO (2002) *Food insecurity: When people must live with hunger and fear starvation. The state of food insecurity in the world 2002.* Rome, Italy: FAO.

Gemo, H., Eicher, C.K. and Teclemariam, Solomon (2003) Mozambique's experience in building a national agricultural extension system, 1987–2003. Maputo: dner, mader. July draft.

Graham, R.D., Welsch, R.M. and Bouis, H.E. (2001) Addressing micronutrient malnutrition through enhancing the nutritional quality of staple foods: Principles, perspectives and knowledge gaps. *Advances in Agronomy*, **70**: pp. 78–142.

Hambly, H. and Setshwaelo, L. (1997) Agricultural research plans in sub-Saharan Africa: A status report. ISNAR research report 11. International Service for National Agricultural Research. The Hague, The Netherlands.

Haug, R. (1999) Some leading issues in international agricultural extension, a literature review. *The Journal of Agricultural Education and Extension*, **5**(4), pp. 263–74.

Hoddinott, J. (2003) Food aid in the 21st century: Food aid as insurance. Paper presented at international workshop, Defining the role of food aid in contributing to sustainable food security, Berlin, September. International Food Policy Research Institute. Washington, DC.

Michelsen, H., Zuidema, L., Hoste, C. and Shapiro, D. (2003) *Improving agricultural research at universities in sub-Saharan Africa: A study guide.* Research management guidelines no. 6. International Service for National Agricultural Research. The Hague, The Netherlands.

Oehmke, J.F. and Crawford, E.W. (1996) The impact of agricultural technology in sub-Saharan Africa. *Journal of African Economies*, **5**(2), pp. 271–92.

Smith, L.C. and Haddad, L. (2000) *Overcoming child malnutrition in developing countries: Past achievements and future choices.* Food, agriculture, and the environment discussion paper 30. International Food Policy Research Institute. Washington, DC.

Social learning in the mainstreaming environment and sustainability education in African universities partnership

Akpezi Ogbuigwe and Heila Lotz-Sisitka

The Mainstreaming Environment and Sustainability in Africa's (MESA) Universities Partnership (see www.unep.org/training) is designed as UNEP's contribution to the UNDESD. It works with the African Association of Universities (AAU), UNESCO, and a broad partnership network to infuse environment and sustainability concerns into universities in Africa in ways that respond to the Millennium Development Goals (MDGs), the African Ministerial Conference on the Environment (AMCEN) and the New Partnership for Africa's Development's (NEPAD) commitments to sustainable development (SD) in Africa. Since its inception in 2004, MESA has adopted a broad based understanding of education for sustainable development (ESD) and social learning. MESA promotes ESD as a networked learning process in itself (that is, a social-learning view of ESD).

The MESA programme recognizes that ESD can support the development of a 'learning society' in which people learn from and with one another and collectively become more capable of withstanding setbacks and dealing with sustainability-induced insecurity, complexity and risks. From this vantage point, ESD as seen and practised in MESA is a process of reflexive change – involving change in the way knowledge is viewed, produced and used in universities, and change in the way universities function in society as 'learning hubs' for learning how to prevent and respond to sustainability issues and risks. The MESA network is therefore constituted as a social learning network.

With this view of learning at its core, MESA has been premised on a concept of ESD innovations, and all its activities support university teachers and professors in learning more about SD and ESD in various ways (that is, there is no one recipe). It seeks to support university lecturers and managers to see that a sustainable society will require new ways of thinking about teaching, learning and knowledge in universities.

A few important characteristics of the MESA programme provide evidence of this view of learning and knowledge:

- MESA is a **transdisciplinary initiative**: it involves university teachers and lecturers from all university disciplines, and encourages an understanding of how individual disciplines can contribute to ESD, but also, and perhaps more importantly, how transdisciplinary knowledge creation is possible at the level of practice – where sustainability issues are experienced in communities, schools and in the day-to-day production and consumption practices in society.
- MESA actively encourages the **development of partnerships and networks** among universities, business, government, civil society and community partners, recognizing that learning for sustainability requires a diverse range of views and different knowledge modalities in society.
- MESA learning also takes account of both the **local and the global dynamics of knowledge** creation and sustainability practices, and actively encourages university lecturers to engage with local and indigenous knowledge *as well as* the latest information available from scientific reports, and other information resources that are available through international knowledge exchange mechanisms, and through mediums such as ICT enhanced learning. Development of new knowledge at local and regional level to enrich local understanding and capacity is also encouraged through research partnerships.
- MESA engages a **reflexive learning and professional development model** which locates the learning of lecturers, student participants and university managers in own 'change project' contexts. This model encourages situated learning of how to go about mainstreaming environment and sustainability in African universities.

Some social learning outcomes that are emerging from this learning framework include:

- **A commitment to situated learning**: For example, in Liberia the Director General of Higher Education has launched a MESA Universities Partnership initiative to mainstream environment and sustainability concerns into research and community engagement in Liberia. Under this initiative, students are assigned to various communities to work and mobilize resources and human knowledge in addressing SD issues during their junior and senior years. The project also aims to create awareness among rural communities on sustainable living and development.
- **A commitment to networked social learning**: African networks supporting the MESA partnership have increased. For instance, the SADC (Southern African Development Community) Regional Environmental Education Programme recently established a funding mechanism to upscale MESA in SADC countries, and in March 2009 launched three university MESA chairs in the Universities of Botswana, Swaziland and Zambia. The Horn of Africa Environmental Network is supporting an Ethiopian MESE network, and is collaborating with UNESCO PEER (Programme for Education for Emergencies and Reconstruction) to take MESA to Somalia, and involve Somalia's universities in MESA activities and networks. This is a perfect example of enhancing social learning processes by upholding the spirit of partnerships and networking for SD. Other examples include the University of Buea in Cameroon, which has established a national network with other universities for ESD. It has also established a regional network with universities in Chad, the Central African Republic, Gabon and the Republic of Congo for ESD training. It also utilizes case studies to consider ways of integrating sustainability into various degree programmes.
- **A commitment to learning in communities of practice**: With communities of practice existing across 80 universities in 40 African countries, the partnership has developed into a best practice in the area of mainstreaming. In 2007 a study was undertaken to establish how to strengthen

a systems approach to MESA (Togo, 2009), and this study noted that the existence of communities of practice is an essential learning mechanism for MESA activities. In various universities, different types of communities of practice focusing on ESD and learning about sustainability exist, with activities ranging from teaching communities of practice, management communities of practice, and/or student communities of practice, with many overlapping constituencies and including communities and other groups that have an interest in learning for sustainability. For example in South Africa, a South East African Climate Consortium has been established to support a climate change teaching, research and student action community of practice across three Eastern Cape Universities. These are now linking to Western Cape Universities, and a Habitable Planet Winter School Workshop is being organized for students interested in ESD and sustainability issues. In the University of Swaziland, a MESA Implementation Committee exists, with links to the Swaziland Regional Centre of Expertise in ESD.

- **A commitment to fostering dialogue and lifelong learning that promotes global solidarity, rather international competitiveness**: The MESA has facilitated a number of international training programmes, linking teachers and managers in African universities to universities and lecturers in the East and in the Global North, with some emerging results. For example, through interactions on an international training programme between African and Swedish universities, a climate change education research network has been formed, and researchers are working on collaborative research to understand climate capabilities and how education can strengthen learning and adaptation responses to complex issues such as climate change, which manifest differently in different settings. Dialogue and lifelong learning possibilities have also been extended through technology-enhanced environmental learning resources such as the resource produced by UNEP for the MESA Universities Partnership – '*Sustainable Societies Africa: Modules for Sustainable Development*'. This flexible resource makes it possible for all universities to offer a foundation course in 'Sustainable Societies in Africa' to all students and other lifelong learners.

SUSTAINABLE DEVELOPMENT CONTRIBUTIONS

The MESA is primarily an edu-centred intervention to engage and involve universities in the process of mainstreaming environment and sustainability into African university curricula, management practices and community engagement. Through these educational activities, there are some tangible contributions to sustainability practices at local level – university lecturers report practical outcomes from some of their research initiatives at community level, and student and management interventions are improving campus management. It is, however, the longer-term societal contributions to SD that are of interest to MESA – in the form of integrating knowledge and practice of SD into a range of societal practices. To date little monitoring and evaluation of this component of MESA has taken place as this would require M&E (monitoring and evaluation) instruments that extend beyond monitoring the educative contributions of the initiative and would involve the complex task of linking educative instruments to actual SD indicators, which by their nature, would have to be context specific. The MESA initiative has recently been upscaled to a global partnership programme under the banner of UNEP's Global Universities Partnership for Sustainability (GUPES).

REFERENCE

Togo, M. (2009) A Systems Approach to Mainstreaming Environment and Sustainability in Universities: The Case of Rhodes University, South Africa. Unpublished PhD thesis, Rhodes University, Grahamstown, South Africa.

GOOD PRACTICES II.1

Higher Education and Sustainability in Africa: Sharing Actions for Change

The following experiences are a selection of good practices on higher education and sustainability. Some of them were presented at the 5th International Barcelona Conference on Higher Education and others are part of the GUNi observatory.

The good practices cover the following institutional areas:

Community and social engagement

Institutional management

Curricula and learning innovation

Research

GOOD PRACTICE 1

Young Congolese university students learn about peaceful conflict resolution

Institutional area(s):

LOCATION: Africa
INSTITUTION: Jeunes et Femmes pour les droits de l'homme et la paix (JFDHOP)

Founded in 2002, the JFDHOP currently organizes educational activities in Rwanda, Angola, the Central African Republic, Burundi and the Democratic Republic of the Congo. Much of its activity involves organizing courses at higher education institutions in order to introduce Congolese university students to the concepts of human rights and the culture of peace. Under the guidance of UNESCO, the JFDHOP teaches sessions on peaceful conflict resolution at public and private higher education institutions. These sessions are open to students of any ethnic group and political affiliation.

Detailed information is available at GUNi HEiOBS:

http://www.guninetwork.org/guni.heiobs/good-practices/young-congolese-university-students-learn-about-peaceful-conflict-resolution

GOOD PRACTICE 2

Greening and sustainable environment: University campuses as a model for Nigerian society

Institutional area(s):

LOCATION: Nigeria
INSTITUTION: University of Ilorin

This good practice was undertaken by two Nigerian universities: University of Ilorin and Gombe State University. The goal of the initiative is to restore nature's equilibrium on the university campuses for sustainable development. Different measures have been implemented among which we can highlight: establishment of an environmental protection committee; engagement of a landscaping workforce; establishment of a biological garden (which houses a zoo and a botanical garden); construction of a dam to supply water for human use and fishing; prohibition of indiscriminate felling of trees and burning of bush on the campuses; and the inclusion of courses relating to conservation in the university curriculum.

Detailed information is available at GUNi HEiOBS:

http://www.guninetwork.org/guni.heiobs/good-practices/greening-and-sustainable-environment-university-campuses-as-a-model-for-the-nigerian-society

GOOD PRACTICE 3

Social responsibility and citizenship for graphic design students

Institutional area(s):

LOCATION: South Africa
INSTITUTION: University of Stellenbosch

With this good practice, the university students form learning partnerships with the high school students, through which they explore relevant social issues, often underlined by deep cultural and material differences, and seek innovative ways of articulating and resolving these problems through the visual medium. The module creates a forum for an ongoing dialogue between the different life-worlds of the parties involved. Last but not least, it aims at the creation of a 'bottom-up' institutional and social transformation.

Detailed information is available at GUNi HEiOBS:

http://www.guninetwork.org/guni.heiobs/good-practices/social-responsibility-and-citizenship-for-graphic-design-students

GOOD PRACTICE 4

Institutionalization of indigenous knowledge research for development: Institute of Indigenous Knowledge (IIK)

Institutional area(s):

LOCATION: Uganda
INSTITUTION: Mbara University of Science and Technology

The Mbara University of Science and Technology (MUST) has recently been working on bringing back traditional knowledge to higher education. It has done so by presenting a model Institute of Indigenous Knowledge (IIK) whose main goal is to enhance universities' role by adding a discipline to the range of universities research and teaching, namely the studies of indigenous systems, science and technologies for development. The IIK pools together expertise within Africa and beyond who will capture, document, research and generate as well as share knowledge of useful IK practices, and their usage in the contemporary context, and thereby preserve the information and promote their wider application: thus, documenting and spreading indigenous knowledge in various fields.

Detailed information is available at GUNi HEiOBS:

http://www.guninetwork.org/guni.heiobs/good-practices/institutionalization-of-indigenous-knowledge-research-for-development-institute-of-indigenous-knowledge-iik

Amplifying grassroots community voices in Vhembe district

Institutional area(s):

LOCATION: South Africa
INSTITUTION: University of Venda

This programme endeavours to 'take the university to its rightful owners – grassroots communities' and create all-inclusive community ventilation platforms where people as young as seven years old have the opportunity to express their views on local development issues. Through reflection circles that are facilitated by students and mediated by peers within the community, issues militating against local development are discussed in a democratic manner and decisions made. The university team of academic staff/faculty and students works closely and co-learns with community-based and run institutions as programme implementation proceeds.

Detailed information is available at GUNi HEiOBS:

http://www.guninetwork.org/guni.heiobs/good-practices/amplifying-grassroots-community-voices-in-vhembe-district

The bright side of Sunnyside service learning centre

Institutional area(s):

LOCATION: South Africa
INSTITUTION: University of South Africa

In October 2008 the Department of Social Work initiated the UNISA Bright Site project in collaborative consultation with the stakeholders and the community of Sunnyside. The programme is currently run by the Department of Social Work in conjunction with students and with input from other academic departments. The mission of the project is: 'Integrating and capacitating the worlds of UNISA and communities by engaging in a mutually beneficial relationship through relevant services, learning opportunities, shared resources, research, and policy.' Establishment of a service learning site provided alternative options for placements of social work students within the community engagement context. Students render services while learning and becoming competent towards the achievement of their qualification.

Detailed information is available at GUNi HEiOBS:

http://www.guninetwork.org/guni.heiobs/good-practices/the-bright-site-of-sunnyside-service-learning-center

---

The reader can also find the following good practices related to sustainability in Africa at the GUNi Observatory:

- Biodiversity conservation through bioprospecting in Madagascar
  LOCATION: Madagascar
  INSTITUTION: Ecole Normale Superieure

- Empirical approach to SD-curriculum transdisciplinary model: curriculum for climate change and gender
  LOCATION: Kenya
  INSTITUTION: University of Nairobi

- Improving community: higher education institutions' interactions for sustainability
  LOCATION: Nigeria
  INSTITUTION: University of Port-Harcourt

- Mainstreaming environment and sustainability at the University of Namibia
  LOCATION: Namibia
  INSTITUTION: University of Namibia

- Raymond Ackerman Academy for Entrepreneurial Development: Integrating sustainability in entrepreneurship
  LOCATION: South Africa
  INSTITUTION: University of Cape Town

- Technology transfer to the community: development of biogas and waste management plants for penitentiary institutions.
  LOCATION: Rwanda
  INSTITUTION: Kigali Institute of Science

http://www.guninetwork.org/guni.heiobs

II.2 Higher Education Commitment to Sustainability in the Arab States

Ramzi Salamé

Abstract

This paper starts with a reminder of the various elements necessary to achieve sustainable development (SD) and the central role of educational institutions in this endeavour. It then provides some details on the various roles that higher education institutions (HEIs) could play to move the SD agenda ahead, particularly in relation to their education, research, and community development functions, and the realization of sustainable campuses, with specific expectations towards these institutions in each of these areas, in addition to the necessary formal commitment towards SD.

The situation concerning the commitment of HEIs in the Arab countries towards SD is then examined in light of these expectations, and a certain number of indicators are provided that show that, except for the establishment of a number of UNESCO chairs relevant to SD, the Arab HEIs are lagging behind in this endeavour in all other modes of action, putting a heavy burden on priorities for future action. The paper ends by providing three promising examples of commitment towards SD shown by three HEIs in Jordan and Saudi Arabia.

INTRODUCTION

Starting from the landmark definition set by the United Nations Brundtland Report (1987)[1] stating that sustainable development is about 'meeting the needs of the present (generations), without compromising the ability of future generations to meet their own needs', sustainable development could be achieved through the conjunction of the following three golden triple dimensions (see Figure II.2.1):

- The three components of the concept of sustainable development, that is, protection of the environment, economic development, and social development
- The three basic principles for action, that is, comprehensiveness of scope, complementarity of actions, and partnerships
- The triangle of actors, that is, the public authorities, civil society, and the media

As a major component of civil society, educational institutions occupy a central role with regard to various aspects that would enhance the chance of achieving SD. Under the leadership of UNESCO, the UN has declared 2005–2014 as the UN Decade of Education for Sustainable Development (DESD) with the goal to integrate the principles, values, and practices of SD into all aspects of education and learning. The mid-decade review of the progress made has led to the adoption by the international community of 'the 2009 Bonn Declaration Agenda for ESD in Educational Institutions'[2] stating the following goals for actions:

- Re-orient education and training systems to address sustainability concerns
- Re-orient curriculum and teacher education programmes to integrate ESD
- Support the incorporation of SD issues in education using an integrated and systemic approach in all forms of education
- Promote ESD's contribution to achieving quality education
- Develop and extend ESD partnerships to integrate ESD into training, vocational education and workplace learning

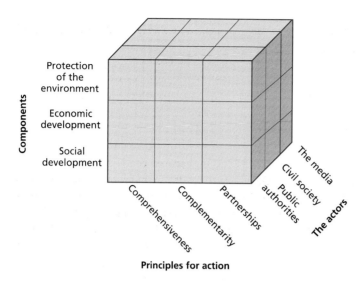

FIGURE II.2.1 The golden elements of sustainable development matrix

- Encourage and enhance scientific research and new knowledge development for ESD through the involvement of HEIs and research networks in ESD
- Intensify efforts in education and training systems to address critical and urgent sustainability challenges such as climate change, and water and food security
- Involve youth in the design and implementation of ESD

THE ROLE OF HIGHER EDUCATION IN SD

HEIs could play a major role in the drive towards the achievement of SD, through their educational role, as well as through their research and community development roles, and their proper action as managers of usually vast property and material assets.

The education role should primarily aim at educating students in all disciplines to respect, promote, and fulfil the requirements of SD, hence the need for an interdisciplinary approach. In this field of action, HEIs should set, as one of the intended learning outcomes of their educational programmes, the acquisition by the students of the generic competences for sustainability:

- Educating for critical and creative thinking, lifelong learning, and for citizenship and democracy
- Educating for sustainable consumption and production patterns, and for sustainable health, population behaviour, and demographic dynamics
- Building capacities for sustainable productive work
- Promoting gender equity and empowering girls and women for full participation in social, economic and political life

In their research role, HEIs must put SD onto the research agenda in an integrated way and adopt comprehensive research approaches, encompassing policy research and strategic analysis, development of methodologies, diagnostic tools, and indicators to monitor SD and assist decision-making. They must also strengthen the science/knowledge base of SD, particularly through empirical research, establishing observatories and databases to monitor SD and report on its various components, as well as documenting best and bad practices.

Specific themes related to the conservation and management of natural resources may include protection of the atmosphere, oceans and freshwater resources, combating deforestation and desertification, managing fragile ecosystems, promoting sustainable agriculture and rural development, conservation of biological diversity, environmentally sound management of biotechnology, and environmentally sound management of toxic chemicals, and hazardous, solid, and radioactive wastes.

In their community development role, HEIs would essentially devote time and efforts to promote the concepts and values and build public understanding and awareness about SD, as well as play the role of social observatory and intervention centre to promote SD and ensure proper respect and fulfilment of its requirements by the higher education community in particular and the public at large.

Finally, HEIs should strive to achieve sustainable campuses through the application of SD principles to the management of these sites.

SPECIFIC EXPECTATIONS TOWARDS HEIs AS REGARDS SD

The commitment of HEIs towards SD is expected to materialize around the following actions:

1. Formal institutional commitment to SD should essentially result in the inclusion of SD in the mission statements of the institutions and of at least some of its most relevant components; the adoption of institutional policy on SD; the establishment of institutional set-ups for SD, such as the creation of a senior position in charge of SD, and the establishment of bodies at various levels with the mandate to promote

and monitor SD, such as a council, a task force, an institutional committee, and so on; the establishment of chairs and/or institutes in SD, in basic sciences as well as in sociopolitical and sociocultural dimensions of SD; and putting SD on national and international cooperation agendas and networking.

2. As for study programmes, HEIs committed to SD are particularly expected to offer study programmes on SD at undergraduate and/or graduate levels in various disciplines or across disciplines; offer courses to teach and learn SD principles and applications throughout the various programmes they offer; integrate SD principles throughout at least some courses; adopt transformative pedagogy/learning approaches in order to achieve the acquisition by the students of generic competences and reflexivity for sustainability.

3. Embedding SD in the research agenda would mean at least the realization of theses and dissertations on SD and on education for sustainable development (ESD); the establishment of observatories on SD and ESD, with baseline, benchmarks, tracking, dissemination of information, and so on; holding conferences, seminars and workshops on SD and ESD; publishing papers, books and periodicals on SD and on ESD.

4. HEIs committed to SD are also expected to enhance the higher education community's involvement in SD. This could particularly be achieved through the establishment of communities of interest and networks on SD among faculty members, staff, and students; building the community members' capacities for responsible citizenship; and establishing internal and external partnerships for SD.

5. Finally, HEIs really committed to SD are expected to strive towards realizing sustainable campuses with zero waste through the implementation of the four Rs (Reduce; Reuse; Recycle; Recover) in all institutional endeavours and activities.

SD ON THE AGENDAS OF HEIs IN THE ARAB STATES

When this paper was first written (October 2010), a Google search with the key words 'sustainable development' resulted in the following hits: in English: 15,900,000; in French: 6,120,000; in Spanish: 462,000; in Arabic: 125,000. If demographic parameters are considered, it appears clear that both Spanish and Arab countries are underrepresented in the number of documents on SD searchable by Google. Moreover, the examination of more than the first 100 documents

yielded by Google in Arabic shows that less than 5% of these documents pertain to the activities of HEIs.

Also, a search on SD (including ESD) in a database called Shamaa (Arab Educational Information Network),[3] which has recorded publications in education over the Arab countries since 2007, including theses and dissertations, books, and articles of periodicals, has yielded only seven hits out of more than 11,000 records the database contained at that time.

On another front, the examination of the signatories of the 1990 Talloires Declaration (University Presidents for a Sustainable Future) shows that only two universities in Lebanon and one in Tunisia (out of 427) have adhered to this declaration.[4] Also, only two Arab universities hold membership of the Association for the Advancement of Sustainability in Higher Education,[5] and no one holds membership in the International Sustainable Campus Network (ISCN).[6] Finally, there is no regional association on sustainability in higher education, whereas there is a parent organization called the Ma'an Arab University Alliance for Civic Engagement, associated to the Talloires Network established following the 2005 Talloires Declaration on the Civic Roles and Social Responsibilities of Higher Education.[7]

It appears that there are no periodicals on SD or on ESD either in Arabic or published in the Arab States. The *International Journal of Arab Culture, Management and Sustainable Development* is, in fact, edited at the Universidad de Oviedo, Spain and published by Inderscience, Switzerland.

In this field, a relatively recent paper about environmental education in the Arab States (Hamzah, 2008)[8] notes the absence of such scientific periodicals on environmental research, in any aspect, while 'the Arab world has relatively recently witnessed the emergence of several non-academic magazines and newsletters that are dedicated to environmental issues and concepts' (p. 211). To this effect, Hamzah notes that 'scientific and environmental contributions of the Arab world to global knowledge [are] very low in comparison with other nations and regions', and he comments on it by writing that 'this is hardly surprising due to the desperate need of universities and research centres for further funding and the need to develop more international alliances and partnerships' (p. 210).

On the other hand, examination of a very large number of Arab HEI websites has shown that there are rare occurrences of the following manifestations of commitment to SD: inclusion of SD in the mission statement of the institution; establishing institutional set-ups for SD; offering courses to teach and learn SD principles and applications; establishing communities of interest on SD among faculty members and students; publishing papers and books on SD; establishing partnerships for SD; putting SD on the international cooperation agenda; implementing some of the four Rs (Reduce; Reuse; Recycle; Recover) as a way to realize sustainable campuses.[9]

However, as may be expected, a certain number of HEIs in the Arab States offer study programmes and degrees in environmental studies at the various cycles. Table II.2.1 summarizes the data on this issue compiled by Hamzah.[10]

TABLE II.2.1
Number of study programmes and degrees offered in environmental studies in Arab universities according to higher education cycles

State	No. of universities concerned	No. of programmes and degrees				
		Bachelor	Master	Ph.D.	Other	Total
Bahrain	1		1			1
Egypt	4	5	4	1		10
Jordan	4	5	2			7
Kuwait	1	1				1
Lebanon	4	4	3	1	1	9
Libya	1	1				1
Morocco	1		1			1
Oman	1	1				1
Total	17	17	11	2	2	32

Source: Compiled by the author from data in Hamzah, Riyad Y. (2008). Environmental Education; in Mostafa K. Tolba and Najib W. Saab, *Arab Environment: Future Challenges*. Arab Forum for Environment and Development (AFED) Report 2008 (Chapter 15, pp. 202–4).

As shown in this table, these programmes relate to 17 universities in eight countries for a total of 33 programmes, most of which (17/32) being at the bachelor's degree level.

An examination of the topics covered by these study programmes shows the following:

- 22 programmes pertain to general environmental sciences, sometimes in relation to biology, chemistry and biochemistry
- 8 programmes pertain to environmental engineering and technology
- 8 programmes pertain to water resources and water management
- 5 programmes pertain to environmental health
- 4 programmes pertain to applied geology and earth sciences
- 4 programmes pertain to respectively SD in general, energy management, land management, and sustainable agriculture

According to the author of the paper, 'these statistics reflect the current deficiencies found in providing higher education in environmental issues', and he argues that 'degree programmes should be expanded to cover all the necessary aspects of environmental education' particularly as concerns 'environmental legislation, environmental management, and environmental risk management'. He also argues that the quality of these programmes should be enhanced in order to 'provide the individual with the tools necessary to transform society into a more sustainable society, taking into consideration the social, economic, cultural, and environmental elements of the place, as well as its history and traditions'.[11]

In parallel to the study programmes in environmental studies, and as shown in Table II.2.2, out of the 57 UNESCO chairs established and still active, as of April 2011, in 16 out of the 22 Arab States,[12] a sizeable percentage (35%) concerns or is related to SD, these chairs being spread over 11 Arab States.

TABLE II.2.2
Number of UNESCO chairs established in Arab universities

State	No. of chairs in SD	Total no. of chairs	State	No. of chairs in SD	Total no. of chairs
Algeria	2	6	Palestine	0	3
Bahrain	2	2	Qatar	0	1
Egypt	0	2	Saudi Arabia	0	1
Jordan	3	6	Sudan	4	7
Lebanon	1	2	Syria	1	1
Libya	1	1	Tunisia	1	6
Morocco	3	14	UAE	1	3
Oman	1	1	Yemen	0	1
			Total	20	57

Source: Compiled by the author from: http://www.unesco.org/fileadmin/MULTIMEDIA/HQ/ED/UNITWIN/pdf/Doc_annexes/TB Chairs 2030042011.pdf (last accessed: 21 May 2011).

Nonetheless, examination of these chairs shows a relatively low level of activities, much of them lacking the human and financial resources to operate in an efficient manner.

As for the inclusion of SD in research agendas, according to the information available on the net, the following themes are present to some extent on the research agendas of various Arab universities, generally with the support of the relevant authority or fund of the State: environment, desertification, renewable energies, fresh water, sustainable agriculture and food security, biotechnologies, economic and social dynamics, nutrition, and chronic diseases.

A certain number of Master's theses and doctoral dissertations on SD are realized in the HEIs of most of the Arab countries, the most frequent of which are in agriculture and rural development.

Also, holding conferences, seminars and workshops on SD is present across the Arab States, although generally dealing with the basics and not addressing the issues of rare occurrences or leading to action plans.

However, out of the 20 national and regional research centres that cover the environmental studies listed by Hamzah (2008, p. 208), only six (30%) pertain to universities in Bahrain, Egypt, Kuwait, Lebanon, and Oman, the great majority being established by relevant ministries or other governmental bodies.

Also, the Commission on Science and Technology for Sustainable Development in the South (COMSATS), established in 1994 with membership of 21 countries from Africa, Asia, and Latin America, among which are five Arab States, has 16 centres of excellence, four of which are in the Arab States, with only one being a higher education institution.[13]

PROMISING EXAMPLES

The first of the promising examples that could be cited as an Arab HEI committed, at least to some extent, to SD, concerns the University of Jordan. This is a typical medium-size (about 1450 faculty members and 32,000 students at all levels and in all fields), governmental university, established in the early 1960s, and encompassing all fields of knowledge.[14]

The examination of the activities undertaken in the recent years by the University of Jordan concerning SD

shows that they encompass, as shown in Figure II.2.2, the inclusion of SD in the mission statements of two departments, the establishment of one community committee and one chair, providing four courses on SD, the realization of three dissertations and theses, the declaration by ten faculty members that one of their main research interests is in SD, the publication of eleven books and papers in periodicals, the presentation of twenty-three papers on various issues of SD in academic conferences.

For instance, the Department of Agricultural Economics and Agribusiness has embedded the following in its mission statement:

> To provide students with economic knowledge, and management and analytical skills for implementing sound economic decision for optimal allocation and proper use of natural resources in the agribusiness sector, and distribution of agricultural products to promote sustainable development of rural communities and protecting environment.[15]

It is to be noted that the mission statement could deal with SD without mentioning it expressively. Thus, more HEIs may have included in their mission statements some ingredients of sustainable development without expressively using the two words. The following example illustrating this matter comes from the ICARDA's (International Center for Agricultural Research in the Dry Areas – Aleppo, Syria)[16] mission statement that reads as follows:

> To contribute to the improvement of livelihoods of the resource-poor in dry areas by enhancing food

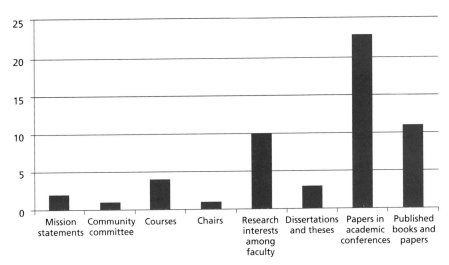

FIGURE II.2.2 Activities of the University of Jordan in recent years as regards sustainable development
Source: Compiled by the author from: http://www.ju.edu.jo/centers/SearchCenter/Pages/Results.aspx?k=sustainable development (last accessed: 21 May 2011).

security and alleviating poverty through research and partnerships to achieve sustainable increases in agricultural productivity and income, while ensuring the efficient and more equitable use and conservation of natural resources.

A second promising example concerns the Madaba University in Jordan.[17] This is a relatively small university under establishment. In the declaration of its objectives, it is said that it aims at achieving an environmentally friendly (green) and self-sustainable campus, through the recycling of the water consumed and reusing it for irrigation, using renewable geothermal resources to generate the energy required for cooling and heating systems, and reserving all internal roads to pedestrians.

A third promising example concerns the King Abdullah University for Science and Technology in Saudi Arabia.[18] This is a recently established university with huge endowment and high expectations. The design of its campus has tried to respect SD in all aspects. For example, in the site planning and architecture, special care was devoted to massing and orientation, using reflective roofs and light-coloured paving and shade, the choice of building materials, water conservation, energy efficiency and using of renewable energy, especially solar energy, adopting energy-saving strategies, particularly in ventilation and lighting, and paying attention to coral reef and mangrove protection.

Also, the university has adopted a community-wide recycling and composting programme to reduce the amount of waste it produces, and an alternative transportation plan to provide fuel efficient transportation options for all residents.

In view of its design, in June 2010, the innovative and sustainable architecture of the KAUST campus earned a Platinum rating on the Leadership in Energy and Environmental Design (LEED) scale, produced by the US Green Building Council. In addition, the International Sustainable Campus Network (ISCN) has awarded KAUST its 2010 Construction Category Award.[19]

It is also to be noted that the research agenda of KAUST focuses on nine themes among which four directly pertain to SD, that is, solar and photovoltaic engineering, water desalination and reuse, clean combustion, the Red Sea milieu.[20]

CONCLUSION

Although the available documentation is quite limited, one can say that, in general, SD and ESD are not really

on the agendas of a significant number of HEIs in the Arab States. In general, these institutions are still at phase 1 according to Leal Filho's (2010)[21] typology, that is, absence of understanding and of efforts and projects to promote sustainability.

In fact, there are in the Arab States some promising endeavours regarding HEIs' commitment to SD. However, in general, these institutions are far from meeting expectations, except, perhaps, as regards the establishment of chairs in SD within the framework of UNESCO UNITWIN Chairs and Networks Programme.

Thus, the actions to advance the cause of SD in HEIs in the Arab States should encompass all areas of interventions, with, perhaps, priorities as regards the sensitization of academic leaders and managers to the need for formal institutional commitment to SD and the establishment of institutional set-ups to promote and monitor progress towards SD in all fields of intervention (study programmes, research agendas, community involvement, realization of sustainable campuses), with substantial participation of faculty members, administrative staff, and students alike.

Also, since best practices are relatively scarce in the Arab region, networking among HEIs, within the Arab countries as well as with the outer world, appears to be indispensable in order to move ahead. Arab institutions have to learn from international experiences in this domain, as well as from each other, particularly by sharing best practices, creating common databases, and developing and implementing exchange programmes and joint initiatives.

Finally, the necessity of engaging in SD activities demands greater synergy and active participation of other relevant stakeholders, such as government, businesses and local communities, in order to jointly develop priorities embedded in policies and programmes of action. And HEIs in the Arab States, supposed to be the main reservoir of high competences in the various domains and disciplines related to SD, should take the lead in this endeavour.

NOTES

1   World Commission on Environment and Development, 1987. Report of the World Commission on Environment and Development: Our Common Future. Published as Annex to General Assembly document A/42/427, Development and International Co-operation: Environment August 2, 1987. http://www.un-documents.net/wced-ocf.htm (Last accessed: 21 May 2011).
2   http://www.esd-world-conference-2009.org/fileadmin/download/News/BonnDeclarationFinalFR.pdf   (Last accessed: 21 May 2011).

3   http://www.shamaanet.org
4   http://www.ulsf.org/programs_talloires_signatories.html
    (Last accessed: 21 May 2011). The concerned universi-
    ties in the Arab countries are the American University
    in Beirut – Lebanon (one of the 19 original signatories),
    the University of Balamand, Tripoli – Lebanon, and the
    Ecole Nationale d'Ingénieurs, Tunis – Tunisia.
5   http://www.aashe.org/membership/members/
    institutional#international (Last access: 21 May 2011).
    The concerned institutions in the Arab countries are the
    American University in Sharjah – UAE, and the Qatar
    Foundation, Qatar.
6   http://www.international-sustainable-campus-network.org/
    index.php?option=com_hotspots&view=all&Itemid=35
    (Last access: 21 May 2011).
7   http://www1.aucegypt.edu/maan/ (Last accessed: 21 May
    2011).
8   Hamzah, Riyad Y. (2008). Environmental Education;
    in Mostafa K. Tolba and Najib W. Saab, *Arab Environ-
    ment: Future Challenges*. Arab Forum for Environment
    and Development (AFED) Report 2008 (Chapter 15, pp.
    199–212), http://www.afedonline.org/afedreport/english/
    book15.pdf
9   For modest examples of higher education contribution
    to ESD, see Oman national experience, in UNESCO
    (2011). National Journeys towards Education for
    Sustainable Development. http://unesdoc.unesco.org/
    images/0019/001921/192183e.pdf (Last accessed: 12
    June 2011).

10 Hamzah, Riyad Y. (2008) op. cit., pp. 202–4.
11 Ibid., p. 206.
12 It is to be noted that, compared to the other regions of the
    world, the Arab region has the least number of UNESCO
    Chairs.
13 COMSATS Centres of Excellence. http://www.comsats.
    org/index.php?LinkID=14 (Last accessed: 12 June 2011).
14 http://www.ju.edu.jo/home.aspx (Last accessed: 21 May
    2011).
15 http://agriculture.ju.edu.jo/AgriculturalEconomicsAgri-
    business/Pages/Missionvision.aspx (Last accessed 21
    August 2011).
16 http://www.icarda.cgiar.org/Mission.htm (Last accessed:
    21 May 2011).
17 http://www.lpj.org/index.php?option=com_content&vie
    w=article&id=601:madaba-university-project&catid=8
    1&Itemid=113&lang=en (Last accessed: 21 may 2011).
    Note that the university has recently changed its name to
    the American University in Madaba.
18 http://www.kaust.edu.sa/about/sustainable/sustainable.
    html (Last accessed: 21 May 2011).
19 http://www.kaust.edu.sa/media/pressreleases/iscnaward.
    html (Last accessed: 21 May 2011).
20 http://www.kaust.edu.sa/research/centers/intro.html (Last
    accessed: 21 May 2011).
21 Leal Filho, W. (2010). Sustainability at Universities:
    Opportunities, challenges and trends. GUNi Website.
    http://www.guni-rmies.net/news/detail.php?id=1593
    (Last accessed: 21 May 2011).

Inside View II.2
Oman's journey towards education for sustainable development in higher education

Ingrid Mulà[1]

INTRODUCTION
Oman was one of the first countries of the Arab States to express a commitment to sustainable development (SD) and education for sustainable development (ESD). As a response to the United Nations Decade of Education for Sustainable Development (UN DESD), Oman formed a national team and appointed a national coordinator to guide the ESD implementation process at the country level. The Sultanate of Oman has emphasized the key role of higher education (HE) as a catalyst for change and has ensured that opportunities exist to engage staff and students in the sustainability agenda. This paper will showcase various practical ESD initiatives implemented by the state university, the Sultan Qaboos University.

In Oman, sustainable development cannot be understood and achieved without consider-ing socioeconomic and environmental dimensions as well as the cultural legacy of the country. The Sultanate of Oman is located in the southeastern corner of the Arabian Peninsula with a total land area of about 300,000 km²

and a population of 2,350,000 (according to the national census of 2003). With its privileged geographical position, the Sultanate of Oman is at the intersection of trading between the East and the West. Its great geographical diversity, consisting of open deserts (gravel plains and areas of sand dunes), large mountain ranges and coastal land, needs to be conserved in order to ensure the nation's prosperity and security.

Since 1970, the Omani government has worked on transforming lifestyles and build-ing a modern nation based on SD principles. Changes in the health, education and economic systems, as well as in the provision of modern infrastructures, have taken place to ensure posi-tive social and economic development.

The Omani government's commitment to environmental preservation is reflected in its policy, as well as in the development of several plans and programmes. In 1970, Oman was the first country within the Arab World to establish a Ministry of the Environ-ment. Since then, the Sultanate of Oman has contributed to the international commitment

towards environmental conservation and sustainability, and has participated in the implementation of many international initia-tives in this domain.

A POLICY CONTEXT FOR ESD DEVELOPMENTS
This review presents policy developments in terms of sustainable development and national responses to the UN DESD. It also showcases the different mechanisms put in place to coordinate ESD in Oman, such as the formation of an ESD national team and the appointment of a national coordinator.

ECONOMIC VISION 'OMAN 2020'
One of the most important national initiatives in which SD is spelled out in Oman, is the Economic Vision 'Oman 2020', which empha-sizes the need to:

• Develop human resources and promote skills and competences that ensure a posi-tive and efficient technological progress with regard to the continuous changes at national and global dimensions

- Create a stable macroeconomic framework in which the private sector is capable of efficiently using human and natural resources, and in ecological friendly ways
- Encourage the establishment of an effective and competitive private sector and to consolidate mechanisms and institutions that will foster shared visions, strategies and policies between the private sector and the government
- Provide appropriate conditions for the realization of economic diversification through the optimal use of natural resources, considering the geo-strategic location of the Sultanate
- Enhance the standard of living of the Omani people by reducing inequalities among regions and among people with different income levels, and to ensure that the fruits of development are enjoyed by all citizens

NATIONAL RESPONSES TO THE DESD

In 2007, the United Nations Educational, Scientific and Cultural Organisation (UNESCO) National Commission (NatCom) of Oman participated in the preparation and development of a draft ESD agenda for the Arab region – a regional response of the UN DESD in association with the UNESCO Beirut Office. Under UNESCO Beirut supervision, the NatCom distributed the first UN DESD Global Monitoring and Evaluation questionnaire to stakeholders who had participated in regional ESD activities during the period 2005–2007, and appointed a national coordinator. At that time, no national team or coordinator existed in Oman to manage ESD and UN DESD activities such that the questionnaire could not be completed accurately.

The Oman Ministry of Education has shown continued support to ESD, recognizing the necessity to strengthen international cooperation in terms of ESD policies and programmes in line with the UN DESD objectives. The NatCom therefore suggested that the Minister of Education assume the role of ESD national coordinator and form a national team.

The Ministerial Decision No. 78/2008, issued in April 2008 and presided over by the Minister of Education, resulted in the establishment of an ESD national team. The team includes representatives from the Oman National Commission for Education, Culture and Science (Focal Point), the Sultan Qaboos University, and the ministries of manpower, health, education, higher education, national economy, environment and climate affairs, agriculture, and social development. The objective of the national team is the coordination of policies, events and activities in the field of ESD at the country level. The ESD national team also delegates functions to other organizations and stakeholders from the private sector as well as non-governmental organizations (NGOs) with expertise on ESD domains. A national coordinator from the Oman NatCom has also been appointed.

The ESD national team has participated in many national initiatives with respect to the national implementation of ESD and the UN DESD. The team participated in the development of a Draft UN DESD National Strategy for the Sultanate of Oman. A national report, entitled *Focus on Education for Sustainable Development in Oman: Towards a Sustainable World* (2009), was prepared and presented at the UN World Conference on Education for Sustainable Development, 'Moving into the Second Half of the UN Decade', held in Bonn, Germany (31 March–2 April 2009).

ESD IN HIGHER EDUCATION

The government provides free higher education to a large group of graduates. Full or part-time scholarships exist for those students unable to enrol to the state university or pay the fees of private universities. In Oman, it is believed that women are key partners in the country's prosperity and development process, which is clearly reflected in the increased number of women enrolling for HE courses.

Several ESD projects, undertaken by the faculties of commerce, education and agriculture at the Sultan Qaboos University (SQU), are presented in this paper as exemplary initiatives in higher education, and include the following.

FACULTY OF COMMERCE

The Faculty of Commerce of the SQU trains and prepares students in areas of business and economics. It offers courses in which the economic dimension of sustainable development is addressed. SD-related courses are intended to:

- Showcase innovative business practices through creative thinking and problem solving
- Promote a close interaction and creation of alliances with the business community through lecture series, field studies and internships
- Promote basic and applied research, which will add to theoretical and practical knowledge in the various fields of specialization
- Train students to develop a number of skills related to problem solving, creative thinking and the application of modern technologies (that is, computer, internet)

Students in their fourth and fifth years are encouraged to develop projects linked to the economic aspects of sustainable development, and present them to colleagues and lecturers. The faculty also organizes ESD initiatives such as the Business Week, Capital Market Forum and Market Day.

FACULTY OF EDUCATION

The Faculty of Education of SQU prepares future teachers and offers quality programmes to achieve the objectives of the DESD. An array of topics in the field of ESD are addressed in these programmes, such as Education For All (EFA), gender equality, the role of education in eradicating poverty and hunger, and peace issues. ESD topics are also addressed in Bachelor's of Arts and Master's programmes.

Field training is one of the most important components in teacher education as it is designed to connect the students with their future working environment. The Faculty of Education offers practical training for undergraduate and postgraduate students. Students can put in place ESD pedagogical approaches and content in real life situations.

FACULTY OF AGRICULTURE AND MARINE SCIENCES

The Faculty of Agriculture and Marine Sciences has introduced themes of sustainable development within its undergraduate programmes, in particular, in areas related to water and fisheries. For instance, in the natural resources and environmental economics course, students are introduced to SD and its importance in terms of natural resources management. Students work on practical projects related to SD and linked to specific issues such as water, fisheries, pollution, population growth and non-renewable resources.

The faculty also undertakes research related to the challenges of sd in Oman, for instance, the scarcity of rainwater.

Student activities within this faculty are considered as major contributions in the field of ESD and include the Day of the Omani Farmer, Tree Day, International Water Day, Economics Forum, and the Green Tide Festival, among others. For example, during the Green Tide Festival, students identify the major environmental problems and risks faced by the community and propose best possible solutions to the authorities concerned. The Green Tide Festival includes a charity market, an educational entertainment evening, workshops, contests and various environmental awareness campaigns.

CONCLUDING REMARKS

Countries across the world are facing many sustainable development challenges. ESD enables people to understand these challenges and to take action for a sustainable future. In Oman, these actions included the formation of a national team, and the appointment of a national coordinator to organize, manage and direct activities, events and projects to respond to the UN DESD call.

The Sultanate of Oman pays considerable attention to higher education, which is a vital pillar in Oman's educational system as it precedes entry into the labour market. Teaching and learning in higher education institutions consists of collaborative and interactive learning, and modern technologies are essential in this process. Practical training is offered by many HEIs in Oman as real-life situations help students apply theory to practice. Partnerships between universities, the government and the private sector are established in order to create work placements and training opportunities for students.

This country review has provided a brief overview of some of the efforts and initiatives of the Sultanate of Oman to integrate ESD with special emphasis on the HE sector. The most important challenges revolve around the lack of financial support, educators' motivation, awareness about the UN DESD goals and provision of material and resources.

NOTE

1   This paper was compiled by Ingrid Mulà. The paper was extracted from the Mulà, I. and Tilbury, D. (2011) *National Journeys Towards Education for Sustainable Development*, Paris: UNESCO. The case study on Oman in this publication was written by Abdullah Khamis Ali Ambusaidi.

Spotlight Issues II.3
Challenges facing the Arab region in education for sustainable development[1]

GUNi Secretariat

INTRODUCTION
The following text is an extract from the *Regional Guiding Framework of Education for Sustainable Development in the Arab Region*, a document prepared by a group of programme specialists and experts from UNESCO, UN Organizations and Arab States, as part of the UN Decade of Education for Sustainable Development (DESD). The Regional Guiding provides a general reference point of the activities that could be implemented by any of the partners such as education and training institutions, production and services, international and regional organizations, civil society and NGOs.

CHALLENGES FACING THE ARAB REGION IN EDUCATION FOR SUSTAINABLE DEVELOPMENT
During the period 2006–2007, the UNESCO Regional Bureau for Education in the Arab States (Beirut) designed, in cooperation with a small group of experts and specialists in the Arab region, a questionnaire to explore member state opinion regarding priorities and mechanisms to be adopted in order to achieve ESD/DESD objectives in the region.

After the discussion and adoption of the draft questionnaires/forms, these were distributed to the National Commissions for UNESCO in the Arab region, to ensure its completion by ministries of education and higher education, universities, and research and development centres, as well as other partners concerned with sustainable development, in order to identify national and regional plans of action.

Fourteen Arab countries completed the questionnaires/forms and nominated a National Focal Point. The Focal Point will ensure coordination and exchange of experiences among institutions at the national and regional levels. The analysis of questionnaires allowed the identification of challenges that are facing sustainable development in the Arab region, and that are consequently generating challenges to the achievement of ESD.

Challenges facing SD in the Arab region as stated in the questionnaires/forms can be classified as follows:

1. **Challenges at the Economic Dimension:**
   * Poverty, unemployment and brain drain (the biggest challenge at the three levels)
   * Role of women in the workplace and in the production sector
   * Desertification, agriculture and water scarcity

- Scarcity of resources in general and the need to develop these resources and to rationalize their use

2. **Challenges at the Social Dimension:**
   - Political, security and demographic stability and sustainability of development efforts
   - Weakness of the role played by youth in social life
   - Weakness of women's participation in social life
   - Need to develop management and organizational patterns and methods in private and public sectors
   - Lack of health awareness, especially as regards infectious and communicable diseases such as AIDS

3. **Challenges at the Environment Dimension:**
   - Lack of environmental awareness, lack of environmental conservation and environmental depletion in a number of cases
   - Increase of environmental pollution rate in all its forms
   - Existence of biodiversity requiring the establishment of multiple systems to preserve it
   - Outbreak of several resources unfair consumption patterns

Education systems in the region are facing common challenges that are negatively influencing their capacity to achieve the desired success. Among these challenges are: the failure to reach the required rates in order to achieve Education for All (EFA) goals; the failure to provide the necessary resources for education development plans and, more particularly, human resources; and the irrelevance of methods used for the provision of appropriate educational materials.

At the same time, ESD/DESD in the Arab region is facing specific challenges that can be summarized as follows:

- The understanding by all parties of *the wide concept of education for sustainable development* and of its nature.
- *The complex nature of education for sustainable development* represents a great challenge to its integration in school materials, making ESD/DESD overlap with other educational materials and activities.

- The consideration of the Arab States' *values and traditions* when planning and implementing ESD. These values and traditions are not used enough in the preparation of ESD curricula and teaching materials.
- The fact that many Arab countries have recently finished completing the development of their policies in the education sector, since it is difficult for citizens to accept the idea of amending these policies after starting their implementation.
- The issue of *regional and subregional cooperation*, due to the lack of previous experience in this field in the Arab region. It is hoped that participating international organizations will assist in the enhancement of such cooperation.
- The provision of the *necessary funding* and training and the promotion of the principle of equal partnership.
- Wars and conflicts still constitute a burden thus constituting a challenge not only for ESD but also for development itself and for the sustainability of large segments of human beings.

In light of the limited available funds and the multiple challenges facing the states of the region, in addition to the fact that the major part of the budgets allocated to education fall under the article related to salaries, the financing issue still constitutes the main obstacle to the achievement of the UN DESD in the Arab region.

BASIS OF THE REGIONAL FRAMEWORK FOR THE ARAB REGION

The Regional Guiding Framework of Education for Sustainable Development is developed according to a set of bases related to the concept of sustainable development in the region, and the approaches to achieve goals of ESD/DESD:

1. Efforts focus on the achievement of *a quantum leap* aimed at triggering change in the behaviour and orientations of individuals, with the participation of all members of society as well as of all public and grassroots institutions.
2. Priority is given to the harmonious and integrated orientation of efforts towards education for sustainable development *through a holistic approach not as an additional component*

3. *Education for sustainable development efforts are complementary to the existing initiatives* – such as Education for All, the Literacy Decade, the MDGs, and so on.
4. By recognizing that it is impossible for one unique party to achieve the ESD objectives by itself, the Framework of Action is based on the hypothesis that *all social categories and institutions should play a role* in the achievement of the objectives.
5. Efforts aimed at achieving the objectives of the Decade put both genders on an equal footing, as well as racial and religious groups, rural and urban areas, and social and economic levels, and so on.
6. Efforts take advantage of *information and communication technologies (ICTs)* in reaching all social categories and in achieving the objectives of the Decade.
7. *Public and grassroots bodies cooperate to provide the necessary funding* to achieve this quantum leap in learning and the international community and organizations contribute whenever needed.

TIMETABLE FOR THE IMPLEMENTATION OF ACTIVITIES

Extensive discussions between specialists have resulted in a proposal suggesting the classification of UN DESD activities and events in the Arab Region into three phases:

Phase One (2005–2007): Launching of Activities and Planning

- It was necessary to raise awareness on the DESD and in developing Arab capacities and expertise. A number of regional activities and training sessions have been organized during this period in addition to the elaboration and dissemination of national and subregional studies.

Phase Two (2008–2011): Commitment and Construction

- This phase concerns the building of activities and programmes for ESD in the Arab region as well as in other regions of the world as planned in Phase One.

Phase Three (2012–2014): Support, Follow-up and Evaluation

- The answers provided by educational institutions in the Arab region to the questionnaire included a limited number of proposed projects and programmes of action for Phase Three.

NATIONAL, REGIONAL AND INTERNATIONAL COOPERATION

ESD is characterized by the breadth of its concept and content and by the fact that it exceeds knowledge to target behaviours. It has hence become impossible for a party, institution or ministry successfully to achieve the DESD objectives by itself.

At the regional level, UNESCO will seek to establish an inter-agency regional consultative team to ensure communication and coordination of joint programmes of action. At the national level, it is necessary to select a coordination body that would be entrusted with the management of the Decade, and at the international level, UNESCO's efforts are aimed to coordinate the efforts of the proposed consultative committee gathering representatives of UN organizations.

MONITORING, EVALUATION AND FOLLOW-UP

The linkage between monitoring and assessment and the planning process related to the implementation of the DESD is of utmost necessity. The achievement of these objectives requires all participating parties to designate responsibility for monitoring, assessment and follow-up and to establish appropriate mechanisms that take the special characteristics of each country as well as the diversity of cultures into account. Considering the diversity of partners, it would be better if each one establishes its own indicators. It is also normal for each country to forge its own appropriate indicators.

UNESCO offices in the region will also seek to ensure maximum integration and coordination between the efforts of UN agencies, international organizations, technical cooperation bodies and NGOs, and to support cooperation and exchange of experiences among Arab States themselves and between the latter and other regions of the world.

BIBLIOGRAPHY

UNESCO (2008) *Regional Guiding Framework of Education for Sustainable Development in the Arab Region.*

UNESCO (2007) *UNESCO Mid-Term Strategy 2008–2013*, www.unesco.org. Paris: Nov 2007.

UNESCO (2007) *Global Monitoring Report 2008.* Paris, October 2007.

United Nations (2007) *Background Note for UN Discussion on the MDGs.* New York: April 2007.

UNESCO (2007) *The UN Decade of Education for Sustainable Development. (DESD 2005–2014) The First Two Years.* Paris: 2007.

UNESCO (2005) *EFA Global Monitoring Report 2005: The Quality Imperative, Regional Overview: Arab States.* Paris: 2005.

SELECTED WEBSITES

www.unesco.org/education/desd
www.unesco.org
www.unesco.org/beirut
www.unescobkk.org/esd
www.unep.org
www.icarda.org
www.fao.org
www.esd.org.uk/esdtoolkit

NOTE

1   This piece is an adaptation made by GUNi of the *Regional Guiding Framework of Education for Sustainable Development in the Arab Region* available at http://unesdoc.unesco.org/images/0016/001619/161944m.pdf

---

Network Experience II.2
Ma'an Alliance: towards more civically engaged Arab universities

Barbara Ibrahim

At a time when change is sweeping the Arab region, universities have a vital mission to prepare young citizens for the tasks of building their societies. Universities themselves are examining ways to become more active 'institutional citizens' as well, by engaging with their immediate communities, offering the expertise of faculty and administrators, and contributing to policy reform projects. The Ma'an Arab University Alliance for Civic Engagement brings together Arab universities with the collective goal of enhancing civic engagement in higher education. Founded in 2008, the Alliance encourages peer learning and sharing of experience and offers resources for curricular development and research in this area. The Alliance currently has twelve member universities in eight countries of the region.

ORIGINS

Decades of overcrowding, inadequate budgets and rote learning had distanced many Arab campuses from the worldwide movement towards a more engaged pedagogy. However students were lobbying for greater participation in the community and some faculties responded by encouraging clubs, class field visits, and community activities. At another level, faculties at national universities have traditionally been called upon by governing bodies to provide their research know-how towards the solution of pressing social problems. Offices of Community Outreach formed at some national universities, but restrictions were enforced on political and civic engagement if seen as threatening to the existing regimes. A further challenge is that some administrators and academics still view civic engagement as an alien idea, and one that interferes with a purely academic environment.

In order to connect those within Arab universities with a commitment to civic engagement, a regional conference was held in October 2008, hosted by the American University in Cairo (AUC) in partnership with Innovations in Civic Participation. Titled 'Tadamunn: Towards Civic Engagement in Arab Education', the conference brought together over fifteen regional universities from Sudan to Palestine to the Arab Gulf for three days of intense discussions and planning. Administrators, faculty members and students attended and worked in parallel groups to devise recommendations for future action. The energy and ideas generated at Tadamunn – especially by the student participants – became the first step towards establishment of a network of Arab universities committed to advancing higher education civic engagement in the region.

Following one of the main recommendations, the Gerhart Center at AUC in partnership with the global Talloires Network launched the Ma'an Arab University Alliance, a network to strengthen the community engagement activities of member institutions. Among the envisioned activities are documenting creative campus programmes; demonstrating impact; advancing dialogue on the civic roles of universities in their environments; and holding seminars for peer learning and skill transfer in areas such as community-based learning pedagogy. One immediate activity was the formation of a website to which members may post useful materials and publications in Arabic and English.

THE VISION AND VALUES

In order to join Ma'an, the president or chancellor of a university within the Arab region writes a letter of commitment that covers the following principles.

The Ma'an Arab University Alliance is a regional association of institutions committed to strengthening the civic roles and social responsibilities of Arab higher education. We work together to implement the recommendations of the Ma'an Declaration in the Arab World, working within the Talloires Network to build a global movement of engaged universities and citizens.

The Ma'an Alliance is unique in that it is a network of universities specific to the region. We work with the knowledge and understanding that civic engagement has multiple facets. In our work we promote the following values:

- Respect for mutual learning between institutions of higher education and communities
- Application of standards of excellence to community-engagement work
- Aspiration for diversity in both our membership and approach to civic engagement
- Empowerment of individuals and groups to strengthen relationships between higher education and society
- Scholarly recognition of the value of service and action in teaching and research

With the establishment of the following goals:

- Promote and expand civic engagement programmes on campus through teaching, research, and community service
- Facilitate the exchange of best practices, as well as educational and financial resources between member institutions
- Encourage students to collaborate with university administrators to increase civic engagement programmes

MAIN ACTIVITIES

The Ma'an Arab University Alliance aims to create a movement of civic engagement and social responsibility among institutions of higher education in the Arab World. Collectively, this can form an effective lobby advocating for civic engagement activities between the university and the community, and supporting the exchange of best practices among its members and with others within the region.

Ma'an's first official event was 'Expanding Civic Engagement in Arab Universities: A Peer Learning Workshop for Faculty' hosted by the American University of Beirut in 2009. The seminar was attended by over 30 academic administrators and faculty members. A subset of Ma'an member universities met in June of 2011 in Madrid during the international Talloires conference on university civic engagement.

MEMBERSHIP

Members of the Alliance commit themselves to action on both institutional and collective levels. Members agree to expand and strengthen their civic engagement and social responsibility work through teaching, learning, research, and service. They also agree to share information on their civic engagement policies and programmes with the membership of the Alliance.

The following institutions have signed their commitment to the goals of the Ma'an Alliance and are therefore simultaneously members of the Alliance and the global Talloires Network:

American University in Cairo
Qatar University
American University in Beirut
Lebanese American University, Lebanon
Notre Dame University-Louaize, Lebanon
Saint-Joseph University, Lebanon
Effat University, Saudi Arabia
Ahfad University, Sudan
Al Quds University, Palestine
Bir Zeit University, Palestine
The Dubai School of Government, UAE
American University of Kuwait
Arab International University, Syria

PARTNERSHIPS

To achieve its goals, the Ma'an Alliance has established partnerships with key actors in civic engagement matters, namely the Innovations in Civic Participation (ICP) and the Gerhart Center.

ICP is a global leader in the field of youth civic engagement whose mission is to facilitate the generation of opportunities for young people to improve their communities and build essential skills for future success through civic engagement. ICP envisions a world where young people in every nation are actively engaged in improving their lives and their communities through civic participation (www.icicp.org, www.tufts.edu/talloiresnetwork).

The Gerhart Center is a university-based institution offering resources for the promotion of philanthropy and civic engagement in the Arab world. Established in 2006, the center aims to further the American University in Cairo's mission to advance social responsibility and active citizenship. The Center promotes social change in the Arab region through building a culture of effective giving and civic responsibility (http://www.aucegypt.edu/RESEARCH/GERHART).

STUDENT ROLES

Students play an important role in the expansion of civic engagement on their own campuses, so the Ma'an Alliance encourages students to participate in active dialogue between higher administration and faculty to share ideas on the implementation of innovative programmes.

During the October 2008 Tadamunn Conference, students discussed a variety of themes. They felt a lack of awareness about civic engagement at institutions in the Middle East and North Africa region. Many described the level of volunteerism at their institutions as low and believed that there is a gap between the faculty and local community. They also mentioned that students lacked creativity due to the curriculum at their university.

Their highest priority recommendations were to incorporate community-based learning courses in the curriculum; providing opportunities for post-graduation work and/or volunteering in public service; for universities to provide funds for student-led civic engagement projects, mentorship and support for student leaders; and more open dialogue and communication with students.

Students felt it important to discuss motivations. They attributed students' participation to several factors including faith, personal experience(s), the sense of belonging to a social movement, and social interaction with peers. In addition, they debated whether volunteerism should be made mandatory in universities, presenting compelling arguments for and against this policy.

CHALLENGES REMAIN

The Ma'an Alliance hopes to become the premier and central resource for the Arab region on civic engagement practices in higher education.

The Ma'an Arab University Alliance brings together resources, experience, and experts from within the region to discuss successes and setbacks that are specific to the region and the culture. While the goals of both the Alliance and the Talloires Network are one and the same, approaches to the success of these goals will vary widely from country to country and region to region. A cultural perspective on civic engagement is vital and absolutely necessary in order to understand civic engagement in the Arab region. Giving and social solidarity are deeply embedded in the culture of the region, but often seen as an individual charitable responsibility rather than a strategic institutional goal.

There are important signs of change. A number of public and private universities are establishing off-campus programmes, career placements and internships. At the same time, student clubs are lobbying for a more engaged relationship to local communities and problems. Community-based learning as a classroom method has over 40 faculty adherents and 56 courses at the AUC alone, with many more coming on board in Ma'an member universities.

Challenges remain in countries that are facing conflict or unfinished political transitions, but increasingly more voices are calling for higher education to live up to its responsibilities as a contributing member of the community and incubator of tomorrow's citizens.

GOOD PRACTICES II.2

Higher Education and Sustainability in Arab states: Sharing Actions for Change

The following experiences are a selection of good practices on higher education and sustainability. Some of them were presented at the 5th International Barcelona Conference on Higher Education and others are part of the GUNi observatory.

The good practices cover the following institutional areas:

Curricula and learning innovation

Community and social engagement

Institutional management

Research

GOOD PRACTICE 1

American University in Madaba Project

Institutional area(s):

LOCATION: Jordan
INSTITUTION: American University in Madaba

The American University in Madaba aims to bring sustained prosperity to the region, coupled with a lifelong sense of belonging that instills peaceful co-existence. It is a higher education institution that utilizes English as its medium of instruction, and which provides quality education based on tolerance, mutual respect, moral fortitude and integrity, to all citizens of the region and beyond. The university's campus will also be environmentally friendly and self-sustainable, and will use geothermal energy for heating and cooling systems.

Detailed information is available at GUNi HEiOBS:

http://www.guninetwork.org/guni.heiobs/good-practices/madaba-university-project

GOOD PRACTICE 2

Bard Palestinian Connection

Institutional area(s):

LOCATION: Palestinian Territories
INSTITUTION: Bard Palestinian Connection

The Bard Palestinian Connection (formerly the Bard Palestinian Youth Initiative) is involved in the building of civil society in the West Bank. Through education, cultural and exchange programmes, sports and literacy camps, the building of children's libraries, and hands-on service and construction projects, Bard students and staff contribute to the creation of a viable and sustainable Palestinian state. One of the conclusions they have reached, and that has been corroborated by many, especially the Palestinians, is that that creating a strong, working Palestinian civil society is the best way to resolve the challenges of the region.

Detailed information is available at GUNi HEiOBS:

http://www.guninetwork.org/guni.heiobs/good-practices/bard-palestinian-connection-formerly-the-bard-palestinian-youth-initiative

GOOD PRACTICE 3

King Abdullah University of Science and Technology (KAUST)

Institutional area(s):

LOCATION: Saudi Arabia
INSTITUTION: KAUST University

Sustainable development is integral to KAUST's overall mission to nurture innovation in science and technology, and support world-class research in areas such as energy and the environment that are important to Saudi Arabia, the region and the world. This emphasis on sustainable practices influences KAUST's research agenda, campus planning, and operations. KAUST integrates sustainable measures into the design of the entire community. The university demonstrates new ways to build in the region, and new ways to live that promote responsible stewardship of energy resources.

Detailed information is available at GUNi HEiOBS:

http://www.guninetwork.org/guni.heiobs/good-practices/king-abdullah-university-of-science-and-technology-kaust

GOOD PRACTICE 4

An approach to institution–wide sustainable engagement with industry to democratize knowledge and experiences in order to understand and respond to the needs of community and society

Institutional area(s):

LOCATION: Oman
INSTITUTION: Middle East College of Information Technology

The Middle East College of Information Technology (MECIT) is an HEI in the Sultanate of Oman. It undertook a project to establish a sustainable relationship between the HEI and the industry. A consultative process between MECIT and captains of industry in the Sultanate of Oman brought to light commonalities in certain objectives and needs. Through it, the role of industry was recognized as an institution of knowledge and it was possible to make effective use of the growth and development in various industrial sectors for the betterment of HEIs. As a result, an approach that was constructed with sustainability and engagement as its guiding principles was adopted in bringing MECIT and industry closer.

Detailed information is available at GUNi HEiOBS:

http://www.guninetwork.org/guni.heiobs/good-practices/an-approach-to-institution-wide-sustainable-engagement-with-the-industry-to-democratise-knowledge-and-experiences-to-understand-and-respond-to-needs-of-community-and-society

GOOD PRACTICE 5

Advancing research, enabling communities: American University of Beirut outreach from the Beqaa Valley

Institutional area(s):

LOCATION: Lebanon
INSTITUTION: The American University of Beirut (AUB)

Following Israel's war with Lebanon in 2006, AUB joined the reconstruction effort to rebuild shattered livelihoods in southern Lebanon. The Land and People relief programme adapted a model from public health: the mobile rural development 'clinic', providing agricultural and business development advice to rural communities. The management of the Land and People programme was recently moved to AREC (Agriculture Research and Education Center). The programme achieved international recognition. It has featured in the Lebanese, Arab, US Dutch and German media and has won a certificate of appreciation from the United Nations Development Programme for its innovative approach.

Detailed information is available at GUNi HEiOBS:

http://www.guninetwork.org/guni.heiobs/good-practices/advancing-research-enabling-communities-american-university-of-lebanon-outreach-from-the-beqaa-valley

The reader can also find the following good practices related to the Arab states at the GUNi Observatory:

- Community College, Social Service Experience
  LOCATION: Sudan
  INSTITUTION: University of Bakhat Alruda

- IWGDS Capacity Building Program
  LOCATION: Sudan
  INSTITUTION: Afhad University

- Processing Student Applications Electronically
  LOCATION: Oman
  INSTITUTION: Oman Ministry of Higher Education

- The UGA -Tunisia Educational Partnerships
  LOCATION: Tunisia
  INSTITUTION: The University of Georgia

http://www.guninetwork.org/guni.heiobs

Sustainability and Higher Education in Asia and the Pacific

Ko Nomura and Osamu Abe

Abstract

Higher education institutions in Asia and the Pacific have endeavoured towards sustainability, which has been propelled by government policies and agencies in many cases, as well as several regional and subregional efforts.

To cope with the complexity and uncertainty embedded in sustainable development, networking, multi-stake-holder approaches and community engagement/outreach are often seen in the region to promote education for it. The region has also witnessed the start of several significant research projects and centres in this field, which tend to emphasize community engagement and outreach as well as action-research. The strong commitment to, and the emphasis on the community-based approach in, sustainability education and research can be considered as a means to respect the region's rich social and environmental diversities that are under threat against the backdrop of rapid globalization. Actions for sustainable management, such as campus greening, are also popular in the region.

For the further progress of sustainability efforts in higher education, this paper highlights the importance of the following points:

- to review the impact of existing policies that have been significant in shaping the current actions
- strategic developments of the community-based approach
- to promote the whole-institution approach in each local context

INTRODUCTION

DIVERSITY AND GLOBALIZATION: CHALLENGES FOR SUSTAINABILITY

Asia-Pacific is such a vast and diverse region. This is particularly so when one follows UNESCO's definition, which encompasses Russia to the north, New Zealand to the south, Turkey to the west and the South Pacific Islands to the east.

Its diversity, which is evident in comparison with other UNESCO regions, is reflected in each of the three pillars of sustainable development – environmental, economic and social sustainability. The climate in the region ranges from tropics to arid and polar, including the world's highest mountains (the Himalayas), the deepest sea (the Mariana Trench), the driest deserts (for example Gobi), rainforests and permafrost tundra. It accommodates the world's largest countries (for exam-

ple China and India) and smallest island nations (for example the Pacific Islands), where one can encounter a large number of ethnic groups with diverse languages, cultures and different religions (for example Hinduism, Buddhism, Islam, Christianity). There is also a significant economic disparity between the highly developed nations (for example Japan), the least developed (for example Nepal), the smallest (for example Tuvalu), and the fastest growing economies. In such a situation, effort to achieve sustainability, including education for it, should require diverse action.

This diversity defies simple generalizations; however, it may be possible to illustrate a map of how the region is advancing with regard to education for sustainable development (ESD) at the higher education level and identify some trends by referring to common challenges among the Asia-Pacific countries. Perhaps the most significant one is the challenge of globalization. In fact, its impacts seem more significant for the Asia-Pacific higher education institutions (HEIs).

Many Asian economies were hit hard by the economic crisis in the late 1990s. Strong demands for recovery increased the drive for rapid industrialization and exploitation of natural resources. Further integration into the global market economy and the introduction of foreign capital damaged local industries in many Asia-Pacific countries, creating various social problems. Accordingly, research and education on the socioeconomic and environmental implications of economic globalization have become significant.

At the same time, the economic crisis forced governments to reconsider their policies on higher education (HE). In many cases, HE policies have shifted to lay more weight on producing human resources that can lead national development in a competitive global economy. Also, guided by market principles, governments have increased the autonomy of the universities (for example Thailand, Indonesia, Singapore) and/or corporatized them (for example Malaysia, Japan, South Korea, Australia, Singapore) to assist flexible management for increasing competitiveness, while cutting government expenditure on them.

These factors have promoted the internationalization of university education. For example, most Australian universities have off-shore programmes in Asia in addition to increasing foreign students in their home campuses. The Japanese and South Korean governments launched a plan for '300,000' and '50,000' foreign students respectively. Malaysian universities are the pioneers of twinning programmes with foreign (mainly Anglo-American) universities, in which students spends a part of their study time in Malaysia to obtain degrees from foreign universities, which can help save on their expenses. 'Boston of the East' programme was launched in Singapore to increase the number of potential foreign students by inviting the world's leading universities to create a centre of brainpower for Asia's industries. Countries in the Asia-Pacific region started UMAP (University Mobility in Asia and the Pacific) in 1991 to promote student exchange programmes. These have promoted the Anglicization of the programmes in many of the countries (for example Japan, South Korea, Thailand, Malaysia, and Indonesia).

In terms of research, many Asia-Pacific governments started establishing Centres of Excellence (CoEs), which are intended to be hubs for world-class research (for example the Chinese '211 Project', the 'Brain Korea 21', the CoE Programmes in Japan and the Philippines). The globalization of the HE market has increasingly pressurized HEI staff members to publish their research outcomes in English regardless of their local languages.

Globalization can also harm social diversity, an essential element in sustainable development. Globalization is more often than not about globalizing Western culture, knowledge and values. Since the universities in the Asia-Pacific have been in the vanguard of Western knowledge in the process of modernization and economic growth, the challenge of sustainability in the era of globalization has required them to reconsider their roles both in local and global contexts.

In other words, the challenge of sustainable development requires significant transformation for educational institutions in Asia-Pacific, for regional diversity and the impact of globalization upon it. Accordingly, the region has shown strong commitment to ESD. For example, the adoption of the United Nations Decade of Education for Sustainable Development (UN DESD) is based on the proposal by the Japanese government and NGOs at the Johannesburg Summit (Nomura and Abe, 2009), and Japanese-Fund-In-Trust is a major resource for UNESCO to promote ESD worldwide. A strong commitment to sustainability in higher education is also established in the region.[1]

This paper first introduces relevant 'policies and international efforts' in the following section, which will illustrate the levels of consciousness about the need to shift HEIs toward sustainable development within the region. Then, the progress in the 'curricula/learning process', 'research' and 'institutional management and operation' are introduced in turns, with reference to the efforts made on community engagement in each aspect, which the authors consider as a regional characteristic. This is followed by a section on 'future directions', which identifies the issues to be addressed for further progress.

POLICIES AND INTERNATIONAL EFFORTS

REGIONAL EFFORTS/NETWORKS

Since UNESCO is the lead agency of UN DESD, its Asia and Pacific Regional Bureau for Education has given guidance for its progress. Although the ESD programme of the Bureau generally works in a comprehensive manner, with regard to HE, the Bureau started the Asia-Pacific Regional Network of Teacher Education Institutes for ESD (ESD-Net) in 2006.[2] It has provided training workshops on reorienting educational programmes as well as opportunities to share information and experiences through the internet. The Bureau's Asia-Pacific Programme of Educational Innovation for Development (APEID) has also hosted several international conferences on ESD, covering the HE sector.

UNEP's Regional Office for Asia and the Pacific (UNEP-ROAP) established UNEP Asia-Pacific Regional University Consortium (RUC) with eight HEIs in the region.[3] It strives for cooperation in inter-disciplinary education and research, and the provision of expertise that can help efforts for sustainable development, with particular attention paid to the Chinese context. RUC started a leadership programme on the environment and sustainable development at Tongji University in China (Niu et al., 2010).

The United Nations University's Institute of Advanced Studies (UNU-IAS), located in Yokohama, Japan, has developed two international networks on ESD, with significant support and commitment from the Japanese Ministry of Environment. One is the Regional Centres of Expertise in ESD (RCEs), a network of formal and non-formal education organizations for promoting and putting into action ESD at the local and regional community level, in which many Asia-Pacific HEIs are involved (Mochizuki and Fadeeva, 2008).[4] The other is the Promotion of Sustainability in Postgraduate Education and Research Network, or ProSPER.Net (Nomura et al., 2011; see Box II.3.1).[5]

SUBREGIONAL EFFORTS

This vast region can be divided into several subregions in many ways. According to international efforts concerning ESD, it can be divided into the following: Southeast Asia, Northeast Asia, the Pacific Islands, Australia and New Zealand, Central Asia and Russia, South Asia and West Asia.

In *Southeast Asia*, the 10 member countries of the Association of South-East Asian Nations (ASEAN) are engaged in ESD based on the ASEAN Environmental Education Action Plan 2008–2012, which replaced the preceding plan for 2000–2005. The Plan features environmental education and is initiated by the ASEAN Senior Officials on the Environment; however, as it is subtitled 'Environmental Education for Sustainable Development', it aims at contributing to the global endeavours of ESD such as UN DESD. This Plan serves as a main reference document for ASEAN member states in developing their national environmental education and ESD plans, which in turn influence their higher education policies.

In *Northeast Asia*, one cannot find an established framework such as ASEAN's plan for ESD. However, there are several subregional efforts on environmental

---

BOX II.3.1: PROSPER.NET

ProSPER.Net is a network of postgraduate institutes in the Asia-Pacific region set up to promote education and research in the field of sustainability. Launched in 2008, it consists of 21 HEIs (as of February 2011) from nine countries in the region, including two regional universities.

In addition to information sharing through various means, the network has conducted joint projects among its members. One of them is the *development of business school curricula*, which is led by the Asian Institute of Technology (AIT). It includes activities such as creating new courses on related topics (for example social business and poverty reduction at AIT; sustainable development and East Asian business at Yonsei University, South Korea; and leadership for sustainable development at Gadjah Mada University, Indonesia), curriculum development (for example MBA curriculum on sustainable development at Universiti Sains Malaysia), and case studies by Shinshu University, Japan.

Another is the *programme in public policy and sustainable development* led by TERI University, India, targeted at mid-career government officials. Three fully developed course modules first became available online between August and October 2009, followed by the second and the third cycle of curriculum delivery. Students completing three separate course modules over a one-year period are awarded a diploma from a ProSPER.Net consortium.

The lead institute for the project of *training of educators (and researchers) on sustainable development* is Universiti Sains Malaysia, which aims to develop a generic model for teaching postgraduate educators and researchers in the field of sustainable development through the development of a model and a manual for SD.

Other network activities include the ProSPER.Net summer school and the 'Prosper.Net-Scopus Young Scientist Award in Sustainable Development' which is to be given annually to a young scientist or researcher in the region who has made significant contributions in the field of sustainable development. It has also started a project to develop an alternative university appraisal system, based on the recognition that the current mainstream assessment and ranking systems are not guiding HEIs in the direction of sustainable development (Fadeeva and Mochizuki, 2010).

education such as the Tripartite Environmental Education Network (TEEN), a major project of the Tripartite Environment Ministers Meeting including China, Japan, and South Korea (TEMM).[6]

For the *Pacific Island Nations*, the Pacific Regional Environmental Programme (SPREP) and the Pacific Island Forum (PIF) provide regional frameworks for ESD. SPREP provided Education and Communication for a Sustainable Pacific Guiding Framework: 2005–2007 against the backdrop of the launch of the UN DESD in 2005.[7] The education ministries of the PIF member countries endorsed the Pacific Education for Sustainable Development Framework in 2006 as the regional response to UN DESD,[8] followed by its Action Plan for Implementing Education for Sustainable Development in the Pacific Islands 2008–2014.[9]

Although *Australia and New Zealand* are in Oceania in a geographical sense, it seems better to deal with them independently when it comes to ESD. As English-speaking developed countries hosting many HEIs, the situation concerning education and sustainable development is considerably different from that of the Pacific Island Nations. In fact, HEIs in these two countries often work closely together, and the governments of Australia and New Zealand do not participate in the PIF frameworks.

The countries in *Central Asia and Russia* tend to promote ESD in relation to the United Nations Economic Commission for Europe (UNECE) Strategy on ESD,[10] instead of Asia-Pacific frameworks. The EU also provides financial assistance to this subregion through the Regional Environmental Centre for Central Asia (CAREC: see CAREC, 2009; Kasimov et al., 2005).

In *South Asia*, the South Asia Cooperative Environment Programme (SACEP) plays an important role in promoting ESD through the 'South Asian Environmental Education and Training Action Plan 2003–2007', and by providing various opportunities for training.[11] Also, the South Asia Youth Environment Network, which was set up in July 2002 with support from the UNEP-ROAP, aims at ensuring the participation of HEIs and university students in the subregion for the progress of ESD at an HE level.[12]

In *West Asia*, regional initiatives for promoting environmental education or ESD are not as evident as in other subregions. However, UNESCO's Teheran Cluster plays a coordinating role in this field for countries such as Afghanistan, Iran, Pakistan and Turkmenistan (although Turkmenistan can be considered a Central Asian country).

Thus, education for sustainability has been initiated and developed considerably in the Asia-Pacific region, although one can see differences with respect to the rhythms of engagement according to the subregions. What seems to be a common factor is that the countries in this region based education for sustainability on environmental education. In fact, it is suggested that environmental educators took the initiative in developing ESD in Asia-Pacific, while people involved in citizenship education play an important role in the UK and Ireland (McKeown and Hopkins, 2007, p. 19). What has facilitated the involvement of environmental educators in the sustainable development education movement may be that environmental education has developed 'ESD-ish' in the region apart from the emergence of the concept of ESD, particularly in the developing part of the world, encompassing other socioeconomic issues such as poverty and population growth (for example Nomura, 2009; Deo, 2005; Chhokar, 2010).

A strong initiative from the environmental sector can also be seen in HE for sustainable development. Nomura et al. (2011) argue that one of the characteristics of cross-border partnership among the Asia-Pacific HEIs regarding sustainability are the initiatives by environmental ministries and organizations, with reference to the cases of ProSPER.Net and RUC, which were initiated by the Japanese Environment Ministry (through UNU-IAS) and UNEP-ROAP respectively. In contrast, many other international HEI networks on sustainability that have appeared so far were initiated by the agencies from the 'education' sector. For example, the Association of University Leaders for a Sustainable Future, the Co-operation Programme in Europe for Research on Nature and Industry through Coordinated University Studies, the Global Higher Education for Sustainability Partnership, and the Baltic University Programme were all initiated by either several HEIs themselves or 'educational' institutions such as the European Universities Association and the Swedish Ministry of Education. In other words, the region is demonstrating the possibility of cross-boarder HEI collaboration through ESD based on the commitment of the agents from the non-educational sectors, in order to support their policies. Another characteristic of sustainability in HEIs in Asia-Pacific could be that HEIs in the region do not seem to be enthusiastic about participating in global ESD networks in comparison with the active intra-regional efforts (Nomura et al., 2011).

POLICY DEVELOPMENTS

Government policies play a critical role in developing ESD, including in the HE sector, in many Asia-Pacific countries. This trend is particularly evident in Northeast and Southeast Asia. In Japan, the Ministry of Education, Culture, Sports, Science and Technology (MEXT) promotes ESD as part of its policies to cope with the challenges facing Japanese HEIs, such as the severe competition from globalization, recruitment pressure due to the decreasing 18-year-old population, and other demands to cope with various social issues (Nomura and Abe, 2010). The MEXT, together with the Ministry of Environment, has provided support to Japanese universities in terms of education and research for sustainability (see below). Interestingly, this kind of top-down approach, which can be found in the Japanese ESD movement in general (Nomura and Abe, 2009), has not only encouraged universities' effort for sustainability, but also guided them in certain directions. For example, the tendency for Japanese universities to emphasize community engagement in their ESD programmes (see below) cannot be understood separately from the selection criteria of the above-mentioned government assistances that mostly require collaboration with local communities (Nomura and Abe, 2010). In Japan, these sectoral developments are coordinated at the Inter-ministerial Meeting on the UN DESD with reference to the National Implementation Plan for the UN DESD.[13]

In Taiwan, sustainability education became an important topic for policymakers in the late 1990s. Since then, the National Council for Sustainable Development and the Ministry of Education have provided significant support to HEIs such as funding for programmes and facilitating module development (Su and Chang, 2010).

In China, ESD policies have been developing since the late 1990s when education was given an important place in the National Agenda 21. This can be seen in the rapid increase of HEIs in China engaging in ESD; since 1997, more than 50% of universities have improved the curriculum for ESD at different levels and in different subject areas (Niu et al., 2010). In 1997, with support from BP plc, the WWF and the Ministry of Education launched an initiative that resulted in the establishment of an ESD network and 21 ESD centres distributed across universities in different provinces (Niu et al., 2010).

In the Philippines, a National Environmental Education Action Plan 2005–2014 was introduced to support the implementation of UN DESD and ASEAN Environmental Education Action Plan (Galang, 2010). In India, the decision of the highest court to mandate environmental education at all levels of formal education, including a compulsory undergraduate course, has encouraged government support to promote ESD (Chhokar, 2010). In New Zealand, the government

identified environmental sustainability as a key national goal in the Tertiary Education Strategy in 2002 (although it is not a priority).

In some countries, the National Commissions for UNESCO take the lead in promoting ESD, including in the HE sector, in collaboration with the governments. One example is Indonesia, especially since the National UNESCO Commission appointed the Senior Rector Deputy for Education, Research and Society Services of Gadjah Mada University as the national ESD coordinator. Another example is South Korea, where the UNESCO National Commission established the National Committee on ESD in 2009. Together with the government bodies, the Korean Committee has made its efforts based on such legal frameworks as the national 'Green Growth' policies, the Environmental Education Promotion Law, and the Basic Law on Sustainable Development.

Not surprisingly, one may not see the same degree of government commitment in a few subregions in Asia-Pacific due to the different socioeconomic and political contexts. For example, the 'issues of ESD as well as sustainable development itself were not appropriately reflected in policy for Central Asian countries' such as Kazakhstan, Kyrgyzstan, Tajikistan, Turkmenistan and Uzbekistan (CAREC, 2009, p. 4). Still, even in such a subregion, there are significant policy developments. Take Kazakhstan HE policies for example, the government indicated that all HEIs must introduce a mandatory subject of 'Ecology and Sustainable Development' for bachelor's degrees (CAREC, 2009).

The Pacific Island Nations are unique in that policy development is generally initiated at the subregional level because of the limited scale of economies for each government to address national needs independently (Corcoran and Koshy, 2010). They include the above-mentioned SPREP's and PIF's frameworks. In fact, the University of the South Pacific (USP), which plays a key role in promoting ESD in the South Pacific, is the regional university of the 12 Island nations.

Thus, there are various policy frameworks for sustainability in HE in this region. In addition to sectoral policies made by the ministries of education and the environment, some countries developed the DESD action plan (for example Japan), environmental education action plan/environmental education promotion laws (for example the Philippines, South Korea). Others base their policies on existing sustainable development strategies (for example China, Taiwan, South Korea), or the regional frameworks (for example Pacific Island Nations). While ministries of the environment play an important role in the ESD policy process in many of the countries in the region as mentioned, regular inter-ministerial meetings in Japan, UNESCO National Committees in South Korea and Indonesia, and the National Council for Sustainable Development in Taiwan have respectively played an intra-government coordination role. Although approaches are different, these policy developments have been significant in shaping sustainability in HE in each university function, as reviewed in this and the following sections.

CURRICULA/ LEARNING PROCESSES

HEI NETWORKS AND MULTI-STAKEHOLDER APPROACHES

Curricula about and for sustainability must deal with the complexity and uncertainty embedded in this issue, which requires a trans/interdisciplinary method. An orthodox approach may be curriculum development by incorporating the relevant elements. However, as Chhokar (2010) reports in the Indian context, there is a lack of capacity among faculty staff to promote inter/ transdisciplinary education against the strong influence of each discipline and the traditional examination/evaluation system that emphasizes information recall rather than understanding and critical thinking. Similar cases are reported from other countries in the region; for example, the analysis made in the Australian context shows there is an opposition to curriculum change due to the lack of organizational and resource support for staff (Thomas, 2004; Tilbury, 2004).

To address this issue, St Petersburg State University (Russia) has offered programmes and lecture courses to improve the qualification of university teachers through its specialized organizations to support the university's structural and curricular changes, including the establishment of a new department in ecological safety and sustainable development within the faculty of geography. Over 23% of the total courses at the university are relevant to sustainable development (Verbitskaya et al., 2002).

Considering the limited knowledge about this complex and uncertain issue of sustainability and the limited resources available for each institution, HEIs in the region are active in sharing experiences, expertise and resources by networking and employing multi-stakeholder approaches. In Japan, a forum of around 20 HEIs, HESD (Higher Education for Sustainable Development), was set up in 2007, which has organized annual meetings, symposiums and online exchange of information on sustainability education. Most of the members are recipients of the MEXT's fund called 'Contemporary GP' (GP stands for good practices), which supports distinctive educational efforts for important contemporary social needs. The funding scheme included 'promoting environmental education for sustainable societies' as one of the six categories in the fiscal years 2006 and 2007 (Nomura and Abe, 2010). As the application guideline stipulated that successful proposals should emphasize student action in society and involve multiple stakeholders, the information exchanged at HESD tends to focus on community engagement in HE.

Several ESD networks concerning HE have also emerged in other countries. In Thailand, for example, the Environmental Education for Sustainable Development Network, consisting of environmental education experts, is actively developing ESD at the field level in collaboration with the Ministry of Natural Resources and Environment. The Teacher Education Network, which is composed of twelve teacher education institutions, is another Thai network contributing to the development of ESD in Thailand.

International networks are also established in the same context. As mentioned earlier, the Japanese Ministry of Environment has supported ProSPER.Net, a regional network of HEIs for sustainable development (21 HEIs in the region are participants as of 2010). UNEP-ROAP's RUC is another example of this kind; its members jointly provide an international Master's programme at UNEP-Tongji Institute of Environment for Sustainable Development, which emphasizes problem-oriented, field-based and interdisciplinary learning for sustainability. In Russia, 19 universities participate in the Baltic University Programme (BUP) and provide students with opportunities of education for sustainability through this cross-border network of HEIs. In the South Pacific, the USP initiated the 'Pacific Network of Island Universities' or NIU project in 2009. The NIU project aims at mainstreaming ESD in teaching and research at HEIs in the region, involving major universities in the subregion such as the University of Papua New Guinea and the National University of Samoa.

In addition to the networks of HEIs, the need for multi-stakeholder commitment is also recognized in the region for improving and supporting the learning process. One of the reasons is that education for sustainability requires connecting curriculum content with social needs and integrating practical and transdisciplinary knowledge from different sources. A series of university summits by Australia's National Environmental Education Council has encouraged the involvement of stakeholders from business, industry and government in sustainability education at a tertiary level (Tilbury and Cooke, 2001).

In Japan, the Ministry of the Environment established a government–industry–academia consortium in this regard, based on the Ministry's 'Vision for University-led Environmental Leadership Initiatives for Asian Sustainability' (Environmental Leadership Vision), in addition to financial support for the inter/transdisciplinary model curriculum development that emphasizes the involvement of various stakeholders. The consortium is aimed not only at supporting the development and implementation of high-quality programmes though facilitating internships, fieldwork and other participatory learning opportunities, but also at serving as an employment matchmaker between the educational institutions that provide human resources and the organizations that employ them in order to facilitate practical environmental leadership training (Ministry of the Environment, Japan, 2008).

COMMUNITY ENGAGEMENT AND OUTREACH

As well as the networking and multi-stakeholder involvement, community engagement and outreach is another common approach that is popular in Asia-Pacific to cope with the obstacles facing the development of curriculum and learning processes towards sustainability. The significance of this approach is recognized by governments and other related agencies in this region, as demonstrated by funding policies of the Japanese government (mentioned above). This has steered the way for many good practices. Interestingly, many of them provide a *certificate* to motivate students to take related modules.

For instance, Ehime University in Japan changed its general education curriculum in 2006 so that students of any faculty and interested members of the public can pursue its 'ESD Leadership Certificate', which highlights fieldwork and action-research with local NGO groups for revitalizing local industries such as agriculture, forestry or fisheries (Nomura and Abe, 2010). Kobe University provides an ESD sub-course within the inter-faculty collaboration of Faculties of Human Development, Letters, and Economics. It emphasizes action-research at a local level, in such fields as disaster reduction and prevention, conservation, community building and the three-Rs of reduce, reuse and recycle (Itoh et al., 2008). The Kushiro campus of Hokkaido University of Education provides a teacher education curriculum with focus on sustainable community development with particular consideration for depopulated areas, the increase of which has thrown up many social problems in Japan. The curriculum features fieldwork and the university works closely with local stakeholders. Graduates are given the certificate of

'ESD planner'. Nishinippon Institute of Technology certifies students who have successfully taken designated modules, which are provided in collaboration with various local stakeholders, as the 'Environmental ESD Coordinator'.

Chhokar (2010) reports that locally situated practices have seen greater success in India, with reference to the case of the Samvardhan project and the curriculum activities linked to the RCE Pune in India. The Samvardhan project was an experiment in rural HEIs in the state of Gujarat, in which community engagement was centrally positioned in the learning process. Together with their teachers, the students of rural development were involved in development projects, which facilitated connecting curricula to real-life experiences. Some of the Samvardhan alumni are now working as successful community entrepreneurs in the villages of Gujarat. As for RCE Pune, instructors at the University of Pune have worked with local NGOs and help them through projects in which students can learn in real-world settings with regard to social issues such as labour and poverty.

The Universiti Sains Malaysia, which is the leader and secretariat of RCE Penang, expresses strong commitment to poverty alleviation as a part of ESD in its mission statement. It has employed an 'inside-out' approach in which the university began implementing ESD in the campus using the metaphor of the 'University in a Garden', and later expanded to the communities involving multi-stakeholders (Sanusi and Khelgat-Doost, 2008). Through this approach, 'the complex and broad concept of sustainability or sustainable development can be translated into concrete practice first by the University and then by the community, thereby leading to better understanding and implementation of the concept' (Sanusi and Khelgat-Doost, 2008, p. 490).

Gadjah Mada University in Indonesia established the Institute for Research and Community Services as one of its efforts made in accordance with its policy to be a world-class research university. It has made significant educational impacts – all the final-year undergraduate students at the university now must take the community service programme. This is an intra-curriculum activity aimed at applying and developing students' knowledge outside campus and sensitizing students to social problems, while contributing to actual problem-solving in the communities in a participatory manner. In cooperation with Gadjah Mada and the National ESD Coordinator, who is the Senior Rector Deputy of the University, the Ministry of National Education is planning to disseminate this kind of community service programme to the other universities in the country.

In New Zealand, in collaboration with the Ministry for the Environment and Local Government New Zealand, the Centre for Continuing Education at the University of Auckland provides a programme designed to improve the decision-making of practitioners within a sustainable resource management context. The programme has accommodated over 1300 lay and professional decision makers since 2004, and it is evaluated as effective (Geertshuis, 2009). The core course of the environmental science programme at the University of Canterbury, New Zealand, incorporates many current local case studies, with the assistance of multiple stakeholders including local councils and local native tribes (Nobes, 2002).

In Australia, the 'Green Steps Program' started by Monash University students in 2000, offers opportunities for university students to link their studies to the environment through work experience and networking by such means as training and internships. The programme has involved other universities and organized 40 courses for more than 500 participants, in collaboration with stakeholders such as private companies and city councils.

RESEARCH

PROJECT-BASED AND INSTITUTIONAL ARRANGEMENTS

Like learning processes, research on sustainability and sustainability education requires inter/transdisciplinary approaches. The general ways to facilitate these approaches include participation in research projects on particular themes (mainly environmental issues) that require multiple disciplines, and institutional arrangements such as establishing interdisciplinary research centres.

In Japan, the MEXT allocated a considerable amount of funding for the University of Tokyo from 2005 in order to support sustainability research. Based on this funding, Tokyo University started the Integrated Research System for Sustainability Science (IR3S) project, involving four other national universities as the main members (Osaka, Ibaraki, Kyoto, Hokkaido) and six other cooperating institutions. The member universities conducted interdisciplinary sustainability research and education on such topics as 'global warming', 'population, water and food supplies', and the 'socio-economic system reform and technology strategy'.

There also emerged several research centres committed to sustainability education in the region, which employ researchers with various backgrounds.

For example, the Australian government established the Australian Research Institute for Environment and Sustainability (ARIES) at the Graduate School of the Environment, Macquarie University, to undertake projects on capacity development for sustainability. The research activities by ARIES include a series of national reviews of environmental education for sustainability in Australia, including the HE sector (Tilbury et al., 2005).

In Northeast Asia, Rikkyo University, Japan, established the Education for Sustainable Development Research Centre (ESDRC) in 2007, with the support of the MEXT's funding. ESDRC consists of four project teams (the Asian regional project team, the Pacific regional project team, the corporate social responsibility project team, and the overall project team), and conducts research and practices in each field. In China, with the help of UNEP-ROAP, UNEP-Tongji Institute of Environment for Sustainable Development was established at Tongji University in Shanghai in 2002 and is a prominent base for sustainability research and education.

In the South Pacific, the Pacific Centre for Environment and Sustainable Development (PACE-SD) based at the USP plays a central role in sustainability education research. Their activities include policy research – PACE-SD played a key role in developing the regional ESD frameworks mentioned above (Corcoran and Koshy, 2010).

In Southeast Asia, the Research and Development Centre on ESD Innovation was established at the Faculty of Education, Chulalongkorn University (Thailand) in 2007. It aims at being the centre of excellence on ESD at a national and regional level through its research and practical activities including material development, workshops, and networking teacher education institutes throughout the country.

COMMUNITY ENGAGEMENT, OUTREACH AND ACTION-RESEARCH

Community engagement is also a popular approach in sustainability research in Asia-Pacific. In fact, there seems to be a high social demand for universities to contribute to local issues through research, particularly in a participatory manner. In New Zealand, some councils are proactive in proposing research projects that are relevant to their needs and concerns for research students at the environmental science programme at the University of Canterbury, which is often accompanied with the councils' financial and logistical support (Nobes, 2002).

In Indonesia, HEIs' contribution to local communities for their livelihood, social development and conservation has been emphasized since long before the term sustainable development gained popularity. The Indonesian government stipulated three missions for universities (*Tridharma*) in the Higher Education Law in 1961, namely education, research and community service. Since then, the universities' function in contributing to addressing various socioeconomic issues has been stressed in Indonesia, where poverty and related issues still prevail. This is reflected in the Environmental Study Centres which have been established at all state universities since the late 1970s. In addition to facilitating environmental studies on campus, the centres have provided various programmes at the community level, as well as training courses for the public such as environmental impact assessment, wastewater management, and forest management.

The USP is also active in community engagement and outreach. For example, given the significant vulnerability of the small island nations in the Pacific to the impacts of global climate change, the USP's PACE-SD and Institute of Applied Science conduct action-research on climate change adaptation targeting local communities in coastal areas, emphasizing the implementation of cost effective adaptation options through community level planning and capacity building.

In Japan, research on sustainability education at the tertiary level is not very popular, in contrast to active practices. In fact, there have been only a few articles on this topic in the Japanese *Journal of Environmental Education* as of yet, and other publications seem to focus on sharing information for practitioners without academic analysis (Nomura et al., 2010). However, the issue of community engagement and outreach has attracted some exceptional attention from researchers, who tend to employ action-research approaches to local issues (Nomura et al., 2010; Oguri, 2010). Like the ESD course mentioned above, Kobe University is active in action-research concerning local issues with the engagement of various stakeholders through its RCE network such as NGOs, the media, and international organizations. In order to facilitate communication with local citizens for the identification of local needs, the university opened a 'Science Shop' in 2007, which provides various events for information exchange as well as daily consultation. The Education and Research Centre for Lifelong Learning at Kagoshima University conducted an action-research project targeting the whole local town. The focal point of the project is the discussion at the Centre's open extension programmes involving town council officials and local residents, leading to comprehensive town planning (Oguri, 2010).

INSTITUTIONAL MANAGEMENT AND OPERATION

CAMPUS GREENING AND LEARNING

For many universities in Asia-Pacific, campus greening is a major approach to sustainability in practice. In fact, it can provide good learning opportunities for staff members as well as students. There are a variety of examples, such as campaigns for recycling and using energy and water efficiently. Interesting practices include an on-campus environmental tax at Kyoto University, Japan, which taxes each department for its use of electricity and water, and this 'tax revenue' is used for introducing eco-friendly facilities. Furthermore, Mie University is set to introduce a carbon-offset programme, in which the university pays 'eco-points' for the reduction of CO_2 at student and staff member households where eco-points can be used for payment at shops on and around campus. It aims not only to mitigate the university's greenhouse gas emissions but also to raise environmental awareness.

In Australia and New Zealand, the Tertiary Education Facilities Management Association, which is the peak university facility management body in both countries, is working towards capacity building of staff through workshops and resource material development (Tilbury et al., 2005). Also in Australia, Australasian Campuses Towards Sustainability provides opportunities for knowledge sharing for HEI staff, students and the wider community (Tilbury et al., 2005).

In Taiwan, the Taiwan Sustainable Campus Project has contributed to curriculum development as well as decreasing the environmental impact of campus operation since 2010 (Su and Chang, 2010).[14] The project involves educational institutions from primary schools to universities nationwide, in total 507 schools as of 2009, which conduct activities such as the changing to renewable energy, rooftop gardening, and creating biotope spaces (Su and Chang, 2010).

In China, following financial support for Tsinghua University's Green Campus Plan, the government launched the 'National Green Campus Project' involving many other universities. Many excellent practices followed from this plan. For example, Tongji University succeeded in its effort for energy and water resource-savings (Niu et al., 2010). In South Korea, more than 20 universities took part in the Korean Green Campus Association, in relation to the motto 'reduce, reuse, recycle' (Park, 2008).

Environmental management systems are often used for campus greening. One of the systems is ISO 14000. The positive educational impacts of the use of ISO

14000 have been reported (for example, see: Fisher, 2003 in the context of New Zealand, and Hayashi and Sakurai, 2005 for Japan). Several universities in Japan have organized ISO student committees, and involved students in the process of environmental management and related actions such as environmental education (Nomura and Abe, 2010). These efforts have resulted in the establishment of the 'Environmental ISO National Student Committee' of Japan. In addition to international systems such as ISO, local systems are also often used by universities. Several Japanese universities have obtained the Eco Action 21, which is the environmental management system organized by the Japanese Ministry of the Environment.

The Environmental Education Network of the Philippines has hosted the Dark Green Schools programme since 2006. It is an accreditation process based on external and internal evaluation involving multiple stakeholders such as communities considering various aspects of university practices such as their policy statements, administration and finance arrangements, academic activities, community outreach and extension programmes/efforts, and income-generating projects (Galang, 2010). Through utilizing this approach, it is expected that it will assist in the 'whole institution' approach towards sustainability, which integrates various functions within the universities, taking into account social demands.

University students are also advocating for a sustainable campus operation. The nationwide environmental society of university students in Japan, called Eco-League, founded a project 'Campus Climate Challenge in Japan' in 2008, following pioneering action in the US and Canada. It has published annual reports on the environmental sustainability ranking of Japanese universities with focus on the emission of greenhouse gases.

FUTURE DIRECTIONS AND CONCLUDING REMARKS

CRITICAL ANALYSIS OF POLICIES AND INTERNATIONAL EFFORTS FOR EDUCATION AND RESEARCH

As we have seen, the Asia-Pacific universities are actively engaged in their efforts towards sustainability, although the degree differs according to subregions and countries, which may be reflecting the socioeconomic and environmental diversity in the region. Their commitments can be illustrated by the emergence of various HEI networks and multi-stakeholder partnerships for achieving sustainability.

The development process of these endeavours has been propelled by several factors including policy arrangement by governments in the Asia-Pacific region. While appreciating such government initiatives, Nomura and Abe (2010) consider the critical analysis and evaluation of them as necessary for the sustainability and effectiveness of university effort in the long run. In other words, it is warned that the universities' dependency on government resources may not always result in an appropriate and long-lasting commitment of universities for sustainability at a local, national and regional level, as government supports could shift to other policy areas at some point.

In fact, government policies do not always match local needs, particularly because of the embedded diversities in the Asia-Pacific context, although the policies have a strong influence in shaping practices. A collection of reports from several countries in the region on HE for sustainability point out that there is often a gap between government policies and the situation at a local level (Ryan et al., 2010). Thus, critical policy analysis together with theoretical/practical research on education for sustainability is important for the future of sustainability in HE in this region.

Against the backdrop of internationalization of HE, several HEI collaborations at the regional level have emerged. They have demonstrated the possibilities of cross-boarder partnership among HEIs through initiatives by environmental ministries and organizations. Based on the research on ProSPER. Net, Nomura et al. (2011) argue that efforts for diversifying sources of funds will be the key to its further development, given the reliance on the resources of one agency so far for the network's operation and core activities. This echoes the situation at a national level as mentioned above.

OPERATION: NEEDS OF THE WHOLE-INSTITUTION APPROACH

Efforts on greening university campuses are popularly initiated in the Asia-Pacific region. However, few cases integrate various functions of universities in the direction of sustainability. Even in Australia, which seems to be a leading country in the region in terms of sustainability at universities, it has been reported that there have been failures to embrace a whole-institution approach (Thomas, 2004; Gudz, 2004). The situation in other countries is more or less the same (see Nomura and Abe, 2010 for the case of Japan), although there are some innovative exceptions.

As Tilbury and Wortman (2008) point out, one of the key elements for the whole-institution approach is multi-stakeholder engagement. The remarks by Corcoran and Koshy (2010), made in the context of Pacific Island Nations, about the importance of situating the whole-institution approach in the local context seem applicable to the other subregions in Asia-Pacific as well, considering the embedded diversity there.

COMMUNITY-BASED APPROACH FOR EDUCATION AND RESEARCH: STRATEGIES TO COPE WITH GLOBALIZATION

It has been argued that community engagement and outreach programmes are a popular approach among Asia-Pacific universities for sustainability. Community engagement should be significant because the concepts of sustainability and sustainable development are so vague that it would be easier for the students to learn about them in real-world local settings. Besides, universities are expected to contribute to the local communities where they are based without being ivory towers; in fact, the challenge of sustainability in general requires active participation from all sectors within society.

In regard to Asia-Pacific, it also seems possible to argue that the stress on 'community' is a reflection of the respect for regional diversity in the face of globalization that can impair it. Sustainable development highlights social as well as environmental and economic elements, requiring respect for local diversity in these regards. Thus, it is not surprising for sustainability educators to underscore local community as the unit to confront the encroachment of globalization. Oguri (2010) remarks that the reaction to the impact of globalization is the main issue in Japanese social education research, which contributes to the emphasis of community engagement and outreach for research and practice for HE in terms of sustainability.

In this context, the challenge of globalization and sustainability requires the reconsideration of the shape of knowledge and the role of universities, resulting in restructuring the HE sector, since the HE sector in many countries in this region has developed under the strong influence of the Western world. In the era of globalization, where globalization very often means Westernization, the internationalization of education and research has increased the demand for the activities of university staff members that meet 'global standard'. Su and Chang (2010, p. 170) argue in the Taiwanese context that the adoption of the worldwide 'research excellence' trend in HE and the global ranking system based on quantitative

publication measures result in the discouragement of academic faculties to orient their commitment to sustainability education, which requires long timescales and qualitative assessment with respect for local values.

In other words, globalization can result in the 'detachment' of universities and their knowledge from the local contexts against the basic concept of sustainability. Concern regarding this point seems to have been the driving force for many university staff to stress local engagement and outreach in their effort towards sustainability. In the Pacific context, Thaman (2002, p. 237) argues that 'Western science and Western economic rationalism continue to dominate the global approach to development, which now pervades the lives of most people everywhere', and universities are facing challenges to incorporate traditional indigenous/local knowledge and perspectives in education and research as a means of achieving a more holistic and interdisciplinary way of thinking towards sustainability. Fadeeva and Mochizuki (2010) argue the need for an alternative university appraisal system with reference to the Asia-Pacific context and the principles of ESD, such as the idea that education must be culturally appropriate and locally relevant, although the current global ranking and appraisal system has failed to include them.

Thus, the active engagement of universities in Asia-Pacific for sustainability seems to be related to embedded local diversity and the impact of globalization, although further research is necessary to understand the relations in detail. This entails the reconsideration of the role of universities between the agency contributing to the local demands and culture, and the institutions that need to survive in the internationalized education and research sector that assists national development. Given the importance of the HE sector in shaping the future of our society, its successful transition to take on a new role, which is still halfway there, is key to sustainable development in Asia-Pacific.

ACKNOWLEDGEMENTS

The authors wish to thank Alex Ryan, Daniella Tilbury, Peter Blaze Corcoran, Kiran Banga Chhokar, H. Jenny Su, Angelina P. Galang and Dongjie Niu, who have worked together with the authors in a research project on higher education in the Asia-Pacific since 2008, for this paper owes much to their inputs.

REFERENCES

CAREC (Regional Environmental Center for Central Asia) (2009) *Legal Acts, Programmes and Regulatory Frameworks of Education in the Central Asian Region: A Review*. CAREC, Almaty.

Chhokar, K.B. (2010) Higher education and curriculum innovation for sustainable development in India. *International Journal of Sustainability in Higher Education*, **11**(2), pp.141–52.

Corcoran, P.B. and Koshy, K.C. (2010) The Pacific way: sustainability in higher education in the South Pacific nations. *International Journal of Sustainability in Higher Education*, **11**(2), pp. 130–40.

Deo, S. (2005) Pacific Island Nations, in *A Situational Analysis of Education for Sustainable Development in the Asia-Pacific Region*, UNESCO Asia-Pacific Regional Bureau for Education, pp. 65–72.

Fadeeva, Z. and Mochizuki, Y. (2010) Higher education for today and tomorrow: university appraisal for diversity, innovation and change towards sustainable development. *Sustainability Science*, **5**, pp. 249–56.

Fisher, R. (2003) Applying ISO14001 as a business tool for campus sustainability: A case study from New Zealand. *International Journal of Sustainability in Higher Education*, **4**(2), pp.138–50.

Galang, A.P. (2010) Environmental Education for Sustainability in Higher Education Institutions in the Philippines. *International Journal of Sustainability in Higher Education*, **11**(2), pp. 173–83.

Geertshuis, S. (2009) Improving decision making for sustainability: a case study from New Zealand. *International Journal of Sustainability in Higher Education*, **10**(4), pp. 379–89.

Gudz, N. (2004) Implementing the sustainable development policy at the University of British Columbia. *International Journal of Sustainability in Higher Education*, **5**(2).

Hayashi, H. and Sakurai, S. (2005) Daigaku ni okeru ISO 14000 Dounyu ni Kansuru Kenkyu 1. (Study on the ISO 14001 Introduction at Universities, No.1). *Otsuma Journal of Social Information Studies*, **14**, pp. 115–25.

Itoh, M., Suemoto, M., Matsuoka, K., Ito Atsuchi, Yui, K., Matsuda, T. and Ishikawa, M. (2008) Contribution of Kobe University to the Regional Centre of Expertise (RCE) on Education for Sustainable Development (ESD) Hyogo-Kobe. *International Journal of Sustainability in Higher Education*, **9**(4), pp. 479–86.

Kasimov, N.S., Malkhazova, S.M. and Romanova, E.P. (2005) Environmental education for sustainable development in Russia. *Journal of Geography in Higher Education*, **29**(1), pp. 49–59.

McKeown, R. and Hopkins, C. (2007) Moving beyond the EE and ESD disciplinary debate in formal education. *Journal of Education for Sustainable Development*, **1**(1), pp. 17–26.

Ministry of the Environment (2008) *Vision for University-led Environmental Leadership Initiatives for Asian Sustainability*. Japan: Ministry of the Environment.

Mochizuki, Y. and Fadeeva, Z. (2008) Regional centres of expertise on education for sustainable development (RCEs): an overview. *International Journal of Sustainability in Higher Education*, **9**(4), pp. 369–81.

Niu, D., Jiang, D. and Li, F. (2010) Higher education for sustainable development in China. *International Journal of Sustainability in Higher Education*, **11**(2), pp.153–62.

Nobes, D.C. (2002) Building on the foundations: environmental science at the university of Canterbury, Christchurch, New Zealand. *International Journal of Sustainability in Higher Education*, **3**(4), pp. 371–9.

Nomura, K. (2009) A perspective on education for sustainable development: historical development of environmental education in Indonesia. *International Journal of Educational Development,* **29**(6), pp. 621–7.

Nomura, K. and Abe, O. (2009) The education for sustainable development movement in Japan: a political perspective. *Environmental Education Research*, **15**(4), pp. 483–96.

Nomura, K. and Abe, O. (2010) Higher education for sustainable development in Japan: policy and progress. *International Journal of Sustainability in Higher Education*, **11**(2), pp. 120–9.

Nomura, K., Natori, Y. and Abe, O. (2011) Region-wide education for sustainable development networks of universities in the Asia-Pacific. In: Sakamoto, R. and Chapman, D. (eds) *Cross-Border Partnerships in Higher Education: Strategies and Issues*. New York: Routledge, pp. 209–27.

Nomura, K., Ota, E. and Takahashi, M. (2010) Research on ESD in higher education: taking stock and moving forward. *Kankyo Kyoiku* (Environmental Education), **20**(4), pp. 25–34 (In Japanese).

Oguri, Y. (2010) How does ESD research deal with 'local community'? *Kankyo Kyoiku* (Environmental Education), **20**(4), pp. 16–24 (In Japanese).

Park, T.Y. (2008) 'ESD of Korean Universities', presentation at international symposium 'Sustainability in Higher Education: Learning from Experiences in Asia and the World', December 2008, Rikkyo University, Tokyo, Japan.

Ryan, A., Tilbury, D., Corcoran, P.B., Abe, O. and Nomura, K. (2010) Sustainability in higher education in the Asia-Pacific: developments, challenges and prospects. *International Journal of Sustainability in Higher Education*, **11**(2), pp. 106–19.

Sanusi, Z.A. and Khelgat-Doost, H. (2008) Regional centres of expertise as a transformational platform for sustainability: a case study of Universiti Sains Malaysia, Penang. *International Journal of Sustainability in Higher Education*, **9**(4), pp. 487–97.

Su, H.J. and Chang, T.C. (2010) Sustainability in higher education in Taiwan. *International Journal of Sustainability in Higher Education*, **11**(2), pp. 163–72.

Thaman, K.H. (2002) Shifting sights: the cultural challenge of sustainability. *International Journal of Sustainability in Higher Education*, 3(3), pp. 233–42.

Thomas, I. (2004) Sustainability in tertiary curricula: what is stopping it happening? *International Journal of Sustainability in Higher Education*, **5**(1), pp. 33–47.

Tilbury, D. and Cooke, K. (2001) *Building Capacity for a Sustainable Future*. Sydney: Macquarie University.

Tilbury, D. (2004) Environmental education for sustainability: a force for change in higher education. In: Corcoran, P.B. and Wals, A.E.J. (eds) *Higher Education and the Challenge of Sustainability: Problematics, Promise, and Practice*. Kluwer Academic Publishers, pp. 97–112.

Tilbury, D. and Cooke, K. (2005) *A National Review of Environmental Education and its Contribution to Sustainability in Australia: Frameworks for Sustainability.* Australian Government Department of the Environment and Heritage and Australian Research Institute in Education for Sustainability.

Tilbury, D., Keogh, A., Leighton, A. and Kent, J. (2005) *A National Review of Environmental Education and its Contribution to Sustainability in Australia: Further and Higher Education.* Canberra: Australian Government Department of the Environment and Heritage and Australian Research Institute in Education for Sustainability.

Tilbury, D. and Wortman, D. (2008) Education for sustainability in further and higher education: reflections along the journey. *Planning for Higher Education*, **36**(4), pp. 5–16.

Verbitskaya, L.A., Nosova, N.B. and Rodina, L.L. (2002) Sustainable development in higher education in Russia: the case of St Petersburg State University. *International Journal of Sustainability in Higher Education*, **3**(3), pp. 279–87.

NOTES

1   See, for example, Vol. 11 No. 2 of *International Journal of Sustainability in Higher Education*.

2   ESD-Net <http://www.unescobkk.org/education/teacher-education-and-training/esd-net-and-teacher-education/>

3   RUC   <http://www.rrcap.unep.org/leadership/about/ruc.cfm>

4   RCE <http://www.ias.unu.edu/efsd/rce>

5   ProSPER.Net <http://www.ias.unu.edu/efsd/prospernet>

6   TEMM < http://www.temm.org/>

7   Education and Communication for a Sustainable Pacific Guiding Framework: 2005–2007 <http://www.sprep.org/topic/pdf/EduCommsFramework.pdf>

8   The Pacific ESD Framework <http://unesdoc.unesco.org/images/0014/001476/147621E.pdf>

9   The Action Plan for Implementing ESD in the Pacific Islands 2008-2014 < http://www.unescobkk.org/fileadmin/user_upload/esd/images/asia_pacific/Pacific_ESD_Regional_Action_Plan.pdf>

10 UNECE Strategy for ESD <http://www.unece.org/env/esd/Strategy&Framework.htm>

11 South Asian Environmental Education and Training Action Plan 2003-2007 <http://www.sacep.org/pdf/SACEP_education%20&%20training%20action%20plan.pdf>

12 South Asia Youth Environment Network < http://www.sayen.org/ >

13 The National Implementation Plan for the UN DESD (in Japanese) <http://www.cas.go.jp/jp/seisaku/kokuren/keikaku.pdf>

14 Taiwan Sustainable Campus Project <http://www.esdtaiwan.edu.tw/>

Inside View II.3
Higher education and sustainability in Australia: transforming experiences

Jo-Anne Ferreira and Daniella Tilbury

INTRODUCTION

In Australia, as in other countries, much has been written about the need for the higher education (HE) sector to contribute towards the development of more sustainable societies, now and into the future (Kelly, 2010; Stewart, 2010; Chambers, 2009; Tilbury et al., 2005a; Tilbury, 2004; Calvert, 2003; Wright, 2002). This literature outlines *why* changes are necessary, *what* changes are required and *how* these are to be achieved. They call for changes to policy and practices in relation to the management and operations of the organization, as well as to research, teaching and community engagement.

However, it is only recently that the sector has understood that these changes cannot occur in a piecemeal manner and that if higher education institutions (HEIs) are to reorient themselves towards sustainability, changes will have to be made to the core of institutional culture. Experience of implement-

ing pilot projects has shown that this is not a matter of making a few 'surface' or 'shallow' changes but requires 'deep' changes to the ways in which those in the organization think and work (Kelly, 2010; Stewart, 2010; Chambers, 2009; Thomas, 2004; Tilbury et al., 2005a). A rethink of organizational principles and realignment of cultural practices is needed. The enormity of the changes required and the resistance current structures and cultures present may explain why the HE sector continues to struggle in its efforts to engage with sustainability, notably in the areas of curriculum and pedagogy.

In this paper, we begin by reviewing the policy environment and efforts of sector bodies. We then provide several examples of progress across a range of areas within the Australian HE sector including: curriculum and pedagogy; research; social and community engagement; and institutional management and operations.

GOVERNMENT AND SECTOR INFLUENCES

The Australian Government has played a key role in advancing efforts to transform the HE sector towards sustainability. A number of government policies, such as *Living Sustainably: The Australian Government's National Action Plan for Education for Sustainability* (Australian Government, 2009), and the *National Vocational Education and Training Sector Sustainability Policy and Action Plan (2009–2012)* (National VET Sector Sustainability Action Group and the Ministerial Council for Vocational and Technical Education, 2009) have been developed to motivate and enhance efforts in the sector.

The *Living Sustainably* policy outlines four strategies and actions to achieve the objective of '[equipping] all Australians with the knowledge and skills required to live sustainably' (Australian Government, 2009, p. 4). One of these strategies relates clearly to the need to encourage and enable system-wide change in the HE sector and HEIs. The strategy outlines the need to reorient education systems to '[achieve] a culture of sustainability in which teaching and learning for sustainability are reinforced by continuous improvement in the sustainability of campus management' (Australian Government, 2009, p. 5). The objectives of this strategy include integrating Education for Sustainability into all university courses/subject areas as well as campus management initiatives. The policy seeks a whole-of-system approach to sustainability (Australian Government, 2009, p. 21). It acknowledges the need to align explicit and hidden curriculum: this means enacting sustainability across the campus as well as teaching it through formal offerings. The *National Vocational Education and Training Sector Sustainability Policy and Action Plan (2009–2012)* similarly provides strategies for aligning the values and practices of this part of the HE sector. Through these policies, and the incentives that accompany them, the Australian Government has demonstrated commitment to reorienting the HE sector in Australia towards sustainability. Its messages are clear and consistent.

Equally, various sector bodies support this movement towards sustainability. The Australian Learning and Teaching Council (ALTC) is an Australian Government funded organization that seeks to enable excellence in the sector (www.altc.edu.au). The ALTC has acknowledged the need to invest in sustainability and to support the sector in the reorientation process. It supported the development of the Learning and Teaching Sustainability portal (http://sustainability.edu.au/) which provides a central resource for accessing the latest news about learning and teaching sustainability in HE; programmes and courses on offer at Australian universities; and a number of resources including videos and presentations on a range of sustainability issues. The ALTC has also funded the development of interdisciplinary courses and programmes that deal with the complexities of sustainability, such as the *Responding to climate change complexity* initiative (http://sustainability.edu.au/news/article/taking-aim-climate-change).

Other peak HE bodies such as the Australian Vice-Chancellors' Committee (AVCC),

which is a committee of Australia's university presidents (now called Universities Australia), have also embraced this agenda, acknowledging that by 2020 the university sector in Australia will play a key role in leading sustainability change across communities (AVCC, 2006). These key sector drivers coincided at the recent Sustainability in Higher Education roundtable (2010) convened by the Australian Government. The event catalysed further support for sector changes through the Green Skills Agreement and the Green Skills Agreement Implementation Plan (2010) (www.deewr.gov.au/Skills/Programs/Work-Develop/ClimateChangeSustainability/Pages/GreenSkillsAgreement.aspx).

A number of networks also support the reorientation process across the Australian HE sector. The Australasian Campuses towards Sustainability (ACTS) network has brought together universities and individuals who are working to ensure the HE sector in Australia and New Zealand becomes sustainable. The network includes academics and administrators, such as environmental and campus managers and sustainability officers, and has enabled inter-university dialogue. The network links together practitioners through their website (www.acts.asn.au), as well as through professional development seminars and annual conferences. ACTS has done much to support champions over recent years and to celebrate good practice in a number of areas, particularly campus greening. It has recently acknowledged the need to provide greater support and incentives in the areas of curriculum and senior leadership for sustainability (ALTC, 2011). To step up their efforts, ACTS is currently adapting the Universities that Count (UTC) index, which has proved to be a powerful tool in the United Kingdom in persuading senior management to incorporate sustainability ambitions in their strategic and corporate plans.

SUSTAINABILITY IN PRACTICE

Several examples of initiatives that address sustainability within the Australian HE sector are showcased in this section. These include initiatives to address sustainability in the curriculum and pedagogy of institutions; in the research efforts of institutions, through

'greening' the operations of institutions; and through social and community engagement within and outside of the institutions.

CURRICULUM

Curriculum and pedagogy remain the least addressed aspects of efforts to reorient HE towards sustainability (Cotton et al., 2009; Hedderman et al., 2009; Thomas, 2004). There is an ageing academic population in the Australian HE sector, which implies that many academics began their academic careers before concerns about sustainability were being raised. This may be why sustainability, given its interdisciplinary, complex and changing nature, is an issue that many feel they are inadequately prepared to address. Such cultural conditions make it particularly challenging to seek to mainstream sustainability. Despite this constraint, there are two key national initiatives that have had impact. The first has been successful in enabling many universities to address the escalating need for business graduates with sustainability skills (Martin and Steele, 2010; Thomas and Benn, 2009; Tilbury et al., 2005b); the second in reorienting teacher education for sustainability (Steele, 2010; Ferreira et al., 2009; Ferreira et al., 2007). Details of these initiatives can be accessed at www.aries.mq.edu.au.

RESEARCH

Australia is not unique in investing heavily in scientific and technological research to identify sustainable solutions to current issues (see, for example, the Renewable Energy Research Institute at the University of Western Australia – www.sustainability.ofm.uwa.edu.au or the CRC Sustainable Tourism – www.crctourism.com.au). Research centres such as the Sustainability Policy Institute at Curtin University (http://sustainability.curtin.edu.au/); the Sustainable Futures Institute at the University of Technology, Sydney (www.isf.uts.edu.au) and The Australia Institute (www.tai.org.au) also undertake social research for sustainability.

Some research projects seek to inform and transform HE practices towards sustainability. A project known as Action Research for Curriculum Transformation Towards Sustainability (ACTS) (www.environment.gov.au/education/publications/pubs/acts.pdf), undertaken by Macquarie University in 2004–05, sought to transform curriculum and pedagogy for sustainability through bringing together colleagues from across the disciplines with varied levels of engagement with sustainability, to develop innovative curricula for sustainability. The project was successful in changing the educational practices of a select number of teaching teams. The project has since been utilized to generate change in other universities (for example the University of New South Wales, the University of Queensland, and Griffith University). It is an example of how research is able to not just inform but also drive change for sustainability.

MANAGEMENT AND OPERATIONS

The greening of operations and management structures has received the most attention in HEIs within Australia. The Australian National University was the first to set up a Green Office in Australia (www.anu.edu.au/anugreen), and most universities in Australia now have similar offices. Another key trend is the development of ecologically sustainable buildings within HE. A good example of this is the Griffith University EcoCentre (see below) and the recent Mirvac School of Sustainable Development at Bond University (www.gbca.org.au/greenstar-projects/project-profile.asp?projectID=146) which were both designed and constructed with a low environmental footprint in mind, and to showcase what technology can offer sustainable development. Griffith University has also begun construction on Australia's first zero-emission, self-powering teaching and research building driven by solar-powered hydrogen energy (http://www.griffith.edu.au/about-griffith/campuses/nathan-campus/facilities/sir-samuel-griffith-building). The ACTS network plays a key role facilitating sharing about such initiatives between HEIs.

SOCIAL AND COMMUNITY ENGAGEMENT

Universities are increasingly recognizing the need to extend beyond the university walls to form partnerships with neighbouring businesses, communities and government agencies. One such example is the Griffith University EcoCentre that is housed within a facility built using eco-design principles (http://www.griffith.edu.au/environment-planning-architecture/ecocentre). The building acts as a showcase for the community at large of a number of design principles and features that can be put into place in people's homes. The EcoCentre houses within it the Toohey Forest Environmental Education Centre (http://www.toohforeeec.eq.edu.au/) whose programmes cater for school-aged students, and which hosts a number of community workshops, forums and talks on sustainability topics and issues determined by the local community.

Another example is the University of Western Sydney's (UWS) *Bringing Sustainability to Life* initiative (http://www.uws.edu.au/sustainability). Through this initiative, UWS works in partnership with a wide range of Greater Western Sydney groups to address those aspects of social, economic and environmental sustainability that most affect this rapidly developing urban area.

CONCLUSION: MAKING PROGRESS

The Australian HE sector shows an increasing commitment to sustainability. This is evident in the number of policy documents and efforts that support such a commitment; the development of networks that assist with the shift from understanding to action; and the notable changes in the discourses and practices that are evident within HEIs themselves. Creating the changes that are required to promote and address sustainability issues within individual institutions and within the HE sector as a whole is a complex and ambitious task, which no doubt explains why few institutions in the sector address sustainability in a systemic way.

Providing incentives as well as professional development opportunities for senior managers to take note of the changes required for HE to make a meaningful contribution in this area will be an important next step. To date, there are no programmes in Australia offering sustainability training for executive and senior management within the HE sector. Such programmes could be the key to scaling up practice and joining up the dots within and across institutions so that sustainability becomes a central component of the culture of all HEIs in Australia.

REFERENCES

Australian Government (2009) *Living Sustainably: The Australian Government's National Action Plan for Education for Sustainability.* Canberra: Department of Environment, Water, Heritage and the Arts.

Australian Learning and Teaching Council (2011) Education for Sustainability Shifting in a Positive Direction. http://sustainability.edu.au/news/article/education-sustainability-shifting-positive-direction (Accessed 27 May 2011).

Australian Vice-Chancellors' Committee (2006) *AVCC Policy on Education for Sustainable Development.* http://www.aries.mq.edu.au/useful_links/education/ (Accessed 1 May 2011).

Calvert, J. (2003) Developing the Deakin advantage. *B-Hert News,* **16**, April, pp. 29–30.

Chambers, D. (2009) Sustainability should be a university's badge of honour. *Education Alliance Quarterly,* **4**, September, pp. 24–6.

Cotton, D., Bailey, I., Warren, M. and Bissell, S. (2009) Revolutions and second-best solutions: Education for sustainable development in higher education. *Studies in Higher Education,* **34**(7), pp. 719–33.

Ferreira, J., Ryan, L. and Tilbury, D. (2007) Mainstreaming education for sustainable development in initial teacher education in Australia: A review of existing professional development models. *Journal of Education for Teaching,* **33**(2), pp. 225–39.

Ferreira, J., Ryan, L., Davis, J., Cavanagh, M. and Thomas, J. (2009) *Mainstreaming Sustainability into Pre-service Teacher Education in Australia.* Sydney: ARIES .

Hedderman, M., Dobson, A. and D'Cruz, B. (2009) Sustainability and global citizenship as part of curriculum design in Higher Education: What approach works in changing the actual behaviour of today's students/tomorrow's decision makers? In: Haslett, S. and Rowlands, H. (eds) *Proceedings of the Newport NEXUS Conference.* Centre for Excellence in Learning and Teaching Special Publication, **1**, pp. 21–6.

Kelly, P. (2010) Can we make the changes? Insights from the edge. *Journal of Future Studies,* **15**(1), pp. 77–90.

Martin, A. and Steele, F. (2010) *Sustainability in Key Professions: Accounting.* Sydney: ARIES.

National VET Sector Sustainability Action Group and The Ministerial Council for Vocational and Technical Education (2009) *National Vocational Education and Training Sector Sustainability Policy and Action Plan (2009–2012).* Canberra: Department of Education, Employment and Workplace Relations.

Steele, F. (2010) *Mainstreaming Education for Sustainability in Pre-service Teacher Education in Australia: Enablers and Constraints.* Sydney: ARIES.

Stewart, M. (2010) Transforming higher education: A practical plan for integrating sustainability education into the student experience. *Journal of Sustainability Education,* **1**, May 2010.

Thomas, J. and Benn, S. (2009) *Education About and For Sustainability in Australian Business Schools Stage 3: An Action Research Program.* Sydney: ARIES.

Thomas, I. (2004) Tertiary or terminal: A snapshot of sustainability education in Australia's universities. *Proceedings of Effective Sustainability Education Conference,* 18–20 February, 2004, University of New South Wales, Sydney.

Tilbury, D. (2004) Rising to the challenge: Education for sustainability. *Australian Journal of Environmental Education,* **20**(2), pp. 103–14.

Tilbury, D., Adams, K. and Keogh, A. (2005a) *A National Review of Environmental Education and its Contribution to Sustainability in Australia: Further and Higher Education.* Canberra: Australian Govern-ment Department of the Environment, Water, Heritage and the Arts and ARIES.

Tilbury, D, Crawley, C. and Berry, F. (2005b) *Education About and For Sustainability in Australian Business Schools.* Canberra: Australian Government Department of the Environment, Water, Heritage and the Arts, ARIES and Arup Sustainability.

Wright, T. (2002) Definitions and frameworks for environmental sustainability in higher education. *International Journal of Sustainability in Higher Education,* **3**(3), pp. 203–20.

Inside View II.4
Education for sustainable development in higher education in India

Kiran Banga Chhokar

THE NATIONAL CONTEXT

In India education has been acknowledged as an important driver of development. The Education Commission appointed by the Government of India in 1964 wrote in the Foreword to its Report titled *Education for Development,* 'No task could be more challenging, more vital and relevant to India's progress and development – economic, cultural and spiritual' (Education Commission, 1966). The essence of these words, that education can lead to economic, cultural and spiritual development, is repeated in all the policy documents on education drafted since then (for example Government of India, 1981, 1998 and 2009).

India has for long suffered from poverty, social inequality, and religious and social strife. These realities ensured that the essential principles of sustainable development, such as social justice, equity, democracy and religious tolerance, were entrenched in India's Constitution and in the idea of development and of education as they evolved. Despite the rapid economic growth and increasing affluence for a growing middle class in the recent past, a large number of Indians continue to live in extreme poverty, and other social and economic ills persist, in contradiction to India's educational and developmental policies and strategies.

EARLY INITIATIVES

The history of efforts to use education as a tool for what is now called sustainable development (SD) goes back almost a hundred years. In 1920, Mahatma Gandhi set up the Rashtriya Vidyapith (National University) to prepare youth of character, ability and dedication for leading the country towards independence and development. Gandhi's university was later renamed Gujarat Vidyapith after the state of Gujarat where it is located. Although its curriculum has changed over the years to respond to the needs of modern times, the university is still committed to Gandhian ideals of equality, nonviolence, peace, dignity of labour, local relevance, social service and rural development.[1]

Another institution worth mentioning in this context is India's first school of social work which was set up in 1936 in Mumbai. The objective of the Tata Institute of Social Studies (TISS) was to study the country's social issues and problems and impart education that would create trained personnel who could respond to those issues and needs. Its stated vision, using the modern language, is:

> To be an institution of excellence in higher education that continually responds to the changing social realities through the development and application of knowledge, towards creating a people-centred and ecologically sustainable society that promotes and protects the dignity, equality, social justice and human rights for all, with special emphasis on marginalised and vulnerable groups.[2]

ENVIRONMENT AND DEVELOPMENT

In India, as in most developing countries, the basic idea of sustainability is not new as people have traditionally lived quite sustainably (GUNi, 2011). Nearly 70% of India's population is still primarily dependent on the natural environment for their livelihoods and daily needs. The degradation of the natural and social environment as a result of processes of economic development directly affects the lives of this majority. Discrimination on the basis of caste, religion, gender and economic status are everyday realities in this culturally diverse and complex society. In this context, environmental education (EE) in India has been more concerned with developmental issues than with environmental issues seen in isolation. The debate over the difference between EE and education for sustainable development (ESD) is thus not very relevant in the Indian context as EE has long dealt with issues for which the more developed countries use ESD as a lens and a tool.

Given this close relationship between environment and development, the Government of India recognizes EE as a key pillar in its development strategy (Government of India, 1981, 1998). The National Education Policy (NEP) of 1986 stressed the significance of environmental orientation to education at all levels. It stated:

> There is a paramount need to create a consciousness of the environment. It must

permeate all sections of society, beginning with the child. Environmental consciousness should inform schools and colleges. This aspect will be integrated in the entire educational process. (Government of India, 1998, NEP: 8.15)

A significant development in India was the response of the highest court in the land to a public interest lawsuit filed by an environmental lawyer on the need to create more environmentally (and hence socially) sensitive and responsible citizens – it directed that EE must permeate all levels of education (Supreme Court of India, 1991). The court gave the responsibility of ensuring the implementation of the directive at the tertiary level to the University Grants Commission (UGC), the apex grant-giving and policymaking body for higher education (HE). Despite some initial delays, most universities introduced an undergraduate course on Environmental Studies from the academic year starting in 2004. The court directive has made EE/ESD a reality in undergraduate institutions throughout India, which account for 85% of the students enrolled in HE.

THE DECADE AS A CATALYST?

Since its launch in 2005, the United Nations Decade of Education for Sustainable Development (UN DESD or DESD) has been a catalyst in India to promote the agenda for change in support of education for sustainable development (Government of India, 2009). Three major international conferences have been held in India since the beginning of the DESD. 'Education for a Sustainable Future', held at the Centre for Environment Education (CEE)[3] in Ahmedabad in January 2005 was the first conference on ESD to be held globally after the launch of the DESD. In November 2007, the 'Fourth International Conference on Environmental Education', subtitled 'Environmental Education towards a Sustainable Future', was also held in Ahmedabad where again CEE was the host agency, while the conference was organized by the Government of India with UNESCO and UNEP as co-sponsors. In November 2010, CEE again played host to an international conference titled 'Ethical Framework for A Sustainable World' held to commemorate 10 years of the Earth Charter.[4] Each of these conferences

had a special workshop and working group on higher education. In December 2010, the Banaras Hindu University organized a seminar on 'Higher Education and Sustainable Development' as part of its Alumni Meet.

The Government of India has recently entered into an agreement with UNESCO to set up a Category I institute of UNESCO in New Delhi called the Mahatma Gandhi Institute of Education for Peace and Sustainable Development. The Institute will undertake peace education and sustainable development-related research and capacity building in order to promote education for peace and sustainable development among member states in the Asia-Pacific region.

It is difficult to say whether the DESD has had much impact on academics in India so far as many academics are still not aware of ESD. As an example, of the 68 articles submitted between 2006 and 2010 by South Asian academics to the *Journal of Education for Sustainable Development*, an international peer-reviewed journal published in India, 47 were either on education or on sustainable development. The focus of most others was on environmental issues without linking them to education or learning or unravelling the social, economic or ethical strands.[5]

On the other hand, independent of the DESD, and in many cases prior to it, a growing focus on sustainable development and its challenges has become evident in HE curricula, perhaps more strongly driven by the emerging needs of industry and society, and the interest of individual teachers or of groups of teachers at universities.

NEW INITIATIVES IN ENVIRONMENTAL AND SUSTAINABILITY EDUCATION

In recent years several higher education institutions (HEIs) have initiated courses and programmes in sustainable development (see Table 1).[6] Certain universities have created special programmes in collaboration with foreign partners while others are offering home-grown initiatives.

All of the programmes and courses in Table 1 claim to have an inter- and multidisciplinary approach. IIM Ahmedabad's Center for Management in Agriculture offers the elective *Shodh Yatra* course (which translates as 'jour-

ney of explorations'), which involves direct local engagement.[7] Students walk approximately 250 km through remote villages learning how local grassroots innovators and other change agents use traditional knowledge and creativity to solve local problems.

Not only does the curriculum at India's premier engineering institutions, the Indian Institutes of Technology (IITs), reflect an increasing focus on sustainable development, in December 2010 a Centre dedicated to sustainability studies was inaugurated at IIT Madras. The Indo-German Centre for Sustainability will conduct interdisciplinary research and undertake projects in areas related especially to rural development, land use, water resources, energy and waste management. The Banaras Hindu University, too, in 2010 launched an Institute of Environment and Sustainable Development. According to its brochure, the Institute, which is 'dedicated to a better understanding of critical scientific and social issues related to sustainable development goals through guided research', will also conduct courses and engage with community for locally relevant sustainable development.

The decade-old TERI University, in addition to offering various courses and three master's programmes with a sustainability focus (see Table 1), is also one of the founding members of ProSPER.Net – the Promotion of Sustainability in Postgraduate Education and Research Network, an alliance of 21 HEIs in the Asia-Pacific region under the auspices of the United Nations University Institute of Advanced Studies (UNU-IAS).

A university recently set up with a clear social purpose 'to facilitate a just, humane, equitable and sustainable society' is the Azim Premji University in Bangalore.[8] It will launch its first three programmes – master's in Education, Development and Teacher Education respectively – in the academic year beginning July 2011. The university plans to offer teaching programmes and conduct research in the fields of Education and Development.

CURRICULA AND LEARNING PRACTICES

While most of the meaningful examples of environmental and sustainability education have generally been initiated by motivated academic faculties, in some cases they have gained impetus under the DESD. An example

TABLE 1
An indicative list of universities offering programmes and courses in sustainable development

Programme	Course/Module	University
Master's in: • Sustainable Development • Sustainable Development for Urban Environments		University of Madras, with University of Staffordshire, UK
Master's in Sustainable Development		Jadavpur University with University of Staffordshire, UK
Master's in: • Sustainable Development • Global Warming Reduction • Green Business • Green Technology		Global Open University, Dimapur, Nagaland
• Postgraduate Diploma in Environmental and Sustainable Development • Appreciation Programme on Sustainability Science		Indira Gandhi Open National University (IGNOU)
Master's in Sociology	• Sustainable Development	University of Hyderabad
Master's in Sociology	• Sustainable Development • Environment and Society	Jammu University
Postgraduate Programme (Public Policy)	• Environment and Development	Indian Institute of Management (IIM), Calcutta
Postgraduate Programme in Management	• Poverty and Governance	Indian Institute of Management (IIM), Ahmedabad
Postgraduate Programme in Management in Agriculture	• Shodh Yatra	Indian Institute of Management (IIM), Ahmedabad
B. Tech Civil Engineering	• Technology and Sustainable Development	Indian Institute of Technology (IIT) Madras
Master's in Development Studies (five-year integrated programme)	• Focus on Sustainable Development	School of Humanities and Social Sciences, IIT Madras
• Master's in Public Policy and Sustainable Development • MBA Business Sustainability • Master's in Sustainable Development Practice		TERI University, New Delhi

is a series student projects facilitated by the Regional Centre of Expertise (RCEs) of ESD in Pune.[9] At the University of Pune, individual instructors have worked with local NGOs (non-governmental organizations) to identify projects that could help students to learn in real-world settings while helping the NGOs with some of their work requirements. A group of students studied the problems and needs of migrant labour in the city. Another group helped slum dwellers to engage in a participatory budgeting exercise that enabled them to inform the municipal corporation about their priorities for allocation of government funds (Menon, 2009).

Opportunities for engaging with the community abound but only a few HEIs require

their students to undertake community and field projects. Recognizing the importance of the learning that happens when students encounter real-life learning situations, several NGOs in India provide internship opportunities to students from both within and outside the country. CEE, for example, has set up a service to facilitate internships by matching the interests of students with the needs of its own varied projects and programmes and those of NGOs associated with it through UNDP's Small Grants Programme.

CAPACITY BUILDING

While there are some self-motivated teachers who are aware of the enormous value of

ESD approaches to learning and make use of them, a majority need to be introduced to the concept of ESD and its approaches and methodology, and be convinced of its relevance, need and importance for them to become willing facilitators of learning. Exposing them to some of the necessary skills is the next step. Capacity building of teachers is therefore a key to the success of ESD. The UGC has set up and funded Academic Staff Colleges (ASCs) at several universities across the country to offer orientation and refresher courses to teachers of colleges and universities with a view to improve the quality of education. Over the past few years the UGC has been funding courses on Environment and Sustainable Development for college and university teachers at many of these ASCs but these tend to focus on content and not on pedagogy. A survey conducted by CEE in 2007 to study how the compulsory course on Environment was being taught revealed that only 2 of the 37 respondents had received training to teach the course. Two-thirds of the respondents reported that they followed the UGC model syllabus and its recommended textbook (or one closely modelled on it), without their own input, that lectures were the predominant teaching method, and field visits and project work, recommended by the UGC as an essential component, were often not included (Chhokar, 2010).

The CEE has been offering orientation programmes to college teachers as part of its own professional development programmes for in-service professionals. These programmes are about the 'what, why and how' of ESD and focus strongly on how to encourage reflection and critical thinking. Towards the end of the programme, the teachers develop course curricula based on what they think can or should be integrated into their own course or courses, to take back with them to implement. This also provides them with a sense of ownership of the curriculum.

A commendable example of curriculum development with the involvement of the faculty, and with support of institution heads, was a three-year project called Samvardhan, initiated by CEE in collaboration with the Field Studies Council, UK, in three rural HEIs in the state of Gujarat. Rural HEIs in Gujarat are based on the

Gandhian philosophy of educating rural youth to bring about development in their villages, The CEE team analyzed the curricula of the selected institutions, identified areas that were amenable to infusion of environmental and sustainability concepts, issues and perspectives; and developed appropriate approaches and methods. The curricula were then developed and refined in discussion with the teachers in the locale-specific contexts of the selected institutions.

Through a series of well-planned, intensive training programmes, field visits, exposure tours and participatory exercises spread over the three years, the capacity of the teachers was built in the subject content, new teaching-learning methods, and in skills and abilities to enable them to transform their rural development programme into a sustainable development programme.

A vital dimension of the capacity building was the reorientation of the extension component of the curriculum which required students to undertake development activities in nearby villages. The teachers worked intensively with students to help them question their understanding of rural realities and needs, identify relevant projects and extension activities in consultation with the community, and develop and implement their projects. (For a detailed discussion see Chhokar and Pandya, 2005, and Chhokar, 2010.)

A key factor that contributed to the success of this experiment was, that in addition to capacity building of teachers, that of HEI heads too was built so that they readily provided the necessary support to the teachers. With this in view, CEE has organized seminars for the heads of HEIs, but what is really needed is a two-tier programme of capacity building for participating institutions.

STUDENTS AS CATALYSTS

While many of the initiatives are due to the efforts of interested and motivated teachers, a lot is happening through the interest and efforts of students. This has taken many educational forms, including learning from campus practice and through student-led actions, and informal and non-formal learning opportunities, often those provided by environmental clubs and youth networks. Members of the South Asia Youth Environment Network[10] in India are working to create 'model green colleges'. They engage with students of vari-

ous colleges to identify major issues, such as energy and water conservation, and to work out action plans for implementation.

In October 2009, students at IIT Madras organized a symposium on SD focused on energy security to mitigate climate change, financing sustainable development and the challenges of urbanization. The symposium aimed to bring together students from various disciplines, to debate, discuss and draft 'smart policy recommendations that can make our markets, technologies and lifestyles sustainable.'[11]

CONCLUSIONS

A review of the stated objectives of courses and programmes, and discussions with teachers of some of the SD programmes indicated that efforts are being made to teach across disciplines, to expose students to real-life situations through field projects and internships, and to encourage critical thinking. Just how effective these efforts are in helping students learn to deal with complexity, uncertainty and change would, however, need a deeper study.

The approaches described above, by and large, do not seem to be the focus in the mandatory undergraduate course in Environmental Studies. The course provides the opportunity to reach a large number of students and introduce them to the concept of sustainable development and the issues of social justice, equity, democracy, participation and sustainable lifestyles. But that requires capacity building of teachers who themselves must understand the concepts and issues and have the skills to help their students learn how to question and reflect on what is going on around them and find out for themselves what needs to be done.

India's current education system is almost like a sleeping giant, and any reform within it needs to be approached from different directions at the same time. In recent years, and especially in 2010–11, the setting up of some of the new universities, institutes and centres committed to sustainable development reflects a greater awareness of the relevance and value of ESD. It offers the prospect for greater dialogue and discussion on SD and the role of HE among academic faculty university and college leaders, and policymakers, which should bring greater clarity, and action, about how ESD is fundamental

to bringing about a new ethos and greater empowerment in society.

REFERENCES

Chhokar, K.B. (2010) Higher education and curriculum innovation for sustainable development in India. *International Journal of Sustainability in Higher Education*, **11**(2), pp.141–52.

Chhokar, K.B. and Pandya, A. (2005) Samvardhan: An experiment in education for sustainable development. *The Declaration*, **7**(2), pp. 20–4.

Education Commission (1966) *Education for Development: Report of the Education Commission 1964–1966* (Education and National Development) (Kothari Commission). New Delhi: Government of India.

Government of India (2009) *Towards a New Development Paradigm: Education for Sustainable Development*, India Report to the World Conference on ESD. New Delhi: Ministry of Human Resource Development.

Government of India (1998) *National policy on education, 1986 (as modified in 1992) with National policy on education, 1968*, Department of Education. New Delhi: Ministry of Human Resource Development. Retrieved on 23 February 2011, from: http://education.nic.in/policy/npe86-mod92.pdf

Government of India (1981) Education (Chapter 21) in the *Sixth five year plan 1980–85*. New Delhi: Planning Commission. Retrieved on 23 February 2011, from: http://planningcommission.nic.in/plans/planrel/fiveyr/welcome.html

GUNi (2011) Interview with Heila Lotz Sisitka. GUNi Newsletter March 2011. http://www.guni-rmies.net/news/detail.php?id=1719 (retrieved on 29 March 2011).

Menon, S. (2009) Participatory Budgeting, http://education-for-change.blogspot.com/search/label/Governance (retrieved on 18 February 2011).

Sarabhai, K.V. and Chhokar, K.B. (2009) Environmental education in India: Evolution of education as a tool for sustainable development. In: Taylor, N., Littledyke, M., Eames, C. and Coll, R.K. (eds) *Environmental Education in Context: An International Perspective of the Development of Environmental Education*. Rotterdam: Sense Publishers, pp. 51–61.

Supreme Court of India (1991) *MC Mehta v Union of India and Others. Writ petition* (civil) No. 860 of 1991, Order, Dated 22.11.1991.

NOTES

1 http://www.gujaratvidyapith.org/ (retrieved on 20 January 2011).
2 http://www.tiss.edu/TopMenuBar/ about-tiss/vision-mission (retrieved on 20 January 2011).
3 The Centre for Environment Education (www.ceeindia.org) is a national organization set up in 1984 by the Ministry of Environment and Forests as a Centre of Excellence in environmental education.
4 The Earth Charter is a declaration of fundamental ethical principles for building a just, sustainable and peaceful global society in the present century. It is a product of a decade-long, cross-cultural dialogue on common goals and shared values held across the world.
5 Data from the *Journal of Education for Sustainable Development*.
6 The universities and courses mentioned here are only indicative of the range and do not present a comprehensive account of this field in HEIs in India.
7 http://www.sristi.org/cms/shodh_yatra1 (retrieved 18 January 2011).
8 http://azimpremjifoundation.org/home. html (retrieved on 20 January 2011).
9 The idea of RCEs was initiated by the United Nations University. It is a network set up to create an enabling environment for organizing activities locally, to enhance collaboration across formal education and between formal education and local actors in ESD such as local government, research organizations and NGOs.
10 http://sayen.org/projects_ongoing.htm (retrieved on 27 January 2011). The network is supported by the United Nations Environment Programme to involve youth in working towards sustainable development.
11 http://www.iitm.ac.in/conferences/371-shaastra-symposium (retrieved on 27 January 2011).

Spotlight Issues II.4
Lifting the fog: towards a racially inclusive academy

Steve Larkin

The topic of this paper 'Lifting the Fog; Towards a Racially Inclusive Academy' will address racial inclusiveness from the perspective of Aboriginal and Torres Strait Islander people in Australia.

The paper looks at the sector from the perspective of both students and staff through an analysis of the less tangible barriers – the 'fog' – that can make the academy seem impenetrable or uninviting to Indigenous people. The paper concludes by advocating for a self-reflective institutional approach which can be used to disperse the fog.

A core indicator of a racially inclusive academy is the number of Aboriginal and Torres Strait Islander people represented as students.

Aboriginal and Torres Strait Islander people continue to be under-represented in Australia's higher education (HE) sector. Drawn from ABS Census data,[1] the dark grey trend line in Figure 1 shows how many Aboriginal and Torres Strait Islander students we would expect to see in HE, if they were represented proportionally to their share of the population.

When it is considered that there are over 800,000 domestic students enrolled in Australia, it means that there are over 14,500 Aboriginal or Torres Strait Islander students who miss out. Under-representation is the entrenched norm.

The Australian academy is no more inclusive of Aboriginal and Torres Strait Islander people as staff than as students. Currently, Aboriginal and Torres Strait Islander people make up less than 1% of the university work-

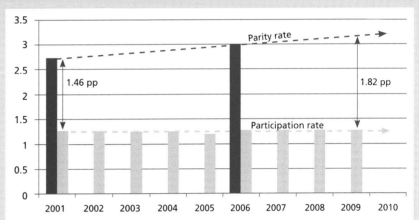

FIGURE 1 Aboriginal and Torres Strait Islander students in HE: calculation of parity and actual participation rates

forces. Yet, Aboriginal and Torres Strait Islander people are 2.5% of the Australian population. Two-thirds of the Aboriginal and Torres Strait Islander HE workforce are employed in general or non-academic roles. The pattern of Aboriginal and Torres Strait Islander people's employment within universities is skewed away from research and teaching positions.

Aboriginal and Torres Strait Islander staff should be regarded highly as institutional assets. Aboriginal and Torres Strait Islander staff bring a wealth of cultural knowledge and perspectives in addition to the academic and professional skills of our field of study. In research, Aboriginal and Torres Strait Islander staff apply both professional and cultural understandings to produce new areas of knowledge.

So, given the benefits that Aboriginal and Torres Strait Islander staff bring to every university, why are there so few of us? In short, why in 2011 do we still struggle to create a racially inclusive academy?

Discussions around education outcomes for Aboriginal and Torres Strait Islander students are also frequently couched in deficit terms looking at the individual students themselves, their families and communities. Time and time again we see the 'usual suspects' rolled out to explain low enrolments, retention and attainment rates for Aboriginal and Torres Strait Islander students: often locating the 'problem' at the family and community level.

To understand this we must consider the 'fog' – the hazy, almost invisible barriers that work to exclude Aboriginal and Torres Strait Islander people as university students and staff.

From the perspective of students, this fog is a form of intellectual exclusion in the academy. This exclusion is institutional in nature and is due to the existence of a dominant epistemology in teaching, assessment and research that serves to disregard and/or devalue Aboriginal and Torres Strait Islander methodologies and ways of knowing. This dominant epistemology – the neo-liberal positivist epistemology – pervades pedagogical approaches, the structure and governance of institutions, staffing and research. Its continued dominance is due to its perceived objectivity and neutrality – but in operation, it is anything but that.

In action, the dominant pedagogical approach, assessment paradigm and research methods converge to devalue Aboriginal and Torres Strait Islander perspectives and perpetuate the deficit approach. Various studies on research methods and knowledge production in colonized countries have demonstrated how the colonial past influences the understanding of what counts as academic research and who can do it (Louis, 2007; Shih, 2010; Hunter, 2002; Goldberg, 1993).

Once we acknowledge the existence of a dominant theory of knowledge based on core claims about the nature of knowledge – including *who* can know, *how* they know and what counts as evidence for claims or of intellect – we can begin to understand how this dominant theory of knowledge operates to devalue and marginalize other 'ways of knowing' and expressions of intelligence.

This has a powerful affect upon students. If the academy presumes that some forms of knowledge are superior, it becomes less likely to consider other forms of knowledge – particularly the knowledge that its students already own through personal experiences and participation within diverse cultural traditions – as valuable. Milner (2007) states that educators should acknowledge and consider their own *and* their student's racial and cultural backgrounds when teaching. He further contends that colour-blind and culture-blind approaches – often pursued in the name of neutrality – can lead to an ignorance of discriminatory institutional practices toward students of colour or of different cultural backgrounds.

Students should not feel that, in order to gain a university education, they must renounce other more subtle forms of cultural knowledge. Instead the academy should be offering forms of knowledge that can co-exist, if not complement each student's existing cultural knowledge.

If we acknowledge, as a starting point, that universities as institutions are based on white non-neutral terms of reference, we can begin to see how institutional characteristics create a fog that discourages or excludes Aboriginal and Torres Strait Islander people. From that starting point, we can enter into a dialogue on how an openness to alternative pedagogies and different ways of thinking and doing in HE might better meet the needs of Aboriginal and Torres Strait Islander students.

A perspective that critically examines the institution, rather than the individuals within those institutions, would also go a long way towards challenging the deficit approach to Aboriginal and Torres Strait Islander education that has for too long provided the loudest explanations for poor student outcomes. With this shift in perspective, from pathological people to pathological institutions, our universities will also become places much more welcoming of different perspectives and experiences; they will become 'culturally safe' for Aboriginal and Torres Strait Islander people.

What I am proposing is not a total rejection of Western theory, research or knowledge, but rather, the promotion and encouragement of Aboriginal and Torres Strait Islander perspectives in the academy. If we acknowledge that innovation and creativity stem from embracing difference, then recognising equivalence between different forms of knowledge is critical to our collective futures.

Aboriginal and Torres Strait Islander people are subject to another set of negative forces in the field of university employment. These forces take the form of the supposedly 'neutral' employment processes that admit people to the academy and promote them once they are through the door.

Feminist scholarship has revealed how workplace practices and processes (which purport to be neutral) can actually exclude women from succeeding within a workplace (Deaux and Emswiller, 1974; Heilman, 2001). In brief, gender-based stereotypes can cloud our assumptions about a person's qualifications and skills, as well as their performance at work.

And bias within these sorts of merit-based professional processes is not confined to issues of gender. Any stereotyped assumptions, including race, can inadvertently influence these decisions, despite processes that claim to be neutral and meritocratic. McKay and McDaniel (2006) found a clear relationship between a lower work rating and the subject's race, particularly when the criteria being assessed required high-level thought processes. These results unequivocally point to a racial bias within these supposed neutral, merit-based performance assessments.

These 'neutral' performance management processes cannot only facilitate racial bias, they can actually mask these inequalities beneath a veneer of meritocracy. Castilla (2008) demonstrated that not only does bias affect the performance ratings given to employees of different races; it also affects the pay and promotion decisions of employees who receive the same rating but are of different races!

These industry studies clearly show that meritocratic HR processes can be systematically undermined by the unexamined prejudices of decision makers and their wider organization. The academy needs to carefully examine its own behaviour to check that its merit-based processes are not clouded by a fog of prejudice and discrimination.

Unfortunately our academies are far from racially inclusive. For students who do not fit the mould, our institutions can appear unfriendly and exclusive. They are spaces in which one cultural form of knowledge is enshrined as normal and natural while others are disregarded or subjugated.

Gusa (2010) has described how the dominant culture can easily come to see itself as entitled to this pre-eminence based upon its own worth. When others challenge this sense of natural ascendency, people within the dominant culture can react to affirm their own power, creating a 'chilly climate' for others beyond the privileged group. This is particularly powerful within education institutions, because here people within this ascendant group are literally judging the quality of the work done by students and colleagues, some of whom – if they can brave the cold – make it to our hallowed citadels to study and work.

Going beyond the effect of race on

students, there is no reason to suspect that employment decisions within the university would be exempt from the powerful effect of unexamined racial prejudice upon decision-making. Sadly, the process of becoming an academic, and earning your stripes within the university do not endow you with any innate power to see through cultural assumptions.

In many ways, this fog is more insidious than explicit instances of discrimination and racism, which unfortunately continue to occur in our universities. How can we work to disperse the fog of discrimination that might be highly visible to a first year Aboriginal or Torres Strait Islander student, but entirely undetectable to a senior academic from an Anglo-Western background?

There are a number of strategies that can delimit and prevent the 'fog'.

One of the most powerful tools is self-reflection. Universities must imagine their behaviour and processes from the perspective of Aboriginal and Torres Strait Islander people. One way to disrupt the hegemonic voices of power is to empower alternative voices that can reveal the deep veins of truth within forms of knowledge previously dismissed as folklore or hearsay. The alternative voices, however, need to be able to garner respect within the stylized conventions of debate within the academy.

In conclusion, my key point – that dominant epistemologies, pedagogical approaches, and ways of knowing combine with subjective merit systems to create an invisible fog that inhibits our ability to create a racially inclusive academy – requires us to examine our own academies, to shine a light on the way we develop and value knowledge to ensure that the sector is not clouded by a fog that is invisible to the majority, but highly discouraging to Aboriginal and Torres Strait Islander people.

Achieving this goal is the aim of all truly great teachers and universities. We work towards it by carefully examining our institutions and ourselves, by dispersing the fog to uncover unconscious forms of discrimination and exclusion. By exposing our hidden assumptions we become better able to acknowledge our own assumptions about race and racism and work to balance them with more inclusive practices.

Through these acts of personal reflection and critique, we become more sensitive to wider epistemological processes within institutions or the wider society that exclude others.

We have the tools to conduct this self-examination; and we know that change is possible. We need to make the invisible visible – to recognize the knowledge assets that Aboriginal and Torres Strait people bring to academia, but also to reveal, and then lift, the subjective fog that clouds our sector and discourages Aboriginal and Torres Strait Islander participation. By doing this, I am confident we can truly achieve a racially inclusive academy.

REFERENCES

Castilla, E. (2008) Gender, race and meritocracy in organizational careers. *American Journal of Sociology*, **113**(6), pp. 1479–526.

Deaux, K. and Emswiller, T. (1974) Explanations of successful performance on sex-linked tasks: What is skill for the male is luck for the female. *Journal of Personality and Social Psychology*, **29**, pp. 80–5.

Goldberg, David Theo (1993) *Racist Culture: Philosophy and the Politics of Meaning*. Cambridge, MA: Blackwell.

Gusa, D. (2010) White institutional presence: The impact of whiteness on campus climate. *Harvard Educational Review*, **80**(4), pp. 464–89.

Heilman, M. (2001) Description and prescription: How gender stereotypes prevent women's ascent up the organizational ladder. *Journal of Social Issues*, **57**(4), pp. 657–74.

Hunter, Margaret (2002) Rethinking epistemology, methodology and racism: Or, is white sociology really dead? *Race and Society*, 5, p. 119.

Louis, Renae Pualani (2007) Can you hear us now? Voices from the margin: Using Indigenous methodologies in geographic research. *Geographical Research*, **45**(2), p. 130.

McKay, P. and McDaniel, M. (2006) A re-examination of black-white mean differences in work performance: More data, more moderators. *Journal of Applied Psychology*, **91**(3), pp. 538–54.

Milner, IV, H. Richard (2007) Race, culture, and researcher positionality: Working through dangers seen, unseen, and unforeseen. *Educational Researcher*, **36**(7), p. 388.

Shih, Cheng Feng (2010) Academic colonialism and the struggle for Indigenous Knowledge Systems in Taiwan. *Social Alternatives*, **29**(1), p. 44.

NOTE

1   An account of how the Department of Education, Employment and Workplace Relations (DEEWR) calculates the Indigenous Parity Rate is available at: http://www.deewr.gov.au/Indigenous/HigherEducation/Pages/PerformanceIndicatorsData.aspx This page also includes the references for the ABS Census data.

NB: As the link shows, DEEWR only provides a parity rate up until 2006 (which was 3.0). The rise in the parity rate from 2006 onward is a projection based on past trends. See the table titled 'Parity Rate by state/territory, Australia; 2001, 2004–2006' in the attached link for details.

INTRODUCTION

For development to be sustainable, mitigation of the destructive effects of natural disasters remains a challenge. Proper application of scientific and technical knowledge on disasters offers an opportunity to reduce the vulnerabilities and risks of various social groups. Disaster education is now recognized as an essential element in formulating the appropriate disaster risk reduction strategies for any country. Over the past few decades, there has been remarkable progress in developing the theoretical basis for disaster management. The advancement in science and technology allows better understanding and presentation of risk and vulnerability issues; application of remote sensing techniques and GIS (geographic information system) has significantly contributed in this regard. Social scientists have been successful in exploring the various social dimensions associated with disaster risks and vulnerabilities. When disaster education is mentioned, the usual focus is more on the school or family or community education. Very little focus has so far been given to higher education (HE). However, HE (in college and university) is the key to developing professionals in the subject. Higher education in disaster is still lacking in most of countries and regions.

Higher education in disaster risk reduction (DRR) is a multidisciplinary issue. It encompasses all faculties of knowledge ranging from science, social science, humanities and so on. The availability of formal degrees in the field of DRR has been only a recent innovation from a few academic institutions worldwide. Before offering academic degrees, many institutions around the world conducted disaster-related research and offered training programmes of varying duration. The objective of these research and training and degree programmes is mainly to foster local or regional need.

It is important to facilitate DRR education at tertiary level through development of a regionally suitable and sufficiently flexible curriculum structure. Before embarking on developing a curriculum structure for DRR education, particularly at the postgraduate level, it is important to differentiate DRR education from DRR training. This is because, prior to the evolution of mainstream DRR education, DRR training either in the form of response and recovery or preparedness was fairly widespread across agencies concerned with it. DRR education is not only about the creation of well-versed professionals in DRR but is also a vehicle for knowledge accumulation and, importantly, knowledge creation. While there are academic programmes that deal with disasters from the perspective of the discipline that hosts them, that is, geology, engineering, geography to name a few, there is yet to visibly emerge DRR as a discipline on its own, which takes comprehensive account of all components.

With the above background, this paper focuses on the importance, evolution and process of HE in the disaster field.

EMERGING ISSUES OF HE IN DISASTER RISK REDUCTION

Being an interdisciplinary subject, DRR has its links to other sectors, such as environment, development, and human security. The link between environment and disaster is prominent in the area where natural and social issues merge, and this is specifically prominent in rural localities where most communities depend on agriculture and natural resources for their livelihood. These issues are linked with the overall concept of human security (Shaw, 2006). Climate change impacts are often regarded as the missing link between environment and disaster. However, the relationship is not clearly reflected in national policies and international and local actions. The following section shows some of the key issues to be reflected in higher education in DRR.

ENVIRONMENT DISASTER LINKAGES

The link between development, environment and disasters is very deeply entrenched. Unplanned, ad-hoc and poor development is directly responsible for a significant part of the vulnerabilities observed in the Asia region. Large-scale industrial developments unmindful of related risks and pollution considerations, the rise of high-density settlements with inadequate infrastructure, non-engineered buildings – all have contributed to high levels of risk. The intermediary in this process is often the environment, as can be seen clearly in the case of climate change that has been established to have arisen out of man-made causes. While there is very popular recent focus on carbon footprints, the concept of ecological footprints has existed for a long time in the academic domain.

HYDRO-METEOROLOGICAL DISASTERS

The most significant increasing trend that threatens vulnerable populations in the mountain regions, river basins, arid swathes and coastal stretches of Asia is one of increasing hydro-meteorological disasters. In terms of climate-change-induced catastrophic events; these threaten us with shocks such as cyclones, cloudbursts, flash floods and urban floods. On the other hand, in terms of prolonged stresses, they threaten us with drought and water stresses. Their impact on urban settlements is also increasing, though not as visible and noticed as the case of catastrophic events.

CCA–DRR SYNERGY

Climate change adaptation (CCA) and disaster risk reduction (DRR), though broadly understood to be linked in some ways, have not yet been taken as a holistically linked complementary set of measures that require collaborative and coordinated action by all concerned stakeholders. The significance of CCA–DRR synergy is a concept without meaning for vulnerable communities who do not feel the impact of climate change or natural disaster sectorally, but it hits them as a combined whole with devastating effects.

NETWORKING OF HE IN DISASTER RISK REDUCTION

The Asian University Network of Environment and Disaster Management (AUEDM: www.auedm.net) is a unique initiative of prominent Asian universities that come together to share knowledge resources related to environment and disaster risk management among themselves and with the larger group of stakeholders working on these issues, in addition to conventional national and thematic boundaries. AUEDM members work in close collaboration to conduct education and research, share findings and find ways forward in a region that is increasingly at threat due to climate change impacts. AUEDM also works closely with governments, international agencies and corporate and civil society organizations to establish collaborations that eventually lead to resilient communities. AUEDM reflects each member's commitment to implementation-oriented education and research in the field of environment and disaster risk reduction.

One of the specific features of the AUEDM is close cooperation with civil society organizations. Non-governmental organizations (NGOs) have direct field access, and experiences in grassroot project implementation. However, these experiences are not properly reflected in the educational curriculum. Thus, the network aims at bridging academic research, education and field practice. Some of the highlights of the university–NGO cooperation are:

- *Quality of knowledge and information:* All participating universities in the targeted countries are esteemed organizations in the field of disaster risk management. Therefore, it brings high quality knowledge and information.
- *Extensive network:* The four universities have the largest networks in the tsunami-affected areas, and thus ensure that the knowledge product will have largest circulation in future.
- *Ensuring sustainability:* Through development of the certificate courses and customized courses, young professional development will be ensured, which is linked to the sustainability of disaster preparedness activities in the targeted countries and communities.

AUEDM STARTED FROM AN IMPERATIVE
AUEDM has been conceived and pursued by its member organizations based on this common understanding and motivation. It has come about from felt needs that appear to be crucial for the survival of millions of poor and vulnerable men, women and children living on the margins of society in Asia. AUEDM members come together for reasons of educational, research and networking imperatives:

- *Educational imperative:* To discuss the status and scope of environment and/or

disaster risk reduction curriculum in the higher studies in each university. Each country has its own perspective. Some countries have full, two-year DRR master's programmes. Some universities have some modules of DRR in their postgraduate programmes. Therefore, the attempt is not to standardize programmes, but to learn and understand the process in DRR. The challenge is how effectively the process can be customized into each context.

- *Research imperative:* To discuss the possibility of climate change adaptation as the key entry point of collaborative research. Each country has a high prevalence of impacts of climate change being borne by the most vulnerable communities. Impacts are most visible in coastal, mountain, urban poor and migrant communities. Since adaptation is a relatively new subject, heavy investments need to be made in research on effective local adaptation as a means for coping with imminent climate change impacts and linked disasters.
- *Network imperative:* To discuss the establishment of the Asian Universities network. While there are integral commonalities in the vulnerability context and the nature of impacts, the local setting and contextual nuances are highly varied across Asian countries. Networking is the only way to share knowledge and experiences, and to draw lessons based on principles derived from practices. The network is thus expected to go a long way in the development of a regional knowledge base, making it accessible for practitioners, and using it to influence the policy environment.

GUIDING PRINCIPLES OF HE IN DRR
In reality, DRR higher education is practised in different departments in the universities, starting from engineering, science, architecture, agriculture, economics, social science and humanities. A comprehensive DRR course is desirable but possibly not a practical solution in many countries, depending on the market mechanism of required professionals. DRR higher education can learn significantly from the process and approaches of sustainable development. The following sections cover some suggested future directions of higher education in DRR.

INCLUSIVE CURRICULUM
Disaster type, nature, intensity, density, frequency, perception, damages, response, relief, recovery, prevention, mitigation, and preparedness vary not only in terms of location but also relate to the socioeconomic conditions, technical capabilities, political priorities, development agenda of particular societies. While each has its own priority, a curriculum structure needs to address issues at a general level that are inclusive of all for a well-rounded foundation in order to proceed to specific issues.

THEORETICAL FOCUS
Curricula will focus on imparting education primarily in the field of disaster risk reduction with climate change adaptation, disaster risk reduction/prevention/mitigation as important components. The theoretical focus will be on the basic concepts and theories of disaster risk reduction climate change adaptation, global warming and scientific understanding of the various types of disasters.

FIELD ORIENTATION
Curricula will not only focus on theoretical knowledge; faculty and students should undertake research on disaster-related issues. Exposing students to real-life situations to assess vulnerabilities, mitigation and preparedness measures will help them to bridge theories with practice.

MULTIDISCIPLINARY
Disaster preparedness and management are multidisciplinary in nature. Various subjects such as Geography, Environmental Sciences, Geology, Economics, Sociology, Social Work, Psychology, Medical Sciences, Civil Engineering, City and Regional Planning, Architecture, Urban and Regional Planning, Agriculture, Forestry, Animal/Plant Sciences and Management Sciences contribute to the field of disaster management. Keeping in view the DRR cycle, it has special areas of interest and research (see www.unisdr.org).

SKILL ENHANCEMENT
The curriculum will focus on producing trained manpower. The training should be based on experiences learned from previous case studies according to market demand. The trained

manpower produced by the university would be engaged in government/non-government/private sector institutions dealing with disaster preparedness and management and thus play an important role in minimizing the losses caused by disasters through better preparation and management.

REFERENCE
Shaw, R. (2006) Community based climate change adaptation in Vietnam: Inter-linkage of environment, disaster and human security. In: *Multiple Dimensions of Global Environmental Changes*, edited by S. Sonak, TERI publication, pp. 521–47.

Network Experience II.3
Alliance for sustainability in higher education

Aurea Christine Tanaka

The reality of our complex problems and the need to transform the way we do things, behave and apply the knowledge that is being generated lead to a necessary process of rethinking, revisiting and reshaping institutional, social, cultural and economical structures. Education and research are fundamental and critical instruments that influence this process and provide the basic foundations for developing human capacity to build a tangible and solidly sustainable world.

Within this context, several initiatives in higher education were established in order to advance the dissemination, awareness, practice and sharing of innovative methodologies and pedagogies that aim to foster responsible citizens, who are conscious of their role in nurturing sustainable practices, as well as transforming structures and processes.

These are part of a broad international agenda that recognized education as one of the instruments to achieve sustainable development (SD), a statement included in Chapter 36 of Agenda 21; that emphasized the importance of partnerships for further promoting and implementing programmes and activities on education for sustainable development (ESD), proposed during the World Summit on Sustainable Development in 2002; and that devised strategies for the planning and implementation of the United Nations Decade of Education for Sustainable Development (UN DESD).

In the Asia-Pacific region, an alliance under the auspices of the United Nations University Institute of Advanced Studies (UNU-IAS) was established among leading universities, focusing on postgraduate education. The alliance, called ProSPER.Net, stands for Promotion of Sustainability in Postgraduate Education and Research Network. Members are higher education institutions (HEIs) based in the Asia-Pacific region, which have ongoing SD or ESD activities. Through this collaborative platform, they pursue opportunities for synergies and share good practices, building upon their strengths and expertise.

ProSPER.Net was launched to focus on postgraduate education, since there are other networks in the region with their respective thrusts, for example distance learning (Asia-Pacific Initiative – API), environmental education for sustainable development (Asia-Pacific Regional University Consortium – RUC), teacher education (ESD-Net, a UNESCO initiative), to mention a few.

As of July 2010, in the two years of its existence, the network has grown to 21 member universities from a wide range of countries: Australia, China, Fiji, India, Indonesia, Japan, Malaysia, the Philippines, the Republic of Korea and Thailand.[1] The plan is to expand to include more institutions and thus create optimal conditions in the region for educational programmes, activities and curricula to be increasingly permeated with sustainability issues.

In Asia, HEIs have a major role in offering knowledge and capacity through education and research, development of innovative approaches, technology and solutions to current and future problems. This is due to the region's rapid economic development and implementation of policies to promote growth and inclusion in global markets without taking into account social development, well-being of citizens and environmental adversities.

In order to enhance transformation in postgraduate education and having in mind a long-term perspective of, among others, educating the future leaders of a sustainable Asia, ProSPER.Net members have been partnering in a number of joint projects with the purpose of broadening the scope of ESD activities and thus stimulating collective responsibility for the region's sustainable development.

The diversity of countries involved ensures on one hand a multicultural approach to sustainability issues that need to be contextualized according to local challenges and needs. This certainly contributes to enriching the exchanges by bringing to the learning process different elements and visions while maintaining an Asian perspective. However, accommodating diverse approaches can also pose a challenge, especially when considering educational standards, regulations, curricula, and calendars, to mention a few institutional issues. Notwithstanding these differences, ProSPER.Net members have been actively collaborating with each other, overcoming institutional particularities internally and on an individual basis, while making efforts to cooperate at the network level through joint projects.

ProSPER.Net is governed by a general assembly comprising representatives of all member institutions and a board elected by the general assembly and having a limited number of members. UNU-IAS and the UNU International Institute for Software Technology (UNU-IIST) are *ex-officio* members of both governing bodies, functioning as the secretariat for the network, responsible for project management, strategic guidance, communication and dissemination, and other organizational matters.

With this governance structure and upon the board's approval, the following projects[2] have been carried out, funded by the Ministry of the Environment of Japan, through their contribution to UNU-IAS:

- Integration of sustainability issues in business school curricula, development of materials on social business, social entrepreneurship and on UN Global Compact principles
- Design and delivery of an e-learning programme on sustainable development practice in public policy
- Faculty training module and resource materials for sustainability

- Researchers' school in sustainable development
- Research on innovative pedagogies applied in regional poverty reduction programmes
- An alternative university appraisal project, that aims to reflect upon and create tools for university evaluation in terms of their ESD activities

Through these projects, it is possible to verify that the network has been focusing on integrating sustainability in specific areas, on influencing such curriculum transformations and development of specific competences through new methods, pedagogies and approaches. For example, with regard to the projects involving business schools and case studies development on social business and social entrepreneurship, a project led by AIT (Asian Institute of Technology), the idea was to influence curriculum development and also, through analysis of established practices, incorporate the necessary curriculum changes so as to provide customized tools and develop skills needed for local businesses to be sustainable.

Through the project that aims to deliver knowledge needed to foster a sustainable approach in public policy, some ProSPER.Net members, with the leadership of TERI University, proposed to offer a short transdisciplinary course that would address pressing issues like natural resource management, economic aspects of public policy and science and policy for climate change, using web-based technology and expertise of partners. The intention was to fill a gap in mid-career public policymakers' education, since they regularly take decisions on complex and cross-sectoral problems that affect local communities and society at large.

A more basic approach as regards the training on SD would be carried out by two of the listed projects: the faculty training module and resource materials for sustainability, an activity developed by USM (Universiti Sains Malaysia) and partners, and the researchers' school in sustainable development. While the first was directed at producing a comprehensive and systematic collation of materials that would provide faculty members tools to inte-

grate SD issues in their teaching and research, the second targets postgraduate students, also with the purpose of exposing them to SD challenges in a particular region, but to study and analyse a specific theme. The researchers' school in sustainable development is to be held annually on a rotational basis among ProSPER.Net members, with a different sustainability-related theme each year that reflects and explores specific characteristics of a determined location. Students will thus be exposed to different realities in Asia and will work together as a team to reflect upon and possibly find solutions to local problems. The first researchers' school was hosted by RMIT University in its Viet Nam campus and focused on developing research projects related to a sustainable future in the Mekong Delta region.

A research project on innovative pedagogies applied in regional poverty reduction programmes was developed to identify new approaches that can guide the transformation of educational practices designed and carried out according to the agenda and needs of poor communities. The purpose of some of these innovative educational platforms is to develop competences and skills that can positively improve and have a major impact on the livelihood of communities in remote and rural areas. In the long run, this project envisions applying the same methodologies and pedagogies to other contexts in different countries. This project was carried out by AIT and selected partners, within the existing Poverty Reduction and Agricultural Management Programme in Southern Laos.

Aiming to create an instrument that recognizes universities' good practices in integrating ESD principles in their operational, institutional and academic activities, some ProSPER.Net members led by Hokkaido University initiated the Alternative University Appraisal project. A self-reflection tool was developed to allow universities to review and critically reflect upon their practices and activities in governance, education, research and outreach from the perspective of ESD. The idea is to identify strengths of ESD initiatives and areas of

improvement. The ultimate goal is to create a community of practice through a peer-consultation system wherein universities will have the opportunity to share and learn good practices, innovative pedagogies and methodologies from each other. A sub-working group that is exploring benchmarking aspects of the project was formed, and the data collected initially from ProSPER.Net members complements the self-reflective exercise, indicating objectively universities' activities in various fields pertaining to SD and their performance in relation to other institutions in specific areas.

Besides these joint projects, ProSPER.Net also created an award for young scientists in SD, a collaborative initiative with Elsevier, responsible for Scopus, the largest database of peer-reviewed literature. The intent is to stimulate and reward research being carried out in different fields and that emphasizes SD achievements. Awards have been given in Business, Economics and Management, Engineering and Technology, Agriculture and Food Security, Energy and Water in the past two years. The areas of research that the award covers are changed every year and award winners have shown that their research makes a real impact and contribution to transform local realities.[3]

This brief account of ProSPER.Net activities shows that the various projects and activities aim to address specific features that are part of the UN DESD's strategies:

- Vision building and advocacy
- Consultation and ownership
- Partnership and networks
- Capacity building and training
- Research and innovation
- Use of information and communication technologies
- Monitoring and evaluation

By building synergies with other networks in the region and beyond, ProSPER.Net members are striving to transform the education scenario in Asia-Pacific, in an attempt to contribute to the region's development within the scope of their mission, through the creation and dissemination of knowledge.

NOTES

1 For more information regarding the members and their ESD programmes and activities, visit www.ias.unu.edu/efsd/prospernet.

2 Joint projects are developed with the leadership of one ProSPER.Net member university in cooperation with at least two others.

3 For more information on the award, areas and winners, see www.ias.unu.edu/efsd/prospernet/ysa.

GOOD PRACTICES II.3

Higher Education and Sustainability in Asia and the Pacific: Sharing Actions for Change

The following experiences are a selection of good practices on higher education and sustainability. Some of them were presented at the 5th International Barcelona Conference on Higher Education and others are part of the GUNi observatory.

The good practices cover the following institutional areas:

Curricula and learning innovation

Community and social engagement

Institutional management

Research

GOOD PRACTICE 1

The ADB-MFU project on capacity building for natural resources management and socioeconomic benchmarking in the Greater Mekong Subregion (GMS)

Institutional area(s):

LOCATION: Asia and the Pacific
INSTITUTION: Mae Fah Luang University

This is a three-year programme started in 2007 by the Mae Fah Luang University (MFU), along with its university network, GMS University Network, on natural resources and environmental management. Their goal is to undertake research on 'socioeconomic benchmarking' and 'integrated land-use planning and management' carried out by graduate students who will be supervised by in-country academic scholars. Then they will analyse and synthesize the livelihood and land-use studies by developing models to identify and recommend 'effective interventions' for livelihood improvement. Eventually, all of these will serve as the foundation of a long-term process of developing intellectual capacity for research and analysis rooted in the GMS.

Detailed information is available at GUNi HEiOBS:

http://www.guninetwork.org/guni.heiobs/good-practices/the-adb-mfu-project-on-capacity-building-for-natural-resources-management-and-socio-economic-benchmarking-in-the-gms

GOOD PRACTICE 2

The university in a garden

Institutional area(s):

LOCATION: Malaysia
INSTITUTION: Universiti Sains Malaysia

The University in a Garden concept as conceptualized by USM in 2001–02 is designed to depict the close affinity between the role and function of the university as an institution of higher learning and nature as part of the global ecological setting. The flora, fauna, aquatic elements and other natural creations are dynamically linked in the exploration of knowledge into the nature of existence. The concept is an invitation to value, preserve and nurture the campus ambience as part of efforts to create and sustain an intellectually conducive setting in order to kindle the spirit and practice of symbiotic co-existence.

Detailed information is available at GUNi HEiOBS:

http://www.guninetwork.org/guni.heiobs/good-practices/the-university-in-a-garden/

GOOD PRACTICE 3

UNEP-Tongji Institute for Environment and Sustainable Development

Institutional area(s):

LOCATION: China
INSTITUTION: IESD

Established in May 2002, one of the main objectives of UNEP-Tongji IESD is to develop educational programmes to build research, technical and managerial skills, and capacity in developing countries. The Institute will introduce and strengthen international environmental education and scientific research, and design its educational programmes for undergraduate and postgraduate students with support from the College of Environmental Science and Engineering and other related colleges of Tongji University. Furthermore, it aims to establish an internationalized educational institution in respect of environment and sustainable development.

Detailed information is available at GUNi HEiOBS:

http://www.guninetwork.org/guni.heiobs/good-practices/unep-tongji-institute-for-environment-and-sustainable-development

Samvardhan – improving the quality of life of tribal communities in south Gujarat

Institutional area(s):

LOCATION: India
INSTITUTION: Centre for Environment Education

The Centre for Environment Education (CEE) is a national institution engaged in developing programmes and material to increase awareness about the environment and sustainable development. CEE was established in 1984 as a Centre of Excellence in Environmental Education. CEE's primary objective is to improve public awareness and understanding of the environment with a view to promoting the conservation and sustainable use of nature and natural resources, leading to a better environment and a better quality of life. To this end, CEE develops innovative programmes and educational material, and builds capacity in the field of education for sustainable development (ESD).

Detailed information is available at GUNi HEiOBS:

http://www.guninetwork.org/guni.heiobs/good-practices/samvardhan-improving-quality-of-life-of-tribal-in-south-gujarat

Innovative teacher training in remote Australian indigenous communities: a sustainable staffing model

Institutional area(s):

LOCATION: Australia
INSTITUTION: Charles Darwin University

Charles Darwin University is delivering its initial teaching degree to indigenous students by sending lecturers out each week to five remote rural communities in Australia's Northern Territory. The students would not otherwise be able to enroll in such a course due to poor housing, few resources, lack of mobility and little internet access. The delivery of the course is integrated into the students' current work as teacher assistants in the classroom, and is designed to allow them to make the shift to being a fully qualified teacher. The communities are indigenous, and some of the schools are bilingual, so the local ways of knowing, doing and being are also embedded into the programme.

Detailed information is available at GUNi HEiOBS:

http://www.guninetwork.org/guni.heiobs/good-practices/innovative-teacher-training-in-remote-australian-indigenous-communities-a-sustainable-staffing-model

A participatory pedagogy for the digital native: the green MBA

Institutional area(s):

LOCATION: Singapore
INSTITUTION: Knowledge Universe Education

In collaboration with a British university, a small tertiary education institution in Singapore is offering a unique degree programme in a unique way. Tapping into the zeitgeist, it has developed a 'Green MBA' to be delivered in a format that is specially designed to appeal to the 'digital native'. The curriculum has been developed by a team of adjunct faculty from all around the globe; a custom-built delivery platform has been constructed that takes full advantage of the social media revolution; and learning design is conducive to a participatory pedagogy, where authentic learning tasks allow students to take centre stage.

Detailed information is available at GUNi HEiOBS:

http://www.guninetwork.org/guni.heiobs/good-practices/a-participatory-pedagogy-for-the-digital-native-the-green-mba

Lakeside Drive Community Garden

Institutional area(s):

LOCATION: Australia
INSTITUTION: Charles Darwin University

The Lakeside Drive Community Garden, is an outreach programme of Charles Darwin University's (CDU) Office of Community Engagement that enables students, staff, community members and organizations and local business to work together to create a demonstration site for tropical food production and sustainable living education in Darwin and regional areas. With the support of CDU's Community Engagement Coordinator, the Talloires Group drafted a plan to submit to the university vice-chancellor. Students had to petition Darwin City Council to allow them to use a two-acre lot that was under lease by the university. Finally, in August 2008 CDU formally recognized the community garden as a student-run project that would be hosted by the University's Office of Community Engagement.

Detailed information is available at GUNi HEiOBS:

http://www.guninetwork.org/guni.heiobs/good-practices/lakeside-drive-community-garden

The reader can also find the following good practices related to sustainability in Asia and the Pacific at the GUNi Observatory:

- A student centred approach to shaping sustainability of teaching within Chemical engineering education
  LOCATION: Malaysia
  INSTITUTION: Nottingham University Campus Malaysia

- Green Office Program
  LOCATION: Australia
  INSTITUTION: Australian National University

- Special course on environmental rehabilitation
  LOCATION: Japan
  INSTITUTION: Okayama University

- Sustainable context of higher education in Kazakhstan: the International IT University
  LOCATION: Kazakhstan
  INSTITUTION: International IT University

- Turning sustainable awareness into practice at the Thai International College
  LOCATION: Thailand
  INSTITUTION: Mahidol University

http://www.guninetwork.org/guni.heiobs/

II.4 Higher Education and Sustainability in Europe

J.H.A.N. Rikers, G.R. de Snoo and M.C.E. van Dam-Mieras

Abstract

As to higher education and sustainability the actual situation in Europe is dominated by the ambition to formulate policies on a European level on the one hand and by the large diversity in policies and educational systems in the European states on the other. The Lisbon Agenda and Bologna Process are dominating the policy landscape regarding these developments in Europe, specifically within the EU. On the national level sustainable development (SD) has been anchored in national policies. The position of higher education (HE) in these policies is however unclear in general. Only a few nations have dedicated policies for education for sustainable development (ESD) in HE. More countries however have a national programme connected to the UN Decade of Education for Sustainable Development (UN DESD).

The general trend in ESD in higher education institutions (HEIs) is towards a focus on an integrated approach and towards education *for* sustainable development, which requires an embedding of ESD in HE on all levels. ESD in practice can only be understood on the local and regional level. Therefore, examples have been collected and need to be collected to aid our understanding of the impact of ESD approaches in sustainable regional development.

Moving towards integration of ESD in higher education requires more and new strategies; this paper elaborates some strategy priorities.

THE EUROPEAN PERSPECTIVE

The word 'sustainable' refers to a situation that can continue. In relation to Planet Earth it implies that the human inhabitants of the planet will have to learn how to live together in peace, dignity and mutual respect on one planet without causing irreversible damage to it by their production and consumption activities.

That which comes to the forefront within the context of SD depends upon where on Earth one lives. In the economically more developed part of the world the ecological aspect may be the most important, while in the less developed parts of the world economic development may have priority. Culture, another important dimension of SD, tends to get less attention than economy and ecology but it too is very important.

If we accept that our present society is a globalizing society, an important point to consider is that globalization exceeds the traditional frames of reference societies have. Every culture has its own specific worldview, which is an important factor in its societal set of norms and values. Asking ethical questions such as 'What is a good life in a moral sense?' in a global society therefore, quickly results in 'defending our values against theirs' (van der Wal, 2003). In a global space a multitude of different, culturally determined moral convictions will be at stake. The challenge is to see that as a source for development rather than as a source for conflict. The Earth Charter (http://www.earthcharter.org) wants to offer a shared vision of essential values based on science, international law, philosophy and religion that can function as a moral basis for an emerging global society.

COMPLEXITY, UNCERTAINTY AND TRANSITION

In order to face the 21st century's problems, society needs path-breaking solutions conceived in terms of fundamentally different sets of technologies, institutions and social arrangements from those we have today. Sustainable development therefore is a challenge at all levels of scale – micro, meso and macro – characterized by the need for longterm approaches and the involvement of many stakeholders with often conflicting interests. The inherent complexity and uncertainty of the challenges asks for fundamental changes, not just for incremental changes leading to optimization within established frameworks. Transitions resulting in structural change and changes in framing conditions are needed. The types of innovations needed cannot be restricted to designing and evaluating solutions, but must also engage with a process of paradigmatic change. This strategic management challenge requires special methods of working. Visions of sustainable futures have to be created, the dynamics of co-evolutionary change on several innovation fronts have to be handled, the inherent uncertainty of change has to be faced and the communication about options and their implications with stakeholders and decisions makers has to be organized. Loorbach and Rotmans (2006) state that such transitions require organization-exceeding innovations at the system level, which are realized by a variety of agents and which fundamentally change both the structure of the system and relations among the agents and other stakeholders.

In seeking new development pathways the focus is no longer just the techno-economic system that delivers economic growth, but the whole social-ecological system embracing the natural world, the cultural world and interactions between the two.

The natural world is inherently complex, which by itself leads to indeterminacy and uncertainty. The interactions between mankind and nature are increasingly mediated through powerful technologies and the social systems that interact with the natural world are, in their own ways, just as complex, unpredictable and unfathomable as the natural system. Social systems are not only complex, but are also 'reflexively' complex (Funtowicz and Ravetz, 2002) and there is no 'cure-all solution' for SD challenges. The combinations of uncertainty, globalization, tensions among nations relating to access to resources, deprivation of nations resulting from poverty gaps, powerful technological interventions, the potential for irreversible ecological change and the limited capacity of humanity to adapt or respond when ecological change undermines the very basis of human survival or quality of life constitute a powerful case for a precautionary approach (Jansen et al., 2008).

There is a need to ensure that understanding of the threats to and opportunities for survival and sustainability are widely diffused into all spheres and levels of development decision-making within society, politics, business and science. This implies that ESD in all its forms and at all levels – formal, non-formal and informal – can be a very important societal change factor.

HIGHER EDUCATION IN EUROPE

THE EUROPEAN LEVEL

In Europe two processes have been dominantly present over the past decade: the EU Lisbon Strategy for Growth and Jobs and the Bologna Process. The objective of the Lisbon agenda is to ensure Europe's wealth and growth through a competitive knowledge economy. The objective of the Bologna Process is to harmonize European HE policies and to create a European Higher Education Area.

The Magna Carta Universitatum, issued in 1988 in Bologna, Italy, at a meeting of university rectors celebrating the 900th anniversary of the oldest European university, can be seen as an early step in the Bologna Process. One year before, the ministers of education from France, Germany, Italy and the UK had committed themselves to 'harmonising the architecture of the European Higher Education System'. In 1999 the ministers of education from 29 European countries signed the Bologna Declaration at the University of Bologna. Since that time follow-up meetings have been organized in Prague (2001), Berlin (2003), Bergen (2005), London (2007) and Leuven (2009); the next meeting is to take place in Bucharest in 2012 (http://en.wikipedia.org/wiki/Bologna_Process).

In a document prepared by the Confederation of EU Rectors' conference and the Association of European Universities (CRE) disseminated by the European Commission (http://ec.europa.eu/education/policies/educ/bologna/bologna.pdf) the Bologna Declaration is described as a binding commitment to an action programme. The objective is to create a European Higher Education Area (EHEA) in order to enhance the employability and mobility of European citizens and to increase the international competitiveness of European HE, which should have been realized by 2010. Specified objectives are:
- a common framework of readable and comparable degrees
- the introduction of undergraduate and postgraduate levels in all countries
- ECTS-compatible credit systems
- a European dimension in quality assurance
- elimination of remaining obstacles to the free mobility of students

In the document it is stated that:

> The Bologna process aims at creating convergence
> and, thus, is not a path towards the 'standardisation'
> or 'uniformisation' of European higher education.
> The fundamental principles of autonomy and
> diversity are respected.

As the EU Treaty states that education falls under national control – the subsidiarity principle – the EU's role is limited to support for and stimulation of the Bologna Process. In European policy the ambition to become a highly competitive knowledge economy – the Lisbon Strategy for Growth and Jobs – is another important driving force behind the Bologna Process.

In her contribution 'The role of higher education for human and social development in Europe' to the Global University Network for Innovation (GUNi) series Higher Education in the World, volume 3, Corbett (2008) comes to the conclusion that, so far, the Bologna debate has been largely about devising policy instruments for recognition and qualification and about exchange and mobility for students and staff. She also states that the Bologna Process could be a good basis on which to work for a more meaningful commitment to the World Conference on Higher Education (WCHE) aims, in association with the EU. Thinking in terms of such a synergy with the WCHE manifesto implies reflection on the European perspective on an interdependent world.

During UNESCO WCHE, held at UNESCO Headquarters in Paris in July 2009, over 1000 participants from 150 countries debated a range of issues including the impact of globalization on education, social responsibility, academic freedom, research and financing. The final communiqué of WCHE (http://www.unesco.org/en/wche2009/) says that:

> At no time in history has it been more important to
> invest in higher education as a major force in building
> an inclusive and diverse knowledge society and to
> advance research, innovation and creativity.

The communiqué also stresses that:

> higher education must pursue the goals of equity,
> relevance and quality simultaneously.

Higher education should lead society in generating global knowledge to address global challenges. It is argued that there is a need for strengthened regional cooperation, for addressing the worldwide shortage of teachers, for offering training and for anticipating societal needs. Meeting these challenges requires new approaches in HE including open and distance learning (ODLs) and information and communication technologies (ICTs). In principle, open educational resources (OERs) can readily be shared by many countries and HEIs. The use of electronic library resources and tools to support teaching, learning and research deserves active exploration. Also the results of scientific research could be made much more available through ICTs in addition to open access to scientific literature. It is stated that for globalization of HE to benefit all, it is critical to ensure equity in access and success, to promote quality and to respect cultural diversity as well as natural sovereignty. The new dynamics call for cross-border cooperation and for partnerships and concerted action at national, regional and international levels.

In April 2009 the ministers responsible for HE in the 46 countries of the Bologna Process convened in Leuven and Louvain-la-Neuve (http://ec.europa.eu/education/news/news1357_eu.htm). The communiqué of this conference starts as follows:

> In the decade up to 2020 European higher education
> has a vital contribution to make in realising a Europe
> of knowledge that is highly creative and innovative.
> Faced with the challenge of an ageing population
> Europe can only succeed in this endeavour if it
> maximises the talents and capacities of all its citizens
> and fully engages in lifelong learning as well as in
> widening participation in higher education.

In the preamble we also read:

> We pledge our full commitment to the goals of the
> European Higher Education Area (EHEA), which is an
> area where higher education is a public responsibility,
> and where all higher education institutions are responsive to the wider needs of society through the diversity
> of their missions. The aim is to ensure that higher
> education institutions have the necessary resources
> to continue to fulfil their full range of purposes such
> as preparing students for life as active citizens in a
> democratic society; preparing students for their future
> careers and enabling their personal development;
> creating and maintaining a broad, advanced knowledge
> base and stimulating research and innovation. The
> necessary ongoing reform of higher education systems
> and policies will continue to be firmly embedded
> in the European values of institutional autonomy,
> academic freedom and social equity and will require
> full participation of students and staff.

It is concluded that over the past decade the EHEA rooted in Europe's intellectual, scientific and cultural heritage has been developed and that the Bologna Process is leading to greater compatibility and comparability of HE systems and is facilitating mobility of students and scholars. The three-cycle structure and the European Standards and Guidelines for quality assurance have been adopted. A European register for quality assurance agencies has been created and national qualification frameworks linked to the overarching EHEA framework based on learning outcomes and workload have been established. However, as not all the objectives set in the Bologna Declaration have been completely achieved, commitment beyond 2010 is necessary.

Higher education priorities for the next decade are a striving for excellence, a focus on quality, the diversity of and within HE systems, and equipping students and staff of HEIs to respond to the changing demands of the fast evolving society. In this context, the provision of equal opportunities to quality education and the integration of lifelong learning opportunities in the educational systems are important aspects. The latter implies that qualifications may be obtained through flexible learning paths, including part-time studies as well as work-based routes. From the employability perspective, both raising initial qualifications and maintaining and renewing a skilled workforce are of major importance. An ongoing curricular reform geared towards the development of learning outcomes, new approaches to teaching and learning, effective support and guidance and more focus on individual learners in all three cycles are important aspects. HE at all levels should be based on state-of-the-art research and development thus fostering innovation and creativity in society. Also the career development opportunities of early stage researchers should be made more attractive.

The European HEIs are also called upon to further internationalize their activities and to engage in global collaboration for SD. Competition on a global scale will be complemented by enhanced policy dialogue and cooperation with other regions of the world. The organization of Bologna Policy Fora should encourage this (http://ec.europa.eu/education/news/news1357_eu.htm). In the context of international openness it is also stated that:

> Transnational education should be governed by the European Standards and Guidelines for quality assurance as applicable within the European Higher Education Area and be in line with the UNESCO/OECD Guidelines for Quality Provision in Cross-Border Higher Education.

From the foregoing it can be concluded that, although the Bologna Process is still mainly about devising policy instruments for recognition and qualification and about exchange and mobility for students and staff in the EHEA, an encouraging agreement with the WCHE ambitions can be seen. However, for facing the 21st century's problems society needs path-breaking solutions conceived in terms of fundamentally different sets of technologies, institutions and social arrangements from those we have today. In other words, paradigm shifts are needed as well.

In 2005 EEAC, the network of European Environment and Sustainable Development Advisory Councils, published the report 'Sustaining Sustainability. A benchmark study on national strategies towards sustainable development and the impact of councils in nine EU ember states' (Niestroy, 2005). The report deals with national strategies for SD in nine EU member states – Belgium, Finland, Germany, Hungary, Ireland, the Netherlands, Portugal, Sweden and United Kingdom – with a focus on the role of national councils for sustainable development in producing and implementing SD strategies. One of the conclusions was that the governance dimension is of great importance for SD policies because the process itself needs much attention. SD strategies cannot be implemented like a 'plan', but need flexible approaches on the governmental side with clear targets and accountable objectives. Such a leading role asks for mechanisms for coordination and improving coherence and for vertical linkages to the regional and local level. Coordination on the 'highest' level is considered beneficial for progress and policy coherence, but at the same time SD strategies need to foster ownership, actions and commitment in all parts of society. According to the report, the lessons to learn for the European level are that the Agenda 21 approach of capacity building, ownership and civil society engagement on all levels seems to be not taken up at the European level. The Commission itself should be more aware of the governance dimension of SD. In particular, horizontal coordination, the styles of cooperation between Directorate-Generals (DGs) and the link between the Lisbon and the SD strategy have to be more clear.

The Commission recognizes that education and training build the critical foundation for sustainable development. The Commission wants to stimulate member states to share knowledge and good practice to stimulate ESD. The report 'Inventory of innovative practices in education for sustainable development' (EC, DG Education and Culture, 2008) presents a range of practices from 27 EU member states and three EEA countries. The selected practices represent different geographical levels and different scales of implementation. Several types of innovation are also covered: innovation in the content, innovation in the delivery method, innovation in forging new partnerships and networks, innovation at the institutional level and innovation in addressing SD.

To illustrate the contemporary position of ESD in European HE, we refer to the good practice database in ESD available on the Copernicus Alliance website (www.copernicus-alliance.net).

THE NATIONAL LEVEL

Currently, a rather extensive overview of national strategies for SD is available for most European countries. The information is available and freely accessible on a web portal (www.sd-network.eu). In general, national strategies for SD connect to themes like poverty reduction, environment protection, biodiversity, innovation towards more sustainable production, climate change, sustainable energy, water management and waste management. National strategies are based on the 1992 Rio Conference outcomes and Agenda 21. Most national strategies have been updated in the past few years taking into account the developments since the World Summit on Sustainable Developent (WSSD) in Johannesburg 2002 (especially the United Nations Decade of Education for Sustainable Development 2005–2014) and the more prominent place on the EU agenda of SD in general. Education is recognized as a main driver for achieving the goals of these national strategies, and especially research is mentioned in connection with innovation, the search for alternative sources of energy and sustainable technologies. On the national level, however, the focus of a policy can vary substantially.

Only a few European countries have released a national strategy specifically addressing HE. Here we give the examples of England and Austria (see Box II.4.1). Only in Sweden has an Act on Higher Education been altered to include the responsibility for HEIs to integrate SD in their research and education.

BOX II.4.1: ESD STRATEGY FOR HIGHER EDUCATION IN ENGLAND AND AUSTRIA

In February 2009 the Higher Education Funding Council for England released its 2008 update to the strategic statement and action plan for SD in higher education. In the foreword, Professor Lord Stern of Brentford (London School of Economics and Political Science), states:

Climate change is the greatest environmental challenge facing the world today. To meet this challenge, the world needs minds capable of creating new possibilities for meeting our basic needs such as energy, water, shelter and food; minds that can transform our daily experiences into ones that allow a sustainable development, safeguarding our opportunities and the environment for future generations.

The higher education sector is where these minds are trained and developed. Therefore, it is crucial that the sector contributes strongly to sustainable development. It can do so by training and expanding these young minds; researching answers to challenges and informing public policy; showing its own understanding and commitment through careful campus management; and by being a responsible employer and active member of the business and local community.

The actual version of the *Austrian Strategy for Education for Sustainable Development* was released in November 2008. A strong relationship with the DESD is the first characteristic to be noticed. Austria is a prominent promoter of the Decade in Europe. In general the Austrian Strategy for ESD aims to support a transformation of awareness toward sustainability among teachers and learners alike. The strategy has the following key elements:
● Establishment within the education system
● Partnerships and networks
● Competence development among teachers
● Research and innovation
● Scenario development
● Monitoring and evaluation

The strategy covers all sectors of education, from formal education to non-formal and informal education. For HE in particular the strategy states that HEIs in Austria have to address the (further) development of interdisciplinary and transdisciplinary approaches in research and education. The institutions are expected to further implement and integrate sustainable development into their core activities. In particular, the education of teachers needs special focus.

For the leading principles for Austrian HE, the strategy refers to the Copernicus University Charter.

ESD in European higher education is more visible on the institutional level and in national and international networks of universities and other knowledge institutions.

CURRICULA AND LEARNING PROCESSES: FROM EDUCATION ON SD TO EDUCATION FOR SD

The United Nations Economic Commission for Europe (UNECE) accepts ESD as an instrument for capacity building for individuals, groups, communities, organizations and countries to make judgements and choices in favour of SD (United Nations Economic Council for Europe, 2005). UNECE member nations are 56 countries located in the European Union, non-EU Western and Eastern Europe, South-East Europe and the Commonwealth of Independent States (CIS), and North America. The adopted strategy stresses the importance of dedicating attention to a broad variety of learning settings indicated as formal, non-formal and informal learning settings. This strategy is the basis for policymaking in the EU countries and other members of UNECE, where these policies will lead to changes in the educational systems of the membership nations.

Learning environments relevant to ESD may be rather different from traditional learning environments. Learners will not only have to experience disciplinary, multidisciplinary and transdisciplinary perspectives, they also will have to take different levels of scale, from local to global, into consideration. Furthermore they will experience that knowledge does not only flow from the disciplinary domain where it is generated in fundamental research to the complex societal context of application. Knowledge to deal with the complexity and uncertainty of societal challenges will also have to be generated, at least partly, in the societal context itself and from there feed back into the university (Gibbons et al., 1994).

The challenges of SD will thus affect the way future professionals are educated and trained in HE. Also the (potential) role of universities in lifelong learning should be reflected upon. During ESD, future professionals need to develop attitudes, knowledge and skills the traditional, mainly disciplinary organized, system of HE often doesn't provide. Professionals should possess integrative competences in addition to disciplinary knowledge. Therefore, in education competence development, a problem-oriented approach, authentic contexts and active, often collaborative, knowledge construction become more and more important in addi-

tion to mastering disciplinary knowledge (de Kraker et al., 2007). A certain degree of disciplinary knowledge remains necessary of course, as it forms the base of inter- and transdisciplinarity knowledge.

In most European educational programmes, awareness raising on SD started with the incorporation of environmental and sustainability issues in separate courses in traditional disciplines such as biology, chemistry and so on. Recently, new master's programmes have been developed specifically aiming the learning *for* sustainable development. For example, Leiden University and Delft University of Technology have developed together an MSc programme in Industrial Ecology for students of both universities (see: http://www.cml.leiden.edu/research/industrialecology). In this programme students are being trained specifically to gather the knowledge, insight and skills required in multidisciplinary efforts to analyse sustainability problems and to contribute to better decision-making in managing the world's natural resources, environmental quality and biodiversity. In other European countries similar developments can be noted, for example at the KTH Royal Institute of Technology in Sweden. Elsewhere in Europe specific educational programmes (bachelor's and master's level) are being developed focusing on the *transition* towards a more sustainable society. One such example is the Creative Sustainability programme at Aalto University School of Economics in Finland. An extensive list of study options being developed by European HEIs can be found at, for example, www.masterstudies.com.

What about students who do not have their primary focus on studying sustainability? They should be able to get at least some basic understanding about SD during their training period. Again as an example, we look at developments at Leiden University. Here a university-wide general multidisciplinary minor on Sustainable Development at bachelor level has recently been developed (30 EC). This minor has an interdisciplinary character and is designed for students from all faculties. This means that it does not matter whether students study humanities, natural sciences or social sciences – they can all join. In addition to more traditional forms of education delivery such as lectures, students are encouraged to learn from each other by the organization of seminars, excursions and working groups for exchanging knowledge between the different disciplines. Here HE focuses on (1) concepts of SD, including environmental problems, drivers behind these problems, innovation of societies and industries; (2) methods for SD, such as planning and visioning, negotiation, participatory research, ecological design principles, economic instruments; and (3) thematic analysis and solutions development, in which students work in groups on a specific theme in SD, such as biofuels.

The Graz University in Austria developed a creative view on ESD by introducing intergenerational learning and ESD (http://www.uni-graz.at/rce/EN/Efocusgroups_lll.htm). In Spain the reputable University of Technology of Catalonia has integrated SD into its teaching programmes and in its principles as a university for innovation (Ferrer-Balas et al., 2004).

On 20 December 2002 the United Nations General Assembly adopted Resolution 57/254, which declared the United Nations Decade of Education for Sustainable Development (DESD 2005–2014). DESD is a global platform that seeks to (1) embed SD into all learning spheres, (2) reorient education and (3) develop initiatives that can showcase the special role of ESD. UNESCO is identified as the international lead agency. In the official DESD documents the objective is formulated as: 'a world where everyone has the opportunity to benefit from education and learn the values, behaviour and lifestyles required for a sustainable future and for positive societal transformation' (UNESCO, 2006).

In chapter 36 of Agenda 21 'Promoting Education, Public Awareness and Training' the four thrusts of ESD were defined (McKeown and Hopkins, 2010):

1. Improving access to quality basic education
2. Reorienting existing education to address sustainability
3. Increasing public understanding and awareness of sustainability
4. Providing training for all sectors of the economy

Because Europe and North America have relatively high literacy rates, it is understandable that access to basic education is not a priority for these nations. An important objective is to give ESD a place in curricula in education. There are many initiatives going on, but the contributions of various disciplines and specific schools' efforts go unnoticed (McKeown, 2002). The challenge is to identify, stimulate and connect these different initiatives within the existing educational system in such a way that individuals are encouraged to use their talents to contribute to a better future for all. Salcedo-Rahola and Mulder (2008) provide an overview of the development of master's programmes across Europe.

To monitor and assess progress over 10 years a UNESCO Global Monitoring and Evaluation Framework for DESD was formulated (Tilbury, 2009). But, as Tilbury remarks:

> success of the DESD will be judged not only by the UN Monitoring and Evaluation mechanisms set in place by UNESCO but also by how it meets the expectations from stakeholders across the globe who strive for more sustainable communities.

RESEARCH

As has been argued in the preceding paragraphs, in order to face the 21st century's problems society needs path-breaking solutions in terms of fundamentally different sets of technologies, institutions and social arrangements from those we have today. This implies not only that the generation of new knowledge through research in natural and social sciences and engineering is needed, but also that new approaches in research methodology have to be established. Innovative approaches in knowledge transfer between research and society and in the way individuals are educated and trained are also needed. The remainder of this section will focus on the research agenda for ESD.

When discussing ESD-related research one can take a wider approach and include SD-related research on, for example, climate change or reusable energies, as well as other interesting research areas such as trying to predict the Peak Oil moment (for example the London Metropolitan University's ACEGES project: http://www.londonmet.ac.uk/lmbs/research/cibs/aceges/home.cfm) or research on sustainable production and consumption. All these research topics have a clear relationship with SD and the research results will find their way to students through teaching at the universities performing this research.

Research on ESD that takes a narrow approach focuses on the changes required in education.

A NEED FOR DIFFERENT APPROACHES

In the search for research approaches addressing SD and ESD problems, one example has already been mentioned. The field of industrial ecology has emerged and is integrated in the teaching offerings of many European universities. The research topics that are typical for industrial ecology show the integrative approach and the interdisciplinarity that is required to study complex ESD-related problems. In Box II.4.2 industrial ecology as a field of research is explained.

BOX II.4.2: WHAT IS INDUSTRIAL ECOLOGY?

Industrial ecology is a relatively new field of research that is rapidly emerging on a global scale. Frosch and Gallopoulos (1989) first introduced the term Industrial Ecology together with the concept of Industrial Ecosystems, referring to the design of production sites in analogy to natural ecosystems.

Industrial ecology as a field of research was first introduced at a colloquium at the US National Academy of Sciences in 1991. The field of industrial ecology has grown fast in recent years and now several initiatives have been taken for education programmes in this area (Van der Voet et al., 2002). The *Journal of Industrial Ecology* (since 1997, published by Wiley, http://onlinelibrary.wiley.com/journal/10.1111/(ISSN)1530-9290) and the International Society for Industrial Ecology (since 2001, http://www.is4ie.org) give Industrial Ecology a strong position in the international scientific community.

THE CONCEPT OF INDUSTRIAL ECOLOGY

Industrial ecology aims at a sustainable co-existence of the technosphere and the environment. The analogy between natural and technical systems and processes is a core concept. Processes in nature, where cycles are closed and waste from one process is input for another, are models for socio-technological processes.

Ayres (1989) elaborated the biosphere–technosphere analogy as a useful image to develop in his description of 'Industrial Metabolism'. In short, the analogy amounts to the following:

- In the biosphere, evolution has resulted in efficient use of materials and energy in systems to build and break down functional materials in a steady state, if we consider planet Earth as one system.
- In the technosphere, resources are exploited and unusable waste streams to soil, water, and air are produced.
- By learning from the biosphere, society may design and manage its socio-technological processes in a more sustainable manner, resulting in speeding up technological evolution towards a state of material use with more efficiency and with fewer unusable side products.

Source: (cf. http://ie.leidendelft.nl/what-is-ie/)

In research on ESD the focus is on understanding the process of learning that is required to comprehend the full impact of SD and how education can contribute to achieving a more sustainable society. This means that for research on ESD new research approaches (or the re-introduction of old approaches) are required. One aspect that stands out when analysing this type of research is that most of this research is context related. This means that this research involves stakeholders, is more participatory or is dealing with real-life situations rather than with controlled laboratory setups.

One approach to research on ESD is to look at research problems from the perspective of systems thinking (Martin, 2005).

Another example of an emerging field of research in SD is the field of social learning (Fadeeva, 2007). Community-based research involving local and regional stakeholders, including universities is seen as a way of building knowledge to understand the complexity of SD. Fadeeva (2007) argues that:

> The emphasis of social learning on bottom-up formulation of the sustainability agenda and the importance of multiple ways of knowing and learning, as opposed to the necessarily consensus driven agenda,

re-emphasises and refines DESD's call for collaboration and the importance of different perspectives.

In her review on ESD processes and learning, Tilbury (2011) concludes that as well as 'gaining of knowledge, values and theories related to SD ... ESD learning also refers to:

- Learning to ask critical questions
- Learning to clarify one's own values
- Learning to envision more positive and sustainable futures
- Learning to think systemically
- Learning to respond through applied learning
- Learning to explore the dialectic between tradition and innovation'

Research focusing on understanding the competences needed to work in the field of ESD as an instructor or as a problem solver is emerging. First examples show a complex set of competences that educational systems need to adopt in order to fulfil the mission (Barth et al., 2007).

Research and development activities in line with DESD objectives need a different organizational structure to incorporate the bottom-up and multi-stakeholder approach to research on ESD. The emergence of Regional Centres of Expertise (RCEs) on ESD (Fadeeva, 2007) is creating regional networks of actors that are looking for alternative approaches and organizing principles. Often universities are the drivers behind these so-called RCEs (see section below, 'Stakeholder collaboration on the regional level' for more information on RCEs). For example, ESADE Business School in Spain (ranking in the top 10 worldwide and a founding member of RCE Barcelona) has developed special programmes to mobilize their research expertise for research targeting corporate social responsibility (CSR), non-governmental organization (NGO) management and leadership, and social initiatives.

Stakeholder involvement in research projects is outside the normal research discipline. This means that researchers trained to perform such research need additional skills and tools. For this purpose and also for learning more on local aspects of effects of climate change the EU-funded project 'The lived experience of climate change' was initiated (http://www.leche.open.ac.uk/). The project will develop online curriculum resources and virtual learning communities. These resources will support master's dissertations in the broad area of the lived experience of climate change – how individuals and organizations conceive and respond to its perceived local impacts, for example extreme weather or biodiversity changes. They can be used flexibly by universities to complement existing postgraduate programmes.

As was mentioned before, not all developments can be classified as 'new'. The concept of *science shops*, for example, emerged in the Netherlands in the 1970s and their main function is to increase both public awareness and to provide access to science and technology to laymen or non-profit organizations. A science shop is a facility, often attached to a specific department of a university or an NGO, which provides independent participatory research support in response to concerns experienced by civil society. It's a demand-driven and bottom-up approach to research. Their work can be described as community-based research (CBR).

Science shops are managed and operated by both permanent staff members and students who screen questions provided by members of civil society. Science shop staff use these questions to provide challenging problems to both research students and university faculty members in hope of finding solutions to the question. Students who participate in science shops can often acquire credits towards their degree. Also, many students do their postgraduate work on problems identified by science shops.

The Dutch system has inspired science shops in nations across Europe such as Denmark, Austria, Germany, Norway, the UK, Belgium and Romania. Moreover, there are currently science shops in countries outside Europe such as Canada (source: www.livingknowledge.org). The EU funded CIPAST (Citizen Participation in Science and Technology) project 2005–2008 renewed the role of science shops in Europe and connected the concept to the interdisciplinary approach in ESD-related research.

INSTITUTIONAL MANAGEMENT AND OPERATIONS

NETWORKING

The ability to work together in teams with persons from different disciplinary, social and cultural backgrounds is a vital aspect of ESD. Future professionals and world citizens should also be able to think, communicate and collaborate across boundaries that divide disciplinary, national and cultural perspectives. Learning environments in traditional curricula have shortcomings in that respect as they tend to focus mainly on disciplinary approaches. Existing networks like the Baltic University Programme (BUP) (http://www.balticuniv.uu.se) show a shift in focus from environmental education to education for sustainable development.

Recently a number of European universities have founded the Copernicus Alliance (CA – www.copernicus-alliance.net), a network connecting European institutions and other networks in HE in Europe to collaboratively spread this message.

BOX II.4.3: THE DATABASE OF BEST PRACTICES IN ESD

The EU-funded project 3-LENSUS (Lifelong Learning Network for a Sustainable Europe, 2009–2010: http://www.3-lensus.eu) developed among others a database to collect best practices in ESD across Europe. The consortium partners, consisting of European universities and several RCEs on ESD connected to their respective networks to collect the first set of projects. Based on the evaluation of the available literature a set of indicators was developed. The projects collected were judged in terms of these indicators. After the end of the project the database was transferred to the Copernicus Alliance and is now available on the website (www.copernicus-alliance.net). In the future this database can grow into a benchmark for best practices on ESD in Europe.

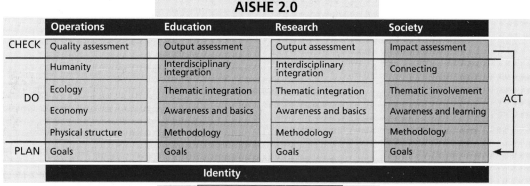

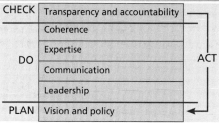

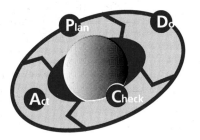

Deming Cycle
Source: http://commons.wikimedia.org/wiki/

The philosophy of the AISHE model is based on the EFQM Excellence model, a model for quality management, developed by the European Foundation for Quality Management (EFQM, 1991). The model is based on the concept of continuous improvement. This process can be described with the so-called 'Deming Cycle' (Deming, 1986).

Applying the AISHE 2.0 instrument means that a university will get a detailed and realistic image of the present situation regarding the integration of sustainability in the university or part of it, in one curriculum or more, depending on the level of the institution where the assessment is applied.

In addition the university will get a description of the desired situation on an agreed upon later date. This description can form the basis for a coherent policy on sustainable development for the university.

Those involved in the assessment procedure can become the champions of the policy developed. If used for that purpose the assessment can result in a certificate.

As the AISHE 2.0 instrument is based on continuous assessment, it is advisable to repeat the assessment every two to three years to document the improvement and to collect empirical evidence to adapt the policy.

Consortia of European universities team up to collaboratively develop new tools and approaches to research. The LECH-e project (http://www.leche.open.ac.uk/) for example:

> brings together nine European Higher Education Institutions across six countries, creating a community of scholars, students and citizens to make a major contribution to sustainable development education and research. Supported by the European Union Lifelong Learning Erasmus Programme, the project will develop online curriculum resources and virtual learning communities. These resources will support Masters dissertations in the broad area of the lived experience of climate change – how individuals and organizations conceive and respond to its perceived local impacts, for example extreme weather or biodiversity changes. They can be used flexibly by universities to complement existing postgraduate programmes. At the end of the project in May 2011 they will become open educational resources for any university to use.

TRANSFORMATION

For those universities that take their responsibility towards ESD seriously and want to include competences for sustainability in their curricula an instrument has been developed to assess their level of achievement. The Assessment Instrument for Sustainability in Higher Education (AISHE) 2.0 Manual is developed to provide such an instrument (Roorda et al., 2009).

BOTTOM-UP OR TOP-DOWN?

The development of European universities into institutions that can be considered sustainable is a long process. But it is not without hope. In Germany for example, Adomssent (2010) concludes that the number of institutions that have introduced environmental management systems is now substantial. Moreover many institutions have moved to producing Sustainable Development Reports.

In this whole development a distinction can be made between the development of educational and research programmes by the academic staff and the academic departments and the emerging of 'green universities'. The latter refers to all the efforts undertaken by universities to become sustainable operations (including greening the campus, sustainable supply chain management, the use of renewable energies or waste management).

The question arises: where did this come from? Was it an individual staff member who started pushing or was it the insight of the executives developing new strategies and policies for the university? In general, research-driven universities cannot be changed by top-down

measures. The 'academic freedom' of the lecturers and researchers is one of the best-protected rights in HE with the Magna Charta Observatory of Fundamental University Values and Rights in Bologna, Italy, as the guardian.

The success of the introduction of SD and ESD in European universities is no doubt based at the roots. Staff members have taken initiatives and have introduced the topic into their research and teaching. The departments and institutes (and their management) have been instrumental in the growth of the number of educational and research programmes. But it is without any doubt that the support of the universities' top management is crucial in mainstreaming SD in universities across Europe.

SOCIAL AND COMMUNITY ENGAGEMENT

VIRTUAL LEARNING ENVIRONMENTS

If ESD asks for innovative learning environments in which learners can experience different perspectives on a problem and different levels of scale, the opportunities of ICT in the design and implementation of learning environments deserves active exploration. ICT should not be considered as a means to replace people, however, but as a means to support human activities. The use of ICT instruments enables people to design, develop and implement learning processes and learning environments that optimally enhance individuals' learning processes. ICT is also most useful for introducing an international component in individual learning environments. This refers not only to the use of the internet for access to information, but also to, for instance, joint curriculum design by universities co-operating in a network. In addition, the availability of and easy access to social software such as Facebook, Hyves, LinkedIn and Twitter can create new opportunities for learning environments and communities. Finally, virtual mobility is just as important as physical mobility in the internationalization of HE. Innovative use of ICT should therefore be placed in the context of how the supportive infrastructure for learning – in the educational system – is presently organized (Cörvers et al., 2007; Dam-Mieras, van et al., 2007).

THE OPEDUCA PROJECT

An example of an approach that emerged outside formal education and follows a bottom-up development of learner-focused learning experiences is presented in the case of OPEDUCA (Dutch acronym for: Open Educatieve Omgeving en Regio – Open Educational Environment and Region).

BOX II.4.5: LEARNING FOR SUSTAINABLE DEVELOPMENT – FUTURE-ORIENTED LEARNING IN A REGIONAL CONTEXT: OPEDUCA

The OPEDUCA concept was developed by a group of teachers, schools, universities, companies and interested experts and individuals in the Netherlands, inspired by the ideas of Mr Jos Eussen, the current director of RCE Rhine-Meuse (Rikers et al., 2010). RCE stands for 'Regional Centre of Expertise on Education for Sustainable Development (ESD)', an initiative of the United Nations University in Tokyo.

The basis for the OPEDUCA concept is to step outside the existing educational structure and imagine a new one, better equipped for future-oriented learning, using the knowledge available in the region across individuals, institutions and organizations. In the OPEDUCA concept the learner and the learner life cycle take the lead. Learning experiences are developed following the ageing of the learner and meeting knowledge demands at different stages in life. Following the learner life cycle 'continuous learning paths' are being developed and offered. In this approach the stepwise educational system (pre-school, primary, secondary, tertiary, post-initial, lifelong learning) disappears and is replaced by the individual who is constantly rewarding his/her learning needs. For the teaching organizations this means that the offerings have to be designed anew, no longer topic-based or following the classical categorization of sciences. The new approach builds on learning offers based on high-level themes that are relevant to the learner. For example, themes such as 'water' or 'energy' or 'money' or 'health and hygiene'.

In this approach teaching institutions on all levels and the private sector collaborate in creating the best possible learning option. Depending on the regional situation and the beliefs of the parties involved, this will allow for a diversity of learning options. What is avoided in this concept is an expensive third-party involvement in the development process. Only those directly involved (teachers, students, parents, schools, universities, government, and companies) or benefiting from the learning process are co-producers. The products delivered by the OPEDUCA formula target the main players in the process, teachers, students and companies. For these target groups dedicated programmes are developed:

- Flight for Knowledge: targeting the learner and organized in themes
- Business Class: targeting the business sector to participate in creating theme-based Flights for Knowledge
- Teacher Empowerment: targeting the teacher who will play a key role in building Flights for Knowledge

STAKEHOLDER COLLABORATION ON THE REGIONAL LEVEL

Collaboration of different stakeholders is a key feature in ESD. Another feature is that this collaboration develops on a regional level. The need for stakeholder collaboration on a regional level is growing, especially in urbanized areas of Europe, where competition for land use and other resources is fierce, or countryside where nature is threatened by growing cities, pollution, mining or other non-sustainable human behaviour. In particular the search for information and/or knowledge is a binding factor for this regional collaboration, creating a natural role for knowledge institutions to step in as a partner.

Several initiatives have developed in Europe, based on the desire to create an interface between academia and society. In existence for over 20 years, the Baltic University Programme (www.balticuniv. uu.se) is one of the oldest initiatives. The BUP is a network of about 225 universities and other institutes of higher learning throughout the Baltic Sea region. The Programme focuses on questions of SD, environmental protection, and democracy in the Baltic Sea region. The aim is to support the key role that universities play in a democratic and peaceful SD. This is achieved by developing university courses, and by participation in projects in cooperation with authorities, municipalities and others.

The growing need on the regional level appeared to be fertile soil for the concept of Regional Centres of Expertise on ESD (in short RCEs) (Fadeeva and Mochizuki, 2010; Rikers et al., 2010). The concept of RCEs was introduced at the WSSD in Johannesburg in 2002 and became one of the instruments for the UN Decade of Education for Sustainable Development (UNESCO, 2006). Launching the concept of RCEs in regions looking for a collaborative model addressing sustainability issues resulted in a fast-growing global network of RCEs. The flagship project engaging several RCEs and candidate RCEs was the EU-funded 3-LENSUS project

(Lifelong Learning Network for Sustainable Development). The project has delivered a database for good practices in ESD that is now integrated in the Copernicus Alliance website (www.copernicus-alliance.org). The second product of the project is a set of indicators to be used to distinguish good practices in ESD. The indicators and background information are available in the 3-LENSUS handbook: *Multi-Actor Learning for Sustainable Regional Development in Europe: A Handbook of Best Practice* (Barton and Dlouhá, 2011). The handbook can be downloaded from the 3-LENSUS website (www.3-lensus.eu).

In Ireland the Campus Engage Network (www. campusengage.ie) started in 2009 and will provide a forum for discussion and sharing of information among HE academics, administrators and students, and people involved in community organizations.

The Partnership for Education and Research about Responsible Living (PERL) is a global initiative that has strong roots in Europe. PERL is a partnership of educators and researchers from over 120 institutions in more than 50 countries – working to empower citizens to live responsible and sustainable lifestyles. PERL aims to advance education for responsible living by focusing on consumer citizenship, education for sustainable consumption, social innovation and sustainable lifestyles.

CONCLUDING REFLECTIONS

For sustainable development, path-breaking solutions in terms of fundamentally different sets of technologies, institutions and social arrangements from those we have today are needed. This calls for awareness of threats to and opportunities for survival in all spheres and levels of development decision-making within society, politics, business and science on the one hand and for creative and innovative solutions on the other. Education in all its forms and at all levels – formal, non-formal and informal – could be an important societal change factor but that calls for critical reflection on the way education is organized.

In Europe, as in many other regions of the world, ESD emerged from environmental research and education that entered the academic world in the 1970s. SD is a much broader field, however, dealing also with economic and cultural aspects. In HE a broad range of relevant approaches to ESD can be identified, but the programmes are increasingly also offered under a label other than sustainable development. For instance, within Leiden University quite a few interfaces with

SD can be mentioned. The multi- and interdisciplinary research domains 'Global interaction of people, culture and power through the ages', 'Interaction between legal systems', 'Political legitimacy: institutions and identities', 'Asia modernity's and traditions' all have ground in common with SD. In the Faculty of Mathematics and Natural Sciences fundamental research on bio-solar energy has a prominent place and the activities of the Institute of Environmental Sciences have been described above. Within the Faculty of Law examples are the investigations in social cohesion, sustainable globalization and poverty and the interface between law and climate change. The tensions between mankind and nature, between the global and the local levels, between poverty and sustainable development and between cultural perspectives are investigated by the Institute of Anthropology and Development Sociology in the context of research on development, global politics and global economy. Because at Leiden University education is research inspired, the findings from these topics will also be fed back into a variety of areas of education. In many other European universities similar trends can be recognized. Most initiatives are still more focused on awareness raising than on path-breaking solutions, but both types are needed of course.

For education to act as a societal change factor, incremental improvements of and within existing formal education are not enough. Innovative solutions have to be found and a fading out of the borders between formal, non-formal and informal education has to occur. The potential contribution of ICTs deserves active exploration. How can we create learning environments in which people from different backgrounds – disciplinary, national, cultural – work and learn together? Do Open Education Resources (OERs) (Mulder, 2010) offer a good approach for working together on the design and development of good quality educational materials on the one hand while remaining competitors on the other? Are social networks – Facebook, Hyves, LinkedIn, Twitter – useful instruments in the innovation of education and learning?

The task ahead for the remaining part of the Decade of Education for Sustainable Development is to come up with research-based answers to the question that Tilbury (2011) describes as 'a direct relationship between processes and outcomes in ESD'. Therefore it was concluded at a workshop at the 5th International Barcelona Conference on Higher Education 'Higher Education's Commitment to Sustainability: from Understanding to Action', Barcelona 23–25 November 2010, Universitat Politecnica de Catalunya

(UPC) that for Europe the following priority strategies are recommended:

- To firmly embed ESD in the curricula and operations of HEIs, it is essential to include SD criteria in their Quality Assurance mechanisms. Instruments like the AISHE model should be considered.
- To show commitment, European universities should engage in publishing an annual report on their SD achievements.
- HEIs should engage in sustainable regional development and, for example, participate in Regional Centres of Expertise on ESD or initiate such centres in their home region.
- EU subsidy programmes should stimulate education *for* sustainable development initiatives.
- EU subsidy programmes should stimulate European-wide collaboration and networking.

REFERENCES

Adomssent, Maik (2010): Hochschule und Nachhaltigkeit. Eine kritische Bestandsaufnahme. In: *ZEP – Zeitschrift fur internationale Bildungsforschung und Entwicklungspadagogik*, **33**(4) pp. 33–4. (University and Sustainability. A critical analyses. In: *ZEP – Journal for international research in education and development pedagogic.*)

Ayres R.U. (1989) Industrial metabolism. In: Ausubel, J.H. and Sladovich, H.E. (eds) *Technology and Environment*. Washington, DC: National Academy Press, pp. 50–69.

Barth, M., Godemann, J., Rieckmann, M. and Stoltenberg, U. (2007) Developing key competencies for sustainable development in higher education. *International Journal of Sustainability in Higher Education*, **8**(4), pp. 416–30.

Barton, A. and Dlouhá, J. (eds) (2011) *Multi-Actor Learning for Sustainable Regional Development in Europe: A Handbook of Best Practice*. Guildford UK: Grosvenor House Publishing.

Corbett, A. (2008) The role of higher education for human and social development in Europe, *Higher Education in the World*, Volume 3. *Higher Education: New Challenges and Emerging Roles for Human and Social Development*, Palgrave Macmillan, pp. 240–58.

Cörvers, R., Leinders, J. and Dam-Mieras, M.C.E. van (2007) Virtual seminars – or how to foster an international, multidisciplinary dialogue on sustainable development. In: *Crossing boundaries. Innovative learning for sustainable development in higher education*, Kraker, J. de Lansu, A., and van Dam-Mieras, R. (eds) Frankfurt am Main: Verlag für Akademische Schriften, pp. 142–87.

Dam-Mieras, M.C.E. van, Lansu, A., Rieckmann, M. and Michelsen, G. (2007) Development of an interdisciplinary intercultural master's program on sustainability: Learning from the richness of diversity. *Innovative Higher Education*, **32**(5).

Deming, W.E. (1986) *Out of the Crisis*. Cambridge: MIT Press.

EC, DG Education and Culture (2008) Inventory of innovative practices in education for sustainable development.

http://ec.europa.eu/education/moreinformation/doc/sustdev_en.pdf).

EFQM (1991) EFQM Model. European Foundation for Quality Management, http://www.efqm.org.

Fadeeva, Z. (2007) From centre of excellence to centre of expertise: Regional centres of expertise on education for sustainable development. In: Wals, A.E.J. (ed.) (2007) *Social Learning: Towards a Sustainable World*. The Netherlands: Wageningen Academic Publishers.

Fadeeva, Z. and Mochizuki, Y. (2010) Roles of regional centres of expertise on education for sustainable development. *Journal of Education for Sustainable Development*, **4**, pp. 51–9.

Ferrer-Balas, D., Bruno, J., de Mingo, M. and Sans, R. (2004) Advances in education transformation towards sustainable development at the Technical University of Catalonia, Barcelona. *International Journal of Sustainability in Higher Education*, **5**(3), pp. 251–66.

Frosch, R.A. and Gallopoulos, N.E. (1989) Strategies for manufacturing. *Scientific American,* **261**(3), 144–52.

Funtowicz, S.O. and Ravetz, J. (2002) Post-Normal Science: environmental policy under conditions of complexity. http//www.nusap.net.

Gibbons, M., Limoges, C., Nowotny, H., Schwartzmann, S., Schott, P. and Trow, M. (1994) *The New Prodcution of Knowledge*. London: Sage.

Jansen, L., Weaver, P. and van Dam-Mieras, M.C.E. (2008) Education to meet new challenges in a networked society. In: Larkley, J.E. and Maynhard, V.B. (eds) *Innovation in Education*. Nova Science Publishers Inc., pp. 1–50.

Kessels, J., Boers, E. and Mostert, P. (2002) *Vrije ruimte. Filosoferen in organisaties*. Amsterdam: Uitgeverij Boom.

Kraker, J. de, Lansu, A. and Dam-Mieras, M.C.E. van (2007) Competences and competence-based learning for sustainable development. In: Kraker, J. de, Lansu, A. and van Dam-Mieras, R. (eds) *Crossing Boundaries. Innovative Learning for Sustainable Development in Higher Education*. Frankfurt am Main: Verlag für Akademische Schriften, pp. 103–14.

Loorbach, D. and Rotmans, J. (2006) Managing transitions for sustainable development, www.ksinetwork.nl/down/output/publications/TM_Itchapter.pdf

Martin, Stephen (2005) Sustainability, systems thinking and professional practice. *Systemic Practice and Action Research*, **18**(2), pp. 163–71.

McKeown, R. (2002) Progress has been made in education for sustainable development. *Applied Environmental Education and Communication*, **1**, pp. 21–3.

McKeown, R. and Hopkins, C. (2010) Moving beyond the EE and ESD disciplinary debate in formal education. *Journal of Education for Sustainable Development*, **1**, pp. 17–26.

Mulder, F. (2010) The advancement of Lifelong Learning through Open Educational Resources in an open and flexible (self) learning context. Paper presented at the handover of the rectorate at the Open Universiteit in the Netherlands on 10 December 2010, www.ou.nl/docs/campagnes/scop/oer_paper_by_fred_mulder.pdf

Niestroy, I. (2005) *Sustaining Sustainability. A benchmark study on national strategies towards sustainable development and the impact of councils in nine EU member states*. Utrecht: Uitgeverij Lemma bv.

Rikers, J., Hermans, J. and Eussen, J. (2010) Building RCE Rhine-Meuse. *Journal of Education for Sustainable Development*, **4**, pp. 93–104.

Roorda, N., Rammel, C., Waara, S. and Fra Paleo, U. (2009) AISHE 2.0 Manual, accessed at: http://www.hu2.se/2010v/AISHE_2.0_Manual_-_2nd_draftswa.pdf

Salcedo-Rahola, B. and Mulder, K. (2008) *Sustainable Development in Higher Education: What has Europe got to offer?* SDPromo Report, Delft University of Technology.

Tilbury, D. (2009) A United Nations Decade of Education for Sustainable Development (2005–14): What difference will it make? *Journal of Education for Sustainable Development*, **3**, pp. 87–97.

Tilbury, D. (2011) *Education for Sustainable Development: An Expert Review of Processes and Learning.* Paris: UNESCO.

UNESCO and UNU (2005) *Proceedings of the International Conference Globalisation and Intangible Cultural Heritage*, 26–27 August 2004, Tokyo.

UNESCO (2006) *Framework for the UN DESD International Implementation Scheme.* Paris: UNESCO.

United Nations Economic Council for Europe (2005) *UNECE Strategy for Education for Sustainable Development*, Adopted at the high-level meeting of Environmental and Education Ministries Vilnius. Geneva: UNECE.

Voet, E. van der, Baas, L., Hendriks, Ch., Kleijn, R., Mulder, K., Roome, N. and Udo de Haes H.A. (2002) Interuniversity Masters curriculum Industrial Ecology. Proceedings Conference Engineering Education in Sustainable Development, 24–25 October 2002, Delft University of Technology.

Wal, K. van der (2003) Globalisierung, Nachhaltigkeit und Ethik. Natur und Kultur. *Tranzdisziplinäre Zeitschrift für ökologische Nachhaltigkeit*, **4**(1), pp. 100–19.

Inside View II.5
Higher education commitment to sustainability in the Mediterranean area: from understanding to action

Michael Scoullos

The current 'state' of education for sustainable development (ESD) in the Mediterranean countries is the result of long and persistent effort by a number of organizations and individuals at both the environmental and educational fronts. It is hard to isolate the commitment to sustainability of higher education from the overall evolution and development of environmental education in its widest context, which includes formal, non-formal, and informal modes and is combined with the flow of information to, and raising the awareness of, the wider public. In fact, the university and research community of the late 1960s and early 1970s, throughout the Mediterranean, was among the first, worldwide, to point out the emerging serious problems linked with marine pollution and loss of biodiversity. Academics at that time had already emphasized the links between the damage caused by pollution and unsustainable patterns of development.

A series of seminars and workshops in the 1970s addressing environment and development issues at university level in France, Greece, Italy, Lebanon and Spain could be identified, while in conferences – such as those organized frequently by CIESM/Commission Internationale pour l'Exploration Scientifique de la Mer Mediterranee (Monaco), the Club of Rome (Italy), the 'Pacem in Maribus'/International Ocean Institute (Malta), the Ekistics/Doxiades Group (Athens), and so on – the issue of the needed education and research was repeatedly discussed. Several discrete initiatives were mentioned for the introduction of relevant issues in much academic teaching, mostly in natural and health sciences (Chemistry, Biology, Toxicology), in City Planning – Architecture and, to a lesser extend, in other disciplines (Law, Social sciences).

The environment movement in the Mediterranean was largely started from these initiatives,[1] which were also the root for environmental education in the region. As it is known, environmental education (EE) was promoted considerably in the 1970s, during the milestone Conference of Stockholm (1972), in which a proposal was made for the official recognition of EE as a policy tool for the protection of the environment in all countries; in Belgrade (1975), where participants formulated the concepts, visions and the characteristics of EE; and in Tbilisi (1977), which resulted in an important reference text for all the effort that followed until today. The Mediterranean academic community was very active in all these fora and provided a considerable, though fragmented, dissemination to, and feedback from, the higher education institutions (HEIs) of the region.

From its first steps, the vision of Tbilisi already embodied a wide spectrum of environmental, social, ethical, economic and cultural objectives which are essential to the understanding and consolidation of the current notion of 'education for sustainable development' (ESD). Thus, the principles of Tbilisi were translated early on into educational policies – and many programmes – in several Mediterranean countries. They helped introduce relevant issues in specific sectors and courses in higher education and set the pace of action at the national and regional level. Subsequent application at the formal schooling system level, however, proved quite difficult.[2]

It is no coincidence that in the Mediterranean, where in the 1970s and 1980s the 'cold war' was still very visible with both the American and Soviet fleets present, EE also attempted to address the risks from armed conflicts. Therefore UNESCO asked a Mediterranean university teacher to prepare the background document 'Environmental Education as a Vehicle for International Comprehension and Peace' for the Moscow '10 years from Tbilisi' Conference (1987).[3] As a consequence, relevant issues were introduced in several Mediterranean universities, mostly under 'International relationships' and 'Law'.

In the year of the Moscow UNESCO Conference (1987), the concept of sustainable development was formally introduced by the Brundtland 'Our Common Future' report involving in a more direct and 'equal' way the sectors of economy, environment and society. This was clearly depicted in the Rio Earth Summit (1992) and especially in its 'Agenda 21', which devoted its 36th chapter to the relevant education.

Meanwhile, throughout the 1980s and early 1990s various 'targeted' types of education were developed in some Mediterranean HEIs, such as 'development education', 'peace education', 'human rights education', 'health education', and 'multicultural education'.[4]

The Rio provisions of Chapter 36 were not easily put into action either by elementary or by higher education. In the Mediterranean, UNESCO, together with the University of Athens and the Mediterranean Information Office for Environment, Culture and Sustainable Development (MIO-ECSDE) organized the 'Re-orienting Environmental Education for Sustainable Development' inter-regional workshop (Athens, June 1995),[5] which made recommendations for the necessary transformations and proposed the organization of the 'Twenty Years from Tbilisi' and halfway between Rio and Johannesburg conference 'Environment and Society: Education and Public Awareness for Sustainability' in the Mediterranean city of Thessaloniki, in December 1997, attended by 1283 participants from 83 countries.[6] The conference also marked the shift from EE to ESD at the higher education level throughout the world, and of course in the Mediterranean region.

After the Thessaloniki conference, it became clear that in order to properly deliver ESD there was a need to do more than include contemporary societal, ecological and cultural parameters in EE. Rather, ESD involves a new mindset, in which these parameters should be understood throughout the curriculum not as being in conflict (as they are commonly portrayed within false dilemmas) but in full synergy. Having this in mind, higher education in the Mediterranean countries had to overcome a large number of serious obstacles. Most of the academic work in the region follows – even today – well established, in some cases, 'monolithic', 'sectoral-disciplinary' approaches with little tradition for inter-cooperation and no 'appreciation' for multi – and intra – disciplinarity, which is still viewed by many academics and university departments as 'soft', 'not solid', or 'superficial', approaches. In the entire period from Rio (1992) to Johannesburg (2002) the vast majority of Mediterranean universities experienced internal hesitations/suspicions and, in some cases, struggle over the effort of some academics to adapt to new realities and introduce ESD or, rather, some aspects of it, in their courses. The existing educational systems were not oriented to SD and the Millennium Development Goals focused on few educational targets, referring to overall basic education viewed in a very 'traditional' way.

There was a need for the Johannesburg Summit to focus more on education and also find ways to promote ESD. To this end, MIO-ECSDE, together with other actors from Mediterranean universities, launched the 'ERA 21' campaign. This campaign for **E**ducation **Re** **A**ffirmation for the 21st century was signed by thousands of academics and asked the Summit to pay attention to the appropriate education for bringing about the required change towards SD. This, together with the launching of MEdIES (Mediterranean Education Initiative for Environment and Sustainability) during the Summit (www.medies.net), as a TYPE II Initiative under the UN and also in synergy with several other important non-Mediterranean Initiatives and efforts had, indeed, some impact.

The conclusions of the Johannesburg Summit (2002) made repeated references to ESD and emphasized the need for inclusion of SD in all educational systems at all levels. During the Summit, the launching of a 'Decade for Education for Sustainable Development' (2005–2014) by the UN (UN DESD) was decided and then proposed unanimously in the UN General Assembly a few months later (Resolution 57/254). The primary goal of this Decade is the promotion of education as a basis for a sustainable society and the diffusion of principles of SD into all forms and levels of education, as requested by ERA 21.

The UN DESD, to a certain extent because of difficulties in promoting and comprehending the concepts of SD and ESD by educators and to a large extent because of inadequate promotion of ESD by the UN system itself, has had 'uneven' results in the various parts (regions and countries) of the world. In the Mediterranean the UN DESD was launched in November 2008 in Athens and at that time a decision was made for the elaboration in the region of a '(Pan-)Mediterranean Strategy on ESD', using as a source of inspiration the 'UNECE Strategy on ESD' (Vilnius, 2005). The latter was the result of a dynamic initiative undertaken by the 56 member states of the UN Economic Commission for Europe (UNECE).[7] Among them, a very active role was played by its 13 Mediterranean member states. It is noted that the Mediterranean Arab countries are not part of UNECE and the scope of a Mediterranean Strategy on ESD is to be accepted by everybody around the Mediterranean Sea. The primary purpose of the UNECE Strategy and, hopefully, of the Mediterranean one is to encourage countries to incorporate ESD into their educational systems, covering all levels from primary to tertiary including vocational and adult, on the basis of both formal and non-formal education. Apart from listing principles and objectives, the Strategy provides the critical components for the setting up of National Implementation Plans, including, *inter alios*: the roles and responsibilities of governments and other stakeholders, such as universities, as well as schemes for international cooperation. In 2007 the baseline data were gathered by the countries based on UNECE and UNESCO forms (indicators), and in 2010 the UNECE's mid-term report showed considerable progress, including at higher education levels.

It is outside the scope of the present short paper to make a full survey of the Mediterranean universities that have introduced SD and ESD themes and courses, lessons or seminars into their curricula but there are many such attempts. Several are made at postgraduate level, and in master's courses, but there are also concrete steps at undergraduate level. A recent programme (TEMPUS RUCAS) led by the University of Crete is trying to stimulate the introduction of SD/ESD at undergraduate level in Mediterranean universities.[8] This programme arose out of the initiative of 18 Mediterranean universities (in the countries of Albania, Bosnia-Hergegovina, Croatia, Egypt, France, Greece, Italy, Lebanon, Morocco, Slovenia, Spain, Tunisia, and Turkey) which together formed the 'Network of Mediterranean Universities for Sustainable Development', focusing on ESD. The Network was launched following a series of initiatives in Athens, on 18–19 November 2008, under the leadership of the University of Athens and facilitated by MEdIES, with the support of UNESCO/BRESCE. One of its main aims was to initiate a common master's on ESD. The process is in progress and also involves the 'greening' of the universities following the so-called 'Whole Institute Approach'. To obtain that, a few universities of the region (for example Technical University of Catalonia) have established special offices or services for promoting SD within the universities. In the same spirit, the Congress of Rectors of the Greek Universities established a Committee for the 'Sustainable/Green Greek University' which has agreed upon a Charter and is moving swiftly with initiatives to implement at all levels (technical, educational, administrative). The initiatives of the Global University Network for Innovation (GUNi), coordinated by a Mediterranean university (Polytechnic University of Catalunia), are expected to facilitate this most needed tendency for a sustainability 'renaissance' of higher education in the Mediterranean region.

NOTES

1   Scoullos, M. and Roniotes, A. (2003) *The Evolution of Environmental Policies in the Mediterranean from an NGO Perspective*. Athens: MIO-ECSDE.
2   Scoullos, M. and Malotidi, V. (2004) Handbook on Methods used in Environmental Education and Education for Sustainable Development. Athens: MIO-ECSDE.
3   Scoullos, M. (1987) *Environmental Education as a Vehicle for International Compre*hension and Peace. International Congress on Environmental Education and Training, UNESCO-UNEP.
4   Scoullos, M. and Malotidi, V. (2004) op. cit.
5   UNESCO-UNEP (1996) *Re-orienting Environmental Education for Sustainable Development, Summary Report of the Inter-Regional Workshop* (Athens, June 26–30, 1995), UNESCO-UNEP, MIO-ECSDE.
6   Scoullos, M. (ed.) (1998) *Environment and Society: Education and Public Awareness for Sustainability*. Proceedings of the Thessaloniki International Conference organized by UENSCO and the Government of Greece, Athens, 8–12 December 1997
7   UNECE Strategy for Education for Sustainable Development, Vilnius 2005 http://www.unece.org/env/documents/2005/cep/ac.13/cep.ac.13.2005.3.rev.1.e.pdf, 23 March 2005.
8   TEMPUS RUCAS (www.uoc.gr).

Inside View II.6
Sustainability in higher education: the Central and Eastern European case

Jana Dlouhá and Bedřich Moldan

DEFINING THE REGION AND POLICY FRAMEWORK

In the UNESCO categorization, Central and Eastern Europe (CEE) includes the Central Group of countries (Poland, Czech Republic, Hungary, Slovenia, Slovakia, Estonia, Latvia, Lithuania, Romania, Bulgaria and Turkey; but not Cyprus and Malta); and some of the Eastern European countries (Albania, Belarus, Bosnia and Herzegovina, Croatia, Republic of Moldova, Russian Federation, Serbia, The former Yugoslav Republic of Macedonia and the Ukraine) (UNESCO, 2011).

Within the UN Decade of Education for Sustainable Development (2005–2014), the UNECE *Strategy for Education for Sustainable Development* (ESD) is the policy document at the European level that should serve as the driving force for policy changes in the field of education. The Strategy provides concrete and measurable goals to be transferred to national policies; it pays special attention to the countries in Eastern Europe, the Caucasus and Central Asia (EECCA),[1] and South-Eastern Europe that face many challenges in the field of ESD. The document concerns all levels of education including higher education institutions (HEIs) that should provide leadership throughout the whole system and that are especially important for teacher education. In 2010, the second evaluation phase of the Strategy based on National Implementation Reports was completed: it identified general trends and differences and found that the subregions EU/West and EECCA[2] follow largely the same pattern in many areas except for 'participation in democratic decision-making' (rated the lowest in the EECCA region and among the highest in the EU/West). All 32 countries[3] that provided a report clearly put the Strategy into action and incorporated ESD into formal systems (UNECE, 2011).

On the other hand, higher education (HE) is too specific to be largely influenced by policies that originate outside academia – HE institutions themselves have the ability to make a greater impact on academic practice within their associations, for example University Leaders for a Sustainable Future (ULSF). To understand the mechanism of (potential) sustainability-oriented transition, the historical tradition and culture of HEIs has to be reviewed.

CEE – TRANSFORMATION OF THE HIGHER EDUCATION SYSTEMS

HE education policy in the countries of Central and Eastern Europe (CEE) faced similar challenges in the period of transition from 1990 until the present, at the same time respecting specific conditions in countries that greatly depend on past policy, and the institutional system and cultural features that form a tradition within the educational sector. Educational systems in CEE countries had to be cleared of ideological ballast and simultaneously the importance of international and global processes increased. In academia, new quality criteria, especially in research, were accepted and the system faced growing demand for mobility (Kohoutek, 2009, pp. 13–16). Reform changes within national higher education systems have taken place since 1989 in three periods (Kohoutek, 2009, pp. 13–16).

In the first period of policy changes (1990–1993), the liberalization and decentralization processes of the system of governance structures were most important. Educational change in HE was characterized by depoliticization, breaking down the state monopoly, and decentralization of management and administration, including recognition of students' rights and the building of democratic structures that allowed autonomy. Liberalization of the HE environment (restoration of academic self-governance, and of the freedoms fundamental to the academic community) was followed by a growing interest in tertiary studies (increasing student enrolments), and also by a shift in the attention paid to different disciplines (growth in interest in humanities, especially economics and law, and a significant decline in interest in technical sciences). The mission of academic institutions also changed: they were initially oriented towards teaching and were not supposed to do research. Higher education and research took place in separate institutions yet competed for the same budget – so an unhealthy rivalry developed between the two systems (Balázs et al., 1995).

In the second phase (approximately 1994–1999), the HE policies of the CEE countries faced challenges of growing numbers of students, a lack of financial resources necessary to increase system capacity, introduction of private higher education providers, and a consequent quality issue demand for accountability and well-defined academic performance (outputs and efficiency). Universities slowly started to replace the 'liberal absolutism' of the first period with civic and market accountability and accepted their role in the 'knowledge society'. The second stage was characterized by emerging pragmatism – the emphasis switched to the need to expand and diversify HE to meet new socioeconomic demands. The CEE countries found that their HE policy priorities were rapidly converging with those of Western Europe but still recognized that their entire education systems were not adjusted to the needs of a market economy (Burnett, 1996).

In the third period, roughly from 1999 until the present, HE policies in Central and Eastern Europe have been changing in certain domains – typically in degree structure and quality assurance – to the extent that they need to accommodate the essentials of the Bologna Process.

SUSTAINABILITY IN HEIs – PRINCIPLES AND INDICATORS
Because of their intellectual capacity and hence their role in the 'knowledge society', universities are considered to be key actors in achieving a sustainable future. But if they want to respond to this challenge they still need radical innovation that concerns thinking, internal organization and operation, and their interaction with other social players beyond academia. To develop a holistic and consistent sustainability-oriented HE system, its 'greening' should be undertaken in a relatively wide area of university life. ULSF in its Sustainability Indicators Project mentions the seven most important areas: professional education requirements in all academic disciplines and research; within the role of the institution in its social and ecological systems; in university management and specific activities such as scholarships; with regard to the student support and campus student life services, outreach and forming partnerships both locally and globally to enhance sustainability; and finally, they need to express sustainability visions in mission statements (Clugston and Calder, 1999).

Besides these visible indicators of change, deeper and more qualitative transformations play a role within the processes of education and research. Daniella Tilbury stresses in particular the role of social learning (which contradicts traditional forms of academic learning in certain respects) and the need for a different view of pedagogy that includes active and participatory learning, pays attention to the management that is spread across educational systems themselves and develops synergies through ESD across schools, communities and universities (Tilbury, 2011). Sustainability-oriented leadership that should be developed in HE requires systemic thinking and transdisciplinary skills on top of existing disciplinary knowledge, and understanding of processes of human change (Jansen, 2003). In teacher education in particular, research into commonly adopted ESD pedagogies is a high priority (see, for example, priorities for action in the UNECE Strategy for ESD, § 58–60). In all these areas, higher education should play a role and 'contribute significantly to ESD in the development of appropriate knowledge and competences' (UNECE, 2005, § 20).

Sustainability-oriented changes in universities may be developed through top-down as well as bottom-up approaches. The top-down approach sets the trends in the management and governance of academic institutions and their systems' borders; the bottom-up approach is widely applicable due to the great autonomy of universities on all (including bottom) levels and their specific educational and research culture. The top-down and bottom-up approaches are complementary, although they need communication between the relevant parties (Jansen, 2003). The bottom-up approach is contributing to an invisible, incremental but more fundamental transition (Stephens and Graham, 2010), but is more difficult to observe while the top-down approach is more appropriate for comparison of universities through exploring the main technological, cultural and structural elements of sustainability transformation (Ferrer-Balas et al., 2008). However, a kind of university ranking based on sustainability criteria does not exist and to get an overall picture, the policies pursued by universities in different areas of sustainability should be examined.

CENTRAL AND EASTERN EUROPEAN SPECIFICS
The introduction of sustainability themes in HE and research in CEE countries depends to a great extent on leadership: the role of personalities that very often do not have a specifically environmental disciplinary background (environmental disciplines due to their interdisciplinary character are not often accredited for habilitation purposes). But even if such 'leadership' exists, it is often based on expertise and aimed at the introduction of sustainability-oriented methods or 'technology' within a specific discipline – complex innovation is difficult to achieve. Under circumstances where universities worldwide are increasingly moving 'beyond the old science driven model', reconsidering their roles in society and increasing their communication and cooperation with other social players (Zilahy and Huisingh, 2009), systemic reorientation of this kind on the HE level in CEE countries still awaits a more stable political and economic situation.

DISCIPLINARY EXCELLENCE IN ENVIRONMENTAL AND SUSTAINABILITY SCIENCES

In some CEE countries, including the former Czechoslovakia, environmental sciences were relatively well advanced before 1990 and were part of the permitted opposition to the regime. During the transition period, environmentally educated experts and citizens contributed significantly to EU accession from a technical point of view; they also promoted civic society through democratic dialogue between NGOs and government. Simultaneously, all CEE countries experienced an increased need for environmental experts due to the environmental burden inherited from the former regimes and new legislative challenges. As a consequence, environmentally oriented disciplines flourished but the values inherent within them started to be perceived as contradictory to the new market culture. In the course of HE development, a narrowing disciplinary orientation reflected the need to raise academic excellence according to accepted criteria. In contrast, integration of SD principles into academic performance that require broader dialogue built upon an inter-disciplinary basis, and theoretical reflection and/or practical output was often lacking. The involvement of universities in social processes was mostly perceived as leadership that could promote 'green' technological progress and economic development, support environmental protection and provide assistance for policymaking purposes from an expert point of view.

CONCLUSION – WHITE SPOTS IN CEE EDUCATIONAL POLICIES

In CEE countries, SD-oriented education at lower levels of the educational system in general capitalizes on interaction with NGOs; and these multi-stakeholder processes on the higher education level are developed mainly in teacher education and within broad educational partnerships that are often part of international projects and/or are funded by European grant schemes within the framework of general EU policies (see relevant ESD case studies or good practices, for example (EC DG, 2008)). Apart from teacher education, the benefits of social learning are not widely recognized and university dialogue with other stakeholders on regional principles in particular is often lacking. If we take the Regional Centres of Expertise model shared worldwide as an indicator of regional cooperation, we see that of 85 RCEs, 26 are in Europe and only 2 in CEE, specifically in Russia (as of March 2011: Fadeeva, 2011).

In the sustainability-oriented transition, reflection is an important process as it provides information for refocusing or altering accepted strategies; however, this level of change is often neglected (Stephens and Graham, 2010). In spite of the fact that all UNECE countries report that they increasingly promote research addressing the content of ESD (see UNECE, 2011), research reflecting ESD transition (aside from statistics based on financial requirements) is not sufficient in CEE countries. For illustration, the number of articles by authors from CEE countries in the *International Journal of Sustainability in Higher Education* over the past three years is half of the total of 115 articles.[4] Thus, HEIs that in general have large potential for ESD transition, as there is considerable expertise in environmental/sustainability science in the CEE region, are still dependent on – or are struggling with – policies that originated outside academia: they could hardly be internalized as ESD-oriented dialogue at the academic level is insufficient. But such 'external' ESD oriented policy pressure might be perceived as ideological by those academics who are not themselves endeavouring to achieve sustainability oriented goals through teaching, management and cooperation within HE institutions and beyond.

REFERENCES

Balázs, K., Faulkner, W. and Schimank, U. (1995) Transformation of the research systems of post-communist Central and Eastern Europe: an introduction. *Social Studies of Science*, **25**(4), p. 613–32.

Burnett, N. (1996) Priorities and strategies for education – A World Bank review: The process and the key messages. *International Journal of Educational Development*, **16**(3), pp. 215–20.

Clugston, R. M. and Calder, W. (1999) Critical dimensions of sustainability in higher education. Sustainability and University Life, 5, pp. 31–46.

EC DG Education and Culture (2008) *Inventory of innovative practices in education for sustainable development.* Final Report submitted by GHK and Danish Technology Institute Technopolis.

Fadeeva, Z. (2011) List of RCEs, e-mail correspondence. April 2011.

Ferrer-Balas, D., Adachi, J., Banas, S., Davidson, C. I., Hoshikoshi, A., Mishra, A., Motodoa, Y. et al. (2008) An international comparative analysis of sustainability transformation across seven universities. *International Journal of Sustainability in Higher Education*, **9**(3), pp. 295–316.

Jansen, L. (2003) The challenge of sustainable development. *Journal of Cleaner Production*, **11**(3), pp. 231–45.

Kohoutek, J. (2009) Setting the stage: quality assurance, policy change, and implementation. In: Kohoutek, J. (ed.) *Studies on Higher Education. Implementation of the Standards and Guidelines for Quality Assurance in Higher Education in the Central and East-European Countries – Agenda Ahead.* Bucharest: UNESCO.

Stephens, J.C. and Graham, A.C. (2010) Toward an empirical research agenda for sustainability in higher education: exploring the transition management framework. *Journal of Cleaner Production*, **18**(7), pp. 611–18.

Tilbury, D. (2011) Education for Sustainable Development An Expert Review of Processes and Learning. Paris: UNESCO.

UNECE (2005) UNECE Strategy for Education for Sustainable Development. Vilnius: CEP/AC.13/2005/3/Rev.1.

UNECE (2011) Learning from each other: Achievements, challenges and ways forward – Second evaluation report of the UNECE Strategy for Education for Sustainable Development. Geneva: Information Paper No. 8.

UNESCO (2011) Institute for Statistics. Key indicators on all levels of the national education system (online) (cit 2011-02-24). Available from http://stats.uis.unesco.org/unesco/TableViewer/document.aspx?ReportId=198&IF_Language=eng.

Zilahy, G. and Huisingh, D. (2009) The roles of academia in Regional Sustainability Initiatives. *Journal of Cleaner Production*, **17**(12), pp. 1057–66.

1. These countries are Armenia, Azerbaijan, Belarus, Georgia, Kazakhstan, Kyrgyzstan, Republic of Moldova, Russian Federation, Tajikistan, Turkmenistan, Ukraine, and Uzbekistan.
2. The SEE subregion was not analysed, as only Croatia submitted a report.
3. The following countries submitted the Report on time: Armenia, Austria, Belarus, Belgium, Bulgaria, Canada, Croatia, Cyprus, Czech Republic, Denmark, Estonia, Finland, France, Georgia, Germany, Greece, Hungary, Iceland, Israel, Kazakhstan, Kyrgyzstan, Latvia, Lithuania, Malta, Moldova, Netherlands, Norway, Poland, Romania, Serbia, Slovakia, Slovenia, Sweden, Switzerland, Turkey, Uzbekistan.
4. Articles from the relevant issues from 2011, 2010, 2009, 2008 were considered, covering the following article categories: 'research', 'case study', 'general review' or 'conceptual'.

Spotlight Issues II.6
Making higher education a key stakeholder of future democratic societies

Claudia Lenz and
Ana Perona-Fjeldstad

In recent years, higher education institutions (HEIs) have been under pressure to act as 'production centres', delivering skilled academics adapted to the quickly changing needs of the economy. Less focus has been put on preparing future citizens for quickly changing social and political realities. Which would be the contributions of university leaders, professors, students and administration workers to democratic development? Do we talk about a democratization of HEIs or about fostering interaction between these institutions and the societies they are part of – or about both?

The European Wergeland Center (EWC) is a resource centre for Education on Intercultural Understanding, Human Rights and Democratic Citizenship which was established as an innovative initiative by the Norwegian government and the Council of Europe in 2008. With its core target group being teacher trainers and teachers but also other educational practitioners (in formal and informal learning environments), the idea of creating links between HEIs and the communities they are situated in has informed EWC activities right from the beginning. Combining a focus on capacity building/training for educators and on research and development, the EWC profoundly shares the vision that HEIs can play a vital role in building tomorrow's sustainable democracies by educating tomorrow's responsible citizens.

This has been expressed in several EWC activities, such as the 'Educators' Consultations', events, in which 'fresh' international research findings have been discussed with educational practitioners regarding the possible impact for learning and teaching on the ground.[1] In these events, small steps towards the realization of the potential of higher education (HE) to contribute to awareness, reflection and the development of solutions for urgent societal challenges have been realized.

Another example is the international conference 'Reimagining Democratic Societies – A new era of personal and social responsibility?' which was held at the University of Oslo 27–29 June 2011, aiming to:

- Strengthen the role of HE in furthering democratic citizenship
- Identify concretely the role that HE can play in reimagining democratic societies
- Stress the importance of the involvement of the different stakeholders: academic, administrations, students, local communities
- Develop further strategies to strengthen this role

So, back to the central question of this article: how can HE's role in renewing and strengthening democratic societies be envisioned?

To start with, some crucial questions on the present 'state' of Western democracies need to be raised: Do we assume that democracy has already been realized and only needs to be kept alive or do we assume that democracy by its nature is an aspiration that by principle cannot be realized (and, thus, constantly needs to be reimagined)? Do we think and talk about one *master version* of democracy or *multiple democracies*? To narrow down the idea of democracy to only one model would turn the idea into ideology. Keeping democracy alive needs, therefore, constant debate and reflection – something citizens need to be trained for in educational institutions.

Another question relates to HEIs as such – are they, with their inherited elitism and conservatism, the least well-suited institutions to promote democracy? Do we need to reinvent *higher education* – its institutional settings, its ethos and practices – in order to promote democratic societal change?

In the following paragraphs we will elaborate four topics:

- The role of higher education facing today's and tomorrow's global challenges
- Social cohesion, 'new work' and citizenship
- Establishing democratic cultures within HEIs
- Involvement in the broader community/society

THE ROLE OF HIGHER EDUCATION FACING GLOBAL CHALLENGES

Which developments at a macro level define the challenges of democratic societies today? In a recent speech, Jan Egeland, Director of the Norwegian Institute of International Affairs, pointed out that the number of armed conflicts and wars has decreased since the 1970s, and that democracy has been introduced in many countries ruled by dictators some decades ago. However, another development contrasts this positive image: today, we observe a growing gap in the distribution of wealth among individuals within societies as well as a growing distance between rich and poor societies. And these societies are more aware than ever, thanks to widely available communication technologies, about these inequalities and other possible realities. This results in social tensions and political instability. As a consequence, sustainable democratic and peaceful development requires a fight against poverty and social exclusion.

These observations coincide with a report recently delivered by the Group of Eminent People of the Council of Europe, 'Combining diversity and freedom in 21st century

Europe'. The report states that Europe is experiencing a rise in xenophobia and intolerance, threatening the core values of Human Rights, rule of law and democracy, and recommends active steps to be taken to fight these tendencies in – among other – all branches of education.[2]

Further aspects might be added to the diagnosis of the present: environmental and demographical changes will lead to an increase in but also a need for immigration in many Western countries. These phenomena will force societies to find solutions that assure inclusion of all members of society, regardless of ethnicity, age or gender.

If HEIs are regarded as one responsible stakeholder of sustainable development among others, the question arises: How can they equip students with knowledge, skills and attitudes that help them to respond as active citizens to the challenges of their time? What do students need to learn, experience and practise in their studies, that empowers them to stand up for equal rights, social justice and peaceful conflict resolution?

SOCIAL COHESION, 'NEW WORK' AND CITIZENSHIP

Facing the strong focus on economy dominating educational policies and reforms during the last decades, universities meet a dilemma: students want to be educated for the workforce (unemployment rates are increasing, competition for jobs is fierce), and demand high-quality professional knowledge and skills. As a consequence, little time and resources are left for universities to act as agents of democratic change. Little attention is paid to letting students develop their vision of a 'good life'. What is needed is a renewed vision of the aim of higher education, which would address students as citizens *and* professionals who will take over social responsibility.

Access to quality education has a crucial impact on social cohesion and democracy. Can we, at all, separate the focus on participation in the labour market from civic participation? In many processes of transformation from dictatorship to democracy worldwide, we can see that educated middle classes are an important bearer of democratization. If the children of migrants and other underprivi-

leged groups are denied access to HE they are denied becoming effective agents of political and social change.

But how welcoming are HEIs to young people who are not raised within a middle-class habitat? Following Pierre Bourdieu's analysis of institutional 'cultures' of high schools and universities, we still can attest that they often preserve the unjust distribution of power and wealth in society by more or less 'invisible' mechanisms of exclusion. In order to contribute to more inclusive societies, HEIs need to open for and actively attract students who traditionally are mistrustful of academic culture – and habitat.

So, what are the signifiers of 'high-quality education'? There seems to be a need to readjust the visions and criteria for 'excellence' from marked orientation towards social responsibility. In order to do so, universities and colleges need to develop democratic cultures 'within' as well as become active stakeholders in developing visions and action for sustainable democratic development at a local and global scale. Moving beyond the image of universities as academic 'Ivory Towers' as well as beyond the neo-liberal notion of HE as a service sector delivering a skilled labour force to the markets, a third visions arises: HEIs as a space where 'civic culture' is experienced and promoted and where *civic professionalism* is developed.

ESTABLISHING DEMOCRATIC CULTURES WITHIN HEIs

What is needed for universities to overcome their inherited conservatism and traditional hierarchies in order to become hubs of democratic culture? Of course, structural changes are required, such as enhanced participation of all stakeholders in the development of vision and decision-making. Importantly, the relations between students and professors need to build on values of mutual respect and a liflong learning culture (in which teachers are also learners, even though more experienced ones). The importance of administration staff for the creation of inclusive and open institutions should also not be underestimated. If we think about diversity issues, many everyday obstacles for foreigners or migrants can be solved by sensitive administration workers.

But HE finds its *raison d'être* in academic training and research. Thus, democratic change within requires the development of a new 'academic ethos' embracing the qualities of critical thinking, engagement and responsibility. So, which are the didactical approaches and necessary curriculum changes needed? What do 'democratic' styles of learning and teaching look like? Some approaches are already practised in many places:

- Student-centred learning – specific perspective on learning, focusing on questions more than answers, gives students opportunities to engage in inquiry-based learning, learning out of interest
- Problem-based learning – starting from real-life problems and creating opportunities to respond to them

This kind of learning culture represents a paradigm shift – not starting from what professors and universities think is relevant for students but relating learning to what is experienced as relevant to students.

What needs to be acknowledged as a challenge, though, is the danger of persuasive and manipulating frameworks: value-based education should not become ideological and indoctrinating education. There is a fine line between inviting and encouraging students to reach highly informed views and persuading them to hold specific views and values. The key to this problem seems to be to root all thinking and action in the art of reflection and self-reflection and to develop a habit of also testing out different possibilities to view and interpret reality. This would be, in the sense developed by Hannah Arendt, the art of judgement which is the precondition of political action.

INVOLVEMENT IN THE BROADER COMMUNITY/SOCIETY

This last point leads to the links between HE and students' community engagement or other types of involvement in social and political activities. How can universities allow students to go through experiences and acquire a set of tools necessary in their lives as responsible citizens? 'Taking the kids out of the classrooms' is one of the options – offering students opportunities to get involved in activities supporting the underprivileged and poor in a community. This is based on the assumption that learning is at its best when learners can apply theoretical concepts and abstract reflections in concrete/real-life environments through activities and if they experience that they 'can make a difference'. However, incentives are needed, such as credit points for a student's 'application' of theoretical knowledge and academic skills in a social and political responsible engagement.

However, too strong a focus on 'activism' needs to be avoided. Universities are unique spaces providing opportunities for 'thinking through' – and to balance action and reflection. In addition, student's needs and interests might vary according to personality and stage of life (not all students are youngsters).

OUTLOOK – HEIs AS AN INTEGRAL PART OF CIVIC SOCIETY

Turning back to the start of this article, it seems evident that HEIs have a role to play in the maintenance, renewal and permanent 'reinvention' of democracy. Universities and colleges can be 'hubs' were a systematic and informed reflection of social reality leads to renewed engagement, initiatives and interventions – which, again, become the object of critical investigation and reflection.

What is needed to realize this vision is a democratic development within and a systematic involvement 'outside': interaction between HEIs and the realities they are surrounded by. Realities which, in fact, are no 'outside' but a vital aspect of all students', professors' and administration workers' lives. Developing academic cultures *as* democratic cultures will, thus, be an important building block in the development of sustainable democracies.

NOTES

1 In 2011 the Educators' Consultations dealt with the findings of the International Citizenship and Civic Education Study (ICCS). See documentation under http://www.theewc.org/ucontent/educators.consultations.2011/ (accessed July 6, 2011).

2 http://book.coe.int/ftp/3667.pdf (accessed July 6, 2011).

Network Experience II.4
The European higher education for sustainable development network – COPERNICUS Alliance – back on stage with Charta 2.0

Friedrich M. Zimmermann, Clemens Mader, Gerd Michelsen and Maik Adomssent

Learning societies as well as knowledge networks are characterized by trust, knowledge exchange and a shared desire for the further development of common visions and aims. Developed by the former Association of European Universities, and focusing on the European Higher Education Area, the COPERNICUS Charta has been signed by more than 300 universities since its launch in 1993. The Charta's aim was to commit European universities to fostering environmental actions within their institutions as well as in cooperation with society. However, although universities committed to a common vision the necessary coordination strategies for reaching it were missing. Initiatives that took place were mainly coordinated in the framework of projects funded by the European Union such as the Virtual Campus for Sustainable Development or the follow-up project Lifelong Learning Network for Sustainable Development. Partners of those projects came together to work on higher education for sustainable development strategies as well as to discuss options for establishing coordination strategies for the COPERNICUS Alliance, the European Network on Higher Education for Sustainable Development. Finally, the COPERNICUS Alliance (CA) has been built up in 2010 to strengthen European university cooperation to contribute to sustainable development in Europe.

Founding partners have agreed on the following COPERNICUS Alliance aims:

- **Policy:** to cooperate with European policy to strengthen the role of sustainability in the future development of European research programmes and higher education policies
- **Service:** to disseminate tools for the integration of sustainability in higher education
- **Outreach:** to promote higher education for sustainable development in Europe
- **Representation:** to represent European higher education in international committees on education for sustainable development
- **Network:** to exchange and enhance knowledge on education for sustainable development between European higher education and student organizations working for sustainable development

These aims are central to the further development of the COPERNICUS Alliance. Additionally, members agreed on the development of an updated COPERNICUS Charta. The COPERNICUS Charta 2.0 stands in the tradition of the 'COPERNICUS University Charter for Sustainable Development', which was announced in 1993 by the European Rectors' Conference (now: European University Association, EUA).

BOX 1: COPERNICUS CHARTA 2.0/2011
EUROPEAN COMMITMENT TO HIGHER EDUCATION FOR SUSTAINABLE DEVELOPMENT

Preamble

The challenges of sustainable development are more and more visible, everyday, everywhere. Universities have the unique combination of teaching, research and service to society to address these challenges in different ways depending on their different orientations, capabilities and quality. To be more effective they need to enhance their individual capabilities by effective cooperation: between disciplines and generations, between theory and practice and between devoted institutions. Together they should contribute to the 'learning society' we need in order to measure up to all the challenges; today, tomorrow and thereafter. This has been on the agenda of the European universities since 1988 when they drafted and signed first the Magna Charta in Bologna and then the CRE-COPERNICUS Program and Charter in Geneva.

Since then, many activities have been developed and sometimes successfully implemented; many of these in the framework of the UN Decade of Education for Sustainable Development. In the 2010 conference held by GUNi (the Global University Network for Innovation) in Barcelona many reports were given on such activities. The European Regional Centres of Expertise on Education for Sustainable Development, formally acknowledged by the United Nations University and the Ubuntu Alliance, provide stimulating examples.

The COPERNICUS Alliance believes that it is time to scale up our efforts based on the experience gained. Humankind must learn to care for the needs of the present, without compromising the ability of future generations, anywhere in this world, to meet their own needs. In the COPERNICUS Charta 2.0 we pledge that the signatories, all universities and other higher education institutions, are firmly committed to play the central role they 'noblesse oblige' are obligated to in contributing to our successful transition towards a sustainable society, which is free, just, equal, solidary and tolerant. A society which is characterized by respect for nature and our fellow humans and by shared responsibility.

Principles of action

The COPERNICUS Alliance aims to promote sustainable development in European higher education by addressing concerted action on the following target levels:

Inside higher education institutions

- sustainable development is given fundamental status in their strategy and all their activities, that is, institutional commitment, sustainability ethics, and dissemination of knowledge;
- the creative development and implementation of comprehensive and integrated sustainability actions is promoted in relation to their functions in learning and teaching, research, and internal and external social responsibility.

In relation to the whole of education

- institutions of higher education pay particular attention to their role(s) in realizing processes of lifelong learning for sustainable development by involving formal, non-formal and informal learning in this direction;
- higher education for sustainable development is promoted in European policymaking.

In relation to society

- universities, against the backdrop of sustainable development, have to envision that, beyond being scientific institutions, they have to act as partners in regional networks;
- closer cooperation with other stakeholders in local communities is aspired to in order to better respond to their needs and requirements as well as to learn lessons from personal and corporate experiences.

In networks of universities

- knowledge on education for sustainable development between European higher education and student organizations that work for sustainability is exchanged and enhanced;
- European higher education for sustainable development is represented in international committees on education for sustainable development.

The COPERNICUS Alliance aims to achieve the above-mentioned goals through a growing network of European higher education institutions and develop a platform to strengthen integration of sustainable development in higher education management, education, research and universities' contribution to society.

Version 2.0, as of 21 April 2011

By 2011 the CA comprises 18 active members from 9 European countries. The Alliance is led by its elected president and vice-president supported by a scientific board. Members pay an annual membership fee for the bulk of which finances members' service in working groups while 15% is allocated to the CA fund which members can apply for, in order to support research contributions to the Alliance aims and principles. Four working groups (WG) have been established in the course of the first CA workshop in 2010. Those working groups aim to support research and development activities in the field of the Alliance principles:

- *WG1: Implementation of Sustainability in Universities:* This WG focuses on sustainability implementation strategies by universities and should support practitioners in the development of such. Participants of this group also investigate new forms for university appraisal incorporating criteria of sustainable development. Therefore in the course of the 2011 annual meeting a special workshop on alternative appraisal systems for sustainability in higher education was held with support of the Austrian Ministry of Science and Research.

- *WG2: Innovative Teaching and Learning:* Web-based learning as well as transformative learning practices are core topics of this working group. By cooperating in the EU-Lifelong Learning Project – 3-LENSUS (Lifelong Learning Network for Sustainable Development) – the group is following up the project outcomes and maintains the LENSUS Good Practice Learning for Sustainable Development Database.

- *WG3: European Interdisciplinary research for sustainable development:* Members of this WG exchange ideas in the field of European research policies as well as inter- and transdisciplinary research methodologies. In a workshop in June 2011, the group explored the potential for developing a research focus on meta-questions of Interdisciplinary Research – with a focus on sustainability.

- *WG4: COPERNICUS Alliance Management:* To ensure a participatory development of the organization's management a WG has been initiated, open for all members to contribute to the development of an innovation network with shared leadership structures and transformative management practices.

The COPERNICUS Alliance believes that it is time to scale up efforts based on the experience gained by the international and European higher education academy for sustainable development community. Aims and management structures including the WGs should contribute to the development of an innovation network to further support European universities and university policies to move towards sustainable development principles and practices. Further information is available at www.copernicus-alliance.org.

GOOD PRACTICES II.4

Higher Education and Sustainability in Europe: Sharing Actions for Change

The following experiences are a selection of good practices on higher education and sustainability. Some of them were presented at the 5th International Barcelona Conference on Higher Education and others are part of the GUNi observatory.

The good practices cover the following institutional areas:

Curricula and learning innovation

Community and social engagement

Institutional management

Research

GOOD PRACTICE 1

Tackling educational disadvantaged, widening participation and enhancing civic engagement between DIT and the wider community

Institutional area(s):

LOCATION: DUBLIN
INSTITUTION: Dublin Institute of Technology

The aim of the Community Links Programme is to help in the alleviation of educational disadvantage at local (inner-city Dublin), national and international levels. This is achieved through initiatives primarily directed at personal development including self-esteem, confidence, motivation and empowerment of individuals and communities. The Community Links Programme is made up of five very different projects, but what they all have in common is a commitment to support communities and individuals to reach their full potential. The programmes are located in the primary, secondary, third level and community sectors. The issues concerned are the alleviation of absenteeism, prevention of drop-out, increases in the attainment in schools, return to education in communities and access to education for all, civic engagement and social change.

Detailed information is available at GUNi HEiOBS:

http://www.guninetwork.org/guni.heiobs/good-practices/tackling-educational-disadvantage-widening-participation-and-enhancing-civic-engagement-between-dit-and-the-wider-community-1

Grassroots cross-boundary innovation in higher education

Institutional area(s):

LOCATION: Netherlands
INSTITUTION: Wageningen University

The Initiative for Transformative Sustainability Education (ITSE) at Wageningen University is a grassroots working group of academics, teachers, and students who have developed a framework for cross-boundary sustainability education that addresses not only theoretical knowledge and practical skills, but also guides students to question their values, attitudes and behaviour, develop leadership skills, learn to empower themselves and others, and learn to facilitate social and collaborative learning among a great diversity of stakeholders. Currently, ITSE is applying this framework to the design of a BSc Minor programme in Sustainable Development: Empowerment for Action.

Detailed information is available at GUNi HEiOBS:

http://www.guninetwork.org/guni.heiobs/good-practices/grassroots-cross-boundary-innovation-in-higher-education-lessons-from-the-process-of-designing-transformative-sustainability-education

Baltic University programme

Institutional area(s):

LOCATION: North America, Europe
INSTITUTION: Uppsala University

The Baltic University Programme (BUP) is a network of about 225 universities and other institutes of higher learning throughout the Baltic Sea region. The network is coordinated by the Baltic University Programme Secretariat, a part of Uppsala Centre for Sustainable Development (Uppsala CSD) at Uppsala University, Sweden. The Programme works mainly through producing and offering courses for studies of the Baltic Sea region, its environment, political change, and sustainable development. All courses have an element of regional studies and are interdisciplinary. Cooperation with other actors in society in applied projects is an important part of studying and developing sustainability strategies, and promoting competence development at large.

Detailed information is available at GUNi HEiOBS:

http://www.guninetwork.org/guni.heiobs/good-practices/baltic-university-programme

The ECOART project

Institutional area(s):

LOCATION: Spain
INSTITUTION: UNESCO Chair on Distance Education

The project starts from the need for conciliating two worlds, two cultures that are being developed with little contact between them: Science and Art. The project arises from the fact that in order to confront the serious environmental problems facing humanity, we need to look at these from multiple perspectives. Therefore, it is necessary, not only to analyse with scientific accuracy, which is totally essential, but also with a creative vision that helps to imagine future scenarios of sustainable life on the planet. Thus, ECOART develops like a 'cross bred' art, born from the shared search in both territories, and offering the opportunity to show how these types of knowledge complement each other.

Detailed information is available at GUNi HEiOBS:

http://www.guninetwork.org/guni.heiobs/good-practices/the-ecoart-project/

Educational innovation in university education: A proposal from the UNESCO Chair in Environmental Education and Sustainable Development

Institutional area(s):

LOCATION: Spain
INSTITUTION: UNESCO Chair on Environmental Education and Sustainable Development

Two projects are presented in this work, which are focused on two educational strategies, respectively: (a) The construction of conceptual maps, which is a technique that enhances analytical and rational thinking, using the editor Cmap tools; and (b) online groups of collaborative learning, which is a technique that promotes teamwork and enhances participation, discussion and divergent thinking. The projects were implemented during the academic years 2006/07 and 2008/09, respectively. Each of them was presented to the students as a pilot experience with an expected workload of 25 hours (equivalent to 1 ECTS credit) and participation was voluntary.

Detailed information is available at GUNi HEiOBS:

http://www.guninetwork.org/guni.heiobs/good-practices/educational-innovation-in-universitary-education.-a-proposal-from-the-unesco-chair-in-environmental-education-and-sustainable-development-uned/

Keeping it Local: Shared Solutions for Sustainability

Institutional area(s):

LOCATION: United Kingdom
INSTITUTIONS: University of Northampton

This project puts partnership working at the centre of sustainable development and recognizes that universities need to demonstrate leadership in a new era of localism. By partnering with local public and private sector organizations, the project will identify common targets, objectives and solutions for sustainability in the county of Northamptonshire as a pilot project, with the aim of identifying the multiplier effects above and beyond that which are achievable by any one organization. 'Shared Solutions for Sustainability' will be created and some trial actions implemented across the county. The learning gained will be developed into toolkits, events and presentations to facilitate the dissemination and encourage adoption of best practice by other higher education institutions in partnership with their local communities.

Detailed information is available at GUNi HEiOBS:

http://beta.guninetwork.org/guni.heiobs/good-practices/keeping-it-local-shared-solutions-for-sustainability

Living and learning sustainability in higher education: a research study on indicators of social learning

Institutional area(s):

LOCATION: United Kingdom
INSTITUTION: University of Gloucestershire

This research looks at the learning that occurs within the social contexts of HEIs. This study refers to this learning as 'social learning'. It was conducted at three universities in the UK that have made an explicit commitment to sustainability and it seeks to capture and document lived experiences of staff (academic, administrative and support) which are informed by social learning opportunities regarding sustainability within these institutions. Furthermore, the research has involved a group of members of staff who have reflected on their stories about social learning for sustainability in each HEI.

Detailed information is available at GUNi HEiOBS:

http://www.guninetwork.org/guni.heiobs/good-practices/social-learning-sustainability-higher-education-indicators-institutional-change

The reader can also find the following good practices related to sustainability in Europe at the GUNi Observatory:

- Awareness and education in sustainability at the University of the Basque Country (UPV/EHU)
  LOCATION: Spain
  INSTITUTION: University of Basque Country

- Challenges for the 21st century: teaching sustainability in the context of higher education
  LOCATION: Spain
  INSTITUTION: University of Burgos

- Curricula innovation of the study programme
  LOCATION: Macedonia
  INSTITUTION: University of St Kliment Ohridski

- Developing a centre to coordinate sustainability efforts at Franklin College Switzerland
  LOCATION: Switzerland
  INSTITUTION: Franklin College Switzerland

- Disciplinary integration in research and teaching to promote sustainability models
  LOCATION: United Kingdom
  INSTITUTION: Kingston University

- Dutch national network for sustainable development in higher education curricula (DHO)
  LOCATION: Netherlands
  INSTITUTION: Dutch National Network

- Educating leadership for sustainable environments: international MSc programme 'Environmental Governance'
  LOCATION: Germany
  INSTITUTION: University of Freiburg

- Environmental design in university curricula and architectural training in Europe (EDUCATE)
  LOCATION: Spain
  INSTITUTION: University of Seville

- Hazardous waste management at the University of Alicante
  LOCATION: Spain
  INSTITUTION: University of Alicante

- Integrating art and education for sustainable development: student seminars in context of a transdisciplinary cooperation project
  LOCATION: Germany
  INSTITUTION: Leuphana University of Lueneburg

- Intergenerational course on methods for sustainable development
  LOCATION: Austria
  INSTITUTION: University of Graz

- Is social networking pedagogically sustainable? Putting social learning objects into action
  LOCATION: France
  INSTITUTION: Université Paul-Valéry Montpellier 3

- Porto Polytechnical Engineering School sustainable development action plan
  LOCATION: Portugal
  INSTITUTION: Porto Polytechnical Engineering School

- Social representations of sustainable development of Polish, French and German students
  LOCATION: France
  INSTITUTION: Université de Provence

- Study programme sustainable development – cross-cutting programme for bachelor's students
  LOCATION: Germany
  INSTITUTION: COAST – Centre for Environment and Sustainability Research

- Sustainable development in higher education through the increased quality of doctoral programmes
  LOCATION: Romania
  INSTITUTION: University Dunarea de Jos of Galati

- Teaching sustainable architecture and urban design
  LOCATION: Poland
  INSTITUTION: Cracow University of Technology

http://www.guninetwork.org/guni.heiobs/

II.5 Canada and USA Regional Report

Tarah Wright and Heather Elliott

Abstract

Canada and the United States of America (USA) have played pivotal roles in the development of the global sustainability in higher education movement. Many North American universities are modelling sustainability on their campuses, rethinking policies that are counterproductive to sustainability, and redeveloping curriculum to be more consistent with the tenets of sustainability. Universities and colleges have also begun to work beyond the borders of their campuses, to form regional, national and Canada–USA collaborations and partnerships. The number of academics working in the field of sustainability in higher education is increasing rapidly in both Canada and the USA, and their scholarly outputs are well represented in English-language journals, grey literature and books. While it is apparent that Canada and the USA have made significant steps towards sustainability in higher education, finances, leadership, communication, geography, a lack of understanding and awareness of sustainability issues among the university population, and a resistance to change remain as challenges to the movement and burgeoning field of sustainability in higher education.

INTRODUCTION

Canada and the United States of America (USA) both have a rich history and have played pivotal roles in the development of the global movement to inspire higher education institutions (HEIs) to take a lead role in creating a sustainable future. However, a North American overview is somewhat daunting, as there are many differences in the HE systems found in each country.

While geographically large, Canada has a relatively small population of approximately 34 million (0.5% of the world's population), 93 degree granting universities and a university student enrolment hovering around 1 million. Canada is dominated by a public university system under the responsibility of each province, but funded through fiscal transfers from the Government of Canada. According to the Government of Canada, the average tuition for a Canadian student enrolled in an undergraduate programme in a Canadian university was $4917 in 2009.

In contrast, the USA has a population of 309 million (4.5% of the world's population) with approximately 4300 colleges, universities and junior colleges and over 18 million students. The USA has a significant percentage of private institutions, including approximately 600 for-profit HEIs and almost 6000 corporate universities and degree-granting educational facilities run directly by companies. In 2009, the average annual tuition for a student enrolled in a public university in their own state was $7020. Tuition for students from outside the state is generally double. The tuition for private universities ranges from $15,000 to $68,000 annually.

While each country has specific laws governing HE, only the USA has legislation that deals specifically with sustainability in higher education (SHE). In August 2008, President Bush signed into law the Higher Education Sustainability Act (HESA), which was part of the new Higher Education Opportunity Act (http://www2.ed.gov/policy/highered/leg/hea08/index.html). The major impact of the legislation is in that it provides for the 'University Sustainability Grants Program' administered through the Secretary of Education, in consultation with the Environmental Protection Agency, which allows colleges and universities to establish sustainability research programmes and implement sustainable measures on campuses.

The budget for 2010 was $50 million. The Council of Ministers of Education, Canada (CMEC) released Learn Canada 2020 (www.cmec.ca/Publications/.../CMEC-2020-DECLARATION.en.pdf) in April 2008 is a framework document that serves as a collective statement of the Ministers' responsibilities in education and their goals for the coming decade. In the document, the Ministers identified education for sustainable development (ESD) as a key activity area on which to focus collaboratively through intergovernmental organization; however, no formal legislation exists.

BOX II.5.1: CANADIAN POLITICAL FRAMEWORK

Canada's government was originally established in the British North American Act in 1867 by the British parliament, but was unable to make constitutional changes without British parliament approval until 1982. The Canadian Constitution provides for a parliamentary system of government, consisting of the monarchy and two legislative chambers: the House of Commons, and the Senate. The Constitution provides for two key levels of government: federal and provincial (there are 10 provinces in Canada and 3 territories). The federal government is led by the prime minister and cabinet and provincial governments by a premier and cabinet. While there are over 16 registered federal political parties, the main five parties are the Liberal Party (generally thought of as in the centre of the political spectrum), the Conservative Party (right of centre, and currently in power), the New Democratic Party of Canada (left of centre), Le Bloc Québécois (a Quebec separatist party), and the Green Party (espousing green values and sustainability as its core mission). The constitutional responsibility for education (other than the education of aboriginal people) rests with the provinces of Canada. As a result, a distinctive system of education has evolved in each region. In 2008, the Council of Ministers of Education (made up of ministers from each province) released a collective statement about ESD in Learn Canada 2020 (www.cmec.ca/Publications/.../CMEC-2020-DECLARATION.en.pdf), but to date no formal legislation exists at the federal or provincial levels.

BOX II.5.2: USA POLITICAL FRAMEWORK

The government of the United States is a federal constitutional republic based on the Declaration of Independence of 1776 and the Constitution of 1789. Power is divided between the federal government and the 50 member states. The Constitution created three separate branches of government, each with their own powers and areas of influence: the Legislative Branch (consisting of Congress which is responsible for making federal laws); the Executive Branch (made up of the president, cabinet and the bureaucracy, with power lying with the president); and the Judicial Branch (the Supreme Court and other federal courts). The modern political party system is dominated by the Democratic Party (generally positioned as left-of-centre and supporting an American liberalism platform) and the Republican Party (generally positioned as right-of-centre and supporting an American conservatism platform) which between them have won all presidential elections in the US since the mid-1850s. As of November 2010, 36.0% of American adults identified themselves as Republicans; 34.7% Democrats, and 29.3% were not affiliated with either major party (Rasmusen, 2010). Higher education in the USA is generally the responsibility of individual states with the exception of the Tenth Amendment, which has the federal government guarding the right of its citizens to equal access to public institutions and equal opportunity within them. The Higher Education Sustainability Act (http://thomas.loc.gov/cgi-bin/query/z?c110:H.R.3637:) is the only legislation related to ESD in the USA. It provides for a grant programme that allows colleges and universities to establish sustainability research programmes and implement sustainable measures on campuses.

HIGHER EDUCATION FOR SUSTAINABILITY MOVEMENT

Higher education for sustainability (HES) is relatively new and emerging movement in both the Canadian and USA educational systems. The roots come from international sustainable development (SD) efforts starting in the 1970s. For example, the Stockholm Conference on the Human Environment in 1972 specifically discussed the role of HE in international sustainable development. Mention of sustainability and HE are also made in the Belgrade Charter (1975), Tibilisi Declaration (1977) and United Nations Conference on Environment and Development (1992). The movement within HE in North America arguably did not begin to solidify until the 1990. At this time some North American scholars were criticizing HE for its inability to be a model of sustainability in both physical operations and curriculum (Clugston, 1999; Orr, 1995). One reaction to these criticisms was the development of sustainability in higher education policies and declarations (see Wright, 2004).

An historic attempt to define and promote SHE was made in the creation of the Talloires Declaration. While the Talloires is an international declaration that now enjoys over 418 signatories worldwide (USA n=163, Canada n=33), its development was American-led. In October 1990 the President of Tufts University, with the help of the Rockefeller Foundation, the US Environmental Protection Agency, and the John D. and Catherine T. MacArthur Foundation, convened 22 university presidents and chancellors to voice their concerns and create a document that outlined key actions HEIs must take to create a sustainable future.

ORGANIZATIONS

The 1990s also saw the proliferation of not-for-profit organizations and non-governmental organizations (NGOs) focused on SHE in North America. University Leaders for a Sustainable Future (ULSF) was officially established as the Secretariat for signatories of the Talloires Declaration in the early 1990s. Established under another name by Dr Tony Cortese, then Dean of Environmental Programs at Tufts University, the organization changed its name to ULSF in 1995 to reflect an emerging focus on all levels of leadership within HE, including senior administrators, faculty, staff and students, and the introduction of a formal membership structure. ULSF maintained an institutional affiliation with Tufts University until 1997 when it moved to Washington, DC to become the HE programme of the Center for Respect of Life and Environment (CRLE). While continuing to serve as Secretariat for signatories of the Talloires Declaration, ULSF expanded its programmes and services to include sustainability assessment, research on theoretical models and case studies of sustainability initiatives in HE, formative evaluation of sustainability initiatives, and forming new international partnerships to advance SHE globally. ULSF became independent of CRLE in 2007, functioning as a virtual organization and continues to maintain its position as Secretariat for signatories of the Talloires Declaration (www.ulsf.org).

Around the same time, the National Wildlife Federation (NWF) established its Campus Ecology programme (http://www.nwf.org/Global-Warming/Campus-Solutions.aspx) which has become a leading conservation programme in HE. Their mission is to assist students, faculty, staff and administrators in transforming colleges and universities in the USA into learning and teaching models of sustainability, by: assisting with the design and implementation of practical conservation projects; providing training and incentives; and, helping to document and share lessons learned nationally and beyond.

In 1991 Learning for a Sustainable Future (LSF) was established in Canada by a diverse group of youth, educators, business leaders, government and community members (www.lsf-lst.ca/). The original purpose of this not-for-profit charitable organization was to integrate sustainability education into Canada's education system at all levels. LSF facilitates the delivery of sustainable development education programmes and resources to teachers and students across Canada. At the end of 2008, LSF achieved the goal of reaching over 200,000 Canadians. LSF, in partnership with Environment Canada and Manitoba Education, Citizenship and Youth, is leading the Canadian response to the UN Decade of Education for Sustainable Development through the implementation of a series of initiatives, some of which are directly targeted at HE.

Second Nature (www.secondnature.org) was founded in Boston in 1993 by a small group of forward-thinking leaders that included Dr Anthony D. Cortese from Tufts University, Senator John F. Kerry (D-MA), Teresa Heinz Kerry, Bruce Droste, and others. This group sought to establish an organization dedicated to bringing about the change in society that is vital to the success and livelihood of every current and future living being: a change for a just and sustainable future. Since its founding, Second Nature has worked with over 4000 faculties and administrators at more than 500 colleges and universities to help make the principles of sustainability fundamental to every aspect of HE. It has helped to advance the higher education for sustainability movement at state, regional, and national levels by serving and supporting HE leaders in making healthy, just, and sustainable living the foundation of all learning and practice in HE.

The Association for the Advancement of Sustainability in Higher Education (www.aashe.org) has arguably become the largest organization for university sustainability in North America. Its roots go back to the Education for Sustainability Western Network (EFS West) established in 2001, which served college campuses in the Western US and Canada by providing resources and support for sustainability efforts. In 2004, EFS West held the first North American Conference on Sustainability in Higher Education, in Portland, Oregon. The success of this conference and increasing demand for EFS West's resources led it to transition from a regional organization to a North American higher education association – the Association for the Advancement of Sustainability in Higher Education. AASHE was officially launched in January 2006, serving as the first professional HE association for the campus sustainability community. AASHE continues to work to advance sustainability in all sectors of HE and support campuses in meeting their sustainability goals.

PARTNERSHIPS

Many partnerships have been established as a result of the higher education for sustainability movement. For example, the Higher Education Association Sustainability Consortium (HEASC) was formed in December 2005 by leaders of several associations, to support and enhance the capacity of HE to fulfil its critical role in producing an educated and engaged citizenry and the knowledge needed for a thriving and civil society. These organizations recognize that fulfilling their mission requires a broader, systemic, collaborative approach to their own work and that of the constituents they serve. HEASC's purpose is to learn from one another, work together on joint projects, get access to the best expertise and information on sustainability, and to keep a collective, ongoing focus on advancing education for a sustainable future over time (http://www2.aashe.org/heasc/index.php).

Established in 2006, ESD Canada (formally the National Education for Sustainable Development Expert Council) brings together a broad range of stakeholders from across the country to support systemic change towards ESD within the formal, non-formal and informal education systems. Made up of representatives from provincial and territorial Education for Sustainable Development Working Groups, Ministry of Education representatives for jurisdictions that do not yet have Working Groups, as well as national and international organizations, the council addresses cross-cutting issues of ESD and promotes research, communication and the sharing of best practices (www.esdcanada.ca).

The United States Partnership for Education for Sustainable Development (USPESD) was first conceived at a November 2003 gathering held in Washington, DC that included almost 100 participants from a diverse range of sectors including K-12 (all primary and secondary education) and higher education, science and research organizations, conservation and environmental NGOs, faith communities, living institutions, youth advocacy organizations, government agencies and others (www.uspartnership.org). Convened by the National Council on Science and the Environment and University Leaders for a Sustainable Future, the group met to respond to the call by the UN General Assembly for a Decade of Education for Sustainable Development (2005–2014). Participants decided that the Partnership would not design or implement programmes of its own. Rather, it would serve as a clearing house and as a catalyst to convene groups and build community to support existing and emerging initiatives. The Decade and the US Partnership provide international and national context for such efforts, helping to promote and strengthen education for sustainable development in the United States.

MAJOR CONFERENCES AND INITIATIVES

The Greening the Campus Conference (known to many as colloquially as 'Ball State') is perhaps the longest running conference focused on SHE in North America. The first conference was held in April 1996 at Ball State University in Indiana. The biannual conference has grown from a participant base of 200 to over 2000 at the 2009 event.

While a relative newcomer, the biannual AASHE conference has become one of the most popular SHE events in North America. The first conference was held in 2006 in Tempe Arizona with over 650 attendees. By its next conference, in Raleigh, NC, in 2008, attendance had almost tripled to over 1700 participants, with even greater numbers attending the 2010 conference in Denver.

A well-established initiative by the Society for College and University Planning (SCUP) is the Campus Sustainability Day (http://www.scup.org/page/csd/mission). Campus Sustainability Day is a satellite broadcast where leaders in HE exchange ideas and challenge colleges and universities to integrate sustainability practices into all areas of campus. Universities across North America choose to celebrate Campus Sustainability Day in different ways – some devoting a whole month to highlighting campus sustainability efforts, some by encouraging sustainability conversations over a week.

An initiative that is gaining great momentum is the American College and University Presidents Climate Change Commitment (ACUPCC) which has now been signed by over 550 HE presidents. By signing the commitment, these presidents are pledging to work towards clean energy, carbon-neutral campuses, and professional development initiatives on sustainability so HE will both model and teach sustainability principles (www.presidentsclimatecommitment.org).

CURRICULUM AND LEARNING PROCESSES

A sustainable society is 'one that can persist over generations, one that is far-seeing enough, flexible enough, and wise enough not to undermine either its physical or social systems of support' (Meadows et al., 1992). While a sustainable future cannot be achieved through changes and actions in one sector alone, education is a key component in working towards this goal. Yet universities have been criticized for their unsustainable behaviour. David Orr (1995) argues that environmental problems are not the work of ignorant people, but 'largely the result of work by people with BA's, B.Sc.'s, LLB's, MBA's and PhD's'. Ecological footprint models show us that it is the well-educated people of industrialized countries who use the majority of the earth's natural resources and who contribute the most to the world's sustainability problems. In fact, many scholars criticize HE for producing disciplinary leaders incapable of addressing critical sustainability problems, because they are blindly contributing to them. Why is this? It seems that the academy is very good at fragmenting and sectoralizing information so that one discipline has no understanding of its impact on the others. For example, a student graduating from a business degree might understand the financial benefits of oil extraction, but not the full environmental, political and social ramifications and costs (and vice versa for a student in political science or biology).

Einstein once observed that 'the significant problems we face cannot be solved at the same level of thinking we were at when we created them'. North American HEIs have been responding to the challenge of educating for sustainability by developing new and interdisciplinary environment and/or sustainability programmes, and/or attempting to infuse sustainability concepts into traditional disciplines.

STAND-ALONE PROGRAMMES
According to the Association of University and Colleges of Canada, there are over 200 degree, diploma and certificate programmes offered in French and English related to the environment across the country. However, there are very few programmes that contain the term sustainability in the title.

Dalhousie University was the first HEI in Canada to launch a College of Sustainability in 2009 (http://sustainability.dal.ca/College_of_Sustainab.php). The College offers a unique interdisciplinary undergraduate programme in environment, sustainability and society and enjoyed a cohort of 325 students in its first year of operation. The University of Alberta has a post-baccalaureate diploma programme in environmental and sustainability education. In fall of 2011, the University of Winnipeg, Manitoba will offer a new graduate degree programme in Development Practice focusing on indigenous development and sustainability, in partnership with the MacArthur Foundation.

In the USA, there are over 20 universities and colleges with undergraduate programmes related to sustainability. One of the best known is the School of Sustainability at Arizona State University (www.schoolofsustainability.asu.edu). The school offers flexible, interdisciplinary, and problem-oriented BAs and BScs in Sustainability. There are also over a dozen universities offering master's degrees, and five universities offering doctoral degrees related to sustainability. For example, Harvard University offers a Master's Degree in Sustainability and Environmental Management, designed to educate working professionals on the two core environmental issues facing the global community: ecological management, and sustainability. Prescott College, an independent liberal arts school dedicated to environment and social justice offers a Doctor of Philosophy (PhD) in Education with a concentration in Sustainability Education (http://www.prescott.edu/academics/phd/index.html).

GENERAL EDUCATION PROGRAMMES
In the USA, many universities have general education (GE) requirements that students are required to take. The intention is to introduce undergraduates to the richness and diversity of the various academic disciplines and have students graduate with a common collective knowledge about the world that enables them to communicate, make informed decisions and participate fully as informed citizens in local, national and global matters. In some cases, the GE requirements are set by the state, in others, the GE requirements are set by the individual school. According to Rowe (2002), a number of colleges and universities have incorporated an in-depth exposure to environmental literacy in their GE requirements. Some have also included topics of social responsibility and/or civic engagement. Others have combined the two. For example, the University of Northern Iowa has required students to take the course Environment, Technology and Society as a GE requirement since 1988.

Two national surveys in the US provide strength to Rowe's claims. In a 2001 survey of 496 four-year institutions in the USA, Wolfe (2001) found that 11.6% had a required GE course in environmental literacy, and 55% had an option of taking an environmentally related course for their GE requirements. In the same year, the National Wildlife Federation published the *State of the Campus Environment: A National Report Card on Environmental Performance and Sustainability in Higher*

Education (McIntosh et al., 2001). This survey of both two- and four-year colleges in the United States showed that 8% of HEIs had an undergraduate programme requirement related to environmental literacy.

Stanford is aggressively working towards sustainability becoming part of the university's GE requirements. In fall 2006 Stanford introduced the pioneering I-Earth curriculum (https://pangea.stanford.edu/courses/i-earth/). This programme helps students to develop an interdisciplinary understanding of the planet and the intersections of its natural and human systems. Proponents of I-Earth becoming a GE requirement argue that an understanding of the planet on which we live is essential for all students and should be considered on par with all students having an understanding of the humanities. Their slogan is 'not yet a requirement for Stanford, but a requirement for life'.

Another interesting example is the Portland State Freshman Inquiry on Sustainability. At this university, students take a year-long sequence of courses that introduce students to Portland State's GE goals. The Sustainability Freshman inquiry explores the interconnectedness of global systems using an interdisciplinary approach to show how sustainability issues can be understood from different perspectives (http://www.pdx.edu/unst/freshman-inquiry-sustainability).

CERTIFICATES AND DIPLOMAS IN SUSTAINABILITY
Some universities in both the United States and Canada have seen the benefit in creating concurrent and post-degree certificates and diplomas in sustainability. For example, the MIT Sloan School of Management has developed a sustainability certificate that can be taken by students enrolled in any of the school's programmes (http://mitsloan.mit.edu/sustainability/). Ryerson University in Toronto has developed a professional development certificate in sustainability for individuals from any disciplinary background (www.ryerson.ca/ce/sustain).

INTEGRATING SUSTAINABILITY ACROSS THE CURRICULUM
While interdisciplinary programmes related specifically to sustainability are most welcome in North America, many feel that sustainability must be integrated into the traditional academic disciplines if we are to create positive sustainable change. As Tony Cortese (2008), President of Second Nature, says, 'rather than being isolated in its own academic discipline, education about the environment must become an integral part of the normal teaching in all disciplines'. The same is true for sustainability. Therefore, instead of adding sustainability on as an additional degree requirement, many HEIs are trying to shift the dominant paradigm and infuse environmental literacy, social responsibility and civic engagement into courses in multiple disciplines.

The Disciplinary Associations Network for Sustainability (DANS) has declared its commitment to education for a sustainable future (http://www2.aashe.org/dans/). DANS recognizes that the engagement of academic disciplines is critical to advancing the overall goals of sustainability, and aims to help HEIs to lead in making education, research, and practice for a sustainable society a reality. York University in Toronto hosts the United Nations Educational, Scientific and Cultural Organization (UNESCO) Chair on Reorienting Teacher Education to Address Sustainability (http://www.unesco.org/en/education-for-sustainable-development/networks/working-group-of-unesco-chairs/canada/).

Well-known models for helping faculty to incorporate environmental sustainability issues into university courses from music to history to mathematics include the Ponderosa Project (Northern Arizona University, 1995–2002), and the Piedmont Project (Emory University, 2001–present). The Association of the Advancement of Sustainability in Higher Education offers the Sustainability across the Curriculum Leadership Workshop for faculty leaders of all disciplines who wish to develop curriculum change programmes around sustainability on their campuses. To date, they have had over 300 faculty members participate in the workshops, who have then returned to their campuses to teach others about infusing sustainability into the curriculum (http://www.aashe.org/profdev/curriculum.php).

BOX II.5.3: COLLEGE OF SUSTAINABILITY, DALHOUSIE UNIVERSITY

The College of Sustainability is the first of its kind in Canada. It launched the innovative Environment, Sustainability and Society (ESS) undergraduate degree programme in 2009 with an incoming class of 300 students. The ESS programme brings students from a wide variety of backgrounds together who share a common passion for the planet. Instead of creating a stand-alone programme (which could be interpreted as another silo), the ESS programme requires students to combine their studies with a more traditional discipline. Depending on their specialty, students work towards a Bachelor of Arts, Bachelor of Science, Bachelor of Management, Bachelor of Community Design, Bachelor of Computer Science or Bachelor of Informatics (sustainability.dal.ca).

INSTITUTIONAL MANAGEMENT AND OPERATIONS

A large step towards recognizing the importance of sustainability in the HE setting is a formal, public commitment to becoming more sustainable. To date, there have been many national and international declarations signed by various institutions. These include the Talloires Declaration, the Halifax Declaration, the Sapporo Sustainability Declaration, and the Earth Charter Initiative. A major part of these declarations includes institutions becoming more sustainable in their internal practices and operations. Implementing changes in physical operations is often considered easier than other changes (Wright, 2009) as institutions may often see a financial return on these investments.

One way that universities have responded to the sustainability challenge is to establish sustainable practices in campus management and operations, attempting to model sustainable behaviour in the development of buildings, dining services, energy, grounds, transportation, purchasing, waste management, water, financing, investing and policy development. Many universities have found campus greening initiatives to be cost-effective in the long run. In recent years, a number of campuses have established staff positions devoted to advancing sustainability on campus. The University of British Columbia was an early adopter of campus sustainability and created its first Sustainability Office with Director in 1998 (www.sustain.ubc.ca). With humble beginnings of one staff member, the office has now grown to a staff of over a dozen, often handling million-dollar budgets. Harvard University was also an early adopter. In 1999 an interfaculty group of faculty, staff, and students met on a number of occasions to discuss how to secure a dedicated staff member to the issue of sustainability. One year later enough funding was raised to begin the Harvard Green Campus Initiative (later becoming the Office for Sustainability in 2008). There are now more than 100 Campus Sustainability Officers working in colleges and universities in Canada and the USA.

To date, the majority of sustainable institutional management and operations has focused on environmental, rather than social, sustainability. The Association for the Advancement of Sustainability in Higher Education (AASHE) has online records concerning best practices and institutions that are currently implementing projects in a wide variety of operational and management aspects. It also provides an annual conference, weekly bulletins, online forums, webinars and train-the-trainer sessions.

Green design or LEED (leadership in energy and environmental design) criteria are often included in many buildings currently being built or planned. While this can have a major impact on the emissions, energy and environmental or social sustainability of the building, the majority of campus structures have already been built. Older buildings have larger environmental footprints. For this reason, retrofitting existing buildings with more efficient energy and water technologies is an important step. In addition, many campuses in North America have begun investigating renewable energy production.

To improve social sustainability, efforts are made to improve campus accessibility for those with low mobility. In terms of management, sustainable procurement policies and waste management have been major focuses. All these efforts are often assessed and reported using assessment tools such as the Sierra Youth Coalition's Campus Sustainability Assessment Framework (CSAF), AASHE's Sustainability Tracking, Assessment and Rating System (STARS) programme, the Princeton Review, NWF Sustainable Campus Report Card, or the Sustainable Endowment Institute's Green Report Card.

In North America, there is a growing trend towards using schools as living laboratories, allowing students to gain hands-on experience while improving their campus or community. David Orr began this movement at Oberlin College in the 1980s but it has since spread out onto many different campuses. For example, the Arizona State University has created the Campus Living Laboratory Network (CLLN) to facilitate work on campus sustainability projects between students, staff and faculty. At the University of British Columbia Farm, students have the opportunity to be involved in various learning and research initiatives (www.landfood. ubc.ca/ubcfarm/). This 24-hectare farm is financially self-sufficient and run by the Centre for Sustainable Food Systems. In 2008, both UBC colleges, 4 of UBC's 11 schools and 8 of UBC's 11 faculties were involved with the farm.

In recent years some companies and organizations have emerged to help facilitate the greening of campus operations. Those to note include: Clean Air Cool Planet (CACP) which partners with campuses to identify and promote solutions to climate change; the College and University Recycling Council (CURC); the Green Power Partnership which is an Environmental Protection Agency programme providing advice and resources to prospective university green power purchasers and publicity to green power leaders; and, the Society for College and University Planning (SCUP) which focuses on the promotion, advancement, and application of effective planning in HE and is a major proponent of universities modelling sustainable behaviour.

As key university stakeholders, students have considerable interest and influence in the management of their institutions. Since students have become more concerned with sustainability, universities have improved their efforts. Most, if not all, HEIs now have student environmental or sustainability groups active on their campus, which may or may not connect to larger national organizations. In Canada, the Sierra Youth Coalition is a branch of the Sierra Club of Canada which focuses on sustainable campuses and high schools (www.syc-cjs.org/ sustainable-campuses). It provides a supportive network for students interested in sustainability and offers training related to multi-stakeholder group building and campus assessments with their tool, the Campus Sustainability Assessment Framework. As of 2009, 72 of approximately 277 Canadian campuses were involved (SYC, 2009). Students in the United States organize through SEAC (pronounced 'seek'), a national network of organizations concerned with various aspects of sustainability (www.seac.org/). On the environmental front, they are involved in the Climate Challenge, but they also focus on indigenous rights and social justice (SEAC, 2008). There is also a Sierra Student Coalition, the youth branch of the US Sierra Club which is involved in SHE, particularly the use of coal energy (Sierra Club, 2010).

BOX II.5.5: GREEN BUILDING FOR COMMUNITY

Education through experiential learning helps students become confident in their skills, and applying this in partnership with local not-for-profits is a win-win situation. The University of Virgina's ecoMOD programme is such an example. It provides teams of students the opportunity to perform interdisciplinary research and design ecological, modular and affordable house prototypes for low-income housing organizations. They then build and evaluate these prototypes in order to provide homes and suggestions for design improvements (University of Virgina, 2010).

BOX II.5.6: INVESTING IN CAMPUS SUSTAINABILITY

The creation of the Green Campus Loan Fund (GCLF) at Harvard has thus far provided funding for 153 greening the campus initiatives (www. green.harvard.edu/loan-fund). The $12 million revolving loan fund provides university groups with capital for projects that will repay the loan amount within five years through reductions in operating costs, waste removal or utility consumption related to the project. By taking a holistic approach to the economics involved, instead of considering the capital and maintenance separately, the GCLF has led to overall savings of $4 million already (Harvard College, 2009).

RESEARCH

Research is a critical tool in developing a sustainable future, and universities have a responsibility to contribute through their scholarly activities. What constitutes 'sustainability' research is still a much-debated topic. A recent attempt by Waas et al. (2010) defines it as 'all research conducted within the institutional context of a university that contributes to sustainable development'. They adopt a comprehensive view, including foundational and applied research in both disciplinary and interdisciplinary contexts. Glasser et al. (2005) distinguish between research that contributes to the sustainable development of society in general, and sustainability in higher education which is an emerging field of inquiry that focuses on incorporating 'sustainability concepts and insights into higher education and its major areas of activity … It also refers to research that treats higher education institutions as complex systems and focuses on the integration of sustainability across all of its activities, responsibilities, and mission'. While both types of research occur in Canada and the USA, for the purposes of this paper, we focus our efforts mostly on the latter.

RESEARCH MEETINGS

A critical step to promoting sustainability in higher education is to develop new modes of collaboration and information sharing. Information sharing, collaboration, and the development of a research agenda were difficult until recently in the United States and Canada. Because of the interdisciplinary nature of sustainability research, scholars come from a variety of backgrounds, which made it difficult for researchers to meet and discuss their work at traditional disciplinary conferences, or to plan for future research priorities. The past decade has seen a change in this with the development of organizations dedicated to sustainability in higher education (see section on Organizations above) and, following from there, some gatherings of scholars in the field.

One of the first gatherings of researchers was in October 2005 in Halifax, Canada. Thirty-five HES experts representing 17 different countries gathered to further intellectual understanding of HES research and to explore the development of research priorities for the future (for full report see Wright 2007). Further, the Association for the Advancement of Sustainability in Higher Education (AASHE) has a sub-group dedicated to sustainability in higher education research who converse online and meet regularly at the AASHE conferences.

RESEARCH CENTRES

Canada and the United States host a multitude of centres dedicated to sustainability research in general (for example the International Institute for Sustainable Development, the Canadian Consortium for Sustainable Development Research at the University of British Columbia, the Earth Institute Colombia University, the Institute for Sustainable Solutions at Portland State University, and the Global Institute of Sustainability at Arizona State University). There are many research centres dedicated to environmental education within HEIs, but few research centres dedicated to SHE. Exceptions are the Centre for Environmental and Sustainability Education at Florida Gulf Coast University, the Robert A. Macoskey Center for Sustainable Systems Educa-

tion and Research at Slippery Rock University, and the Center for Environmental Sustainability Education at the University of Wisconsin-Milwaukee.

PUBLICATIONS

In North America, the majority of the research dedication to SHE is disseminated through traditional academic means such as journal articles, books, and newsletters.

In a bibliometric study of English-language journal articles related to education for sustainable development (ESD) from 1990 to 2005, Wright and Pullen (2007) found that approximately 70% of the manuscripts published resulted from individuals working at a Canadian or US university. Given this apparent dominance in research output, it is surprising that the two countries do not play host to more journals dedicated to the subject. Wright and Pullen (2007) found that the majority of North American authors published in the *International Journal of Sustainability in Higher Education*, which is supported in part by the University Leaders for a Sustainable Future in the USA, but produced and published in Europe. The only North American journal that focuses almost exclusively on SHE is *Sustainability: The Journal of Record* which launched in March 2008.

Grey materials in the field include: the *AASHE Bulletin* which offers a weekly compilation of news, opportunities, new resources, and events related to sustainability in higher education; *AASHE Digest*, an annual review of campus sustainability efforts; and the *Campus Ecology Yearbook* which provides case studies about campus environmental projects.

Seminal books that have been produced by North American authors include (but are not limited to) the following:

- *Ecodemia: Campus Environmental Stewardship at the Turn of the 21st Century* by Julian Keniry, National Wildlife Federation, 1995.
- *The Campus and Environmental Responsibility* by David Eagan and David Orr (eds), Jossey Bass Publishers, 1992.
- *Greening the Ivory Tower: Improving the Environmental Track Record of Universities, Colleges, and Other Institutions* by Sarah Hammond Creighton, MIT Press, 1998.
- *Educating Citizens: Preparing America's Undergraduates for Lives of Moral and Civic Responsibility* by Anne Colby, Thomas Ehrlich, Elizabeth Beaumont, and Jason Stephens, Jossey-Bass, 2003.
- *Sustainability on Campus: Stories and Strategies for Change* by Peggy F. Barlett and Geoffrey W. Chase, MIT Press, 2004.

- *Higher Education and the Challenge of Sustainability: Problematics, Promise, and Practice* by Peter Blaze Corcoran and Arjen E.J. Wals (eds), Springer, 2004.
- *Planet U: Sustaining the World, Reinventing the University* by Michael M'Gonigle and Justin Starke, New Society Press, 2005.
- *The Green Campus: Meeting the Challenge of Environmental Sustainability* by Walter Simson (ed.), APPA, 2008.
- *Teaching Environmental Literacy: Across Campus and Across the Curriculum* by Heather L. Reynolds, Eduardo S. Brondizio, and Jennifer Meta Robinson (eds), Indiana University Press, 2009.

FUNDING AGENCIES

The development of the fifty million dollar 'University Sustainability Grants Program' allows scholars in US universities to engage in research dedicated to sustainability and to implement sustainable measures on campuses. Further, academics in both Canada and North America can apply to national granting bodies for work related to sustainability in higher education, although none of the granting agencies are focused exclusively on sustainability research. In the USA, the National Science Foundation (NSF) is an independent federal agency with an annual budget of $7 billion (financial year 2010). The NSF dedicated additional funding from 2006–2011 for research that improves humanity's ability to live sustainably on the earth. In Canada, researchers can apply to the Canadian Institutes of Health Research, the National Science and Engineering Research Council, or the Social Sciences and Humanities Research Council of Canada (SSHRC) for funds to support sustainability research. In 2008, SSHRC created four funding programmes dedicated to developing and building on capacity for research, talent development and knowledge mobilization on Canadian environment and sustainability issues.

SOCIAL AND COMMUNITY ENGAGEMENT

Higher education plays an important role in educating citizens, but also has a role to play as a key community member, at both local and global levels. Partnerships between community stakeholders, including HEIs, can lead to positive results for all.

Universities can contribute to their communities in a variety of ways, including questioning the role of society and its members. Their campuses have long been thought of as a safe refuge for inquiry and reimagining.

Some campuses are making an active effort to renew this discussion of society's role, for example Walden University in Minnesota, USA. This advanced degree distance education institution hosts an annual conference on social change issues that people attend in person and virtually. In addition, Walden University promotes volunteerism with its Service Network that links students and alumni with not-for-profits and the Global Day of Service when members of its community, past and present, get involved in the greater world.

It is important to ensure that everyone feels comfortable engaging in dialogue and speaking of their experiences in order to generate the best ideas. Through transcultural dialogue and mutual understanding, people and organizations with differing viewpoints are able to come together and produce fascinating results. In Saskatchewan, Canada, grassroots mobilization of municipalities, HEIs, Aboriginal communities, not-for-profit organizations and businesses led to the formation of a Regional Centre of Expertise (RCE) on Education for Sustainable Development through the United Nations University-Institute for Advanced Studies (UNU-IAS) (Dahms et al., 2008).

Many HEIs understand the benefits of working with their communities and forming links with civil society. This often involves working together on research or community planning. Students at Carleton University in Ontario, Canada, gain considerable experience through the Carleton-Batawa Initiative. The goal is for students to transform the community of Batawa, making it a sustainable city (Boyle, 2009). Students themselves have been forging partnerships with their broader communities through the creation of Public Interest Research Groups (PIRGs) across Canada. While these not-for-profit organizations are student-run and student-funded, the focus is on broader community issues including social and environmental justice, and non-students are invited to participate in the working groups (APIRG, 2005). In the United States, the not-for-profit organization Campus Compact has been working with presidents of HEIs since 1985 to promote civic engagement. More than a quarter of all American HEIs are now involved and, since the beginning, over 20 million students have volunteered and formed partnerships in their local communities, representing more than $5.7 billion in service (Campus Compact, 2010).

Local circumstances are often influenced by global happenings, making the latter just as important. Various networks of HEIs, professors, not-for-profits and other stakeholders have sprung up to explore global problems and innovate solutions. As mentioned in a previous section, AASHE facilitates bringing together

HEIs from primarily the United States and Canada, though institutions in other countries are beginning to join as well. Its focus is on making campuses more sustainable through management, operations and teaching. In Canada, the World University Service of Canada (WUSC) links post-secondary institutions and individuals together to focus on human development and education through partnered projects overseas. Some of the development projects focus specifically on strengthening civil society and promoting human rights (WUSC, n.d.). The United States Partnership for Education for Sustainable Development (USPESD) is a network to bring together different groups and sectors on various initiatives related to sustainability. The sectors include K-12 education, higher education, faith communities, business and communities (USPESD, n.d.).

Many members of the professoriate are involved with sustainability in their communities, via professional or personal life. AASHE hosts Teach-the-Teacher sessions through which faculty and staff are able to share their experiences and wisdom with members of other universities, so that they might learn and be able to implement change on their own campuses. Ann Dale, recipient of a Canada Research Chair position at Royal Roads University in British Columbia, Canada, is a leader in sustainable community development. Her research has focused on interactions between the environment and society, social capital and sustainable community development. She also chairs the Canadian Consortium for Sustainable Development Research (Royal Roads University, 2010). Harry C. Boyte, co-director of the Augsburg College Center for Democracy and Citizenship in the United States, has published a number of books on citizen engagement and education for democracy and has actively been involved in community groups focused on community renewal (Augsburg College, 2010).

Sometimes the greatest contribution that HE can make is to deliver knowledge back into the hands of society and help create positive social change. The Centre for Research on Work and Society (CRWS) at York University in Canada focuses on labour issues and research partnerships between unions, the university and the community (CRWS, n.d.). In an effort to inspire social change internationally, Brown University has been hosting a social change workshop for graduate students in the summers for 80 students in top graduate programmes from around the world (Institute for Humane Studies at George Mason University, 2009). Students and faculty alike

present research and facilitate dialogue on democracy, society and the economy.

BOX II.5.7: THE GOGGLES PROJECT

The non-profit Goggles Project, an initiative of the fictitious ReThink University, launched its inaugural cross-Canada campus tour in September 2010. A cast of four lively characters engaged university audiences in experiential theatrical performances that asked them to rethink the role that their institution should play in building a more sustainable planet. The energy and ideas generated by the tour are harnessed by the Goggles Project website (www.gogglesproject.org). By using positive and fun messaging, the tour has initiated increased dialogue on campuses about sustainability in higher education.

ANALYSING THE PRESENT AND LOOKING TO THE FUTURE

While it is apparent that Canada and the US have made significant steps toward sustainability in higher education, the challenges and barriers to advancing individual universities toward sustainability (for example financial, leadership, communications) as identified by Leal Filho and Wright (2002) are still very real in Canada. A recent study of 23 Canadian university presidents revealed that the most significant constraints to moving toward SHE were seen as financial, lack of understanding and awareness of sustainability issues among the university population, and a resistance to change (Wright, 2010). These challenges are ubiquitous for the movement in both Canada and the USA. The problems are further exacerbated by the large geography of the two countries, and the relatively recent development of the scholarly field. Finally, many of the metrics needed to determine the advance of the SHE movement are unavailable. Currently, though anecdotal information is rich, there are no agencies that officially collect information on the quantity or quality of sustainability curriculum in these countries, the numbers of and initiatives of sustainability officers and offices on university campuses, the progress of campuses in developing green buildings and modelling sustainability through operations, and the amount of research funding dedicated to sustainability in higher education research.

The following strategies and actions are suggested
to advance sustainability in higher education in Canada
and the USA:

- **Develop indicators to assess the progression of
  sustainability in higher education at national
  and international levels.** It is not enough to have a
  collection of case studies and anecdotes about SHE
  initiatives. In order to understand the advancement
  of the movement, a set of basic indicators that can
  be easily collected and understood is essential.

- **Develop innovative and creative initiatives to
  engage the university community in discussions
  about the role the university can play in creating
  a sustainable future.** Sustainability in higher education over the long term requires the integration of
  community involvement, stakeholder identification,
  institutional collaboration, and communication.
  Although several advances have been made, some
  of the major stakeholders (administrators, faculty,
  staff and students) have remained largely absent in
  discussions regarding the role universities can play in
  creating a sustainable future. Public outreach, through
  environmental communication, is an effective vector
  in social change and should be used to help make
  sustainability a cultural norm on campuses.

- **Promote a deeper understanding of sustainability
  among societal leaders.** While most educated people
  in Canada and the United States have heard of the
  term sustainability or sustainable development, for
  the majority, their understanding is vague. If we

are to advance sustainability in higher education,
the public's understanding must go beyond the
Venn diagram conceptualization of sustainability
to a deeper and more meaningful comprehension.
Scholars should focus their efforts on societal leaders
including politicians, spiritual leaders, and teachers.

- **Promote the development of university-wide
  undergraduate academic programmes that allow
  students to learn for a sustainable future.** While
  classes focused on sustainability are a wonderful
  addition to the curriculum choices for undergraduate students, sustainability concepts must be infused
  into all disciplines or else the notion that environment and sustainability are special interests rather
  than something for all to consider will be reinforced.

- **Promote the development of an active and
  empowering curriculum focused on creating
  change for a sustainable future.** Studies show that
  the didactic delivery of information about sustainability may teach students about the issues, but
  lecture rarely leads students to action. Universities
  need to accept and adopt news ways of teaching that
  incorporate experiential and transformative learning
  techniques which often leads to students translating
  knowledge into positive action.

- **Support the development of tenure criteria that
  acknowledge and honour cross-disciplinary work
  in sustainability.** The current tenure and promotion
  system in Canada and the United States tends to
  favour scholars who engage in research and teaching
  in a single aspect of a single discipline. Sustainability in higher education moves beyond disciplinary
  boundaries and requires academics to engage in the
  scholarship of integration. Academics must work with
  faculty associations, university presidents and provosts
  to promote a new understanding that values interdisciplinary, cross-disciplinary and trandisciplinary work.

- **Create campus sustainability officer positions
  at each university in Canada and the USA.** The
  number of campus sustainability officers in Canada
  and the United States has skyrocketed since the
  1990s, but the number of staff dedicated to sustainable campus operations is still minimal compared
  to the number of universities. Just as a Health and
  Safety Officer is now standard at every university and
  College, a Sustainability Officer should be as well.

- **Develop regional, national, and international
  networks of scholars engaging in research in
  the field of sustainability in higher education.**
  Sustainability in higher education is a relatively new
  and emergent area of inquiry, yet not without strong
  foundations in education, policy analysis, manage-

ment theory, environmental studies, sociology ecology, psychology and philosophy. Despite the initial success of SHE scholarship, to date there is a lack of cohesion among researchers. A critical step in making SHE research effective is the encouragement of collaborative partnerships and intellectual exchange among researchers. SHE research is naturally interdisciplinary, and researchers are housed in a variety of disciplines. This often makes it difficult for researchers to meet and discuss their research at traditional conferences, or to plan for future research priorities. A critical step in promoting SHE research is to develop new modes of collaboration and information sharing at regional, national and international levels.

● **Further develop the list of research priorities for the field.** Due to the emerging nature of the field, SHE scholars must continue to develop an understanding of the critical questions necessary to advance sustainability in higher education. Scholars must define priorities for SHE research and develop comprehensive research strategies for the future.

If you are thinking ten years ahead, plant a tree. If you are thinking one hundred years ahead, educate the people. – Kuan Tzu, c.500 BCE

REFERENCES

APIRG (2005) About APIRG and what we do. http://www.apirg.org/whatwedo/ (Accessed May 31, 2010).

Augsburg College (2010) Center for Democracy and Citizenship – Harry Boyte. http://www.augsburg.edu/democracy/boyte.html (Accessed 1 June 2010).

Boyle, S. (2009, August) New Shoes for Batawa. Canadian Architec thttp://www.canadianarchitect.com/issues/story.aspx?aid=1000339062&PC= (Accessed 31 May 2010).

Campus Compact (2010) About us. http://www.compact.org/about/ (Accessed 1 June 2010).

City of Cleveland (n.d.). Sustainable Cleveland 2019 FAQ. http://www.city.cleveland.oh.us/CityofCleveland/Home/Community/ThingsToDo/AISummit/FAQ (Accessed 1 June 2010).

Clugston, R. (1999) Introduction. In: Leal Filho, W. *Sustainability and University Life*. Frankfurt/M., Germany: Peter Lang.

Cortese, A. (2008) *Sustaining God's Creation: The Role of Higher Education*. Broomfield, Colorado: American College & University Presidents Climate Commitment. National Association of Schools and Colleges of the United Methodist Church, Annual Meeting, 28 July, 2008.

Council of Ontario Universities (2009) Ontario universities committed to a greener world. http://www.cou.on.ca/content/objects/GreenPledge-forWeb&internalxeroxing.pdf (Accessed 1 June 2010).

CRWS (n.d.). What is the CRWS? http://www.yorku.ca/crws/ (Accessed 1 June 2010).

Dahms, T., McMartin, D. and Petry, R. (2008) Saskatchewan's (Canada) Regional Centre of Expertise on Education for Sustainable Development. *International Journal of Sustainability in Higher Education*, **9**(4), pp. 382–401.

Glasser, H., Calder, W. and Fadeeva, Z. (2005) Definition: Research in Higher Education for Sustainability. Document prepared for the Halifax Consultation. Halifax, Nova Scotia.

Harvard College (2009) Green campus loan fund. http://green.harvard.edu/loan-fund (Accessed 31 May 2010).

Institute for Humane Studies at George Mason University (2009) Social Change Workshop. http://www.theihs.org/ContentDetails.aspx?id=824 (Accessed 1 June 2010).

Leal Filho, W. and Wright, T.S.A. (2002) Barriers on the path to environmental sustainability: European and Canadian perspectives in higher education. *International Journal of Sustainable Development and World Ecology*, **9**(2), pp. 179–86.

McIntosh, M., Cacciola, K., Clermont, S. and Keniry, J. (2001) *State of the Campus Environment: A National Report Card on Environmental Performance and Sustainability in Higher Education*. National Wildlife Federation, Reston, VA.

Meadows, D.H., Meadows, D.L. and Randers, L. (1992) *Beyond the Limits: Global Collapse or a Sustainable Future*. London: Earthscan.

NWF (2010) Campus Ecology. http://www.nwf.org/Global-Warming/Campus-Solutions.aspx (Accessed 1 June 2010).

Orr, D. (1995) *Earth In Mind*. Washington: Island Press.

Rasmussen, Scott. Rasmussen Reports. http://www.rasmussenreports.com/public_content/politics/mood_of_america/partisan_trends (Accessed 1 December 2010).

Rowe, D. (2002) Environmental Literacy and Sustainability as Core Requirements: Success Stories and Models. In: *Teaching Sustainability at Universities*. Walter Leal Filho (ed.). New York: Peter Lang.

Royal Roads University (2010) Profile: Ann Dale. http://www.royalroads.ca/media-directory/ann-dale-phd (Accessed 1 June 2010).

SEAC (2008) About SEAC. http://www.seac.org/about (Accessed 28 May 2010).

Second Nature (2010) Mission. http://www.secondnature.org/about/index.html

Sierra Club (2010) About the SSC. http://ssc.sierraclub.org/about/index.html (Accessed 1 June 2010).

SYC (2009) Sierra Youth Coalition Annual Report 2008–2009. http://www.syc-cjs.org/sites/default/files/Annual%20Report%202008-2009.pdf (Accessed 1 June 2010).

UBC Farm. http://www.landfood.ubc.ca/ubcfarm/faq.php (Accessed May 2010).

University of Virginia (2010) About ecoMOD. http://ecomod.virginia.edu/about/ (Accessed 31 May 2010).

USPESD (n.d.) USPESD: A brief history. http://www.uspartnership.org/main/show_passage/2 (Accessed 1 June 2010).

Walden University (2010, April) Walden University's new service network Advances its mission of social change. http://www.waldenu.edu/News-and-Events/35145.htm (Accessed 31 May 2010).

Webster, A. (2008, April) SSCC 2008 Live: Turning a University/College into a Living Laboratory. http://www.aashe.org/blog/sscc-2008-live-turning-universitycollege-living-laboratory (Accessed May 2010).

Waas, T., Verbruggen, A. and Wright, T. (2010) University research for sustainable development: Definition and characteristics explored. *Journal of Cleaner Production*, **18**(7), pp. 611–18.

Wolfe, V. (2001) A survey of the environmental education of students in non-environmental majors at four year institutions in the USA. *International Journal of Sustainability in Higher Education*, **2**(4), pp. 301–15.

Wright, T. (2004) The Evolution of Environmental Sustainability Declaration in Higher Education. In: Argen Wals and Peter Blaze Corcoran (eds) *Higher Education and the Challenge of Sustainability: Promis, Practice, Contestation, and Critique*. Kluwer Academic Press.

Wright, T. (2007) Developing research priorities with a cohort of higher education for sustainability experts. *International Journal of Sustainability in Higher Education*, **8**(1), pp. 34–43.

Wright, T. (2009) Sustainability, Internationalization and Higher Education. In: *Internationalizing the Curriculum in Higher Education*. Carolin Kreber (ed.). Toronto: Jossey Bass Publishers.

Wright, T. (2010) An assessment of university presidents' conceptualizations of sustainability in higher education. *International Journal of Sustainability in Higher Education*, **11**(1), pp. 61–73.

Wright T. and Pullen, S. (2007) Examining the literature: A bibliometric study of ESD journal articles in the ERIC database. *International Journal of Education for Sustainable Development*, **1**(1), pp. 77–90.

WUSC (n.d.) About us. http://www.wusc.ca/en/about/about_us (Accessed June 1, 2010).

Spotlight Issues II.7
Renewable energies and sustainability education in the United States

Debra Rowe and Aurora Winslade

INTRODUCTION

Higher education is in a stage of transformation. Human civilization is threatened as climate change, loss of biodiversity, increasing resource consumption and other ecological stressors become ever more dangerous to our future. The continuing poverty of so many of the world's people is further evidence that our worldviews, our mental maps, and our actions that were born largely out of the industrial revolution need to be updated to reflect current realities, limits on natural resources, and nature's cycles. In the United States there is no national plan for how to reduce the nation's greenhouse gases and build a sustainable energy future. Federal regulations are lacking for climate change and incentives for renewable energy and energy efficiency are inconsistent and insufficient to build a stable and robust movement away from fossil fuels. There is no national plan for sustainability education. Despite this, there are positive indicators in higher education (HE) at both the community college and four-year university level. Networks of national organizations that include HE faculty, staff, and students in the US are taking actions to build a green and sustainable future, and actions at individual institutions and within these networks are growing in number and scope. Sustainability is increasingly being incorporated into the core competences required of today's and tomorrow's leaders. Progress is being made in curricula, research, community partnerships, and the business operations at our colleges and universities.

VISION FOR SUSTAINABILITY IN HIGHER EDUCATION

In the US, education for a sustainable future requires more than training renewable energy and energy efficiency technicians. We also need education that helps all students understand our sustainability societal challenges and engages them in building solutions. We need managers, policymakers, investors, consumers, and community members involved in creating a robust green and sustainable economy. In addition to technical know-how, we also need effective team members and leaders who are able to work together to create systemic changes to support a sustainable energy future.

Effective sustainability change agents are continually developing skills that allow them to work collaboratively with others to envision and create new ways of doing business and relating to one another. They assess the challenges, and act systemically to address problems at their source. The American College Personal Association's Presidential Task Force on Sustainability includes change agent skills as an essential learning outcome for sustainability education, and describes change agents as:

Resilient, optimistic, tenacious, committed, passionate, patient, emotionally intelligent, assertive, persuasive, empathetic, authentic, ethical, self-aware, competent, [and] curious … Change agents help envision, articulate and create positive scenarios for the future of society. [They] see the paths, small steps, for changes needed for a more sustainable future, convert it into a task list and timeline, and follow through effectively.[1]

Many people are aware, at some level, of how dire the situation is, but feel hopeless and helpless. Change agents help people move from fear and resistance to change and engagement in solutions. Svanström et al. found in a comparison of sustainability learning outcomes in multiple countries that there is increasing international concurrence regarding the importance of moving beyond critical thinking and a good analysis to learning how to make positive change in the real world.[2]

The higher education sustainability (HES) movement has been growing rapidly in the US over the past decade. More and more institutions are integrating sustainability into mission and planning, curriculum, research, student life, operations and business practices via sustainability committees, positions, and policies, and inclusion into existing job descriptions. Higher education is also working with the students and the regional stakeholders to build more sustainable communities. Colleges and universities in the US are also increasingly participating in developing and endorsing sustainability-oriented legislation.

CURRICULA FOR SUSTAINABILITY IN THE UNITED STATES

In the US, employers are asking HE to graduate students who are able to solve real-world sustainability challenges and who are able to work effectively in teams. College graduates are increasingly required by potential employers to understand basic sustainability principles. In a survey of over 1300 business professionals conducted by Hart Research Associates in 2010, 85% of respondents viewed sustainability knowledge as valuable and 78% believed that it would become even more important over the next five years.[3]

Colleges and universities are responding to this shift. New sustainability minors, majors, and concentrations are emerging throughout the

US. In addition to more opportunities to focus on sustainability through newly created or modified environmental studies programmes, work is being done to integrate the triple bottom line perspectives of sustainability into a wide variety of existing disciplines and courses. Learning outcomes often include both technical sustainability theories and the interpersonal skills required to think systemically and be effective change agents. The complex challenges related to sustainability cannot be solved by theory alone, and students are learning to apply these problem-solving and interpersonal skills to real-world sustainability issues in their assignments, through student organizations, and internships. There is a convergence of thought that a core pedagogy for sustainability education is to give students the opportunities to help solve sustainability challenges in the real world as academic assignments. One key outcome of such learning is to develop a self concept and skill set to contribute to solutions to our sustainability challenges in their adult roles as workers, citizens or community members, consumers, investors and family members. Campuses and local communities are becoming living, learning laboratories for sustainability.

Institutions are partnering with government agencies, businesses, non-profits, and kindergarten to 12th grade (K-12) schools. Faculty and students are looking to campus and community organizations for potential sustainability projects and using them in and out of the classroom. Some institutions, such as the University of British Columbia in Canada[4] and the University of California, Santa Cruz[5] in the US, have created web-based databases to document ongoing, completed, and/or potential projects. The Society for College and University Planning has worked with the US Partnership for Education for Sustainable Development to create an open source, free online matchmaking website where colleges and communities can post sustainability-related projects and faculty and students can integrate them into assignments and student life. Students are more engaged when they are working on real problems and when the solutions they help create may actually contribute to making a measurable positive difference. Many of today's students are learning how to work collaboratively, think systemically, and be effective change agents.

The American College and University Presidents' Climate Commitment published a document describing how hundreds of institutions are integrating sustainability into curricula. This document describes a number of useful approaches and strategies, from adding a credit hour to any course to include a real-world sustainability project to integrating the principles of sustainability into the course requirements of all degrees.[6]

The US Department of Education has funded a few projects on sustainability education. One of these projects combines the expertise Project Kaleidoscope, Mobilizing STEM Education for a Sustainable Future, and the Disciplinary Associations Network for Sustainability (DANS). The project is entitled 'Mobilizing Disciplinary Societies on Behalf of our Students … and our Planet' and it convenes the following academic disciplinary associations to collaborate on multiple projects that will help educators better prepare students to help solve the real-world 21st century 'Big Questions' that relate to real-world issues, and the project is expected to expand to other academic disciplinary associations in the third year:

American Association of Physics Teachers (AAPT)
American Chemical Society (ACS)
American Institute of Biological Sciences (AIBS)
American Psychological Association (APA)
American Society for Engineering Education (ASEE)
Association for Career and Technical Education (ACTE)
Mathematical Association of America (MAA)
National Association of Biology Teachers (NABT)
National Association of Geoscience Teachers (NAGT)
National Numeracy Network (NNN)
Special Interest Group on Computer Science Education (SIGCSE)

The HES efforts in the US are complemented by the increasing number of K-12 efforts. Over a dozen national K-12 associations are catalyzing sustainability education efforts across the country via the K12 National Associations Network for Sustainability. The US Partnership for Education for Sustainable Development, which facil-itates both higher education and K12 networks, has created sustainability education standards, compiled a wealth of curricular resources and offers catalytic professional development to educators and staff.[7] Finally, most of the major textbook publishers are making efforts to update their textbooks to include sustainability in multiple academic disciplines. They have recognized that including sustainability issues and perspectives in textbooks can be a distinct competitive advantage and increase adoptions. Such textbook revisions can have a dramatic impact on reaching the classrooms of many instructors, professors and adjunct professors who are not yet engaged in sustainability.

CURRICULA FOR RENEWABLE ENERGY AND ENERGY EFFICIENCY IN THE US

There are approximately 1200 community colleges in the US educating about half of all undergraduate students. In the area of renewable energies and energy efficiency, in the past three years dozens of community colleges have received money from the federal stimulus funds, from the US National Science Foundation, from the US Department of Energy, and from other sources to develop curricula in renewable energies and energy efficiency. Most of this has been specifically targeted at technician training. Yet the availability of training funds was not accompanied by a national education for sustainability plan or a national curricular framework. Many colleges are creating their curricula independently of each other in an uncoordinated manner.

In the past year, there have been efforts by federal agencies to create national workforce standards and competences (that is, in energy auditing and weatherization in the residential sector) and national 'train the trainer' programmes (that is, in solar thermal and solar electricity). The US Small Business Administration has developed an online course to help contractors see how they can successfully move into the business of energy efficiency. The US Department of Energy has created a robust online platform for advanced curricular materials. Additionally, a national inter-federal agency committee has started to meet at the US Department of Education to coordinate sustainability education efforts across federal agencies. These strategic actions on a national level are helping to build a more coordinated educational capacity for renewable energies and energy efficiency.

Another challenge is that federal legislation is needed to fix a marketplace that is presently skewed towards fossil fuels and away from renewable energies (for example stable tax credits for renewable energies, regulation of carbon emissions, a national renewable portfolio standard or feed in tariff). The US Congress failed to pass such legislation in 2010.

Despite the inconsistent and incomplete marketplace incentive structures, educators are increasingly teaching renewable energies, energy management and sustainability education into core competences and skills. They are using three main strategies:

- integration into existing technology programmes (for example electronics, automotive, manufacturing, agriculture, construction, architectural design, heating and cooling)
- creation of new energy technology programmes
- inclusion of the basic knowledge regarding the urgent need for renewable energies and conservation into core requirements for all degrees

Given the skewed marketplace, it has become increasingly clear that the traditional strategy of waiting for the energy employers to show up at the door is not moving fast enough to build a robust green economy that can transition to more energy efficiency and renewable energies. Successful workforce, certificate, and degree programmes are utilizing effective strategies that are grounded in partnerships with government, non-profits and businesses. Efforts are being made to educate contractors and other businesses, government, community planners, non-profits, and all consumers to help grow the green economy.

Colleges and universities are both responding to market demand and being catalytic in helping to build demand for clean energy technicians and greener employees. Many institutions are convening stakeholders from government, business associations, local non-profits and other community sectors to produce a more coordinated effort to build a sustainable economy that produces more employment opportunities. For example, the College of

Lake County held a green communities conference that was open to all parts of the community. Participants brainstormed and envisioned more livable and sustainable communities and then created next steps to move in that direction. An increasing number of colleges have developed institutes and programming for sustainable living, such as Gateway and Flint Hills Community Colleges. Oakland Community College and other colleges have held targeted seminars for contractors and other business owners, showing how they can build their businesses and improve their profits by going green while creating new job openings for graduating students.

Additionally, since outdated regulations and policies are artificial market barriers to a green economy, partnerships are forming to update regulations and policies to support the growth of the green economy. For example, over the past few years, community stakeholders have come together to pass state renewable portfolio standards and remove outdated codes, increasing the numbers of renewable energy installations and building green energy activity. Progress has been made but more work need to be done.[8] The American Association of Community Colleges[9] has developed a policy toolkit to help colleges work with other stakeholders to inform and align policies at the organizational, local, state and national levels for more renewable energies implementation. Without appropriate marketplace policy revisions, the existing regulations make it much more convenient for consumers to use artificially inexpensive fossil fuels and the shift to renewable energies will be hampered, which could cause an inappropriately cynical and negative evaluation by the public and key decision makers of the prospects for a green economy.

In the 10 campus University of California system, students in 2002-2003 successfully built partnerships with staff, faculty, and the Regents to pass a landmark green building and renewable energy policy. Several of the key student organizers of this effort have since been hired as sustainability professionals and are continuing to build the partnerships that have allowed it to grow and expand as technology changes and opportunities become available. Now known as the UC Policy on Sustainable Practices (http://www.universi-

tyofcalifornia.edu/sustainability/policy.html), it has expanded several times to include additional sustainability indicators such as waste, procurement, transportation, and food. Since the establishment of the policy, the California investor-owned utility companies, under legislative and financial pressure to reduce greenhouse gases and improve efficiency, have partnered with both the University of California and the California State University system to invest hundreds of millions of dollars in energy efficiency for new and existing buildings that have resulted in tremendous cost savings and reduced environmental impact.

To assist community colleges, the American Association of Community Colleges has created the Sustainability Education and Economic Development (SEED) online resource centre (www.theSeedCenter.org). This resource centre includes hundreds of resources vetted by industry experts in the areas of solar energy, wind power, energy efficiency, green building, and sustainability education. (Additional sectors will be added soon, probably in the areas of sustainable agriculture, water, and/ or biotechnologies.) Each area covers the topics of: innovative practices and partnerships to build sustainable local economies; skills, competences and career pathways; industry projections; and materials for curricular development. In addition, there are listings of college programmes and success stories, a sharing community for instructors and educational administrators to share curricula, and a place to post questions as an online learning community for educators. Materials for presidents and professional development webinars for educators and staff about how to build a quality programme and catalyze a greener and more sustainable regional economy are key components of the centre. 'Colleges in Action' vignettes about new energy and sustainability programmes and a wiki of curricular resources uploaded by specific colleges is also included.

CONCLUSION

Higher education has the opportunity, and the obligation, to train graduates who are able and empowered to create a world that builds a higher quality of life for present and future generations. Particularly at the community college level, institutions in the US are increasingly developing curricula and programmes for students to learn the technical skills required for renewable energy and energy efficiency, and there is a national growing trend to teach about sustainability throughout higher education. This is happening despite the lack of a coherent national agenda and policies. National networks and resources exist to guide educators, support students, staff, and faculty, and share best practices. The campus itself is proving to be a valuable laboratory for practising the skills required of our leaders.

Beyond, and equally important as, the technical skills, more and more institutions and individuals are realizing the importance of interpersonal and change agent skills to create a more sustainable future. Higher education is transforming as the need for informed and active citizens becomes clearer. Throughout the US, there are signs of progress in the development of new curricula, greener operations, and innovative partnerships between higher education, government, business, non-profits, and the local communities.

WEBSITES

http://dans.aashe.org/content/participating-associations, Disciplinary Associations Network for Sustainability Participating Associations (accessed 2011).

http://heasc.aashe.org/content/resource-center, Higher Education Associations Sustainability Consortium Resource Center (accessed 2011).

http://secondnature.org/SNPrograms.html, Second Nature Programs (accessed 2009).

NOTES

1   ACPA's Presidential Taskforce on Sustainability, Change Agent Abilities Required to Help Create a Sustainable Future. http://www.myacpa.org/task-force/sustainability/docs/Change_Agent_Skills.pdf (accessed 2009).

2   Svanström, Magdalena, Francisco Lozano and Debra Rowe (2008) Learning outcomes for sustainable development in higher education. *International Journal of Sustainability in Higher Education*, 9(3), pp. 339–51.

3   Hart Research Associates (2010) *Raising the Bar: Employers' Views on College Learning in the Wake of the Economic Downturn: A Survey Among Employers Conducted On Behalf Of: The Association Of American Colleges And Universities*. 20 January, pp. 1–2.

4   University of British Columbia SEEDS Library, http://www.sustain.ubc.ca/seeds-library (accessed 2010).

5   University of California Santa Cruz, Sustainability Website, http://sustainability.ucsc.edu (accessed 2010).

6   The American College and University Presidents' Climate Commitment, ACUPCC Publications, http://www.presidentsclimatecommitment.org/resources/publications #guidance (accessed 2010).

7   The US Partnership for Education for Sustainability Development Resources for K-12 and highter education, http://www.uspartnership.org.

8   See http://www.dsireusa.org/ for a database of incentives for renewable energies and efficiency that reflect both the progress and the need for more work in this area.

9   American Association of Community Colleges, Sustainability Education and Economic Development Resource Center, http://www.aacc.nche.edu/Resources/aaccprograms/sustainable/Pages/default.aspx (accessed 2010).

Network Experience II.5
AASHE: a US-based campus sustainability network

Paul Rowland

The Association for the Advancement of Sustainability in Higher Education (AASHE) has become one of the largest campus sustainability organizations in the world. Founded in 2005, it has grown to more than 850 higher education institutional members and 250 affiliate members that include businesses, non-government agencies, and government agencies.

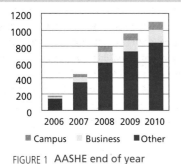

FIGURE 1   AASHE end of year membership

THE ORIGINS OF AASHE

AASHE was formed following the 2004 Education for Sustainability – West (EFS-West) Sustainability and Higher Education Conference. EFS-West was one of several regional campus sustainability organizations in the US at that time. The major function of the regional organizations was to provide opportunities to network and share a sense of belonging among those individuals in HE who were interested in sustainability in terms both of teaching and learning and of the operations of the campuses. The EFS-West conference, along with biennial Greening of the Campus conferences being held at Ball State University, indicated the need for a national/continental organization that could provide both support and a professional home for campus sustainability advocates. During the conversations following the conference,

the board of directors of EFS-West (a group of higher education leaders from the Western US and Canada) decided to move forward with the formation of a national/continental organization. By January 2006 AASHE was fully incorporated as a non-profit company and the transfer of the electronic resources that had been developed by EFS-West along with the initial staffing of AASHE was begun.

FINANCING AASHE

One of the important decisions made by the new leadership of AASHE was to base its financing on institutional membership. By 1 July 2006, 47 colleges and universities had paid membership dues to AASHE. In addition, several business and higher education associations had joined and were publicizing AASHE throughout the US.

In January 2007, the AASHE board of directors hired a full-time executive director and at that time decided to locate in an independent office (that is, not located on a university campus) in Lexington Kentucky where the executive director was located. The original staff located in Portland, Oregon continued to work from their homes while additional staff were hired to work at the Lexington office.

As AASHE grew, the organization became more involved in various external sources of grant and contract funding. Particularly, as a collaborator in founding the American College and University Presidents' Climate Commitment, AASHE found a significant amount of its fiscal support coming from sources other than membership dues. Conference income became a large source of revenue and expenditures.

BOUNDARY ISSUES

Throughout the discussions that formed AASHE (and even today) have been issues about defining boundaries. One early boundary issue was who on a campus is included in AASHE? Following the model of EFS-West, AASHE decided to be inclusive of any and all members of the campus community who were interested in sustainability. In fact, EFS-West made the following claim regarding its work: 'We do this through collaboration among members to share strategies and resources that will assist them in making sustainability central to all teaching, research, professional development, campus operations, facilities, investments, and community outreach.' [1]

Another ongoing issue has been that of geographic boundaries. EFS-West had explicity defined itself as a Western US and Canada association. The AASHE board of directors did not explicitly include geographic boundaries in its incorporation documents or in its bylaws but remained silent in these respects. Although the staff and some board members have referred to the organization as a North American association, there has been little effort to work with institutions in Mexico. Despite the lack of boundary designation there is an implicit recognition of the North American geography in the membership dues structure. Perhaps the best way to describe the current situation is that AASHE is a US-based association with most of its members in the US (91%) and Canada (7%).

PARTNERSHIPS

From its formation, AASHE has recognized the need to form partnerships with other organizations to accomplish its goals. The issues of boundaries have influenced some of the discussions about partnerships. How AASHE works with US regional organizations and how AASHE works with other campus sustainability organizations outside North America are ongoing and complex discussions that are both operational as well as philosophical. The operational issues are often about contextual and fiscal differences. The philosophical issues are often based on differences in how sustainability is framed: that is, the US sustainability movement (with origins in environmental activism) differs from the 'education for sustainable development' movement (with origins in a critique of economic development).

In 2010, AASHE hosted an International Luncheon at its conference to discuss these relationships. In 2011, a similar discussion will be held with the leaders of the US regional groups.

As AASHE has honed its definition of purpose and audience, it has become more strategic about forming partnerships. Some partnerships are clearly connected to the higher education community while others are more connected to environmental NGOs. Determining the appropriate groups to work with is challenging because partnerships can have unintended consequences for a member-based organization. Establishing partnerships is often difficult and time consuming but it also can be very rewarding.

MAJOR PROJECTS

From its inception, AASHE has played a major role in helping the campus sustainability community publicize their successes and create a collection of lessons learned and good practices. The web-based resource centre pulls together information about a wide spectrum of campus sustainability information ranging from directories of sustainability degree programmes to lists of solar photovoltaic installations on campuses. Staff are regularly engaged in developing new collections of information.

Some of the information is drawn from the weekly *AASHE Bulletin* that is distributed to about 11,000 individuals each week by email. A special *AASHE Bulletin: Global*

Edition is produced twice a year to highlight stories from outside the US and Canada. In addition, AASHE Announcements and AASHE Events inform thousands of subscribers about sustainability activities.

AASHE also has been directly engaged in the production of publications both with and without partners. In 2010, AASHE's *Sustainability Curriculum in Higher Education: A Call to Action* was widely distributed and generated important conversations throughout the US. *Accelerating Climate Initiatives: Breaking through Barriers* was produced in partnership with the Rocky Mountain Institute and continues to be a widely used resource.

AASHE staff and resource centre are often used as sources of information for articles about campus sustainability. In 2010, more than 150 newspaper articles cited AASHE as an information source. AASHE staff also produce writings and disseminate them through magazine articles, the AASHE Blog and entries on various discussion lists.

Like other aspects of AASHE, its conference has continued to grow. In 2006 the conference attracted about 600 delegates; in 2008 more than 1700 delegates; and in 2010, about 2100 delegates. As the largest campus sustainability conference in North America, it has become an important meeting for sharing successes, presenting challenges, and enjoying the camaraderie of other campus sustainability advocates and professionals. The Student Summit held prior to the conference draws more than 500 college and university students.

Almost since its inception, AASHE has provided professional development workshops to the campus community. Each year AASHE holds two Sustainability Across the Curriculum Leadership workshops that provide faculty members with preparation to return to their campus and become campus leaders in education for sustainability. More than 300 individuals have participated in these workshops and most have returned to their campuses and provided workshops or other means of support for their colleagues in the integration of sustainability across the curriculum. AASHE has also held Sustainability Officer Workshops prior to its annual meeting to provide opportunities for campus sustainability staff to learn from one another.

Soon after AASHE was begun, it was asked by the Higher Education Associations Sustainability Consortium to develop a coherent, comprehensive campus sustainability assessment system. After three years of development, piloting and public comment from more than 300 individuals, the Sustainability Tracking, Assessment and Rating System (STARS®) was launched. STARS is a transparent, self-reporting framework for colleges and universities to measure and report their sustainability activities. Participating institutions may receive a Bronze, Silver, Gold or Platinum rating or may simply ask for Reporter status and track their progress over time. More than 250 institutions have become participants.

AASHE'S FUTURE

AASHE's mission is to 'empower higher education to lead the sustainability transformation.' During the rest of this decade AASHE will need to increase its influence among the thousands of US institutions that have not become members. In addition, it will need to intensify its efforts in curricular discussions and change to ensure that all graduates of its member institutions understand the principles of sustainability and the challenges of creating a global sustainable society. Finally, AASHE will be examining and developing its role as a member of a global community of higher education sustainability organizations.

NOTE

1   Education for Sustainability Western Network (n.d.) EFS West's Sustainability and Higher Education conference. http://www2.aashe.org/cpmf2004/program.php (accessed May 2010).

GOOD PRACTICES II.5

Higher Education and Sustainability in North America: Sharing Actions for Change

The following experiences are a selection of good practices on higher education and sustainability. Some of them were presented at the 5th International Barcelona Conference on Higher Education and others are part of the GUNi observatory.

The good practices cover the following institutional areas:

Curricula and learning innovation

Community and social engagement

Institutional management

Research

GOOD PRACTICE 1

North America's top campus sustainability project

Institutional area(s):

LOCATION: Canada
INSTITUTION: University of Northern British Columbia

The University of Northern British Columbia has officially opened a bio-energy plant on campus that is making the university a national leader in renewable energy. The UNBC bio-energy plant takes wood waste that is already being produced at a local sawmill and converts it to enough energy to heat the university and reduce fossil fuel consumption by 85%. The new facility joins a wood pellet system on campus, which opened in 2009. Construction of the bio-energy plant involved local companies and was only the second building in Prince George built to LEED gold standard.

Detailed information is available at GUNi HEiOBS:

http://www.guninetwork.org/guni.heiobs/good-practices/north-americas-top-campus-sustainability-project

GOOD PRACTICE 2

Fostering the renewal of learning and teaching in the field of aboriginal issues

Institutional area(s):

LOCATION: Canada
INSTITUTION: Nomadic University

The Nomadic University is an innovative training programme created in 2007 by the DIALOG network – a research and knowledge network relating to aboriginal peoples. It is one of several knowledge mobilization initiatives developed over the years to encourage the sharing of knowledge, skills and learning between the academic and aboriginal milieus. Through the Nomadic University's activities, DIALOG offers interactive and dynamic teaching that fosters the development of a reflective and comprehensive understanding of aboriginal issues. The training team for each session includes DIALOG researchers, students, and aboriginal partners and reflects the inter-institutional, interdisciplinary and intercultural collaboration that characterizes DIALOG. The hands-on learning experience offered by the program occurs within the context of recognized academic curricula and enables students to obtain academic credits. The Nomadic University welcomes students from various universities, researchers, stakeholders, practitioners, civil society actors and the general public.

Detailed information is available at GUNi HEiOBS:

http://www.guninetwork.org/guni.heiobs/good-practices/fostering-the-renewal-of-learning-and-teaching-in-the-field-of-aboriginal-issues-dialog2019s-nomadic-university

GOOD PRACTICE 3

Go green initiative

Institutional area(s):

LOCATION: United States
INSTITUTION: University of Phoenix

The University of Phoenix purchases nearly 47 million kilowatt hours of green energy annually – the equivalent of powering more than 4000 average American homes per year. At the University of Phoenix, there is a special emphasis on taking care of the earth for future generations. The Go Green initiative is designed to help fulfill the university's environmental commitment by involving students, faculty members, employees, alumni and facilities in locations around the world. The university highlights the importance of sustaining the natural resources we all share. As an institution of higher learning, it plays a vital role in educating the environmental stewards of today and tomorrow.

Detailed information is available at GUNi HEiOBS:

http://www.guninetwork.org/guni.heiobs/good-practices/go-green-initiative-university-of-phoenix

GOOD PRACTICE 4

Green purchasing program

Institutional area(s):

LOCATION: North America
INSTITUTION: Duke University

Duke's Green Purchasing Program helps university purchasers and employees make environmentally responsible purchasing decisions to reduce negative effects on human health and the environment. In July of 2004, Duke adopted a set of environmentally preferable purchasing guidelines to reduce its environmental impact in six strategic areas: source reduction, forest conservation, recycled content, landscaping, energy and water, and toxics and pollution. Furthermore, Duke University gives preference to environmentally friendly products whose quality, function, and cost are equal or superior to more traditional products.

Detailed information is available at GUNi HEiOBS:

http://www.guninetwork.org/guni.heiobs/good-practices/green-purchasing-program

GOOD PRACTICE 5

The sustainability tracking, assessment and rating system

Institutional area(s):

LOCATION: United States and Canada
INSTITUTION: AASHE

The STARS® framework is intended to engage and recognize the full spectrum of colleges and universities in the United States and Canada – from community colleges to research universities, and from institutions just starting their sustainability programmes to long-time campus sustainability leaders. STARS encompasses long-term sustainability goals for already high-achieving institutions as well as entry points of recognition for institutions that are taking first steps toward sustainability. Furthermore, the aim of this programme is to help HEIs set and meet sustainability goals and will foster information sharing about practices and performance among the campus sustainability community.

Detailed information is available at GUNi HEiOBS:

http://www.guninetwork.org/guni.heiobs/good-practices/the-sustainability-tracking-assessment-and-rating-system

GOOD PRACTICE 6

Designing and implementing a pan-university commitment to sustainability

Institutional area(s):

LOCATION: United States of America
INSTITUTION: Global Institute of Sustainability, ASU

The Global Institute of Sustainability (GIOS) is a practice for leading, supporting and coordinating Arizona State University's (ASU) wide commitment to sustainability. According to the University of Arizona, GIOS is a good practice unlike any other university structure in the US. As a result of this practice, the institute manages a comprehensive School of Sustainability, promotes sustainability-focused research, helps public decision makers deal with sustainability challenges, prioritizes university-wide efforts toward sustainable practices, and builds global partnerships. The institute and the school were established to transcend conventional academic boundaries by leading and supporting all ASU learning, research and operations units to engage in sustainability. The institute also works 'horizontally' to inspire and infuse sustainability across ASU'S entire curriculum.

Detailed information is available at GUNi HEiOBS:

http://www.guninetwork.org/guni.heiobs/good-practices/designing-and-implementing-a-pan-university-commitment-to-sustainabilty

Canadian Consortium for Sustainable Development Research

Institutional area(s):

LOCATION: Canada
INSTITUTION: Royal Roads University

The overall goal of CCSDR is to promote interest in the greater understanding of sustainable development through the production of useful knowledge and the promotion of strategic alliances. Members bring perspectives at the micro, meso and macro levels; their expertise and research is applied, interdisciplinary and normally involves some community outreach. Their purpose is to work together as a consortium in order to further the process of sustainable development through support for interdisciplinary research and application of that research to societal needs.

Detailed information is available at GUNi HEiOBS:

http://www.guninetwork.org/guni.heiobs/good-practices/canadian-consortium-for-sustainable-development-research

The reader can also find the following good practices related to sustainability in North America at the GUNi Observatory:

- The Ponderosa Project
  LOCATION: United States
  INSTITUTION: Northern Arizona University

- The Combination of Diverse Cultural Experiences and Sustainability in Higher Education Design
  LOCATION: United States
  INSTITUTION: University of Wisconsin

- Sustainability and Architectural History Curriculum
  LOCATION: United States
  INSTITUTION: University of Florida

- Portland State University – Toward sustainability program excellence and institutional distinction
  LOCATION: United States
  INSTITUTION: Portland States University

- Center for Sustainable Building Research (CSBR)
  LOCATION: United States
  INSTITUTION: University of Minnesota

http://www.guninetwork.org/guni.heiobs/

II.6 Higher Education, Environment and Sustainability in Latin America and the Caribbean

Orlando Sáenz and Javier Benayas

Abstract

This paper describes the historical process and current status of environmental mainstreaming in higher education institutions (HEIs) in Latin America and the Caribbean (LAC).

By taking a historical perspective, this paper shows how the process has evolved in three stages over more than six decades. Over the course of this period, environmental higher education (HE) focused initially on natural resources, later on the environment and finally on sustainable development. Throughout this process, a very important role has been played by the promotional programmes of various international agencies, as well as the national environmental education policies of some of the region's countries. Nevertheless, credit for the achievements in the long process of greening HE belongs primarily to the universities themselves.

To describe the current situation of environmental HE in LAC, this paper will present some of the best-known experiences in the areas of training, research, outreach and environmental management at the region's universities. This overview will shed light on the great diversity of practices and approaches that Latin American HEIs have developed with regard to sustainability. However, the available knowledge about this complex process remains fragmented and superficial. To overcome these limitations, it is essential that the scientific community dedicated to studying environmental HE agree on and develop a common research programme.

EARLY STAGES OF ENVIRONMENTAL HIGHER EDUCATION IN LAC

The first stage in the process of greening HEIs was the emergence of technical and vocational training in the use of natural resources and the conservation of nature. At the international level, this process began in 1948 with a UNESCO-convened conference that resulted in the creation of the International Union for Conservation of Nature and Natural Resources (IUCN) and marked the first use of the term *environmental education*. The Education Committee set up by the IUCN in 1949 was the first entity to promote the incorporation of education for nature conservation in HEIs (UNESCO, UNEP and ICFES, 1988, p. 11).

The initial stage was dominated by the environmental education trends that Sauvé referred to as *naturalistic* and *conservationist or resourcist*. As its name implies, the naturalistic trend generally focused on the relationship with nature, but it comprised several different educational approaches, which emphasize 'learning *in* nature', 'learning *from* nature' and 'learning *about* nature'. The conservationist or resourcist trend, meanwhile, focused on the conservation of resources (Sauvé, 2004, pp. 1–4).

A recent study on the historical emergence and early stages of the development of environmental HE in Colombia (Sáenz, 2011a) showed that, starting in 1950, the country's universities began to offer the first technical and vocational training programmes on the use and conservation of natural resources. In the 1950s and 1960s, a total of 26 academic programmes on environmental issues were created at 14 different Colombian HEIs.

Equal or greater advances could certainly be found if similar studies on this initial stage were to be carried out in other LAC countries, but at present very little is known about this stage in the region's process of environmental mainstreaming in HE.

The environmental education (EE) stage, as currently understood, began twenty years later, with a series of international events including the Biosphere Conference, held in Paris in 1968, and the United Nations Conference on the Human Environment, held in Stockholm in 1972.

LAC participated actively in all of the international meetings that took place in the 1970s and 1980s, including the International Seminar on Environmental Education in Belgrade (1975), the Intergovernmental Conference on Environmental Education in Tbilisi (1977) and the International Congress on Environmental Education and Training in Moscow (1987). In 1976, Bogota was the site of one of the regional meetings hosted by UNESCO and the United Nations Environment Programme (UNEP) as part of the International Environmental Education Programme in the run-up to the Tbilisi Conference.

Under the banner of 'Environmental Education in Latin America and the Caribbean', the 1976 meeting resulted in two important papers: a preliminary study of the region entitled 'Needs and Priorities in Environmental Education' (UNESCO, 1976) and a consultancy report entitled 'Overview of Trends and Activities' (De Teitelbaum, 1976). Both documents stressed the importance of EE at the HE level in the region, as compared to other levels and types of EE in general.

ENVIRONMENTAL HIGHER EDUCATION AND INTERNATIONAL ORGANIZATIONS IN LAC

Starting in 1976, many of the new developments of HEIs in the field of EE were the result of regional promotion by various international organizations. But the organizations that did the most to promote EE in LAC during that period were UNEP and the International Centre for Training in Environmental Sciences (CIFCA).

CIFCA was created in 1975 through an agreement between UNEP and the Spanish government. From the outset, its work focused on the promotion of EE at the HE level in Spanish-speaking countries. In 1977, CIFCA published a study entitled 'Overview of Environmental Higher Education in Latin America', which marked the first attempt to catalogue the region's progress in environmental mainstreaming at HEIs and was therefore considered a significant milestone in the process.

After CIFCA was shut down in 1983, the task of cataloguing and promoting environmental HE in LAC fell to UNEP's Regional Office for Latin America and the Caribbean (ROLAC). This work intensified with the creation of the Coordinating Unit (UCORED) and the Environmental Training Network for Latin America and the Caribbean (RFA-LAC) in 1981 and 1982, respectively, which worked in close cooperation with CIFCA during their first two years of existence.

Proposals for the creation of networks of this sort in other regions of the world had been circulating for ten years, but LAC was the only region that actually managed to create an Environmental Training Network. The creation of the RFA-LAC was made possible by the interest and effort of numerous people and institutions dedicated to this goal (Sejenovich and Ángel, 1982).

The first activities of the RFA-LAC's Coordination Unit focused on the construction of the network (Sejenovich, 1981b). In several countries, environment-related government agencies were designated as focal points in the regional network, and national networks were set up to bring together different types of institutions, including universities. Their main task was to diagnose, plan and promote the development of environmental education and research in their respective countries and coordinate their actions with UCORED. Since its establishment in 1982, the Environmental Training Network primarily oriented its tasks towards the transformation of knowledge in university education in LAC (Leff, 2009, p. xvii).

One of the main objectives of UCORED was to determine the level of development achieved by environmental HE in the region. In 1984, it published 'Diagnosis of Environmental Mainstreaming in Higher Education in Latin America and the Caribbean', the results of which were presented at the first Seminar on Universities and the Environment in Latin America and the Caribbean, held in Bogota in late 1985.

The study found that, in general, universities in LAC were already carrying out many environmental activities as part of their teaching, research and outreach programmes (UNESCO, UNEP and ICFES, 1988, p. 22), but that the process of environmental mainstreaming in HE still faced serious obstacles in the region. Several of these obstacles arose from the traditional academic structure, which is ill-suited to meeting demands for changes in the epistemological approach and organizational model at HEIs that would enable the incorporation of environmental aspects.

HIGHER EDUCATION FOR SUSTAINABLE DEVELOPMENT IN LAC

The third and current stage focuses on concepts such as *education for sustainable development*, *education for sustainability* and *education for sustainable societies*. This stage began with the United Nations Conference on Environment and Development, held in Rio de Janeiro in 1992. Since then, according to Sauvé, promoters of the sustainable development proposition have advocated the reform of all education for these purposes, giving rise to the sustainability trend (Sauvé, 2004, p. 19).

In the current stage, the process of incorporating environmental and development-related issues into HE in LAC has accelerated considerably, as compared to the two earlier periods. Unfortunately, there have been no recent regional studies that would enable a comparison with the progress reports of the 1970s and 1980s. If such a study were carried out, it is almost certain that the comparison would show tremendous quantitative and qualitative increases in terms of training, research and outreach related to the environment at the region's HEIs over the past twenty years.

One clear indicator of the significant progress made during this most recent stage of the process can be seen in Colombia. Since its participation in the early studies conducted by the UNEP-affiliated entities CIFCA and ROLAC, Colombia has occasionally conducted new studies and reports on the incorporation of environmental and development-related topics in HE (Ángel, 1989; ICFES, 1990; Morales, 1998; Pabón, 2006; RCFA, 2007; and Carrizosa, 2009). According to the two most recent quantitative studies, Colombian HEIs offered 465 programmes of this sort in 2006, up from 190 in 1999.

It is highly likely that similar increases in the supply of HE in environmental and development-related subjects are now taking place in other LAC countries. This is the case, for example, in Mexico, where in 1993 the Environmental Training Sub-directorate, a unit of the Ministry of Social Development's Environmental Education Directorate, published a study entitled 'Supply of Environmental Courses in Higher Education Institutions in Mexico' (Bravo, 1993). Later, in 2000 and 2001, the Mexican National Association of Universities and Higher Education Institutions (ANUIES) sent its members a questionnaire entitled 'Educational Actions Related to the Environment and

Sustainable Development in Higher Education Institutions in Mexico'. A comparison of the findings of the two studies reveals explosive growth in the number of academic programmes in the field of environmental studies, which shot up from 290 in 1993 to 1399 in 2001 (ANUIES, 2002, p. 4).

Within the frame of the Ibero-American Congress on Environmental Education held in Guadalajara (1992) a document was developed that included experiences and initiatives from different countries, which incorporated environmental education in the university context (Curiel, 1993). The Latin American congresses held in Mexico (1997), Venezuela (2000), Cuba (2003), Brazil (2006) and Argentina (2009) have continued to expand this subject.

ENVIRONMENTAL EDUCATION POLICIES IN SELECTED LAC COUNTRIES

HEIs play the leading role in the integration of environmental and sustainability-related issues in HE in LAC. Various UN agencies and international organizations – including UNESCO, UNEP and CIFCA – have also played an important part in this process. Starting in the 1970s, these institutional players were joined by the national governments of some countries, which began to formulate specific policies to guide and promote EE in all its forms and levels, including at the HE level.

An early case was that of Brazil. In 1999, the country adopted a National Environmental Education Policy with the ratification of Law 9795, whose direct precursor was Law 6938 of 1981, which established the National Environment Policy, and the Federal Constitution of 1988, which obliges the state to promote environmental education at all educational levels and raise public awareness on environmental conservation. Brazil's National Environmental Education Policy invokes this constitutional principle and makes explicit reference to the HE level, in which it promotes environmental mainstreaming in the training, specialization and continuing education of educators and professionals in all areas, as well as the preparation of professionals for environmental management activities.

In 2004, Brazil updated its National Environmental Education Programme (ProNEA), which currently spearheads the country's various actions in the field of EE. Although ProNEA does not have a special area dedicated to HE, many of its objectives and courses of action are directly related to this level. To make even further headway in this direction, Brazil is proposing the formulation of an Environmental Education Policy in Higher Education (Brazil, MMA – MEC, 2005, p. 29).

Since 2002, Colombia has had a National Environmental Education Policy, which provides explicit guidelines for HEIs in this area. In fact, Article 4.9 of this policy is devoted exclusively to addressing the issue of universities, training and environmental education (Colombia, MMA – MEN, 2002, p. 27). In its section on HE, Colombia's National Environmental Education Policy begins by acknowledging the progress of the country's universities and the work done by the Colombian Network for Environmental Training (RCFA), but goes on to identify a number of shortcomings that still persist. To overcome these problems, the policy recommends that HEIs take a holistic view that will enable them to assist in the search for alternative solutions to the environmental crisis (Colombia, MMA – MEN, 2002, p. 28).

Another LAC country that has a National Environmental Education Policy is Guatemala. This policy, formulated in 2004, can be understood as a result of a process that began in 1986 with the approval of the Law on the Protection and Improvement of the Environment, which led to the creation of Guatemala's National Environment Commission (CONAMA). In 1991, the Congress of Guatemala passed a Law on Environmental Education, which identifies the value of respect for nature as one of the aims of education.

One important feature of Guatemala's National Environmental Education Policy is the fact that it identifies various ministries as governing bodies: the Ministry of the Environment and Natural Resources; the Ministry of Education; the Ministry of Health and Welfare; and the Ministry of Agriculture, Livestock and Food. Something similar happened in Brazil and Colombia, where cooperation between the environment and education ministries facilitated the approval of each country's national policies on environmental education. In contrast, the case of Mexico shows that a lack of coordination between government agencies makes it difficult for public policies of this sort to be adopted in practice. In Mexico, EE has been promoted mainly by environmental-sector institutions, while remaining under-recognized by the education sector (González, 2003, p. 8).

NATIONAL UNIVERSITY NETWORKS ASSOCIATED WITH THE RFA-LAC

Within just a few years of its creation, UNEP's RFA-LAC managed to create national networks in a few different Latin American countries. The first of these was Colombia's RCFA. In 1982, Colombia's National Institute for Natural Resources and the Environment (INDERENA) was designated as one of the country's focal points. In general, INDERENA failed to meet expectations. Nevertheless, it did support a few activities, in particular academic events to promote environmental mainstreaming in HE.

The most important of these events was the Seminar on Universities and the Environment in Latin America and the Caribbean, held in Bogota in 1985. This event brought together 59 universities and environmental institutions from 22 of the region's countries. According to one of the organizers, the seminar heightened awareness of the scope of the environmental perspective in higher education (Ángel, 1989, p. 60). The participants in the seminar adopted a document entitled 'Ten Theses on the Environment in Latin America', better known as the Charter of Bogota. In the following years, these theses had a great influence on environmental education processes in the region's HEIs (Tréllez, 2006, p. 3).

In 1986, coordination of the RCFA was handed over to the Colombian Institute for the Promotion of Higher Education. For 10 years, this Institute, a unit of the Ministry of National Education, worked as a tireless advocate of EE in the country's HEIs. In 1996, the newly created Ministry of the Environment (MMA) took over the coordination of the RCFA. This institutional move from the education sector to the environmental sector entailed a reduction in the resources available to finance the RCFA's activities, resulting in a loss of momentum.

Finally, in 2004, the RCFA member universities decided to form a non-profit legal entity linked to the UNEP network programme but with the autonomy to make its own decisions and manage its own resources. The overall objective of this entity is to promote the creation of opportunities for cooperation, exchange and communication between the various members of the network through processes of communication, training, research, participation and management, in pursuit of sustainable development and environmental conservation in Colombia. The RFCA's roster of active members currently includes 40 Colombian universities, the Colombian Association of Universities, seven state institutions and five NGOs.

The other national networks created under UNEP's RFA-LAC programme were much less successful. In 1986, national networks and focal points were created in Argentina, Brazil, Cuba, Mexico, Nicaragua and Venezuela (Tréllez, 198, p. 9), but none of these have proved as enduring as the RCFA.

The network created by UNEP in Mexico was one of these unfortunate cases. In 1985, 25 representatives of various Mexican institutions – mostly universities – held a meeting. These institutions decided to create a coordinating committee composed of representatives of various offices of the Ministry of Urban Development and Ecology (SEDUE), the Ministry of Public Education (SEP) and the National Council of Science and Technology (CONACyT), as well as the six regional networks around which the country's HEIs are organized. However, due to various problems, in particular the failure to define a national focal point, the network failed to consolidate and its activity was suspended (ANUIES, 2002, p. 3).

Between 1988 and 1990, the networks and focal points of Argentina, Brazil and Venezuela held a series of National Seminars on Universities and the Environment on different topics. The first seminar, held in Argentina in 1988, left a series of papers on conceptual approaches in various disciplines, while the second, held in October 1989, was devoted to educational strategies (Ángel, 1990, p. 4). The seminars in Brazil and Venezuela focused on designing strategies for the development of environmental activities at HEIs.

Another national network was created under the RFA-LAC a few years later, with quite different results. In 1996, a group of Guatemalan institutions and universities decided to create the National Network for Environmental Research and Training (REDFIA), whose main purpose was to promote training and environmental research programmes by building on existing capacities and seeking international support (Rodriguez, 2010).

One last national network linked to the RFA-LAC is the Cuban Network for Environmental Management in Universities (RC–GAU). In 1994, a network under the Cuban Ministry of Science, Technology and the Environment was created to oversee EE activity at all levels of education, including the university level. In 2003, the RC–GAU was created in coordination with the Centre for Environmental Management, Information and Education (CIGEA), which acted as the focal point. In 2007, the network merged with the Cuban University Network for Ecodesign and Sustainable Consumption, which collaborates with CIGEA and the UNEP regional office (Ruiz, 2010).

NEW ENVIRONMENTAL UNIVERSITY NETWORKS IN LAC

The past few years have seen a boom in the formation of new environmental university networks in LAC, both nationally and internationally. The number of networks is large and continues to grow, to the point that it is impossible to mention all of them; instead, we will highlight some of the region's best known networks.

One of the most recently created networks is the Mexican Consortium of University Environmental Programs for Sustainable Development (Complexus), which was created in December 2000 when a group of HEIs joined forces with the Centre for Education and Training for Sustainable Development (CECADESU), which is a unit the Mexican Ministry of the Environment and Natural Resources (SEMARNAT), and with ANUIES (Ortiz, 2010).

Another experience is Brazil's Networks for Environmental Education. In 1988, Brazil began the process of institutionalizing the practice of networked communication and social organization, with the first steps being taken by the Paulista Environmental Education Network (REPEA) and the Capixaba Environmental Education Network. In 1992, the Brazilian Network for Environmental Education (REBEA) was created, with the Treaty on Environmental Education for Sustainable Societies and Global Responsibility serving as the new organization's declaration of principles. Various state-level Environmental Education Networks were subsequently created throughout the country. In 2001, Brazil's National Environment Fund (FNMA) called for REBEA and the REPEA to be strengthened and for other regional networks to be set up. These networks were later joined by the University Network of Environmental Education Programmes (RUPEA), as well as by the National Association for Postgraduate Studies and Research in Education (ANPEd), which works specifically in the field of HE (Brazil, MEC – MMA, 2005, pp. 22, 28 and 29).

More recently, international networks have sprung up that mostly involve HEIs from the LAC region. One example is the International Organization of Universities for Sustainable Development and the Environment (OIUDSMA). Created in 1995, this network is focused on developing education and research programmes in the environment and sustainable development fields. Since 2007, OIUDSMA has been linked to the Alliance of Ibero-American University Networks for Sustainability and the Environment (ARIUSA), of which it is a founding member (Rosúa, 2010).

An even more important experience is the Environment Committee of the Association of Universities of the Montevideo Group (AUGM). This AUGM was created in 1991 with the primary purpose of leading the integration process in the Southern Cone through the creation of an expanded shared academic space based on the scientific, technological, educational and cultural cooperation of its members (Grupomontevideo.edu.uy, 2011). The AUGM has various academic committees, including the Environment Committee, created in 1993, which aims to encourage the interaction of AUGM members dedicated to the environment and promotes joint activities involving research, outreach and teaching as appropriate means of achieving the objectives of the partner universities through the products resulting from this interaction (UNLP.edu.ar, 2011).

In northern South America, the Continental Association of Universities for Sustainable Development (ACUDES) was created in Bogota in 2009, primarily by private HEIs, with the aim of raising awareness about the importance of preserving the environment by reducing global pollution. With a total of 11 university members in Ecuador and Colombia, in addition to Harvard University, ACUDES has plans to launch several activities, including the Knowledge Network University Chairs (Barriga, 2010).

In late 2009, the Argentine Network of Universities for Sustainability and the Environment (RAUSA) was created as a result of a decision by the national universities of the Norte Grande region to promote the shared environmental and sustainability policies of the region's universities. Also in 2009, RAUSA became a member of ARIUSA (Basterra, 2010).

Finally, in early 2010, seven universities from the metropolitan area of Santiago, Chile signed the protocol of collaboration to boost the Sustainable Campuses initiative in Chile.

ALLIANCE OF IBERO-AMERICAN UNIVERSITY NETWORKS FOR SUSTAINABILITY AND THE ENVIRONMENT

ARIUSA is essentially a network of university environmental networks mainly comprising HEIs in LAC and Spain. It was created in Bogota in 2007 when representatives of the RFA-LAC, OIUDSMA, the RCFA, REDFIA, Complexus and the RC–GAU signed its articles of association.

This founding group of networks has expanded over the past two years with the addition of other university networks such as ACUDES, RAUSA, the Southern Brazilian Network for Environmental Education (REASul), the Sectoral Committee on Environmental Quality, Sustainable Development and Risk Prevention (CADEP) of the Conference of Rectors of Spanish Universities (CRUE), and the Mexican Network of Multidisciplinary Postgraduate Courses on the Environment and Sustainability (REMEPPAS).

An interesting unplanned phenomenon has emerged: new networks have arisen from within ARIUSA. These new networks are considered operational or affiliate networks.

The first of these networks – the University Network for the Environment and Sustainable Development, led by the University of Granada in Spain – was created in late 2008 by the Organisation of Ibero-American States (OEI) and the Government of Andalusia as a means of participating in the Programme for Academic Exchange and Mobility (PIMA).

The second network to be created under the umbrella of ARIUSA – the Network for Research on Science, Technology, Innovation and Environmental Education in Ibero-America (IETC-AMB) – was formed in order to participate in the 2010 edition of the Ibero-American Programme for Science, Technology and Development (CYTED). The network's first joint research project was a comparative analysis entitled 'Incorporation of Environment and Sustainability Issues in Science and Technology Systems and Higher Education in Ibero-America'.

The third operational network to emerge from ARIUSA was created in 2011 as part of a project to develop an Ibero-American Master's Degree in Environmental Science and Technology. The formal creation of this network involved six universities from Colombia and one each from Spain, Mexico and Bolivia. For its upcoming activities, it will be enjoying the support of the Postgraduate University Association (AUIP), the Inter-American Organisation for Higher Education (OUI-IOHE) and the Spanish Agency for International Development Cooporation (AECID) (Sáenz, 2011b).

CURRENT STATUS OF THE GREENING PROCESS IN HIGHER EDUCATION INSTITUTIONS IN LAC

Throughout most of the environmental mainstreaming process in HE in LAC, the primary focus has been on teaching activities. This has resulted in the creation of courses and academic programmes related to the environment in one sense or another, as well as the reform of conventional curricula to include these new topics. These new training activities have not always been accompanied by the appropriate research and outreach activities, but projects of the latter sort have also gradually become more common at universities. Since the late 1990s, in addition to implementing environmental actions in the three traditional university functions, the region's HEIs have also introduced new institutional environmental-management practices.

Unfortunately, this important and rich greening process in the region's HE system over the past few decades has been poorly documented. Recent studies have only been conducted in a handful of countries, and it is from these that we must infer the characteristics of the region's current situation.

Given the importance attributed to environmental HE, progress in the process of greening HEIs has often been measured in terms of the number of environment-related academic programmes created by universities during a given period. This figure has been used in almost all progress reports on environmental mainstreaming in HE at both the national and regional levels.

No updated information on EE programmes in LAC has been made available since the UNEP report of 1985. One attempt to catalogue progress was made in 2003 and 2004, but it was limited to postgraduate environmental programmes in Latin America. Although the study enjoyed the logistical and institutional support of the UNEP regional office, its results were very poor: information was requested from 432 universities in 21 Latin American countries, but just 80 of them responded. With those responses, the study was able to identify just 97 postgraduate-level EE programmes in 13 Latin American countries (Eschenhagen, 2009, p. 174).

Mexico and Colombia offer more useful statistics from the same period. ANUIES identified 1399 environment-related programmes in Mexico in 2001 (ANUIES, 2002, p. 4), while the RCFA reported 465 environment-related university programmes in Colombia as of late 2006 (RCFA, 2007).

Taking these national-level data as a reference, we can estimate that the region's universities currently offer several thousand EE programmes. The environmental-research and university-outreach projects in this field are likely to be even more numerous. The number of HEIs in LAC that have undergone a significant degree of greening can probably be counted in the hundreds.

These estimates give a rough idea of the general magnitudes of the most important variables in the process of greening HE in LAC, but they fall far short of providing good knowledge of the current situation. Therefore, there is an urgent need at the regional level for further studies on various aspects of environmental mainstreaming at the region's HEIs.

In the absence of precise figures that paint a complete picture of the current situation in LAC, we can point to some of the most significant achievements of the region's universities in this field. The remainder of this article will describe a few dozen of these achievements. We must bear in mind, however, that the sheer number of HEIs in the region that carry out training, research, outreach and environmental-management activities makes it impossible to mention all of them in a short article.

ENVIRONMENTAL EDUCATION PROGRAMMES AT HIGHER EDUCATION INSTITUTIONS IN LAC

Environmental HE is understood as a set of pedagogical discourses and educational practices related to the environment – in other words, HE that makes reference to the relationship between humans and nature, undertaken amid an increasing diversity of meanings. In environmental HE, various ideas and actions are put forth and organized into specialized training programmes on issues related to the environment and sustainability.

In LAC, there is no official classification of areas of emphasis or knowledge into which EE programmes can be grouped. Even the few researchers who work in this field have reached no consensus as to what categories should be commonly used. It is possible to use the conventional classification of areas of knowledge, as was done in the ANUIES study of 2002. Nevertheless, this classification has been seriously questioned by the community of environmentalist scholars and scientists in LAC because it does not recognize environmental sciences as a new area of knowledge (RCFA, 2007).

Given these circumstances, it seems logical to classify environmental training programmes on the basis of their different objects of knowledge and intervention. Using this criterion, training programmes can be classified according to area of focus: natural resources, habitat or land, terrestrial and marine biota, pollution problems, natural hazards, or various specific environmental issues.

To provide a general overview, we can divide the thousands of environmental HE programmes currently offered by HEIs in LAC into the proposed categories and focus on representative programmes selected from each group. The programmes can be chosen arbitrarily or using a database. At present, only two databases are known to be available: a list of environmental postgraduate programmes in the region developed by ROLAC in 2004, and a database on environmental programmes in Colombia developed by RCFA in 2006.

Using the proposed classification, the two aforementioned information sources and quick internet searches, the environmental HE programmes shown below can be identified as a small sample of the huge academic offering available at the region's universities in this new area of knowledge.

Within the group of programmes focused on knowledge and use of natural resources, the following subcategories are clearly distinguishable:

Area	Programme
Natural resources in general	Master's Degree in Management of Natural Resources, State University for Distance Education, Costa Rica
Forest resources	Forest Engineering, Mayor University, Chile (UMAYOR. cl, 2011) Master's Degree in Management and Conservation of Tropical Forests, Tropical Agronomic Centre for Research and Teaching
Water resources	Specialization in Environmental Management of Water Resources, Central University, Colombia
Soil resources	Master's Degree in Management and Conservation of Water and Soil, University of Cuenca, Ecuador
Fish and fishery resources	Fishery Engineering, National University of Callao, Peru

Within the group of programmes focused on knowledge and use of land, the following three subcategories are distinguishable:

Area	Programme
Watershed management	Master's Degree in Comprehensive Watershed Management, Autonomous University of Querétaro, Mexico (UAQ.mx, 2011a)
Land and habitat studies	Master's Degree in Human Settlements and Environment, Catholic University of Chile
Regional planning	Master's Degree in Urban and Regional Planning, University of Buenos Aires

Within the group of programmes focused on knowledge and conservation of biota, the following two subcategories are distinguishable:

Area	Programme
General biology	Undergraduate Degree in Environmental Biology, Jorge Tadeo Lozano University, Colombia
Ecology	Master's Degree and PhD in Ecology, University of Brasilia

Within the group of programmes focused on knowledge and management of marine environments, the following three subcategories are distinguishable:

Area	Programme
Marine science	Specialization in Marine and Coastal Environmental Management, Naval Academy of Colombia
Marine biology	Bachelor's Degree in Marine Biology, University of the Sea, Oaxaca, Mexico
Oceanography	Master's Degree in Oceanography, University of Valparaiso, Chile

Within the group of programmes focused on knowledge and management of pollution, at different historical moments, two subcategories of programmes have emerged that are closely related but which receive different names. A widespread trend in recent years is to offer programmes that integrate the two approaches.

Area	Programme
Sanitary engineering	Central American Master's Degree in Sanitary Engineering, San Carlos University, Guatemala
Environmental engineering	Undergraduate degree in Environmental Engineering, Catholic University of Asunción, Paraguay
Sanitary and environmental engineering	Master's Degree in Sanitary and Environmental Engineering, Santo Domingo Institute of Technology, Dominican Republic (INTEC.edu.do, 2011)

More recently, we have seen the emergence of environmental training programmes focused on the management of natural hazards. The first programmes of this sort to be offered were those relating to hazard management in general, such as the Master's Degree in Socio-natural Hazard Management, offered by the University of the Andes in Venezuela (ULA.ve, 2011). In recent years, we have begun to see programmes related to climate change, such as the Advanced Specialization in Climate Change and the Development of Clean Mechanisms, offered by the Simón Bolívar Andean University in Ecuador (UASB.ec, 2011).

It can also be useful to classify environmental HE programmes according to whether they are primarily monodisciplinary or interdisciplinary. Of the programmes that are primarily monodisciplinary, some are rooted in the social and human sciences whereas others focus mainly on the physical and natural sciences.

The programmes rooted in the social and human sciences are intended to train environmental educators; one example is the Specialization in Environmental Education offered by the Pedagogical and Technological University of Colombia. Programmes like this are offered at all levels of HE and are among the most common types of environmental programmes. In a closely related field of knowledge and action, the region's universities have recently begun to offer environmental communication programmes, one example being the Specialization in Environmental Communication offered by the National University of Rosario in Argentina (UNR. edu.ar, 2011).

Latin American HEIs also offer EE programmes focused on many other social and human sciences. For example:

Programme	Institution
Master's Degree in Environmental Geography	University of Panama
PhD in Environment and Society	Federal University of Campinas, Brazil
Master's Degree in Environmental Psychology	National Autonomous University of Mexico
Master's Degree in Environmental Law	University of Palermo, Argentina (PALERMO.edu, 2011)
Master's Degree in Environmental Economics and Natural Resources	Autonomous University of Baja California Sur, Mexico
Master's Degree in Environmental and Regional Policy	Bolivian Centre for Multidisciplinary Studies (CEBEM.org, 2011)

Monodisciplinary EE programmes are also offered in the physical and natural sciences. Examples include the following:

Programme	Institution
PhD in Applied Environmental Geology	Autonomous University of Nuevo León, Mexico
Bachelor's Degree in Environmental Chemistry	University of Chile
Master's Degree in Geochemistry and the Environment	Federal University of Bahia
Technical Degree in Environmental Physics	National University of Tucumán (ELDIARIO24.com, 2011)

More recently, HEIs in LAC have begun to offer programmes in environmental sciences with a clear interdisciplinary approach. The concept has encountered some resistance to recognition in the HE systems of certain countries, including Colombia. Nevertheless, in addition to seeking formal recognition (RCFA, 2007), Colombian universities are offering a growing number of educational programmes in this new area of knowledge. Colombian institutions already offer programmes of this sort at all levels of HE; examples include the Joint PhD offered by the University of Valle, the University of Cauca and the Technological University of Pereira; the Master's Degree offered by the University of Antioquia; and Undergraduate Degree offered by the University of Applied and Environmental Sciences. A similar rise in environmental-sciences programmes is being seen in other Latin American countries.

The largest number of EE programmes offered by universities in LAC fall into the category of environmental management and planning and, consequently, the study of the relationship between development and the environment. Examples of programmes of this sort include the following:

Programme	Institution
Master's Degree in Environmental Planning and Management	University of Chile
Advanced Studies Programme in Sustainable Development and the Environment	The College of Mexico
PhD in Planning and Sustainable Development	Autonomous University of Baja California (UABC.mx, 2008)
Specialization in Ecology, Environment and Development	INCCA University, Colombia
PhD in Environment and Development	Federal University of Paraná, Brazil

In this group of programmes, the Master's Degree in Environmental Management offered by Bogota's Pontifical Xavierian University stands out from the pack. Due to its interdisciplinary approach, it is recognized as one of the leading environmental postgraduate courses in Colombia and in LAC as a whole (Eschenhagen, 2009). The programme also has a very interesting history. It was launched in 1982 under the name of Master's Degree in Sanitation and Environmental Development, and in the early 1990s it was renamed the Master's Degree in Environmental Management for Sustainable Development (Sáenz, 1997). However, following the latest curricular reform, the term 'sustainable development' was eliminated from the programme's name. This case is fairly representative of a school of thought – increasingly popular among the region's academic community – that calls into question the notion of sustainable development.

ENVIRONMENTAL RESEARCH AND OUTREACH EXPERIENCES IN THE REGION

In addition to providing HE, the other two traditional functions of universities are research and community outreach.

Environmentalism emerged in the mid-20th century as a response to the serious problems that societies began to perceive and to experience directly in their relationship with the natural environment. In order to address the global environmental crisis, society first needed to gain knowledge of the new situations they faced. To do this, they called on the scientific community, which in LAC is concentrated in the universities. This was the beginning of the greening of university research – a process that is still ongoing.

The number of researchers, projects, research groups and research centres are the indicators most frequently used to keep track of the research activities taking place at HEIs. Unfortunately, no reliable information is available on scientific activity in the environmental field. As with other aspects of the greening of HEIs, the available data are sparse and incomplete.

Under these conditions, if we wish to provide an overview of the status of environmental research at the region's universities, at present we can only draw on the information provided by one or two national cases and reviews of a handful of particular experiences that circulate among interested parties or can be found on the internet.

Another aspect of interest is the close link between environmental research and HEIs' environmental and sustainable-development outreach activities. The vast majority of scientific and technological activities at these institutions target specific environmental situations or problems. Research on environment-related subjects tends to be applied research, as it almost always aims to provide the knowledge necessary to manage situations or solve problems. This applicability is intrinsic to technological development and innovation in this field. This is not to say that there is no basic research carried out in environmental subjects, whether in the humanities and social sciences or in the physical and natural sciences; however, it is clear that the basic research in this area is indeed limited.

This strong link between environmental research and environment-related university outreach is seen clearly in the practices of researchers, research groups and research centres working in this field. In addition to strictly conducting research, in LAC many of these entities often engage in consultancy and advisory projects, both for government agencies and for private companies. Others complement their activities with or specialize in support projects aimed at solving the environmental problems that communities face or improving their quality of life. As a result, research/action/participation projects in environmental and sustainable development fields are common at universities.

Although the environmental research/outreach activities carried out at the region's HEIs have yet to be exhaustively quantified, some orders of magnitude can be indicated: research centres number in the hundreds; research groups number in the thousands; researchers number in the tens of thousands; and research/extension projects are even more numerous.

By way of example, in 2007 in Colombia, there were 574 research groups linked to the National Environmental Science and Habitat Programme, which is part of the National Science and Technology System (Parra and Vásquez, 2007, p. 167). From this data we can infer that, in Colombia alone, there were close

to 2000 environmental researchers and a somewhat smaller number of active research projects at that time. If this figure is extrapolated to countries such as Brazil and Mexico, we can expect a total of close to 10,000 researchers to be working on environmental subjects in each country.

Because these figures are so large, it would be unrepresentative to cite particular examples of researchers or research projects, or even research groups. A better way to get an idea of the current status of this aspect of the greening of the region's HEIs is to present a handful of research centres specialized in environmental subjects. Although well known, these centres are not necessarily the largest of their kind, nor are the research/outreach experiences the most interesting on record. This is merely a small sample intended to illustrate some of the environmental science practices that have been developed at universities and other research centres in LAC.

The Centre for Environmental Sciences at the University of Concepción is a multidisciplinary and interdisciplinary academic unit focused on research, training, outreach and technical assistance in environmental subjects. The EULA-Chile Environmental Sciences Centre debuted in the 1990s with a research project, conducted in cooperation with Italian universities, entitled 'Management of Water Resources in the Biobío River Basin and the Adjacent Coastal Area'. Its research units are specialized in aquatic systems, regional planning and environmental engineering (EULA.cl, 2011).

The Institute of Ecology, based in Xalapa, forms part of Mexico's science, technology and HE systems. Established in 1975, it was the first institution of its kind in the country devoted exclusively to ecological research. Although not a university, since 1994 the Institute of Ecology has provided training at the master's and doctoral levels for small groups of students. It is primarily involved in research oriented towards the optimal use of natural resources and the conservation of biodiversity in Mexico. It also provides counselling services for some industries, such as tourism, and carries out research projects with international cooperation. It is described as perhaps the most important research and HE institution in its field in Latin America (ANUIES.mx, 2011b).

Colombia boasts several environmental research centres that have extensive experience and enjoy international recognition. One such centre is the Institute for Environmental Studies (IDEA), a unit of the National University of Colombia. The IDEA is an interfaculty institute involved in research, interdisciplinary teaching and outreach at four locations in different regions of Colombia. Its current work focuses on economics and the environment, culture and environmental education, transport and the environment, urban environmental management, and agricultural environmental studies (IDEA.UNAL.edu.co, 2011).

Another important centre is the Institute for Research and Development in Water Supply, Environmental Sanitation and Water Conservation (CINARA), which opened in 1985. It is attached to University of Valle's Engineering Department and defines itself as a transdisciplinary research institute for development in the field of environmental management, with a focus on water management (CINARA.UNIVALLE.edu.co, 2011). CINARA is well known throughout LAC and other regions for its work in this field.

In Ecuador, the Socio-Environmental Studies Programme, organized by the Latin American Faculty of Social Sciences (FLACSO), aims to promote analysis, debate and interpretation of the interrelationships between the environmental and social aspects of Latin America's socioeconomic dynamics (FLACSO.org.ec, 2011). Although it offers a Master's Degree in Social and Environmental Studies, the Programme's team is devoted primarily to research. Its projects include the Socio-Environmental Observatory, which is dedicated to monitoring the social and environmental impacts of certain economic activities, such as those of the oil industry, and the resulting socio-environmental conflicts brought about in Ecuador and the Andean subregion.

Finally, the Federal University of São Paulo is currently working to create an Institute for Marine and Environmental Sciences, which it hopes will emerge as a major centre of national and international excellence. In addition to offering undergraduate and postgraduate courses, this new institute will primarily carry out research and outreach activities in the following fields: health and the environment; ecotoxicology and environmental monitoring; physical, chemical and biological oceanography; marine sciences, marine biology and biotechnology; fishing and agriculture; and port affairs (César, 2011).

This last case illustrates the fact that the greening process of university research and outreach activities in LAC continues unabated. In fact, the process seems to be accelerating, as the region has seen quite a boom in environmental research.

Events such as Mexico's National Congress of Environmental Sciences have helped to spread the results of this work to society. In Colombia, the Congress of Environmental Sciences and Technologies has provided a similar venue since 2010.

INSTITUTIONAL ENVIRONMENTAL MANAGEMENT EXPERIENCES AT HIGHER EDUCATION INSTITUTIONS IN LAC

In recent years, the universities of the region have grown increasingly concerned with their own environmental performance. In 1999, the Union of Universities of Latin America and the Caribbean (UDUAL) published its 'Declaration on Latin American Universities in the 21st Century'. In this Declaration, 170 universities from 22 LAC countries, all affiliated with UDUAL, pledged to exercise leadership in caring for and preserving the many dimensions of our natural environment (UDUAL.org, 2011). UDUAL has fulfilled its promise in recent years by participating in the Decade of Education for Sustainable Development (DESD). As part of the DESD, UDUAL proposed a working agenda that urged the region's universities to reflect on sustainable development and listed the steps that must be taken, including each institution taking responsibility for its own environmental impacts.

In 2011, OUI-IOHE published its 'Declaration for Sustainability of and from Universities', which was signed by 52 HEIs, the vast majority from LAC countries; numerous other universities and university networks have subsequently voiced their support for the Declaration. In the 'Declaration of the Americas', the OUI-IOHE universities pledged to strengthen the capacity of institutions and of the inter-American university community to move towards sustainable modes of thought, knowledge and action that bolster their commitment to sustainability (OUI.IOHE.org, 2011).

Adhering to their commitments, many LAC universities have progressively implemented various institutional environmental-management practices. One example is given by the members of Complexus. This Mexican consortium only admits universities that have a thematically and institutionally cross-cutting programme expressly created to promote educational activities focused on the environment. These programmes take many forms, mainly due to the varying degrees of importance that authorities ascribe to the need to coordinate efforts in this area (Bravo, 2003, p. 2).

The diversity of the actions undertaken by LAC universities to meet their environmental commitments first came into focus at the Fourth International Seminar on Universities and the Environment. This event, held in Bogota in 2007, focused specifically on the environmental management and planning of university campuses. The Seminar's purpose was to shed light on the most important experiences in environmental management and planning at HEIs in LAC and other regions of the world.

On the basis of the reports received, a systematic analysis and reflection on environmental management and planning on university campuses was carried out. One of the main conclusions of the study was that there is no common model for the organization of environmental management at HEIs in Latin America and the Caribbean or in any other region (Sáenz, 2007). On the contrary, in this area universities have shown a great capacity for invention and innovation, which is embodied in the myriad names given to the environmental management systems they implement.

One of the best-known examples of this phenomenon is provided by the Autonomous University of San Luis Potosi (UASLP). The UASLP's Environmental Management System forms part of the institution's Environmental Agenda, which contains two other strategic elements: the Multidisciplinary Postgraduate Programme in Environmental Sciences, which conducts research and trains high-level human resources, and the University Academy for the Environment, which works to incorporate environmental perspectives in curricula and teaching methods. The UASLP's Environmental Agenda is overseen by a unit attached to the rector's office that was created in 1998. This environmental management system was implemented in 2002 (UASLP.mx, 2011) with the specific aim of bringing the UASLP's environmental performance up to an appropriate level. The system comprises three components: the Environmental Audit and Assessment, the Environmental Management Plan and the Performance Indicator System (Medellín and Nieto, 2007).

Also in Mexico, the Autonomous University of the State of Morelos (UAEM) adopted a University Environmental Management Programme in 2002 with the aim of promoting an environmental policy that respects and preserves the university environment through an approach that runs from corrective to preventative. This programme's actions cover five areas: integrated waste management, efficient management of water and energy, hazards and safety, the natural environment and landscape architecture, and environmental education. Among other activities, UAEM has enrolled in the National Environmental Audit of the Federal Environmental Protection to achieve in the future of the Environmental Complicance Certificate (Ortiz et al., 2007).

In Colombia, the University of Applied and Environmental Sciences (UDCA) is one of the HEIs that has made the greatest progress in institutional environmental management. In 2000, the UDCA Governing Board adopted its first environmental policy, which was subsequently revised in 2007. In the text of the policy, the UDCA pledged to continually improve the institution's environmental performance by preventing pollution and reducing environmental impacts (Anzola and Espinosa, 2007). The UDCA's Environmental Management and Sustainable Development Unit, which is attached to the Department of Planning, is responsible for implementing the policy (UDCA.edu.co, 2011). Since late 2005, the UDCA has been committed to implementing an environmental management system in accordance with ISO Standard 14001:2004. For its work in this field, the UDCA was recognized for its progress towards environmental excellence by the Bogota city environmental authority.

As a local state university, the District University of Bogota was required to develop and launch an Institutional Environmental Management Plan. The environmental policy adopted by the university's rector in 2007 provided the general outline for the Plan, which is intended to improve environmental conditions in the university's facilities, enhance quality of life, raise the university community's levels of health and welfare, comply with laws responsibly, contribute knowledge and practices in environmental management, use resources efficiently, recycle and reuse materials, and properly treat and dispose of waste (Sánchez, 2007).

In Brazil, the University of São Paulo started a programme called Recycle USP in 1993. Still in effect today, this programme addresses issues related to the USP's solid waste management and also provides EE. By means of educational, informational and integrated waste-management initiatives, the programme aims to make the USP a point of reference in terms of responsible consumption and proper waste disposal. The programme is in effect on all USP campuses and directly involves nearly 700 faculty, staff and students (USP.br, 2011). Since 2007, the USP has been collaborating with the ECOCAMPUS Office of the Autonomous University of Madrid on a project intended to enhance the environmental performance of the two universities, both of which are sustainability-oriented (UAM.es, 2011).

The HEIs of LAC are home to many other environmental-management experiences. Space limitations prevent us from describing them all; the projects mentioned are among the best known but not necessarily the most advanced. An exhaustive study would surely find that the great diversity of approaches and practices in this field make it impossible to identify a single model. Such a study would also show that the region's HEIs are continually undertaking a broader and more effective environmental commitment.

TOWARDS COLLECTIVE RESEARCH: A STRATEGY GOING FORWARD

By describing some current experiences in training, research, outreach and university management related to the environment and sustainability, this paper has presented a very general outline of the historical process of environmental mainstreaming at HEIs in LAC. This process is undoubtedly much more complex than what can be captured in a brief review.

To appreciate the full magnitude and importance of the progress HEIs in LAC have made in terms of greening, a research programme needs to be designed and implemented in order to investigate the historical process and the current status of environmental mainstreaming. Owing to the complexity of the endeavour, such a programme can only be undertaken collectively and over the long term.

Similar proposals have been put forth by other researchers focused on EE, as well as by leaders of the Latin American environmental thought movement. One such leader is Enrique Leff, who in the preface of a recent book (Eschenhagen, 2009) proposed the creation of a true research programme in the field of EE at the university level. Leff advocates a programme of this sort as a means of assessing and scrutinizing the many projects that are cropping up at universities in LAC (Leff, 2009b, p. xxi).

As made clear in this paper, predecessors of such a research programme on the greening of HEIs date back at least as far as the early 1970s. The programme should take into account all international, Latin American and national EE programmes at the university level that have been referenced, mentioned or reintroduced here, as well as in the work of writers from Latin America and other regions.

Without a doubt, this line of research has already made significant progress, but a genuine research programme has yet to be established. In fact, the proposed object of study has received far less attention than other lines of research on EE. According to the most recent available assessment, environmental HE in LAC has not been widely investigated because many more studies on EE have focused on the primary and basic levels, as well as non-formal EE (Eschenhagen, 2009, p. xxiv).

This lack of research on the greening process of HEIs stands in contrast to the subject's importance to contemporary societies. It is these university programmes that are training professionals capable of meeting the challenge of environmentalism, with first-hand experience and a future-oriented outlook in the constitution of sustainability (Leff, 2009, p. xxi).

Since the UNEP report published in 1985, there has been no systematic monitoring of the emergence, configuration or institutionalization of research and EE programmes in LAC. To correct this shortcoming, a systematic process for monitoring and evaluating university greening must be put into place (Leff, 2009, p. xvi). At the regional level, this need is being partially addressed by means of a comparative research project on the incorporation of environmental and sustainability-related issues in the HE systems of several Latin American countries (Sáenz, 2010).

Nevertheless, this and other projects are just the beginning of what needs to be a much broader research programme. The research should complement and go beyond the reports that have been published with some regularity in countries such as Colombia and Mexico. In addition to taking inventory and developing creation timelines, researchers must analyse and evaluate the existing programmes. After having partially catalogued the emergence, establishment and institutionalization of new environmental and sustainable development (or sustainability) programmes at universities, researchers should undertake a thorough investigation of the strategies and contents thereof and record the various ways in which environmental aspects and environmental knowledge are incorporated in these programmes (Leff, 2009, p. xix).

This assessment should take into account the objectives, curricular structure, syllabuses and specific content of programmes offered by HEIs in LAC. But this, by itself, is not enough. Researchers should also evaluate the teaching methods and educational practices being developed in the region.

This assessment of the curricula and teaching methodologies of university programmes must necessarily lead to consideration of their epistemological basis. Epistemological vigilance is unavoidable when examining, for example, the ways in which these programmes approach interdisciplinarity and the dialogue of knowledge, or the various environmental concepts on which they are based (Leff, 2009, p. xvii).

Only once we have gained broad, in-depth knowledge of the multiple aspects of the current EE situation in LAC will we be able to justify making recommendations aimed at correcting shortcomings, building on strengths or proposing a reorientation of the current process. It is better to know and understand before rushing into action. In any event, for some guidance in this area, readers are referred to the very recent 'Declaration for Sustainability of and from Universities' (OUI.IOHE.org, 2011), which features entirely valid statements and proposals.

REFERENCES

Ángel, Augusto (1989) *Programas Ambientales Universitarios. Diagnóstico.* Instituto Colombiano para el Fomento de la Educación Superior (ICFES) e Instituto Nacional de Recursos Naturales y Ambiente (INDERENA). Bogota.

Ángel, Augusto (1990) *Diagnóstico de la Calidad de los Estudios Ambientales en Colombia.* Trabajo presentado a la 'Misión de Ciencia y Tecnología' organizada por COLCIENCIAS en 1988, con relación al tema 'Ciencia, Tecnología y Medio Ambiente'. Bogota.

Ángel, Augusto (2001) *Medio Ambiente e Interdisciplina. Utopías y Realidades.* En: PARRA, Álvaro del Campo (Compilador). *Memorias del Segundo Seminario Universidad y Medio Ambiente en América Latina y el Caribe.* Realizado el 24, 25 y 26 de noviembre de 1999. Corporación Universitaria Autónoma de Occidente. Cali, pp. 75–92.

ANUIES (2002) *Acciones ambientales de la IES de México en la perspectiva del desarrollo sustentable: Antecedentes y situación actual.* Asociación Nacional de Universidades e Instituciones de Educación Superior. México D.F.

ANUIES – SEMARNAP (2002) *Plan de Acción para el Desarrollo Sustentable de las Instituciones de Educación Superior.* Asociación Nacional de Universidades e Instituciones de Educación Superior y Secretaría de Medio Ambiente, Recursos Naturales y Pesca. Gobierno de México. México D.F.

Anzola, Germán and Espinosa, Marco Tulio (2007) Gestión Ambiental en la U.D.C.A. Hacia el Desarrollo Humano Sostenible. En: RCFA *Gestión Ambiental Institucional y Ordenamiento de Campus Universitarios.* Memorias del Cuarto Seminario Internacional Universidad y Ambiente. Red Colombiana de Formación Ambiental – RCFA. Universidad de Ciencias Aplicadas y Ambientales – U.D.C.A. Bogota, pp. 127–47.

Barriga, Pablo (2010) *Presentación de la Asociación Continental de Universidades de Desarrollo Sustentable – ACUDES.* Reporte entregado para el informe sobre las Redes constituyentes de la Alianza de Redes Iberoamericanas de Universidades por la Sustentabilidad y el Ambiente – ARIUSA. Quito.

Basterra, Indiana (2010) *Presentación de la Red Argentina de Universidades por la Sostenibilidad y el Ambiente – RAUSA.* Reporte entregado para el informe sobre las Redes constituyentes de la Alianza de Redes Iberoamericanas de Universidades por la Sustentabilidad y el Ambiente – ARIUSA. Corrientes – Argentina.

Brazil, MEC (2007) *Educación Ambiental: Aprendices de Sustentabilidad.* Ministerio de Educación. Gobierno Federal del Brasil.

Brazil, MMA – MEC (2005) *Programa Nacional de Educación Ambiental – ProNEA.* Ministerio del Medio Ambiente y Ministerio de Educación. Gobierno Federal del Brasil. Brasilia. 3rd edn.

Bravo, María Teresa (1993) *Oferta educativa de estudios ambientales en instituciones de educación superior en México.* Directorio INE/Sedesol. México.

Bravo, María Teresa (2003) Las instituciones de educación superior se organizan para participar en el cambio ambiental: El Complexus. En: Revista *Agua y Desarrollo Sustentable.* No 8, Octubre. Gobierno del Estado de México, pp. 22–4.

Carrizosa, Julio (2009) *La Universidad Colombiana y las Políticas para el Desarrollo Sostenible.* Universidad de Ciencias Aplicadas y Ambientales. Biblioteca Universidad y Ambiente. Vol. V. Bogota.

César, Augusto (2011) *Informe sobre la creación del Instituto de Ciencias del Mar y Ambientales de la UFSP.* Reporte entregado para un documento de la Alianza de Redes Iberoamericanas de Universidades por la Sustentabilidad y el Ambiente – ARIUSA. Sao Paulo.

CIFCA (1977a) *El CIFCA y la Formación Ambiental.* Cuadernos del CIFCA No. 1. Segunda Edición. Centro Internacional de Formación en Ciencias Ambientales. Madrid.

CIFCA (1977b) *Informe de la Reunión sobre Estudios Superiores Medioambientales en América Latina.* Centro Internacional de Formación en Ciencias Ambientales. México D.F. RE. 2 DOC.

CIFCA (1978a) *La Formación Ambiental en América Latina.* Cuadernos del CIFCA No. 8. Centro Internacional de Formación en Ciencias Ambientales. Madrid.

CIFCA (1978b) Panorama de los Estudios Superiores Medioambientales en América Latina. En: CIFCA, 1978a. *La Formación Ambiental en América Latina.* Cuadernos del CIFCA No. 8. Centro Internacional de Formación en Ciencias Ambientales Madrid. pp. 55–139.

CIFCA (1980a) *Necesidades científico – técnicas del medio ambiente.* Cuadernos del CIFCA No. 21. Centro Internacional de Formación en Ciencias Ambientales. Madrid.

CIFCA (1980b) *La Formación Ambiental Universitaria.* Cuadernos del CIFCA No. 20. Centro Internacional de Formación en Ciencias Ambientales. Madrid.

Colombia, MMA – MEN (2002) *Política Nacional de Educación Ambiental.* Ministerio de Ambiente y Ministerio de Educación Nacional. República de Colombia. Bogota.

Curiel, Arturo (1993) *Educación ambiental y Universidad.* I Congreso Iberoamericano en Educación ambiental. Universidad de Guadalajara.

De Teitelbaum, Mirta (1976) *Educación y Medio Ambiente en América Latina. Panorama General de las Tendencias y Actividades Actuales.* Organización de las Naciones Unidas para la Educación, la Ciencia y la Cultura. Programa de Educación Ambiental UNESCO – UNEP. Paris. Noviembre. Septiembre. 29 pp. ED-76/CONF655/Col Documento preparado para la UNESCO y presentado en la Reunión regional sobre Educación Ambiental en América Latina y el Caribe.

Eschenhagen, María Luisa (2009) *Educación Ambiental Superior en América Latina. Retos Epistemológicos y Curriculares.* Red Colombiana de Formación Ambiental. Biblioteca Universidad y Ambiente. Vol. IV. Bogota.

González, Edgar (1999) Otra lectura a la Historia de la Educación Ambiental en América Latina y el Caribe. En: *Tópicos en Educación Ambiental.* 1(1) pp. 9–26.

González, Edgar (2003) Atisbando la construcción conceptual de la educación ambiental en México. En: Bertely Busquets, María (ed.). *Educación, Derechos Sociales y Equidad. La investigación educativa en México*

1992–2002. Tomo 1: Educación y diversidad cultural y Educación y medio ambiente. México, Consejo Mexicano de Investigación Educativa, pp. 243–75.

Guatemala, MARN – MINEDUC (2004) *Política Nacional de Educación Ambiental.* Ministerio de Ambiente y Recursos Naturales. Ministerio de Educación. Gobierno de Guatemala.

ICFES (1990) *Programas y Actividades Ambientales en la Educación Superior.* Instituto Colombiano para el Desarrollo de la Educación Superior. Subdirección Académica. Red de Formación Ambiental. Bogota.

LEFF, Enrique (2009) Prólogo. En: Eschenhagen, María Luisa, *Educación Ambiental Superior en América Latina. Retos Epistemológicos y Curriculares.* Red Colombiana de Formación Ambiental. Biblioteca Universidad y Ambiente. Vol. IV. Bogota, pp. xv–xxi.

Medellín, Pedro and Nieto, Luz María (2007) El Sistema de Manejo Ambiental de la Universidad, Autónoma de San Luis Potosí, México. En: RCFA *Gestión Ambiental Institucional y Ordenamiento de Campus Universitarios.* Memorias del Cuarto Seminario Internacional Universidad y Ambiente. Red Colombiana de Formación Ambiental – RCFA. Universidad de Ciencias Aplicadas y Ambientales – U.D.C.A. Bogota, pp. 95–110.

Morales, Tito (1998) *Programas Académicos en Ciencias Ambientales a nivel de Pregrados y Posgrados ofrecidos actualmente en las universidades públicas y privadas de Colombia.* Facultad de Ciencias Ambientales. Universidad Tecnológica de Pereira. Convenio GTZ – UTP. Pereira.

Novo, María (1995) *Educación Ambiental. Bases éticas, conceptuales y metodológicas.* Editorial Universitas, Madrid.

Ortiz, Laura, Sánchez, Enrique and Lara, Julio (2007) La Gestión Ambiental en la Universidad Autónoma del Estado de Morelos, México. En: RCFA *Gestión Ambiental Institucional y Ordenamiento de Campus Universitarios.* Memorias del Cuarto Seminario Internacional Universidad y Ambiente. Red Colombiana de Formación Ambiental – RCFA. Universidad de Ciencias Aplicadas y Ambientales – U.D.C.A. Bogota, pp. 77–90.

Ortiz, Laura (2010) *Presentación del Consorcio Mexicano de Programas Ambientales Universitarios para el Desarrollo Sustentable – COMPELXUS.* Reporte entregado para el informe sobre las Redes constituyentes de la Alianza de Redes Iberoamericanas de Universidades por la Sustentabilidad y el Ambiente – ARIUSA. Cuernavaca.

Pabón, Morelia (2006) Instauración de la Formación Ambiental en la Universidad Colombiana. En: *Revista Palabra.* Universidad de Cartagena. Cartagena, pp. 51–4.

Parra, Álvaro del Campo and Vásquez, Fredy (2007) La investigación en Ciencias Ambientales en la República de Colombia. En: RCFA *Las Ciencias Ambientales: Un nueva Área de Conocimiento.* Red Colombiana de Formación Ambiental. Bogota, pp. 167–87.

RCFA (2007) *Las Ciencias Ambientales: Un nueva Área de Conocimiento.* Red Colombiana de Formación Ambiental. Bogota.

Rodriguez, Germán (2010) *Presentación de la Red de Formación e Investigación Ambiental – REDFIA.* Reporte entregado para el informe sobre las Redes constituyentes de la Alianza de Redes Iberoamericanas de Universidades por la Sustentabilidad y el Ambiente – ARIUSA. Guatemala.

Rosúa, José Luis (2010 *Presentación de la Organización Internacional de Universidades por el Desarrollo Sostenible y el Medio Ambiente.* Reporte entregado para el informe sobre las Redes constituyentes de la Alianza de Redes Iberoamericanas de Universidades por la Sustentabilidad y el Ambiente – ARIUSA. Granada.

Ruiz, Lourdes (2010) *Presentación de la Red Cubana para la Gestión Ambiental en las Universidades (RC–GAU).* Reporte entregado para el informe sobre las Redes constituyentes de la Alianza de Redes Iberoamericanas de Universidades por la Sustentabilidad y el Ambiente – ARIUSA. La Habana.

Sáenz, Orlando (1997) Maestría en Gestión Ambiental para el Desarrollo Sostenible. Trayectoria Académica y Reforma Curricular. 1982–1997. En: *Ambiente y Desarrollo.* Año 4, Nos. 6–7. Instituto de Estudios Ambientales para el Desarrollo. Pontificia Universidad Javeriana. Bogota, pp. 201–18.

Sáenz, Orlando (2007) La Gestión Ambiental y el Ordenamiento de Campus Universitarios. Análisis y reflexiones a partir de algunas experiencias relevantes. En: RCFA *Gestión Ambiental Institucional y Ordenamiento de Campus Universitarios.* Memorias del Cuarto Seminario Internacional Universidad y Ambiente. Red Colombiana de Formación Ambiental – RCFA. Universidad de Ciencias Aplicadas y Ambientales – U.D.C.A. Bogota, pp. 233–89.

Sáenz, Orlando (2010) *Proyecto Red de Investigación sobre Ciencia, Tecnología, Innovación y Educación Ambiental en Iberoamérica.* Programa de Ciencia y Tecnología para el Desarrollo – CYTED. Bogota.

Sáenz, Orlando (2011a) *La Formación Ambiental Superior. Surgimiento histórico y primeras etapas de desarrollo. 1948–1991.* Trabajo de Investigación para el Doctorado en Educación y Sociedad. Universidad Autónoma de Barcelona. Barcelona.

Sáenz, Orlando (2011b) *Máster Iberoamericano en Ciencias y Tecnologías Ambientales. Contexto, antecedentes, gestiones y retos. 2007–2011.* Universidad de Ciencias Aplicadas y Ambientales. Alianza de Redes Iberoamericanas de Universidades por la Sustentabilidad y el Ambiente – ARIUSA. Bogota.

Sánchez, Fernando (2007) Experiencia en la formulación y puesta en marcha del Plan Institucional de Gestión Ambiental – PIGA – en la Universidad Distrital Francisco José de Caldas. En: RCFA *Gestión Ambiental Institucional y Ordenamiento de Campus Universitarios.* Memorias del Cuarto Seminario Internacional Universidad y Ambiente. Red Colombiana de Formación Ambiental – RCFA. Universidad de Ciencias Aplicadas y Ambientales – U.D.C.A. Bogota, pp. 159–72.

Sauvé, Lucie (2004) Una cartografía de corrientes en educación ambiental. En: Sato, Michele and Carvalho, Isabel (eds) *La Investigación en Educación Ambiental: Cartografías de una identidad narrativa en formación.* Porto Alegre. Armted.

Sejenovich, Héctor (1981a) *Antecedentes a nivel mundial y regional de la Red de Formación Ambiental en América Latina y el Caribe.* Unidad de Coordinación de la Red. Oficina Regional para América Latina y el Caribe. Programa de las Naciones Unidas para el Medio Ambiente. México.

Sejenovich, Héctor (1981b) *Metodología para la elaboración de un proyecto sobre el establecimiento de una red de instituciones de formación ambiental en América Latina y el Caribe.* Unidad de Coordinación de la Red. Oficina Regional para América Latina y el Caribe. Programa de las Naciones Unidas para el Medio Ambiente. México.

Sejenovich, Héctor and Ángel, Augusto (1982) *Proyecto de la Red de Formación Ambiental.* (Versión resumida). Programa de las Naciones Unidas para el Medio Ambiente (PNUMA/UNEP) y Centro Internacional de Formación en Ciencias Ambientales (CIFCA). Bogota. Presentado en el Seminario sobre 'Ciencia, Investigación y Medio Ambiente' Realizado en Bogota del 25 al 30 de enero.

Soares, Silvia Helena and Wainer, José (2007) *Asociación de Universidades Grupo de Montevideo. 15 años de Historia.* Asociación de Universidades Grupo de Montevideo. Montevideo.

Tréllez, Eloísa (1986) *La Red de Formación Ambiental en Colombia. El Icfes, Punto Focal de la Red. Propuesta para un plan de acción.* Instituto Colombiano para el Fomento de la Educación Superior. Subdirección Académica. Bogota.

Tréllez, Eloísa (2006) Algunos elementos del proceso de construcción de la educación ambiental en América Latina. En: *Revista Iberoamericana de Educación.* No. 41, pp. 69–81.

UNEP/ORPALC (1985) *La Incorporación de la Dimensión Ambiental en América Latina y el Caribe.* Primer Seminario sobre Universidad y Medio Ambiente para América Latina y el Caribe. Bogota, 28 de octubre a 2 de noviembre. Programa de las Naciones Unidas para el Medio Ambiente. Documento UNEP/WG 138-2. México D.F.

UNEP/ORPALC (2003) *Propuesta de Revisión de la Red de Formación Ambiental para América Latina y el Caribe: Balance y Perspectivas.* Oficina Regional para América Latina y el Caribe. Programa de las Naciones Unidas para el Medio Ambiente. Panamá. Documento UNEP/LAC-IGWG.XIV/9/Rev.1 presentado al XIV Foro de Ministros de Medio Ambiente de América Latina y el Caribe. Panamá, 20 al 21 de Noviembre.

UNESCO (1976) *Necesidades y Prioridades de la Educación Ambiental. Estudio preliminar de la región de América Latina y el Caribe.* Organización de las Naciones Unidas para la Educación, la Ciencia y la Cultura. París. Noviembre. ED-76/CONF.655/COL1.

UNESCO, UNEP and ICFES (1988) *Universidad y Medio Ambiente en América Latina. Seminario de Bogota.* Realizado del 28 de octubre al 1 de noviembre de 1985. Organización de las Naciones Unidas para la Educación, la Ciencia y la Cultura, Programa de las Naciones Unidas para el Medio Ambiente e Instituto Colombiano para el Fomento de la Educación Superior. México. D.F.

INTERNET REFERENCES

ANUIES.mx, 2011a (accessed 18/07/2011)

ANUIES.mx, 2011b, http://www.anuies.mx/servicios/d_estrategicos/ afiliadas/234.html (accessed 22/07/2011)

AUGM.edu, 2011, http://www.grupomontevideo.edu.uy (accessed 29/07/2011)

CEBEM.org, 2011, http://www.cebem.org/cursos.php?seccion=55&id=335&tip=pa&tipc=1 (accessed 18/07/2011)

CINARA.UNIVALLE.edu.co, 2011, http://cinara.univalle.edu.co/index.php?seccion=MISION (accessed 22/07/2011)

CONGRESODECIENCIASMABIENTALES.com, 2011, http://www.congresodecienciasambientales.com/comite.htm

ELDIARIO24.com, 2011, http://www.eldiario24.com/nota.php?id=212674 (accessed 18/07/2011)

EULA.cl, 2011, http://www.eula.cl/index.php?option=com_content&view=article&id=7&Itemid=95 (accessed 22/07/2011)

FLACSO.org.ec, 2011, http://www.flacso.org.ec/html/program.php?id_programa=1002&ID=DC_00 (accessed 22/07/2011)

GRUPOMONTEVIDEO.edu.uy, 2011, http://www.grupomontevideo.edu.uy/medioambiente/ (accessed 18/07/2011)

IDEA.UNAL.edu.co, 2011, http://www.idea.unal.edu.co/ (accessed 22/07/2011)

INTEC.edu.do, 2011, http://www.intec.edu.do/pdf/pensa/postGrado/ (accessed 18/07/2011)

OUI-IOHE.org, 2011, http://www.oui-iohe.org/es/images/declaracion.pdf (accessed 18/07/2011)

PALERMO.edu, 2011, http://www.palermo.edu/derecho/maestrias/ m_derecho_ambiental_plan.html) (accessed 21/07/2011)

PNUMA.org, 2010, http://www.pnuma.org/educamb/QuienesSomos.php (accessed 04/12/2010)

UABC.mx, 2011, http://www.uabc.mx/iis/pds/ (accessed 21/07/2011)

UAM.es, 2011, http://www.uam.es/servicios/ecocampus/especifica/inv_cooperacion.htm (accessed 19/07/2011)

UAQ.mx, 2011a, http://www.uaq.mx/FCN/fcn_cuencas.htm (accessed 21/07/2011)

UAQ.mx, 2011b, http://aeropuerto.uaq.mx/maestrias/mca/anca2011.html (accessed 23/07/2011)

UASB.ec, 2011, http://www.uasb.edu.ec/contenido_oferta_academica.php?cd_oferta=91&swpath=oaespsup (accessed 21/07/2011)

UASLP.mx, 2011, http://ambiental.uaslp.mx/ (accessed 21/07/2011)

UDCA.edu.co, 2011, http://www.udca.edu.co/es/departamento-planeacion/gestion-ambiental-desarrollo-sostenible.html (accessed 19/07/2011)

UDUAL.org, 2011, http://www.udual.org/Asamblea/sigloxxi.htm (accessed 18/07/2011)

ULA.ve, 2011, http://www.ula.ve/prensa/index.php?option=com_ (accessed 18/07/2011)

UMAYOR.cl, 2011, http://www.umayor.cl/um/ingenieria-forestal-umayor/ (accessed 20/07/2011)

UNESCO.org/iau, 2011, http://www.unesco.org/iau/sd/sd_dkyoto. html (accessed 18/07/2011)

UNLP.edu.ar, 2011, http://www-old.unlp.edu.ar/comitemedioambiente/ (accessed 18/07/2011)

UNR.edu.ar, 2011, http://www.unr.edu.ar/evento/344/especializacion-en-comunicacion-ambiental (accessed 18/07/2011)

USP.br, 2011, http://www.inovacao.usp.br/recicla/index.php (accessed 18/07/2011)

THE CARIBBEAN REGION

The Caribbean is located between the Atlantic Ocean and the Caribbean Sea and is composed of islands and the mainland countries of Belize, Guyana and Suriname. To the north are the Bahamas and the Turks and Caicos, to the south are the Lesser Antilles and in the centre are the Greater Antilles. The Greater Antilles include the countries of Cuba, Jamaica, Haiti and the Dominican Republic (*Hispaniola*), and Puerto Rico. The Lesser Antilles comprise the Leeward and Windward islands. As a result of its history the Caribbean is a mix of English, Spanish, French and Dutch-speaking countries with a population of approximately 40 million.

Many countries in the Caribbean have a fairly strong tradition of environmental education (EE). The concept of sustainability or education for sustainable development (ESD) was formally addressed in the region at the launch of the UN DESD in 2005 in Kingston, Jamaica. As a result, many countries have begun to widen their concept of EE to include that of 'sustainability'. The three paradigms illustrated in the UNESCO review of ESD structures are in operation in the region (Figure 1).

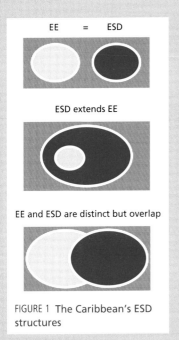

FIGURE 1 The Caribbean's ESD structures

So implementation of sustainability varies. This is often dependent on individual stakeholders who are driving the implementation.

SOCIAL MOVEMENTS

There are a number of social movements and organizations in higher education in the region that are helping to advance a greater awareness of sustainability and encouragement of sustainable practices. These include:

1. MESCA: Mainstreaming Environment and Sustainability in Caribbean universities. This movement is based on MESA (Mainstreaming Environment and Sustainability in African universities) and was initiated in 2009. It is a movement comprising ten universities in the region.
2. Projects: for example the Infusion of Biodiversity Education in Teacher Education in Jamaica, and the Sustainable Teacher Environmental Education Project from as early as 2000. Among the projects' outcomes were (a) the development of courses in EE, through the Joint Board of Teacher Education, for primary and secondary pre-service teachers in teachers colleges in Jamaica, Belize, Turks and Caicos Islands, and (b) and the piloting of whole-college approaches to environmental ESD with an emphasis on environmental stewardship.
3. Networks: for example the Caribbean Network of Teacher Educators for Sustainability.
4. Institute for Sustainable Development, the University of the West Indies (UWI): The main functions of the Institute are research, project development and management, graduate teaching and consultancy. The main areas are strategic development and business planning, foresighting, technology roadmapping, technology and innovation studies, economic development and trade, integrated assessment, risk assessment and management, disaster preparedness and resilience. Some of the present projects include:
   –0 Zero net energy/energy plus building
   – Reform of Jamaica's planning system
   – Reform of Jamaica's environmental regulatory system
   – Reform of Jamaica's national squatter policy
   – Reform of Jamaica's national security system
5. Centre for Resource Management and Environmental Studies (CERMES) located at the Cave Hill campus, UWI, Barbados: The Centre promotes and facilitates sustainable development in the Caribbean through graduate education, applied research, innovative projects, professional training and involvement in national, regional and global initiatives. The focus seems to be primarily on the physical environment.

CURRICULA AND LEARNING PROCESSES

The strengths in this area are connecting the curriculum content with one's own life, social learning and service learning programmes, field-based programmes, teacher capacity building, educating citizens with civic awareness, participatory and problem-oriented pedagogical methods and educating for global and local contexts.

Schools of Education, for example, in the three campuses of the University of the West Indies, have strong field-based programmes. Teaching practicum is conducted in schools and students are generally encouraged to explore what is taking place in communities. Field-based programmes are seen as essential in the pure and applied sciences as well as in social sciences.

Service learning or community action projects also form part of the teaching and learning process in a number of courses, for example, in the Literature and Education for Sustainable Development course for graduate students. Here each student is required to develop a small project in a community. Some students undertake projects such as recycling, greening, or vegetable gardening.

At Northern Caribbean University, Manchester, Jamaica, every course in the core of a student's programme has a service-learning component that focuses on addressing the social, financial and environmental challenges affecting the society. Additionally, as a policy of the university, each lecturer's teaching load for the academic year must include a service activity and the university has a vice-president whose mandate is to oversee all university community projects.

Participatory and problem-oriented pedagogical methods and educating for global and local contexts are emphasized, especially in courses that focus on the theme of sustainability. These courses include EE courses at the undergraduate and graduate levels.

Although some attempts have been made in linking the humanities and the sciences, more work needs to be done in the areas of transdisciplinary and interdisciplinary approaches generally. Teaching and learning in universities in the region tend to be situated firmly within disciplinary boundaries.

The development of teacher capacity is recognized as key. Universities in the region, working through their Ministries of Education and the Joint Board of Teacher Education, have focused on developing this through their engagement with teachers' colleges. This work has centred on quality assurance as well as in assisting lecturers with the development of curricula. At present, lecturers are encouraged to infuse the theme of sustainability in the curricula. There is also in the Joint Board of Teacher Education (JBTE) programme in Jamaica a core course on Education for Sustainable Development.

Additionally, universities like the UWI attend to teacher capacity building through specially designed programmes, for example the Instructional Development Unit aimed at improving pedagogy of lecturers. ESD, however, needs to be integrated into these programmes.

Values clarification and values analysis are processes that are increasingly used in the Environmental Education, Literature and Education for Sustainable Development and citizenship courses in the School of Education. Also, more recently, linking thinking has become a focus of these courses. Case studies of ESD in other parts of the world help to expose students to what is possible in bringing about environmental action and change.

STUDENT INVOLVEMENT

A recent audit of four universities in the region indicated that students are aware to some extent of sustainability issues as students began and implemented sustainability initiatives in halls of residence by themselves. There were, however, no student groups or organizations

with an environmental or sustainability focus at the four universities audited in the recent MESCA activity, although this is not the case in all institutions of higher learning. Moneague College, St Ann in Jamaica provides an example of student environmental groups.

> ### BOX 1: STUDENT INITIATIVES
> At Moneague College, students in the Environmental Club and the 4H Leaders Club participate in a range of sustainability activities, from field trip exercises to campus tree naming and maintenance of the waste management and food security initiatives. The clubs operate with executive members and with representatives from all college programmes, for example, Teacher Education, Management Information, Pre-University Science and Arts and Environmental Studies (CCCJ) programme.
>
> (Reported by *Desmond Campbell, Senior Lecturer and Coordinator of Environmental projects and Environmental Studies*)

RESEARCH

Research on different aspects of sustainability is undertaken in various faculties of the universities in the region. The research is linked to global and local needs. At Northern Caribbean University, for example, research is conducted on the bauxite industry in watershed management, water harvesting, topsoil management, music and learning, and the use of natural products to treat diseases. Generally, research in higher education is, however, discipline-specific. There are, as a result, very limited transdisciplinary and interdisciplinary research approaches. Additionally, new models of research with a clear focus on the ethics and value implications of research and knowledge are needed.

INSTITUTIONAL MANAGEMENT AND OPERATIONS

The formal commitment to sustainability needs to be strengthened. There is general support for sustainable practices in the region but greater attention and focus are needed. Energy conservation and waste management are seen as critical and have been addressed in various ways – in practice and research. The UWI, Mona, for example, has a campus recycling programme.

At the University of Technology, Jamaica, an energy audit has been done, and solutions provided for greater conservation. Some actions have taken place, for example, solar water heaters now replace traditional electric ones.

> ### BOX 2: INSITUTIONAL INITIATIVES
> Moneague College has been working on waste and water management initiatives over the past four years. We have procured grant funding from the Environmental Foundation of Jamaica to build an organic waste management facility for the controlled decomposition of biodegradable wastes from our chicken-rearing project and from shredded paper and plant matter. The shredded material is used as litter for the chicken project and as food for the worms used in the Vermicompost project. Students are actively involved in these projects. Manure produced is used to enhance the fruit tree crop project. Some 4 acres are covered with fruit trees.
>
> (*Desmond Campbell, Senior Lecturer and Coordinator of Environmental projects and Environmental Studies*)

SOCIAL AND COMMUNITY ENGAGEMENT

There is a strong link between universities and the region, even as we acknowledge the need for a greater community interface. The University of the West Indies, Mona, for example, has created a 'Township Project' that aims to build a stronger relationship between the university and its immediate environs. Meetings with the citizens in these communities are held regularly to discuss community needs and possible interventions with the help of the university. The matter of literacy needs has been one of the issues discussed and an intervention determined.

Public lectures, which provide opportunities for the sharing of knowledge and dialogue between the universities and the wider society, foster important links with civil society.

Involvement of lecturers and departments on the whole, in community service, is also encouraged. Community service involvement is expected to form part of the annual report of each lecturer and each department. Promotion, contract renewal and tenure all take into account this aspect of a lecturer's work.

STRATEGIES AND ACTIONS NEEDED

More cross-disciplinary work in sustainability is needed both intra- and inter- institutions of higher education. Opportunities for the sharing of ideas, practices, research, the development of common understandings of sustainability and general collaboration between faculties in these institutions, as well as between institutions, need to be created. This could be done through university forums in which faculties' departments share their work in sustainability and develop a university-wide approach to sustainability.

In effect, a whole-university approach to sustainability is needed, one in which all categories of staff are able to identify and develop their contribution to sustainability locally and regionally.

Greater connection with NGOs working in the field of sustainability is also an action that would help to advance sustainability in the region.

THE CHALLENGES

- Faculties and departments are too discipline-bound, narrowly focused in their discipline area.

- Sustainability has often been conceived narrowly as the purview of the sciences and, therefore, the reach to other areas has been limited.
- The specific demands of each discipline and department often do not allow time for forging links outside departments and faculties.

CONCLUSION

Since the launch of the UN Decade for Education for Sustainable Development in 2005 in the Caribbean, much has been done in practice and research for sustainability. Much more could be accomplished, however, if there were an overall strategic plan with a sustainability focus for HEIs on both a national and a regional level. At the very least, there needs to be ongoing dialogue on sustainability within and across faculties in our universities.

Inside View II.8
Brazil needs ESD to create a safe path to a more sustainable future

Zióle Zanotto Malhadas

Sustainability, as a new paradigm that will generate new forms of relationships and understanding of citizens' responsibilities, is facing serious difficulties of implementation in the higher education system, mainly because Brazil does not yet have a political framework that supports education for sustainability (EfS) in higher education institutions (HEIs).

Great expectations are evident, since the HEIs should lead the way to develop innovative advanced research in order to offer contribution to the community and institutional managerial efforts, but it is a slow moving process in the Brazilian HEIs. Curriculum transformation is one of the main objectives to be achieved in EfS, but it is considered a very difficult goal to achieve, since most academics stand against changes.

Some steps forward were taken at the International Conference on Education for Sustainable Development – ESD-2010, promoted by the RCE-Curitiba-Paraná (May 2010) in partnership with the United Nations University (UNU-IAS), the Federal University of Paraná, the Catholic University, the Federal Technological University and the Federation of Industries of Paraná (SESI-SENAI), which brought together about 800 people from the region, plus representatives from 72 countries. The main objective was to encourage and enhance innovative teaching approaches to integrate education for sustainable development (ESD) in the university, primary school and community.

Meanwhile, significant activities are taking place all around the university grounds, where some teachers and researchers are working in partnership with community leaders and industry representatives, like the National Confederation of Industries (CNI, Confederaçao Nacional da Industria) and its regional partners – the state federations of industries,[1] which sum up efforts to persuade their affili-

ates to implement the Brazilian Strategic Map of Industry (2007–2015) that defines sustainable development as the industry's overall goal. It represents a complex challenge to a society deeply marked by inequalities and by the need to grow and promote the social inclusion of a considerable portion of its population, as well as to contribute towards the solving of environmental issues and to promote excellence in professional training and qualification through dynamic partnerships with universities.

As ESD is meant to be transformative, a need to create alternative models of development that could co-exist alongside existing models is imperative. This would involve invention, innovation and implementation of projects in the community with the cooperation of HEIs, as well as analysis of what is occurring in terms of sustainability all over the world and the driving forces that are making it happen.

NOTE

1 National Confederation of Industries – Present in all 26 States and the Federal District, the State Federations of Industry comprise over one thousand associated employers' unions and 196 thousand companies.

INTRODUCTION

Report of progress in overcoming poverty in Latin America and Caribbean (LAC) has been heralded recently by international institutions. While relative progress in poverty and inequality has been achieved in some countries, the poorest countries are still very poor and others have seen increases in their poverty despite economic growth. The first part of this article analyses the persistence of poverty in spite of economic growth, the second analyses inequality, income distribution and equity gains. The third analyses trends in education, access and the pervasiveness of exclusion and its consequences on regional development. The fourth recommends some policy options towards sustainable development in the region.

POVERTY TRENDS AND THE LIMITS OF GROWTH

At the beginning of the 21st century, overcoming poverty, inequality and exclusion as a strategy for taking the path toward sustainable development is perhaps the most urgent and important goal for countries and institutions in the context of globalization and the new perspective of constructing knowledge societies.

PERVASIVE POVERTY: TRENDS AND GAINS

LAC's poverty rates (percentage of total income) are lower than in most other developing regions in the world. However, the region's extreme poverty rates are relatively high given the level of development of most countries (ECLAC, 2008).

According to 'growth' indicators, one person of every three in the Latin American and Caribbean region is poor, with insufficient income to satisfy daily basic needs, and one of every eight is extremely poor and unable to meet daily needs for food even if they spend all their income on nutritional needs. Poverty levels vary among and within countries as seen in Figure 1.

UNEQUAL DISTRIBUTION AND INEQUALITY

Latin America and the Caribbean remains the most unequal region in the world. Inequality is due substantially to the concentration of income at the top of the income scale, and its absence at the bottom. The richest fifth of

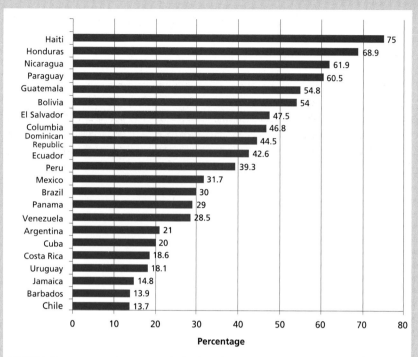

FIGURE 1 Poverty rates by country in LAC region 2007–2008
Source: ELAC (2008) *Social Panorama of Latin America.* Santiago, Chile: ELAC/UN

LAC population receives nearly 60% of the total income, while the poorest fifth receives around 3%. In every other region of the developing countries, the poor receive a higher share of total income. The inequality income indeces (Gini) vary from country to country, but are very high compared to other regions. For some countries like Venezuela, Costa Rica and Uruguay, inequality has increased or remained static (Figure 2).

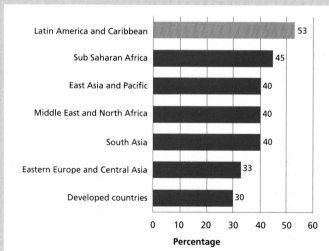

FIGURE 2 Inequality in the world by regions 2004–2008
Source: López-Calva, L.F. and Lustis, N. (2009) *Declining Inequality in Latin America: A Decade of Progress?* New York: Brookings Institution Press and United Nations Development Programme

UNEQUAL EDUCATION, EXCLUSION AND UNDERDEVELOPMENT

Latin America and the Caribbean has revealed the continuity and deepening of inequality and the exclusion of strata and groups in most of the countries of the region.

Primary education has become almost universal in the region, but timely progression and completion for the most vulnerable groups have become elusive and limited. The ratios for access to and timely progression through the secondary levels are lower than for the primary level and vary widely from country to country, within regions (Aponte, 2008). Only a small percentage (8.3%) has access to post-secondary education and this is concentrated in the population's richest quintile at a ratio of 27 to 1, as shown in Figure 3.

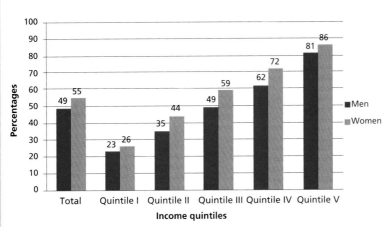

FIGURE 3 Latin America and Caribbean population age group 20 to 24 with complete secondary education by per capita income and sex-selected countries 2008
Source: ELAC (2010) *Social Panorama of Latin America.* Santiago, Chile: ELAC/UN

ability of future generations to satisfy their needs and to seek the well-being of all in all the forms of human existence as a whole' (WCED, Brundtland Commission, 1987). Sustainability is a conceptual counterposition to 'modernization', a paradigm that has dominated the social sciences since the early 1940s, but that has increasingly been questioned after the 1970s' world crisis. While 'modernization theory' is about growth and societal development, sustainability is about human needs, knowledge and the interactions among society, the economy and environment. Development indicators have been and still remain under the assumption that society's development is equivalent to economic growth. Gross national product and per capita income are still the core indicators used to determine how 'developed' a given country is. During the past two decades,

Conditions of persistence poverty, increasing inequalities between rich and poor, between living in urban and rural areas, and between those disadvantaged by geographic location, gender, age, disability, race and ethnicity, or by lack of education, health and education services remain as the main obstacles for overcoming poverty and marginalization. Policy trends towards sustainability to overcome ongoing poverty, inequality and exclusion should be reviewed in order to:

1. Increase investment and improve access to, and the quality of primary and secondary education levels, particularly in the rural schools. Increase investment and access to higher education where learning and research must embrace knowledge transdisciplinary systems thinking to address economic, social and environmental action on local and global scales over short, medium and intergenerational time periods in terms of limits to growth, production and consumption; and the use and preservation of resources according to the needs and rights of future generations in relation of diversity and the interdependence of systems.

2. Improve poor people's access to financial markets by inducing saving and investment. The high costs of borrowing from formal institutions and lack of collateral are factors limiting the capacity of the poor to borrow, obtain finance for capital investments, purchase land, establish cooperatives, and to access education services. Reduction to finance costs could make possible savings and reinvestment of residual income in sufficiency economic activities.

3. Reduce poverty with policies (subsidies and cash transfers) that can also protect lower-income families from falling into poverty. Subsidies should be conditioned to remain in schools, to enter job training programmes, and create self-deployment initiatives.

4. Incorporate learning technologies (ICTs) in schools as critical opportunity efforts for a more equitable education. This would be an essential step in reducing inequality and poverty and in enhancing social integration in the region.

5. Existing educational policies and learning strategies should depart from a 'pluralistic' approach to educational opportunities instead

TOWARDS SUSTAINABLE DEVELOPMENT

The UN Millennium Declaration represents a very important step to support the world's most vulnerable people. Policies and programmes for sustainable development will have to be more focused in order to reduce the persistence of poverty, inequality and exclusion of millions of people in the globe and the LAC region.

The notion of sustainable development refers to: 'the effort of societies to satisfy current life needs without compromising the

efforts to broaden the scope have incorporated indicators such as the human development index, environmental factors, and others, to determine the impact of economic growth on income distribution, prosperity and quality of life. The limits of this approach led to an emerging alternative paradigm of thinking about the future, where societal, economic and environmental considerations are balanced in the pursuit of development for satisfying human needs and improved quality of life.

of adapting diversity to mainstream education programmes (creating new inequalities) in order to pursue the 'equality of differences' and the 'differentiation of inequalities' where there are different 'talents' and different 'merit criteria' for an inclusive sustainable education for all, and for building sustainable democratic knowledge societies in the region.

6. Universities and higher institutions will play a central role in knowledge production, dissemination and professional training and development towards the sustainable endogenous development paradigm, and for supporting local and regional economic, social and environmental development.

Although progress has been made, it is uneven and without a major push forward, many of the Millennium Development Goals' targets for 2015 are likely to be missed in many countries in the LAC region. Old and new challenges threaten further progress in some areas or even to undo the success achieved so far.

Economic, social, cultural and ecological policies of governments, institutions and international organizations directed to enhance endogenous sustainable development with inclusion and equity cannot be focused solely on economic growth. They should be guided by principles for reducing poverty and inequality, and increasing social justice, self-sufficiency and effectiveness both in the short and the long term.

To meet this challenge, it will be necessary to reorient plans of study and programmes in basic education and higher education in order to address the need for more sustainable production and consumption patterns.

BIBLIOGRAPHY

Aponte-Hernandez, Eduardo (2008) Inequality, Inclusion and Inequality Trends in Higher Education in Latin America and the Caribbean: Towards An Alternative Scenario for 2021 in America. In: *Trends in Higher Education in Latin America and the Caribbean*, Ana L. Gazzola, Axel Didriksson (eds). Caracas, Venezuela: IESALC/UNESCO.

Becker, Egon, Jahn Thomas, Stiess, Immanuel and Wehling, Peter (1997) *Sustainability: A Cross-Disciplinary Concept for Social Transformations*. Management of Social Transformations (MOST) Policy Papers 6 UNESCO-Paris and Institute for Social-Ecological Research (ISOE) Frankfurt, Germany.

Birdsall, Nancy and Sabot, Richard (1994) Inequality as a Constraint on Growth. *Development Policy. Inter American Development Bank*, **3**(3), September, pp. 1–5.

Bowles, Samuel, Durlaf, Steven, Hoff, Karla (eds) (2006) *Poverty Traps*. Princeton, NJ: Russell Foundation.

Denninger, Klaus and Squire, Lyn (1998) Inequality as constraint to growth in Latin America. In: Mitchel, A. Seligson, John and Passen-Smith, T. (eds) *Development of Underdevelopment: The Political Economy of Global Inequality*. Colorado: Lynne Reinne Publishers.

ECLAC (2010) Statistical Yearbook for Latin America and the Caribbean for Santiago, Chile: ECLAC UN.

ECLAC (2010) *Social Panorama of Latin America*. Santiago, Chile: ECLAC.UN.

ECLAC (2008) *Social Panorama of Latin America*. Santiago, Chile: ECLAC, UN.

ECLAC (2007) *Social Panorama of Latin America*. Santiago, Chile; eclac.

Heiwege, Ann and Birch, Melissa B.L. (2007) Declining Poverty in Latin America: A Critical Analysis of New Estimates by International Institutions. Global Development and Environment Institute. Working Paper No. 07-02. http://ase.tufts.under/2dae

Kuznets, Simon (1955) Economic growth and income inequality. In: Mitchell, A., Seligson, John and Passen-Smith, T. John *Development of Underdevelopment: The Political Economy of Global Inequality*. Colorado: Lynne Reinne Publishers.

López-Calva, Luis F. and Lustis, Nora (2009) *Declining Inequality in Latin America: A Decade of Progress?* New York: Brookings Institution Press and United Nations Development Programme.

Loaiza, Norman, Fajnzyber, Pablo, and Calderon, Cesar (2005) *Economic Growth in Latin America and the Caribbean*. Washington, DC: The World Bank (www.worldbank.org).

Portes, Alejandro and Castells, Manuel (eds) (1989) *The Informal Economy*. Maryland: The John Hopkins University Press.

Puryear, Jeffrey and Malloy-Jewers, Marie (2009) How Poor and Unequal is Latin America and the Caribbean? Inter American Dialogue, Policy Brief 1. November. (ww.thedialogue.org).

Tokman, Victor (1992) *Beyond Regulation the Informal Economy in Latin America*. New York: Lynne Rienne Publishers.

UN (2010) Millennium Goals Report. New York: United Nations Millennium Goals 2015 (www.un.org).

UN (2005) *Hand Book on Poverty Statistics*. New York: United Nations.

UN (2007) *Untie Nations Human Development Report*. New York: United Nations.

UNESCO (2010) *EFA Global Monitoring Report Reaching the Marginalised*. Paris: UNESCO.

World Bank (2010) *World Development Indicators*. Washington: World Bank. www.worldbank.org

WCED (1987) *Our Common Future* (Brundtland Commission Declaration). Oxford, UK: Oxford university Press.

Spotlight Issues II.9

Contributions of intercultural higher education to sustainable development and well-being: Experiences in Latin America

Daniel Mato

This paper provides an overview of the main intercultural forms of higher education (HE) developed in recent decades in Latin America in response to the needs, demands and proposals of indigenous and Afro-descendant peoples. There are currently more than 100 intercultural experiences of HE in the region, each with its own unique characteristics. Nonetheless, they all are guided by concepts related to sustainable development or community well-being. These intercultural initiatives provide contextualized training for professionals and specialists, give value to the knowledge and languages of indigenous and Afro-descendant peoples and aim to improve the quality of life of indigenous and Afro-descendant communities.

HIGHER EDUCATION, INTERCULTURAL COOPERATION, SUSTAINABLE DEVELOPMENT AND WELL-BEING

The belief that knowledge production corresponds to two worlds, one in possession of supposedly 'universal' truths and the other in possession of merely 'local' truths, underlies the claim to superiority of Western civilization, whose knowledge is claimed to be 'universal'. Encounters, conflicts and negotiations between 'universal' and 'local' kinds of knowledge have become more frequent in recent decades due to the expansion and deepening of relations between social actors who operate on a global level, in contrast to those who operate at a more local level. In this context, an analysis of the limitations and consequences of belief in the existence of 'universal' and 'local' kinds of knowledge is increasingly feasible and necessary – and indeed, increasingly urgent, given the environmental disasters resulting from the prevalence of the contemporary Western model.

These circumstances require a review of HE in terms of the prevailing institutional models, content, teaching-learning methods and the relationship between conventional higher education institutions (HEIs)[1] and society. Valuable contributions have been made by intercultural HE experiences in the past couple of decades in Latin America, where both conventional HEIs and other openly intercultural HEIs (IHEIs) have developed novel institutional models, curricula and teaching and learning methods. The starting point for these institutions is to acknowledge the existence of unequal intercultural relations in their societies and to seek to establish equitable intercultural relations in which all sides cooperate in mutual recognition of the value of the other and accept world views different to the prevailing contemporary Western vision. This has significant implications for the production of knowledge and the kind of education offered by HEIs.

The recognition of these other world views suggests, among other things, adopting a perspective on the future of our societies in terms of 'well-being', rather than in terms of 'development', which is still considered – for all that it is qualified by the adjective 'sustainable' – as synonymous with progress and economic growth. Well-being is used as an alternative term to sustainable development because it represents social transformation horizons that are more consistent with the world views of many American indigenous peoples. These other world views understand humans to be part of what modern Western societies call 'nature' – and not as a superior species that views and manages the planet as a source of natural resources.

The intercultural HE experiences being developed in Latin America should be appreciated not only for their role in training people from indigenous and Afro-descendant communities but also for their ability to foster critical reflection on contemporary societies and their future, higher education types, HEI models, curricula and learning styles.

INTERCULTURAL HIGHER EDUCATION IN LATIN AMERICA

In 2007, the UNESCO International Institute for Higher Education in Latin America and the Caribbean (UNESCO-IESALC) launched the Cultural Diversity, Interculturality and Higher Education Project (hereinafter, the Project). With the participation of over 50 researchers from 11 Latin American countries, the Project has published three books, which contain, in addition to a number of thematic chapters, some 40 studies on intercultural higher education experiences (Mato, 2008, 2009, 2010). The description below is based on these studies and on information on 80 other experiences in a register compiled from responses to a questionnaire to representatives of HEIs in 2009. The Project currently holds information on about 120 experiences, although it is estimated that another 50 remain undocumented.

We can classify the experiences identified by the Project in five different groups:

1. PROGRAMMES FOR THE INCLUSION OF INDIGENOUS AND AFRO-DESCENDANT STUDENTS IN CONVENTIONAL HEIs
Scholarship programmes, quotas and academic and psychosocial support for indigenous and Afro-descendant students in conventional HEIs are 'inclusion of individuals' approaches about which there are conflicting views. One view is that they foster inclusion and help to train indigenous and Afro-descendant experts who, in one way or another, serve their communities; these programmes also constitute a first step in the transformation of conventional HEIs. However, an alternative view is that such programmes offer limited possibilities for intercultural cooperation in research and learning, lead to brain-drain from remote communities to large cities and result in the loss of values, languages and knowledge to communities. Although there are numerous programmes aimed at the inclusion of individuals in Latin America, they are not a focus of the Project, which is more concerned with exploring experiences that integrate the knowledge of indigenous and Afro-descendant communities.

2. INTERCULTURAL COOPERATION IN EDUCATION PROGRAMMES IN CONVENTIONAL HEIs
This group includes a wide variety of experiences, some with little intercultural cooperation and others in which the teachers, languages, knowledge and modes of knowledge production and learning of indigenous and Afro-descendant organizations and communities are well represented. Many of the experiences are geared to training teachers for bilingual intercultural education programmes offered at various educational levels.

Of the many such experiences, 15 have been studied by the Project. Examples include the Insikiran Indigenous Teacher Training Programme at the Federal University of Roraima (Brazil); the degree in Ethnic Education at the University of Cauca (Colombia); the Teaching Qualification Programme in Afro-Colombian Ethno-Education at the University of the Pacific (Colombia); the Advanced Community Justice Programme at the University of San Andrés (Bolivia); the Cotopaxi Programme for Bilingual Intercultural Education at the Salesian Polytechnic University (Ecuador); and the Training Programme for Bilingual Intercultural Education in Andean Countries, with the participation of indigenous organizations and universities from several Andean countries and the support of some of the Andean governments.

3. INTERCULTURAL COOPERATION IN RESEARCH OR IN DEVELOPING LINKS WITH COMMUNITIES BY CONVENTIONAL HEIs

The Register of Experiences compiled basic information on dozens of these experiences, very different from each other. So far only six of them have been studied, and, due to limitations of space, just two are described here. Through the Traditional Medicine Teaching and Research Programme of the National Polytechnic Institute in Mexico, an interdisciplinary team recruited from this institution works with primary teachers and children, traditional healers and farmers in the state of Oaxaca. Also in Mexico, community members and academics, researchers and students from different departments participate in the Human Development Interdisciplinary Research Programme of the Metropolitan Autonomous University, which combines research with vocational training and community service.

4. INTERCULTURAL COLLABORATION BETWEEN HEIS AND INDIGENOUS AND AFRO-DESCENDANT ORGANIZATIONS IN JOINT TRAINING PROGRAMMES

Only four experiences of this type have been identified, all offering degrees recognized by national education authorities. The Indigenous Education Institute of the Indigenous Organization of Antioquia in Colombia, in cooperation with the Pontifical Bolivarian University and the University of Antioquia in Colombia offers a degree in Ethno-Education, a degree in Mother Earth Education and a diploma in Indigenous Government and Administration. Two other initiatives are co-sponsored by the Interethnic Association for Development of the Peruvian Rainforest (AIDESEP), based in Peru. One is the Peruvian-Amazon Bilingual Teachers' Programme, developed in cooperation with the Loreto Higher Teaching Institute; the other is the Intercultural Health Nurse Training Programme developed in cooperation with the Public Higher Technological Institute in Atalaya. Finally, the Manuel Zapata Olivella Education and Research Institute and the University of La Guajira in Colombia offer degrees in Afro-Colombian Ethno-Education.

5. INTERCULTURAL COOPERATION IN IHEIs

IHEIs in Latin America are characterized by their goal of integrating the knowledge, knowledge production modes and learning modes from a range of cultural traditions. Although these IHEIs were created to respond to the demands and proposals of indigenous and Afro-descendant communities, they also include a smaller proportion of representatives from other cultural traditions, including those generally referred to as 'white' or 'mestizo'. Examples of some such institutions created by indigenous and Afro-descendant organizations include the Kawsay Indigenous Intercultural University, the initiative of a network of indigenous organizations in Bolivia, Peru and Ecuador; the Amazon Centre for Indigenous Education, an initiative of the Coordination of Indigenous Organisations of the Brazilian Amazon; the Intercultural, Indigenous and Autonomous University, an initiative of the Regional Indigenous Council of Cauca in Colombia; the Amawtay Wasi Intercultural University of Indigenous Nationalities and Peoples, created by sections of the Confederation of Indigenous Nationalities of Ecuador; and the University of the Autonomous Regions of the Caribbean Coast of Nicaragua and the Bluefields Indian and Caribbean University, created in Nicaragua on the initiative of indigenous and Afro-descendant community leaders.

IHEIs have also been created by state agencies. For example, the Research and Training Centre for Aboriginal Teachers was created by the Chaco provincial government in Argentina. Mexico has ten intercultural universities, all members of the intercultural university network of the Secretariat of Public Education, some founded by the Secretariat itself (for example the Intercultural University of Chiapas), others created by agreement with a conventional university (for example the Intercultural University of Veracruz) and yet others created by previous state governments and subsequently assimilated into the national system (for example the Indigenous Autonomous University of Mexico). Two other IHEIs are the Intercultural Indigenous University, established by the Fund for the Development of the Indigenous Peoples of Latin America and the Caribbean (a multilateral body representing governments and indigenous organizations) and the Intercultural Ayuk University in Mexico, created by the Ibero-American University, a Jesuit university.

ACHIEVEMENTS OF INTERCULTURAL HIGHER EDUCATION IN LATIN AMERICA

The main achievements of intercultural educational experiences as studied by the Project are as follows:

- They improve the possibilities for indigenous and Afro-descendant people to access higher education and successfully complete their studies.
- They are adapted to the needs, demands and projects of communities and to regional and local opportunities for employment, productive initiatives and community service.
- They develop participatory approaches to learning, often focused on applied research.
- They integrate learning, research and service to communities.
- They include and combine different types of knowledge and knowledge production modes.
- They promote and foster the valorization of the languages and knowledge of peoples and communities and conduct research and contribute proactively to strengthening these languages and knowledge.
- They undertake teaching and research guided by criteria based on cultural diversity, interculturality, equity, inclusion, democratic governance, sustainable development and well-being.
- They train graduates who contribute to local and regional sustainable development and to improving the quality of life of their communities.

REFERENCES

Mato, Daniel (ed.) (2008) *Diversidad cultural e interculturalidad en Educación Superior. Experiencias en América Latina*. Caracas: UNESCO-IESALC.

Mato, Daniel (ed.) (2009) *Instituciones Interculturales de Educación Superior en América Latina. Procesos de Construcción, Logros, Innovaciones y Desafíos*. Caracas: UNESCO-IESALC.

Mato, Daniel (ed.) (2010) *Educación Superior, Colaboración Intercultural y Desarrollo Sostenible/Buen Vivir. Experiencias en América Latina*. Caracas: IESALC-UNESCO.

1   The term 'conventional' is used to refer to HEIs that were not specifically founded to respond to the needs, demands and proposals of indigenous and Afro-descendant communities.

Network Experience II.6
Higher education institutions' efforts towards sustainability: experiences in Mexico

M. Laura Ortiz Hernández

INTRODUCTION

Today, we cannot deny the process of environmental degradation caused by the activity of the Earth's nearly 7 billion inhabitants. The efforts being made in various sectors to counteract this process are therefore very important. Higher education institutions (HEIs) play a crucial role in promoting sustainable human development and in changing society's attitudes towards the environmental crisis, because, in addition to educating citizens, their main responsibilities include generating knowledge and developing technologies that have an impact on various sectors.

If HEIs are to comprehensively educate students in the principles of sustainability, they should – in addition to imparting discipline-specific information – practise what they preach. The activities of university campuses have undeniable environmental impacts, such as the generation of hazardous waste and sewage, as well as energy use and other impacts. Universities should therefore aim to minimize the negative effects of resource consumption in the fulfilment of their primary and secondary functions, so that they are able to support society in a transition towards more sustainable lifestyles.

In Mexico, HEIs have made significant contributions by developing proposals to solve environmental problems in the areas of teaching, research and extension. Traditionally, these proposals have materialized independently or through strategic alliances formed to promote positive results and impacts.

One important experience has been the work of various universities – both public and private – under the umbrella of the Mexican Consortium of University Environmental Programs for Sustainable Development (Complexus). These universities share an interest in influencing educational programmes, research, services and non-formal education,

as well as the goal of integrating, organizing and coordinating the efforts of each of the participating institutions to address problems at the local, regional and national levels.

The Consortium's abbreviated name was chosen for how it encapsulates and reflects the spirit of the network from educational, organizational and environmental perspectives. Derived from the Latin word meaning 'to weave together', *Complexus* conveys the idea of adopting the perspective of complexity, as in woven fabric. Complexity is the fabric of events, actions, interactions, feedback, determinations and vicissitudes that make up our world (Morin, 1990).

Complexus was created in 2000 when a group of HEIs joined forces with the Centre for Education and Training for Sustainable Development (CECADESU), which is a unit of Mexico's Secretariat of the Environment and Natural Resources (SEMARNAT), and with the National Association of Universities and Higher Education Institutions (ANUIES) (Bravo-Mercado,

2003). As part of the creation of Complexus, an agreement was signed by the presidents of the participating universities. Another agreement was signed by ANUIES and SEMARNAT, and yet another established the Action Plan for Sustainable Development in Higher Education Institutions. As of August 2010, Complexus was made up of 17 Mexican HEIs, each with its own environmental plans or programmes (http://www.complexus.org.mx).

The mission of Complexus is to improve the quality of academic processes related to the environment and sustainable development by enabling the institutional directors of environmental programmes and offices to collaborate with one another. By working together, universities enjoy advantages such as the opportunity to share experiences and optimize the available human and physical infrastructure at HEIs, as well as the possibility of implementing integration and cooperation strategies (Figure 1). The HEIs that belong

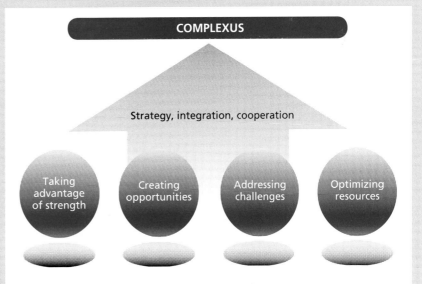

FIGURE 1 Strategies cor cooperation among the HEIs belonging to Complexus

to Complexus share their experiences with environmental management systems, including the management of hazardous waste and urban solid waste, park planning, sustainable procurement, bioclimatic construction, environmental education strategies, and cooperation for advanced educational programmes (undergraduate and postgraduate levels).

The objectives of Complexus are as follows:

1. To improve the environment-related academic work of HEIs.
2. To encourage members to set up programmes that favour the development of the necessary knowledge, aptitudes, competences, skills, values and attitudes for sustainable development.
3. To promote the incorporation of environmental aspects in higher education curricula.
4. To strengthen the environmental and sustainable development content of teacher training and refresher programmes.
5. To spread information about sustainable development among HEIs.
6. To promote the creation of environmental programmes at universities.
7. To promote the creation and strengthening of environmental management systems at HEIs.

ORGANIZATIONAL STRUCTURE
The organizational structure of Complexus was established by the collaboration agreement signed by the presidents of the participating universities. It consists mainly of the Council of Presidents, the Consortium's highest authority; the Executive General Secretariat, which is responsible for coordinating the Consortium's operations; and the Committee of Representatives, which includes one representative of each HEI, appointed by the respective president. Agreements are reached by the Committee of Representatives, which meets at least once a year to draw up a work plan. After the annual meeting, the Committee works via virtual media.

MAIN ACCOMPLISHMENTS
As mentioned above, each of the HEIs that make up Complexus has its own environmental plan or programme, which in most cases includes the following:

- Planning and implementing the university's environmental policy
- Establishing environment-related strategic areas and actions
- Establishing links between the university and social, private and governmental organizations
- Contributing to the comprehensive education of students

In the course of implementing their environmental plans or programmes, the people at each HEI have acquired experience consistent with the peculiarities of their institution. They later share this experience by teaching courses and workshops and by publishing materials such as books, magazines and articles, with the goal of extending their good practices and experiences to other universities.

are the internal means of environmental management at HEIs. This includes compliance with requirements for comprehensive waste management, efficient water and energy use, park management, sustainable procurement and bioclimatic construction.
3. The implementation by universities of a system of sustainable performance indicators, which Complexus considers an appropriate tool for assessing the environmental performance of HEIs. A system of indicators has been drawn up and adapted for use by Mexican HEIs.
4. The generation of theoretical and methodological proposals for the incorporation of environmental education for sustainability at HEIs.

In addition to the annual meetings of the Committee of Representatives, Complexus has

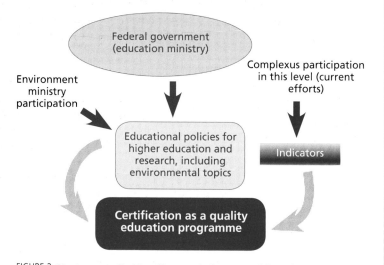

FIGURE 2 Strategy applied in efforts to influence public policies on higher education in Mexico

The following are Complexus's main strategic lines (Súcar-Súcar et al., 2009):

1. The greening of curricula, which entails the integration of sustainability criteria into all advanced-level education programmes, regardless of discipline, to ensure that students are capable of developing appropriate skills for environmentally and socially sustainable human development.
2. The implementation and strengthening of environmental management systems, which

organized various face-to-face academic activities, including workshops, courses, lectures, forums and seminars. From 2001 to 2010, Complexus has held more than 20 academic events aimed at encouraging HEIs to adopt sustainability strategies.

One of the needs we have identified is for HEIs to include environmental aspects in their educational programmes with a view to comprehensively educating their students. In Mexico, in order for an educational programme to be considered high quality, it must be accredited by one of the accreditation bodies recognized by the Ministry of Education. In the accreditation process, a series of indicators are used to verify that educational programmes meet certain minimum standards, and Complexus is working to have environmental indicators included in this process (Figure 2).

INSTITUTIONAL SUPPORT
The work done by each member university through the Committee of Representatives enjoys the support of the respective institution. CECADESU has provided economic support for several Complexus academic events. Additionally, the universities provide economic support for events, especially those held at their own facilities, and provide funds to allow their representatives to attend national meetings or Complexus-organized events.

LINKS TO INTERNATIONAL NETWORKS
Complexus is interested in sharing its experiences with other networks at the interna-

tional level. It is a member of the Alliance of Ibero-American Networks of Universities for Sustainability and the Environment (ARIUSA), which develops academic cooperation activities oriented towards the coordination of shared-interest events, carries out collaborative research projects, and supports the creation and strengthening of postgraduate programmes in subjects related to sustainability and the environment. By participating in this organization, Complexus is consolidating valuable strategic alliances that will help to strengthen sustainable universities.

CONCLUSIONS
The work strategy of Complexus has had a positive impact, both regionally and nationally, by establishing collaborations that share the strengths of each university, by identifying challenges and opportunities for improvement, and above all by optimizing the use of resources in collaboration proposals to ensure a positive impact on higher education policies in Mexico.

REFERENCES
Bravo-Mercado, M.T. (2003) Las instituciones de educación superior se organizan para participar en el cambio ambiental: El Complexus. *Agua y Desarrollo Sustenta-ble.* **8**, pp. 22–4.
Morin, E. (1990) *Introducción al pensamiento complejo* (ed.) Gedisa, Barcelona, p. 166.
Súcar-Súcar, S., Medellín-Milán, P. and Nieto-Carabeo, L.M. (2009) *Consorcio Mexicano de Programas Ambientales Universitarios para el Desarrollo Sostenible.* Report presented at the 5th World Environmental Education Congress. Montreal, Canada. 10–14 May 2009.

GOOD PRACTICES II.6

Higher Education and Sustainability in Latin America and the Caribbean: Sharing Actions for Change

The following experiences are a selection of good practices on higher education and sustainability. Some of them were presented at the 5th International Barcelona Conference on Higher Education and others are part of the GUNi observatory.

The good practices cover the following institutional areas:

Curricula and learning innovation

Community and social engagement

Institutional management

Research

GOOD PRACTICE 1

Integral community action programme in vulnerable neighbourhoods

Institutional area(s):

LOCATION: Argentina
INSTITUTION: University of Buenos Aires

This good practice aims at the construction of communal spaces called 'Centros de Extensión' which promote social integration. The programme creates Extension Centres, which are established in order to generate stable ties with the communities in which they are inserted. They give the programme an organizational structure, centralizing the efforts of the various projects, allow the exchange of information and create stability. In each centre there is an information office staffed with university personnel, who guide activities and later also collect demands and concerns of the neighbourhood arising from the interests and needs of various stakeholders.

Detailed information is available at GUNi HEiOBS:

http://www.guninetwork.org/guni.heiobs/good-practices/integral-community-action-program-in-vulnerable-neighborhoods

The Brazilian example of the new Afro-Brazilian University: foreign policy, innovation and south–south cooperation

Institutional area(s):

LOCATION: Brazil
INSTITUTION: University of International Integration of Brazil-Africa Lusophony

This good practice has as its theme curricula innovation through the first Brazilian public university (tuition free) of Brazil and Africa Integration: UNILAB, currently under construction. Its proposal is pioneering and innovative: within the context of Brazilian higher education policy, to establish a university that promotes south–south cooperation in the field of higher education. Located in northeast Brazil, UNILAB responds to demands from Portuguese language-speaking African countries, and is an expression of Brazil's cooperation policy towards Africa: half its students will be Brazilians, while the other half will be Africans subsidized by Brazil. Its innovative curricula aims at sociocultural integration, interdisciplinary, flexible study programmes, university–society relationships, sustainable development and intercultural dialogue, where teaching is the practice of freedom and citizenship affirmation, training professionals able to be active agents in the present and to indicate directions towards a future of solidarity.

Detailed information is available at GUNi HEiOBS:

http://www.guninetwork.org/guni.heiobs/good-practices/the-brazilian-example-of-the-new-afro-brazilian-university-foreign-policy-innovation-and-south-south-cooperation

'Building Sustainable Schools' the UNAM's strategy for a sustainable university for high schools

Institutional area(s):

LOCATION: Mexico
INSTITUTION: Universidad Nacional Autónoma de México

The 'Building Sustainable Schools' programme is the section of EcoPuma that aims at implementing the UNAM's Strategy for Sustainable Development in high schools, including the 14 public schools that are part of the UNAM, as well as the close to 300 private schools that have decided to join the UNAM educational system. The programme's objectives are: to promote sustainable management in daily school operation, so that schools reduce the environmental impact of their activities while also being seen as models of environmental responsibility by their communities and, above all, by their students; and to provide, to bachelor degree students and students of schools incorporated to the UNAM, information that will raise their awareness of the present environmental situation and make them able to translate this knowledge into individual and collective actions and activities, both in their immediate environment and daily life.

Detailed information is available at GUNi HEiOBS:

http://www.guninetwork.org/guni.heiobs/good-practices/201cbuilding-sustainable-schools201d-the-unam2019s-strategy-for-a-sustainable-university-for-high-schools

Vidas Móviles Program

Institutional area(s):

LOCATION: Colombia
INSTITUTION: Javeriana Pontificial University

In the 'Vidas-Móviles' programme of the Javeriana Pontifical University, the School of Medicine leads a reintegration programme for internally displaced persons (IDPs) that is based on much more than just curing the ill. This university/community-oriented programme helps armed conflict refugees from other, usually rural areas of the country, to integrate into Bogota city life, and all that that can necessitate. From direct clinical healthcare via health brigades, to workshops in community-feeding centres on developing ecology-conscious citizens, along with, for instance, microbiology students analysing the chemical/bacteriological characteristics of a nearby creek to improve water quality. It converts the university from being an elite institution on the sidelines, to an area of active agency in terms of resolving the country's main long-standing problems.

Detailed information is available at GUNi HEiOBS:

http://www.guninetwork.org/guni.heiobs/good-practices/vidas-moviles-program

PuentesUC

Institutional area(s):

LOCATION: Chile
INSTITUTION: Pontifical Catholic University

PuentesUC is a programme of the Pontifical Catholic University of Chile. PuentesUC creates a formal link between the university and the local community by assigning programme managers to work directly with members of municipalities to address local issues by means of academic disciplines. The municipalities themselves state their requirements based on their daily experience and permanent contact with the communities they serve. These requirements are then translated into academically approachable resources by the university and each institution's programme manager. This direct link allows students to engage in highly effective service programmes in the local communities. Once service projects are completed, participants from both the university and the municipality share their experiences and knowledge gained.

Detailed information is available at GUNi HEiOBS:

http://www.guninetwork.org/guni.heiobs/good-practices/puentes-uc

GOOD PRACTICE 6

Literature to address the problem of violence

Institutional area(s):

LOCATION: Jamaica
INSTITUTION: The University of West Indies

This programme has introduced major issues of sustainability and focused on that of violence in Jamaican society. Additionally, this project has aimed to infuse education for sustainable development (ESD) into the curricular content of the largest teacher training college in Jamaica, thus providing a potential long-term impact via the elucidation of the country's youth – Jamaica's future hope for any struggles to come, or even its stability. It started with the reorientation of the Literature programme for student teachers who were preparing to teach English literature and language to secondary school students.

Detailed information is available at GUNi HEiOBS:

http://www.guninetwork.org/guni.heiobs/good-practices/literature-to-address-the-problem-of-violence-infusing-education-for-sustainable-development-esd-into-the-curriculum

The reader can also find the following good practices related to sustainability in Latin America and the Caribbean at the GUNi Observatory:

- Human rights and sustainability: experiences from a higher education programme in Mexico
  LOCATION: Mexico
  INSTITUTION: Universidad Veracruzana Intercultural

- Juchimán, green and gold. Environmental programme for sustainable development
  LOCATION: Mexico
  INSTITUTION: Universidad Juárez Autónoma de Tabasco

- Social commitment projects in the environmental agenda of UASLP
  LOCATION: Mexico
  LOCATION: Autonomous University of San Luis Potosi

- Sustainable good practices in the University of Sonora
  LOCATION: Mexico
  INSTITUTION: University of Sonora

- Sustainable management of wastes
  LOCATION: Mexico
  INSTITUTION: Autonomous University of the State of Mexico

- The green network
  LOCATION: Mexico
  INSTITUTION: University of Colima

http://www.guninetwork.org/guni.heiobs

PART III
MOVING FROM UNDERSTANDING TO ACTION: BREAKING BARRIERS FOR TRANSFORMATION

Finding an adequate response to the challenges posed by (un)sustainability is a major challenge for higher education institutions (HEIs). The aim of this paper is to discuss the barriers, or difficulties, that prevent HEIs from finding such a response and to suggest ways of overcoming them. We first look at the general meaning of sustainability and the related, but in some ways more contested, sustainable development (SD). We will argue that the inevitable impreciseness of sustainability and SD combined with the need to give it meaning in a specific context involving multiple stakeholders makes these concepts attractive from an educational perspective as they require joint meaning-making, co-creation of new knowledge, collaborative learning and, indeed, critiquing. Education in the context of sustainability is briefly explored to contextualize the challenges faced by HEIs in this emerging domain of research, education and science and society in general. The second part of the paper presents the main findings from a study on barriers and solutions identified in two GUNi polls and discussed in parallel workshop sessions at the Fifth International Barcelona Conference on Higher Education. The last part summarizes and reflects upon the barriers in addressing sustainability challenges faced by HEIs and offers some possible solutions to overcoming these barriers.

INTRODUCTION

In response to a growing environmental crisis and vast inequalities in global development, the international community and its political leadership adopted sustainable development as a leading development model by the end of the 20th century. Contemporary society considers it the best way to address the vast, complex and interrelated environmental and development issues for the sake of current and future human well-being and for the integrity of the planet (Waas et al., 2011).

Tilbury (2007) argues that to succeed in the transition towards a society that is more

sustainable begs the question of what sustainability and/or SD might encompass and whether we can identify any principles that describe and characterize these concepts.

The most popular definition of sustainable development comes from the report *Our Common Future* by the World Commission on Environment and Development (WECD). Sustainable development is defined as 'development that meets the needs of the present without compromising the ability of future generations to meet their own needs' (WCED, 1987). Some scholars have introduced 'sustainability' as a better alternative to SD in that, they argue, sustainable development might be regarded as conceptually flawed as it suggests that continuous development is needed while it can be argued that it is equally important to sustain our resources by stopping forms of development deemed unsustainable. In this view sustainable development can be seen as a contradiction in terms or an oxymoron (Jickling, 1992; Jickling and Wals, 2008).

There is considerable agreement among sustainability scholars and practitioners about some fundamental principles underlying sustainability or 'rules of action towards sustainable development'. They represent the 'sustainability arena' or some kind of 'common ground' that anyone who justifies a line of action with an appeal to sustainability should respect and take into account (Hugé et al. 2011; Waas et al., 2011). Fundamental sustainability principles include (Hugé et al., 2011):

● Global responsibility (in tackling global socio-ecological issues), which refers to international cooperation in a spirit of 'shared but differentiated responsibility'.

● Integration (of ecological, social and economic impacts and their interactions), which refers to the reconciliation and integration of environmental and developmental objectives.

● Inter- and intra-generational equity, which refers to the needs and preferences of current and future generations (inter-generational equity), and also includes

III.1

SUSTAINABILITY IN HIGHER EDUCATION: MOVING FROM UNDERSTANDING TO ACTION, BREAKING BARRIERS FOR TRANSFORMATION

Jesús Granados-Sánchez, Arjen E.J. Wals, Dídac Ferrer-Balas, Tom Waas, Mireia Imaz, Stefan Nortier, Magdalena Svanström, Hilligje Van't Land and Gerardo Arriaga

The authors wish to thank Carolina Cortes for her remarkable contribution in both the workshops and the poll on which this document is based.

geographical (global North-global South) and social intra-generational equity.

- Precaution (in the face of uncertainty): the precautionary principle states that the lack of full scientific certainty shall not be used as a reason for postponing measures to prevent environmental degradation.
- Participation, which refers to the involvement of all concerned stakeholders in decision-making for sustainable development.

A complementary way to understand and operationalize sustainable development is through 'mental models' (Rosner, 1995) or metaphors (Scott and Gough, 2003). It is common practice to model sustainability in a number of pillars or dimensions, and most commonly there are three (economy, environment and social), depicted in the form of an equilateral triangle or as three intersecting, equally sized circles. Each angle/circle stands for one of the three dimensions with sustainability in the middle (Lozano, 2008; Waas et al., 2011). There is also the model proposed by Hart (2000) comprising concentric or nested circles. But, criticized alternative models are proposed, that is, those by Granados (2011), Lozano (2008) and Giddings et al. (2002). Granados (2011) proposes that sustainability can be metaphorically compared to a three-lens telescope (see Figure III.1.1). In this model, each lens represents a different dimension of sustainability: the environment, society and its institutions and the socio-economic dimension. Considering that we need to look at things from a new point of view, Granados (2011) suggests that we must reverse our viewpoint and look through the biggest lens first. Just as a telescope only functions well when each lens works in conjunction with the other, sustainability is only viable if these three cruxes exist in equilibrium as they are interrelated and interdependent upon each other. Each lens affects and reacts to the others, and is also equally affected by the others, in simultaneous co-evolution, visualizing the principle of intergenerational equity (Lozano, 2008). The telescope metaphor also enables us to envision the dynamic time dimensions. Depending on how much we extend or contract the telescope we will put more emphasis on the present or in the future (short, mid or long term). Additionally, this model takes into account space and scale, so it allows us to look at the big picture of global sustainability while at the same time affording the opportunity to focus on the local context, where action comes easier (Granados, 2011).

Since the 1990s, universities worldwide have increasingly embraced sustainable development and the more recent and overarching sustainability movement. More than 1000 academic institutions worldwide have signed international declarations towards implementing sustainability through environmental literacy initiatives; curriculum development; research; partnering with government, non-governmental organizations and industry in developing sustainability initiatives; and 'greening' physical operations (Wright, 2004; Barlett et al., 2004). Such actions, however, are only a beginning. Much remains to be done for sustainability to become genuinely and fully implemented at universities and for universities to become true sustainability leaders (Waas et al., 2010). Catalysts towards this objective are the United Nations Decade of Education for Sustainable Development (2005–2014) (DESD) (UNESCO, 2011) and, related to the DESD, the establishment of Regional Centres of Expertises (RCE) (UNU, 2011). The objective of the DESD is

FIGURE III.1.1 The telescope metaphor for describing and interpreting sustainability (Granados, 2010)

to integrate the principles, values and practices of sustainability into all aspects of education and learning (UNESCO, 2011), including universities, whereas RCEs are networks of existing formal, non-formal and informal education organizations, mobilized to deliver education in the context of sustainability to local and regional communities (UNU, 2011).

Only recently have scholars attempted to define sustainability in higher education (SHE) research. For example, Glasser et al. (2005) define it as:

> any research that is directed at advancing our ability to incorporate sustainability concepts and insights into higher education and its major areas of activity: policy, planning, and administration; curriculum/teaching; research and scholarship; service to communities; student life; and physical operations/ infrastructure. It also refers to research that treats higher education institutions as complex systems and focuses on the integration of sustainability across all of its activities, responsibilities, and mission.

SHE is an emerging field and up until now has mainly focused on the integration of sustainability in (1) education (curricula/teaching), and (2) physical operations/management, in particular the environmental management of institutions (Waas, et al., 2010). In this paper we explore the barriers or difficulties that prevent HEIs from achieving sustainability and offer some propositions to overcome them.

BARRIERS AND SOLUTIONS FOR TRANSFORMING HEIS TOWARDS SUSTAINABILITY

One area in which GUNi works is to establish what barriers and possible solutions higher education institutions (HEIs) encounter when they try to implement sustainable development in their performance. For this purpose, participative channels have been created to involve all those experts interested in this transformation of HE. There are four working phases in the process:

- The GUNi First-Round Poll: Breaking Barriers for Transformation.
- The parallel workshops: Moving from Understanding to Action: Breaking Barriers for Transformation, held at the Fifth International Barcelona Conference on Higher Education, Higher Education's Commitment to Sustainability: from Understanding to Action (Fifth IBCHE Conference).
- The GUNi Second-Round Poll: Breaking Barriers for Transformation.

- The creation of a working group within the knowledge community that is being nurtured through GUNi's virtual platform. This forum enables a group of professionals invited from all over the world to discuss and share innovative ideas, experiences and knowledge regarding barriers to and solutions for the implementation of sustainable development in HE. Additionally, this virtual platform aims to provide a future open forum for professionals in the field for the continuous exchange of ideas on the most pressing issues facing HE in the world.

THE GUNI FIRST-ROUND POLL: BREAKING BARRIERS FOR TRANSFORMATION

The rationale behind setting up the first poll was to identify the main barriers preventing HEIs from transforming so that they can contribute to the sustainability paradigm.

The poll consisted of a list of 14 proposed barriers (see Table III.1.1) that referred to the introduction of ESD; the centrality of technology vis-à-vis social knowledge; short-term market needs; unconscious unsustainability; the lack of sustainable ethics and values; compartmentalized thinking; overall system redesign; social responsibility; isolation; the pedagogical approach; diverse knowledge integration; HE's influence on governments; and breaking inertia.

The poll was distributed to different experts in HE worldwide. A total of 200 of them sent in their answers. The participants included 36% from Europe; 15% from Latin America and the Caribbean; 9.5% from Asia and the Pacific; 6.5% from Arab states; and 4% from North America. The rest, 22%, did not specify their nationality.

The methodology of the poll was the following: the participants were instructed to rate the level of relevance for each barrier (1 to 5, where 1 is not important and 5 is very important); they then had to mark the level of difficulty in overcoming each barrier (low, medium and high) and finally they had to choose the most relevant barrier according to their own context. Additionally, there was a space for the inclusion of other barriers that each participant could add. Table III.1.1 shows the results of the GUNi First-Round Poll.

One of the poll's main conclusions is that there was a general perception – among the 200 participants – that all 14 barriers are relevant given the fact that they all have an average rating of between 3 and 4. As can be seen from Table III.1.1, the highest rating was 3.93 whereas the lowest was 3.02. The results are a clear signal of a common ground regarding the relevance of sustainable development in HEIs and, thus, of the

TABLE III.1.1
GUNi First-Round Poll results: barriers to change according to their relevance and the difficulty in overcoming them

Scope	Barriers to transforming HE towards sustainability	Average according to level of importance	Difficulty in being overcome
Introduction of ESD	It is difficult to identify what content should be introduced in a transversal curriculum at the HE level.	3.93	H
Technology-centred, socially ignored	High recognition of technology and instrumental knowledge to the detriment of human and social knowledge.	3.77	H
Short-term market needs	High pressure to orient HE activity (teaching offer, content and research) to short-term labour and market needs and to profitable activities.	3.70	H
Unconscious unsustainability	There is a hidden agenda of unsustainable practices.	3.64	M
Lack of sustainable ethics and values	There is a lack of analysis of the values that are transmitted in the educational process and a lack of reflection on the ethics and values that should be introduced in HE.	3.63	H
Compartmentalized thinking	Structures in HE strengthen compartmentalized thinking, leaving little space for integrative thinking and trans-boundary learning.	3.60	M
Overall system redesign	Sustainability continues to be seen as an 'add-on' rather than as a 'built-in' or as requiring a 'whole system re-design'.	3.57	M
Social responsibility	Greater emphasis is placed on science for impact factors in research than on science for impact (societal relevance).	3.52	M
Isolation	HEIs have become far removed from their communities' knowledge needs and are perceived as ivory tower institutions of experts.	3.46	M
Pedagogical model	The pedagogical model strengthens the separation of knowledge from experience.	3.41	M
Pedagogical approach	The pedagogical perspective is still one of transmission (knowledge transfer) rather that one of transformation.	3.22	M
Diverse knowledge integration	The mismatch between a mono-cultural model of knowledge in a multicultural and diverse society.	3.28	M
HE's influence on governments	There are no adequate bridges that allow the transfer of knowledge to political decision-making on local and global issues, such as the ones that exist to meet the needs of industry and the market.	3.20	M
Breaking inertia	The dynamics of academia make it difficult to deal with deep transformational needs.	3.02	M

implicit need for finding solutions. This could be explained because all participants were professionals involved in this field.

Furthermore, according to the results of the poll, there is a clear relationship in the top three barriers between their level of importance and the difficulty in overcoming them. Thus, it could be said that respondents of the poll highlighted that the greatest barriers were those related to the content and knowledge that needs to be prioritized in curricula.

PARALLEL WORKSHOPS: MOVING FROM UNDERSTANDING TO ACTION: BREAKING BARRIERS FOR TRANSFORMATION

The results obtained in the GUNi First-Round Poll were used as a starting point for the discussions in the workshop sessions during the Fifth IBCHE Conference. The aim of the workshops was to offer a forum for collective discussion and proposals for overcoming the main barriers in the transformation of HE systems towards sustainability. The discussions at the workshops were based on an interactive and participative methodology: the 115 participants from across the world were divided into seven groups and they were then asked to work on three barriers and to identify the solutions that they considered most important. Each workshop's facilitator and participants developed diagrams, tables and lists of the barriers to change, in which they identified the different links between them and outlined various critical reflections.

It is worth highlighting that there was an active exchange of ideas on the thematic areas in which the barriers could be classified during the workshops. The classification made could be summarized as follows: education; research; service and outreach; and management. However, after further analysing the barriers, it was found that encapsulating them all in only four areas, instead of broadening their understanding, would limit and reduce their scope. Given the fact that barriers extend across several sectors and often fall into different areas, each barrier was assigned a thematic area (see Table III.1.2). It is acknowledged that the barriers are often transversal (that is, have an impact on one or more sectors), but for analytical reasons the classification described above was deemed useful.

Afterwards, the facilitators and participants were asked to choose three to five barriers that they considered the most relevant and to propose appropriate solutions. Largely based on the debates, and the sharing of ideas and experiences during the parallel workshops, the outcomes made it possible to reach a general consensus about the most urgent barriers that had to be overcome in order to properly implement sustainable development in HEIs. New barriers were added to the first proposal, and a final list of 21 barriers and 28 solutions was defined (see Table III.1.7).

However, it is worth mentioning that the list was based on general criteria and not on a 'one-to-one' principle. Thus, the list of solutions does not necessarily provide an ultimate answer on how to fit them in with the list of barriers. Rather, the two lists are a manifestation of a general understanding among professionals involved in promoting the pressing need to target sustainable development in HEIs, the most urgent barriers faced by them and finding feasible, adaptable and sustainable solutions. Nevertheless, the set of solutions covers most of the barriers, but three of them – barriers Ba2, Ba4 and Ba11 – do not have an associated solution. Table III.1.2 summarizes the possible relationship between the barriers defined and the proposed solutions, which are shown in Tables III.1.6 and III.1.7. It should be noted that some solutions can help overcome more than one barrier. This is the case of solutions So6, So11, So20, So24 and So25, which apply to three or more barriers. The barriers related to a common understanding of ESD, the integration of diverse knowledge, the introduction of ESD, new institutional set-ups, interdisciplinarity, research versus pedagogy and the influence of HE on governments are linked to just one concrete solution, whereas the following barriers are related to two solutions: the pedagogical approach, leadership, breaking inertia, avoiding unconscious unsustainability, the pedagogical model and government sustainability policies. For the rest of the barriers (short-term market needs, social responsibility, funding for ESD, isolation versus networking, training in ESD), three or more solutions were proposed.

TABLE III.1.2		
Possible relationship between barriers and solutions		
Thematic areas	Barriers	Solutions
Common Understanding of ESD	Ba1	So1
Technological vs Social	Ba2	–
Integration of Diverse Knowledge	Ba3	So5
Frame of mind	Ba4	–
Pedagogical Approach	Ba5	So3/So5
Leadership	Ba6	So6/So11
Introduction of ESD	Ba7	So2
New Institutional Set-ups	Ba8	So8
Interdisciplinarity	Ba9	So8
Breaking Inertia	Ba10	So10/So11
Unsustainable structures	Ba11	–
Research vs Pedagogy	Ba12	So7
Short-term Market Needs	Ba13	So20/So23/So24/So25
Avoiding Unconscious Unsustainability	Ba14	So2/So11
Theory vs Practice	Ba15	So5/So22
Social Responsibility	Ba16	So6/So7/So10/So20/So22
Funding for ESD	Ba17	So16/So17/So18/So19
Government Sustainability Policies	Ba18	So24/So25
Isolation vs Networking	Ba19	So22/So23/So24/So25/So27/So28
Influence of HE on Governments	Ba20	So26
Training in ESD	Ba21	So4/So06/So11/So13/So14

GUNI SECOND-ROUND POLL: BREAKING BARRIERS FOR TRANSFORMATION

The GUNi Second-Round Poll was conducted based on the final list of barriers and solutions. The goal of this second poll was to evaluate the degree of relevance given to each of the barriers and solutions by all respondents. Furthermore, it aimed to shed some light on the general trends that lead to the inclusion of sustainable development in HEIs. The process for answering was similar to that of the first poll: each barrier and solution was rated according to its level of importance (1 to 5, where 1 is not important and 5 is very important) and then the respondents were asked to choose the five most relevant barriers and solutions they considered as a priority in their own particular context. The poll was redistributed to experts, of whom 201 completed it. By professional posts, the biggest group of respondents were professors. In second place were the group of researchers, directors and vice-chancellors. Each of the three groups had about thirty respondents. There was a lower rate of participation by administrative staff, practitioners and students (see Table III.1.3).

TABLE III.1.3
Number of participants

Number of participants according to professional posts		
Professional posts	Number of participants	%
Vice-Chancellor/Rector	27	13.4
Director	30	14.9
Professor	73	36.3
Administrative Staff	18	8.9
Researcher	36	17.8
Practitioner	11	5.5
Student	6	2.9
Total	201	100

The poll was not intended to be proportionally representative of all regions, but rather to engage experts from all around the world and gather their professional views on sustainable development in HEIs. However, an analysis of participation by regions (Table III.1.4) shows that specialists from Europe predominate in the total number of respondents. Asia-Pacific and Latin America and the Caribbean are other regions whose contribution was significant, while in the case of Africa, the Arab States and North America, the participation was lower.

TABLE III.1.4
Participants by region

Regions	Number of participants
Africa	18
Arab States	14
Asia and the Pacific	37
Europe	80
Latin America and the Caribbean	33
North America	19
Total	201

From the GUNi Second-Round Poll, it can be concluded that the overall rating given to all the barriers during the Second-Round Poll was higher than the First-Round Poll. Additionally, the difference between the highest- and the lowest-rated barrier was narrower in the second poll than in the first one, and thus all barriers considered for this analysis have

been taken as relevant. This could be explained by an increase of awareness among participants as a result of their participation in the First-Round Poll, the workshop and the Second-Round Poll. However, given the fact that participation during both polls was anonymous, this explanation cannot be said to be conclusive.

As can be seen in Table III.1.5, there appears to be a relationship between the barriers that were voted a highest number of times as priorities and the mean response they received on the level of importance in overcoming the barrier. Thus, there seems to be a general agreement among the participants about the barriers that most urgently need to be broken down.

The priority barriers, as shown in Table III.1.5, are difficulties in attaining integrative thinking; transdisciplinary learning and interdisciplinary cooperation in universities; sustainable development is felt to be an 'add-on' to education, not as a built-in aspect of HE; the lack of vision and prioritization of sustainable development at the leadership level of HE; the lack of a common understanding of ESD in HE; and lack of coordination and vision to change sustainability policies and education at government level.

In the case of the solutions, given that the results are similar to those of the barriers, the same process of classification used with the barriers was followed. The top five solutions considered a priority as a starting point at the respondents' institutions are: developing an institutional understanding, vision and mission on sustainable development in HEIs taking into account faculty, students, and external parties, and engaging in open dialogues with all of them; changing the incentive system and quality indicators for encouraging and promoting multidisciplinary work, interdisciplinary teaching, theses and projects; building a culture of sustainability by involving and engaging the local community, universities, families, schools and other stakeholders in sustainability issues and projects, including active learning courses and action research with local community projects that take students out of the classroom; involving internal stakeholders in a way that leads to ownership, empowerment, participation and willingness to contribute to and be responsible for change by communicating and sharing more information (for example through team-building, coffee breaks, awareness-raising of ESD issues, and so on); and promoting sustainable development in universities, monitoring the design and implementation of sustainable development content in curricula, offering awareness-raising and/or training programmes on sustainable development for all university academic and administrative staff.

TABLE III.1.5
Priority barriers

	Barrier	Number of votes	Mean response
	Priority barriers		
1	**Ba9:** Difficulties in attaining integrative thinking, transdisciplinary learning and interdisciplinary cooperation in universities.	78	3.92
2	**Ba4:** Sustainable development is felt to be an 'add-on' to education, not a built-in aspect for HE.	73	3.98
3	**Ba6:** Lack of vision and prioritization of sustainable development at the leadership level of HE.	67	3.87
4	**Ba1:** Lack of common understanding of ESD in HE.	59	3.67
5	**Ba18:** Lack of coordination and vision to change sustainability policies and education at government level.	54	3.92

In Table III.1.5 and Table III.1.6, it can be seen that both the priority barriers and the priority solutions match the five most rated barriers and solutions on the level of importance in overcoming or applying them.

If we compare the relationship between the priority barriers and the priority solutions, it can be seen that they more or less focus on the same issues, the first of which is related to the transformation of HEIs through leadership. Such leadership should introduce and monitor sustainable development as a priority by reaching a common understanding and facilitating interdisciplinarity and transdisciplinarity. The second priority is related to policy change at the government level that would encourage and promote the transformation of the way HE works.

TABLE III.1.6
Priority solutions

	Solution	Number of votes	Mean response average
	Priority solutions		
1	**So1:** Developing an institutional understanding, vision and mission on sustainable development in HEIs taking into account faculty, students, and external parties, and engaging in open dialogues with all of them.	82	4.21
2	**So8:** Changing the incentive system and quality indicators to encourage and promote multidisciplinary work, interdisciplinary teaching, theses and projects.	74	4.19
3	**So22:** Building a culture of sustainability by involving and engaging the local community, universities, families, schools and other stakeholders in sustainability issues and projects. Including active learning courses and action research with local community projects that take students out of the classroom.	56	4.15
4	**So4:** Involving internal stakeholders in such a way that leads to ownership, empowerment, participation and willingness to contribute to and be responsible for change. Communicating and sharing more information.	55	3.85
5	**So11:** Promoting sustainable development in universities, monitoring the design and implementation of sustainable development content in curricula, offering awareness-raising and/or training programmes on sustainable development for all teaching, research and administrative staff.	51	3.92

TABLE III.1.7
List of barriers and solutions

Barriers	Solutions
Ba1: Lack of a common understanding of ESD in HE.	So1: Developing an institutional understanding, vision and mission on sustainable development in HEIs, taking into account faculty, students, and external parties by engaging in open dialogues with all of them.
Ba2: Supremacy of technological/instrumental knowledge versus human/social knowledge.	So2: Designing a management mechanism for organizations as a whole to create a comprehensive vision of sustainable development, based on which experts (teachers) will be able to work on projects to develop competences in interdisciplinary, integrated social relationships.
Ba3: Absence of culture-specific knowledge, indigenous knowledge and knowledge of traditional ecological systems.	So3: Encouraging analysis, synthesis, process and critical thinking as well as action-oriented competences by using sustainable development tools for learning and communication on issues from a problem-solving perspective.
Ba4: Sustainable development is felt as an 'add-on' to education, not a built-in aspect in HE.	So4: Involving internal stakeholders in such a way that leads to ownership, empowerment, participation and willingness to contribute to and be responsible for change. Communicating and sharing more information (for example through team-building, coffee breaks, awareness-raising about ESD issues, and so on).
Ba5: Pedagogical processes focused on the transmission perspective (knowledge transfer) rather than on the 'transformation' perspective.	So5: Opening up the learning process to base sustainability on different cultures and perspectives. Knowledge of native, indigenous and marginalized cultures. Integrating alternative courses (drama, arts, yoga); introducing service-learning activities and running accredited extracurricular activities for students.
Ba6: Lack of vision and prioritization of sustainable development at the leadership level of HE.	So6: Having educated and selected leaders at all management levels to facilitate and support collaborative and democratic dialogue processes on the social responsibility of HE.
Ba7: Lack of consensus in HEIs about the way to introduce education for sustainable development.	So7: Carrying out volume-based research into sustainable development education, focusing both on processes and outcomes.
Ba8: HEIs are too compartmentalized. Lack of departmental autonomy and coordination, and too many offices and units.	So8: Changing the incentive system and quality indicators to encourage and promote multidisciplinary work, interdisciplinary teaching, theses, projects, and so on.
	So9: Developing institutional policies to appraise the approach to sustainability in HEIs by means of compulsory indicators.
	So10: Reviewing the mission and vision statements of universities.
Ba9: Difficulties in acquiring integrative thinking, transdisciplinary learning and interdisciplinary cooperation in universities.	So11: Creating leadership units to help reduce bureaucracy and its processes; create common physical and intellectual spaces where interaction becomes possible; act as an expert and consultancy unit; help integrate sustainable development in universities; monitor the design and implementation of sustainable development content in curricula; offer awareness-raising and/or training programmes on sustainable development for all university teaching, research and administrative staff.
Ba10: The dynamics of academia hinder change, which gives rise to gaps between mission and vision and reality.	So12: Overhauling selection criteria and the recruitment of senior managers/leaders in universities; recognizing transformative leadership in a global context using the global interconnectivity of technology in such a way that injects new blood into institutions.
	So13: Having an 'active institution–good ESD practices' assessment mechanism or indicator to evaluate universities. Promoting good practice institutes.
Ba11: Difficulty of sustainable processes in non-sustainable civilizations, institutions and organizations.	So14: Having scheduled sustainable development meetings at universities (for example, starting working days with project presentations, holding an annual meeting of university faculties to discuss the development of sustainable development at the university).
Ba12: The educational system tends to make teachers prioritize research and publications over education and pedagogical practices.	So15: Running new programmes on sustainability that include extra-curricular activities.
	So16: Linking research to sustainability.
Ba13: High pressure to focus HE activities on short-term labour and market needs and on profitable activities, thus making HEIs factories for degrees and publications.	So17: Applying for government funding.
	So18: Making research grants available for cross-disciplinary research.
Ba14: Unconscious introduction of unsustainable practices in curricula.	So19: Securing financial resources from the business sector that can be earmarked for HE activities related to sustainability.
Ba15: The pedagogical model strengthens the separation of knowledge from experience.	So20: Offering services that are beneficial to society and at the same time generating financial resources to invest in sustainability projects at the institutional level.
	So21: Ensuring the proper management and use of financial resources at the institutional level.
Ba16: Science for impact factors places more emphasis on research than on science for impact.	So22: Building a culture of sustainability by involving and engaging the local community, universities, families, schools and other stakeholders in sustainability issues and projects. Including active learning courses and action research with local community projects that take students out of the classroom.
Ba17: HE has been confined to devoting financial support to science and technology, thus making it difficult to finance ESD.	So23: Creating academic programmes that help the interrelationship between society and HEIs.
	So24: Submitting policies on sustainable development to governments and organizations through university research and partnerships with local communities.
Ba18: Lack of coordination and vision to change sustainability policies and education at government level.	So25: Developing joint initiatives and having direct communications at the national, international and local level (NGOs, HEIs, civil society, RCEs, other universities, and so on).
Ba19: Isolation between universities and between universities and their communities.	So26: Drawing up guidelines for governments and organizations for developing policies and programmes that promote the role of universities as change agents for sustainability.
Ba20: Absence of HE stakeholders who influence governments on development and innovation.	So27: Having international agencies and committees to implement and monitor national levels of ESD accreditation and that also have an influence on national governments.
Ba21: Absence of professional resources and pedagogical training.	So28: Sharing knowledge with other HEIs and with the government on which they depend.

CONCLUSIONS

Given that thus far HE has contributed to the generation of knowledge and actions that have led to the crisis situation we are currently experiencing, we must start to reconceptualize our understanding of universities in a way that will bring about sustainable development in society. This alternative way of doing things must integrate changes in internal organization, knowledge creation, educational models, information technologies, social responsibility and knowledge transfer.

We can conceptualize sustainability from different standpoints. Based on the reflections in this study and taking into account the different stages of sustainability (O'Riordan, 1996, 2004) and the ideas of the transition movement (Chamberlin, 2009; Hopkins, 2008), it is fair to say that the future of HEIs can be seen from three different perspectives: continuity, transition and radical change (see Figure III.1.2).

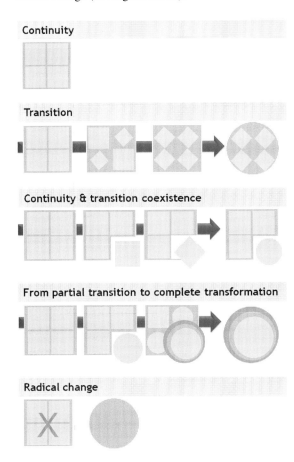

Continuity

Transition

Continuity & transition coexistence

From partial transition to complete transformation

Radical change

FIGURE III.1.2 Pathways towards sustainability (considering time, degree of change and level of institutional commitment)

Continuity refers to a situation in which the status quo prevails and things remain the same as they are.

Business as usual is the rule and ignoring the evidence of unsustainability is the mandate.

Radical or complete change, as its name suggests, is about the total restoration of how we conceive universities, namely, a situation in which their mere existence is not taken for granted. This *tabula rasa* would entail the reconceptualization of universities, the reformulation of their mission in current society, and the design of adaptable and malleable institutions that reflect changing contexts. A new start! However, such an approach would mean turning a blind eye to contextual factors and power relations, which makes it unfeasible.

In view of these two antagonistic scenarios, we are faced with a third approach consisting of a gradual reform of the current system. Thus, transition is about a process in which sustainable development is progressively included in HE, which seems to be the more plausible option. Given this situation, it makes sense to talk about the 'transition university' whereby universities are able to design their own sustainability strategies to suit their multiple needs. It also can be acknowledged that one or more of the three above-mentioned approaches can coexist in a single HEI. Thus, part of a university community may call for continuity, whereas another part may push for the introduction of changes (continuity and transition coexistence). In the case that a transformative part can influence and break resistances from the continuity part of the community, then the scenario moves to a change of the whole institution (from partial transition to complete transformation).

Spaces have opened up around the world to turn universities into more responsive institutions – more responsive in the sense of more in tune with pressing societal issues, with the local community and with the new direction taken by research and education in response to sustainability challenges. After responding to environmental issues in the 1970s through the launching of environmental engineering programmes and greening campuses in the 1990s and the turn of this century, a third wave can now be seen to be affecting some, although certainly not all, universities around the globe. This third wave (Wals and Blewitt, 2010) is a convergence of the environmental, social and economic spheres and the blurring of disciplines on the one hand, and the reconceptualization of teaching and learning, on the other. In sync with this, as was seen at the Fifth International Barcelona Conference on Higher Education, universities are repositioning themselves by becoming partners in knowledge co-creation with multiple societal actors in what some refer to as 'hybrid learning configurations'. There is no longer one truth, if there ever was one, but rather a socially constructed reality in which knowledge is co-created through dialogical interaction in specific contexts.

However, it appears that there are a number of barriers in HE that affect its ability to respond to the challenges posed by sustainability. Taking this as a starting point, this study falls within the transition approach. If it had focused on reimagining the sustainable university, it would lean towards the radical change approach.

This study, entitled *Breaking Barriers for Transformation*, has had the support of hundreds of professionals from all around the world. It had no intention of being proportionally representative of regions and the biggest group of respondents to the polls and contributors to the workshops and the knowledge-community working group were professors, namely, those who are already interested in advancing sustainability in HE.

In this study, 21 barriers and 28 solutions have been identified. There is no straightforward equivalence among them. Thus, different solutions may fall within more than one barrier, and one barrier may be linked to more than one solution (Figure III.1.3).

There seems to be a general consensus among participants on the relevance of sustainable development as well as the most urgent barriers, which are:

- Difficulties in acquiring integrative thinking, transdisciplinary learning and interdisciplinary cooperation in universities.
- Sustainable development is felt as an 'add-on' to education, not a built-in aspect of HE.
- Lack of vision and prioritization of sustainable development at the leadership level of HE.
- Lack of a common understanding of ESD in HE.
- Lack of coordination and vision to change sustainability policies and education at government level.

The solutions considered as priorities on which work should start are:

- Developing an institutional understanding, vision and mission on sustainable development in HEIs, taking into account faculty, students, and external parties, and engaging in open dialogues with all of them.
- Changing the incentive system and quality indicators for encouraging and promoting multidisciplinary work, interdisciplinary teaching, theses and projects.
- Building a culture of sustainability by involving and engaging the local community, universities, families, schools and other stakeholders in sustainability issues and projects. Including active learning courses and action research with local community projects that take students out of the classroom.
- Involving internal stakeholders in such a way that

leads to ownership, empowerment, participation and willingness to contribute to and be responsible for change. Communicating and sharing more information (for example through team-building, coffee breaks, awareness-raising of ESD issues, and so on).
- Monitoring the design and implementation of sustainable development contents in curricula, offering awareness-raising and/or training programmes on sustainable development for all university academic and administrative staff.

If we compare the relationship between these priority barriers and solutions, it can be seen that they more or less focus on the same issues, the first of which is related to the transformation of HEIs through leadership. Such leadership should introduce and monitor sustainable development as a priority by reaching a common understanding and facilitating interdisciplinarity and transdisciplinarity. In her analysis of the status of sustainability in HEIs in Africa (Chapter II.1 of the *Regional Perspectives* report), Heila Lotz-Sisitka also states that leaders should be targeted to further the agenda of sustainable development in universities. The second priority is related to policy change at government level that would encourage and promote the transformation of the way HE works.

The continuity approach is a hegemonic movement in HEIs that tends to close spaces for dialogical interaction, cross-boundary learning and knowledge co-creation. Peters and Wals (2011) refer to this as 'science as commodity', which very much pushed universities to think more in business-like terms of efficiency, market shares, rankings, impact factors, profitability and productivity. As the survey clearly shows, it is quite a challenge for many HEIs to find innovative ways of teaching, learning and researching that require boundary-crossing, experimentation and creativity that lead to societal impact and a more sustainable world. A multi-stakeholder dialogue for creating an inspiring and energizing vision involving all actors in HE, including those who represent the communities of which the institutions are part, the changing of the incentive systems and the indicators used to judge performance and, indeed, building a culture of sustainability involving the local community, are strongly supported by the respondents. A transition from 'science as commodity' to 'science as community' or at least a strengthening of the latter is needed to allow for community building and a change in culture (see Table III.1.8).

The continuity and transition approaches will probably continue to coexist for a while, but for sustainability to become ingrained in HE in a meaningful way

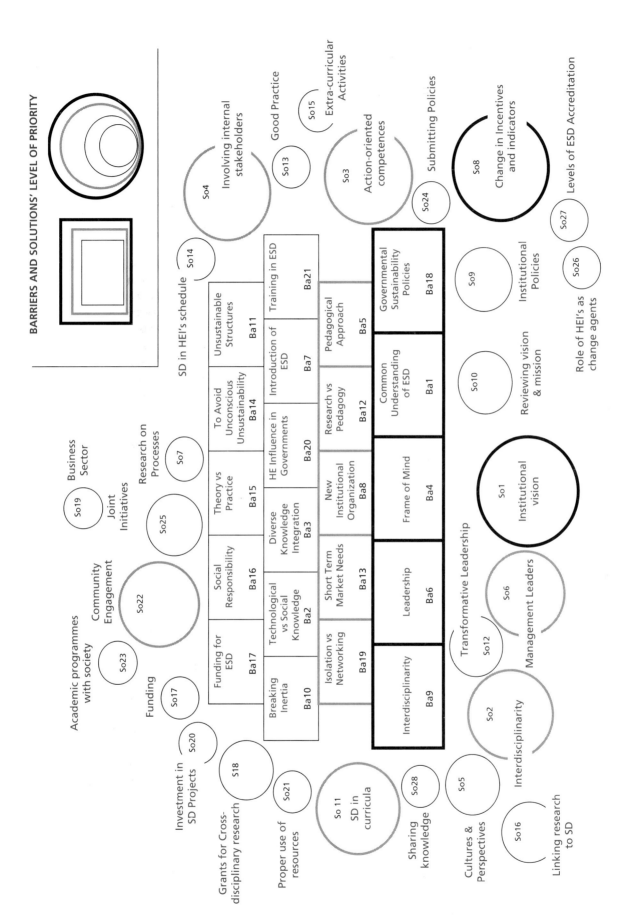

BARRIERS AND SOLUTIONS' LEVEL OF PRIORITY

FIGURE III.1.3 The relationship between barriers and solutions

TABLE III.1.8
Juxtaposing two conceptualizations of science in the context of higher education (Peters and Wals, 2011)

	Science as commodity	Science as community
Research orientation	Science for impact factors Strong emphasis on publication targets to be met by publishing in ISI journals, preferably with a high impact factor.	Science for impact Strong emphasis on societal relevance targets to be met by positive feedback from extended peers who include those who are to benefit from the research.
Educational orientation	Efficiency Students are viewed from an economic perspective as clients, input, throughput and output, who need to obtain their diplomas within the time allocated at a minimal cost. Instrumental – transfer of predetermined and relatively fixed outcomes.	Authenticity Students are viewed from a human development perspective as citizens who want to develop and engage in meaningful learning based on authentic educational materials. Emancipatory – high degree of self-determination, space for transformation, co-creation and emergent outcomes.
Business orientation	Focus on continuous growth The university wants or is forced (as governments withdraw public funding) to obtain more money from the market. Faculty is given acquisition targets and 'billable days' targets.	Focus on dynamic quality The university invests in community relations and community outreach, thus seeking to become an indispensable and integral part of the community, which in return is willing to support the university.
Epistemological orientation	Empirical rationalism Finding an objective truth. Establishing causality. Single truth exists and can be known. Maximizing predictability, management and control. Minimizing uncertainty.	Socio-constructivism Co-creation of knowledge, inter-subjectively validated. Pluralist. Not one single 'truth' but many subject to interpretation. Uncertainty as a given. Facts and values are inseparable.
Type of knowledge generated	Scientific and technical knowledge that can (allegedly) be generalized across contexts to inform attempts by various social actors to predict, control, and/or intervene for specific instrumental ends.	Not only scientific and technical knowledge, but also phronesis: ethically practical knowledge that is indispensable for the task of making context-specific value judgements about ends and means.

the science-as-community perspective will need to gain ground. Fortunately, there is evidence that this is happening: many exemplary practices are presented in this report that support this claim. In research, all kinds of niche journals have emerged that are transdisciplinary and cross-boundary in nature with sustainability as a normative guiding framework. An increasing number of students and academics are engaged in a range of innovative methods and new forms of learning that appear to be particularly fruitful for working on contextual sustainability issues. These methods include transdisciplinary learning (for example Klein, 2000; Sommerville and Rapport, 2000), transformative learning (for example Cranton, 2007; Mezirow and Taylor, 2009), cross-boundary learning (for example Levin, 2004), anticipatory learning (for example Tschakert and Dietrich, 2010), action learning (for example Marquardt, 2009; Cho and Marshall Egan, 2009), social learning (for example Pahl-Wostl and Hare, 2004; Keen et al., 2005; Wals, 2007), and participative learning (Reid, et al., 2008). These forms of learning show a high family resemblance in that they (Peters and Wals, 2011; Wals and Dillon, 2011):

- Consider learning as more than merely knowledge-based.
- Maintain that the quality of interaction with others and of the environment in which learning takes place is crucial.
- Focus on existentially relevant or 'real' issues essential for engaging learners.
- View learning as inevitably transdisciplinary, 'transperspectival' and trans-boundary in that it cannot be encapsulated in a single discipline or in a single perspective.
- Regard indeterminacy as a central feature of the learning process in that it is not and cannot be known exactly what will be learned ahead of time and that learning goals are likely to shift as learning progresses.
- Consider such learning as cross-boundary in nature in that it cannot be confined to the dominant structures and spaces that have shaped education for centuries.

Finally, further evidence comes from the emerging multi-stakeholder community-based networks around the world, which tend to have HE representatives among their members (students, staff or both). The revival of university science shops as conceptualized in the 1970s (www.livingknowledge.org) is testimony to this, as is the birth of a number of new networks of community-engaged universities (for example Centro Boliviano de Estudios Multidisciplinarios, Commonwealth Universities Extension and Engagement Network, Global Alliance of Community Engaged Research, PASCAL International Observatory, Participatory Research in Asia). Likewise, this is reflected in the rapid growth of regional centres of expertise (RCEs) in which universities are partners in a network of NGOs, civil society organizations, community groups, schools, and so on (Mochizuki and Fadeeva, 2008). Within these networks and centres, a range of participatory forms of research can be found, such as action research (Reason and Bradbury, 2007), community problem-solving (Stapp et al., 1996), and citizen science (Irwin, 1995). They also include different conceptualizations of science and scientific inquiry, such as Mode 2 science (Gibbons, 1994; Nowotny, 2005; Nowotny et al., 2001), post-normal science (Funtowicz and Ravets, 1993), sustainability science (Clark and Dickson, 2003; Komiyama and Takeuchi, 2006) and transdisciplinary research (Hirch-Hadorn et al., 2008).

The question is whether these movements towards ingraining sustainability in HE and the strengthening of 'science as community' with its associated forms of teaching, learning, research and community organization will move from the margins to the mainstream. In times of accelerating change in which the science–technology–society relationship will inevitably need to be reconceptualized in order for HE to remain relevant and trusted, there may be a move away from the commoditization of knowledge towards a new vision and mission of HE that is more congruent with the challenges of our time. That is why this study must continue to lead the way forward and try to go into the proposed solutions in greater depth through concrete actions to be implemented in HEIs.

BIBLIOGRAPHY

Bartlett, P.F. and Chase, G.W. (2004) *Sustainability on Campus*. Cambridge, MA: MIT Press.

Bonnet, M. (2002) Education for sustainability as a frame of mind. *Environmental Education Research,* **8**(1), pp. 9–20.

Cachia, R., Anusca, F., Ala-Mutka, K. and Punie, Y. (2010) *Creative Learning and Innovative Teaching. Final report on the study on creativity and innovation in education in EU members states*, Joint Research Centre (JRC), European Commission, Luxembourg (JCR 62370) (http://ftp.jrc.es/EURdoc/JRC62370.pdf).

Chamberlin, S. (2009) *The Transition Timeline for a Local, Resilient Future*. Devon: Green Books.

Chitty, C. (2002) *Understanding Schools and Schooling*. London: Rouledge Falmer.

Cho, Y. and Marshall Egan, T. (2009) Action Learning Research: A Systematic Review and Conceptual Framework, *Human Resource Development Review*, **8**(4) 431–62.

Clark, W.C. and Dickson, N.M. (2003) Sustainability science: the emerging research program. *Proceedings of the National Academy of Sciences* (PNAS) USA, 100:8059–61.

Cranton, P. (2007) Transformative learning theory as a framework for acquiring knowledge for social sustainability.

In: Willis, P., Harris, R., Gelade, S. and McKenzie, S. (eds) *Rethinking work and learning: Adult and vocational education and social sustainability*. New York: Springer.

Delanty, G. (2006) *Community. Comunidad, educación ambiental y ciudadanía*, Barcelona, Editorial Graó.

Dobson, A. (1998) *Justice and the Environment. Conceptions of Environmental Sustainability and Dimensions of Social Justice*. Oxford: Oxford University Press.

Dobson, A. and Bell, D. (ed.) (2006) *Environmental Citizenship*. London: The MIT Press (Massachusetts Institute of Technology, University of Edinburgh).

Dobson, A. and Quilley, S. (2010) Sustainability as competitive advantage in higher education in the UK. *International Journal of Environment and Sustainable Development,* **9**(4).

Erias, A. and Álvarez-Campana, J.M. (2007) *Evaluación ambiental y desarrollo sostenible*, Ediciones Pirámide, Madrid.

Ferrer-Balas, D., Lozano, D., Huisingh, D., Buckland, H., Ysern, P. and Zilahy, G. (2010) Going beyond the rethoric: system-wide changes in universities for sustainable societies, *Journal of Cleaner Production*, 18, 607–10.

Fien, J. (2005) Teaching and learning geography in the UN decade of education for sustainable development. *Geographical Education*, 18, pp. 6–10.

Funtowicz, S.O. and Ravetz, J.R. (1993) Science for the Post-Normal Age, *Futures*, 25/7 September 1993, 739–55.

Gibbons, M. (1994). *The New Production of Knowledge: The Dynamics of Science and Research in Contemporary Societies*. London: Sage Publications.

Giddings, B., Hopwood, B. and O'Brien, G. (2002) Environment, economy and society: fitting them together into sustainable development. *Sustainable Development*, **10**(4), 187–96.

Glasser, H., Calder, W. and Fadeeva Z. (2005) Definition: Research in Higher Education for Sustainability. Document prepared for the Halifax Consultation. Halifax, Nova Scotia.

Goldberg, M. (2009) Social conscience. The ability to reflect on deeply-held opinions about social justice and sustainability. In: Stibbe, A. (ed.) (2009) *The Handbook of Sustainability Literacy. Skills for a changing World*. Devon: Green Books, pp. 105–10.

Granados, J. (2010) *L'Educació per la Sostenibilitat a l'Ensenyament de la Geografia. Un estudi de cas*. Doctoral thesis (https://www.educacion.es/teseo/imprimirFicheroTesis.do?fichero=18803).

Granados, J. (2011) Teaching Geography for a Sustainable World: A case study of a secondary school in Spain, *Review of International Geographical Education Online* (RIGEO), 1(2).

Hart,M: (2000) A better view of sustainable community (http://www.sustainablemeasures.com/node/26)

HE21 (1999) *Sustainable Development Education: Teacher Education Specification*. London: Forum for the Future.

Hirsch-Hadorn, G., H. Hoffmann-Riem, S. Biber-Klemm, W. Grossenbacher, D. Joye, C. Pohl, U. Wiesmann und E. Zemp (2008) The Emergence of Transdisciplinarity as a Form of Research. In: G. Hirsch-Hadorn, H. Hoffmann-Riem, S. Biber-Klemm, W. Grossenbacher, D. Joye, C. Pohl, U. Wiesmann and E. Zemp (eds) *Handbook of Transdisciplinary Research*. Springer: Dordrecht, pp. 19–39.

Hopkins, R. (2008) *The Transition Handbook: From oil dependency to local resilience*, Dartington: Green Books Ltd.

Huckle, J. and Sterling, S. (1996) *Education for Sustainability*. London: Earthscan Publications Ltd.

Hugé, J., Waas, T., Eggermont, G. and Verbruggen, A. (2011) Impact assessment for a sustainable energy future – Reflections and practical experiences. *Energy Policy*, doi:10.1016/j.enpol.2011.07.023

Inman, S. and Rogers, M. (2008) *Teachers for a Better World: Education for sustainable development/globalcitizenship in initial teacher education*. London: CCCI, WWF and London South Bank University.

Innerarity, D. (2010) Incertesa i creativitat. Educar per a la societat del coneixement, *Debats d'Educació*, no. 18, Fundació Jaume Bofill, Barcelona.

Irwin, A. (1995). *Citizen science: a study of people, expertise, and sustainable development*. London: Routledge.

IUCN (2006) El Futuro de la Sostenibilidad (http://cmsdata.iucn.org/downloads/iucn_future_of_sustainability_sp.pdf)

Jensen, B.B. (2005) *Building Capacity and Empowerment through ESD*. Vienna: SEED and Austrian Federal Ministry of Education, Science and Culture.

Jickling, B. (1992) Why I don't want my children to be education for sustainable development. *Journal of Environmental Education*, 24(4), 5–8.

Jickling, B. and Wals, A.E.J. (2008) Globalization and Environmental Education: Looking beyond sustainable development. *Journal of Curriculum Studies*, 40(1), 1–21.

Kates, R.W., Parris, T.M. and Leiserowitz, A. (2005) What is sustainable development? Goals, indicators, values and practice. *Environment: Science and Policy for Sustainable Development*, 47(3), pp. 8–21 (http://www.heldref.org/env.php).

Keen, M., V.A. Brown and R. Dyball (2005). *Social learning in environmental management. Towards a sustainable future*. London: Earthscan.

Klafki, W. (1998) Characteristics of critical-constructive Didaktik. In Gundem, B.B. and Hopmann, S. (eds) (1998) *Didaktik and/or Curriculum. An International Dialogue*. New York: Peter Lang.

Klein, J.T. (2000) Integration, evaluation and disciplinarity. In: Somerville,, M. and D. Rapport (eds) *Transdisciplinarity: Recreating Integrated Knowledge*. Oxford: EOLSS Publishers.

Komiyama, H. and Takeuchi, K. (2006) Sustainability science: building a new discipline, *Sustainability Science*, 1: 1–6.

Levin M. (2004) Cross-Boundary Learning Systems—Integrating Universities, Corporations, and Governmental Institutions in Knowledge Generating Systems, HYPERLINK "http://landbouwwagennld.library.ingentaconnect.com/content/klu/spaa" \o "Systemic Practice and Action Research" *Systemic Practice and Action Research*, 17(3), 151–9.

Linz, M. (2007) Sobre suficiencia y vida nueva, in: RIECHMANN, J. (2007) *Vivir bien con menos. Sobre suficiencia y sostenibilidad*, Icaria Editorial, Colección Más Madera, Barcelona.

Lozano, R. (2008) Envisioning sustainability three-dimensionally, *Journal of Cleaner Production*, 16, 1838–46.

Mallarach, J.M. (1999) *Criteris i Mètodes d'avaluació del Patrimoni Natural*, Documents dels Quaderns de Medi Ambient, No. 2, Generalitat de Catalunya, Barcelona.

Marquardt, M. J. (1999) *Action learning in action*. Palo Alto, CA: Davies-Black.

Mezirow, J. and Taylor, E.W. (eds) (2009) *Transformative Learning in Practice: Insights from Community, Workplace, and Higher Education*. San Francisco: Jossey-Bass.

Mochizuki, Y. and Fadeeva, Z. (2008), Regional Centres of Expertise on Education for Sustainable Development (RCEs): an overview, *International Journal of Sustainability in Higher Education*, 9(4), 369–81.

Morin, E. (2000) *Les Sept Savoirs Nécessaires à l'Éducation du Futur*, Paris: UNESCO.

Morin, E. (2009) *Para una Política de la Civilización*, Paidós, Madrid.

Nowotny, H. (2005) 'The increase of complexity and its reduction: Emergent interfaces between the natural sciences, humanities and social sciences', *Theory, Culture and Society*, 22(50), pp. 15–31.

Nowotny, H., Scott, P. and Gibbons, M. (2001) *Re-thinking Science: Knowledge and the Public in an Age of Uncertainty*, Cambridge: Polity Press.

O'Riordan, T. (1996) Democracy and the sustainability transition. In: Lafferty, W. and Meadowcroft, J. (eds) (1996) *Democracy and the Environment: Problems and Prospects*, Cheltenham: Edward Elgar, pp. 140–56.

O'Riordan, T. (2004) Beyond Environmentalism. Towards sustainability. In: Matthews, J.A. and Herbert, D.A. (eds) (2004) *Unifying Geography. Common Heritage, Shared Future*. Abingdon: Routledge, pp. 117–43.

Orr, D. (2004) *Earth in Mind: On Education, Environment and the Human Prospect* (2nd edn). Chicago: Island Press.

Pahl-Wostl, C., and M. Hare (2004) Processes of social learning in integrated resources management. *Journal of Community and Applied Social Psychology* 14:193–206.

Peters, S. and Wals, A.E.J. (2011, in press) Learning and Knowing in Pursuit of Sustainability: Concepts and Tools for Trans-Disciplinary Environmental Research. In: Krasny, M. and Dillon, J. (eds) *Transdisciplinary Environmental Education Research*. London: Taylor and Francis.

Porritt, J. (2005) *Capitalism: As if the World Matters*. London: Earthscan.

Prensky, M. (2009) *Digital Wisdom*, (http://www.innovateonline.info/pdf/vol5_issue3/H._Sapiens_Digital-__From_Digital_Immigrants_and_Digital_Natives_to_Digital_Wisdom.pdf).

Purvis, M. and Grainger, A. (eds) (2004) *Exploring Sustainable Development. Geographical Perspectives*. London: Earthscan.

Reason, P., and Bradbury, H. (2001). HYPERLINK "http://bookshop.blackwell.co.uk/jsp/display_product_info.jsp?isbn=9780761966456" *Handbook of Action Research: Participative Inquiry and Practice*. London: Sage Publications.

Reid, A., Jensen, B., Nikel, J. and Simovskal, V. (eds) (2008) *Participation and Learning. Perspectives on Education and the Environment, Health and Sustainability*. London: Springer.

Rosner, W.J. (1995) Mental models for sustainability. *Journal of Cleaner Production*, 3(1-2), 107–21.

Sachs, W. (1991) Environment and development: the story of a dangerous liaison. *The Ecologist*, 21(6), p. 252.

Scott, W. and Gough, S.R. (2003) *Sustainable Development*

and Learning: Framing the Issues. London/New York: Routledge Falmer.

Somerville, M. and D. Rapport (eds) T*ransdisciplinarity: Recreating Integrated Knowledge.* Oxford: EOLSS Publishers.

Stapp, W.B., Wals, A.E.J. and Standkorb, S.L. (1996) *Environmental Education for Empowerment.* Dubuque, Iowa: Kendall-Hunt Publishing.

Sterling, S. (2001) *Sustainable Education: Revisioning Learning and Change*, Schumacher Briefings 6. London: Green Books Publishers.

Tilbury, D. (2007) Learning based change for sustainability: perspectives and pathways. In: Wals, A.E.J. (ed.) (2007) *Social Learning, Towards a Sustainable World. Principles, Perspectives, and Praxis.* The Netherlands: Wageningen Academic Publishers.

Tschakert, P., and Dietrich, K.A. (2010) Anticipatory learning for climate change adaptation and resilience. *Ecology and Society*, **15**(2): 11.

UN (2001) *Indicators of sustainable development: guidelines and methodologies.* New York: United Nations Department of Economics and Social Affairs, Division for Sustainable Development; 2001 (http://www.un.org/esa/sustdev/publications/indisd-mg2001pdf).

UN (2002) *The Johannesburg Declaration on Sustainable Development*, 4 September 2002 (http://www.housing.gov.za/content/legislation_policies/johannesburg.htm).

UN (2000) *Declaración del Milenio* (http://www.un.org/spanish/millenniumgoals/).

UN (1992) *Agenda 21* (http://www.un.org/esa/sustdev/documents/agenda21/htm).

UNESCO (1996) *Educació: Hi ha un tresor amagat a dins,* Centre Unesco de Catalunya, Barcelona.

UNESCO (2002) *Education for Sustainability. From Rio to Johannesburg: Lessons learnt from a decade of commitment.* Paris: UNESCO.

UNESCO (2008) Education and the Search for a Sustainable Future, *Policy Dialogue 1: ESD and Development Policy* (http://unesdoc.unesco.org/images/0017/001791/179121e.pdf).

UNESCO (2009a) Bonn Declaration. UNESCO World Conference on Education for Sustainable Development, 31 March–2 April, Bonn, (http://www.esd-world-conference-2009.org/fileadmin/download/ESD2009_BonnDeclaration080409.pdf)

UNESCO (2009b) *Trends in Global Higher Education: Tracking an Academic Revolution*, (http://unesdoc.unesco.org/images/0018/001831/183168e.pdf).

UNESCO, 2011 http://www.unesco.org/new/en/education/themes/leading-the-international-agenda/education-for-sustainable-development/about-us/

UNU, 2011 http://www.ias.unu.edu/sub_page.aspx?catID=108&ddlID=183

Waas, T., Hugé, J., Verbruggen, A. and Wright, T. (2011, in press) Sustainable development: A bird's eye view. *Sustainability.*

Waas, T., Verbruggen, A. and Wright, T. (2010) University research for suatinable Development: definition and characteristics explored. *Journal of Cleaner Production* (18) 629–36.

Wals, A.E.J. (ed.) (2007) *Social Learning, towards a Sustainable World. Principles, Perspectives, and Praxis.* The Netherlands: Wageningen Academic Publishers.

Wals, A.E.J. and Dillon, J. (2011, in press) Learning theories and their implications for environmental education research. In: Stevenson, R., Brody, M., Dillon, J. and Wals, A.E.J. (eds) *International Handbook of Environmental Education Research.* New York: Lawrence Erlbaum/AERA.

Wals, A.E.J. and Blewitt, J. (2010) Third wave sustainability in higher education: some (inter)national trends and developments. In: Jones, P., Selby, D. and Sterling, S. (eds) *Sustainability Education: Perspectives and Practice Across Higher Education.* London: Earthscan?

WCED (1987) *Our Common Future.* Oxford: Oxford University Press.

WCED (1998) Conferencia de la Naciones Unidas sobre el Medio Ambiente y Desarrollo. Río 92. Programa 21. Acuerdos, Serie Normativas, Ministerio de Medio Ambiente, Madrid.

Wright, T. (2004) The evolution of environmental sustainability declarations in higher education. In: Wals, A. and Corcoran, P. (eds) *Higher Education and the Challenge of Sustainability: Problematics, Promise, and Practice.* Dordrecht: Kluwer Academic Press, pp. 7–19.

PART IV
VISIONS FOR TRANSFORMATION

IV.1 Learning for Living with the Earth

Perceiving the Earth as a living being that is sensitive, remembers and is alive, and learning to treat it with respect, not as something external and objective, but as a complex being that includes us and which has its own mechanisms of balance, interaction and self-organization – these are important aspects of the sustainability paradigm.

It is therefore important to reflect on the educational purpose of higher education (HE) as it relates to the requirements of the sustainability paradigm. If we agree that the purpose of HE is the development and acquisition of competences and skills for learning how to live a 'considered life' within the context of the times, to be a globalized citizen, to coexist with others, to act respectfully and to transform oneself and society, then HE should be preparing people to deal with the contemporary issues that, in their complexity, represent clear threats to sustainable ways of being.

This purpose implies the need to learn a variety of skills and values: a deep understanding of human beings and life; sustainable development as a collective social process to be learned and applied; a need for mutual recognition, understanding and respect between cultures for intercultural relationships and support for diversity; the ability to deal with the exponential expansion of technology without losing the human capacity to put it to common human service; and the ability to set aside fear in order to confidently cooperate on peace building and justice at all levels of activity.

Such a change would abandon a model that places most of its attention on 'content' in favour of one that develops itself in a 'context', preparing people to apply knowledge instead of just accumulating it. This would be an educational model based on 'knowing how to be'.

IV.1a EDUCATING TO LIVE WITH THE EARTH

Moacir Gadotti

The data disseminated in recent years by the United Nations Intergovernmental Panel on Climate Change (IPCC), have led to a worldwide discussion. There is no other issue of such great concern as global warming and climate change. But this is nothing new – warnings have been raised by ecologists since the 1960s. At the Earth Summit in Rio de Janeiro in 1992, 173 heads of state and government leaders adopted a document, Agenda 21, to set the world on the road towards sustainable development, a commitment towards future generations. The Global Forum held at the same time adopted two important and complementary documents for a sustainable society: the Earth Charter and the Treaty on Environmental Education for Sustainable Societies and Global Responsibility. In 1999, UNESCO issued an appeal for Education for a Sustainable Future (UNESCO, 1999) and, in 2002, the United Nations launched the Decade of Education for Sustainable Development (2005–2014).

The world is on the move in different ways, in an attempt to prevent the worst case scenario. However, there are still concerns and the major challenges are yet to be met. What can education do in such a context?

I had the opportunity to take part in the drafting of the first version of the Earth Charter, at the Global Forum in Rio de Janeiro in 1992. The Charter starts explicitly with a declaration of love to the Earth, considered as a living being in constant evolution, with which we share an essential identity. It starts by asserting 'we are the Earth'. Whenever someone is born, it is usually said that such a person has 'come to Earth'. In truth it is not a question of coming to Earth, but rather 'from' Earth. We are all the children of Mother Earth. Whatever we do will fall back upon us. And as children we need to learn to live 'with' her. That is why we need education to live with the Earth.

The Earth Charter was adopted by the Global Forum of Non-Governmental Organizations, representing over 1300 organizations active in 108 countries. It enshrines the so-called 'Rio spirit' that is worded into the preamble of the Charter:

> We are Earth, the people, plants and animals, rains
> and oceans, breath of the forest and flow of the seas.
> We honour Earth as the home of all living beings. We
> cherish Earth for her beauty and diversity of life. We
> welcome Earth's ability to renew as being the basis
> of all life. We recognize the special place of Earth's
> Indigenous Peoples, their territories, their custom and
> their unique relationship to Earth. We are appalled
> at the human suffering, poverty and damage to Earth
> caused by inequality of power. We accept a shared
> responsibility to protect and restore Earth and to allow
> wise and equitable use of resources so as to achieve
> an ecological balance and new social, economic and
> spiritual values. In all our diversity we are one. Our
> common home is increasingly threatened. We thus
> commit ourselves to the following principles, noting
> at all times the particular needs of women, indigenous
> peoples, the South, the disabled and all those who are
> disadvantaged ... [followed by 10 principles]. http://
> habitat.igc.org/treaties/at-03.htm

Today we are aware that the *meaning of our lives* is not detached from the meaning that we build for the planet itself. As we face the degradation of our lives on the planet, our current environmental concerns place us at a crossroads between a 'Technozoic' path that places all its faith in the capacity of technology to bail us out of the environmental crisis without having to change our polluting, consumerist lifestyle, and an 'Ecozoic' path founded on a new, healthy relationship with the planet that acknowledges that we are a part of the natural world and that we can live in harmony with the universe.

SUSTAINABILITY AND LIVING WELL

In such a context, it seems more appropriate to speak of *educating to live with the Earth*, educating for sustainability, rather than of 'education for sustainable development' (UNESCO, 2005). The concept of 'sustainable development' is an ambiguous one. In my opinion, sustainability is the *dream of living well*, of living well with the Earth, sharing the planet with other living beings, human and non-human. Sustainability is the dynamic balance with the other and with the environment; it is harmony among the different. Educating to live with the Earth is educating for a sustainable life and not just educating for a new kind of development. In the meantime, even though it is ambiguous, the concept of sustainable development, seen from a critical viewpoint, holds a formidable educational component: the preservation of the environment depends on environmental awareness and raising such awareness depends on education.

Sustainability is more than just sustainable development. While the prevailing model of development on the planet today points towards planetary unsustainability, the concept of sustainable development points towards planetary sustainability. Here lies the driving force of this concept. The challenge is to change the route and walk towards sustainability for another kind of globalization, for an 'alter-globalization'.

We may split sustainability along two main axes, the first one relevant to nature and the second to society:

1. **Ecological, environmental and demographic sustainability** (natural resources and ecosystems), which refers to the physical basis of the development process and to the capability of nature to support human action, with a view to its reproduction and the limits of population growth rates.
2. **Cultural, social and political sustainability**, which refers to maintaining diversity and identities, directly related to quality of life for the people, distributive justice and the process of building citizenship and participation for the people in the development process.

The category of sustainability is central to the 'ethics of the human being', as Paulo Freire defends in his book *Pedagogy of Autonomy* (Freire, 1997). A new model for development requires a new ethical support, also inspired by the practical experience of traditional peoples who live in a sustainable manner and by the social groups who take the personal choice of a healthier, environmentally sound life. Thus, educating towards a *sustainable life* is educating for voluntary simplicity and for quietness. Our lives need to be guided by new values: simplicity, austerity, quietness, peace, serenity, knowing how to listen, how to live in community, sharing, discovering and doing things together.

The simplicity that we defend is not to be mistaken for simpleness, nor is quietness to be mistaken for a culture of silence. Simplicity must be voluntary and the change in our consumer habits too, by reducing our demands. Quietness is a virtue, conquered through inner peace and not through imposed silence. Quietness is to do with hearing, listening, knowing, learning with the other; much different from one who arrives talking, with a ready-made speech, dictating the rules, imposing a single discourse. Quietness is to do with setting the conditions for many narratives that are silenced today, in order to regain life. Educating to live with the Earth is also training towards understanding. Training in the ethics of humankind, not for the instrumental, utilitarian ethics of the marketplace. Educating to communicate with one another, not communicating to exploit, to draw benefit from the other, but to better understand the other.

The concept of sustainability in education may have a positive impact, not only on individuals, but also on the necessary changes to the educational system. Hence, we may speak of impact at the legal level, in educational reform, curricula and content, and at the personal level of commitment to and engagement with a more sustainable life. Educating for sustainability implies *changing the system*; it implies respect towards life, caring for the planet every day and caring for the entire community of life, of which human life is but a chapter. This means sharing fundamental values, ethical principles and knowledge such as respect towards the Earth and all the diversity of life; caring for the community of life with understanding, sympathy and love; and building democratic societies that are fair, participative, sustainable and peaceful. Sustainability is a core concept in an educational system that looks towards the future.

Educational systems in general are based on predatory principles and instrumental rationality, which reproduces unsustainable values. In order to introduce a culture of sustainability into the educational system we need to re-educate the system: it is a part both of the problem and of the solution. I am convinced that sustainability is a powerful concept, an opportunity for education to renew its old systems, which are grounded on principles and values of competition.

Changing systems and changing people are interdependent processes. The Fourth International Conference on Environmental Education, held in 2007 in Ahmedabad (India), highlighted the importance of changing our *lifestyles*. The Ahmedabad Declaration reflects this debate that includes the economy, education, development, production and consumption:

> Our vision is a world in which our work and lifestyles contribute to the well-being of all life on Earth. We believe that through education, human lifestyles can be achieved that support ecological integrity, economic and social justice, sustainable livelihoods and respect for all life. Through education we can learn to prevent and resolve conflicts, respect cultural diversity, create a caring society and live in peace. (http://www.ensi.org/media-global/downloads/Updates/49/Declaration.pdf)

Since lifestyle was the main theme at Ahmedabad, *sustainable consumption* was highly relevant. We cannot speak about educating to live on planet Earth without speaking of educating for sustainable consumption. Much was said there about consumerism and nutritional habits based on animal protein. We concluded that the nutritional model of rich countries cannot be generalized for the simple fact that we would need more than one planet (in fact, 2.6 planets) to feed everyone that way. The agricultural model is under question. It is necessary to invent another, more sustainable model, one that refers to human health as well as to protecting the environment.

We need to eat in order to survive; however, as opposed to animals, we do not feed out of pure instinct only. We feel pleasure in eating and we may make choices. We have transformed eating into a very significant act. It is not the mere satisfaction of an instinctive necessity. Eating is also a cultural act. Societies have turned it into a social event. There is an enormous variety of foodstuffs and there is enough food for all the inhabitants on Earth. What remains to be done is to distribute food equitably.

The best choice for food is that which is produced locally and the worst is that which comes in a package from far away, generating more waste (industrial products) as well as greater social and environmental costs. It is a question of knowing, of learning how the product that we consume has been produced, of getting to know the entire system of food production.

EDUCATING FOR PLANETARY CITIZENSHIP

We are ever more conscious that we are all inhabitants of one single dwelling, one only home. We have a terrestrial identity; we are earthlings, citizens of a 'single nation', as was insisted upon in Rio in 1992. And just like us, the planet, as a living organism, has its history. Our history belongs to the planet's. We are not in the world; we are actually a part of it. We did not come into the world; we came from the world. We are the Earth and all that lives on Earth. Our destiny is a common one. Hence, educating to live on Earth is also educating for *planetary citizenship*.

The *Ecopedadogy Charter* of 1999 (Gadotti, 2010, pp. 75–8) expressly mentions in its article seven that education for planetary citizenship is a prerequisite, a demand for a planetary society that must be approached pedagogically starting from everyday life, from subjectiveness, that is, starting from people's interests and needs:

> Educating for planetary citizenship entails developing new skills, such as: feeling, intuiting, vibrating emotionally; imagining, inventing, creating and recreating; relating and interconnecting, self-organizing; seeking information, communicating, expressing oneself; locating, processing and making use of the enormous amount of information in the global village; seeking the causes and foreseeing the consequences; criticizing, assessing, systematizing and making decisions. Such skills must lead the people to think and act accordingly, in fullness and transdisciplinarity.

In its article nine, the *Ecopedagogy Charter* evidences the relationship between 'education for planetary citizenship' and the quest for a 'culture of sustainability':

> The aim of education for planetary citizenship is to build a culture of sustainability, i.e. a bioculture, a culture for life, for harmonious coexistence among human beings and with nature. The culture of sustainability must lead us to learn to choose what is really sustainable in our lives, in contact with the lives of others. Thus only will we be involved in the processes to promote life and we will walk with meaning. To walk with meaning is to provide a meaning to what we do, to share meaning, to impregnate day-to-day practices with meaning and to understand the meaninglessness of many other practices that openly or stealthily try to impose themselves and take over our lives every day.

A new understanding of education necessarily ties in with a new understanding of pedagogy. This was how in the 1990s ecopedagogy emerged as a kind of pedagogy oriented towards education for planetary citizenship, although we think it would be more appropriately called 'pedagogy of the Earth' (Gadotti, 2001). The history of ecopedagogy initially started as the 'pedagogy of sustainable development' in a study carried out by the Latin-American Institute of Communication Pedagogy (ILPEC) of Costa Rica and signed by Francisco Gutiérrez (1994). It already contains a reference to a holistic approach, to the dynamic balance between human beings and nature, and to the category of sustainability that are the essential assumptions of ecopedagogy.

Francisco Gutiérrez and Cruz Prado soon realized that the pedagogy of sustainable development was not broad enough to become a great breakthrough in education theory. In their book *Ecopedagogy and Planetary Citizenship* (Gutiérrez and Prado, 1999), they speak about planetary citizenship that goes beyond environmental citizenship. They see ecopedagogy as promoting learning of 'the meaning of things starting with everyday living'. The concept of 'everyday living' is essential to the way in which both authors understand ecopedagogy. Later on they gave a new name to this pedagogy, calling it 'biopedagogy', a pedagogy of life (Prado, 2006), using the same theoretical references and giving the theme more spiritual depth. Cruz Prado and Francisco Gutiérrez were the first to prepare the ground for the potential of ecopedagogy. The Paulo Freire Institute of São Paulo (Brazil) translated the book into Portuguese and it continues to be a major reference for this pedagogy.

The movement for ecopedagogy grew and continued to unfold. As I see it, ecopedagogy can no longer be considered as yet another pedagogy that we may and must build up. It is only meaningful as a global alternative project wherein the concern lies not only in the preservation of nature (natural ecology) and the impact of human societies on natural environments (social ecology), but in a new model of sustainable civilization seen from an ecological viewpoint (integral ecology) that implies changing social, economic and cultural structures. It is therefore connected to a utopian project: changing the human, social and environmental relations that we have today.

The word 'pedagogy' comes from Greek and it literally means 'guide to lead children'. In Classical Greece, the pedagogue was a slave who took the children of freemen to school. The reference for the word 'pedagogy' is an anthropocentric paradigm. All classical pedagogies are anthropocentric. On the other hand, ecopedagogy is a part of a planetary awareness (genera, species, kingdoms, formal, informal and non-formal education, and so on). We expand our viewpoint from an anthropocentric vision to planetary awareness, from the practice of planetary citizenship to a new social and ethical reference: planetary civilization.

Gaia equals life. There are many who believe that it is illegitimate to consider the Earth as a living organism, as that is a quality the Earth lacks. We see life only through the perception that we have of our own lives and that of animals and plants. It is true that we lack the distancing that astronauts have from outer space, but we may have the same distancing of astronauts in time, far longer than our own life span. The Gaia hypothesis, which conceives the Earth as a complex super-organism, alive and in constant evolution, is backed by the Earth's billions of years of history. The first life form appeared over 4 billion years ago. From then onwards the evolutionary process of life has not ceased to become ever more complex, conforming interdependent ecosystems within the macrosystem that is the Earth, which in turn is a microsystem when compared to the macrosystem of the universe. We may only reach an understanding of the Earth as a living being by distancing ourselves from her in time and space.

In order to understand our scale as members of an immense cosmos, and to assume new values based on solidarity, affection, transcendence and spirituality, to overcome the logic of competition and capitalist accumulation, we must journey along a difficult path. No change is ever a peaceful one. But it will not be brought about just by praying, preaching or simply out of our pure desire to change the world. As Paulo Freire (1997) taught us, to change the world is something urgent, difficult yet necessary. But in order to do so we also need to know and to read the world scientifically, not only emotionally. And above all, we must act upon it in an organized manner.

Rationalism must be condemned without condemning the use of reason. The rationalist logic has led us to plunder nature, to death in the name of progress. But reason has also led us to the discovery of *planetarity*. The poetic and emotional statement of astronauts in that 'the Earth is blue' was possible after millennia of rational domination of the laws of nature herself. We must condemn rationalization without condemning rationality. When the astronaut Neil Armstrong first set foot on the Moon he declared: 'one small step for a man, one giant leap for mankind'. In saying this, he was representing us all.

This has been possible through a colossal collective human effort that took into account all the technical, scientific and technological knowledge accrued up until then by humankind. This is something that is not to be ignored. If we are capable today, through the internet, of establishing a web of networks within the entangled planetary communication system, it has been possible thanks to the use of our imagination, our intuition, our emotions, as much as our reasoning; through the gigantic and long-suffering human effort to discover how we may live better on this planet, how we may interact with it. We have done all of the above, oftentimes the wrong way, that is true. We consider ourselves to be 'superior' for our rationality and we exploit nature carelessly, without any respect for her. We do not relate to the Earth and to life with emotion, with affection, with sensitivity. In this field, we are but toddlers, though we learn.

EDUCATING FOR SUSTAINABILITY

In this day and age of converging crises, with the onset of global warming and profound climate change, ecopedagogy has everything to do with *education for sustainability*. Gro Harlem Brundtland states in the foreword of the report by United Nations *Our Common Future:* 'If we do not succeed in putting our message of urgency through to today's parents and decision makers, we risk undermining our children's fundamental right to a healthy, life-enhancing environment. Unless we are able to translate our words into a language that can reach the minds and hearts of people young and old, we shall not be able to undertake the extensive social changes needed to correct the course of development'. To develop the necessary theoretical and practical premises towards this education for sustainability is the task of another pedagogy to complement the pedagogy of the Earth, the 'pedagogy of sustainability' (Antunes, 2002). The category of 'sustainability', as put forward by Leonardo Boff (1999), is central to an ecological worldview, and it is possibly one of the foundations of our new civilizational paradigm that seeks to harmonize human beings, development and Earth understood as Gaia.

Ecopedagogy and education for sustainability are developing either as a *pedagogical movement* or as a *curricular approach*. Like ecology, ecopedagogy may also be understood as a social and political movement. Like any new movement, under way, undergoing evolution, it is a complex one and may take different directions. Ecopedagogy also entails a reorientation of curricula in order that it may bring on board certain principles and values.

Educational systems were born in Europe in the 19th century, amidst the age of industrial revolution, and, despite the current diversity of nations that adopted them later on, they are still very similar to one another today. During the 20th century they were strengthened with the extension of the right to education, enshrined in the Universal Declaration of Human Rights of 1947. Despite this consolidation and the appearance of international assessment schemes for school performance, such as the Programme for International Student Assessment (PISA), we have started the 21st century questioning their ability to promote peace and understanding. UNESCO has very rightly supported the need to *reorient education*, across the board, towards a culture of peace and sustainability. Such is the core concern of the Decade of Education for Sustainable Development (2005–2014) and of recent studies such as that of Peter Blaze Corcoran (2009). UNESCO focuses on the 'reorientation of curricula and current formal education'. The literal quote of the reference document for the Decade states that its main aim is to:

> Integrate the principles, values and practices of sustainable development in all aspects of education and learning. This educational effort will encourage changes in behaviour that will create a more sustainable future in terms of environmental integrity, economic viability and a just society for present and future generations (…). Education for Sustainable Development requires a re-examination of educational policy, in view of a re-orientation of education from nursery school to university and continuing adult learning. (UNESCO, 2005, p. 57)

There are several practices to help us integrate the principle of sustainability at all *levels of teaching*. At the primary-school level, for instance, our children need to enjoy the life experience (experiences are assimilated more than discourse) and they need to learn about the needs of plants and animals, and their habitats, as well as to use less, to reuse and to recycle used materials, and to preserve the ecosystems linked to forests and waters. At a more advanced level we ought to discuss biodiversity, the preservation of the environment, alternative energies and global warming. At the university level we must not only disseminate information on the environment, but also generate new knowledge and research into the quest for a new, more sustainable paradigm of development. If universities become truly committed to sustainability they may educate people to live in harmony with the Earth. And then, this may also contribute much towards developing studies and research into the theme of sustainability and living well, placing such knowledge at the service of social change and preservation of the environment.

The concept of sustainability and of sustainable societies entails a whole new civilizational project, and if applied to pedagogy, it may be unfolded across all fields of education, not only in environmental education (Gadotti, 2009a). Hence, it becomes a key concept to understand the education of the future. It means new principles and values as well as suggesting new symbols, such as the 'garden' in the views of the North American educator Emily DeMoor. She takes the garden as a metaphor and as a physical reality. In an article for the journal *Pátio*, she speaks of educational values for sustainability, of understanding the garden as curriculum (DeMoor, 2000). The idea of the garden embodies the new, emerging values of sustainability. The garden allows us to work with the Earth, to perceive planet Earth through earth. To watch the seed become a plant and the plant become food, the food that gives us life. It teaches us patience and to handle earth carefully from sowing to reaping. To learn that things do not reach us ready-made, that they must be cultivated and cared for. The garden also teaches us that the world is not made, but in the making, it is making us too, and this construction process requires persistence, patience and expectation towards the seed that will eventually become a seedling, and then a plant that blooms and bears fruit.

Emily DeMoor (2000) quotes Paulo Freire's *Pedagogy of the Oppressed* and explains how he was a pioneer of this pedagogy, asserting that he warned more than 40 years ago that life systems on Earth were suffering from great harm and were on the verge of losing the capacity to sustain life on the planet. 'If we wish to adopt a pedagogy that produces sustainability values, Freire's thinking must be extended to include freeing the natural world' (ibid., p. 12). She then quotes another passage from *Pedagogy of the Oppressed*: 'The oppressor consciousness tends to transform everything surrounding it into an object of its domination. The earth, property, production, the creations of people, people themselves, time – everything is reduced to the status of objects at its disposal.' Paulo Freire had an extended awareness towards the world, as we may construe from the same book (Freire, 1975, p. 94) when he states that 'love is a commitment with humankind. Wherever the oppressed may be, the act of love is to commit oneself to their cause'. Emily DeMoor (2000, p. 14) concludes by saying that 'this curricular model is of the essence if we wish to give students the knowledge, the skills and the critical awareness necessary not only for justice or social efficiency, which are important concerns for curricular theory, but also to realize the true freedom, community and sustainability of the Earth and its life forms'.

EDUCATING FOR ANOTHER POSSIBLE WORLD

Diversity is the fundamental characteristic of humanity, and as a result there can be no single way of producing and reproducing our existence on the planet. Human diversity imposes the need to build a diversity of worlds (Gadotti, 2007). We must not respond to one unitary mindset with another. To *educate to live with the Earth* is to educate for another possible world – that is, to make visible that which had been hidden due to oppression, to give a voice to those who are not heard. The feminist struggle, the environmental movement, the Zapatista movement, the landless movement and others have revealed things that had remained invisible throughout centuries of oppression.

To educate for another possible world is to educate to raise awareness, to dealign, to de-fetishise. To *fetishize* neo-liberal ideology is to fetishize the bourgeois, capitalist logic that has managed to solidify itself to the point of making people believe that the world is naturally immutable. Fetishism transforms human relationships into static phenomena, as if they could not be modified. When fetishized, we are unable to do anything because the fetish destroys our ability to act. When fetishized, we can only repeat what has already been done or said, what already exists.

To educate for another possible world is to educate for the emergence of that which does not yet exist, for the 'not yet', for utopia. Thus, we are accepting history as possibility rather than as fatality. This is why educating for another possible world is educating for breakthroughs, for rebelliousness, for rejection, for saying 'no', for yelling, for dreaming of another possible world. Denouncing and announcing. The core of the neo-liberal conception of education is the negation of dreams, of utopia. Therefore, an education for another possible world is, above all else, an education for dreams, an education for hope.

The commercialization of education is one of the major challenges of contemporary history, because it overvalues economic factors to the detriment of human concerns. This logic can only be inverted by an emancipatory education that trains people for critical awareness and dealignment. Educating for another possible world is educating for human quality 'beyond capital', as István Mészáros (2005) put it in his opening remarks at the third edition of the World Education Forum in Porto Alegre in July 2004 (Gadotti, 2009b). Capitalist globalization has stolen away the time we need to live well and the space we need to have an inner life; it has stolen our capacity to build our lives with dignity. More and more people are being reduced to machines for producing and reproducing capital. Capitalism is essentially unsustainable, as asserted in the *People's Agreement*, reached at the World People's Conference on Climate Change and the Rights of Mother Earth, held on 22 April 2010 in Cochabamba (Bolivia):

> The capitalist system has imposed on us a logic of competition, progress and limitless growth. This regime of production and consumption seeks profit without limits, separating human beings from nature and imposing a logic of domination upon nature, transforming everything into commodities: water, earth, the human genome, ancestral cultures, biodiversity, justice, ethics, the rights of peoples, and life itself.

Educating for another possible world means making education – both formal and non-formal – a space for *training critical minds* rather than just training a workforce for the market. It means inventing new spaces as alternatives to the formal educational system and rejecting its hierarchical form in a structure of command and subordination; it means educating to *articulate different forms of rebelliousness* that reject today's capitalist social relations; it means educating to radically change our way of producing and reproducing our existence on the planet; it means, therefore, educating for sustainability (Gadotti, 2009a).

We cannot change the world without changing people: to change the world is to change people – the two processes are interrelated. Changing the world depends on all of us: individuals must become aware and organize themselves in new 'multitudes', in the words of Antonio Negri and Michael Hardt (2005). Educating for another possible world is educating to overcome the dehumanizing logic of capital based on individualism and profit; it is educating to radically transform the current economic and political model.

The Earth is our first great educator. To educate for another possible world is also to educate to find our place in history, in the universe. It is educating for peace, for human rights (including the *Rights of Mother Earth*), for social justice and for cultural diversity, and against sexism and racism. It is educating for planetary awareness. It is educating each one of us to find his or her place in the world, to belong to a planetary human community, to feel the universe deeply.

It is education for *planetarization*, not for globalization. We live on a planet, not a globe. The globe represents the surface, the geographic divisions, the parallels and meridians – in short, cartographic aspects. In contrast to this linear vision, the planet is a whole in motion. Our destiny as human beings is linked to the destiny of this being called Earth – now yet another oppressed creature. To educate for another possible world is to educate for a sustainable relationship with all of the Earth's living things, human or otherwise.

Educating for life in the cosmos – planetary, cosmic and cosmological education – broadens our understanding of the Earth and the universe. It is education for a cosmic perspective. Only thus will we better understand climate change, desertification, deforestation, and other problems that affect both humans and non-humans. The *classical paradigms* – arrogantly anthropocentric and industry-oriented – are lacking in scope to explain this cosmic reality. In the absence of a holistic vision, they are unable to show how to steer the world away from the path leading to extermination and to cruel differences between rich and poor. The classical paradigms are draining the planet of its natural resources. Today's convergence of crises is the result of a deeper crisis: the crisis of the civilizing paradigm. To educate to live with the Earth, therefore, is to educate for another possible world, a task that requires a new paradigm: a holistic paradigm.

REFERENCES

Antunes, Ângela (2002) *Leitura do mundo no contexto da planeterização: por uma pedagogia da sustentabilidade.* (Doctoral Thesis) São Paulo: FE-USP.
Boff, Leonardo (1999) *Saber cuidar: ética do humano, compaixão pela terra.* Petrópolis: Vozes.
Corcoran, Blaze, Peter and Osano, Philip M. (eds) (2009) *Young people, education, and sustainable development: exploring principles, perspectives, and praxis.* The Netherlands: Wageningen Academic.
DeMoor, Emily (2000) O Jardim como currículo. In: Revista *Pátio.* Porto Alegre, no. 13, May–July 2000, pp. 11–15.
Freire, Paulo (1975) *Pedagogia do oprimido.* Rio de Janeiro: Paz e Terra.
Freire, Paulo (1997) *Pedagogia da autonomia: saberes necessários à prática educativa.* São Paulo: Paz e Terra.
Gadotti, Moacir (2001) *Pedagogia da Terra.* São Paulo: Peirópolis.
Gadotti, Moacir (2007) *Educar para um outro mundo possível: o Fórum Social Mundial como espaço de aprendizagem de uma nova cultura política e como processo transformador da sociedade civil planetária.* São Paulo: Publisher Brasil.
Gadotti, Moacir (2009a) *Educar para a sustentabilidade.* São Paulo: Instituto Paulo Freire.
Gadotti, Moacir (2009b) *Fórum Mundial de Educação: Pro-posições para u outro mundo possível.* São Paulo: Instituto Paulo Freire.
Gadotti, Moacir (2010) *A Carta da Terra na Educação.* São Paulo: Instituto Paulo Freire
Gutiérrez, Francisco and Cruz Prado (1999) *Ecopedagogia e cidadania planetária.* São Paulo: Cortez/Instituto Paulo Freire.
Gutiérrez, Francisco (1994) *Pedagogia para el Desarrollo Sostenible.* Heredia, Costa Rica: Editorialpec.
Hardt, Michael and Negri, Antonio (2005) *Multidão: guerra e democracia na era do Império.* Rio de Janeiro: Record.
Mészáros, István (2005) *A educação para além do capital.* São Paulo: Boitempo. Available at http://resistir.info/meszaros/meszaros_educacao.html
Prado, Cruz (2006) 'Biopedagogia'. In: Guadas, Pep Aparício, Dolors Monferrer, Isabel Aparício Guadas and Pascual Murcia Ortiz (eds). *Fórum Paulo Freire – V Encuentro Internacional: Sendas de Freire: opresiones, resistencias y emancipaciones en un nuevo paradigma de vida.* Xátiva: Institut Paulo Freire de España y Crec, pp. 169–211.
UNESCO (1999) *Educação para um futuro sustentável: uma visão transdisciplinar para uma ação compartilhada.* Brasília: UNESCO/Ibama.
UNESCO (2005) *Década das Nações Unidas da Educação para o Desenvolvimento Sustentável (2005–2014).* Brasília: UNESCO.
UN World Commission on Environment and Development (1987) *Our Common Future.* Oxford: Oxford University Press.

IV.1b THE UNIVERSITY AND EDUCATION FOR LIFE

Edgar González-Gaudiano

Ever since environmental education was recommended for inclusion in the school curriculum at all levels and in all educational modalities by the Intergovernmental Conference on Environmental Education held in Tbilisi (Georgia) in 1977, the issue of how to ensure this inclusion has been a recurring problem. This recommendation was enunciated, furthermore, in the context of the proposal for interdisciplinarity that had been developing in the decade of the 1970s.

The debate on interdisciplinarity, which was bolstered by the Nice conference of 1970, has made valuable contributions to theory and has pointed to the need to reshape an outdated curriculum paradigm centred on disciplines. However, given discipline-based curricula and teachers who are trained in disciplines, interdisciplinarity has not been easy to implement in practice. In the decades since the 1970s, approaches have been launched that have given rise to a few successful experiences, although they have not changed the institutional modus operandi as a whole.

The last quarter of the 20th century and the first decade of the new millennium have witnessed the efflorescence of further discussion on the need for a shift in the learning paradigm in academia (Bawden, 2003), particularly with the general dissemination of complex systems theories and post-normal science (Funtowicz and Ravetz, 2000). Both of these approaches foreground fundamental questions about self-organizing living systems in conditions of complexity, diversity and uncertainty, where facts are multiple and uncertain and where values are in dispute, risks are high and decisions are urgent (Funtowicz and Ravetz, 2000).

However, in general, the structure of the conventional curriculum, with the usual exceptions, has remained intact despite the exhaustion of its heuristic possibilities. The most important of the many difficulties can be summarized as follows:

1. Epistemological and theoretical difficulties deriving from the complexity of changing the substantive structure of disciplines in order to foster interdisciplinary approaches and knowledge dialogues from within knowledge categories.
2. Methodological difficulties associated with the complexity of developing operational strategies within a framework of systemic uncertainty and multiple articulations with a number of related fields.
3. Institutional difficulties related to the many forms of internal resistance, given that any curricular reform will shift the balance of power between scientific communities and academic groups and will affect budgetary allocations and spheres of influence.

Thus, rather than respond to a specific epistemological proposal, the current classification of knowledge by disciplines – and the resulting structure of the curriculum – has acted as a conveyor belt for the historically constructed interests of different scientific communities and, as pointed out by Gass (Apostel et al., 1972), is an eloquent reflection of social values. Today's structuring of knowledge in disciplines is one of the main obstacles to educating for life and transmitting an understanding of the network of life's inherent processes of autopoiesis (Maturana and Varela, 1984), resilience, interaction and exchange. These processes acquire great importance in the sustainability paradigm. In other words, the disciplinary structure of knowledge is part of the problem rather than of the solution.

Apart from any controversy over the concept, sustainability represents interdisciplinarity par excellence, with its – perhaps naive – aspiration to holistically confront the hitherto unheard-of systemic complexity of contemporary problems. It is increasingly patent that many of the difficulties in strengthening the sustainability dimension in education processes stem from the disciplinary structure itself, which tends to fragment reality.

Interdisciplinarity is not proposed as the philosopher's stone of education but as a way of reorganizing knowledge so as to better respond to the problems of society. It is based on the premise that although reality is severable from theory for study purposes, the different cognitive components that give rise to the various disciplines are inextricably linked. Disciplines as fields of study have overlapping and permeable boundaries. When these boundaries are openly acknowledged and explored, they pose new questions that have significantly added to the available knowledge, most particularly in the case of environmental and sustainability issues.

From a political perspective, interdisciplinarity questions knowledge production and reproduction practices, the very concept of science, the ethical and social dimensions of science, the notion of the epistemic subject and, naturally, the consequences of their application to nature and life as a whole.

But what interdisciplinarity does not necessarily confront is the essentialist foundation of scientific discourse in Western thinking, that is, the relationship between scientific knowledge, truth and objective reality as opposed to the knowledge that inhabits the territory of appearances and that presents deformed or distorted realities. Arditi (1991) notes that the perception of knowledge understood as a mimesis of reality – that is, the process of knowledge that assumes knowing subjects who seek to represent reality as such in their thinking – has been in crisis since it was formulated in the post-Descartes period. The search for the essence of reality in order to protect the truth and, therefore, the assumption that there is only one true reality, will not be quelled by the interdisciplinarity proposal or by a dialogue of knowledge unless we radically question the aspiration – a development of the Enlightenment – to search for the unity of reality and for all-encompassing knowledge as an explanation for all discrete phenomena and, instead, begin to take into account the diversity of the world.

EDUCATION FOR LIFE

In the current education system, with the university at its apex, it is easier to educate for life from informal processes, that is, using strategies that view education as a social process rather than as a curricular process. In the education system as it has developed in modernity, we are cultivating forms of collective ignorance and of mass destruction through strategies that plant the seeds of unsustainable lifestyles in the minds of subjects. Hence, much of the content and practices of educational institutions need to be unlearned as a prerequisite to reconnecting with the life processes around us.

Some of the most fruitful experiences that have developed in this critical period marking the end of the industrial age have commenced with analyses conducted outside educational institutions, reflecting community-based approaches that overcome the breakdown of socio-cultural norms and values propagated by marketing and the media. One such example is the Transition Movement in the UK led by Rob Hopkins, which promotes the reduction of energy consumption, community self-organization focused on local solutions, the use of goods produced in a sustainable manner, the primacy of the group, the relearning of life skills and harmony with the rest of nature.

What, then, does education for life mean? There is no easy answer, firstly, because it is not enough for students to learn about the processes, cycles and dynamics of life on the planet. If this were all, natural scientists would be committed to the defence of such processes in all areas of daily life – and unfortunately this is not necessarily the case. In other words, the amount of information that is available is not enough to change values and attitudes. This is very evident from the media focus on scientific literacy regarding climate change, which has failed to produce a transformation of lifestyles and consumption patterns among the public (González-Gaudiano and Meira, 2010).

Secondly, the problem is not resolved by educating people *in* contact with the dynamics and processes of nature. I do not deny the important contribution of outdoor education programmes, especially in developing sensitivity to the processes that sustain life on the planet. However, we have to recognize that, in general, there is a disconnection between the learning experiences of children and their personal lifestyles (Brookes, 2004). In other words, the experiences of children do not lead to analysis of, and much less change in, the unsustainable habits that characterize people's everyday lives. The concept of 'the good life' continues to be centred on the notion of a level of comfort that is fuelled by high levels of energy consumption.

The problem lies, then, in educating *for* life, and not in educating *about* and *in* the environment. This still relevant discussion regarding environmental education was broached back in 1972 in a doctoral thesis by Lucas (1979). The most valid approach to building a proposal for educating for life lies in the critical pedagogy of place (Gruenewald, 2003), a synthesis of two trends that have developed along separate pathways but which share common goals and approaches that are not only compatible but mutually complementary. Critical pedagogy proposes an agenda of cultural decolonization and place-based education that emphasizes the spatial aspects of social experience strengthened by an environmental dimension.

Gruenewald's approach concurs with situated environmental learning (O'Donoghue and Lotz-Sisitka, 2006), which advocates for environmental education practices consistently acquiring deeper meanings coherently situated in their own contexts, particularly in frameworks of poverty, vulnerability and risk. This is particularly relevant to the projects for adapting to climate change that are so urgently needed worldwide. In this regard, I draw on the valuable contributions of Donna Haraway (1995), a primatologist who has made major contributions to feminist scholarship and to developmental philosophy and biology – a model, indeed, of the interdisciplinary interfaces mentioned above. Haraway points out that objects of study must explicitly point to the place of departure, since – leaving aside the research method used – we cannot escape our subjectivity and socio-cultural context. This approach is key, as educating for life is not possible from abstraction but can only take place in specific situations holding meaning for our lives. It also defines our political and ethical stance regarding the problems encountered, because positions and meanings are never neutral, no more than education for life can be politically or ethically neutral.

REFERENCES

Apostel, L. et al. (1972) *Interdisciplinariedad. Problemas de la enseñanza y de la investigación en las universidades.* México: ANUIES, 1975 (Biblioteca de la educación superior).

Arditi, B. (1991) Conceptos. *Ensayos sobre teoría política, democracia y filosofía.* Asunción-Paraguay: Centro de Documentación y Estudios (CDE) y RP Ediciones.

Bawden, R. (2003) Engagement, reflexive scholarship and the learning turn with the academy. Keynote speaking presented at *6th Congreso Mundial ALARPM.* Durban, South Africa 21–24 September.

Brookes, A. (2004) Can outdoor education be dispensed with? A critical review of some common rationales for outdoor education. Paper presented at *Connections and Disconnections: Examining the reality and rhetoric. International perspectives on outdoor education theory and practice,* La Trobe University Bendigo, Australia.

Funtowicz, S.O. and Ravetz, J.R. (2000) *La ciencia posnormal. Ciencia con la gente.* Barcelona: Icaria.

González-Gaudiano, E. and Meira-Cartea, P. (2010) Climate change education and communication: a critical perspective on obstacles and resistances. In: Kagawa, F. and Selby, D. (eds) *Education and Climate Change. Living and Learning in Interesting Times*. New York/London: Routledge, pp. 13–34.

Gruenewald, D.A. (2003) The best of both worlds: A critical pedagogy of place. *Educational Researcher*, **32**(4), pp. 3–12.

Haraway, D. (1995) Conocimientos situados: La cuestión científica en el feminismo y el privilegio de la perspectiva parcial. En: Haraway, D. (ed.) *Ciencia, cyborgs y mujeres. La reinvención de la naturaleza*. Madrid, Spain: Cátedra, pp. 313–45.

Lucas, A. (1979) *Environment and environmental education: Conceptual issues and curriculum implications*. Melbourne: Australian International Press & Publications.

Maturana, R.H. and Varela, G.F. (1984) *El árbol del conocimiento*. Santiago, Chile: Editorial Universitaria.

O'Donoghue, Rob and Lotz-Sisitka, Heila (2006) Situated environmental learning in Southern Africa at the start of the UN Decade of Education for Sustainable Development. *Australian Journal of Environmental Education*, **22**(1), 105–13.

IV.1c FOR THE HUMANIZATION OF EDUCATION

Claudio Naranjo

In order to build a more sustainable world with greater solidarity and justice, new generations must learn to be human. I think we need a re-humanizing education, because we are suffering from an accelerating process of dehumanization. People are disappearing, becoming nothing more than numbers, and education is being transformed into an information-transmission process in which people work like robots. The human factor, which is precisely what should be transmitted, is going to waste. It's the treasure of humankind, and it should be a priority. Education deals with pure content rather than relationships and the living relationship. UNESCO put it well: we need to learn to be, learn to learn and learn to live together. But when you think about sustainability, you think that something specific to sustainability is needed, without realizing that what sustainability needs is the same as what education needs, what humanity needs, and what the world needs as a remedy for its problems, because deep down they are all the same. Sustainability is a result of greed; it is a consequence of that which is today referred to as capitalism but which is in fact derived from cannibalism.

It's time we had education for human development. Without it, it will be tough to build a better society. If we want a different kind of society, we will need more complete human beings: something of this nature cannot be built without the proper elements. I think human development is essential not only to achieving a viable society, but also for individual happiness. I don't think we're in this world just to survive.

We need to introduce instinctual emotional education in order to counterbalance the excessive importance attributed to rationality. As for higher education, in order to provide students – future teachers who will go into the vital field of secondary education – with the necessary teaching tools, which are considered instinctual at that level, we should focus not only on the free expression of ideas, but also on the freedom to make room for what I call organismic wisdom, which is closely linked to spontaneous desires and psychotherapy.

The problem of our education is that it is essentially patriarchal. This means not only that it is at the service of an implicit authoritarianism – one which corrupts our democratic intentions – but also that it entails the tyranny of the rational over the emotional and the instinctual. Ours is a predominantly intellectual education, from which the other aspects of human beings are excluded. Education is patriarchal and, like the law, it is heavily influenced by the strict father model because everything is built by men, even though teaching is a female vocation. It is a calling that attracts women, because it attracts people who want to serve and help others; it is a specialized function of mothering. But these people with a mothering vocation find themselves under an administration made up of committees of men, experts on something or another, who know little about teaching or human relationships but quite a lot about content and abstract thinking.

Educators must have the right or the freedom to say what is happening to them. People are not very good at communicating what is happening to them. They don't dare make the leap; it's as if it were prohibited, as if it were dangerous to communicate. For example, nowadays it is seen as improper for a teacher to tell a student, 'I don't feel all that good today' or 'I don't like what you're saying to me' or 'What you're telling me makes me feel insecure'. But generating such a relationship would change things a great deal, since there would be a point of contact – a human relationship would replace a robotic one. We must teach people to speak in the first person, from their own experience, to bring spontaneity to adult experience.

The prevailing education is akin to brainwashing; it is a very established way of understanding things and it is difficult to change. Teachers always face a huge task because they have to re-teach people in order to change acquired habits. What's more, teachers are no longer seeking anything; they are teaching what they worked so hard to learn, because they had to spend many years to learn it. More and more human things are being academicized, including teaching. Even primary education is looking more like secondary education – as if it were necessary to hold admissions interviews for students to enter preschool. The concept of education should be that one cannot teach without being taught, but not in the academic sense. A person cannot be expected to teach humanities without first receiving a humanizing education – which should not be confused with learning psychology or learning humanities.

Nowadays we're hearing a lot about a crisis in education, because young learners do not want the education that is being offered. Existential issues are being systematically stifled by a situation that lacks human contact and dialogue about what goes on in students' minds, families and surroundings. Families are forced to stay on the sidelines; they are trained to be obedient. I think that going to school today is like eating sand – something that is not nourishing – while intuitively understanding that there is something else that would be relevant. What we need is something else: something that helps human development.

Our ability to survive the current worldwide crisis depends very much on whether we can achieve a slightly higher dose of benevolence, a more substantial level of compassion and simple kindness. Without this kindness, all the technical information in the world won't go very far.

We need to bring human development to the heart of all professions – a core of human development in which one learns to be a person, to develop these three levels of instinctual liberation, the transformation of the lower emotions, the low passions in emotions, the types of love. And then comes the transformation of the instrumental and practical mind – typical of our civilized society – into a mind capable of understanding greater things, such as wisdom. Then, the place where one goes for human development is the same place that trains people who excel in transmission capacity – in other words, educators.

There is a big problem in academic education: it is assumed that anyone who takes a course and passes the exams is ready to practise. This is true perhaps for an engineer. In the field of psychotherapy, where I've worked for much of my life, a psychotherapist is not considered to be trained simply because he or she took a course, passed an exam or completed a given number of courses. Psychotherapists must show that they are able to heal others, and to do that they need to have been cured themselves – to have reached a sufficient level of mental health. Some people are emotionally shaky, while others are awkward in their personal relationships. Such people cannot be good therapists. But universities train them as therapists because the system says that if they complete a course and pass the exams, that's it. This is because university education is not experiential. Testing in education deals with writing and the communication of content. It cannot, however, offer evaluations of the sort undergone by a pianist in a competition – that would be something like a good educator. A positive change in this regard would be to verify that educators are capable of educating not because they possess the skill in a particular rigid sense, but rather to analyse what they know how to do, and what they do well.

All professions should essentially be focused on the individual. My first job at the medical school in Chile, at the Institute of Medical Anthropology, was to introduce the human element in medical education. In medical education, the idea is that you begin with cadavers and test tubes and then move on to patients. As a result, you want the patients to look like cadavers or pure chemistry, and you don't feel very comfortable if they do not. And I was a victim of that. When I was in medical school, I remember that one of my first patients said to my instructor, 'This doctor really understands my illness, but he doesn't understand me; he doesn't listen to me.' I didn't feel any connection. I had already felt the impact of the dehumanization of medical studies during the four-year course prior to dealing with patients.

In the past, I have been invited to reflect on educational issues, but never on the concept of the university. I have not been close enough to the university world, especially since I rebelled against academicism and left Chile for Esalen,[1] in California. There, people talked about the nonverbal humanities, and I adopted an alternative position that was somewhat disdainful of academia. Nevertheless, I am interested in the idea of transforming universities into so-called transitional universities that seek to create grassroots learning communities, and where part of university life is required to be community-related.

SEEKERS AFTER TRUTH

The final and most recent stage of the Seekers After Truth (SAT) programme is based on the inspiration of applying it to education. I was encouraged by a conference I was invited to in Argentina, where there were about 2000 attendees. There, I felt like I was talking to a mass of humanity that was breathing with me, like there was resonance. And that was a new experience for me. I thought, What am I doing, teaching things to therapists? These therapists are very successful, they are helping in some circles, and they have created schools that are doing well. But if this were in the schools, would this happen in the world? Everyone goes through school, so we must reach out to educators. I know I can do this with therapists, so why can't I do the same with educators? In the end, it may be the same thing. And thus began my experiment to apply this to educators, as explained in my book *Cambiar la educación para cambiar el mundo* [Changing education to change the world].[2] However, I didn't realize that it was one thing to form groups of educators and quite another to change the institution or to be accepted by education, by the institution.

I have had formal acceptance. The SAT programme is recognized as an educator-training programme in Barcelona, Catalonia, as well as in many parts of Italy. However, the programme has not been adopted at either universities or schools. At universities, it has not been adopted because there is 'no room for it' – all subjects are important and no one wants to step aside to make room for something new. There's a famous true story of a German professor of philosophy who was invited to Japan by a teacher. The teacher starts to serve tea to the German professor – and keeps pouring tea and keeps pouring tea, until the cup is overflowing and the tea spills out onto the saucer. Undaunted, the teacher keeps pouring the tea, which overflows from the saucer onto the tray, until his guest says, 'I believe you want to tell me something.' And the teacher replies: 'Yes. You come to me with your head full of so much infor-

mation and knowledge, and you want to learn from me, but how can I give you anything when you're so full of knowledge?' Something similar happens at universities, and in schools.

It is also an economic issue. How should it be funded? There is also some fear of presenting such a sincere process to university faculties. There are many people who donate money for education, but not for change in education. You can't ask for money to bring wisdom into education, to bring freedom into education, to bring such debatable things into education. But there's enough money to get more computers, because that's where the future lies for these people. More education is supposedly going to save the world, but you can't convince people that it shouldn't be more education of the sort we already have. The education we have simply maintains the world we have.

Instead of helping people to be good people so that we can have a good world, so-called educational institutions go about teaching subjects that supposedly will be useful to us in our professional lives or that supposedly will educate our minds. However, these subjects are not very useful in preparing students for a future life of service – they only serve to educate certain aspects of the mind at the expense of others. Education needs to once again concern itself with the deepest dimension of human beings: the spiritual dimension.

NOTES

1   The Esalen Institute is a centre for experimental education founded in 1962. It is devoted to the exploration of what Aldous Huxley called 'human potential'. More information can be found here: http://www.esalen.org/info/general.html
2   Naranjo, Claudio (2004) *Cambiar la educación para cambiar el mundo*. Vitoria: Ediciones La Llave.

IV.1d NOW IS THE TIME TO ABANDON SUBJECT-BASED EDUCATION

Roger C. Schank

Learning begins with a goal. However, when we think about education and school we often forget this. Someone, somewhere, decides that a student must learn about Napoleon but they fail to ask how such learning might conform to a goal that the student consciously holds. We don't forget this when we try to teach a child to walk or talk because we know that the child does want to learn to do these things. When we teach a child

to hit a baseball we usually determine beforehand that the child wants to learn to do this. But, we forget this simple idea of goal-directed learning as soon as we design curricula for schools. Who cares if the child wants to learn long division? Make them learn it. It is very important. Full speed ahead!

Somewhere along the way, many students get lost. They may get lost in high school, or in college, or in job training. But somewhere they learn to shut off their natural learning instincts, the ones that drive them to improve because they really want to accomplish something. Instead they try hard to do what they were told to do – they study, they pass tests, and eventually their love of learning is gone. The feedback that they have previously gotten from accomplishing a real goal, one that they had truly held, has been replaced by pleasing the teacher, or getting a good grade, or progress in their goal of getting into a 'good college.'

Why can't we just let students learn what interests them? Are the people who run schools simply out of touch with how learning really works, or how actual students behave when faced with something they don't want to learn, or is something else more complex going on?

School is subject-based and further, those subjects are predefined and agreed upon by those in charge. Without giving a history of how this state of affairs came to be, or why it is an issue, it is first necessary to note that it is the case. I say this because when we were students in school we accepted the fact that school is the way it is, and we assumed that it was the way it was supposed to be. We may not think each subject we learn is valuable or interesting and perhaps we long to learn different subjects, but never do we hear people suggest that there shouldn't be subjects in school at all. This is a very difficult idea to swallow. There have always been subjects. What else would there be? First universities had them and then schools copied the subjects that universities taught. But research universities don't teach these subjects as much as they do research in those subjects. Research is always the *raison d'etre* of the modern university.

Universities won't change their research emphasis any time soon. But because scholars criticize literature should that mean that students should be encouraged to be literature majors or required to take literature courses? Because scholars try to prove new theorems in mathematics, does that mean we should encourage mathematics majors or require students to take mathematics courses?

Students go to university, typically because it is rite of passage into the adult world of work. But unless they really want to be scholars, they typically are poorly served by the university faculty.

If school had been designed around something other than subjects what would it have been designed around?

No matter what students do in life they will need to form relationships, assess their own abilities, gain confidence through practice, need to learn to listen, need to learn to love, need to try things out and see how well they work, and need to learn why they do what they do. Algebra relates to none of this and students know.

Students need to learn about how other people behave and why, and they need to learn how to interact with different kinds of people.

Students need to learn how to listen to others and really hear what they are saying.

Students need to learn how to express themselves effectively.

Now let's consider the cognitive science behind this. Everything we do as human beings is goal-directed. We go for a walk for a reason, we shower for a reason, we get a job for a reason, we talk to people we meet for a reason. We pursue goals as soon as we are born. We try hard to learn to walk, talk, get along with our family, get our needs satisfied, and find out what we like and what we don't like. We do this from birth. If school related to the goals that children actually have, that they were working on at the very moment that they enter formal education, school would seem like a natural and helpful experience. Students wouldn't stress about satisfying their teachers any more than they stress about satisfying their parents when they are learning to walk and talk. Yes, they want to please their parents, but that is not exactly the same thing.

People know what their goals are and they know when something they are being offered, a parasailing lesson or a pomegranate, for example, doesn't fit with their goals. They can be convinced to try out a new activity that they believe will not satisfy any of their goals, but for the most part, it is difficult to convince them that weird things that were not on their goal list actually should be on the list. We say things to students like 'you will need this later'. But this is usually a bold faced lie. You don't need algebra later. Making up nonsense convinces nobody.

When we hear an outcry about the need to make children learn science no one ever asks why. The standard answer, if this were ever asked, is that Science is important in tomorrow's world or some such nonsense. Push harder and you might get some remarks about soon all the scientists will be Indians and Chinese, which may be the real fear of those who push science in the US. To address this question properly one has to ask what exactly is meant by 'science.'

When science means learning facts about science we are talking about useless information that is readily forgotten after the test. I have no idea why anyone learns to balance chemical equations or apply physics formulas or learns about biology classifications in high school. None of it is of any use to most adults. (It is easy to test however.)

When the stuff that is being taught does not relate to the inherent goals of the students it will be forgotten. You can count on it. Why this stuff is taught is simply that it derives from a conception of science prevalent in the 1890s that has not been since modified. It is defended by people as a way to produce more scientists, which makes no sense since it probably deters more students from entering science then it encourages.

Scientific reasoning, on the other hand *is* worth teaching.

Why?

Because car mechanics, plumbers, doctors, and crime investigators, to name four random professions, all do scientific reasoning on a daily basis. As a society we only anoint doctors with the glory of doing actual scientific reasoning. The other professions get less glamorous interpretations. But they are all doing the same stuff. This is what they are doing:

> They are taking a look at evidence and trying to determine the probable causes of the conditions that they have found.

To do this one must know what causes what in the real world, which is science, what counts as evidence of known conditions, which is science, and previous cases that are similar which any good scientist must know. So while we may not see a plumber as doing scientific reasoning, that is exactly what he is doing.

Science is about creating hypotheses and gathering evidence to support or refute those hypotheses. Children are natural scientists. They often try stuff out – skipping rocks on the water or dropping stones from the roof or lighting things on fire – to see what happens. But, there is more to science than trying stuff out. One must seek explanations and make sure those explanations are correct. Knowing what constitutes a correct explanation is really the essence of what scientific knowledge is about. But notice that there are correct explanations for hypotheses in plumbing as well as in medicine and that these explanations exist for repairing a faulty engine and for understanding who committed a crime. It is all scientific reasoning.

The difference between plumbing and medicine is in the complexity of the science. Not a lot of invention goes on into plumbing and there aren't all that many explanations to choose from. The degree of difficulty in understanding what is going on and why is what separates those fields and makes one science and one not. But, the basic thought processes are the same.

School needs to be organized around fundamental cognitive activities. A properly designed school system needs to focus on cognitive abilities not scholarly subjects. Kids will recognize instantly that these activities are the ones they know how to do that they need to get better at them. If we allow them to choose what areas of knowledge they would like to focus on while learning these skills, they would be attentive and interested students.

A society that organizes schools around cognitive abilities would become one where people were used to thinking about what they do and how and why they do it. They would not find school stressful or boring.

What are the cognitive processes that make up learning? I have divided twelve types of processes into three groups: *Conceptual processes, Analytic processes* and *Social processes.*

All these processes require practice in order to master them. You cannot learn to master a process without practising it again and again. Feedback and coaching help one learn.

CONCEPTUAL PROCESSES

1. *Prediction: Making a prediction about the outcome of actions*
   Experiential learning about every day behaviour in its most common form – it includes learning about how to travel or eat or get a date, for example. In its complex form it is how one learns to be a battlefield commander or a horse race handicapper. One learns through experience by trial and error. The cognitive issue is building up a large case base and indexing that case base according to expectation failures as I described in *Dynamic Memory*.[1] We learn when predictions fail.

2. *Modelling: Building a conscious model of a process*
   We need to learn how things work. A citizen knows, presumably, how voting works. Someone looking for venture capital should know how fund raising works. Processes need to be learned in order to effectively participate in them and in order to propose changes in them. Building a conscious model of a process matters a great deal if you want to make the process work for you.

3. *Experimentation: Experimentation and re-planning based on success and failure*
   This is probably the most important learning process we engage in while living our lives. We make life decisions and we need to know when we need to change something. There are big decisions – like

getting married or how to raise a child or whether to change jobs – and little decisions such as changing your diet or your sleep habits. We make our decisions on the basis of what has worked before and what has failed to work. We tend to make life decisions without much knowledge. We don't know all that well how our bodies work and we don't really know how the world works or what it has in store for us. Thinking about these issues and learning from failure is a pressing need all through life. Learning to analyse what has worked out and what has not and why is part of living a rational life.

4. *Evaluation: Improving our ability to determine the value of something on many different dimensions*
There are no rights and wrongs in what we like. But there is general agreement about what makes a work of art great. The factors to be considered are not necessarily conscious, although for experts they typically are. In these more subjective and subconscious areas of life, it is more a matter of trying to understand what feels right than understanding why it feels right. There is a difference between being someone who can make an artistic judgement and being an art expert. One might learn to notice things that one had failed to notice, if someone takes the time to point them out. Learning to make artistic judgements is about learning to notice, to describe, and to appreciate.

We need to learn to make value-based judgements. Doing this requires understanding what our values are. Confronting a person with their own value system (one that they have unconsciously adopted) can help them think things out, but change is never easy.

ANALYTIC PROCESSES

1. *Diagnosis: Making a diagnosis of a complex situation by identifying relevant factors and seeking causal explanations*
Diagnosis is a very important skill and one that needs to be learned both in principle and separately for each domain of knowledge. Diagnosis of heart disease isn't a different process in principle from diagnosis of a faulty spark plug in a car engine. Nevertheless one wants a specialist to do the diagnosis in each case. Why is this? Diagnosis is both a matter of reasoning from evidence and understanding what to look for to gather evidence. Given all the evidence, it is easy to make a diagnosis in an area of knowledge you don't know very well. So,

the gathering of the evidence is the most important part. Crime analysts and gardeners all do diagnosis. They all reason from evidence. What separates them is knowing what constitutes important evidence and what does not. Here again this comes from experienced cases.

We learn to do diagnosis and to understand what causes what consciously. This is knowledge that can be taught to us by experts, but it needs to be taught as part of the process of diagnosis. To learn diagnosis one must practise more and more complex cases in one area of knowledge.

2. *Planning: Learning to plan; needs analysis; conscious and subconscious understanding of what goals are satisfied by what plans; use of conscious case based planning*
People plan constantly. Often their plans aren't very complicated. Let's have lunch is a plan after all. Sometimes they make much more complex plans. A football coach makes plans to fool the defence. They are called plays. A general makes battlefield plans. A businessman writes business plans. An architect draws up architectural plans. All these more complex plans have a lot in common with the let's have lunch plan. Namely, they have been used before or something quite similar has been used before. People rarely make plans from scratch. When they do, they find the process very difficult and often make many errors.

Learning to plan therefore has two components: being able to create a plan from scratch (which almost never actually happens) and being able to modify an existing plan for new purposes. The first one is important to learn how to do, but it is the latter ability that makes one proficient at planning. Planning from first principles is actually quite difficult. Normally people just modify an old plan. Acquiring a case base of plans is critical.

3. *Causation: Detecting what has caused a sequence of events to occur by relying upon a case base of previous knowledge of similar situations (case based reasoning)*
All fields of knowledge study causation; biology, physics, history, economics – they are all about what causes what. The fact that this is an object of study by academics tells us right away that it is not easy and no one knows for sure all of the causes and effects that there are in the world.

Because of this, acquiring a set of known causes and effects tends to make one an expert. A plumber knows what causes sinks to stop up and knows where to look for the culprit. A mechanic knows what causes gas lines to leak and knows where to look. A detective knows what causes people to kill and knows where to start when solving a murder case. Causal knowledge is knowledge fixed to a domain of inquiry.

4. *Judgement: Making an objective judgement*

There are two forms of this, both involving decisions based upon data. The first is deciding if you prefer Baskin Robbins or Ben and Jerry's. There is no right answer. We make judgements and then record them for use later. We find ways to express our judgements. (Ben and Jerry's is too sweet, for example.) We learn what we like by trying things out.

The second form is reasoning based on evidence. A jury does this but it doesn't learn much from it. Judges however learn in this way, as do psychiatrists and business people. They collect evidence, they form a judgement and later they may get to see if their judgement is correct. When asked they can tell you clear reasons (typically post hoc justifications) as to why they decided the way they did.

SOCIAL PROCESSES

1. *Influence: Understanding how others respond to your requests and recognizing consciously and unconsciously how to improve the process*

Human interaction is one of the most important skills of all. We regularly interact with family, friends, colleagues, bosses, romantic interests, professors, service personnel and strangers. Communicating effectively is very important to any success we might want to have in any area of life. But, we do not know why we say what we say, nor do we really understand how we are perceived by others. We just talk and listen and go on our way. Some people are loved by everyone and others are despised.

How do we learn to become conscious of inherently unconscious behaviour? One can learn to behave differently if one becomes consciously aware of the mistakes one is making. Watching others, watching oneself, thinking about how to improve; all this helps one make subconscious behaviour into conscious behaviour.

2. *Teamwork: Learning how to achieve goals by using a team, consciously allocating roles, managing inputs from others, coordinating actors, and handling conflicts*

It is the rare individual who works all alone. Most people need to work with others. Children are not naturally good at this and are taught to 'share.' Then

they sometimes do what is called 'parallel play' where they play near each other doing different things. Getting kids to cooperate to do something together is not easy. Usually one wants to dominate the other. There is nothing wrong with this per se. People are who they are and they need to assume roles in any team that are consistent with their personalities. People learn to work in teams by working in teams and receiving helpful advice when a team is dysfunctional.

3. *Negotiation: Making a deal; negotiation/contracts*

Contracts, formal and informal, are the basis of how we function. We reach agreements in business, in marriage, in friendship, in a store, and at school. Parties to those agreements have the right to complain if obligations are not met. Learning to make a contract, legal or not, is a big part of being a rational actor. To make a contract one must negotiate it. Negotiation is often seen as something only politicians and high-powered business leaders do. But, actually, we negotiate with waitresses for good service and we negotiate with our children when we give them an allowance. Learning how to negotiate can only be done by trying and learning from failures.

4. *Describing: Creating and using conscious descriptions of situations to identify faults to be fixed*

When problems exist in any situation we need to be able to describe and analyse those problems. We need to be able to describe them in order to get help from people who may know more about the situation than we do. We need to learn to focus on the critical issues. In order to do this we need also to be able to analyse these situations to see what was supposed to happen and why it isn't happening. Learning to create a careful description of a situation is a skill that can only be learned through practice.

All the cognitive processes require constant practice. Getting better at them throughout one's life is very important. I define learning as improvement in one's cognitive processes. Lifetime learning does not mean the continual acquisition of knowledge so much as it means the improvement in one's ability to do these processes by means of the acquisition and analysis of experiences to draw upon. Will universities ever transform themselves along these lines? Harvard and Yale, Oxford and Cambridge, and similar top-ranked schools feel no need to change. But there are thousands of universities all of whom have adopted the scholarship-driven, subject-based model given to us by the best universities. The advent of line education will change all this. Not right away of course. The current model is too entrenched and on line education typically just replicates the existing model. But new paradigms,[2] based on learning by doing and simulated experience are beginning to emerge. These models rely heavily on students working out situations for themselves and having to actually think hard in order to accomplish what is being asked of them. One doesn't teach thinking explicitly. There should be no courses in prediction or evaluation. Every project students work on must involve each of the twelve cognitive processes. Project-driven education will eventually drive out subject-driven education because it provides what students really want, namely real-world skills they can practise and then use in real life.

NOTES

1 Roger C. Schank, *Dynamic Memory*. Originally published by Cambridge University Press in 1982, revised edition 1999.
2 See for example the Masters programmes at Carnegie Mellon University's Silicon Valley Campus or the new experiential MBA at La Salle BES in Barcelona.

On the Road IV.1
Innovative teaching for sustainable development – approaches and trends

Clemens Mader and
Marlene Mader

New challenges require innovative methodologies. People around the globe are facing challenges in the fields of climate change, poverty, economic crises and many more in social, environmental and economic fields. What actually we have to understand is that many of those challenges are strongly interrelated and it is within the responsibility of higher education institutions (HEIs) to do research on innovative solutions and to prepare future decision makers (students) in a way they can face those challenges and act responsibly and sustainably in their life and future career.

The UN Decade of Education for Sustainable Development is calling in its mission for new approaches of teaching and learning. HEIs are tackling the challenge facing traditional learning environments within their institutions. Therefore lecturers face a new field for the testing and research of innovative methodologies for teaching and learning method-

ologies. Innovative trends in HE teaching methodologies are taking place in the following fields and will be exemplarily described (see Figure 1).

- **What:** Education for sustainable development does not only mean to learn about definitions of sustainable development, it also incorporates to educate and support students to understand aspects of how to manage complex challenges facing interdisciplinarity and the unpredictability of sustainable development. Creativity and innovation management are crucial aspects in learning to 'think outside the box' in holistic systems. Working and living in societies with strong global interrelations of cultural migration, trade, politics and often friendships, requires social competences that have changed tremendously during the past decades. Facing today's social, environmental or economic challenges such as poverty, natural hazards,

economic crisis and so on, system borders are global. Therefore today's and future decision makers need to understand and tackle diverse cultural and personal values.

- **How:** To make students understand such complex interrelations of disciplines, cultures, values and so on, innovative ways of teaching have been tested and developed during the past years. Of course not only is theory being communicated but the aspect of testing in interactive sessions becomes more and more important. Students learn by doing in interdisciplinary case study-oriented sessions. Learning to do and interact with other disciplines and cultures helps to understand others' values and prepares students for later professional environments. Transdisciplinary teaching and research take up challenges brought up by society and contribute to a mutual learning effect by the strong involvement of societal

What?	How?	Where?	Who?
• Managing complexity of interdisciplinary and unpredictability • Creativity and innovation • Social competences • Sustainable development	• Interactive • Multidisciplinary • Interdisciplinary • Transdisciplinary • Case study-oriented learning • Intergenerational • Intercultural • E-learning	• Higher education curricular programmes • Lifelong learning programmes • Formal and informal systems	• Teachers and researchers • Students • Social actors

FIGURE 1 Characteristics of innovative higher education methodologies for sustainable development

actors. Hereby students come into direct contact with society and work on real-life cases to improve their social competences. Transdisciplinary methods also provide an ideal playground for intergenerational learning where elderly or younger generations may directly interact with students in order to work together on learning tasks. E-learning supports not only learning from home but learning without geographical barriers in particular. In international e-learning courses students get the opportunity for intercultural communication. As sustainability is an intergenerational concept concerning today's and future generations such learning environments may play a more and more important role in higher education.

- **Where:** Aspects already mentioned lead us to the assumption that higher education for sustainable development may not only take place within the confines of higher education curricula programmes: barriers to lifelong learning programmes may blur and new educational environments appear (see case described later). Opening and stepping out of the 'ivory tower' consequently also engenders more society-oriented research and education that leads to the active involvement of societal actors into educational and research programmes. Offering lifelong learning programmes for 'non-traditional' learning groups such as non-academics is just one example of contributing to a learning society. Therefore barriers between formal and informal education also blur. As a result, universities may also become part of 'learning regions' contributing to sustainable regional development, especially in peripheral areas where, because of the lack of opportunities open to them, young people migrate to urban areas. By contributing to the development of the knowledge economy also in peripheral areas, young academics may also get the opportunity to move back to their home regions.
- **Who:** New higher education teaching paradigms not only incorporate a one way learning path from teacher to student but, in interactive sessions, contribute to the exchange of knowledge between teachers and students and, if involved, also societal actors.

Consequently HEIs and lecturers have the opportunity to screen their educational programmes for opportunities to incorporate innovative teaching methodologies for sustainable development. Many HEIs in Europe and internationally have already initiated similar programmes during the past years and decade. Some examples are worth mentioning here.

Also presented at GUNi conference 2010, the intergenerational course for 'Methods for sustainable regional processes' has been held for the past four years at the University of Graz. This blocked seminar with approximately 30 participants invites one half students from the university and the other half elderly people from the region. Participants are partly retired or work in any field of job. Coming together with students, they exchange interactively and learn in workshops how to develop regional sustainability processes, where they need to interact with people from various disciplines, professions and ages. The exchange, taking place during the seminar, is of great value not only for the students, and elderly people but also for the 'lecturer' moderating the sessions, who provides short inputs on methodologies and theoretical backgrounds but then becomes part of the group, learning from both the experience of the elderly and the creativity of the students. Cases come from participants, the region or internationally. Learning outcomes are methods for system analysis, process development and interdisciplinary communication.

Another case, especially relevant for intercultural and interdisciplinary case study-oriented learning, is that of the 'European Virtual Seminar' (EVS). The aim of EVS is to foster an international, multidisciplinary dialogue on sustainable development among students from all over Europe by using modern ICT and the internet. Students build groups of different disciplines and work on common topics with a common aim. The learning format, coordinated by Open Universiteit Nederland in cooperation with 13 partner universities across Europe, is based on the following key components:

- a learning community of students (and staff) of different nationalities and from different cultural and disciplinary backgrounds
- a learning process that supports collabo-

ration between geographically distributed students

- a learning content that consists of authentic, current scientific or societal problems
- a learning technology based on modern ICT and the internet that facilitates collaboration, communication and interaction between students (and staff)

Those two cases demonstrate only two of many opportunities to transform higher education towards sustainable development. In 2011, UNESCO published its UN DESD report *Education for Sustainable Development – An Expert Review of Processes and Learning* authored by Daniella Tilbury. In this report Professor Tilbury identifies key processes that underpin education for sustainable development. These include 'processes which innovate curriculum as well as teaching and learning experiences as well as processes of active and participatory learning' (Tilbury, 2011, p. 104). Cases concerning identified characteristics of innovative higher education methodologies therefore contribute to education for sustainable development and will receive more and more importance when planning new curricula, designing course syllabuses or just thinking out of the box when modernizing traditional courses and universities.

Social, economic and environmental challenges caused by humankind's egocentric and/or profit-oriented decisions are driven by educational systems neglecting their responsibility to sustainable development. This universal understanding of irresponsibility needs to be changed fundamentally, by adopting all educational programmes following education for sustainable development principles.

REFERENCE

Tilbury, D. (2011) UNESCO Report on *Education for Sustainable Development – An expert review on processes and learning*, Paris: UNESCO.

WEB ADDRESSES

www.rce-graz.at (accessed March 2011), Regional Centre of Expertise on Education for Sustainable Development Graz-Styria, University of Graz.

www.ou.nl/evs (access 04/2011), European Virtual Seminar for Sustainable Development, Open Unversiteit Nederland.

On the Road IV.2
Collaborative curriculum innovation as a key to sprouting transformative higher education for sustainability

Lisa Schwarzin, Arjen E.J. Wals and Irena Ateljevic

THE 'END' OF PUBLIC EDUCATION

Around the world we are witnessing a shift in public education in general and higher education in particular. This shift is, at least in part, the result of hegemonic neo-liberalistic thought, which not only dominates the world of commerce but has, during the past two decades or so, forcefully entered the world of the public good (for example education, health-care, pensions, elderly care, nature conservation, environmental protection). Privatization, commercialization, and a strong belief in the power of market mechanisms and competition are some characteristics of this type of thinking. Many economists, and indeed politicians and legislators, believe these features of neo-liberalism to be essential drivers of innovation and improved efficiency. Without the latter, they suggest, companies and (formerly) public institutions simply cannot survive in a rapidly globalizing economy. In order for countries (that is, their economies) to remain viable and vital, the 'workforce' needs to be flexible and adaptable, making lifelong learning a necessity, as jobs can change or disappear overnight. At the same time, 'consumers' need not be afraid to spend, even if such spending requires taking out loans or absorbing debt, and their expenditure is fuelled by instant exposure to products (preferably ones that break down quickly or become out of fashion or outdated within a few months or a year at the most).

This shift, which we deliberately caricature, has several implications for the public education system. First, the end of public education is more and more framed in terms of preparing students for work, often under the disguise of 'lifelong learning'. The Lisbon Declaration illustrates this, as it makes a plea for higher education institutes to respond to the emerging 'knowledge economy' by stimulating lifelong learning and linking formal education to work-based learning (European University Association, 2007). One could argue that the original purpose of public education was to prepare students for life rather than for work; after all the term 'education' comes from the Latin word *educare*, which means 'to lead into' life. Just like the role of citizens is today

framed narrowly as one of consumer, the role of education is narrowly framed as serving the economy or, put differently, singly serving the P for Profit in the triple bottom line of People, Planet, Profit.

Second, the world of business has entered the world of public education, sometimes in subtle ways. Neo-liberalistic thinking has led to a rise of so-called 'marketed solutions' to educational problems, bolstering corporate agenda under the guise of disinterested scientific knowledge, benevolent technology and innocent entertainment (Goodman and Saltman, 2002). 'While your local high school hasn't yet been bought out by McDonald's, many educators already use teaching aids and packets of materials, "donated" by companies, that are crammed with industry propaganda designed to instil product awareness among young consumers' (Ross 2000, p. 12, cited in Jickling and Wals, 2008).

We are also witnessing an exponential growth of private education both in Western and, increasingly, in non-Western contexts. Private schools and universities are popping up everywhere, creating pockets of excellence for those who can afford it and who consider public education inadequate or mediocre at best. A common response by ministries of education has been to reward public schools that do well and to punish those who do not, mandating some kind of national testing scheme. These kinds of management tools have in some cases led to improvement of public schools, but they can also be criticized for homogenizing the educational landscape (Goodman and Saltman, 2002) and creating a 'culture of accountability' rather than a 'culture of learning'. Oftentimes teachers find themselves 'teaching to the test', at the expense of investing in learning domains that are not captured by standardized tests. Schools now pride themselves on how they rank in terms of their average test performance, and universities compete worldwide to score as high as possible on rankings like the Academic Rankings of World Universities (ARWU) and the *Times Higher Ed*. As a result they singly focus on the criteria used by these

rankings (for example number of Nobel Prize winners, number of citations, number of journal articles in ISI-journals, percentage of international students and staff, and so on).

These consequences of the wave of neo-liberalism rolling over the public education landscape have major implications for teaching and learning, and dramatically limit the potential of education to respond to the major challenge of our time, which is not to sustain continuous economic growth but to sustain life, including human life, on this planet. In this paper, we argue that in order to reinvigorate (public) education with a heartfelt commitment to learning for change, we need to create social learning networks in educational institutions that involve both teachers and students and that work towards educational change from the personal to the institutional level. We will first consider theoretical insights on integrating sustainability into the higher education curriculum, and then move on to report on an initiative we have been involved with at Wageningen University, which has developed a framework for transformative sustainability education that is currently being translated to the design of a BSc minor programme. Going beyond describing the outcomes of this working group, we also adopt a process-oriented perspective to conceptualize the initiative as a social learning network, and to draw lessons from reflecting on our joint endeavours.

SUSTAINABILITY AND HIGHER EDUCATION

At the beginning of the 21st century, humanity is facing a range of momentous challenges. The doom and gloom of climate catastrophes, shortage of resources, economic exploitation, financial instability, poverty, religious and civil wars, and so on calls for people who are able to deal with pressing issues in which both stakes and uncertainty are high (Funtowicz and Ravetz, 2003).

Education that prepares for work carries instrumental connotation; we might say that it breeds compliance, fostering the learner's ability to fit into the system, unquestioningly. The very institutions of education can turn inquisitive, curious, creative children into result-driven, unimaginative, extrinsically motivated adolescents who see higher education as nothing but a means to receiving the necessary documentation to be granted access to the 'professional' world. On the contrary, by promoting an emancipatory approach to education for life, we echo Haigh's call for (higher) education that promotes planetary citizenship (2008); a form of democratic participation characterized by a heartfelt responsibility to 'act as though the future mattered' (Devall, 1988).

This call is also reflected in policy initiatives like the UN Decade of Education for Sustainable Development, for which UNESCO has been designated the lead agency in promotion and implementation and which encourages the development of curriculum that enhances value-based learning and critical thinking and fosters changes in thinking patterns and behaviours (UNESCO-DESD, 2009). Essentially then, sustainability education needs to depart from an emancipatory standpoint that intends to trigger a transformation in which learners integrate new information, perspectives and practices into their own worldview, and thereby cause shifts in deeply rooted frames of reference (King, 2004). Moreover, as sustainable development is increasingly seen as an emerging property of collaborative learning, the creation of a more sustainable world above all requires learning that leads to co-created, creative solutions, co-owned by more reflexive citizens, living in a more reflexive and resilient society.

Learning for change therefore means to engage in discourse and activities that challenge students on cognitive, attitudinal, emotional, interactive, and practical levels in a context of multiple perspectives and practices. While this might result in confrontation between perspectives and worldviews, discipline-based outlooks and academic cultures (Godemann, 2008), as well as between different types of knowledge (Lawrence and Després, 2004), educators should not impose values or pressure for consensus among learners from different backgrounds (cf. Osberg and Biesta, 2008). Indeed, a focus on consensus would disrespect the diversity of learners and contexts. Instead, contested perceptions need to be exposed and studied to promote

understanding of how differences in views and practices can be utilized for constructive interaction and promising pathways to solutions.

Over the past decades, several forms of education have emerged that foster capacities and qualities necessary for individuals, groups and communities to start walking the talk of sustainability (that is, to match words with action). Transdisciplinary learning, transformative learning, anticipatory learning, and collaborative learning – just to name a few – all show a high family resemblance in that they:

- Consider learning as more than merely knowledge-based
- Focus on existentially relevant or 'real' issues essential for engaging learners
- Maintain as crucial the quality of interaction with others, and of the environment in which learning takes place
- View learning as inevitably transdisciplinary and even 'transperspectival' in that it cannot be captured by a single discipline or by any single perspective
- Regard indeterminacy as a central feature of the learning process, in that it cannot be known ahead of time exactly what will be learnt, and that learning goals are likely to shift as learning progresses
- Consider learning as cross-boundary in nature, in that it cannot be confined to the dominant structures and spaces that have shaped education for centuries

This list shows that learning in the context of sustainability requires 'hybridity' and synergy between multiple actors in society, and the blurring of formal, non-formal and informal education. In other words, learning for change needs to bring together a wide range of societal actors with different interests, perspectives and values but with similar challenges, so that they can participate in processes of social learning.

Social learning in the context of sustainable development builds upon several of its predecessors, like action research and community problem-solving (Wals et al., 1990; Wals, 1994), grassroots learning, collaborative learning, and experiential learning, but it sees the cultivation and utilization of pluralism as essential for the emergence of transformative disruptions. Educational psychologists for long have

argued and shown that learning requires some form of (internal) dissonance (Berlyne, 1965; Festinger, 1957; Piaget, 1964), and exposure to alternative ways of seeing, framing and interpreting can be a powerful way of creating such 'conflict'. Admittedly, excessive dissonance may trigger a defensive response of holding even more tightly to established perspectives. However, dissonance can, when introduced carefully and dealt with in a proactive and reflective manner, lead to what Martin Scheffer calls a tipping point (2009) in one's thinking, in which learners reconsider their views and adopt or co-create new ways of looking at a particular issue. Such tipping points appear necessary in order to generate new thinking that can unfreeze minds, and break with existing routines and systems – a key assumption being that pluralism and heterogeneity offer more promise in finding creative solutions to the stubborn issues of our times, than 'singularism' and homogeneity (see also Page, 2007).

A process that seems central to making sense of pluralism and dissonance is that of *Gestaltswitching* (Wals and Blewitt, 2010). *Gestalswitching* is derived from the German concept of *Gestalt* or 'mindset' and the related *Gestaltungskompetenz* which some use to articulate the kinds of qualities, competences and attributes learners need to develop when engaging in sustainability issues (Barth et al., 2007). Gestaltswitching then refers to the switching back and forth between different mindsets. In the context of sustainability there is a multitude of 'Gestalts' in play, four of which are identified in Figure 1: the temporal Gestalt (past, present, future and intergenerational mindsets), the disciplinary Gestalt (a range of social science and natural science mindsets), the spatial Gestalt (local, regional, global and beyond global mindsets) and the cultural Gestalt (multiple cultural mindsets whereby culture is broadly understood).

It can be argued that a 'trans-human' Gestalt still needs to be added, which suggests we also need to be able to imagine the world from the perspective of the more than human world, allowing ecocentric and biocentric mindsets to enter our thinking and acting. Transformative social learning towards sustainability hence needs to cultivate the competence of switching back and forth

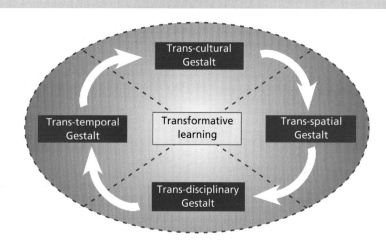

FIGURE 1 Four key Gestalts at play for transformative learning towards sustainability

between various Gestalts, mindsets or lenses, and integrating them in responses to sustainability challenges.

This switching and 'mirroring' or 'relating to' different perspectives requires empathy, or a willingness to open up to and sympathize with 'otherness', as well as the ability to cope with uncertainty. This is a major challenge for higher education, as many scientists consider minimizing uncertainty and maximizing predictability one of their key quests. Instead, in the context of sustainability, it might be more fruitful to put our energy towards *living with* uncertainty, and developing a 'precautionary reflexivity' that can steer us clear of the inaction, paralysis and apathy that come with the prevailing 'wait and see' attitude, which suggests that as long as there is disagreement among scientists and policymakers about what is happening to the planet, we have no reason to break with business as usual. In their edited volume on education and climate change, Kagawa and Selby write: 'As a fundamental contribution to climate change [prevention and adaptation], it seems that educational spaces should build a culture of learning awash with uncertainty and in which uncertainty provokes transformative yet precautionary commitment rather than paralysis' (Kagawa and Selby, 2010, p. 243).

How then can we create emancipatory learning environments that promote these competences of Gestaltswitching, and proactive engagement with dissonance, pluralism and

uncertainty? In our work with the Initiative for Transformative Sustainability Education (ITSE) at Wageningen University we try to actively engage with this question. Please refer to On the Road IV.10, where you find a concise description of ITSE's efforts to create a transformative educational programme in sustainability.

SOCIAL LEARNING FOR EDUCATORS

Here, however, we would like to draw your attention to the central role of educators in facilitating learning for change. Oftentimes they have themselves experienced many years of receiving and distributing passive and outcome-oriented education; so in order to design and facilitate emancipatory processes of learning, educators need first to transcend the prevailing instrumental education practices.

After some time of being engaged in ITSE, it dawned on us that we were actually engaged in a process of social learning that was transforming our take on education. Let us illustrate this by comparing the process of establishing and collaborating in our working group with what Harold Glasser (2007) defines as the key characteristics of social learning:

- the value of difference and diversity in energizing people, introducing dissonance and unleashing creativity
- the importance of both reflection (becoming aware of how one experiences something and being able to articulate this) and reflexivity (gaining awareness of how

actions are embedded in certain values, structures, and patterns)
- the power of social cohesion and social capital in creating change in complex situations loaded with uncertainty
- the power of collaborative action that strengthens the (unique) qualities of each individual

The ITSE initiative was brought into life when an inspired MSc student invited teachers and students to a talk about how education could contribute more 'holistically' to fostering sustainability. The people who gathered represented several of the university's departments and study programmes, including environmental sciences (biology, alternative energy), life sciences (animal and plant sciences, health sciences), social sciences (environmental education, communication, organizational psychology), applied philosophy, and interdisciplinary subjects (sustainable development, international development, human geography).

Initially, this diversity across boundaries of discipline, experience and age caused a considerable amount of misunderstanding and confusion – for instance regarding what sustainability actually is, and what students need to learn to contribute to it. However, through reflexive and open engagement with each other, we were able to suspend our initial feelings of dissonance, learn from each other's perspectives, and create a shared vision on what we came to call 'transformative sustainability education'. Admittedly, the group has since reduced in size somewhat, which might have been partly due to an inability or unwillingness of some to challenge existing assumptions and attitudes. Nevertheless, once we had gained a meta-level understanding of our perspectives, we were able to jointly shape the framework presented here, and then translate it into programme design through a number of workshops in which we defined elements, principles, and tools for transformative sustainability education. Of course this was not always a smooth process, and we experienced a whole range of challenges throughout, for instance when negotiating university course development restrictions. However, facing challenges together also led to growing cohesion and a more amicable atmosphere in our working group, which slowly turned into a community of learners, as we developed ways to draw upon and learn from each other's diverse skills and expertise.

LESSONS LEARNED

While writing this paper, we reflected upon the process of establishing ITSE and collaboratively innovating sustainability curriculum. We would like to share some key lessons that emerged from these reflections, and which might serve to support other initiatives for learning for change.

START WALKING THE TALK

Working together has made us realize that to promote learning for change we need to start in our home institutions. It is interesting that as scholars, what we publish and present internationally on prestigious platforms is rewarded, not the work we do locally, in our own institutions. The increasing neo-liberalization and commodification of academia and higher education creates major barriers to participating in local committees, think-groups, and initiatives to improve our own teaching and learning environment. However, if we want to truly start walking our talk, we need to develop strategies that allow us to make contributions where we can have a sustained impact.

BUILD A SOCIAL LEARNING NETWORK

For some of us, the experience of joining ITSE felt like 'coming home'. We believe that there is a growing body of concerned and dedicated students and faculty who feel that higher education has to break with existing routine practices of teaching, learning and research that tend to lack an integrated perspective. Admittedly, in our group there are differences with respect to the amount of uncertainty we can handle, regarding the belief in science and technology, with respect to the value of intuition and spirituality in moving towards a more sustainable world, and concerning what we see as 'sustainable' and 'transdisciplinary'. But these differences are mostly generative: they sharpen our thinking, they make us become aware of our own assumptions and they heighten our awareness of other ways of 'seeing' and 'being'.

It follows that we need to (re)conceptualize ourselves as learners as well as educators.

Challenging ourselves to develop a constructive meta-awareness of our different perspectives and approaches required becoming more reflexive about our own teaching practices and routines, and co-creating new ways of approaching education. Support structures for academics to become better educators are far from abundant. However, we can use the power of our own agency to create the support we need: it might start with getting a group of likeminded people together for a chat.

INVOLVE STUDENTS

Students are one essential 'resource' for making initiatives in higher education work. Without students driving the effort and playing a key role in maintaining momentum, ITSE would have experienced an early death. Of equal importance are the enriching insights students can provide for linking educational design to learner experience, a topic that is easily overlooked from the 'front stage' perspective of teachers. The students involved in ITSE have become leaders in developing sustainability competence at their institution, and it is in student empowerment that universities can have an impact far beyond publications in high impact factor journals.

DREAM BIG AND STAY WITH THE PROCESS

One challenge for ITSE has been to shift gears between scopes of vision. Our initial 'big dream' was to make sustainability and transformative learning the grounding principles of all educational programmes at our university. Obviously, we needed to break this vision down into achievable steps, of which the framework is the first, and the minor the second. In such stepwise implementation, it is however important to keep the 'big dream' alive, and reflect regularly whether current actions are still working towards the larger vision. It is important to stay with the process, especially when challenges appear. In ITSE, while striving to adopt more integrative ways of thinking and acting, we need to continuously remain aware of our habitual tendency to revert back to 'mono-disciplinary' perspectives. We need to accept that roadblocks are part of the journey, and, rather than despair, approach them with reflexive enthusiasm.

REFERENCES

Barth, M., Godemann, J., Rieckmann, M. and Stoltenberg, U. (2007) Developing key competencies for sustainable development in higher education. *International Journal of Sustainability in Higher Education*, 8(4), pp. 416–30.

Berlyne, D.E. (1965) Curiosity and education. In: Krumbolts, J.D. (ed.) *Learning and the Educational Process*. Chicago: Rand McNally & Co.

Cranton, P. (2008) The resilience of soul. In: Leonard, T. and Willis, P. (eds) *Pedagogies of the Imagination: Mythopoetic Curriculum in Educational Practice*. New York, USA: Springer, pp. 125–36.

Devall, B. (1988) *Simple in Means, Rich in Ends*. London, UK: Green Print (Merlin).

European University Association (2007) *The Lisbon Declaration: Europe's Universities beyond 2010: Diversity with a Common Purpose*. Available: http://www.eua.be/fileadmin/user_upload/files/newsletter/Lisbon_declaration.pdf

Festinger, L. (1957) *A Theory of Cognitive Dissonance*. New York: Harper & Row.

Funtowicz, S. and Ravetz, J. (2003) *Post-Normal Science*. International Society for Ecological Economics. Internet Encyclopaedia of Ecological Economics: http://www.ecoeco.org.publica/encyc.htm.

Glasser, H. (2007) Minding the gap: The role of social learning in linking our stated desire for a more sustainable world to our everyday actions and policies. In: Wals, A.E.J. (ed.) *Social Learning towards a Sustainable World*. Wageningen, the Netherlands: Wageningen Academic Publishers, pp. 35–62.

Godemann, J. (2008) Knowledge integration: A key challenge for transdisciplinary cooperation. *Environmental Education Research*, 14(6), pp. 625–41.

Goodman, R.T. and Saltman, K.J. (2002) *Strange Love or How We Learn to Stop Worrying and Love the Market*. Oxford, UK: Rowan and Littlefield.

Haigh, M. (2008) Internationalisation, Planetary Citizenship and Higher Education Inc. *Compare*, 38(4), pp. 427–40.

Jickling, B. and Wals, A.E.J. (2008) Globalization and environmental education: Looking beyond sustainable development. *Journal of Curriculum Studies*, 40(1), pp. 1–21.

Kagawa, F. and Selby, D. (eds) (2010) *Education and Climate Change. Living and*

Learning in Interesting Times. London, UK: Routledge.

King, K.P. (2004) Both sides now: examining transformative learning and professional development of educators. *Innovative Higher Education*, **29**(2), pp. 155–74.

Lawrence, R.J. and Després, C. (2004) Futures of transdisciplinarity. *Futures*, **36**(4), pp. 397–406.

Osberg, D. and Biesta, G. (2008) The emergent curriculum: navigating a complex course between unguided learning and planned enculturation. *Journal of Curriculum Studies*, **40**(3), pp. 313–28.

Page, S. (2007) *The Difference: How the Power of Diversity Creates Better Groups, Firms, Schools and Societies*. Princeton, NJ: Princeton University Press.

Piaget, J. (1964) Development and learning. *Journal of Research in Science Teaching*, **2**, pp. 176–86.

Scheffer, M. (2009) *Critical Transitions in Nature and Society*. Princeton, NJ: Princeton University Press.

UNESCO-DESD (2009) 'Education' – Homepage of UNESCO Education for Sustainable Development (http://cms01. unesco.org/en/esd/programme/educational-dimensions/).

Wals, A.E.J., Beringer, A.R. and Stapp, W.B. (1990) Education in action: A community problem solving program for schools. *Journal of Environmental Education*, **21**(4), pp. 13–19.

Wals, A.E.J. (1994) Action research and community problem solving: Environmental education in an inner-city. *Educational Action Research*, **2**(2), pp. 163–82.

Wals, A.E.J. and Blewitt, J. (2010) Third wave sustainability in higher education: Some (inter)national trends and developments. In: Jones, P., Selby, D. and Sterling, S. (eds) *Green Infusions: Embedding Sustainability across the Higher Education Curriculum*. London, UK: Earthscan, pp. 55–74.

IV.2 The Role of Knowledge in a New Paradigm

In today's context, there is a need for deeper understanding of the differences between information, knowledge and wisdom. In most classical definitions, information is any kind of event that affects the state of a dynamic system; knowledge is defined as expertise and skills acquired by a person through experience or education; and wisdom is the correct way to apply knowledge. To imagine a different world, then, we need to consider what knowledge needs to be generated for what kind of society.

We also need to understand the relationships between scientific knowledge and other forms of knowledge, and the ways in which ethics and values should be addressed to become an inherent force within higher education's contribution to sustainability. We must conceive a way of uniting and organizing the different types of knowledge. Furthermore, we need to reconsider the value we attribute to different types and sources of knowledge and to move towards a conception of knowledge as human heritage.

The epistemological conflict that underlies the various traditions of knowledge production, dissemination and use has become one of the main causes of the dissociation between the production of knowledge and its application to solving society's problems. A feasible university project should be created to recover the idea of universities as spaces for dialogue and meeting places for different kinds of knowledge, perspectives, interests, cultures and peoples.

IV.2a KNOWLEDGE FOR A NEW PARADIGM: CHALLENGES TO SCIENCE AND TECHNOLOGY

Gilberto C. Gallopín

INTRODUCTION

The prevailing mindset is showing critical inadequacies. It is increasingly recognized as not accidental that in a number of important cases, the very success of classical compartmentalized approaches (in understanding and in action) has led to the aggravation of the environmental and developmental problems addressed. The problématique of sustainable development, in particular, highlights both the need for a new paradigm and the deep epistemological challenges to science and technology (S&T) involved in such a quest.

In this paper, the characteristics of the new situation confronting humankind, the challenges it poses to scientific and technological knowledge and some of their implications for education will be briefly discussed.

THE NEW SITUATION

The world is moving through a period of extraordinary turbulence reflecting the genesis and intensification of deep economic, social, political, and cultural changes. In addition, the speed and magnitude of global change, the increasing connectedness of the social and natural systems at the planetary level, and the growing complexity of societies and of their impacts upon the biosphere, result in a high level of uncertainty and unpredictability, presenting new threats (and also new opportunities) for humankind.

Unfortunately, many of the current trends are seen to be unsustainable environmentally, socially, and economically. Environmentally, the need for a change in direction was officially recognized at the Earth Summit in June 1992; however, the situation continues to deteriorate globally as evidenced in UN reports and other studies. Socially, the Millennium Development Goals (United Nations, 2008), including prominently poverty in its different facets, are not being reached in many regions of the world. Economically, the current global economic crisis is still unfolding and no one can predict what will happen.

The current globalization (economic, cultural, political, and so on) process is interacting with global ecological interdependency, leading to a situation that is unprecedented in the history of human civilization, with consequences very difficult to anticipate (Young et al., 2006).

THE ROLE OF S&T IN THE SUSTAINABILITY TRANSITION

The sustainability (or unsustainability) of development is influenced by a number of fundamental driving forces. Some of these are *proximate*, immediate causal processes directly impinging upon society and the environment, but behind them lie the deeper, *ultimate* drivers that condition human choice by determining the direction taken by the proximate drivers. Knowledge and understanding belong to the latter.

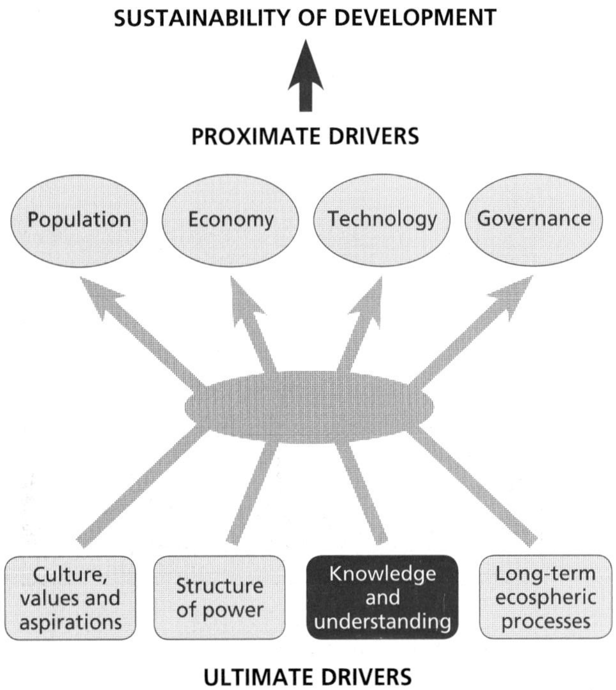

A transition to a development trajectory that is intrinsically equitable and harmonious with the environment requires the implementation of deep changes in the ultimate drivers and not only in the proximate ones. The ultimate drivers of the global system include the foundations of human motivation and social structure (Figure 1). Thus, the role of S&T in the sustainability transition is very important, but there are other, equally or more important, drivers of social and ecological changes.

Knowledge also plays an important role In terms of the actions required to move towards sustainability: the major obstacles to sustainable development being *understanding*, *capacity*, and *willingness* (Gallopín, 2002).

A compartmentalized perception of reality, a scientific tradition and training that is still largely reductionist, and a lack of understanding of the behaviour of complex systems, lead to the first stumbling block; not only lack of knowledge and understanding, but often also the use of inappropriate knowledge. Inadequate institutions, scarcity of financial resources, unskilled human resources, weak infrastructure, plain poverty, and other limitations, contribute to the second obstacle: insufficient capacity to perform the actions and changes needed, affecting notably (but not exclusively) the developing world. Asymmetrical power structures, vested interests, and a conception of humankind emphasizing antagonism, competition and individualism over cooperation and solidarity lie at the heart of the third and arguably major obstacle: lack of political will to implement those changes that are glaringly necessary. The three are required to produce the appropriate actions and changes (Figure 2). This paper focuses on challenges associated with the category of understanding, focusing on its S&T dimensions (albeit recognizing that this is only one of the forms of knowledge humans cultivate).

FIGURE 1 Proximate and ultimate drivers of sustainability of development
Source: Raskin et al., 2002

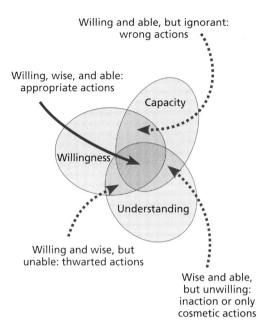

Willing and able, but ignorant: wrong actions

Willing, wise, and able: appropriate actions

Capacity

Willingness

Understanding

Willing and wise, but unable: thwarted actions

Wise and able, but unwilling: inaction or only cosmetic actions

FIGURE 2 The basic conditions for moving towards sustainable development
Source: redrawn from Gallopín, 2002

CHALLENGES POSED BY SUSTAINABLE DEVELOPMENT TO S&T

One major reason for the difficulties encountered by S&T when facing the problématique of sustainable development is that the complexity of situations and problems has been rapidly increasing in recent decades (Gallopín, 1999; Munn et al., 2000; Gallopín et al., 2001). This has occurred in at least three dimensions:

1. *Ontological changes*: human-induced changes in the nature of reality, proceeding at unprecedented rates and scales and also resulting in growing connectedness and interdependence at many levels.
2. *Epistemological changes*: changes in our understanding of the world related to the modern scientific awareness of the behaviour of complex systems, including the realization that unpredictability and surprise may be built into the fabric of reality.
3. *Changes in the nature of decision-making*: a more participatory style of decision-making is gaining space, superseding the technocratic and authoritarian styles. This, together with the widening acceptance of additional criteria such as the environment, human rights, and gender, among others, as well as the emergence of new social factors such as non-governmental organizations and transnational companies, leads to an increase in the number of dimensions used to define issues, problems, and solutions, and hence to higher complexity.

Scientific research about complex, self-aware systems such as those typical of sustainable development problems may have to deal with a compounding of complexity at different levels (Gallopín et al., 2001):

- Physical reality, where the properties of self-organization, irreducible uncertainty, chaos, emergence, and others, come into play (see Figure 3).

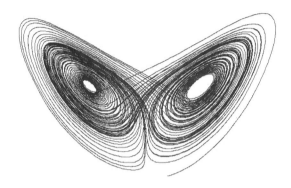

FIGURE 3 The Lorenz attractor, a paradigm of chaotic behaviour (the source of the popular expression 'the butterfly effect')
Source: author's computer simulation

- The need to consider different 'epistemologies' (a plurality of perceptions or viewpoints must be acknowledged and respected, even if not always accepted as equally valid), as symbolized in Figure 4.

FIGURE 4 The fable of the six blind men attempting to describe an elephant, here used as a metaphor for the importance of combining different perceptions
Source: Illustrator unknown; From Martha Adelaide Holton & Charles Madison Curry, 1914, Holton-Curry readers, Rand McNally & Co. (Chicago), p. 108. Available at http://commons.wikimedia.org/wiki/File:Blind_men_and_elephant.png

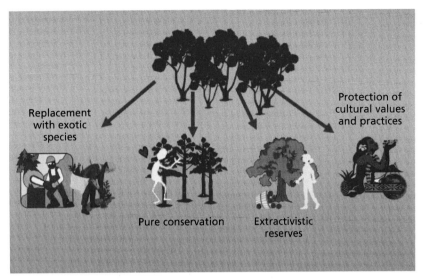

FIGURE 5 Differing goals of social actors
Source: Adapted from a presentation by Roberto Guimaraes

and ecological subsystems (Gallopín, 1991) at different scales, represents the fundamental unit of sustainable development (see Figure 7) and hence the unit of analysis of choice.

INTEGRATED RESEARCH

The fact that the unit of analysis includes both human and natural subsystems means its investigation must be integrative. Integration of scientific research requires a holistic approach (looking at wholes rather than only at their component parts), and an interdisciplinary research style (ICSU, 1999; Kates et al., 2001).

There is a large gap between the rhetoric and the practice of interdisciplinary (not to be confused with multidisciplinary) research. It is not enough to put together a group of researchers from different disciplines

- The need to consider different 'intentionalities' (differing goals) of the involved social actors (Figure 5).

In synthesis, the problématique of sustainable development poses challenges to science of two kinds: those of the first involve challenges to the practice of science (utilization of interdisciplinary teams, inter-institutional – sometimes international-integrated research projects, and so on); the challenges of the second kind are deeper, impinging on the epistemology of science, its methods and fundamental criteria.

This suggests that changes (or at least serious re-examination) of some fundamental aspects of scientific research will be needed in order to improve the capacity of the S&T systems to better contribute to sustainable development. The following, shown in Figure 6, are some of the challenge areas that might be called 'nodal' in the sense that advances made in them would reverberate through many strands of the fabric of scientific knowledge (Gallopín, 2004).

UNIT OF ANALYSIS

Human communities and ecosystems are strongly coupled systems and therefore jointly determined. Besides, they are nonlinear, complex, and self-organizing. A clear implication of this for S&T for sustainable development (S&TSD) is the choice of the appropriate unit of analysis (the basic entity being analysed by a study and for which data are collected in the form of variables). It has been argued (Gallopín et al., 2001) that the socio-ecological system or SES) composed by coupled human

FIGURE 6 Challenges posed to S&T by the problématique of sustainable development
Source: modified from Gallopín, 2004

to work in a project; it is also necessary to establish a true dialogue between the disciplines, an iterative and interactive process of mutual education and learning (Thompson, 1990). Education and training in how to perform interdisciplinary research is often lacking in most education systems; and this is an area in which changes are required.

CRITERIA OF TRUTH

The criteria used to decide what is 'true' or 'valid' need to be re-examined for the adequacy for S&TSD. Occam's Razor ('one should not increase, beyond what is necessary, the number of entities required to explain

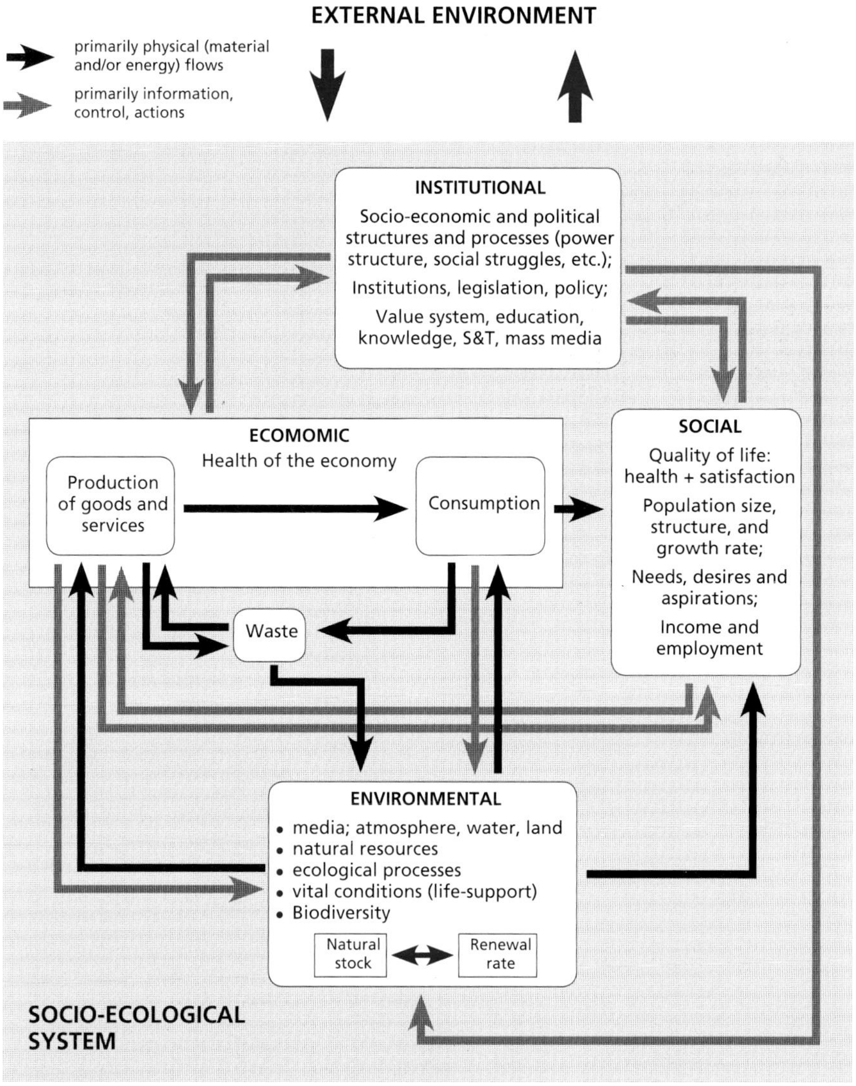

EXTERNAL ENVIRONMENT

primarily physical (material and/or energy) flows

primarily information, control, actions

INSTITUTIONAL

Socio-economic and political structures and processes (power structure, social struggles, etc.);

Institutions, legislation, policy;

Value system, education, knowledge, S&T, mass media

ECOMOMIC
Health of the economy

Production of goods and services

Consumption

Waste

SOCIAL

Quality of life: health + satisfaction

Population size, structure, and growth rate;

Needs, desires and aspirations;

Income and employment

ENVIRONMENTAL
- media; atmosphere, water, land
- natural resources
- ecological processes
- vital conditions (life-support)
- Biodiversity

Natural stock ↔ Renewal rate

SOCIO-ECOLOGICAL SYSTEM

FIGURE 7 A representation of the socio-ecological system.
Source: author's elaboration

quantified, and others (such as cultural processes) may not be quantifiable even in principle. But qualitative factors can be as or more important than quantitative ones in determining the behaviour of the SES.

Two comments are relevant here. First, in a number of cases rigorous (even mathematical) analysis of qualitative factors can be performed (Petschel-Held et al., 2000; Gallopín, 1996; Puccia and Levins, 1987). See also Creswell (2009), and Stake (2010) for examples in the social sciences. Second, even when a rigorous treatment of qualitative factors cannot be performed, they can and should be included (at least in narrative form) in the overall conceptualization of the problem or issue, insofar as they are deemed causally important.

anything') is a good example of a scientific guideline that might be changed in the new complexity context, in line with Einstein's aphorism 'Everything should be made as simple as possible, but not simpler.' Different criteria are evident in the comparison between the analytical and the integrative or systemic approaches in different fields (Holling, 1998; Saner, 1999; De Rosnay, 1975).

INCLUSION OF QUALITATIVE VARIABLES

Too often, especially in the natural sciences, non-quantifiable factors are excluded from consideration, because the methods used cannot incorporate qualitative factors or worse, sometimes non-quantitative information is simply rejected as non-scientific.

However, the dynamics of the SES depends on a large number of complex processes, many of which are not yet

DEALING WITH UNCERTAINTY

S&TSD confronts many sources of uncertainty; some of them are reducible with more data and additional research (that is, those due to random processes, amenable to statistical or probabilistic analysis, or those due to incomplete knowledge, which can be reduced through more data and research). Given the complexity of the SES, those sources of uncertainty can be insurmountable in practice, even if they may not be so in principle. Moreover, fundamental, irreducible uncertainty may arise from non-linear processes (for example chaotic behaviour), in the processes of self-organization (for example Nicolis and Prigogine, 1977) and through the purposeful behaviour of human agency. Furthermore, in complex 'self-aware' (or 'reflexive') systems, which include human and institutional subsystems, another source of 'hard' uncertainty arises; a sort of 'macro Heisenberg uncertainty' effect, where the acts of observation and analysis become part of the activity of the system under study, and so influence it in various ways (Gallopín et al., 2001).

Therefore, the scientific quest for even better understanding and predictive capacity must be complemented by new research and priority-setting strategies that do not merely recognize uncertainty, but even embrace it, becoming part of the process of change as well as probing its transformational possibilities.

ADDRESSING MULTIPLE SCALES
Many complex systems are hierarchic, in the sense that each element of the system is a subsystem of it, and the system itself is a subsystem of a larger order 'supra-system'. Often, there are strong functional couplings between the different levels and therefore the system must be analysed or managed at more the one scale simultaneously. But systems at different scales have different sorts of interactions, and also different characteristic rates of change. Therefore it is impossible to have a unique, correct, all-encompassing perspective on a system at only one system level (Giampietro, 2004). The challenge involves the treatment of cross-scale dynamics, as well as the need to articulate (or at least make compatible) actions at different scales from the local to the global.

ARTICULATION OF KNOWLEDGES
Reaching a useful and usable understanding of SES will require a strong push to advance focused scientific research, including building up classical disciplinary knowledge from the natural and the social sciences, and an even stronger development of interdisciplinary and transdisciplinary research (Schellnhuber and Wenzel, 1998; Kates et al., 2001; ICSU et al., 2002; Gallopín, 1999).

But the challenge goes beyond scientific knowledge itself; many discussions and consultations on the role and nature of S&TSD emphasize the importance of incorporating knowledge generated endogenously in particular places and contexts of the world, including empirical knowledge, knowledge incorporated into technologies, into cultural traditions, and so on. (ICSU et al., 2002).

The participation of other social actors, in addition to S&T professionals, at the different phases of the scientific and technological research process and in related decision-making, can be crucial for ethical, political, pragmatic, and epistemological reasons (ECLAC, 2003).

The need to include other knowledges and perspectives in the S&T enterprise poses important methodological challenges to S&TSD (Gallopín and Vessuri, 2006), as it requires the adoption of criteria of truth and quality that are broader than those accepted today by the S&T community, yet not less solid and rigorous.

SCIENCE-POLICY INTERFACE
For S&TSD to be used effectively in the quest for sustainability, the interface between science and policy needs to be better understood (Gallopín, 1999). An important requirement for an effective dialogue is the realization, by scientists and policymakers, that both communities have much to learn from each other in addressing problems involving sustainable development, and that both are required in the quest for sustainable development. The basis for the dialogue must be the recognition of the real differences in criteria and constraints exhibited by the two communities.

STAKEHOLDER INVOLVEMENT
The possibility of the S&T community to contribute critically to the sustainability transition is connected to its capacity (and willingness) to incorporate the perspectives and concerns of the major stakeholders involved, to ensure the relevance of the orientation of research to collective decision-making.

This requires the involvement of scientists and technologists in processes of consultation and dialogue with the relevant stakeholders. One model has been the Intergovernmental Panel on Climate Change (IPCC), involving sustained bi-directional interactions between the S&T community and the policy community. Also, the joint construction of alternative scenarios of the future (Schwartz, 1991; Gallopín et al., 1997; Cosgrove and Rijsberman, 2000) can be a powerful approach.

CONCLUDING REMARKS

Each of the nine challenges to S&T identified above points to a corresponding need for improvement in educational systems. It is clear that, if taken seriously, the necessary changes would lead to a profound transformation of universities and other educational and training institutions. Today, there are very few learning centres in the world that stimulate interdisciplinary education (in the sense of teaching and experimenting on how to do interdiscipline – not mention the more elusive transdiscipline – as opposed to merely fostering students to work in groups). Fewer still are the universities that study and practise the incorporation of non-scientific knowledges, and science–policy dialogues, or use the integrated SES as a unit of analysis for research and education when dealing with problems associated to sustainable development. The same can be applied to the other challenges to greater or lesser degree.

In a world that is increasingly complex, in rapid process of change, more and more interconnected and interdependent, increasingly unpredictable and uncertain, as is the modern world, the current fragmentation of knowledge has emerged as one of the main obstacles to understanding (Myers, 1984). Paradoxically, often the very success of analytic thinking has contributed to sow the seeds of many of the current problems, to alienate humans from the rest of the universe, and to promote the proliferation of reactive anti-rationalist movements.

The resolution of the complex problems facing humankind in its present stage, requires a transition from a 'structure-oriented' scientific attitude towards a 'processes-oriented' attitude (Jantsch, 1980), from analytic-reductionist to systemic, from fragmented-compartmentalized to holistic, from a vision centred on equilibrium and linear causality towards one focused on change, non-equilibrium systems and nonlinear causal complexes, from the emphasis on the static to the evolutionary processes of self-organization.

In this context, the importance of introducing to education systems elements of a systemic, evolutionary vision, pointing to the understanding (and, better still, to the experience) of the interrelations and coherent totalities is clear.

But even more profound changes are needed, towards integrating the abstract and quantitative knowledge with the understanding and information obtained through the direct, intuitive, sensual and sensory experience of the world. There are other knowledges besides quantitative knowledge, and there are other ways to learn than reading the needle in a dial. These two forms of knowledge are complementary and each one is incomplete by itself. As happened in modern physics with the complementarity wave-particle in the subatomic domain, the approximation to the truth could only be obtained through the broadening of the universe of discourse to include both complementary models of reality, the potential of both brain hemispheres, of the two basic modes of conscience.

This position is solidly argued and developed by Blackburn (1971) in an article in the prestigious journal *Science*. He argued that what is urgently needed is a science able to understand complex systems without, or with a minimum of, abstractions; to 'see' complex systems as a whole requires an act of trained intuition. According to Blackburn, the intuitive knowledge that is essential for a complete understanding of complex systems can be stimulated and trained by:

- the training of scientists to become conscious of the sensorial signs of their surroundings
- insisting in the idea of sensorial knowledge as part of the intellectual structure of science, rather than as a concept added secondarily
- the open approach to complex systems, respecting

their organic complexity before choosing an abstract quantification space where to project them.

He concluded that if we are able to learn to know complexity through the complementary modes of sensorial intuition and logical abstraction, and if we can transmit and describe the first as reliable as we are doing with the latter, then there are hopes for a rebirth of the whole of science comparable to what happened in physics between 1900 and 1930.

But the most formidable challenge is the need for a new *ethics*, different from the presently dominant self-interested, antagonistic and consumeristic one. Its seeds may (or may not) emerge from the current economic, social, and environmental turmoil; but a new ethics would be the ultimate guide for the transition to sustainable development.

REFERENCES

Blackburn, T.R. (1971) Sensuous-intellectual complementarity in science. *Science*, **174**, pp.1001–7.

Cosgrove, W.J. and Rijsberman, F.R. (2000) *World Water Vision: Making Water Everybody's Business*. London, UK: Earthscan Publishing.

Creswell, J.W. (2009) *Research Design: Qualitative, Quantitative, and Mixed Approaches* (3rd edn). London, UK: SAGE.

De Rosnay, J. (1975) *Le Macroscope: Vers Une Vision Globale*. Paris, France: Edition Du Seuil.

ECLAC (2003) Latin American and Caribbean Regional Workshop on Science and Technology for Sustainable Development. *Serie seminarios y conferencias,* No. 25, 5–8 March, 2002. Santiago de Chile, Chile: Economic Commission for Latin America and the Caribbean.

Gallopín, G.C. (1991) Human dimensions of global change: linking the global and the local processes. *International Social Science Journal,* **130**, pp. 707–18.

Gallopín, G.C. (1996) Environmental and sustainability indicators and the concept of situational indicators: A systems approach. *Environmental Modeling and Assessment,* **1**, pp. 101–17.

Gallopín, G.C. (1999) Generating, sharing and utilizing science to improve and integrate policy. *International Journal of Sustainable Development,* **2**(3), pp. 397–410.

Gallopín, G.C. (2002) Planning for resilience: scenarios, surprises, and branch points, pp. 361–92. In: Gunderson, L.H. and Holling, C.S. (eds) *Panarchy. Understanding Transformations in Human and Natural Systems*. Washington, DC, USA: Island Press.

Gallopín, G.C. (2004) What kind of system of science (and technology) is needed to support the quest for sustainable development? Chapter 18, pp. 367–86. In: Schellnhuber, H.J., Crutzen, P.J., Clark, W.C., Claussen, M. and Held, H. (eds) (2004) *Earth Systems Analysis for Sustainability*. Cambridge, USA: M.I.T. Press.

Gallopín, G. and Vessuri, H. (2006) Science for sustainable development: articulating knowledges, pp. 35–51. In: Guimarães Pereira, A., Guedes Vaz, S. and Tognetti, S. (eds) (2006) *Interfaces between Science and Society*. Sheffield, UK: Greenleaf Publishing Ltd.

Gallopín, G.C., Funtowicz, S., O'Connor, M. and Ravetz, J. (2001) Science for the 21st century: from social contract to the scientific core. *International Journal of Social Science*, **168**, pp. 219–29.

Gallopín, G., Hammond, A., Raskin, P. and Swart, R. (1997) *Branch Points: Global Scenarios and Human Choice*. Stockholm, Sweden: Stockholm Environment Institute.

Giampietro, M. (2004) *Multi-scale Integrated Analysis of Agro Ecosystems: An Integrated Assessment*. Boca Raton, USA: CRC Press.

Holling, C.S. (1998) Two cultures of ecology. *Conservation Ecology* (online), **2**(2), p. 4 (http://www.consecol.org/vol2/iss2/art4).

ICSU (International Council of Scientific Unions) (1999) *Special Issue of Science International*. Paris, September 1999. ICSU.

ICSU, ISTS, and TWAS (2002) Science and Technology for Sustainable Development: Consensus Report and Background Document for the Mexico City Synthesis Conference. 20–23 May. *Series on Science for Sustainable Development*, No. 9. Paris, France: ICSU.

Jantsch, E. (1980) *The Self-Organizing Universe. Scientific and Human Implications of the Emerging Paradigm of Evolution*, Oxford, UK: Pergamon Press.

Kates, R., Clark, W.C., Corell, R., Hall, J.M., Jaeger, C.C., Lowe, I., McCarthy, J.J., Schellnhuber, H.J., Bolin, B., Dickson, N.M., Faucheux, S., Gallopín, G.C., Grübler, A., Huntley, B., Jäger, J., Jodha, N.S., Kasperson, R.E., Mabogunje, A., Matson, P., Mooney, H., Moore III, B., O'Riordan, T. and Svedin, U. (2001) Sustainability science. *Science*, **292**, pp. 641–2.

Munn, T., Timmerman, P. and Whyte, A. (2000) Emerging Environmental Issues. *Bulletin of the American Meteorological Society*, **81**(7), pp. 1603–9.

Myers, M. (ed.) (1984) *GAIA: An Atlas of Planet Management*. New York, USA: Anchor Books.

Nicolis, G. and Prigogine, I. (1977) *Self-organization in Non-equilibrium Systems: From Dissipative Structures to Order Through Fluctuation*. New York, USA: Wiley.

Petschel-Held, G.A., Block, M., Cassel-Gintz et al. (2000) Syndromes of global change. A qualitative modelling approach to assist global environmental management. *Environmental Modeling and Assessment*, **4**, pp. 295–314.

Puccia, C.J. and Levins, R. (1987) *Qualitative Modeling of Complex Systems*. Cambridge, MA, USA: Harvard University Press.

Saner, M.A. (1999) Two cultures: Not unique to ecology. *Conservation Ecology* (online), **3**:2 [http://www.consecol.org/vol3/iss1/resp2].

Schellnhuber, H.J. and Wenzel, V. (eds) (1998) *Earth System Analysis: Integrating Science for Sustainability*. Heidelberg, Germany: Springer.

Schwartz, P. (1991) *The Art of the Long View*. New York, USA: Currency Doubleday.

Stake, R.E. (2010) *Qualitative Research: Studying How Things Work*. New York, USA: Guilford Press.

Thompson, K.J. (1990) *Interdisciplinarity. History, Theory and Practice*. Detroit, USA: Wayne State University Press.

United Nations (2008) *The Millennium Development Goals Report 2008*. New York, USA: United Nations.

Young, O.R., Berkhout, F., Gallopín, G., Janssen, M.A., Ostrom, E. and van der Leeuw, S. (2006) The globalization of socio-ecological systems. An agenda for scientific research. *Global Environmental Change*, **16**, pp. 304–16.

IV.2b HIGHER EDUCATION, MODERNITY AND A NEW PARADIGM

María Novo

THE STATE OF THE ART: A WORLD MOVING TOWARDS SUSTAINABILITY

These are difficult times for the environment and for people and societies aspiring to sustainability. Economic globalization has led to the development of production conditions, capital movements and consumption patterns that, as never before, prioritize short-term profits and disregard ecological, social and human constraints.

From an environmental standpoint, this situation of planetary-scale changes in the Earth's cycles and processes is referred to as *global change*. Two features of global change in particular make its impact unique in world history: first, the speed with which the process is unfolding, with significant changes occurring in the short space of a few decades (for example in atmospheric CO_2 levels); second, the fact that a single species, namely, *Homo sapiens*, is the main driver behind all these changes (Duarte, 2006).

These problems led the Dutch chemist Paul Crutzen, Nobel prizewinner in 1995, to propose the term 'Antropocene' to refer to the current period in the geological history of the planet. In this new era, humanity has emerged as a force capable of altering key biosphere processes (Crutzen and Stoermer, 2000).

The current crisis also affects knowledge structures. Indeed, how could it be otherwise? Wallerstein (2005, p. 48) sees humanity as being faced with not one but two great social uncertainties: the nature of the new system that we are building and the epistemology of our new knowledge structures.

How can we educate people in these circumstances? What should we teach the young people in our universities? What criteria and values should we apply? Can we build new lifestyle models inspired by a new sustainability paradigm? These and similar questions daily assail those of us who work in higher education institutions. The challenge is to respond to them consciously and positively, even if we can only do so partially.

UNIVERSITIES AND THE SUSTAINABILITY CHALLENGE

The current crisis is systemic, that is, ecological, financial, political and social. The dawning of a new millennium simultaneously represented a challenge and an opportunity: to reconsider our vision of the world (and of education) by acknowledging previous errors and excesses and developing the necessary criteria to rectify them. The current crisis is also epistemological, in that it affects knowledge and how we produce and transmit it.

What can we ask of higher education in these circumstances? As a priority, higher education needs to be open and creative so that new challenges can be viewed from a fresh perspective; as Mayor Zaragoza (2009, p. 9) has said, we need to leave behind our impassiveness and cowardliness and take charge of our own destiny. The university system needs to decidedly make a contribution to the development of a new ethical, social and ecological scientific paradigm that is capable of taking on board and giving expression to new forms of knowing, doing and being.

This emerging paradigm is already being built on the kind of knowledge and values that can help society make the transition towards greater ecological equilibrium and social equity. A UNESCO-backed environmental education movement, whose ultimate aim is to contribute to sustainable development, has become increasingly active in the last 30 years, particularly through conferences held in Tbilisi (1977), Moscow (1987), Thessaloniki (1997) and Ahmadabad (2007).

Within this movement, higher education recognizes that education is not just about teaching science in whatever of its forms, whether physical, social or human, but also about enhancing deep and broad learning, aimed ultimately at making sense of things and understanding about, and learning for, life. It therefore requires a mobilization of humanity's intellectual, social, affective and spiritual dimensions (Hargreaves and Fink, 2006). The most important issue, in my opinion, is to help people rethink the world – no easy task, but crucial if we want universities to take on board the challenges of a global and plural civilization.

For the university system to contribute to sustainability, the first priority is to adopt a position regarding the problems affecting nature and humanity. Universities need to convincingly demonstrate the non-viability of a growth model that recognizes no limits and that is in dire need of change. They also need to be able to do this at a time when the West – or at least its leadership – lacks a worldview that is capable of providing the necessary guidance.

The Bonn Declaration, which concluded the 2009 UNESCO World Conference on Education for Sustainable Development, called for sustainable development principles to be incorporated across all university disciplines and sectors, with a view to demonstrating ecological, economic, social and cultural interdependence in the construction of the kind of knowledge that, of necessity, must be systemic and integrated. It also emphasized the need for higher education to appeal not only to intellects but also to values, with a view to developing aptitudes and attitudes in students that would enable them to deal with the problems of their time.

The World Conference on Higher Education, held at UNESCO's headquarters in Paris in 2009, also called for progress towards a multidimensional (scientific, economic, environmental, and so on) understanding of global challenges and for the generation of knowledge aimed at solving the associated problems.

Against this background, the universities of the 21st century are faced with a complex, demanding mission: to generate and transmit knowledge that promotes innovation, quality, equity and respect for the environment, while ensuring congruency in the means and methods used for this purpose. The ultimate goal has to be to contribute to social progress with knowledge that addresses the real problems facing humanity, improves our relationship with the environment and promotes social justice. This task implies risk, but, as Mayor Zaragoza (2008) has stated, if risk without knowledge is dangerous, then knowledge without risk is useless.

THE CAUSES OF UNSUSTAINABILITY: THE MODERN GLOBAL MODEL

A principle in law states that whoever is responsible for the cause is also responsible for the damage. Applying this principle to our discourse here, we need to seek the origins of our unsustainability not so much in our actions as in the thought models and mindsets that have historically guided us. We need, therefore, to reflect on and possibly rectify the roots of modern Western thinking as disseminated throughout the world.

Any complex process shaping the modern world is defined by light and shadows, so it would seem fair to consider both of these aspects. Nonetheless, restrictions of space mean that I shall only refer to the latter here, as the roots of our unsustainability lie in the errors and the excesses of the contemporary Western world vision.

From the beginnings of modernity, thinkers and scientists such as Galileo, Descartes, Bacon and

Newton contributed to shaping an understanding of the world and of science that would have an enormous influence on the future of societies. In general terms, the assumptions of Renaissance humanism were abandoned and four kinds of practical knowledge were gradually displaced: the oral, the particular, the timely and the local (Toulmin, 1990).

The problem was that reason as a form of approaching the truth gradually developed into a dangerous rationalism. True rationality is open and dialogues with a reality that it struggles to understand. It knows the limits of logic, determinism and mechanism and it knows that reality has an element of mystery (Morin and Kern, 1993). My criticism is not of science but of scientism, that is, of the idea that science is disinterested and extra-social, that its truth statements stand in isolation from more general philosophical affirmations and that it is the only legitimate form of knowledge (Wallerstein, 2005).

Rationalism was also reinforced by an emerging empiricism. Both are the pillars of a pattern of thought that believes that life and all things that exist can be described with total objectivity and separating the observer from the observed, with a view to obtaining general laws. These laws have governed, over several centuries, a mechanistically ordered worldview – nature is viewed as if by a watchmaker – in the framework of a deterministic physics that admits no randomness or uncertainty.

Under these premises, the paradigm that explains the world as it has developed in the modern era is based on overlooking or ignoring certain notions:

- The complexity of ecological, social and human systems
- The systemic interdependence between all things that exist
- The subject playing a dual role: as the observer-researcher who conditions the experiment and as the person responsible for establishing moral links with the non-human living world
- The context, greatly confused in terms of map and territory
- Time and the irreversibility of processes unfolding in the living world (thermodynamic processes that imply an increase in entropy)

This model is based on the spirit of transformation, on the idea that knowledge is power, on human domination of nature and on an obsession with making and transforming. In this context, the deification of technology and utility relegates ethical issues and questions to the background. As stated by Berman (1981), we have gone from asking if something is good to asking if something serves a function.

In a nutshell, it could be said that technoscience and conscience did not develop at the same pace, nor did they take due account of each other (Novo, 2006). Technoscience has advanced like a high-speed train and, having been left in the hands of the economy, now knows no limits. Individual and collective conscience, meanwhile, has been subsumed by an idea of 'progress' that, based as it is on unlimited economic growth, has led to the current situation of unsustainability.

However, we need to bear in mind that the constitution of modern thought is not only a process whereby scientists seek solutions to problems or knowledge is applied to technology. The phenomenon is a broader one: the principles, theories and laws emanating from the physical sciences are being used to serve economic and political ideologies. The application of such principles outside the field where they were developed has shaped a modern Western worldview that is cloaked in an apparent rationality that conceals its dominant nature.

As would only be expected, the scenario of conflict and change that I describe has affected our higher education system. Universities are implicated in the design, construction and deployment of this modern world paradigm, in a model of knowledge organization – emerging as novel in the context of modernity – that divorces the two cultures of science and philosophy (Snow, 1959).

The expansion of science and of scientific progress through specialization led to a dissection of reality so that the scientific method could be applied. This dissection was indeed necessary – but no thought was given to the equally necessary subsequent reconstruction of the whole. The academic counterpart was the segregation of knowledge into disconnected disciplines and the proliferation of what were generally watertight departments and faculties, as opposed to diversified sources of knowledge that needed to be viewed in relation to other sources of knowledge, which consolidated the compartmentalization of knowledge still further. All of this gradually distanced us from the search for integrated knowledge.

A curious paradox is that, since the early 20th century, Einstein, Bohr, Heisenberg and many other scientists have revealed the limited validity of the mechanistic and deterministic paradigm, thereby opening the way for a more systemic and complex vision that substantially changes the concept of knowledge. This new paradigm takes account of randomness, uncertainty, disorder as the source of order, the self-organization capacity of living systems and an emotional, sensory, artistic dimension that goes beyond pure rationality. However, this new vision has, as yet, had limited influence on what is taught in our universities and how it is taught. Even with the collapse of the boundaries between the disciplines of the 19th century and even though advanced knowledge today occurs in 'the ecotones of knowledge' (biochemistry, psychobiology, and so on), our teaching continues to be anchored – more frequently and more profoundly than is desirable – in an epistemological and methodological structure that continues to reflect reality as compartmentalized and disconnected.

Fortunately, however, the exceptions are many and increasing in number, even though the pace of change is slow. Some areas of academia are making progress in radical epistemological restructuring that brings together different knowledge fields. The dual-culture debate is being increasingly heard and new transdisciplinary networks and research communities, consisting of participants of very different academic origins working together to generate and integrate knowledge, are beginning to proliferate.

Thus, a renewed vision of *scientia* is being constructed as a renewed vision of *philosophia*, whose epistemological centrepiece is not the possibility but the need to be located in the 'unexcluded middle' (Wallerstein, 2005, p. 73).

Nonetheless, these advanced networks and groups tend to develop under the auspices of interdisciplinary institutes and centres and, as yet, few have materialized as university departments and faculties in their own right. Will the 21st century be the historical scenario in which higher education decisively addresses these problems? On this depends not only the effectiveness of our universities as knowledge producers, but also their social utility in promoting a new worldview that fosters sustainability.

THE SCIENTIFIC REVOLUTION AND THE PARADIGM SHIFT

The dynamics of the historical process described above are affected by one crucial fact: science has self-correcting mechanisms of its own that facilitate its transformation. As noted by Kuhn (1962), this natural process allows new scientific findings to replace previous findings or reveal their limited validity. Thus does knowledge develop.

The new science that emerged in the early 20th century opened entirely novel perspectives. It acknowledged, for example, Heisenberg's uncertainty principle, which debunked positivism's claim to complete objectivity by pointing to the possibility of the observer becoming part of the observed system. Today it is accepted, as pointed out by Maturana (1989), that everything that has been said has been said by an observer.

This new vision is of a science that combines determinism and indeterminism, a science whose laws express, as pointed out by Prigogine (1997, p. 109), what is possible, not what is true. Feynman (2000) said that we could have 'approximate answers and possible beliefs' and 'different degrees of certainty about things', but we could not be 'absolutely sure of anything'. Hence, the question regarding any statement is not whether it is true or false, but rather how likely it is to be true or false. At the very least, we have to concede that most of our actions are based on incomplete knowledge.

This *conjectural science* is configured as learning through dialogue with nature. It accepts that our measurements (prior to the generation of knowledge) may be affected by something alien – whether ourselves as observers, our instruments or changed conditions. Contrasting with the notion that knowledge faithfully mirrors reality is that of the 'mapper', that is, the active observer. The mind does not create its laws from nature alone but also on the basis of expectations of what it wants to know, instrumental limits and the influence of context. Thus, knowledge of reality is more than simply a matter of reproducing, but is also a creative process.

We are fortunately witnessing the emergence of science with a conscience (Morin, 1984), which reaches beyond timeless laws to describe events in which both time and historical sequence are important. This science accepts the irreversibility of living processes and incorporates the incomplete, the imperfect and the chaotic.

This science embraces *fuzzy thinking*. It contemplates reality not in black and white but as a palette of greys, with connectedness between the interior and exterior (as between the self and the non-self, the individual and nature). This science does not try to dominate nature, but tries to understand it and understand ourselves 'within' and 'with' the natural world surrounding us. As Habermas (1968) pointed out, we now seek 'a fraternal nature' rather than an exploited nature.

In this evolution, Cartesian rationalism and positivism are not dismantled but are repositioned in terms of their limited validity (Lévy-Leblond, 1996). And this is how, in the field of knowledge, we move from clocks to clouds, to use the beautiful metaphor coined by Popper (1965, cited in Prigogine, 1997), that is, from the mechanical and predictable to the elusive and uncertain.

From this standpoint, living systems are viewed as open systems whose trajectories are constrained by their bonds with the changing environment. Changes in the context require adjustments in the system, with chance, uncertainty and contingency entering into play. As noted by Morin (1984), all self-organization is actually eco-organization by the self, converting the human being into an eco-dependent being. We should not forget that 'the greater our interventions in the natural world, the less we can forecast or modify their effects and the more significant will be their unintended outcomes' (Toulmin, 2003, p. 128).

This model of knowledge emphasizes the circular cause–effect relationships (feedbacks, loops, synergies, and so on) that are fundamental to understanding and interpreting our environmental and economic crisis. Similarly, thresholds and tipping points have acquired new significance, especially as any changes there may be qualitative as well as quantitative. For this reason, it is crucial to consider adaptive models that allow for *resilience*, that is, systems using negative events to their advantage and converting challenges into opportunities.

The science of complexity is being forged in a systemic model that views reality in terms of relationships rather than isolated objects. This non-reductionist vision takes account of the unity of reality, of the union of mind and body, of emotions participating in the reasoning loop (Damasio, 2008). It posits a non-dualistic worldview, in which apparent opposites are viewed as complementary, not antagonistic. This is how we can make the transition from the delusion of uniformity to the celebration of diversity and, along the way, to sustainability.

REFERENCES

Bauman, Z. (2007) *Tiempos líquidos.* Barcelona: Tusquets. [*Liquid Times. Living in an Age of Uncertainty.* Gius, Laterza & Figli]

Beck, U. (1986) *Risikogesellschaft. Auf dem Weg in eine andere Moderne.* Frankfurt am Main: Suhrkamp Verlag.

Berman, M. (1981) *The Reenchantment of the World.* Ithaca: Cornell University Press.

Crutzen, P.J. and Stoermer, F. (2000) The 'Anthropocene'. *Global Change Newsletter,* **41**, pp. 12–13.

Damasio, A. (2008) *El error de Descartes.* Barcelona: Crítica. [*Descartes' Error.* Penguin Books]

Duarte, C.M. (2006) (Coord.) *Cambio global. Impacto de la actividad humana sobre el sistema Tierra.* Madrid: Consejo Superior de Investigaciones Científicas.

Feynman, R.P. (2000) *El placer de descubrir.* Barcelona: Crítica. [*The Pleasure of Finding Things Out.* Perseus Books]

Habermas, J. (1968) *Technik und Wissenschaft als 'Ideologie'.* Frankfurt am Main: Suhrkamp Verlag.

Hargreaves, A. and Fink, D. (2006) *Sustainable Leadership.* San Francisco: John Wiley & Sons Inc.

Kuhn, T.S. (1962) *The Structure of Scientific Revolutions.* Chicago: University of Chicago Press.

Lévy-Leblond, J.M. (1996) *Aux contraires. Le exercice de la pensée et la pratique de la science.* París: Éditions Gallimard.

Maturana, H. (1989) Todo lo dice un observador. In: Thompson, W.I. et al. *Gaia. Implicaciones de la nueva biología.* Barcelona: Kairós, pp. 63–79. [*Gaia: a Way of Knowing.* Lindisfarne Association]

Mayor Zaragoza, F. (2008) La verdad más incómoda todavía: la gente. In: Mesa, M. (ed.) Anuario CEIPAZ 2008: *Escenarios de crisis: fracturas y pugnas en el sistema internacional,* pp. 15–44. Barcelona: Icaria.

Mayor Zaragoza, F. (2009) Todas las personas tienen derecho a la educación y la cultura (prologue). In: Caride, J.A. *Los derechos humanos en la educación y la cultura.* Rosario (Argentina): Homo Sapiens.

Morin, E. (1984) *Ciencia con consciencia.* Barcelona: Anthropos. [*Science avec conscience.* Librairie Arthème Fayard]

Morin, E. and Kern, A.B. (1993) *Tierra-patria.* Barcelona: Kairós. [*Terre-patrie.* Éditions du Seuil]

Novo. M. (2006) *El desarrollo sostenible: su dimensión ambiental y educativa.* Madrid: Pearson/UNESCO.

Popper, K.R. (1966) *Of clouds and clocks.* Washington University Press.

Prigogine, I. (1997) *Las leyes del caos.* Barcelona: Crítica. [*Le leggi del caos.* Bari (Italy): Laterza]

Snow, C.P. (1959) *The Two Cultures.* Cambridge: Cambridge University Press.

Toulmin, S. (1990) *Cosmopolis: The Hidden Agenda of Modernity.* Chicago: University of Chicago Press.

Toulmin, S. (2003) *Regreso a la razón.* Barcelona: Península. [*Return to Reason.* Harvard University Press]

UNESCO (2009) World Conference on Education for Sustainable Development: Bonn Declaration. Bonn (Germany), 31 March–2 April. Available from: www.esd-world-conference-2009.org/.../ESD2009_BonnDeclaration080409.pdf (Accessed 12 July 2009).

UNESCO (2009) World Conference on Higher Education. The New Dynamics of Higher Education and Research for Societal Change and Development, 5–8 July 2009: Communiqué. Unesco. Doc. ED 2009/CONF. 402/2. Available from: unesdoc.unesco.org/images/0018/001832/183277e.pdf (Accessed 20 April 2011).

Wallerstein, I. (2005) *Las incertidumbres del saber.* Barcelona: Gedisa. [*The Uncertainties of Knowledge.* Temple University]

Cristina Bolívar

I seek not to know the answers, but to understand the questions (Oriental wisdom)

This article proposes an epistemological neo-Renaissance worldview of wisdom as the basis for a new sustainable education paradigm. Proposed is an enabling role for the teacher-coach as a facilitator in developing human potential and wisdom, adopting an essential coaching perspective. This is proposed as a way of fostering a shift from educating 'to have' to educating 'to be'.

THE PRESENT MOMENT

We are living in a postmodern epoch, with the 'post' indicating that an era has come to a close. The modern era, with its notions of progress and freedom for humanity, definitively ended with the Holocaust.

I have decided to use the word postmodern to describe [the condition of knowledge in the most highly developed societies]. The word is in current use on the American continent among sociologists and critics; it designates the state of our culture following the transformations which, since the end of the nineteenth century, have altered the game rules for science, literature, and the arts. (Lyotard, 1969)

The rational ideal of modernism and the utilitarian ideal of postmodernism are no longer self-sustainable. Hazard (cited in Berlin, 2002) considered the crisis in Western conscience to be the hallmark of an era in which reason is replaced by darkness. Tenzer (1982) believes that the radical and globalized awareness of a Western crisis is perceived to be simultaneously cultural, social and political.

We can no longer call on the great worldviews of yore that gave clear answers to questions on the meaning of life; nowadays, humanistic values are trivialized. Even conceding that there may be moments when we intuit a search for harmony with the world, we have a sensation of lives lacking in meaning, mainly due to the impact of two factors: first, advertising and information, and second, compulsive purchasing. As Baudrillard (cited in Berlin, 2002) pointed out, we are living in a time of objects, in a culture of simulacrum, in a world of pseudo-events.

The field of education is no exception to the impact of postmodernism. Research and teaching, based on reason and positivist empiricism, sought certain apodictic, irrefutable truths that were of necessity circumscribed by knowledge fragmented into poly-chromatic disciplines. The aim was to encounter a useful truth to teach in a model that domesticated and trained its participants for a control-oriented world and that sought results in certainty and pragmatism.

The crisis in society coincides with a crisis in thinking and in the desire to think – the essential element in communication between humans. Humanity has lost its bearings. Metaphysics[1] seems to be dead. Hence, the outcome of postmodernism is a loss of all values and ideals. This is well described by Vattimo (Vattimo and Rovatti, 1990) in his vision of a weak nihilism that experiments with the experience of the dissolution of being and is also referred to by Rorty (1995, 1998), who defines postmodern society as a postphilosophical society – which only underlines the existence of a thinking vacuum: human beings can know nothing other than their relations with each other and with other finite beings. According to Daniel Ben Itzjak[2] – rabbi and director of the Virtual University of Judaism[3] and translator of a number of books on the Kabbalah – postmodern humans understand nothing and want to understand nothing. Postmodern humans are in denial: they do not wish to confront existentialism or understand that existentialism enables us to understand life and be better humans.

To leave behind postmodernism and forge a new way forward, education needs to facilitate the development of awareness and knowledge so as to recover metaphysical values and the values of being.

THE NEW SUSTAINABILITY PARADIGM IN EDUCATION

Does the current model of education continue to be valid as postmodernism draws to a close? The answer is no. We need a new sustainable education paradigm based on holistic-systemic knowledge and on transdisciplinarity that educates for uncertainty and for paradigmatic change. This paradigm would transform the role of education, which would no longer prepare professionals to compete in the market but switch to educating aware citizens who add value to society through their professional practices and their relationships.

This challenge poses new questions: How to advance towards a new sustainable education paradigm? Should we educate to do or educate to be? We need to change our perspective to focus on being, on generating wisdom and on educating not to have but to be – as the only way to be able to remake economic, political, cultural and social systems in the framework of a sustainable, equitable and inclusive future.

A NEO-RENAISSANCE PROPOSAL

NEO-RENAISSANCE

This leads me to propose an alternative neo-Renaissance worldview, as an emerging paradigm that marks the end of enlightened and postmodernist rationality. As with the Renaissance, it reflects influences from the East (not to mention the suppression of that capitalist by-product, New Age) and the recovery of the Greek and Roman classical origins of Western culture. It integrates and values knowledge from all eras and cultures. It values knowledge of the self as subject (Socrates), the pursuit of wisdom (as object) and contemplation-nous; it is based on a belief in human potential (Aristotle) and in the rational and creative human (Nietzsche's Apollonian and Dionysian principles). We can label it as a new Renaissance, thereby alluding to and making explicit the value of true Aristotelian knowledge and wisdom, which is holistic and intuitive but does not displace nous in favour of science and reason (higher levels of awareness in Beck and Cowan's spiral dynamics).[4] It recovers metaphysical values that make sense of reality, of the existential and of the essential: to use Wilber's term, values are postmetaphysical.[5]

SILENCE

Silence allows us to connect to inner wisdom and the essential being. Silence is the main entry point to the inductive life and to insight, to understanding in a profound sense and to a better worldview. This new worldview comes equipped with a postmetaphysical framework that gives new meaning to reality.

THE EPISTEMOLOGICAL MODEL OF A NEO-RENAISSANCE WORLDVIEW

This epistemological holistic approach combines science and spirit and is well grounded in history and theory. It builds on reasoning that is coherent and contextual and it integrates input from philosophy, psychology and mysticism (Plato, Aristotle, the Kabbalah, Descartes, Kant, Wilber, and so on).

This epistemological model aims to recover and validate the spirit of the Renaissance but passing it through the filter of the advances of the past two centuries. Its main values – the importance of knowledge and the pursuit of well-being – are based on a belief in an integrated human being who reconciles rationality, emotions and spirituality. It is not a question of eliminating the rational or techne, which have their uses, but a question of advancing on the path of integration.

My new proposal for the postmodern era is neo-Renaissance. Wisdom is the fruit of truly holistic knowledge. It is not mere scientific knowledge but the superior dianoetic faculty referred to by Aristotle. The neo-Renaissance worldview encompasses all faculties and levels of knowledge including humanities, arts, science, philosophy, spirituality, and so on.

It seeks to learn to learn (a process referred to as generative or third-order learning) and to raise awareness following an upward spiral fuelled by a quest: its ultimate goal, indeed, is the quest itself. At every turn of this dynamic spiral, awareness and wisdom (whether technical, creative, moral, and so on) grows.

We gradually develop into holistic and meaningful beings for whom reason or intuition alone is insufficient; the two, rather, need to be integrated. As Jung pointed out, intuition is the ability to look through the eyes of the unconscious; it does not value or judge, it takes account of phenomena beyond the palpable, the here and now. And it provides solutions that emerge once we abandon the conscious effort to think. It integrates the traditional scientific way of learning (which primarily relies on language, logic, linear thinking, the masculine, alpha waves, the if-I-don't-see-it-I-don't-believe-it school, the left brain) with another equally valid way of learning: intuition and nous (the feminine, lateral thinking, beta waves, the way of art, the right brain). Learning is a quest in a worldview of perspectives. Truth remains outside our range; it is inaccessible because we are finite beings. As Wilber puts it, it is simply a question of perspectives.

As Arendt (1993) pointed out, a world built by man and not the world in itself appears before the human. It is not a matter of deciding the best or most suitable representation or of constructing a synthesis, but one of preserving diversity and so making the entirety of representations common to all. Science holds that there is a truth known to all that is both homogeneous and immutable and that transmits a sense of security. This is not true, however, as we can merely intuitively invent metaphors of the world (worldview, postmetaphysics) that give meaning to our reality. Truth is merely truth, a perspective that gives meaning to knowledge.

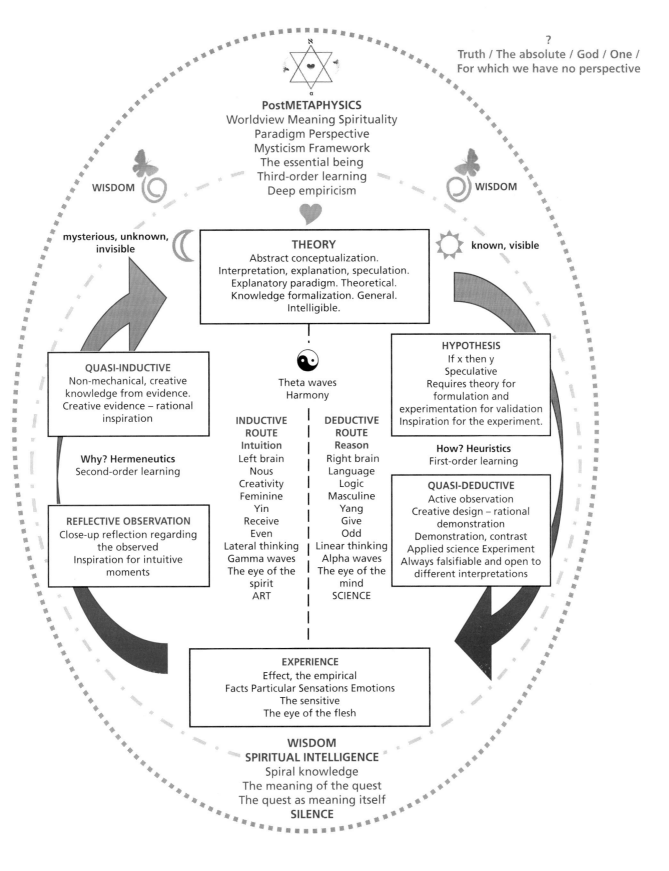

PostMETAPHYSICS
Worldview Meaning Spirituality
Paradigm Perspective
Mysticism Framework
The essential being
Third-order learning
Deep empiricism

WISDOM   WISDOM

mysterious, unknown,   known, visible
invisible

THEORY
Abstract conceptualization.
Interpretation, explanation, speculation.
Explanatory paradigm. Theoretical.
Knowledge formalization. General.
Intelligible.

QUASI-INDUCTIVE
Non-mechanical, creative
knowledge from evidence.
Creative evidence – rational
inspiration

HYPOTHESIS
If x then y
Speculative
Requires theory for
formulation and
experimentation for validation
Inspiration for the experiment.

Theta waves
Harmony

Why? Hermeneutics
Second-order learning

How? Heuristics
First-order learning

INDUCTIVE ROUTE	DEDUCTIVE ROUTE
Intuition	Reason
Left brain	Right brain
Nous	Language
Creativity	Logic
Feminine	Masculine
Yin	Yang
Receive	Give
Even	Odd
Lateral thinking	Linear thinking
Gamma waves	Alpha waves
The eye of the spirit	The eye of the mind
ART	SCIENCE

REFLECTIVE OBSERVATION
Close-up reflection regarding
the observed
Inspiration for intuitive
moments

QUASI-DEDUCTIVE
Active observation
Creative design – rational
demonstration
Demonstration, contrast
Applied science Experiment
Always falsifiable and open to
different interpretations

EXPERIENCE
Effect, the empirical
Facts Particular Sensations Emotions
The sensitive
The eye of the flesh

**WISDOM
SPIRITUAL INTELLIGENCE**
Spiral knowledge
The meaning of the quest
The quest as meaning itself
SILENCE

FIGURE 1 An epistemological model of the neo-renaissance worldview

EDUCATING FOR BEING

As Cristina Escrigas says,[6] we must educate to be, that is, educate people so that they develop their potential, awareness, critical thinking and wisdom. As Freire (1969) expressed it, we should educate to 'critically reflect upon existence' and 'critically act upon it.' That means, as is evident in the epistemological neo-Renaissance worldview model, we should educate by developing deductive–inductive pathways and by recovering art, emotions, and so on,

in short, by promoting the development of spiritual intelligence; this includes emotional intelligence, which, in turn, subsumes emotional–cognitive–pragmatic intelligence.

To paraphrase Claudio Naranjo (2004) in referring to an inclusive education of the body, emotions, mind and spirit, we need a new education, of the whole person for the whole world so as to understand what is happening to us and around us. The ultimate goal is the collective construction of knowledge from the expansion of awareness and wisdom.

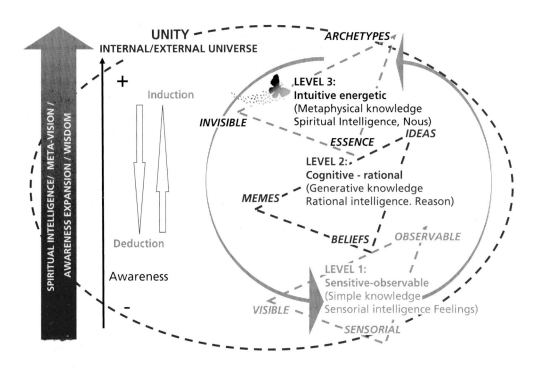

FIGURE 2 Dynamic model of levels of knowledge

FACULTIES

The inductive pathway is characterized by the faculty of nous, the deductive faculty is characterized by science, and the postmetaphysical faculty is related to wisdom.

It could also be said that the postmetaphysical stage is reached from level three (see Figure 2), the level of intuitive-energetic knowledge, since knowledge is not empirical (Kant) but immediate.

If we take the essentialist wisdom of Aristotle, who had an integrated vision of the comprehensive, coherent and complete being, personal development is associated with developing the potential to draw on all one's resources, with the goal being to develop the five dianoetic faculties by means of which the soul realizes truth by affirmation or negation (Figure 3).

BOX 1: ARISTOTLE'S DIANOETIC FACULTIES

Dianoetic faculties	Description
Intellect	**Nous**. Understanding. The human capacity par excellence. Evidence does not need words, it is contemplated.
Wisdom	**Theory**. Science + understanding. Sophia. Philosophy. The human is not pure understanding, but aspires to being godlike and needs science-demonstration.
	This is the most certain (rigorous) mode of knowledge because it not only knows scientific causes but seeks to understand principles. It asks the questions that science overlooks.
Prudence	**Action**. Praxis. Phronesis. Human action, how we build our life in common.
	Acquired through particular experiences.
Science	**Demonstration**. Syllogism. Episteme. Can be taught and understood. Part of a principle and so is science and a per se demonstration of this principle. It is hypothetical, not dogmatic.
Art	**Production**. Techne, technique. Poiesis The production of something that is usually material. A characteristic of Homo faber. More material. More concretion.

More form
More abstraction

More material
More concretion

Knowledge is given in a continuous movement between two extremes – theoretical knowledge and conclusions – that are the starting point for each other. Each extreme requires different abilities that do not occur simultaneously but at different times.

DEVELOPMENT OF POTENTIAL

Educating to be also means helping people develop their potential, helping people unlearn, helping people to overcome the constraints on developing polarity and facilitating the development of authenticity. People thus can be what they do not know that they are, what they do not accept that they are and, definitively, can be all they already are. It is a matter of recovering essence and internal wisdom based on both deductive and inductive knowledge. As Mario Saban (2011) has said, we are apprenticed to wisdom.

THE NEW TEACHING ROLE: THE TEACHER-COACH

Socrates said that it is impossible to teach anything; people can only be helped to discover things for themselves. As is widely known, Socrates (Athens, 470–469 BCE) is considered to be the first coach and the best teacher, given his attitudes and what we would nowadays call competences and also given his maieutic method of questioning and discussion, which was the inspiration for modern-day coaching.

Knowledge is born through maieutic dialogue and joint analysis (in his *Theaetetus* Plato draws an analogy with Socrates' mother, a midwife). The process is a form of obstetrics of the soul: truth blooms through dialectics, through a continuous dialogue based on short questions and answers (*katá brachy dialéghesthai*), on giving and asking for the reason behind statements (*didónai kái déchesthai lógon*), on asking for critical intervention by the interlocutor, on exercising criticism, on working together in the pursuit of truth and good and on striving to understand the other's point of view.

One can say that the roles of master and student are interchangeable and neither has primacy. Education is the joint search for knowledge and truth, with each element recognizing the special position of the other. This is behaviour pointed to as the greatest good and is the role of the teacher-coach. Socrates said that there was no such thing as teaching, only learning. Bringing back Socrates means bringing back the Socratic question and philosophical debate as educational instruments.

According to Brenifier (2011), the focus on incorporating the philosophical practice of Socratic maieutics implies a genuine Copernican turn in teaching and in the concept of education.

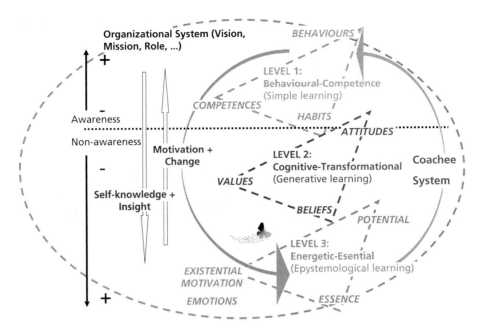

FIGURE 3 Dynamic coaching intervention model

ESSENTIAL COACHING

BOX 2: ESSENTIAL COACHING MODEL

According to the neo-Renaissance stance, the teacher-coach, intervening from an essential coaching perspective, can help rediscover the uniqueness of being, facilitate the development of potential, raise awareness and develop the wisdom necessary to achieve meta-results.

Essential coaching facilitates the third-order learning that accompanies the development of a holistic neo-Renaissance human being, capable of recovering his/her potential for self-awareness and world awareness and exploring the depth and completeness of his/her faculties. We are nowadays constrained by a focus on short-term results, hurriedness and the internal and external noise in our lives. We are blinded by the promise of technological and material well-being.

Essential coaching aims to develop the deepest level of human potential by tackling the essence and uniqueness of humans, breaking the boundaries of the ego to recreate ego and generating knowledge through the expansion of awareness. It is about developing the potential and the spirituality of the person through their inner power to feel, think and do from a higher level of consciousness and coherence.

The teacher-coach facilitates a person's learning and development by introducing them to the teach-

ing role of philosophy and to the style of the coach. It is thus necessary to develop the attitudes and competences of the coach and those specific to what is referred to as the essential coach.

COMPETENCES OF THE ESSENTIAL TEACHER-COACH

Within the essential coaching model we can define the seven core essential coaching competences that need to be developed by the teacher-coach who teaches.

BOX 3: SEVEN CORE COMPETENCES OF THE ESSENTIAL COACH

The essential teacher-coach, to be effective, will start by developing their own wisdom from an orientation to love (acceptance of others and their life and learning processes) and from inner silence and humility. The essential teacher-coach seeks to take education to be beyond teaching theory and academic knowledge. It focuses on the development of whole, critical persons in the context of a sustainable education model that replaces the post-modern world with an alternative neo-Renaissance worldview and thereby makes higher awareness possible (Beck and Cowan, 1999).

1. **Authenticity**
   Integrate being
   Connect with the essential being

2. **Presence**
   Connect with the here and now
   Be energettically open in innser silence

3. **Plasticity**
   Learn to unlearn and learn to read
   Be proactively flexible and consistent

4. **Tenderness**
   Have unconditional love for the human being. Adopt and energetic presence inspired by love

5. **Humility**
   Accept the self in the current process
   Be human

6. **Wisdom**
   Connect with intuition and lateral thinking
   Connect with rationalism and linear thinking

7. **Spirituality**
   Transcend the self
   Connect with the flow and the whole

BOX 4: WISDOM AND LOVE ARE THE BASIS OF THE ESSENTIAL COACH

The coach does not know.
The coach does not interpret.
The coach does not judge.
The coach does not resolve.
The coach is not.

All I know is that I know nothing (Socrates)

BIBLIOGRAPHY

Arendt, H. (1993) *La condición humana*. Barcelona: Paidós.

Aristotle *Ética a Nicómaco*, libros I, VI y X. Textos.

Aristotle (1995) *Física*. Madrid: Gredos.

Aristotle (2000) *Metafísica*. Madrid: Alianza Editorial.

Aristotle (2004) *Tratados de lógica (Organon)*. Méjico: Porrúa.

Beck, D. and Cowan, C (1999) *Spiral Dynamic*. UK: Blackwell Publishing.

Berlin, I. (2002) *El fuste torcido de la humanidad*. Barcelona: Ediciones de bolsillo.

Bermudo, J.M. (2001) *Filosofía política, I. Luces y sombras de la ciudad*. Barcelona: del Serbal.

Bolívar, C. (2007) Coaching esencial. *Rev Capital Humano*, No. 213, September.

Bolívar, C. (Próxima edición) *Ser desde el silencio interior*. Barcelona: Kairós.

Brenifier, O. (2011) *Filosofar como Sócrates: introduccion a la práctica filosófica*. Valencia: Dialogo.

Descartes, R. (1987) *Meditaciones metafísicas*. Madrid: Gredos.

Descartes, R. (1989) *Reglas para la dirección del espíritu*. Madrid: Alianza Editorial.

Freire, P. (1969) La educación como práctica de la libertad. Madrid: Siglo XXI.

Giannantoni, G. (1973) *Qué ha dicho verdaderamente Sócrates*. Madrid: Doncel.

Jung, C.G. (2009) *La vida simbólica*. Madrid: Trotta.

Jung, C.G. (2010) *Sobre el desarrollo de la personalidad*. Madrid: Trotta.

Kant, I. (1787) *Crítica de la razón pura*, prólogo segunda edición.

Lyotard, J.F. (1969) *La condición postmoderna*. Madrid: Cátedra.

Naranjo, C. (2004) *Cambiar la educación para cambiar el mundo*. Barcelona: La Llave.

Newton, I. (1998) *Principios matemáticos de Filosofía Natural*. Madrid: Alianza Editorial.

Palomar, A. (2010) Conformismo, banalidad y pensamiento: imágenes de la alienación en las sociedades de masas según el pensamiento de Arendt. *Jornadas Filosofía Política*, November. Facultad de Filosofía, UB.

Rorty, R. (1995) *Filosofía y el espejo de la naturaleza*. Madrid: Cátedra.

Rorty, R. (1998) *El pragmatisme, una versió*. Barcelona: Eumo editorial.

Saban, M. (2011) *Sod22: el secreto*. Buenos Aires: Ghione Impresores.

Tenzer, N. (1982) *Sociedad despolitizada*. Barcelona: Paidós.

Vattimo, G. and Rovatti, P.A. (eds) (1990) *El pensamiento débil*. Madrid: Cátedra.

Vera, J. (2010) La tarea de cambiar los propios paradigmas. *El arte de dirigir*, **75**, November–December.

Wilber, K. (2000) *Una teoría del todo*. Barcelona: Kairós.

Wilber, K. (2007) *Espiritualidad integral*. Barcelona: Kairós.

NOTES

1 Metaphysics: the branch of philosophy concerned with ontology (the science of being and of its transcendental attributes) and epistemology (the science of wisdom and knowledge). Metaphysics, which refers to things that are 'out there' or beyond physical reality, currently refers to the theory of a suprasensitive world.

2 Personal communication with the author.

3 Universidad Virtual de Judaísmo: http://www.universidad-virtualdejudaismo.com/index.html

4 Beck and Cowan's (1999) spiral dynamics considers that human development progresses through eight general stages, called memes. From the spiral dynamics perspective, a meme is a basic developmental stage that can be expressed in any activity. They are not rigid levels but flowing, overlapping and interrelated waves that create a complex dynamic spiral of the development of conscience. As Beck states: 'The spiral is messy, not symmetrical, with multiple admixtures rather than pure types. These are mosaics, meshes and blends.'

5 Wilber's work focuses mainly on studies of human evolution and the integration of science and religion, as experienced by meditators and mystics, by analysing common elements in Western and Eastern mystic traditions. He has published mainly on philosophy, psychology, anthropology, sociology and religion. Wilber himself is influenced by thinkers such as Nāgārjuna, Huston Smith, Ramana Maharshi, Jürgen Habermas, Jean Gebser, Teilhard de Chardin (with whom Wilber shares the aspiration to a theory that unifies science, art and morality), Plato, Hegel and Buddhism. With Wilber we break definitively with traditional metaphysics and advance towards postmetaphysics.

6 Personal communication with the author.

IV.2d CHALLENGES AND OPPORTUNITIES IN SUSTAINABILITY SCIENCE: A PERSPECTIVE BASED ON RESEARCH AND EDUCATIONAL EXPERIENCES

Masaru Yarime

ACADEMIC, INSTITUTIONAL, AND SOCIETAL CHALLENGES IN SUSTAINABILITY SCIENCE

The emerging field of sustainability science is facing the serious challenge of establishing it as an academic field through the development of concepts and methodologies, institutionalization and networking and collaboration with stakeholders in society. As sustainability science is aimed at understanding the fundamental characteristics of complex and dynamic interactions between natural, human, and social systems, it is crucial to make effective use of knowledge and information on diverse aspects of sustainability. That necessarily requires a broad range of academic disciplines, including natural sciences, engineering, social sciences, and humanities. Thus many concepts and methodologies have been proposed in sustainability science, which poses a significant challenge to establishing it an academic field. In developing sustainability science as a new academic field, it is important to investigate what kinds of conceptualization can be possible or desirable. On the one hand, sustainability science could be considered a new field of science, that is, an emerging scientific branch analysing new phenomena with new approaches, as is the case with nanotechnology and bioinformatics. On the other hand, as different disciplines are involved in addressing many issues related to sustainability, the concept of interdisciplinarity or transdisciplinarity has been emphasized by many researchers in sustainability science. That means it is considered to be a field of meta-science, the science of connecting, integrating, or transcending sciences. We then need to investigate how that could be possible theoretically and to elaborate how transdisciplinarity can actually be implemented in research and education. The same issue could be tackled with different approaches, which, however, are not necessarily connected or integrated, let alone transcended. There is an urgent need to develop concepts, methodologies, and practical tools to implement inter-/transdisciplinarity in education and research.

MULTI-/INTER-/TRANS-DISCIPLINARITY OF SUSTAINABILITY SCIENCE

Global sustainability concerns long-term constraints on resources, including, among others, food, water, and energy. The challenge of sustainability is the reconciliation of society's development goals with the planet's environmental limits over the long term (Clark and Dickson, 2003). The new field of sustainability science now being developed aims at understanding the fundamental character of interactions among natural, human, and social systems (Kates et al., 2001; Clark and Dickson, 2003; Komiyama and Takeuchi, 2006; Komiyama et al., 2011). Sustainability science concerns various domains, including nature (for example climate, ocean, rivers, plants, and other components of the natural environment), technology (for example machinery, chemicals, biotechnology, materials, and energy), and society (for example economy, industry, finance, demography, culture, ethics, and history). The academic landscape of sustainability science likewise consists of clusters of diverse disciplines (Kajikawa, et al., 2007).

It is of critical importance that these diverse types of scientific knowledge be integrated effectively in sustainability science by establishing interfaces with a certain degree of affinity to disciplinary boundaries. There are, however, technical, economic, legal, and institutional barriers and obstacles discouraging such knowledge integration (Maurer, 2006). Researchers are under increasing pressure to publish articles in scientific journals in their own specialties, without much incentive to collaborate with researchers working in different academic fields. As one of the prime motivations for scientific collaboration is to assemble the appropriate expertise for tackling cross-cutting problems Shrum et al., 2007), it is crucial to identify and elaborate the problems and challenges that we intend to tackle in order to promote collaboration in the emerging field of sustainability science. What would be needed are careful analysis and a solid understanding of the institutional conditions for research collaboration.

To examine the patterns of research collaboration in sustainability science, a preliminary bibliometric analysis has been conducted by regions as well as by academic fields (Yarime et al., 2010). The findings suggest that the creation, transmission and sharing of knowledge on sustainability tends to be confined within these regional clusters. Research collaboration in the newly emerging field of sustainability science, which aims at utilizing diverse types of information and knowledge related to sustainability, thus requires organizational and institutional arrangements for more effective collaboration. Field specialization in sustainability research conducted through international collaboration was also found. Research collaboration between Japan and China, for example, tends to be mainly aimed at addressing research needs in China, with support in the form of knowledge and expertise coming from Japanese researchers. Since each country has its own particular focus among the research fields related to sustainability, the existence of regional clusters could pose a serious obstacle to collecting, exchanging, and integrating diverse types of knowledge, which is of critical importance in establishing the transdisciplinary field of sustainability science. Given these patterns of international collaboration, one way of promoting the creation, transmission, and sharing of knowledge on sustainability science could be to encourage research collaboration within existing regional networks at the initial stage and try to establish interregional linkages later.

CONCEPTS, METHODOLOGIES, AND PRACTICAL TOOLS

In the development of academic disciplines in the past we can observe at least two types of evolution: one is concept-oriented, as in chemical engineering, and the other is problem- or use-oriented, as in agricultural science and health science. In the case of establishing chemical engineering as an academic discipline, it was of critical importance that diverse chemical processes were conceptualized in 1915 into 'unit operations' such as drying, distillation, separation, extraction, evaporation, absorption, and adsorption (Rosenberg, 1998). Based on this intellectual foundation, the School of Chemical Engineering Practice was established at the Massachusetts Institute of Technology, followed by establishment of an independent academic department in 1920. Then a standard textbook, *Principles of Chemical Engineering*, was published in 1923. The conceptualization of unit operations effectively functioned as a 'focusing device' in elaborating the purposes of research in chemical engineering. Concepts, tools, and methodologies were applied to actual problems in industry, and the knowledge and experiences obtained were fed back to education and research at universities, leading to the development and institutionalization of chemical engineering.

We can see a significant influence of systems science in the existing literature in the field of sustainability science. Liu et al. (2007) identify some of the most prominent characteristics of inter-systemic interactions, including reciprocal effects and feedback loops, nonlinearity and thresholds, surprises, legacy effects and time lags, resilience, and heterogeneity. While these characteristics certainly represent the complexity of coupled human and natural systems, the mechanisms that explain why these characteristics emerge through complex interactions have not yet been clearly elucidated. The influence of science and technology studies can also be observed to a significant degree in its conceptualization and terminology, including, notably, boundary organization/spanning, co-production of knowledge, and hybridization of scientific and local knowledge. Also, case studies so far mainly concern geographically limited areas in such regions as Africa, Asia, and Latin America. On the other hand, a detailed analysis of sustainability in industrialized countries, where industries are highly advanced and sophisticated technologies play a crucial role, has been relatively lacking in past literature on sustainability science. It would be very useful to conduct case studies in countries such as Japan by taking a specific technology or industrial sector as a boundary condition.

HOW KNOWLEDGE IS TRANSFORMED IN SOCIETY

Scientific knowledge has been utilized extensively for the exploration of territory and utilization of materials on the earth (Yoshikawa, 2006). That process, however, has resulted in the fragmentation of knowledge into different scientific disciplines or fields, leading to deterioration of natural as well as artificial environments without a systemic understanding of the whole. To address this challenge, 'sustainability science' has been proposed since the 1990s by leading scientific organizations such as the International Council for Science (ICSU). This emerging phase of science is aimed at generating knowledge of the processes of change in the interactions of nature, humans, and society. Novel approaches to collecting and analysing various large data sets are required to understand the rules and mechanisms of these complex, long-term processes of interaction.

Sustainability science can be considered as an academic field that analyses the processes of production, diffusion, and utilization of various types of knowledge with long-term consequences for society (Yarime, 2010). Three components can be identified in a process of knowledge transformation in society: knowledge, actors, and institutions. Knowledge itself has aspects of content, quantity, quality, and rate of circulation. Important aspects of actors are their heterogeneity, linkages and networks, and interactions among them. Institutions cover a diverse set of entities, ranging from informal ones such as norms, routines, and established practices to more formal ones including rules, laws, and standards. Sustainability science thus deals with dynamic, complex interactions among diverse actors creating, transmitting, and applying various types of knowledge under specific institutional conditions. There are many phases that can be identified in the production, diffusion, and utilization of knowledge by different actors, without necessarily involving coordination with one another. Gaps and inconsistencies inevitably exist among different phases in terms of the quantity, quality, and rate of knowledge processed. This effectively constitutes a major challenge in pursuing sustainability on a global scale.

A social process of knowledge transformation includes different phases. First of all, a problem affecting sustainability emerges. In this phase, knowledge of the natural sciences is essential to investigating and understanding the causes and mechanisms of the problem. Next, the problem is recognized by many people in society. The way that the problem is reported in the media, including newspapers and TV, significantly influences how the problem is recognized and interpreted in society. Knowledge of methodologies such as discourse analysis is useful in understanding this process. As the problem becomes widely recognized in society, research activities are initiated by scientists at universities and research institutes. The behaviour of scientists will be heavily influenced by the norms and incentives in their communities, which could be significantly different from those in industry. Studies of the sociology of science (Merton, 1973) and economics of science (Dasgupta and David, 1994) have accumulated valuable findings about their behaviour. Scientific investigation of the problem is followed or accompanied by technological development. In this phase, private companies play a major role in inventing and diffusing technological solutions to the problem. Research and development activities of private companies have been studied extensively in the field of the economics of technological change and innovation studies. The technologies developed by industry are introduced in society and subsequently used by different stakeholders. This will cause a variety of impacts, some of them unexpected. Assessments of environmental protection and safety, energy/materials flow analysis, and lifecycle assessment are useful in tracing and understanding the impacts on society. Following these impacts, there will be feedback from the stakeholders in society. Reactions of various actors to scientific and technological developments have been studied in the field of science and technology studies. Thus there are many phases of the knowledge transformation process with feedback among different actors, not necessarily with much coordination with each other.

FOR RECOGNITION AND PROMOTION

To gain peer recognition of sustainability science as an academically established field, institutionalization through establishing programmes, societies/associations, and journals would be helpful. The University of Tokyo initiated an alliance on research and education on sustainability science, the Integrated Research System for Sustainability Science (IR3S) with leading Japanese universities, including Kyoto University, Osaka University, Hokkaido University and Ibaraki University, as well as prominent research institutes in Japan. The University of Toyko started in 2007 the Graduate Program in Sustainability Science (GPSS) with a master's course, and its doctoral course also started in 2009. Similar programmes on sustainability science emerged in other universities around the world in the same period. the academic journal *Sustainability Science* has been launched by IR3S and the United Nations University (UNU). As normally it takes time for a new journal, particularly in a novel field such as sustainability science, to gain a certain degree of recognition, an effective approach is to make an association to a prominent journal which has been already established in academia. For example, a new section devoted to sustainability science has been created in the Proceedings of the National Academy of Science (PNAS) in the United States. Researchers' incentives need to be adjusted to promote cooperation and collaboration between those in different faculties, which would require changes in the criteria for performance evaluation. Promotion and tenure structure need to be adjusted in many universities and research institutes for promoting mobility and developing long-term career paths. It would also be important to create and maintain effective feedback loops with diverse stakeholders in society. Involving various stakeholders in society, however, might pose difficulties in producing rigorous results in the traditional sense. The process of collaborating with stakeholders needs to be credited appropriately in education and research in sustainability science. For graduates of programmes on sustainability sciences, it will be of critical importance to explore their career paths, not only in academia, but also in industry and the public sector. Without having promising opportunities for young people entering this field, sustainability science may not be able to establish its sustainability.

OPPORTUNITIES FOR COLLABORATION

We have identified several opportunities for future collaboration to promote educational and research activities in sustainability science. Students, fellows, and researchers could be exchanged between different universities, possibly with portable scholarships and fellowships. Coordination of academic programmes through bilateral/multilateral schemes could also be pursued. Joint workshops or summer schools for doctoral and young researchers would be a valuable opportunity to exchange and learn from different approaches to conducting rigorous research in this diverse field. Career paths for graduates and researchers need to be explored, with interviews, surveys, and continued dialogues with industry and government. Also it would be useful to have a scheme for exchanging university students and faculty members with employees and researchers in industry. Coordinated efforts for effective outreach to decision makers and stakeholders in international communities would contribute greatly to establishing sustainability science.

EMERGING INITIATIVES FOR INTERNATIONAL PARTNERSHIP

Several initiatives have already been launched to set up global schemes for research collaboration on sustainability science. Among the new types of organizational and institutional arrangements are the Alliance for Global Sustainability (AGS), an inter-university research collaboration between the University of Tokyo in Japan, Massachusetts Institute of Technology in the United States, Federal Institute of Technology in Switzerland, and Chalmers University of Technology in Sweden, and the Forum on Science and Innovation for Sustainable Development hosted by the American

Association for the Advancement of Science (AAAS). The International Conference on Sustainability Science (ICSS) has also been established to encourage communication and knowledge exchange on diverse issues linked to sustainability science. The First ICSS was held at the University of Tokyo in February 2009. In that conference a workshop was organized to provide an international forum to exchange, share, and discuss diverse ideas, concepts, and methodologies in developing doctoral programs on sustainability science and to explore opportunities for mutual collaboration in institutionalizing the academic field of sustainability science. Leading experts working in the field of sustainability science were invited to learn from experiences gained through existing and prospective doctoral programmes on sustainability science at different universities and research institutes around the world. Partners for future networking activities would include the Kennedy School of Government of Harvard University in the United States as well as the School of Sustainability of Arizona State University in the United States, Centre for Sustainability Studies of Lund University in Sweden, International Centre for Integrated Assessment and Sustainable Development of Maastricht University in the Netherlands, and the Sustainability Institute of Stellenbosch University and the Council for Scientific and Industrial Research in South Africa. The second ICSS was held at the Sapienza University of Rome in Italy in June 2010, and the third ICSS will be organized by the Arizona State University in the United States in February 2012. Close collaboration has also been promoted through the AAAS Forum on Science and Innovation for Sustainable Development for information exchange on publications, programmes, projects, researchers, and institutions in sustainability science. These emerging organizational and institutional arrangements will have significant implications for global sustainability, which requires the production, communication, and integration of diverse types of knowledge and expertise.

REFERENCES

Clark, William C. and Dickson, Nancy M. (2003) Sustainability science: The emerging research program. *Proceedings of National Academy of Science*, **100**(14), pp. 8059–61.

Dasgupta, Partha and David Paul A. (1994) Toward a new economics of science. *Research Policy*, **23**, pp. 487–521.

Kajikawa, Yuya, Junko Ohno, Yoshiyuki Takeda, Katsumori Matsushima, and Hiroshi Komiyama (2007) Creating an academic landscape of sustainability science: An analysis of the citation network. *Sustainability Science*, **2**, pp. 221–31.

Kates, Robert W., Clark, William C., Corell, Robert, Hall, J. Michael, Jaeger, Carlo C., Lowe, Ian, McCarthy, James J., Schellnhuber, Hans Joachim, Bolin, Bert, Dickson, Nancy M., Faucheux, Sylvie, Gallopín, Gilberto C., Grubler, Arnulf, Huntley, Brian, Jager, Jill, Jodha, Narpat S., Kasperson, Roger E., Mabogunje, Akin, Matson, Pamela, Mooney, Harold, Moore, Berrien III, O'Riordan, Timothy and Svedin Uno (2001) Sustainability science. *Science*, **292**(5517), pp. 641–2.

Komiyama, Hiroshi and Takeuchi Kazuhiro (2006) Sustainability science: Building a new discipline. *Sustainability Science*, **1**(1), pp. 1–6.

Komiyama, Hiroshi and Kazuhiro Takeuchi, Hideaki Shiroyama and Takashi Mino (eds) (2011) *Sustainability Science: A Multidisciplinary Approach*. Tokyou: United Nations University Press.

Liu, Jianguo, Dietz, Thomas, Carpenter, Stephen R., Alberti, Marina, Folke, Carl, Moran, Emilio, Pell, Alice N., Deadman, Peter, Kratz, Timothy, Lubchenco, Jane, Ostrom, Elinor, Ouyang, Zhiyun, Provencher, William, Redman, Charles L., Schneider, Stephen H. and Taylor, William W. (2007) Complexity of coupled human and natural systems. *Science*, **317**(14 September), pp. 1513–16.

Maurer, Stephen M. (2006) Inside the anticommons: Academic scientists' struggle to build a commercially self-supporting human mutations database, 1999–2001. *Research Policy*, **35**, pp. 839–53.

Merton, Robert K. (1973) *The Sociology of Science: Theoretical and Empirical Investigations*. Chicago: University of Chicago Press.

Rosenberg, Nathan (1998) Chemical engineering as a general purpose technology. In: Helpman, Elhanan (ed.) *General Purpose Technologies and Economic Growth*. Cambridge, MA: MIT Press.

Shrum, Wesley, Genuth, Joel and Chompalov, Ivan (eds) (2007) *Structures of Scientific Collaboration*. Cambridge, MA: MIT Press.

Yarime, Masaru (2010) Sustainability innovation as a social process of knowledge transformation. *Nanotechnology Perceptions*, **6**(3), pp. 143–53.

Yarime, Masaru, Takeda, Yoshiyuki and Kajikawa Yuya (2010) Towards institutional analysis of sustainability science: A quantitative examination of the patterns of research collaboration. *Sustainability Science*, **5**(1), pp. 115–25.

Yoshikawa, Hiroyuki (2006) Academic reform and university reform: Sustainability science (in Japanese). *IDE-Contemporary Higher Education*, **5**, pp. 24–32.

CONNECTING THE DISCONNECTED. SCIENCE AND ART IN THE KNOWLEDGE ADVENTURE

The challenge facing a new systemic, complex paradigm in our universities is to connect the disconnected. To do this we need to escape from the maze created by the separation between elements whose original vocation was and continues to be unity in diversity.

Addressing the relationship between science and art requires these two forms of knowledge to be understood as the two extremes of a continuum. The nomothetic sciences occupy the position of the highest possible objectivity, whereas art occupies the position of minimum objectivity and maximum subjective involvement. Located in between are the idiographic sciences, with philosophy, in its own right, occupying the midpoint of the continuum.

The possible link between them all is to be found in, for example, María Zambrano's concept of *poetic reason* – the wisdom born from the merging of the visible and the invisible and the encounter between intuition, creativity and reason. Poetic reason incorporated in knowledge theory is reconciliatory: it reintegrates and restores the human unity long lost to European culture (Zambrano, 1987, p. 54).

THE ASSUMPTIONS OF SCIENCE

Let us begin by talking about science. To build scientific knowledge in any of its variants, we must be as objective as possible, yet aware that there will always be an element of subjectivity in this knowledge. This necessary application of the precautionary principle to our conclusions is no less than a lesson in humility. As mentioned above, objectivity varies between the nomothetic (natural) sciences and the idiographic (social and human) sciences. In either kind of science, however, we are forced to acknowledge what is undoubtedly one of the greatest contributions of contemporary epistemology: the knowledge that knowledge has limits.

One of the most important of these limits is a blind faith in the congruency and rigour of mathematical language. In 1932, Gödel stated that it was impossible to prove the congruency of a mathematical system from its axioms and that theoretical mathematics was therefore open to uncertainty and indecision. This does not mean we have to renounce mathematical description, but we do need to recognize that even the rigour of description has its limits and that uncertainty flourishes even where we thought there was certainty (Mayer, 2002, p. 71).

Not to feel very secure in our certainties seems to be, then, the road that lies ahead. This does not mean we must deny scientific truths, but we must recognize that they can be superseded and that our knowledge is incomplete. Indeed, complexity invites us to take account of the fact that the greatest certainty of the 20th century is the impossibility of eliminating uncertainty not just in actions but also in knowledge (Morin, 2003, p. 72).

This change in vision, this opening up of perspective that comes from complex thought, suggests that our universities, in their task of explaining the world, need to rely on an equally complex approach, based on interdisciplinary and transdisciplinary models that not only link the various sciences but also link these with art and ethics. It is a question of gradually integrating scientific knowledge with the arts of living, philosophizing and imagining, and of reconstituting compartmentalized knowledge as an integrated whole. Boundaries no longer separate; they are interstitial areas that promote more fruitful encounters. It is a question of accepting the proposition that 'life is a work of art' as a statement of fact, not as an assumption or an admonition (Bauman, 2008, p. 68).

With a view to seeking points of encounter, let us examine some of the features of science and art, taken as the two extremes of a fuzzy continuum. Science, in its most nomothetic version, has four fundamental pillars:

1. The search for the greatest possible objectivity.
2. The establishment of laws or general principles.
3. The need for intelligibility.

4. The principle of falsifiability or dialectics.

The first three laws express, in a synthetic or compressed manner, the systems or phenomena they represent. Thus, the more compression, the better the understanding. As for the fourth law, knowledge, being scientific, runs the risk of being falsified, that is, of being dismantled by new experiences, theories or laws that better explain a phenomenon.

However, not even the faithful application of these principles can lead to irrefutable certainties. Science can point us to closed-off directions, but never to mandatory directions; as Max Weber said, science tells us how to get from one place to another, but it cannot tell us where to go.

Thus, when science lays claim to the universality of its laws or principles, we need to remind ourselves that the laws of nature are fundamentally probabilistic: they express what is possible, not what is true (Prigogine, 1997, p. 109). As Bateson (1982, pp. 24, 26) pointed out, science may improve or refute, but it 'can never prove some generalization'; because it investigates but cannot prove, its truths are, by definition, temporary and susceptible to improvement. Herein lies one of the outstanding features of the scientific endeavour: it is probably the only human activity that is based on the systematic recognition of errors and on criticism and improvement.

THE ASSUMPTIONS OF ART

Art is another form of knowledge, different from but complementary to science, and vital to accounting for the world in all its complexity. With art it is possible to feel, grasp, express, imagine and communicate complexities that are incomprehensible from a scientific perspective (Wagensberg, 1985).

Art, like science, is inspired by wonder, questioning, doubts and fears, but it departs from a different hypothesis and seeks results that cannot be objectified. In essence, art is based on the principle of the subjectivity and communicability of artistic creation. Beyond its revelatory function, art as film, literature, painting, and so on enables us to create, and not just know, reality. It is, in fact, the only human activity where there is creation in the pure sense of the word. For this reason it is said that art imitates nature.

Paul Klee (1976) said that art makes the invisible visible. Art enables us to see what is there but is not immediately evident. It facilitates a reorganization of the imaginary with the real. It enables us to connect reason to feelings, intuitions and emotions.

In contrasting art and the artist with science's drive for universality (the construction of general laws and principles), we see that art, unlike science, seeks the expression of what is diverse, unique and unrepeatable. The work of art is not subject to any law, but rather creates a law unto itself. In that sense it is original.

With regard to the necessary scientific separation between the observer and the observed, in art, unlike science, this is based on the artist's involvement with his/her work, whether from a position of distance or creative silence or when the artist as creator-sender seeks communication with the interpreter-receiver. This link reflects what is known as reception or reader-response theory: the viewer, reader or listener is dynamically involved in the realization of a work of art and his/her answers and interpretations are an essential part of its meaning (Steiner, 2001, p. 72).

As for the scientific notion of intelligibility (and compression), art does not attempt to reduce complexity; rather, it accepts, expresses and transmits complexity. Art derives from the complexity of the artist and his/her unique perception of the complexity of the environment. A work of art is not constructed once and for all (like laws and theories) but is built each time anew, and explanation is left to the unique encounter with the interpreter. A work of art is, therefore, always alive and never finished.

Finally, because it lays no claim to the truth, art, unlike science, is not falsifiable. A work of art is, by definition, evocative; unlike science, which is denotative, art is connotative. This means that a work of art can be recreated, that it can have more or different meanings to those attributed to it by the artist (it is one and manifold at the same time, hence its complexity). Art is thus a sphere where diversity flourishes, where initial chaos gives rise to a certain order.

If, as has been said, the artist is someone who brings order to a disordered cosmos, a work of art functions as a dissipative structure that self-organizes in non-equilibrium conditions and resists increasing entropy (Novo, 2002). The emergence of order from initial chaos is an experience familiar to every artist, from the moment the act of creation commences until the moment when – as expressed by Heidegger (1973) – 'towering up within itself, the work opens up a world, and keeps it abidingly in force.'

SCIENCE AND ART AS COMPLEMENTARY FORMS OF KNOWLEDGE

As part of a new paradigm of complexity, our universities today have the opportunity to view science and art, not as in conflict, but as complementary forms of knowledge and language. As a starting point, we can accept, for example, that our knowledge of even scientific reality is full of exercises in intuition and even metaphor – a semantic transposition mechanism that confirms that meaning is a semantic burden that can be shifted (Chamizo, 1998). Therefore, recognizing the imprint of metaphor across different fields leads us to accept that creativity, imagination and intuition, as constitutive qualities of art, can be recognized and appreciated in other systems of understanding the world (Rábade, 2002, p. 61).

The acknowledgement, then, that our knowledge of even scientific reality is replete with intuition and metaphor opens doors to a model of transdisciplinary knowledge in which the guiding metaphor for truth is not an incomplete attempt to capture or map reality but the fact of living itself (Vattimo, 1997). The act of knowing is shaped, not just by its scientific dimension, but also as a moral and poetic act. As Hölderlin (1977) appropriately stated, man dwells poetically on this Earth.

The reconciliation of science and art, facilitated by the emergence of a new paradigm, is undoubtedly an innovative approach that can and is functioning as a proposal for higher education in the 21st century, a road that leads towards a new vision of the world that no longer appears to be a prosaic program-operated machine, but a complex interweave of intricate relationships. The encounter between science and art will, for once and all, break down the walls raised by modernity between subject and object, humans and the biosphere, cognition and emotion.

Developing an educational model for our universities based on these premises is an opportunity to recover what seemed lost: the unity of knowledge. In this context, the transdisciplinary fusion between scientific and artistic vision opens the door to a model of knowledge (and of teaching and learning) based on the recognition that science and art are not separate, watertight compartments; instead, the points of encounter and reciprocal influences between them are many. Science solves problems, improves our quality of life and enhances human and social development. Art shows us how to imagine, create and interpret reality beyond the limits of reason. Combined, science and art can build and deliver the innovative and creative systemic knowledge necessary to move towards sustainability.

But the encounter between science and art goes even deeper. It occurs within the emerging post-Cartesian paradigm that recognizes and validates other forms of reasoning and of knowledge that, throughout history, have formed the basis for sustainable living. In a decisive transition from fragmentation to cohesion, it articulates what for centuries have been disconnected, namely, logos and pathos.

Higher education in the 21st century can thus be encouraged to embrace the certain and the uncertain and to accept the complexity of the world. In many cases, this is already happening. We have the conceptual, ethical and artistic tools that will enable us to redraw our paths. Our institutions have endless possibilities for ensuring that education – the adventure of teaching and learning – is a point of encounter and a celebration of diversity and of a scientific and artistic awareness or conscience.

TOWARDS A SYSTEMIC AND COMPLEX HIGHER EDUCATION MODEL

It is evident that we need to rethink higher education both in terms of epistemological criteria for generating and constructing knowledge and in terms of methodological approaches and the organization of university structures in the 21st century.

The challenge of educating from a paradigm of complexity – in which scientific, ethical and artistic visions are given equal weighting – may seem well nigh impossible, given the changes required; yet groups that have embarked on this task confirm its viability and relevance. Promoting a culture of complexity would lead to an exploration of issues relevant to the educational process but, unfortunately, often absent from the classroom. For whom and with whom do we build knowledge? What are its limits? How do we identify and create links? How can we make decisions in risk societies? How can we educate in socially and environmentally responsible action?

To do this, we need to step beyond the kind of simplistic thinking that is incapable of conceiving a conjunction between the one and the many (*unitas multiplex*), and develop a more complex thinking that can absorb knowledge from many different dimensions. But from the outset, we need to be aware that complete knowledge is impossible: one axiom of complexity is the impossibility, even in theoretical terms, of omniscience. Complex thinking implies the recognition of incompleteness and uncertainty (Morin, 1994, p. 23).

Accepting these proposals means developing an open epistemology in which object and subject are no longer isolated entities and where the norm is not perfect balance but order from fluctuation; the play between balance and imbalance, irregularity, randomness or uncertainty (Novo, 1997, p. 39). This view greatly complicates the educational task, but it should not be taken as an impediment. It should, rather, be viewed as a stimulus that guides teaching and learning for integrated knowledge, built, like any living process, through advances and setbacks and through impulses and attractions between and across disciplines.

Developing this kind of knowledge is no easy task. Deepening specialist knowledge is unavoidable in a scientific panorama as complex as that of today, where the hold of discipline-based organization is powerful. We can, however, aspire to interdisciplinarity – recognizing that we can be interdisciplinary precisely because we have disciplines (Toulmin, 2003, p. 208). But it is crucial, not to mention truly innovative, to create the mecha-

nisms that will establish and take account not only of epistemological relationships and links but also of social, ecological and moral interactions. Analysing the parts while failing to reconstruct the whole is no longer a valid approach. The interdisciplinary model does not posit an overnight dismantling of educational systems, but it does require that compartmentalized and disciplinary knowledge not be confused with reality. As Paul Klee (1976, p. 79) said, the knowledge of laws is precious, provided we guard against any simplification that confuses naked law with reality.

FROM EPISTEMOLOGY TO METHODOLOGY: SOME KEYS TO CHANGE

A prerequisite for progress is the establishment of cohesive interdisciplinary teams composed of professionals from different knowledge fields combining their efforts in the common endeavour of achieving an integrated view of research or teaching topics. But we must bear in mind that interdisciplinarity is not the product of a major science plus subordinate sciences; rather a primordial feature of this approach is that all disciplines are given the same rank (Sinaceur, 1983).

Knowledge, perfect or imperfect, can thus be woven together in an interstitial area that effectively acts as an intellectual no man's land. It is important to recognize that this knowledge at the boundaries (Gusdorf, 1983) poses its own challenge: the need to locate conceptual and linguistic isomorphisms above and beyond the simple juxtaposition of knowledge or proposals.

Interdisciplinary teams and processes are most effective when their encounters take place under the same paradigmatic umbrella and when cooperation occurs with a common vision of knowledge, of science and of what it means to create and share knowledge. When this happens, a transdisciplinary product emerges from a common framework for understanding the world that is based on the use of an integrating meta-language.

We need to underline the need for higher education to encourage the contextualization of knowledge. A problem, a system or a fact is only intelligible when it is related to its environment. This relationship is much more

than mere dependency: it is constitutive of the system. Logically, the system cannot be understood without including the environment – simultaneously intimate and strange, and simultaneously part of and outside the system. This linkage is absolutely crucial (Morin, 1994). Indeed, in the various manifestations of our educational work, we should always remember that 'all communication necessitates context, that without context, there is no meaning, and that contexts confer meaning' (Bateson, 1982, p. 16).

A welcome practice, in my opinion, and one that is becoming increasingly widespread in the university system, is that of opening up to the real world. The Bologna Process for the construction of the European Higher Education Area encourages approaches in which universities relate to their environment. But this also means that universities must create knowledge that reflects the interests, problems and needs of the communities in which they operate. This 'local' aspect, in conjunction with 'global' aspects, challenges universities to practise 'glocal' thinking.

In adopting a systemic approach to addressing issues, we need to emphasize relationships, starting with internal relationships in our own higher education models – which, in my view, need urgent reassessment. This requires developing seminars, postgraduate programmes and interdisciplinary courses that enable students to reconstruct holistic knowledge from knowledge parcelled out in different disciplines. This is a matter of either rebuilding the whole from the parts (in full awareness that the whole is both more and less than the sum of the parts) or acquiring knowledge of the parts starting from the whole. Whatever the approach, what is fundamental is to develop a holographic model in which the whole and the parts are inextricably linked.

Carrying out these and other innovations requires imagination, creativity and congruency from the academics who teach and organize knowledge in the higher education system. A major challenge is managing resilience. Provided we understand sustainability to be the ability to create, innovate, test and ensure the adaptability of a system (in this case, higher education) in changing societies, the principle of resilience will guide us in encouraging innovations, minimizing inhibitions, reducing resistance to change, enhancing training and information networks, adapting timelines to realities and ensuring lasting change in the medium and long term.

Here again the artistic and ethical dimensions come into their own. The innovations required in our universities need to be addressed, in my opinion, by adopting a multifaceted view. We need to recognize that any problem has not one but many solutions, to foster the joy of discovery in students (Feynman, 2000) and to bring values and ethical principles into play that minimize the allure of scientific neutrality – as blind as it is impossible. Our universities need to understand that any effort to imagine a different, sustainable world is at the heart of any educational process (whatever its content) and is, of necessity, linked to creativity and moral reflection. We need to encourage and stimulate, not merely observe, experience and do, and, above all, we need to foster a creative imagination and the development of ethical criteria on what to observe, what to experience and how to do.

Only in this way can we move ahead towards the kind of education that will bring about a transformation of society and humanity. In this task, we are already closer to being able to make proposals for sustainable living and contribute to the latent challenge, which is to master our mastery, as Morin (1984, p. 54) expressed it. We need, ultimately, to revitalize one of the goals of higher education, which is to seek true wisdom, not just information or knowledge.

REFERENCES

Bateson, G. (1982) *Espíritu y naturaleza.* Buenos Aires: Amorrortu Editores. [*Mind and Nature. A Necessary Unity.* New York: E.P. Dutton]

Bauman, Z. (2008) *El arte de la vida.* Barcelona: Paidós. [*The Art of Life.* Polity Press]

Chamizo, P.J. (1998) La metáfora en los procesos cognitivos. In: *Metáfora y conocimiento,* Analecta Malaciana. Universidad de Málaga, pp. 95–118.

Feynman, R.P. (2000) *El placer de descubrir.* Barcelona: Crítica. [*The Pleasure of Finding Things Out.* Perseus Books]

Gusdorf, G. (1983) Pasado, presente y futuro de la investigación interdisciplinaria. In: Apostel et al. *Interdisciplinariedad y Ciencias Humanas.* Madrid: Tecnos/UNESCO.

Hölderlin, F. (1977) *Poesía completa.* Barcelona: Ediciones 29.

Heidegger, M. (1973) El origen de la obra de arte. In: *Arte y poesía.* México: Fondo de Cultura Económica. [*Der Ursprung des Kunstwerkes*]

Klee, P. (1976) *Teoría del arte moderno.* B. Aires: Ediciones Calden.

Mayer, M. (2002) Reglas y creatividad en la Ciencia y en el Arte. In: Novo, M. (ed.) *Ciencia, arte y medio ambiente.* Madrid: Mundi Prensa, pp. 67–90.

Morin, E. (1984) *Ciencia con consciencia.* Barcelona: Anthropos. [*Science avec conscience.* Librairie Arthème Fayard]

Morin, E. (1994) *Introducción al pensamiento complejo.* Barcelona: Gedisa. [*Introduction a la pensée complexe.* Paris: ESF Editeur]

Morin, E. (2003) *La mente bien ordenada.* Barcelona: Seix Barral. [*La téte bien faite. Repenser la réforme. Réformer la pensée.* Éditions du Seuil]

Novo, M. (1997) El análisis de los problemas ambientales: modelos y metodología. In: Novo, M. and Lara, R. (eds) *El análisis interdisciplinar de la problemática ambiental I.* Madrid: Fundación Universidad-Empresa, pp. 21–59.

Novo, M. (2002) Descubrir, imaginar, conocer: ciencia, arte y medio ambiente. In: Novo, M. (ed.) *Ciencia, arte y medio ambiente.* Madrid: Mundi Prensa, pp.13–26.

Prigogine, I. (1997) *Las leyes del caos.* Barcelona: Crítica. [*Le leggi del caos.* Bari (Italia), Laterza]

Rábade, M. (2002) El pensamiento metafórico en el Arte y en la Ciencia. In: Novo, M. (ed.) *Ciencia, arte y medio ambiente.* Madrid: Mundi Prensa, pp. 61–5.

Sinaceur, M.A. (1983) ¿Qué es la interdisciplinariedad. In: APOSTEL et al. *Interdisciplinariedad y Ciencias Humanas.* Madrid: Tecnos/UNESCO.

STEINER, G. (2001) *Gramáticas de la creación.* Madrid: Siruela. [*Grammars of Creation.* Gifford Lectures for 1990]

Toulmin, S. (2003) *Regreso a la razón.* Barcelona: Península. [*Return to Reason.* Harvard University Press]

Vattimo, G. (1997) La reconstrucción de la racionalidad hermenéutica. In: Fischer, H.R. et al. *El final de los grandes proyectos.* Barcelona: Gedisa. [*Das Ende der groBen Entwürfe.* Frankfurt am Main: Suhrkamp Verlag]

Wagensberg, J. (1985) *Ideas sobre la complejidad del mundo.* Barcelona: Metatemas.

Zambrano, M. (1987) *Pensamiento y poesía en la vida española.* Madrid: Endymión.

On the Road IV.4
Organizational learning and creativity as means to foster sustainability in universities

Rodrigo Lozano

INTRODUCTION

This chapter questions higher education institutions' (HEIs) reliance on traditional Newtonian and Cartesian mental models,[1] when dealing with education for sustainable development. It proposes that new ways of learning are required, where HEIs actively engage in fostering 'metanoia', that is, a shift of mindset (Senge, 1999), for sustainability.

The paper starts with a discussion on sustainability, still considered as an innovation in HEIs. The second part reviews how organizational learning can question underlying assumptions, norms, and objectives, and help to create new processes and methodologies. The final part of the chapter focuses on creativity and 'Eureka' moments, as a means to challenge and break current unsustainable mental models, and thus help to create knowledge that would lead to more sustainable societies.

The paper is based on the premise that learning and creativity follow an iterative process, where creativity breaks the knowledge barrier of current mental models, and then learning helps to consolidate the new mental models. These mental models would, in turn, have to be questioned by creative people.

SUSTAINABILITY, AN INNOVATIVE IDEA IN HEIs

For centuries, universities have been at the forefront in creating and breaking paradigms, and educating future decision makers, entrepreneurs, and leaders (Cortese, 2003; Elton, 2003; Lozano, 2006). However, universities have remained traditional (Elton, 2003), where modern education has relied on Newtonian and Cartesian mental models, which relegate things to mechanistic interpretation and reductionist[2] thinking (Lovelock, 2007; Nonaka and Takeuchi, 2001), the conquest of nature (Cortese, 2003), industrialization (WCED, 1987), and overspecialization and disciplinary isolation (Cortese, 2003).

During the past decade an increasing number of HEIs have engaged in incorporating and institutionalizing the principles of sustainable development (SD) into their systems (Calder and Clugston, 2003; Ferrer-Balas et al., 2010; Lozano, 2006). However, SD is still considered as an innovative idea in most universities (Lozano, 2006), and has not yet permeated all disciplines, scholars, and university managers (Fien, 2002), or throughout the curricula (Matten and Moon, 2004). Several authors (see Cortese, 2003; Orr, 1992; Rosner, 1995) have called for *new ways of learning*, where students are actively and consciously engaged in the use and protection of natural resources, and the safeguarding and improvement of societies' quality of life and well-being for this and future generations. Thereby fostering metanoia for SD.

TOWARDS INQUISITIVE LEARNING

In any organization, such as a university, learning[3] takes place in the different units: individuals, groups, and the organization. Individual learning includes managing mental models by passing through a temporal process to expose assumptions, examining their consistency and accuracy, and seeing how different models can be brought together (Argyris, 1977; Lozano, 2008; Rosner, 1995; Senge, 1999).

In group learning, individuals collaborate to learn (Lozano, 2008; Senge, 1999). The combined intelligence of the team exceeds the sum of the intelligence of its composing individuals, and the team develops extraordinary capacities for collaborative action (Basdur et al., 1986; Senge, 1999; Woodman et al., 1993).

Organizational learning is a complex and iterative process, where organizations acquire knowledge through experiential processes involving action–outcome relationships, and the effects of the environment upon these (van de Ven et al., 1999).

According to Senge (1999), in some cases, individual learning induces organizational learning; however, individual learning does not guarantee organizational learning. Lozano (2008) complements Senge (1999) by indicating that individual learning can facilitate group learning, which in turn facilitates organizational learning. Organizational learning, in turn, facilitates group learning, and thus in turn individual learning. He also argues that congruence plays a key role in this process.

Learning typologies have been proposed by: Argyris (1977), who divides learning into Single-loop (detecting and correcting errors), Double-loop (questioning underlying assumptions and norms), and Triple-loop (developing new processes, or methodologies); and Doppelt (2003), who separates learning into Adaptive learning (searching for direct solutions to immediate problems), Anticipatory learning (identifying potential events and preparing for them), and Action learning (learning from real problems or tasks' experiences). The approaches taken by Argyris (1977) and Doppelt (2003) appear to be independent, yet they can be complementary. This presents the possibility of combining them to offer a more complete typology that would consider the loops and the processes, as shown in Table 1. For a detailed explanation of each type please refer to Lozano (2010).

Processes	Loops		
	Single	Double	Triple
Adaptive	Passive	Proactive	*
Anticipatory	Forecasting	Backcasting	Discerning
Action	Coaching	Experiential	Inquisitive

TABLE 1
Learning typologies according to their loops and processes

Note: * Not applicable, since triple-loop learning focuses on developing new methods and approaches to arrive at re-framings, whilst adaptive learning involves the search for direct solutions to immediate problems.

Learning is a key element in helping to change mental models and behaviour (see Doppelt, 2003; Lozano, 2008; Senge, 1999).

Lower types of learning (for example passive learning) that do not question the underlying principles of the organization, tend to increase bureaucracy, and curtail response to internal and external stimuli. Higher types of learning (that is, discerning and inquisitive learning) can facilitate SD metanoia and consolidate it, for example by including more realistic classroom experiences when teaching SD (Davis et al., 2003).

Although learning is an important part of any change process, it cannot be expected that individuals, groups, or the organization would change their habits after a few days of education (Kotter, 1996); instead, learning needs to be continuous to facilitate changes in the other types of mental attitudes.

'EUREKA', NEW ORGANIZATIONAL MENTAL MODELS

The evolution from passive to discerning and inquisitive learning tends to be cumulative and owes its success to solving problems with techniques close to those already in existence, which reinforces current disciplines and knowledge (Kuhn, 1970).

From the myriad human abilities, creativity may be one of the most powerful and useful ways to break old mental models, and create and institutionalize new ones.

Sternberg and Lubart (1999) argue that creativity is the ability to produce work that is novel (for example original and unexpected) and appropriate (for example useful, and adaptive in task constraints); yet, novelty in a product does not constitute a sufficient condition for defining creativity (Kaufmann, 2001). Csikszentmihaly (2001) proposes that creativity involves a change in memes.[4] For Amabile (1983), creativity refers to products or responses that are novel and appropriate, useful, correct or valuable to the task at hand, where the task is heuristic rather than algorithmic. Woodman et al. (1993) define it as the creation of a valuable, useful new product, service, process, or idea by individuals working together in a complex social system.

The aforementioned creativity definitions present some analogies with innovation, defined as anything (for example a product, a process, or an idea) that is new to a person, organization, or institution (Rogers, 1995). However, innovation refers to the implementation of new products, services, or ideas produced through creativity, or through adaptation of pre-existing products or processes, or those created outside the organization (Woodman et al., 1993).

Basadrud et al. (1982) propose that individual creativity follows a sequential application of divergent thinking (ideation) and convergent thinking (problem finding, solution generation, and solution implementation). Woodman et al. (1993) posit intrinsic motivational orientation as a key element in creativity, in addition to contextual social influences, and antecedent conditions. McNally (cited by Shaw, 1989) proposes that creativity follows four stages:

1. Immersion (experiential inputs from internal and external sources).
2. Incubation (the unconscious development of the process).
3. Illumination (the moment or phase when the pieces of the puzzle fall into place, the 'Eureka' moment).
4. Explication (the phase of self-explanation); and creative synthesis (when the full nature of the experience is revealed.

Woodman et al. (1993) and McNally (cited by Shaw, 1989) provide integrative frameworks

where cognitive and non-cognitive traits tend to come together to create 'Eureka' moments. Thus, creativity could be said to be when the individual's rationality and the emotional psyche connect to create a new product, response, or mental model.

Creativity and the changes it involves cannot be adopted unless they are sanctioned by some group (Csikszentmihalyi, 2001). Woodman et al. (1993) posit that group creativity is a function of individual creativity, the interaction of individuals, group characteristics (for example norms, size, degree of cohesiveness), group processes (for example approaches to problem solving), and contextual influences (for example the larger organization, characteristics of group task).

Organizational creativity is a function of the creative outputs of its component groups and contextual influences (organizational culture, reward systems, resource constraints, the larger environment outside the system, and so on) (Woodman et al., 1993). Organizations create new knowledge and information from the inside out, and do not simply process external information (Nonaka and Takeuchi, 2001).

Once creativity has been accepted in the organization, it might then be transferred to

society. Creativity, once accepted by groups, organizations, and finally society, leads to the development of new mental models. Once the transition to the new paradigm is complete (Kuhn, 1970), then the new paradigm can be said to have been institutionalized (Lozano, 2006; Rogers, 1995; Sherry, 2003). Nonetheless, the institutionalization might not be a clear break from previous mental models.

Figure 1 illustrates the process where creativity breaks the knowledge barrier of current unsustainable mental models. It shows that when the individual 'Eureka' is accepted by a group, then by an organization, and finally by society, new mental models are created. These new mental models, more sustainability oriented, are then consolidated through organizational learning. In the beginning, passive learning helps to expand the reach of the mental models, then this begins to be questioned by individuals (such as students, scholars, academics, and experts), thus moving toward inquisitive and discerning learning. Once the new mental models have been institutionalized, these become the norm, and then the process would recommence.

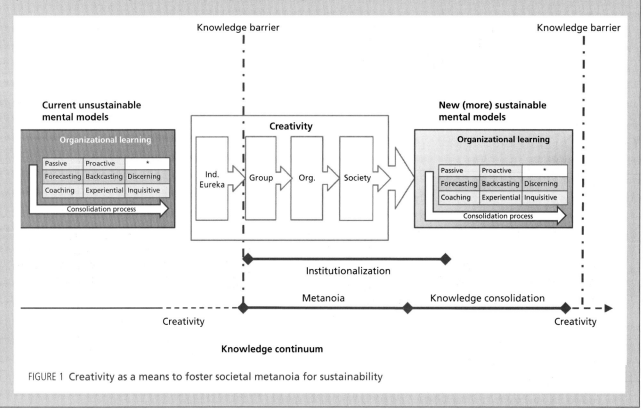

FIGURE 1 Creativity as a means to foster societal metanoia for sustainability

CREATIVITY, 'GAIA', AND SUSTAINABILITY

This section uses Lovelock's (Lovelock, 2007) concept of 'Gaia'[5] to illustrate creativity and learning as means to foster sustainability.

Lovelock started the immersion process, or 'brewing his ideas', of 'Gaia' theory in the 1960s, but the 'Eureka' moment did not appear as a theory until about 1970, when he started sharing it with individuals. The conception of Gaia proposes that the Earth has self-regulating systems of climate and chemistry. From the beginning his ideas of self-regulation were unpopular with Earth and life scientists. Gaia theory took decades before it was partially accepted, because evidence had to appear to confirm it (Lovelock, 2007). In a recent Google Scholar search the term 'Gaia theory' yielded over 24,000 hits (Google scholar, 2010). This could be considered to be group sanctioning as aforementioned. Another important step towards Gaia's adoption was the Amsterdam Declaration (EESP, 2001).

Gaia theory offers an alternative to Newtonian/Cartesian mental models by proposing systems thinking and science, interrelations, and holistic perspectives. However, a question remains: how could Gaia theory, and in turn the sustainability meme and its mental models, be further propagated, and thus foster metanoia? The answer lies in the discussion on learning. When a theory, or mental model, is first developed, such as Gaia, its learning would, unavoidably, have to be through passive learning, whilst the individuals involved comprehend it, for example the teaching of Gaia theory in high-schools in Brazil (see Do Carmo et al., 2009). Then a process of questioning the theory through double-loop learning would take place, for example the reflective learning of Gaia theory (Haigh, 2001), or its questioning through thermodynamics (Karnanin and Annila, 2009). Both positions could be considered as Proactive learning. The questioning of the theory in order to develop new processes and methodologies could lead to Discerning and Inquisitive learning.

CONCLUSIONS

HEIs' reliance on traditional Newtonian and Cartesian mental models, although they have considerably advanced societies, has resulted in unsustainable education and practices.

'Unlearning' old models and providing new ones are part of the solution in moving towards more sustainable societies. This includes students not only learning to pass a test, but also questioning current methods and theories, and developing new methodologies.

Creativity can be a powerful force to foster metanoia for sustainability, by breaking the knowledge barrier of current unsustainable mental models. When the individual 'Eureka' is accepted by a group, then by an organization, and finally by society, then new mental models are created. Thus they begin the consolidation process through organizational learning, beginning with passive learning, which helps to expand the reach of the mental models. Then passive learning is questioned by individuals (such as students, scholars, academics, and experts), thus moving towards inquisitive and discerning learning. Once the new mental models have been institutionalized, these become the norm, and then the process would start again.

This mental models metanoia would help us to depart from education based on causality, mono-disciplinarity, reductionism, and over-specialization, by continuously moving towards education that is systems-oriented, holistic, collaborative, long-term oriented, and interconnected.

Individual learning and creativity for sustainability will fall into the knowledge abyss, if they cannot be transferred to groups, organizations, and finally to society. Therefore, individuals who are working on SD must share their knowledge, and engage in collaboration with different sectors of society.

REFERENCES

Amabile, T.M. (1983) *The Social Psychology of Creativity*. New York: Springer-Verlag.

Argyris, C. (1977) Double loop learning in organizations. *Harvard Business Review*, September–October, 115–25. doi: 10.1225/77502.

Basadur, M., Graen, G.B. and Green, S.G. (1982) Training in creative problem-solving: Effects on ideation and problem finding and solving in an industrial research organization. *Organizational Behaviour and Human Performance*, **30**, 41–70. doi: 10.1016/0030-5073(82)90233-1.

Basadur, M., Graen, G.B. and Scandura, T.A. (1986) Training effects on attitudes toward divergent-thinking among manufacturing engineers. *Journal of Applied Psychology*, **71**, pp. 616–17. doi: 10.1037/0021-9010.71.4.612.

Calder, W. and Clugston, R.M. (2003, March–May) International efforts to promote higher education for sustainable development. *Planning for Higher Education*, **31**, 30–44.

Cortese, A.D. (2003, March–May) The critical role of higher education in creating a sustainable future. *Planning for Higher Education*, **31**, 15–22.

Csikszentmihalyi, M. (2001) A systems perspective on creativity. In: Henry, J. (ed.) *Creative Management* (2nd edn). London: Sage Publications Ltd.

Davis, S.A., Edmister, J.H., Sullivan, K. and West, C.K. (2003) Educating sustainable societies for the twenty-first century. *International Journal of Sustainability in Higher Education*, **4**(2), 169–79.

Dawkins, R. (1978) *The Selfish Gene*. London: Oxford University Press.

Do Carmo, R.S., Nunes-Nieto, N.F. and El-Hani, C.N. (2009) Gaia Theory in Brazilian High School Biology Textbooks. *Science & Education*, **18**(3–4), pp. 469–501.

Doppelt, B. (2003) *Leading Change Toward Sustainability. A Change-management Guide for Business, Government and Civil Society.* Sheffield: Greenleaf Publishing.

EESP (2001) The Amsterdam Declaration Retrieved 6 July, 2010, from http://www.essp.org/index.php?id=41

Elton, L. (2003) Dissemination of innovations in higher education: A change theory approach. *Tertiary Education and Management*, (9), pp. 199–214. doi: 10.1023/A:1024472813449.

Ferrer-Balas, D., Lozano, R., Huisingh, D., Buckland, H., Ysern, P. and Zilahy, G. (2010) Going beyond the rhetoric: system-wide changes in universities for sustainable societies. *Journal of Cleaner Production*, **18**(7), pp. 607–10. doi: 10.1016/j.jclepro.2009.12.009.

Fien, J. (2002) Advancing sustainability in higher education: issues and opportunities for research. *Higher Education Policy*, **15**, pp. 143–52. doi: 10.1108/14676370210434705.

Google scholar (2010) Gaia theory search

Retrieved 27 July, 2010, from http://scholar.google.co.uk/scholar?q=gaia+theory&hl=en&btnG=Search&as_sdt=2001&as_sdtp=on

Haigh, M.J. (2001) Constructing Gaia: using journals to foster reflective learning. *Journal of Geography in Higher Education, 25*(2), pp. 167–89.

Karnanin, M. and Annila, A. (2009) Gaia again. *Biosystems,* **95**(1), pp. 82–7.

Kaufmann, G. (2001) Creativity and problem solving. In: Henry, J. (ed.) *Creative Management* (2nd edn). London: Sage Publications Ltd.

Kotter, J.P. (1996) *Leading Change.* Boston: Harvard Business School Press.

Kuhn, T.S. (1970) *The Structure of Scientific Revolutions* (2nd edn). Chicago: The University of Chicago Press.

Lovelock, J. (2007) *The Revenge of Gaia.* London: Penguin Group.

Lozano, R. (2006) Incorporation and institutionalization of SD into universities: breaking through barriers to change. *Journal of Cleaner Production,* **14**(9–11), pp. 787–96. doi: 10.1016/j.jclepro.2005.12.010

Lozano, R. (2008) Developing collaborative and sustainable organisations. *Journal of Cleaner Production,* **16**(4), pp. 499–509. doi: 10.1016/j.jclepro.2007.01.002

Lozano, R. (2010) *Organisational learning as a means to foster societies metanoia for Sustainability.* Paper presented at the Engineering Education in Sustainable Development, Gothenburg, Sweden.

Matten, D. and Moon, J. (2004) Corporate social responsibility education in Europe. *Journal of Business Ethics,* **54**, pp. 323–37. doi: 10.1007/s10551-004-1822-0

Nonaka, I. and Takeuchi, H. (2001) Organizational knowledge creation. In: Henry, J. (ed.) *Creative Management* (2nd edn). London: Sage Publications Ltd.

Orr, D.W. (1992) *Ecological Literacy.* New York: State University of New York.

Rogers, E.M. (1995) *Diffusion of Innovations* (4th edn). New York: Free Press.

Rosner, W.J. (1995) Mental models for sustainability. *Journal of Cleaner Production,* **3**(1–2), pp. 107–21. doi: 10.1016/0959-6526(95)00057-L

Senge, P.M. (1999) *The Fifth Discipline. The Art and Practice of the Learning Organization.* London: Random House Business Books.

Shaw, M.P. (1989) The Eureka process: A structure for the creative experience in science and engineering. Creativity Research Journal, **2**, pp. 286–98. doi: 10.1080/10400418909534325

Sherry, L. (2003) Sustainability of innovations. Journal of Interactive Learning Research, **13**(3), pp. 209–36.

Sternberg, R.J. and Lubart, T. (1999) The concept of creativity: prospects and paradigms. In: Sternberg, R.J. and Lubart, T. (eds) Handbook of Creativity. Cambridge: Cambridge University Press.

van de Ven, A.H., Polley, D.E., Garud, R. and Venkataraman, S. (1999) The Innovation Journey. Oxford: Oxford University Press.

WCED (1987) Our Common Future (1st edn). Oxford: Oxford University Press.

Woodman, R.W., Sawyer, J.E. and Griffin, R.W. (1993) Toward a theory of organizational creativity. *Academy of Management Review,* **18**(2), pp. 293–321. doi: 10.2307/258761

NOTES

1   Such as schemata, paradigms, perspectives, beliefs, and viewpoints which help individuals to perceive and define their world (Nonaka and Takeuchi, 2001).

2   According to Lovelock (2007), reductionism refers to the analytical dissection of a thing into its ultimate component parts, followed by regeneration through the reassembly of the parts. In contrast, the holistic view analyses a thing from outside and asks it questions while it works.

3   For a discussion on learning refer to Lozano (2010).

4   Dawkins (1978) defines a meme as 'a noun which conveys the idea of a unit of cultural transmission, or a unit of imitation.'

5   The concept of 'Gaia' used in this chapter is the original one posited by Lovelock (2007) and not the radical position taken by some fanatic environmentalists.

IV.3 Open up to Society: Building Sustainability Together

Making substantial changes in higher education, enhancing its quality and relevance, and solving the major challenges it faces will require the committed involvement of all stakeholders, including students and their families, teachers, business and industry, the public and private sectors of the economy, parliaments, the media, the local community, professional associations and society at large.

There is a need for real engagement between universities and society, and this engagement may well extend far beyond national boundaries. The nature of such engagement needs to be debated and deliberated intensively, drawing on real examples, practices and experiences. There is also a need to understand the role that universities will play through this engagement, particularly in the ways that they engage with citizens – both individuals and groups.

University–society dialogue must be part of internal institutional dynamics, since it is from society that the demand for knowledge comes and to society that it is addressed. We need to create a true knowledge-based society through engagement with a broad set of social actors and provide expert advice in dealing with the problematic issues of the day. We need to explore new, more integrated routes of knowledge transfer to citizens that are related to problems rather than disciplines and are comprehensible enough for application.

The relationship between scientific research and political decision-making as it relates to collective well-being and topics of general interest needs to be explored and analysed in order to build bridges between the two. This is an emerging challenge and an imperative both in local contexts and for global problems that can only be addressed under a public-service perspective with the support of society.

IV.3a THE POLITICS OF BUILDING SUSTAINABILITY TOGETHER

Scott J. Peters

INTRODUCTION

In conversations about the engagement of higher education (HE) and society to build sustainability, people tend to focus their attention on one of two main themes: the development and transfer of new technologies and knowledge, or the transformation of teaching, learning, and research in ways that reflect ecological and participatory principles, theories, and methods. Both of these themes are important. But comparatively little attention is given to an additional theme: the political nature of the engagement process.

To ground this theme in something specific, consider agricultural sustainability. In March of 2011 Olivier De Schutter, the United Nations' Special Rapporteur on the right to food, issued a report that urges countries across the planet to make their agricultural systems more sustainable by enacting public policies that support the scaling-up of 'agroecology' (De Schutter, 2011). Agroecology involves the integration of agricultural and ecological sciences with local and/or indigenous knowledges and ways of knowing. Importantly, it isn't just about developing and implementing environmentally sustainable methods of agricultural production. Its practitioners aim not only to solve technical problems for material ends, but also to advance cultural and political values and ideals like democracy and food sovereignty (Altieri, 1995; Warner, 2007; Vandemeer, 2011). And there's evidence it's been effective in advancing these aims. As De Schutter shows in his report, agroecology has been put into practice in many places in ways that have improved not only the sustainability and ethics of food systems, but also their productivity. It's a promising and proven approach to advancing food security.

Calls to scale-up the adoption of agroecology reinforce calls to transform HE in ways that enhance its contributions to the work of building sustainable societies (Corcoran and Wals, 2004). The nature of the transformation in the case of agroecology is not mainly about improving HE's willingness and ability to develop and transfer new scientific knowledge and technologies. Rather, it's about its willingness and ability to engage academic professionals and students from many disciplines in deep, reciprocal, and sustained partnerships with external groups (Peters et al., 2005). By definition, the pursuit of agroecology calls for participatory modes of learning and research that involve the face-to-face engagement of and close working relationships between scientists, farmers, educators, and others (Uphoff, 2002). It calls on participants to honour and interweave different ways of knowing (Pimbert, 2006). It calls on them to engage in discussion, deliberation, and research not only about what can be done to address technical problems (for example insect pests and diseases in crops), but also what should be done to pursue particular values, ideals, and interests (for example local ownership and control of resources). And it requires them to break out of either/or understandings of their main identity and role. Instead of viewing themselves as *either* knowledge producers *or* knowledge consumers/users, it requires all participants to become knowledge co-producers. It requires academic professionals and students to move beyond campus-based work in order to conduct community-based work. And it requires them to break out of disciplinary silos in order to embrace epistemological and methodological pluralism (Norgaard, 1992; Miller et al., 2008).

These are profound changes and transformations for academic and community participants alike. They're much easier to proclaim and advocate for than they are to practise. In large part, that's because engagement isn't just an instrumental technique or method. It's a form of public work that has political dimensions. Whether it's about building sustainability or addressing some other public issue or problem, the engagement process is *inherently and inescapably* political. When academic professionals and students choose to move from understanding to action in building sustainability together with their non-academic partners, they inevitably become engaged in politics.

Unfortunately, the political nature and dimensions of the engagement process are rarely acknowledged. This isn't an accidental oversight. It's partly a reflection of most people's tendency to think about and name interactive and relational work across lines of difference in everyday settings as something other than 'politics' (for example as collaboration, partnering, planning, and so on). More importantly, it's a reflection of a combination of two prevailing views that are held both inside and outside the academy. The first holds that politics is an evil we should try to avoid, overcome, or transcend. The second holds that it's something only politicians do.

These views about politics are highly problematic. We need to get over and beyond them if we wish to understand and improve the work of building sustainability together, where 'together' includes HE and its external partners. We need to acknowledge and embrace the political nature of the engagement process. And we must learn to do so in ways that enhance our appreciation of the *positive* dimensions and value of politics.

POLITICS

A good place to begin is by raising a fundamental question: What is politics? In light of the efforts people make to distance themselves from it, one might think that it's some kind of disease. At best, it's viewed as a necessary evil. But this negative conception of politics is misguided. Instead of being an evil, necessary or not, politics is actually a *good*. It's a positive rather than negative activity. To see it this way, consider its main alternative. As the British political theorist Bernard Crick (1992) points out in his important book, *In Defense of Politics*, the main alternative to politics in much of human history has been tyranny. And tyranny, in each of its various forms, is marked by a rejection of politics in favour of coercion and violence.

A positive view of politics as a good rather than an evil holds that it is an activity people engage in when they are free to work together across lines of difference to advance their interests and values. The work of politics includes naming and framing common problems; expressing and examining values, interests, and desired ends and goals; considering what can and should be done to address common problems and pursue interests and ends; building and exercising power; and acting together in ways that involve reconciliation and negotiation over different and often conflicting values, worldviews, interests, and ends (Forester, 2009).

Beyond understanding politics as good work that involves the above activities, we also need to see that it's not just about elections, or government structures and processes. It's not located only in the state. It's not just what politicians and political parties do, and it's not only about government policymaking. It's an activity people from all walks of life can and do engage in as they come together to name and discuss their problems and aspirations, figure out what can and should be done about them, and act together to pursue their values, interests, and ends (Mathews, 1999). This activity is what Harry Boyte (2004) refers to as 'public work,' and it's taken up in many everyday settings, formal and non-formal, by diverse groups of people.

Importantly, the public work of politics isn't just talk. It includes the collaborative production of material and cultural goods that have broad public value and significance. Such goods include knowledge, wisdom, technologies, methods, and relational power.

To see politics as a positive form of collaborative work is not to say that it's always and everywhere practised and pursued in good and effective ways. Nor is it to say that it's always and everywhere 'democratic'. It isn't. It can be more or less good, more or less effective, and more or less democratic. To view politics as public work in everyday places involving all kinds of people is to accept that it will always be imperfect, and more importantly, that it will always reflect the dynamics and realities of particular contexts.

Like all kinds of work, politics needs to be learned and practised. But practice alone is insufficient, especially when it comes to a kind of politics that warrants being referred to as 'democratic'. Democratic politics involves more than skills and capacities that are developed through practice and experience. It also involves dispositions, ethics, values, and virtues that must be embraced and lived out (Macpherson, 1977; Held, 2006). In other words, the practice of democratic politics isn't just a matter of skill. It's also a matter of character.

One crucial aspect of the view of politics I've sketched here is that it's not just instrumental. It's more than a way for people to solve problems and advance their self-interests, common interests, and larger public interests. It also can be and often is a means for human and community development – including the development of civic agency skills and consciousness among people who have been conditioned to think of themselves as passive consumers, clients, bystanders, or victims. This makes politics something that is good in and of itself. It gives it cultural meaning and significance, beyond any material or economic measurement of its outcomes. This is not to say that it doesn't also have potentially positive connections to economic development. As Amartya Sen (1999) and Martha Nussbaum (2011) have argued, freedom, as expressed through people's engagement in everyday politics (that is, their civic agency), is an indispensible ingredient in the development process.

It's important to recognize that there are many threats to politics, beyond the obvious one of violent and coercive tyranny. Two of the most important threats are especially relevant to the conversation about the engagement of HE and society in the work of building sustainability. The first of these is a form of 'service' that avoids the work of acknowledging and dealing with differences in interests, ends, worldviews, values, and power. Proponents of service often see service as an alternative to politics, or even as something that's *better than* politics. The second threat – often referred to as 'scientism' – is the idea that science offers the only legitimate way of knowing (Sorell, 1991). Further, it holds that all human and environmental problems are basically technical in nature, and that the development and application of scientific knowledge and engineering expertise are all that is needed to understand and address them. Like proponents of service, proponents of this idea see science and engineering as being superior to politics. For well over a century, they have espoused a technocratic ideology centred on the utopian dream of overcoming politics through the development and exercise of scientific and technological expertise (Fischer, 1990; Jordan, 1994).

POLITICS AND HIGHER EDUCATION

Is the kind of politics I'm speaking of here really relevant to and appropriate for HE professionals and institutions? Aren't there real dangers to the move of trying to 'politicize' higher education?

There are, indeed, serious worries about the effects

of HE's engagement in politics. The main worry has to do with the ways political engagement might damage academic freedom, and the trustworthiness of academic work. Another worry, less frequently voiced, has to do with the ways academics who engage in politics might damage democracy by exerting their expertise and authority in disrespectful ways that sideline so-called 'ordinary citizens' from the work of politics. Linked mainly to the former of these worries, in the dominant discourse of academic culture academic professionals and institutions are frequently positioned outside of or above politics. The normative stance with respect to politics is often framed as one of detached, neutral, unbiased, and disinterested objectivity.

Despite the dominant discourse, the question of whether, in what ways, and for what purposes academic professionals and institutions have been, are, or should be engaged in politics is – and has long been – a matter of serious debate (Hammersley, 1995; Peters, 2010). Against the grain of the apolitical, unbiased, disinterested norm and ideal, there is a vast literature on the ways science and other aspects of academic work are political, biased, and interested (for example, Jacob, 1994; Harding, 2000). The concept of the 'traditional intellectual' who is supposed to be free of class allegiances and interests has been exposed as a mirage (Fink et al., 1996). More or less in line with Antonio Gramsci's alternative concept of the 'organic intellectual' (Forgacs, 2000), scholars have established traditions of political engagement in the academic profession that are meant to advance the interests of particular classes and groups. These traditions include public intellectuals who speak and write for broad public audiences as social critics (for example Mills, 1959), and action researchers and public scholars who work with specific publics to facilitate social change as educational organizers, activists, and/or civic educators (Peters et al., 2005; Greenwood and Levin, 2007; Hale, 2008; Peters, 2010).

While many practitioners in 'organic intellectual' traditions work in highly partisan ways, others do not. I want to stress that in this paper I'm not advocating for the 'politicization' of HE in ways that situate its teaching and research functions inside partisan electoral politics, or that involve academic professionals in openly taking sides in specific policy debates as a part of their official academic work. Rather, I'm advocating for an embrace of a set of democratic ideals, dispositions, and methods that enable academics and their community partners to work respectfully across lines of difference, and to do so in ways that reflect a non-neutral embrace of civic learning, development, and action aimed at

advancing not only people's self-interests and common interests, but also larger public interests. In writing of the politics of building sustainability together, my focus is on the political nature of interactive and relational work that involves the face-to-face engagement of academic professionals and students with people and organizations that are external to academic institutions. In calling attention to the politics of the engagement process, my aim is to encourage participants to illuminate, examine, and most importantly improve the politics of building sustainability together.

RELATIONAL ORGANIZING

So how can this be done? There are, of course, many different answers to this question, each in some way tuned to the dynamics and situational realities of context, and each reflective of particular cultures' views and philosophies of politics and public life. Here I want to argue that the first and most important element in a strategy for illuminating, examining, and improving the politics of building sustainability together is to embrace and invest in a broad-based relational organizing approach to engagement. Relational organizing has roots in the American Civil Rights Movement (Payne, 1995; Boyte, 2009) and the Industrial Areas Foundation (IAF), the latter of which was founded by Saul Alinsky in the 1940s and continues into the present (Rogers, 1990; Gecan, 2002; Chambers, 2003). It also has roots in the American land-grant university system's extension work (Peters, 2010).

Relational organizing is a distinct variety and tradition of organizing, different from those that focus on mobilizing people for protests and demonstrations. As its name suggests, it involves the establishment and ongoing development of public relationships among a broad base of people. Instead of protests and demonstrations, the focus of relational organizing is engaging people in productive public work aimed at addressing public issues and problems. Relational organizers are skilled at identifying people's values, motivations, and self- and common interests through the discipline and craft of one-on-one interviews. These interviews have been referred to as the single most important component of organizing (Rogers, 1990). Organizers use them to identify leadership for public work. Organizing in the relational tradition is viewed as a means of education that develops people's civic skills, agency, dispositions, and capacities. It's also viewed as a means of developing collaborative leadership (Longo and Gibson, 2011). It taps and engages people's core values and interests, which are deeper and more sustaining than their concerns about particular issues and problems.

Relational organizing is difficult work. While it can be learned and practised by a wide variety of people, including academic faculty, staff, and students, it must be consciously invested in if it is to succeed. In most institutions of higher learning, however, relational organizing is deeply countercultural. It has been pushed to the margins by allegedly apolitical concepts of 'service', technocratic tendencies and patterns of practice, and an activist, advocacy politics of protest and social criticism. Despite these challenges, it has been increasingly embraced, pursued, and invested in during the past few decades in many colleges and universities (Avila, 2010; Saltmarsh and Hartley, 2011).

One key point must be stressed here. A relational organizing approach to the engagement of HE and society should not be viewed as being limited to the provision and/or application of academic expertise and knowledge. As Sandra Harding (2000) has argued, democratic varieties of engagement offer avenues for transforming research agendas and practices. The conversation about the politics of building sustainability together must therefore be broad enough to attend to the ways reciprocal engagement can do more than simply help to direct who gets access to and who benefits from the results of academic work. It must also attend to the question of how engagement can be organized in order to also inform and shape which questions and problems are taken up by scientists and scholars, and how they are pursued.

Rather than being seen as threatening, this deeper dimension of the engagement process should be viewed as a path for breaking new ground in academic fields, and for vastly enhancing the public meaning and significance of academic work. To be sure, pursuing this path is not easy. It depends on the availability of skilled organizers who can help people learn how to see and attend to differences in interests, power, and ways of knowing. And this kind or organizing isn't likely to be available unless and until higher education institutions invest in it as a means of developing a respectful, constructive, and productive politics of building sustainability together.

REFERENCES

Altieri, M.A. (1995) *Agroecology: The Science of Sustainable Agriculture* (2nd edn). Boulder, Colorado: Westview Press.

Avila, M. (2010) Community organizing practices in academia: A model, and stories of partnerships. *Journal of Higher Education Outreach and Engagement*, **14**(2), pp. 37–63.

Boyte, H.C. (2004) *Everyday Politics: Reconnecting Citizens and Public Life*. Philadelphia: University of Pennsylvania Press.

Boyte. H.C. (2009) Repairing the breech: Cultural organizing and the politics of knowledge. *Partnerships: A Journal of Service-Learning and Civic Engagement*, **1**(1), pp. 1–21.

Chambers, E.T. (2003) *Roots for Radicals: Organizing for Power, Action, and Justice*. New York: Continuum.

Corcoran, P.B. and Wals, A.E.J. (2004) *Higher Education and the Challenge of Sustainability: Problematics, Promise, and Practice*. Dordrecht, The Netherlands: Kluwer Academic Publishers.

Crick, B. (1992) *In Defense of Politics* (4th edn). Chicago: University of Chicago Press.

De Schutter, O. (2011) Agro-ecology and the right to food. United Nations Human Rights Council (published online at www.srfood.org).

Fink, L., Leonard, S.T. and Reid, D.M. (eds) (1996) *Intellectuals and Public Life: Between Radicalism and Reform*. Ithaca, New York: Cornell University Press.

Fischer, F. (1990) *Technocracy and the Politics of Expertise*. Newbury Park, California: Sage Publications.

Forester, J. (2009) *Dealing with Differences: Dramas of Mediating Public Disputes*. New York: Oxford University Press.

Forgacs, D. (ed.) (2000) *The Antonio Gramsci Reader: Selected Writings, 1916–1935*. New York: NYU Press.

Gecan, M. (2002) *Going Public*. Boston: Beacon Press.

Greenwood, D.J. and Levin, M. (2007) *Introduction to Action Research: Social Research for Social Change* (2nd edn). Thousand Oaks, California: Sage Publications.

Hale, C.F. (ed.) (2008) *Engaging Contradictions: Theory, Politics, and Methods of Activist Scholarship*. Berkeley, California: University of California Press.

Hammersley, M. (1995) *The Politics of Social Research*. Thousand Oaks, California: Sage Publications.

Harding, S. (2000) Should philosophies of science encode democratic ideals? In: Kleinman, D.L. (ed.) *Science, Technology and Democracy* (pp. 121–38). Albany, New York: SUNY Press.

Held, D. (2006) *Models of Democracy* (3rd edn). Stanford, California: Stanford University Press.

Jacob, M.C. (ed.) (1994) *The Politics of Western Science, 1640–1990*. Amherst, New York: Humanity Books.

Jordan, J.M. (1994) *Machine-Age Ideology: Social Engineering and American Liberalism, 1911–1939*. Chapel Hill, North Carolina: University of North Carolina Press.

Longo, N.V. and Gibson, C.M. (2011) *From Command to Community: A New Approach to Leadership Education in Colleges and Universities*. Medford, MA: Tufts University Press.

Macpherson, C.B. (1977) *The Life and Times of Liberal Democracy*. New York: Oxford University Press.

Mathews, D. (1999) *Politics for People: Finding a Responsible Public Voice* (2nd edn). Urbana, Illinois: University of Illinois Press.

Miller, T.R., Baird, T.D., Littlefield, C.M., Kofinas, G., Chapin, III, F. and Redman, C.L. (2008) Epistemological pluralism: reorganizing interdisciplinary research. *Ecology and Society*, **13**(2), p. 46 (online).

Mills, C.W. (1959) *The Sociological Imagination*. New York: Oxford University Press.

Norgaard, R.B. (1992) Coordinating disciplinary and organizational ways of knowing. *Agriculture, Ecosystems, and Environment*, **42**: pp. 205–16.

Nussbaum, M.C. (2011) *Creating Capabilities: The Human Development Approach.* Cambridge, MA: Harvard University Press.

Payne, C.M. (1995) *I've Got the Light of Freedom: The Organizing Tradition and the Mississippi Freedom Struggle.* Berkeley, CA: University of California Press.

Peters, S.J. (2010) *Democracy and Higher education: Traditions and Stories of Civic Engagement.* East Lansing: Michigan State University Press.

Peters, S.J., Jordan, N.R., Adamek, M. and Alter, T.R. (eds) (2005) *Engaging Campus and Community: The Practice of Public Scholarship in the State and Land-Grant University System.* Dayton, Ohio: Kettering Foundation Press.

Pimbert, M. (2006) *Transforming Knowledge and Ways of Knowing for Food Sovereignty.* London: International Institute for Environment and Development (IIED).

Rogers, M.B. (1990) *Cold Anger: A Story of Faith and Power Politics.* Denton, Texas: University of North Texas Press.

Saltmarsh, J. and Hartley, M. (eds) (2011) *'To Serve a Larger Purpose': Engagement for Democracy and the Transformation of Higher Education.* Philadelphia: Temple University Press.

Sen, A. (1999) *Development As Freedom.* New York: Anchor Books.

Sorell, T. (1991) *Scientism: Philosophy and the Infatuation with Science.* New York: Routledge.

Uphoff, N. (2002) *Agroecological Innovations: Increasing Food Production with Participatory Development.* London: Earthscan.

Vandemeer, J.H. (2011) *The Ecology of Agroecosystems.* Sudbury, MA: Jones and Bartlett.

Warner, K.D. (2007) *Agroecology in Action: Extending Alternative Agriculture through Social Networks.* Cambridge, MA: MIT Press.

IV.3b THE SOCIAL RESPONSIBILITY OF ENGINEERS[1]

Karel F. Mulder

INTRODUCTION

Technology has often been blamed as the culprit that created a wasteful and over-consuming society, addicted to fossil fuels and poisoning all the Earth's inhabitants. In this view, the 'progress' that engineers and natural scientists claimed to produce by creating new technologies was 'futile' or even a road to collapse: consumer societies had to give up their wasteful lifestyles. New technologies could not play a role in this transition because technology was regarded as the root cause of the problem (Braun, 1995; Sale, 1995).

But in the past 10 years, the mood has changed. Technological options like wind turbines, PV cells, hybrid cars, recycling systems and improved thermal insulation are embraced by green trendsetters (Pernick and Wilder, 2007). Various green products, claiming to have similar functionality as conventional products, are on the market: from green roads to green underwear. But is sustainable development (SD) merely a technological challenge to develop cleaner equivalents of current products?

This paper digs into the relation between the processes of technological change and its social context. The aim of that analysis is to show how scientific and technologic change is intimately intertwined with society and societal change. However, in natural science and engineering, this interconnection is often denied. Instead, one emphasizes the role of new scientific knowledge in societal 'progress'. As a result, the grand challenges that emerge in society and that require new scientific research and new technological developments are often neglected.

Therefore, in order to create the technologies that we need for a more sustainable development, we need engineers who are responsive to society, and are able to understand and interact with a wide range of stakeholders. But how to accomplish this? In the final paragraph, some principles for curriculum reform in engineering education are given.

TECHNOLOGY FOR SD

Sustainable development has been welcomed by large parts of the engineering community as it often promotes the development of more environmentally efficient technologies. But often, the options to 'green' current technologies are limited: sometimes there are inherent upper limits. New systems will have to be created in order to deliver more radical solutions for our problems. However, new systems eventually might create problems of a new nature. Tarr and McShane (1997) offer an example from history:

> In the 19th century horse manure, urine, and horse carcasses left in the streets of cities, created giant

problems. It contributed to the spreading of various diseases. With our current biases, we easily tend to underestimate these problems. In 1908 there were 20,000 New York victims from manure related diseases. The solution of this problem was not found in technologies to prevent manure disposal on the streets but by the introduction of motorized public transportation systems and automobiles.

Nowadays, motorized transport is one of the world's main sustainability problems. With almost 1 billion motorized vehicles, fuel consumption exceeds renewable levels about 1 million times, the annual death toll is more than 1 million and more than 50 million people are injured each year. Air quality, especially in cities, is bad and many people suffer from traffic noise.

Solutions for SD problems will be found in the introduction of new socio-technical systems: not just new technologies, but the combined introduction of new technologies, new ways of organizing, new institutional structures and new behavioural patterns of citizens. These transitions (Rotmans et al., 2001) are often the unplanned result of the interplay of various social, organizational and technological changes. However, transitions bring more than just the changes that are intended. It is not technology alone, but the interplay of social and technological factors that plays a decisive role in transitions. Transitions do not just require technology; they also require cultural, organizational and policy analysis to achieve success. This is not something that engineers are trained for.

Very often, people think in terms of greening existing technologies. However, the range of options to solve sustainability problems widens enormously if one abandons this limit to creativity: the solution to the problems created by cars is not necessarily a cleaner car. It could also be teleworking, easily accessible car rent systems or improved public transport.

Changes at the level of technological systems can potentially create leaps in environmental performance. But this requires much more than the ability to improve the characteristics of an existing technology. It requires thinking in terms of fulfilling the needs of consumers, communities, companies and authorities.

THE ROLE OF SCIENCE AND ENGINEERING

Why is so little attention paid to the social embeddedness of technologies in engineering education? The answer to this can in part be found in the history of modern engineering.

In the 17th and 18th centuries, engineering was a craft and engineers were trained as apprentices. The design of ships, fortifications, bridges and waterworks and the supervision of the construction of these works were carried out by men who learned this craft from more experienced colleagues. At this time, the natural sciences at universities did not aim at solving practical problems. Natural sciences were deemed 'natural philosophy' that is, mainly reflecting on specific natural phenomena. However, engineering and natural sciences increasingly became alike. In the 19th century, the engineer changed into a scientifically trained professional. Engineering Schools were established throughout Europe and the USA. Their curricula were natural science based. This was mainly caused by the high status of the sciences. Many engineering schools had to fight prolonged struggles in order to obtain the same recognition as their university-trained colleagues. In this engineering emancipation struggle, the engineering schools moved away from the engineering core as being problem solvers to making engineering an 'applied science', formulating it in terms of mathematical formulas.

However, engineering has a character different from natural science. Walter Vincenti (1993) asserts that engineering research deals with areas in which the basic science is well understood, but the complexity of the practical problems is large. Historically, one could even say that engineers dealt with complex practical problems of which the basic scientific principles were not even understood.

Science is about analysing and understanding nature, but engineering is about creating new systems that 'work'. By this demand, 'systems that work', the social aspect enters engineering: is an 'unsafe system' a 'system that works'? Or is a 'polluting system' a 'system that works'?

What do we consider to be a 'system that works'? It is interesting to analyse how systems that did not work as intended were produced. For example, was the Concorde a failure, and if so was it a technological failure? The Concorde, developed with heavy support of the French and British governments, entered service in 1976, but was only used by Air France and British Airways. It remained operational for 27 years. Many of its planned routes were unattainable as the aircraft produced too much noise to fly over land. Moreover, its fuel consumption had not been a main issue in design, but was gigantic in comparison to the wide-body aircraft that came into operation in the early seventies. The oil price increases of the 1970s made fuel consumption the main drawback of the Concorde. The aircraft flew without major accidents until a Concorde crashed in Paris in 2000 (Winchester, 2005). Was Concorde a failure? There is no way to judge that by inherent technological standards; we can only judge that by developing consensus on the performance standards that society requires.

THE DIVISION OF RESPONSIBILITIES IN ENGINEERING DESIGN

Most engineers will probably deny that Concorde was an engineering failure. In their eyes, it is probably an economic, commercial and/or political failure but not an engineering failure. Most engineers delimit engineering responsibilities rather strictly. The technological design is theirs but the requirements and evaluations are not their responsibility. They often adhere to a model that sets strict boundaries between engineering design, its commissioning and its use.

The technological design process is seen as one link in a chain of steps:

1. An organization commissions a new process or product.
2. The engineer who accepts the task to deliver the design receives a programme of requirements, which the product should ultimately adhere to.
3. Later, this list of requirements is also used to evaluate the design that the engineer has produced. If the design is accepted, the job of the designing engineer has come to an end.

This view of engineering design is characterized by three activities:
- Commissioning
- Design
- Application

The programme of requirements separates the design process from the commissioning and the application of the design. It therefore has a paramount importance: the designer is supposed to question neither the nature of the design, nor its application.

The sharp division between the design and its commissioning and application can create ethical problems:

> Consider the engineering firm that had agreed to design the living quarters for workers in a country under dictatorship. During the design process, it became clear that there were some rather peculiar requirements that led the engineers to a clear conclu-

sion: this building was going to be a prison! The country's reputation did not suggest that the engineers were contributing to stop crime. Should they just do their designing job, within the limits of the programme of requirements?

The strict separation of engineering design from commissioning and application is a barrier to productive interaction and to responsible behaviour. This model serves to limit the responsibilities of engineers in case of failure. In the case of a successful design, engineers are proud to show their ingenuity. The model is also not in accordance with practice: a programme of requirements cannot be imposed on the engineer by outsiders. It is something that can only be created in interaction between engineer and commissioner, as only in this way can a balance between various requirements be set. In practice, one can often observe engineers advertising the options that they are able to realize at commissioning organizations. A similar phenomenon holds for the use phase: no design is perfect right away even if the design meets the programme of requirements. In the use phase, new requirements might emerge that might lead to a redesigning process.

Despite the shortcomings of this model, engineering embraced the three-stage model and developed a paradigm that disconnected its praxis from its social environment. Efficiency was what counted and new emerging societal demands were often denounced as being 'fashion', or 'misguided by ideology'. The destruction of nature was regarded as 'the price of progress'.

TECHNOLOGICAL PROGRESS

In the 1950s, there was a strong trust in technological progress: electricity would become 'too cheap to meter' and the car was almost an outdated technology as it would probably soon be replaced by the flying car. In the 1960s new problems emerged: pollution, ecological destruction, resource depletion and the technologically driven arms race were issues of strong technology criticism. Various new technologies met fierce resistance (Bauer, 1995).

'Progress', an omnipresent word in the 1950s, was in the 1970s regarded by many as a road to total collapse. The philosophers Marcuse (1964) and Habermas (1968) criticized the ideological nature of technology: technology involves the supremacy of man over nature, of one human over his fellow humans. Several engineers started to engage for an 'alternative technology': a technology that should contribute to a democratic society, and to a use of planet Earth for the benefit of all living species (Dickson, 1974). However, the gap with traditional engineering was tremendous. Alternative technologies had their teething problems, and were ridiculed by traditional engineers as kindergarten technology.

By and large, engineering practice and engineering education were hardly affected by the uproar of the 1970s. However, society had changed, and engineers felt widely misunderstood in society. They were no longer seen as the heroes who produced progress. Instead some regarded engineers as dangerous nerds who were chasing their own weird ideas, neglecting societal interests or even taking unprecedented risks.

CLOSING THE GAP BETWEEN ENGINEERING AND SOCIETY?

The technological criticism of the 1970s led to new areas of study:
- 'Science & Technology Studies (STS)' units at universities aimed at analysing the dynamics of science and technology in society. What is the role of science in public discourse? What affects the course of technological change and could it be influenced (Bijker, 1995), or even (how) could technology be geared towards socially desired outcomes? Gradually theories emerged that conceptualized the relation between society and technology as a co-evolution (Rip, 2002).
- 'Technology Assessment' (TA) aimed at providing decision makers with a societal cost–benefit analysis of new technologies. TA started in the USA in the early 1970s. In Europe it was implemented in various countries in the 1980s (Smits et al., 1995). Gradually TA went beyond being a desk-research activity and became more interactive. Public debates and stakeholder dialogues were facilitated regarding various technologically driven issues such as genetic screening, energy policy, privacy and identification tags, and so on.

Both STS and TA were focused on the interplay of science and technology and policy. They hardly affected the core of engineering praxis. Active participation of engineers in societal debate was often limited to those engineers who found themselves in the 'eye of the tornado': nuclear physicists and reactor engineers, biochemists, and nanotechnologists to mention a few. However, none of them felt comfortable in that position.

SUSTAINABLE DEVELOPMENT

When SD emerged as a new issue, it had far more impact on the engineering community. Many engineers understood that Brundtland's message was not just another form of the environmental message of the 1970s. Sustainable development did not only imply refraining from interference with the environment. It also meant to do more with less, that is, to develop more efficient technologies and systems.

But working on more sustainable technologies generally also implied switching to new lines of research. Instead of making 'sustainability' an add-on requirement for the technologies that researchers were already involved in, they often had to switch to other options.

Successfully developing sustainable transitions requires not only new technologies but also new organizations and rules and even understanding cultural innovation. Working towards transitions means that one has to understand the needs that are to be satisfied. These needs can sometimes be hidden: for example, clothing is not just about keeping people comfortable, it is also a means of self-expression.

New technologies can produce various impacts. Inadequate insight regarding these impacts might lead to technological failures and social conflict. Equipping an engineer with all the knowledge and capabilities to determine and design optimum solutions is probably more than one person can cope with. As a consequence, communication is a key requirement for a new engineer. Not just communication in a technical sense, that is, being able to transmit messages and receive them, but also being able to understand that different people might have different perceptions of reality, and that jointly one might reach better solutions by learning from each other.

An engineer working towards SD should not only take different decisions; decisions should also be taken differently. The designing engineer should be far more involved in interaction with stakeholders.

In order to have real interaction with stakeholders regarding longer-term impacts, the processes should be carefully planned and managed. Various options should be elaborated and their consequences be clarified as input to stakeholder meetings. Scenario exercises are useful tools to provide participants with the data regarding future trends and clarify value conflicts.

ENGINEERING EDUCATION

Academic education always had a dual character: it created the social elite of the industrialized nations but it also trained students to work in the front line of a scientific discipline. Engineering had a somewhat different character: it trained students to design the products and systems by which natural resources are converted to sustain our societies. And exactly at this point the sustainable development challenge started: providing for all on this planet, now and in the future.

Engineering was challenged and it responded. Throughout the industrial world SD was added to the engineering curriculum. But understanding the grand challenges that we face, and just producing more efficient machines is not enough (cf. Mulder et al., 2010).

Sustainable development needs socially committed engineers. We need engineers who can guide the design of new systems and interact with stakeholders to include their stakes into the designing process. That requires major changes from engineering educators, changes that go far beyond adding an SD course to the curriculum. The main elements for curriculum reform should be:

- Combining the social and natural world instead of applying science
- Communicative
- Relativistic
- Reflexive
- Interaction with stakeholders
- Problem-based learning

REFERENCES

Bauer, M. (1995) *Resistance to New Technology*. Cambridge: Cambridge University Press.

Bijker, W.E. (1995) *Of Bicycles, Bakelites and Bulbs*. Cambridge, MA: MIT Press.

Braun, E. (1995) *Futile Progress Technology's Empty Promise*. London: Earthscan Publishing.

Dickson, D. (1974) *Alternative Technology and the Politics of Technical Change*. London: Fontana.

Habermas, J. (1968) *Technik und Wissenschaft als Ideologie*. Frankfurt: Suhrkamp.

Marcuse, H. (1964) *One-Dimensional Man: Studies in the Ideology of Advanced Industrial Society,* Boston: Beacon. Text available at: http://www.marcuse.org/herbert/pubs/64onedim/odmcontents.html

Mulder, K.F., Segalas-Coral, J. and Ferrer-Balas, D. (2010) Educating engineers for/in Sustainable Development? What we knew, what we learned, what we should learn, *Thermal Science*, **14**(3). Special issue on Dubrovnik Conference on Sustainable Development of Water and Energy Systems, 2009.

Pernick, R. and Wilder, C. (2007) *The Clean Tech Revolution: The Next Big Growth and Investment Opportunity.* Collins.

Rip, A. (2002) Co-evolution of science, technology and society, *Enschede*, 7 June, An Expert Review for the Bundesministerium Bildung und Forschung's Förderinitiative Politik, Wissenschaft und Gesellschaft (Science Policy Studies), as managed by the Berlin-Brandenburgische Akademie der Wissenschaften, availablehttp://www.sciencepolicystudies.de/dok/expertise-rip.pdf

Rotmans, J., Kemp, R. and van Asselt, M. (2001) More evolution than revolution, transition management in public policy. *Foresight*, **3**(1), pp. 15–32.

Sale, K. (1995) *Rebels Against the Future: The Luddites and Their War on the Industrial Revolution,* Reading, MA: Addison Wesley.

Smits, R., Leyten, A. and den Hertog P. (1995) Technology Assessment and technology policy in Europe: new concepts, new goals, new infrastructures. *Policy Sciences,* **28**, pp. 272–99.

Tarr, J.A. and McShane, C. (1997) The Centrality of the Horse in the Nineteenth-Century American City. In: Mohl, Raymond A. (ed.) *The Making of Urban America*. New York: Scholarly Resources, Inc.

Vincenti, W.G. (1993) *What Engineers Know and How They Know It: Analytical Studies from Aeronautical History*. Johns Hopkins University Press.

Winchester, J. (2005) *'BAC Concorde.' The World's Worst Aircraft: From Pioneering Failures to Multimillion Dollar Disasters*. London: Amber Books Ltd.

NOTE

1 'Engineers' in this paper refers not only to those professionals who have obtained an engineering degree, but also to all those who determine the design, development, maintenance and/or operation of technological (sub)systems.

IV.3c SOCIAL RESPONSIBILITY OF HIGHER EDUCATION IN ADDRESSING MAJOR GLOBAL ISSUES

Sonia Bahri

The commitment of higher education to sustainable development must be seen in the broader context of social responsibility, a theme highlighted at the 2009 World Conference on Higher Education (WCHE) and in its final communiqué. Since the Global University Network for Innovation (GUNi) chose for its fifth International Conference, and in connection with the follow-up of the WCHE, to emphasize understanding and action, the question which naturally arises is that of defining the social responsibility of higher education. Is there a definition of the social responsibility of higher education as there is for corporate social responsibility? (Corporate social responsibility is generally defined as a 'business contribution to sustainable development'.) The answer is no. At least, as yet, there is not a commonly accepted definition.

DEBATE ON THE SOCIAL RESPONSIBILITY OF HIGHER EDUCATION

Although a common definition of social responsibility of higher education does not exist, debate, writings and publications, and even research on the topic have proliferated in recent years. While this suggests a marked interest in the question, it also suggests that we are far from a consensus or common understanding on exactly what we mean by social responsibility of higher education.

It is the role of a global forum for exchange on innovation in higher education such as GUNi to encourage and stimulate philosophical and political dialogue on this theme, in particular by collating the diversity of viewpoints and approaches. What we can expect from such a forum is to be brought closer to a common understanding of the concept of social responsibility of higher education that would culminate in an internationally recognized definition.

The debate on the social responsibility of higher education is relatively recent. It began in the early 1990s shortly after the advent of the concept of sustainable development in 1987, the collapse of the USSR and the European socialist bloc, the rise of the internet, and the globalization of the economy and of information. This debate, therefore, surfaces with the perception that the world we live in is undergoing rapid economic, social and technological change; that a thorough knowledge and an understanding of these changes are required; and that we have to respond.

Two different approaches are seen in the debate, even though they ultimately merge: the approach that concerns the social responsibility of the university as an institution (the micro-level) and the approach that concerns the issue of the social responsibility of higher education as a system (the macro-level). The distinction has to be made here since the point is not to compare individual universities with one another in their work but to compare them with the other public service systems and economic and social stakeholders in their respective functions.

IS SOCIAL RESPONSIBILITY THAT OF THE INSTITUTION OR OF THE SYSTEM?

In the first approach that focuses on the Institution, the social responsibility of the university is often perceived as an inclusive stance seeking to give as many students as possible access to higher education (equity). The intent is to reach through the academic community to the local communities and notably to the marginalized as a whole, those who have the greatest need of it, namely the marginalized groups (outreach), in relation to whom the university reckons it has a civic engagement obligation as met by community service programmes. Social responsibility is also perceived in connection with the responsibility the university is said to have towards its own students to ensure their welfare and employment opportunities in keeping with whatever the economic and social situation happens to be, or to express the potential response of the particular institution's training and research programmes to economic, social and environmental needs, and contribution to managing political, ethnic or religious conflicts in the area in which it is located. This is what could be called local social responsibility, integrated into territorial development and citizenship approach on the local scale. Here we move closer to the definition of corporate social responsibility since the university is perceived as an entity acting and reacting responsibly in its environment. This does not mean that the university in question will not take an interest through its training and research programmes in global matters and in the major ethical, economic, social and scientific challenges that concern all of us and extend well beyond national or regional boundaries. But what we are talking about here is the task assumed on a voluntary basis by the concerned university and not the broader issue of higher education as a system.

For in the latter case what is involved is higher education perceived in its role as a key player in the public space beside politics, civil society, the media and the production sector. The concept of social responsibility of higher education then comes within a more theoretical and conceptual framework which would be that of a new mission of higher education as a system. The question arising is that of the place higher education must find in relation to the other players in the public space on account of what could be defined as its own 'comparative advantage'.

What sets higher education apart from other institutions is certainly not just its capacity to produce knowledge and human capital but, above all, its capacity to reason and work over the long term. This is not the case of political institutions that have to work under short-term pressure. In an ever more complex world, it is crucial to rely on and give its full place to higher education and more specifically to academic research in the process of decision-making with respect to the building of a sustainable world and thinking ahead to the major global challenges and to the Millennium Development Goals (MDGs).

There are thus differing degrees in perception, reflection, analysis and conceptualization, including by the universities themselves, of what must be the social responsibility of higher education. When taken further, this even includes research programmes on this specific theme where higher education explores the question not just of its own role in an approach that is both epistemological and forward-looking, but also of its own responsibility. This introduces an ethical dimension into such questioning. What is and what should be the mission of higher education in the world of today and tomorrow, given the deep and rapid changes our societies are experiencing and the major challenges they face? To what extent do we possess a comparative advantage and to what extent have we broken with the past?

WHAT MISSION FOR HIGHER EDUCATION?

This transformation of the traditional model of higher education of production and transmission of knowledge is recognized in international debate as necessary for providing, at both the local and the global level, a response to the profound and rapid changes in society and the major challenges facing today's world, and more particularly that of sustainable development.

The fact that the World Conference on Higher Education (Paris, UNESCO, July 2009) gave a prominent place to the theme of the social responsibility of higher education, including in its final communiqué, is very significant in this respect. It means that, over and maybe above the more 'traditional' or more 'technical' themes of access, mass higher education, internationalization and financing of higher education, the international community acknowledges that 'new dynamics' (this was the title of the 2009 WCHE) are transforming higher education functions to 'lead society in generating global knowledge to address global challenges' and promote 'critical thinking and active citizenship', which 'would contribute to sustainable development, peace, wellbeing and the realization of human rights' (UNESCO, 2009).

A big step has thus been taken in the debate towards

recognition of the importance of the social responsibility of higher education in the new mission of this education system regarding major global issues.

WHAT MUTATION FOR THIS NEW MISSION?

While higher education has an active role to play in addressing the social changes and major challenges of our time, it cannot do this without a number of mutations needed for the task. These mutations rest upon four main requisites.

1. NETWORKING/PARTNERSHIPS
In view of the complexity of knowledge and of the world in which we live, universities not networking with other higher educational institutions at national, regional or international levels would be inconceivable. The pooling of knowledge and expertise is indeed essential for good-quality training and research regarding specific sets of themes. Such pooling is nowadays greatly facilitated by the use of ICTs. At the regional level, UNESCO encourages, South–South cooperation especially within its UNITWIN/ UNESCO Chairs Programme, the establishment of subregional poles of excellence, particularly in the countries of the South where the need to pool knowledge and expertise is more keenly felt given the shortage of funds for higher education and bearing in mind the best possible management of available resources. Poles of excellence as defined by UNESCO will enable the creation of 'a critical mass of capacity and expertise to ensure quality' over a given geographical area. At both the national and the subregional levels, universities will need to work in synergy and build bridges between the other stakeholders of the public space: policymakers, whose decisions must draw upon research findings, civil society, industry and the media, and not forgetting local populations. This synergy must ensure complementarity and sharing for the sake of greater impact.

2. TRANSDISCIPLINARITY
The complex challenges of sustainable development require higher education to become the spearhead of transdisciplinarity. With the training of future teachers through an interdisciplinary approach, the next generations need to be instructed in transdisciplinarity and learn to think and work accordingly in their day-to-day activity. Teachers and students, in common with politicians, are at present still much too given to silo thinking. It is to be hoped that in the long run this type

of training will limit those barriers between disciplines which today leave their traces in schools and ministries.

The transformation of higher education towards trandisciplinarity therefore depends on breaking boundaries between faculties and the acquisition of skills for training and research in interdisciplinary teams. Recognition goes today to the importance of the human sciences in the understanding of the natural sciences such as oceanography, where human behaviour patterns explain instances of coastal erosion or loss of biodiversity. Even within the same faculty, research in favour of sustainable development is sometimes conducted in ways that can result in perverse effects regarding the MDGs and sustainable development. If one takes as an example the goal of achieving universal access to education and information, the use of fossil energy in access to the necessary ICTs may thwart the target of reducing carbon dioxide emissions. The same goes for access to safe drinking water through the desalination of seawater, which also uses fossil energy. Transdisciplinarity in research and training is therefore all-important and remains closely tied in with the stimulation of creativity, innovation and anticipation within higher education.

3. CREATIVITY, INNOVATION AND ANTICIPATION

Creativity and imagination should be stimulated in all fields. Einstein said that imagination is more important than knowledge. Indeed, imagination and creativity are the foundation of innovation that will, more specifically in science and technology, help to address adequately major global challenges for sustainable development. Nevertheless, we can address the questions: Are our universities promoting creativity or even allowing creativity? Is creativity quoted in the mission statement of universities?

As highlighted in the conclusion of the European University Association Report on Creativity in Higher Education (EUA, 2007), 'so far relatively little attention has been paid on how creativity and innovation can be enhanced within and by academe', while higher education institutions (HEIs) should promote a culture that is tolerant of failure and thus encourages the members of the university community to question established ideas, to go beyond conventional knowledge and to strive for originality.

Universities should also look towards the future. Indeed, the high level of expertise of the university community in various fields and the fact that they have the time factor on their side (long term) uniquely qualify HEIs to adopt forward-looking orientation, not only to solve current problems but also to anticipate issues of future relevance and prevent important crisis

or disasters. It is clear that inventions and innovations do not happen in one day. They are the result of long efforts of researchers, scientists, engineers and inventors working in R&D in universities and the industry. The *UNESCO Science Report* issued in November 2010 shows that scientific power is now shifting increasingly from industrialized countries (the triad of Japan, USA and the EU) to a number of emerging countries such as China, India and Brazil. It will be part of the social responsibility of higher education in these countries to ensure that efforts in science and technology innovation are oriented towards sustainable development and green economy and to move from a 'reactive' attitude to an anticipatory one. It means in terms of impact that the universities of these countries will make the difference.

4. ENTREPRENEURSHIP EDUCATION

To ensure that research and innovation will have a tangible impact on sustainable development, universities should work on providing students with the appropriate entrepreneurship education programmes. Entrepreneurship could be considered today as 'the missing link' between research outcomes and development. A lack of entrepreneurial cultural spirit and skills could explain the fact that some technical innovations developed within universities in line with sustainable development will never reach the stage of manufacturing and will therefore not be put at the disposal of the concerned populations to reduce poverty or to improve their quality of life.

The workshop on Entrepreneurship held during the 2009 WCHE highlighted the fact that more synergies between teaching, research/innovation and entrepreneurship are necessary, and that entrepreneurship education is not only necessary for business, for economists and engineers; it is a way of thinking. The emerging concept of *social entrepreneurship*, supported by several world-leading universities and foundations is not only about wealth creation. The social entrepreneur participates in profit-seeking business ventures if only to use the profits generated to further social and environmental goals. Cultural change has therefore to take place and all disciplines at universities are relevant to entrepreneurship: communication, languages, and graphic arts and many other fields.

CONCLUSION

All these elements will not be easy to implement or will be insufficient to enable a transformation of higher education to be socially responsible in fulfilling its mission to address major global challenges without adequate leadership. Visionary and strategic leadership in HEIs is crucial. Without it nothing will be achieved. Change will require too much time and energy, if faculty members do not benefit from the understanding and support of the leadership team. This requires national training and coaching strategies towards equipping current and future leaders in higher education with the skills and awareness of good practices to help ensure this change and respond to future challenges.

Finally, if we admit that higher education has to play a major role to 'lead society in generating global knowledge to address global challenges' and to train citizens in this respect, how are the efforts and impacts of each individual HEI going to be measured? Which indicators should be developed to reflect social responsibility of higher education and how to include them in a ranking system that will be entrusted to measure not only the quality of an institution but also its relevance and its capacity to address the major challenges our world is facing?

REFERENCES

EUA (2007) *Creativity in Higher Education – Report on the EUA Creativity Project 2006–2007.*
UNESCO (2009) World Conference on Higher Education: The New Dynamics of Higher Education and Research for Societal Change and Development, Paris, 5_8 July 2009. *Communique.* ED.2009/CONF.402/2. Paris: UNESCO.
UNESCO (2010) *UNESCO Science Report 2010.* Paris: UNESCO

On the Road IV.5
New organizational structures for new challenges: the example of working in networks

Josep M. Vilalta,
Nadja Gmelch and
Alicia Betts

INTRODUCTION
The problems we face on our planet today are becoming more and more complex. To respond to current challenges – such as climate change, the need for alternative energies, hunger, and other humanitarian problems – and to find solutions, more complex answers are necessary. Universities are key actors in this sense. Due to the nature of their activities, universities are institutions that search for solutions to today's challenges. On the one hand, universities are responsible for creating and applying new knowledge and transferring it to society. On the other hand, they train future citizens capable of living and working in this complex world. Although in recent years universities have increased their collaboration with private- and public-sector actors through an interdisciplinary approach ('mode 2' knowledge production, according to Gibbons et al., 1994), individual institutions lack the potential and critical mass to find solutions to today's highly complex and all-encompassing global problems. The latest trend, therefore, is that many higher education institutions (HEIs) and other organizations are increasingly using networks for different purposes and objectives.

THE PROLIFERATION OF NETWORKS
The creation of networks is an example of a new trend in organizational structure. In recent years, networks have proliferated in many different areas and at all levels. For example, cities and local governments all over the world are working together in the United Cities and Local Governments (UCGL) network, non-governmental organizations all over Europe belong to the European NGO Confederation for Relief and Development (CONCORD), and Catalan producers and consumers of fair-trade organic products work together through a local network called Xarxa de Consum Solidari. Online social platforms like Facebook can in certain ways be understood as a reaction to the proliferation of these networks, as they help people and institutions from around the world to get connected and create networks on topics that interest them.

WHY NETWORKS?
Networks offer the possibility of working in a coordinated, coherent, transversal and interdisciplinary way and therefore contributing more effectively to the challenges we face today. Coordination is the key word and main objective of today's organizational discussions. Coordinated work can have many benefits, if done properly. This means that all the institutions that want to coordinate must be convinced of the value of the collaboration and work to foster it. The advantages of coordinated work are well understood. Working in a network makes it possible to avoid repeat or duplicate work. Putting together specialists from different knowledge areas fosters transversality and interdisciplinarity. Coordination improves the division of labour and enables network members to achieve high-level synergies and economies of scale. It also promotes the specialization and differentiation of member institutions.

NETWORKS IN HIGHER EDUCATION
The advantages of cooperating and collaborating in networks are also apparent in the field of higher education. One rising trend in recent years has been the proliferation of higher education networks with a wide variety of forms and aims. Many of these networks – like the Global University Network for Innovation (GUNi), for example – are organized by thematic areas. But there are also numerous examples of geographical networks of HEIs. At the international level universities are brought together by the International Association of Universities (IAU), and at regional level we find

organizations such as the European University Association (EUA) and the Association of African Universities (AAU). At the local level, we are also seeing more and more university networks. Examples include Universities Scotland, the representative body of Scotland's 21 universities and colleges; Universität Bayern, which represents the 11 public universities of Bavaria in Germany; and the Catalan Association of Public Universities (ACUP), which brings together the eight public universities of Catalonia in Spain. The Academic Cooperation Association (ACA) provides a good overview of all the different kinds of networks in its *Handbook of International Associations in Higher Education: A Practical Guide to 100 Academic Networks World-Wide* (Schneller et al., 2009).

Over the past 15 years, the European Union (EU) and individual European countries have illustrated the importance of higher education by generating growth and prosperity. They have therefore designed policies to further develop and modernize the higher education sector (Bologna Process, Lisbon Strategy, Modernization Agenda, EU 2020, and other policies). Regions are key players in the knowledge society and economy and in contributions to research activities and innovation systems: the EUA's *The Rise of Knowledge Regions: Emerging Opportunities and Challenges for Universities* (Reichert, 2006); the Regions of Knowledge initiative of the 7th EU Framework Programme; and the OECD programme on the role of HEIs in regional development, among others. In this context, regional higher education networks have the opportunity (and the challenge) to play an active role not only in the development and cooperation of the higher education sector, but also in their region's economy, culture and society.

WORK AREAS AND INSTRUMENTS: THE EXAMPLE OF THE CATALAN ASSOCIATION OF PUBLIC UNIVERSITIES (ACUP)

Since 2006–2007, the ACUP has greatly intensified its activities and public presence, gaining experience that has established it as a model European university association. This is illustrated by the ACUP's considerable number of relationships and projects at the international level. Since creating an Execu-

tive Secretariat and drafting a joint strategy (ACUP, 2008) aimed at transforming the Catalan university system into a leading system in southern Europe, the ACUP has created a series of initiatives to improve member universities and the university system as a whole in different areas: training, research, knowledge transfer to society, and internal management. The *White Paper on the University of Catalonia*, published in June 2008, was a significant milestone in this direction. This document proposes a future model for Catalan universities: modern, innovative, and at the service of society and social progress. The model is based on a series of strategies and specific projects in the coming years aimed at transforming universities into innovative institutions at the service of society.

The ACUP is currently working in the following areas to foster collaboration among its member institutions as a means of contributing to the modernization of higher education in Catalonia and Spain:

- *Strategy and institutional relations:* Analysis and design of policies for the public university system of Catalonia in collaboration with other institutions and organizations, and promotion of institutional relations with the creators of university and research policies in Catalonia and the rest of Spain.
- *International relations:* Fostering international relations with countries, regions and university systems around the world and promoting Catalan public universities abroad.
- *Monitoring and research:* Preparation and coordination of studies, reports and statistics on the main areas of university activity (teaching, research, knowledge transfer and university management) and collaboration with other organizations and countries.
- *University management:* Promotion of initiatives and projects for the improvement and innovation of university management for the Catalan public university system as a whole, as well as for each of the ACUP's member universities.
- *Formation of society–university links:* Promotion of far-reaching programmes and projects that bring universities and society together with the aim of promoting social, cultural, economic and technological progress.

To achieve its goals, the ACUP works with various instruments, including joint strategies encompassing all member universities, coordination units, and joint programmes and projects. Some specific examples can be found in the above-mentioned *White Paper on the University of Catalonia* published in 2008, the *Internationalization Plan of the Catalan Public Universities 2010–2015* published in 2011, and the *University Development Cooperation Plan* published in 2012. These three publications are the physical materialization of the discussions, compromise, consensus and work of the ACUP's eight member institutions.

DIFFICULTIES AND CHALLENGES

Working in networks is a new way of working for many universities, and it is sometimes quite difficult to advance in the coordination and creation of a common understanding and a vision for the future. Universities as individual institutions traditionally have not worked in collaboration with other universities; quite to the contrary, higher education policies and globalization generally foster competition between HEIs. Collaboration among universities has usually taken the form of cooperation between researchers and professionals in a particular discipline, and has therefore had a discipline-specific (that is, non-institutional) focus. Hence, there is no working tradition that fosters collaboration between HEIs. In many cases, institutional interests are stronger and more immediate than system-wide interests. Universities tend to prioritize institutional autonomy, which makes it difficult to develop and promote common, system-wide visions and objectives for the future.

Another important challenge when working as networks is the management of information. For a network to function, a good flow of information is absolutely necessary. Because institutional interests sometimes prevail over the long-term strategic interests of the system, good information management is not always easy to accomplish and remains one of the greatest challenges that networks face.

CONCLUSION

We are at the beginning of a new trend. Globalization and other global challenges have led to the increasing proliferation of networks. These organizational structures have become *sine qua non* for the higher education sector. We have reviewed the major advantages of working in networks, as well as many of the challenges that networks face. These challenges must be overcome in order to do better work and obtain better results for our society and its future. As the Brazilian bishop Hélder Câmara once said, 'When we are dreaming alone it is only a dream. When we are dreaming with others, it is the beginning of reality.'

REFERENCES

ACUP (2008) *White Paper on the University of Catalonia: Strategies and Projects for the Catalan University*, Barcelona.

ACUP (2010) *Construint un sistema universitari innovador al servei de la societat*, Barcelona.

ACUP (2011) *Internationalization Plan of the Catalan Public Universities 2010–2015*, Barcelona.

ACUP (2012) *University Development Cooperation Plan*, Barcelona.

Schneller, C., Lungu, I. and Wächter, B. (2009) *Handbook of International Associations in Higher Education: A Practical Guide to 100 Networks World-Wide*. Brussels: Academic Cooperation Association.

Gibbons, M., Limoges, C., Nowotny, H., Schwartzman, S., Scott, P. and Trow M. (1994) *The New Production of Knowledge*. London: Sage.

Reichert, S. (2006) *The Rise of Knowledge Regions: Emerging Opportunities and Challenges for Universities*. Brussels: European University Association.

On the Road IV.6
Higher education and peacebuilding in transition societies in Africa: core issues

David J. Francis

Education must rise on the agenda of peacebuilding. We know the wrong type of education can fuel conflict. The use of education systems to foster hatred has contributed to the underlying causes of conflicts, from Rwanda to Sri Lanka, but also in Guatemala and Sudan. (Irina Bokova, Director General, UNESCO. 1 March 2011)

'If University is so important how comes we have this terrible and bloody civil war.' (Market Woman in Freetown, Sierra Leone, July 2001)

INTRODUCTION

One of the crucial and most pressing challenges facing the higher education (HE) sector in Africa today is how to make universities relevant to the evident needs and aspirations of their societies, especially in transition societies including conflict-prone, war-torn and post-conflict communities. Across Africa, the majority of African universities, both public and private, have not taken their social responsibility mandate seriously, beyond the rhetoric of corporate social responsibility and policy prescriptions by the governments of the day (that is, teaching, learning and service). As one African university vice-chancellor poignantly stated, 'Universities in Africa have occupied the space between God and Man, remaining impervious to the socioeconomic and development realities of their societies'.

Given the enormity of the socioeconomic, development and political challenges faced by contemporary Africa and aggravated by the ever increasing pressures of neo-liberal globalization, including the current global financial crisis and the corresponding negative impact on the HE sector, how can African universities take advantage of the opportunities provided by the challenges facing Africa to reinvent themselves, and develop and set strategic priorities that will put universities and the HE sector at the centre of national and continental development and socio-political progress?

More than ever before, and particularly in countries emerging from decades of brutal wars and armed conflicts or post-conflict societies, communities are clamouring for a more visible, practical, active and long-term involvement of universities and the HE sector in finding answers to and responding to the issues and challenges that affect their daily lives and societies. In bitterly divided communities and war-torn societies, there is increasing disappointment, if not a sense of rejection, of the traditional forms, focus, objectives and philosophy of university education systems. From Sierra Leone to DR Congo, South Africa to Egypt and from Senegal to Ethiopia, people and communities now want to see and expect education and, in particular, the HE sector, to serve as a channel to build peace, reconcile bitterly divided societies, resolve intractable conflicts, reduce poverty and to mitigate the perpetual depressing socioeconomic and development indicators such as HIV/AIDS.[1] In these transition societies, the individual educational development and advancement for 'societal good' focus of HE is not only increasingly being questioned but also universities and the HE sector are now expected, and in some cases demanded, to respond and engage with urgent survival/existential issues such as achieving the Millennium Development Goals (MDGs) as well as broader societal and international concerns around peace, democratic governance, human rights, durable security and stability, long-term economic growth and sustainable development, climate change and environmental threats, mitigating the impact of global financial crisis and international terrorism. There seems to be a rejection of the 'Ivory Tower' preoccupation of universities in these war-torn societies. In these transition societies, the emerging expectation is that universities should be instrumental for peace, democratic empowerment, scientific innovation, economic development and socio-political change.

At this critical juncture, no university, government, global governance institution such as the UN, IMF and World Bank or international cooperation partners can afford to neglect these concerns or remain deaf to the call for a radical transformation of universities and HE in Africa today. To respond to these challenges, it would require a fundamental reshaping of the traditional and dominant

HE philosophy and educational system. The general view, in the particular context of post-conflict societies, is that the dominant philosophy and education system of universities have either failed or not produced the desired results. In effect, the traditional relevance and philosophy of universities and the HE sector are being called into question in war-ravaged societies, and in turn there is the emerging expectation that universities should be central to the peacebuilding and development agenda.

FROM HISTORIC NEGLECT OF AFRICAN UNIVERSITIES TO REVITALIZATION OF THE HE SECTOR

But why have universities failed in most African societies to create an environment conducive to durable peace and long-term development? Historically, universities were established and developed in Africa with a focus on social responsibility, especially with the advent of political independence. Universities, at independence, were expected to have a responsibility to society, a commitment and obligation towards the greater good. In effect, universities were part and parcel of the national and continental development and social progress agenda in that they were expected to train and educate current and future leaders of Africa, and contribute to the welfare, quality of life and well-being of society as well as assist in finding answers to issues of peace, war and conflict, security, development, safety, health, human rights and environmental problems.[2] Despite the initial relative progress and development of universities in the 1960s and 1970s due to committed state and external funding support, the African crises invariably affected African universities and hence the HE sector faced difficulties in continuing to fulfil its social responsibility mandate. Part of the problem was that the majority of the universities created in Africa, especially in the post-independence period, were largely patterned on the philosophy, modus operandi, ethos and systems of universities in the West/North. This 'imported' notion of what a university is supposed 'to be' and 'to do' had limited relevance to the context and reality of the African situation. Universities across Africa promoted a rather traditional,

rigid and elitist education that catered mainly for the needs and aspirations of the few ruling and governing elites in post-colonial Africa.

Although there was general agreement that university education could play a catalytic role in peacebuilding, democratic consolidation, scientific innovation, poverty elimination and development, there was however no consensus on the type and level of education for this transformative role and its long-term impact. This privileged education system and philosophy failed to problematize education in terms of 'education for whom', 'by whom' and 'for what purpose', in particular, the type of education for socio-political change. Across much of the African HE sector, there has been little or no serious debate to move beyond the dominant and rather narrow formal education system to broaden the scope of education to include language of instruction that uses indigenous languages, with the exception of Swahili in East Africa, Arabic in North Africa and Amharic in Ethiopia. In effect, millions of Africans have been denied the empowerment and self-actualization opportunities of education in their own indigenous languages. As the former UN Secretary General, Kofi Annan, once remarked 'Education is quite simply peacebuilding by another name'.[3] But some scholars and practitioners argue that education still remains largely an underutilized resource and tool to promote peace, prevent, manage and resolve conflicts.[4]

But the neglect of African universities and why it has been difficult to fulfil their social responsibility had more to do with the internal and external problems and challenges faced by Africa in the 1980s and 1990s. In particular, the 'African crises' of this period were manifested by continent-wide economic crisis and declining economic productivity, depressing socioeconomic and development indicators, and general political instability orchestrated by military coups and dictatorships, civilian one-party authoritarian regimes, political repressions, rampant corruption, inter-state and civil wars and armed conflicts. These developments meant that public universities and the HE sector were systematically starved of funding while either academic freedom was stamped on or academics were co-opted into the neo-patri-

monial systems of governance. The 'Africa crises' not only undermined the willingness and capacity of African scholars to undertake meaningful social science research, but also led to a massive brain drain of the continent's most productive intellectual capital. The internal context and international conditions such as the impact of the imposition of Structural Adjustment Programmes (SAPs) on African economies eroded the viability and contribution of African universities, and further weakened their capacity to fulfil their social responsibility. During this period, universities were largely perceived as separate from society, though a few became the only platform to challenge repressive political regimes in Africa.

However, a new global trend in the late 1990s has seen the revival of international interest and commitment to support African universities and the HE sector, recognizing them as relevant agencies for the attainment of peacebuilding, security, democracy and development agendas in post-cold war Africa. Some of these international initiatives include the former UK prime minister Tony Blair's Commission for Africa and the UK-DFID's £3.5 million funding pledge to support the Association of African Universities (AAU) programme on 'Mobilizing regional capacity for revitalizing Higher Education in Africa' in 2006; the 2005 G8 Gleneagles commitment to support Africa's development; the World Bank initiative on HE in Africa and the African Union's higher education 'Plan of Action for the Second Decade of Education in Africa (2006).

While this revival of international interest in African universities and recognition of the role and contribution of the HE sector to broader issues of development, peacebuilding and socio-political change (and may have seemed to set African universities on the irreversible course of reform), however, the generic theme in all these diverse programmes emerging from within Africa or prescribed for Africa simply talks about and excessively focuses on 'reform', 'revival', 'renewal' and 'revitalization'. This focus is reflected, for example, in the African Union's First (1997–2006) and Second Decade of Education for Africa (2006–2015) Plan of Action documents and its proposed Pan-African University concept;[5] *Our Common Interest: Report of the Commission for Africa* (March 2005); the United Nations University project report *Revitalising Higher Education in Sub-Saharan Africa* (2009) – all of which geared towards integrating Africa into the global knowledge and market economy. The emerging reform and revival of African universities is part of the African Union and NEPAD (New Partnership for Africa's Development) much-touted 'African solutions to African problems'.

Although these international initiatives implicitly acknowledge that universities and the HE sector are critical to Africa's future development, they however excessively focus on mere 'reform' and 'revival'. This is at odds with the increasing call across much of Africa, especially in transition societies, for the imperative to fundamentally transform universities to make them relevant to the needs and aspirations of the peoples and communities. What is more, the international renewal of interest in African universities and emerging process of reform raises several concerns. First, this renewed interest largely focuses on perpetuating the dominant patterns of north–south relations, hence tendentially reinforcing the traditional pattern of unequal power and resource relationship between Africa and the North. Second, in all the reports and initiatives advanced for the revival of international interest in Africa universities, not much effort or strategic planning is invested into supporting intra-African collaborations and building of networking and strategic partnerships among African universities. Third, the international renewal primarily focuses on science and technology in terms of institutional capacity building and funding. Social science research, despite its obvious and often acknowledged importance, is still struggling to gain prominence and to secure sustained funding beyond the usual donor-driven short-term, quick fix and exit, strategy-oriented funding opportunities. Fourth, the revival has led to increasing international HE links and partnerships but not increased levels of donor funding or external support. Fifth, there is a noticeable lack of investment to critically understand the existing context, constraints and capacity

gaps that hinder African universities and the HE sector in terms of their long-term contribution to peacebuilding and development. The important issue of the relevance of universities is aptly reinforced by Goolam Mohamedbhai, Secretary General of the Association of African Universities, in that 'The new dynamics of higher education in the South, especially Africa, must therefore be governed by a complete re-think of the relevance of universities to their communities'.[6] Universities across Africa are increasingly encouraged to take seriously their social responsibility and, according to Judith Rodin, President of the Rockefeller Foundation, 'knowledge, innovation and talent are critical currencies needed to thrive in today's interconnected world, and Africa's universities are increasingly looked upon to generate the ideas and talent necessary to address Africa's challenges on Africa's term'.[7]

HE AND PEACEBUILDING IN AFRICA: ILLUSTRATING THE POTENTIAL

If the African HE sector is to play a catalytic and transformative role in peacebuilding on the continent, then we need a paradigm shift in the philosophy and educational system. What is required is not a half-hearted process of reform or a mere tinkering with the dominant HE philosophy. This traditional approach has not helped Africa in the past 50 years of political independence and will not continue to be of much relevance to the continent. Based on field research in more than 30 transition countries in Africa in the past decade, the message is simple and clear from communities faced with the harsh realities of war, perpetual violence, grinding poverty, daily insecurity and underdevelopment, that universities in Africa have to transform and reinvent themselves to make them relevant to the needs and aspirations of the peoples and communities. This is the emerging social responsibility mandate of universities in 21st century Africa.

The recognition of this peacebuilding challenge in transition societies led directly to the initiative to develop peace education and a conflict resolution curriculum as well as staff development capacity-building programme interventions by the University

of Bradford's Africa Centre for Peace and Conflict Studies (now the John and Elnora Ferguson Centre for Africa Studies) in partnership with African universities in the past decade. In developing this continental initiative, the Africa Centre's collaborative partnerships with African universities in transition and post-conflict societies have focused on three key areas including:

- Securing external funds
- Curriculum development and staff capacity building
- Policy-relevant support to institutionalize education for peace

In collaboration with African partner universities and the HE sector, we raised an estimated £2.3 million income relating to research, training and capacity building for peace and conflict studies from research councils, development cooperation partners and donor agencies. As a Centre, we have been instrumental in securing external funds to develop and introduce peace and conflict studies, human rights and democratic governance studies and development studies curriculum and staff training programmes in nine African countries.[8] Furthermore, we have led the introduction, development and implementation of 13 undergraduate and postgraduate degree programmes in peace and conflict studies, development studies and education for peace at African universities, including the establishment of four specialist Peace and Conflict Management Institutes. In addition, we have led the establishment of the policy-relevant mainstreaming and institutionalization of peace and conflict studies/Education for Peace curricular in these 'traditional/rigid' universities. The curriculum reform, staff development programmes, teaching, learning and skills development have contributed to consolidating and building peace in these post-war countries. The collaborative partnership with African universities for education for peace research and capacity building has been informed by the need to work with and assist our African partners to respond to the pressing needs and aspirations of their war-torn and traumatized communities.

NOTES

1 In 2005, the newly elected President Helen Johnson-Sirleaf of Liberia, at the University of Liberia convocation, mandated the university as the main institution and driver for the achievement of the targets of the UN Millennium Development Goals for Liberia.

2 It is important to note that the practice of social responsibility is both an ethical and ideological concept accepted as part of the mandate of all universities. This social responsibility concept and practice has both a 'negative' (that is, refrain from actions or decisions that may cause harm, suffering, difficult human and societal conditions and so on) and a 'positive'

dimension (that is, to act – be proactive – to improve quality of life, welfare and well-being of society and so on).

3 Secretary General in Address to 'Learning Never Ends' Colloquium, Calls for Education Investment which yields Highest Profit, Press release SG/SM/7125, 10 September 1999, p. 2.

4 W. Potter, 'A new agenda for disarmament and non-proliferation education' Disarmament Forum 2001 <www.unidir.org/pdf/articles/

5 African Union, Second Session of the Bureau of the Conference of Ministers of Education of the AU (COMEDAF III),

18–20 November 2008, Addis Ababa, AU/HRST/ED/BUREAU/PROG (1)

6 WCHE-Forum@communities.unesco.org Subject: Internationalization and Africa Sent: Saturday, 6 June 2009, 12:45.

7 Quoted in G. Furniss, Launch of British Academy Africa Panel Nairobi Report entitled 'The Nairobi Report: Frameworks for Africa-UK Research Collaboration in the Social Sciences and Humanities' The British Academy, London, 27 March 2009.

8 The partner countries include: Sierra Leone, Liberia, Nigeria, DR Congo, The Gambia, Ethiopia, Zimbabwe, Botswana and Sudan.

On the Road IV.7
Universities and communities can build sustainable coexistence: an African perspective
Peter Kanyandago

WE ARE PART OF A BIGGER PICTURE

If higher education is to contribute meaningfully to sustainability, it should help us to situate humanity in a wider perspective. We humans are recent arrivals on the globe but we sometimes forget this in the way we use resources (Brandt, n.d.). Universities have the means, capacity and responsibility to make all this known and to open up to the communities they serve so that the knowledge available can be used as a springboard for action and for building sustainable coexistence. This requires factoring diversity and interconnectedness into higher education programmes. The link between human, animate and inanimate matter must be seen as that of coexistence. This will require some humility on the part of us humans. As Anton (1995, p. 110) notes, promoting uniformity to the detriment of diversity leads to death. However, we should go beyond the fostering of biodiversity and include cultural diversity and diversity in inanimate objects because between these and the animate beings there is a link.

The call for promoting sustainability has been heard in Africa. However, the efforts in this area, especially in different universities, have tended to remain too academic or too much focused on the environment, without being sufficiently translated into tangible action on the ground. Sustainability is not just an environmental issue. It also touches on

questions of equity, fighting against poverty, and promoting gender equity and social justice. Fortunately some good practices do exist in some communities and positive initiatives are being taken in some education institutions in Africa. We will look at a few of these but let us first turn our attention to the interest that is being shown in traditional societies and other communities that promote sustainability and good practices.

LEARNING FROM TRADITIONAL SOCIETIES AND OTHER COMMUNITIES

Some communities have managed to maintain a good balance in relation to using resources. These are people whom we usually call traditional or 'primitive' when we want to demean them. They are found in forests that have survived our thirst for wood in Latin America, Asia and Africa. They are also found in some deserts in Southern Africa. They still have a sustainable way of living, with very good knowledge and science about their environment. Even outside these regions, we find groups and organizations in the Western world concerned about rethinking our relationship with nature. These people, and all those who still have a strong link with the Earth (Fornet-Betancourt, 2009) use religion and spirituality to promote sustainability. Universities that have the mission and ability to research must concentrate their resources on these people

in an open way. The science and technology available should be used to valorize how the Khoisan in the Kalahari desert, the Baniwa in the Brazilian Amazon forest and the Batwa in Bwindi forest in Uganda have managed to coexist with their surroundings without compromising sustainability for so many years. Universities not only should open up to the indigenous people and their knowledge and science, but also need to learn from and with the communities which they serve and from which they emerge.

Over the past few years, the importance of traditional knowledge and practices has been recognized. One initiative in this regard has centred on promoting endogenous development and bio-cultural diversity and has been spearheaded by the Compas Network. In early October 2006, an international conference was organized on the above-mentioned theme. In their Statement of Commitment Supporting Endogenous Development and Bio-cultural Diversity, the participants, representing different community-based organizations, NGOs, universities and peoples from Latin America, Africa, Asia and Europe, expressed their concern about the global environmental, social, economic and cultural crises as well as the way biological and cultural diversity is being eroded and destroyed by human activities. We recognize that there are important and valuable initiatives for bio-cultural diversity: national and international policies and conventions, initiatives by grassroots organizations and social movements. Yet, not enough is being done to prevent further erosion and destruction of bio-cultural diversity (http://www.bioculturaldiversity.net/statement.htm).

The 34 papers addressing diverse issues ranging from traditional medicine to food sovereignty that were presented during the conference are worth reading (http://www.bioculturaldiversity.net/papers.htm). The efforts of this conference were supplemented by the Declaration on Endogenous Development and Bio-cultural Diversity of the Compas Network, at Lezajsk, Poland, on 27 September 2006. With regard to initiatives and activities, among other things, the Declaration recommends:

1. [To] Develop methodologies for working with indigenous and traditional institutions.
2. That in engaging with communities, outside agents identify and work with existing institutions rather than establish new organizations.
3. The promotion of empowerment of traditional authorities through training, networking and exchanges.
4. The recognition and use of traditional structures as channels through which traditional authorities and their communities influence the development process.
5. Initiation and support for policy dialogues amongst stakeholders from different cultural backgrounds on cultural rights and local management of natural resources.
6. Coordination of initiatives for promoting local resources such as indigenous seeds and animal breeds in different parts of the world.
7. [That] Dominant religions respect local spirituality, religions and belief systems. (http://www.bioculturaldiversity.net/compas%20declaration.htm)

The Worldwatch Institute's *State of the World 2010: Transforming Cultures. From Consumerism to Sustainability* comes out strongly with more than 50 contributions to recognize the role of religion, traditional knowledge and practices in promoting sustainability (http://www.blogs.worldwatch.org/transformingcultures).

An important research study conducted by the Nijmegen Institute for Mission Studies with collaborators from Africa, Asia and Latin America culminated in the publication of the book, *Indigenous voices in the sustainable discourse. Spirituality and the struggle for a better quality of life*, with very interesting articles on indigeneity, spirituality, gender, land issues and conflict resolution (Wijsen and Marcos, 2010). Let us now look at a few examples of some good practices in Africa.

EXAMPLES OF SOME GOOD PRACTICES IN AFRICA

Here below I present a few examples which illustrate how some institutions of higher learning have managed, either to include concerns of the community directly in their academic programmes and/or have foreseen linking up with the community and focusing on imparting relevant skills.

UNIVERSITY FOR DEVELOPMENT STUDIES (UDS), GHANA

The UDS (n.d.) (http://www.ghanaweb.com/GhanaHomePage/education/tamale.html) is a multi-campus institution. It runs six faculties and two centres of excellence. During the third trimester, 'Eight weeks ... are devoted to a practical work and extension among the local communities. During this period, the students live in the local communities, conduct research and interact with the populace.' Students then present their findings and recommendations to the communities. Traditional rulers, Members of Parliament, District Assembly members, opinion leaders and the general public are invited to the forums and participate in the discussions.

GREAT LAKES UNIVERSITY OF KISUMU (GLUK)

GLUK (n.d.) (http://www.gluk.ac.ke/) is located in Kisumu, Kenya, near Lake Victoria. It uses a community partnerships concept in its academic programmes. This entails 'collaboration between communities, service providers, private sectors and the training institutions, and is based on strengths and mutual benefits, not on needs. The partnership covers comprehensively all areas of health and development in order to break the vicious circle of poverty and ill-health.' GLUK created seven sites around Lake Victoria.

KIGALI INSTITUTE OF SCIENCE AND TECHNOLOGY (KIST)

KIST (n.d.) (http://www.kist.ac.rw) was established in 1997 with the assistance of the United Nations Development Programme (UNDP) with a clear mandate to train technical and scientific graduates of high calibre. The mission of KIST clearly spells out its uniqueness and includes the following:

1. To equip students with advanced skills with a view to increasing manpower and capacity for national development.
2. To provide consultancy services to government, industry, the private sector and the community at large.
3. To engage in income-generating activities with a view to creating awareness of lucrative investment.
4. To develop and promote close collaboration with the private sector and the community so as to enrich KIST's programmes.
5. To contribute to the cultural, civic and moral training of its students and to participate actively in the economic and socio-cultural development of the country.

THE AFRICAN SCHOOL OF OPEN EDUCATION (ASOE) PROJECT

The concept

ASOE is an educational project of the African Volunteers Association (AVA) (http://www.africa.upeace.org/dpsa/institution.cfm?id_institution=104&listar=1) which aims at putting in place frameworks for sharing resources within the context of communities (Kanyandago, 2010). The programmes are based on the experience of the learner and inspired by African values. The academic programmes are skills and practice-oriented and are primarily intended for the disadvantaged. ASOE puts in place and revises academic programmes with the participation of the learner. ASOE uses distance learning and open education so that the learners can study at home using their environment and the community as a source of their learning, thus cutting costs and making what is learned more relevant. The learners are urged to share what they learn with those around them and the method of assessment involves the community's participation.

Some operational principles

Taking into account the concept of open education and the objectives that ASOE has set for itself, the school has chosen the following principles to guide it in implementing this education project.

- *Affordability and accessibility:* ASOE has put in place measures to reduce costs, for example by using existing buildings and services of volunteers.
- *Relevance:* The challenges facing Uganda and Africa as a whole in the area of higher education include relevance. This is why ASOE deliberately encourages its students to find an interface between their environment, their experience and their work so that education can directly improve their livelihoods.
- *Flexibility:* By being flexible in its approach, ASOE makes it possible for people to access higher education.
- *Contextuality:* Context is a vital aspect in ensuring the relevance of education. This implies taking into account the context of the learner and the teacher.

From these few examples we can see that innovation is found in focusing on answering the needs of society, concentrating on practical and technical issues, and involving the community.

SEARCH FOR SUSTAINABLE COEXISTENCE

The future of the planet, and indeed of the universe, will depend on how much universities will have the humility to accept that they have created dualisms which are hurting the Earth and human relations, that knowledge has been separated from action, and that sometimes this knowledge has been stolen from the communities and commercialized. Universities need to open up to and work with the communities, and especially with traditional ones, to promote sustainable coexistence. This calls for a rethinking not only of how universities should open to the outside, but also ofo how they should be open and flexible in their programmes and approach.

The threats that humanity and the globe face today have not always been like this. While humans have appeared rather belatedly on Earth, our activities have in a very short period become a threat to ourselves and to the globe. The paradox is that while science claims to have solved a lot of problems, and no doubt it has, at the same time it has created other dangers and risks which are not sufficiently addressed. The *tsunami* in Japan in March 2011 and the nuclear crisis that followed are an illustration of how science is not capable of foreseeing everything, especially in the area of nuclear energy. The threats from climate change are essentially coming from how we humans have impacted on climate because of a style of life that compromises sustainability. In all this, it is imperative that our actions be rethought in light of how we are interconnected and depend on one another. Science needs to be rethought and situated within its limits. In the framework of Western culture, which has globally influenced the world positively and negatively, belief in what science can do is almost unquestionable. Canadell (2010) notes that this 'classical model of science grew through the development of a mathematical and technological interpretation of the world, which has provided man with numerous benefits but is now reaching the limits of its own potential, revealed as deficient in its interaction with society and with nature. One of the principal flaws of this model is its regard for the intangible risks and consequences of its application'.

The temptation of globalization is grounded in the search for uniformity, which, as we have seen, leads to death and violence. The differences we find in nature and cultures must be celebrated and promoted. The belief that the more people get to know each other and advance in history the more security and development they will enjoy is not borne out by historical or anthropological facts. We need to invest more in institutions and organizations that help people to know, and above all, to respect each other. The resurgence of extreme right-wing groups in the West that promote xenophobia and racism must be brought under control if humanity is to rediscover the beauty and importance of celebrating and living cultural diversity.

Sustainable coexistence can and must be built by universities opening up to and learning from the community. This can only be achieved if we promote and celebrate diversity, interconnectedness and interdependence while taking on board the necessary ethical requirements.

REFERENCES

African School of Open Education, consulted 28 April 2011 (http://www.africa.upeace.org/dpsa/institution.cfm?id_institution=104&listar=1).

Anton, Danilo (1995) *Diversity, Globalisation and the Ways of Nature*, Ottawa, Canada: International Development Research Centre.

Brandt, Niel (n.d.) Evolutionary and Geological Timelines, consulted 3 July 2010 (http://www.talkorigins.org/origins/geo_timeline.html).

Canadell, Àngels (2010) Sustainability: An Integrative Vision, consulted 4 July 2010 (http://www.guni-rmies.net/news/detail.php?id=1595).

Conference on Endogenous Development and Bio-cultural Diversity (2006) Statement of Commitment Supporting Endogenous Development and Bio-cultural Diversity, consulted 28 April 2011 (http://www.bioculturaldiversity.net/statement.htm).

Conference on Endogenous Development and Bio-cultural Diversity, consulted 28 April 2011 (http://www.bioculturaldiversity.net/papers.htm).

Compas Network (2006) Declaration on Endogenous Development and Biocultural Diversity, consulted 28 April 2011 (http://www.bioculturaldiversity.net/compas%20declaration.htm).

Fornet-Bentacourt, Raúl (ed.) (2009) The Place 'Earth' Occupies in he *Various Cultures. A Dialogue Between Cosmologies in the Face of Ecological Challenge*, Aachen, Germany: Verlag Mainz.

GLUK (n.d.) consulted 2 July 2010 (http://www.gluk.ac.ke).

Kanyandago, Peter (2010) Valuing the African Endogenous Education System for Community-based Learning: An Approach to Early School Leaving. In: Jacques Zeelen et al., *The Burden of Educational Exclusion: Understanding and Challenging Early School Leaving in Africa*, Rotterdam, The Netherlands: Sense Publishers, pp. 99–113.

KIST (n.d.) consulted 2 July 2010 (http://www.kist.ac.rw).
UDS, (n.d.) consulted 2 July 2010 (http://www.ghanaweb.com/GhanaHomePage/education/tamale.html).

The Worldwatch Institute, *State of the World 2010: Transforming Cultures. From Consumerism to Sustainability*, consulted 28 April 2011 (http://www.blogs.worldwatch.org/transformingcultures).

Wijsen, Frans and Marcos, Sylvia (eds) (2010) *Indigenous voices in the sustainable discourse. Spirituality and the struggle for a better quality of life*, Zürich-Berlin: LIT Verlag.

On the Road IV.8
The quest for sustainable suburbs: blurring boundaries between architecture, planning and social sciences[1]

*Carole Després,
Geneviève Vachon and
Andrée Fortin*

INTRODUCTION

'Sustainable development' and 'green buildings' are popular locutions in the discourse of many politicians in developed countries. Best practices are borrowed from around the globe, green certifications are becoming the norm in architecture, public transportation systems are being built, and eco-communities developed. We are witnessing a unique momentum in urban research with a gush of studies that stem from important societal and urban transformations, as well as major theoretical, methodological and technical development. Yet, in Canada, greenhouse gas emissions and energy consumption per capita continue to increase, while the bulk of citizens drive a car to work and either own or dream about a single-family house in a suburb. We suggest that this failure is in part due to the persistent gap between scientific, professional and artistic knowledge, to the sectoral division of professional responsibilities in architecture and urban planning, and to the rigidity of established disciplinary academic traditions.

This chapter presents the programme of research and action of GIRBa – the Interdisciplinary Research Group on Suburbs – at Université Laval, in Quebec, Canada, as an attempt to stimulate and improve collaboration between scientists, professionals and policy decision makers, as well as to train urban planners, architects and social scientists to become 'agents of change'. It illustrates how the group was able to bypass the rigidity of academic disciplinary training and narrow the gap between research and practice by conducting in an intertwined manner empirical research, design, and participatory processes on ageing suburbs, within the sustainability paradigm.

BRIDGING THE DISCIPLINES OF ARCHITECTURE, PLANNING AND SOCIAL SCIENCES

In this section, we argue that urban planning and architecture are both disciplines capable of a constructive dialogue with other domains of knowledge, including the natural and social/human sciences, due to their multidisciplinary position and action-oriented identity aimed at transforming the built and natural environment.

Urban planning is a multidisciplinary discipline for three main reasons: first, the initial academic training of urban planners is often completed in various disciplinary programmes; second, planning programmes are themselves characterized by multidisciplinary curricula taught by faculty members trained in diverse disciplines; and last, several urban planners work in multidisciplinary teams (Pinson, 2004). This capacity of urban planners to bring together knowledge from multiple disciplines in order to define complex urban problems should be highlighted. Working with citizens is also part of the responsibilities of planners. Collaborative methods are designed to empower stakeholders by actively involving them as legitimate decision makers, along with public agencies, in the planning process (Elzinga, 2008; Edwards and Bates, 2011). This competency of urban planners to handle mediation tasks, mixing scientific and political interests, is a disciplinary strength. On the other hand, urban planning went from being considered an art, 'applied' or 'practical', to its replacement in the 1960s by a definition of cities as systems of interrelated activities, including social and economic activities (Taylor, 2007). With this conception of planning as science rather than art, specific train-

ing to support rational decision-making with empirical modes of investigation was required and urban planning gradually lost its expertise on the physical aspects. Hence planners gradually made a more limited contribution to physical interventions and became most commonly dedicated to regulations and master planning. As a result, an enduring tension between architecture and planning over their respective interest in design has revolved around two main notions: while planning is viewed essentially as a process-oriented discipline grounded in social science, architecture (and design, by extension) is largely about 'product' (Anselin et al., 2011).

This situation gave way to a theoretical and professional reorientation of architecture towards urban planning in the past two decades or so, with a specific interest in project making. It gave birth to urban design as a specific area of academic training now taught in various programmes around the world, including Université Laval in Quebec City, Canada. As a field of professional practice, an important share of the contributions from urban design have been carried out by architects and architect-planners (and also landscape architects), owing to their capacity to conceptualize, formalize and materialize projects through the design process. Thanks to the development of systems theory (Simon, 1969), complexity paradigm (Morin, 1990) and constructivist epistemology (Piaget, 1967), design is now recognized as a legitimate mode of inquiry that requires specific skills, knowledge and intuition to translate multidimensional problems into design solutions. Design is interdisciplinary by its very nature, the smallest project making connections between a variety of factors, calling for different types of knowledge and involving several actors (Lawson, 2001). The sequence with which knowledge is integrated into the design process is iterative, involving several loops during which hypothetical solutions are constantly adjusted with additional information brought by clients, users, decision makers, and experts. This implies that architects develop skills for working with others and assure that effective decision-making includes being able to hear what others are saying and respond constructively to one another. Another specific skill of designers in their collaborative work is their use of drawings and models, both physical and digital, to not only convey their ideas and converse with others, but also serve as a tool for problem solving.

Although scientific and multidisciplinary knowledge is essential to the definition of complex design problems with regard to sustainability, architecture students have less opportunity compared with their planning counterparts to interact with researchers from the social sciences and learn to interpret scientific data during their education. Faculty members are, with few exceptions, trained as architects (although their post-professional degrees might be in related disciplines). Indeed, because design studios constitute the heart of an architect's education, as a means for developing students' 'proficiency in using specific information to accomplish a task, correctly selecting the appropriate information, and accurately applying it to the solution of a specific problem' (NAAB, 2009, p. 21), educators must be able to teach such processes. As a result, few students have the appropriate training for searching scientific databases for specific cutting-edge knowledge and translating it appropriately to support or verify decision-making, and most do not experience working in close collaboration with social scientists.

In contrast, social scientists are generally trained to conduct and interpret empirical research early in their education. However, those involved in urban studies (for example urban sociology, urban geography, urban anthropology, environmental psychology) are often disconnected from the applied world of planning and urban design, except for the expert opinions and research they might be

required to understand. Again, academic institutions might have contributed to the situation. On the one hand, even though multidisciplinary training is valued and encouraged in reality, programmes are often competing for students, namely with regard to annual budget calculation methods, thus discouraging mobility across disciplines. On the other hand, topics taught in the social sciences often fluctuate according to both faculty research interests and the priorities of research funding agencies. This situation adds to the challenge of bringing together architects, planners and social scientists to work together on complex urban problems. However, a growing number of architects and planners are seeking specialties beyond their professional education and, for this purpose, engage in a complementary higher education programme. In this manner, they are combining their competences for collaborative multidisciplinary work and problem solving with a capacity to conduct and interpret 'scientific' research. They are becoming privileged knowledge translators, able to interact with social scientists and interpret research data in terms that can be understood by designers.

Together, architects, urban planners and urban researchers hold complementary sets of competences that allow for implementing research and action programmes that, in turn, could lead to identifying creative solutions to complex urban problems. To reach this goal, however, we need to train the next generations of professionals and researchers to work closely together, and to show mutual respect for each other's knowledge and skills. How is it possible to do so within the disciplinary limits and constraints of architecture, planning and social sciences education?

TOWARD MORE SUSTAINABLE SUBURBS: THE CONTRIBUTION OF GIRBa

This section tells the story of how GIRBa – the Interdisciplinary Research Group on Suburbs – successfully trains architects, planners and social scientists to work together around sustainability issues with regard to urban planning and development. GIRBa put in place a 'transdisciplinary'[2] programme of research and action, with the intention of identifying solutions for retrofitting existing and ageing suburbs as a sustain-

able alternative to ongoing urban sprawl. As an academic research group, GIRBa annually comprises around 25 members – professors, postdoctoral fellows and graduate students trained in architecture and planning but also in sociology, rural engineering, geography, political science, and environmental psychology. By bringing together architects, planners and social scientists, the group is able to intertwine publicly funded interdisciplinary research and contractual applied research, as well as architectural and urban design projects, all anchored by a common object of investigation and context of action. The research and action programme is formally organized around three types of research: *empirical or scientific research* on suburban demography, and urban and architectural morphology, as well as daily uses and social representations of the territory; *architectural and urban design research* conducted in advanced studios; *collaborative* planning projects with municipalities, and government housing and planning agencies, as well as with the population.

As part of this programme, GIRBa orchestrates major collaborative design processes involving a large number of stakeholders representing diverse fields of interest, expertise and knowledge. The shared objective of each process is to build consensus, throughout numerous interactive activities, around a strategic and sustainable plan for retrofitting and consolidating different types and scales of suburban environments in Quebec City. The process of consensus building typically involves generating a diagnosis, defining general planning orientations, and designing a strategic planning and development plan. As an example, one of these participatory processes involved the consultation of close to 500 citizens in face-to-face interviews, focus groups and through an internet survey, as well as close collaboration between 100 stakeholders through 45 activities during 18 months.[3] GIRBa's graduate students were involved at all stages of each collaborative process. Their specific contribution varied according to their own disciplinary training, such as conducting relevant research and literature reviews and developing exploratory design hypotheses, identifying appropriate collaborative activities and organizing planning sessions, and building the communication plan. They also participated in the collaborative activities themselves, which could involve presenting their own research and hypotheses, taking and transcribing meeting minutes, redrawing in-progress diagnoses, visions and design hypotheses, preparing the final reports, and also taking care of logistical aspects (Després et al., 2008; Vachon et al., 2007).

The results of an internet survey addressed to evaluate participants' perception of the strengths and weaknesses of one of the collaborative processes, as well as of the success of its outcome (Gatti, 2011; Després et al., 2008) were very positive. Several key actors indicated that the general orientations, objectives and design criteria had made their way into their government agency, something that GIRBa was able to verify in their official documents and websites (Després et al., 2008). A debriefing meeting also confirms that the GIRBa's students were very satisfied with what they had learned throughout the process. First of all, they had learned a lot about suburbs. Also, they saw at work the respective rationalities and types of knowledge held by different stakeholders, and realized how they can be complementary but also contradictory, thereby revealing the complexity of the problem. They learned about the orchestration of a collaborative process through concrete experience. Students in social sciences learned to read maps and drawings, and to relate research data to specific geographical locations and intervention scales. For their part, designers learned to translate research data into design objectives, criteria or spatial concepts. Finally, they all built up a multidisciplinary professional network.

Over the years, GIRBa has become a real incubator for interdisciplinary research and creative design, as well as a training centre that initiates future social scientists, architects and planners to collaborative planning and design processes. Our students are trained to work differently, understanding the need for scientific evidence, and technical and aesthetic knowledge, as well as ethical considerations. Our experience convinced us of our definite capacity to empower future generations of architects, planners, and social scientists as well as decision makers to take advantage of their respective skills and knowledge in order

to further their understanding of the complexity of urban problems with regard to sustainability and work in a collaborative manner to identify solutions.

Our experience also allows us to make the following more general observations. First, *scientific research* is not performed in the same way when conducted in *close and constant collaboration between researchers from different disciplines*. Second, *design research* is a legitimate and autonomous way of producing knowledge for a given problem, one that accepts *intuition* and *uncertainty*. Finally, *action research* has proved to be an alternative mode of knowledge production that recognizes *practical reasoning*, *material* and *organizational constraints*, and that values *public debate*. GIRBa's approach allows for blurring the frontiers not only between academic disciplines and designers, but also between academia, practitioners, decision makers and citizens, which is the essence of the transdisciplinarity paradigm.

CONCLUSION

GIRBa's work exemplifies how a group of university professors teaching architecture, planning and social sciences are able to contribute in advancing with the introduction of sustainability in the curriculum and learning methodologies of future professionals. It illustrates how academic institutions can play a leadership role in training future professionals to tackle sustainable development with approaches adapted to the complexity of urban problems. In *Les sept savoirs nécessaires à l'éducation du futur*, Edgar Morin (2000) invites us to challenge and revise pedagogic models in order to deal with the complexity of our contemporary world. GIRBa's work is an example of what can be done within existing academic structures, reminding us that universities are not only the locus of knowledge production but also of knowledge transmission; they are institutions where one learns to produce knowledge and to apply it (Lawrence and Després, 2004, p. 398). Our transdisciplinary programme of research and action is a good example of the potential contribution of universities in training professionals and researchers with different disciplinary backgrounds to work together,

which may very well have positive effects on all levels of society.

REFERENCES

Anselin, L., Nasar, J.L. and Talen, E. (2011) Where do planners belong? Assessing the relationship between planning and design in American universities. In: *Journal of Planning and Education Research*, **31**(2), pp. 196–207.

Després, C., Brais, N. and Avellan, S. (2004) Collaborative planning for retrofitting suburbs: transdisciplinarity and intersubjectivity in action. In: Lawrence, R.J. and Després, C. (eds) *Futures*, **36**(4) (special issue), pp. 471–86.

Després, C., Fortin, A., Joerin, F., Vachon, G., Moretti, G.P. and Gatti, E. (2008) Retrofitting postwar suburbs: a collaborative planning process. In: Hirsch Hadorn, G. et al. (eds) *Handbook of Transdisciplinary Research*. Heidelberg: Springer.

Edwards, M.M. and Bates, L.K. (2011) Planning's core curriculum: Knowledge, practice, and implementation. In: *Journal of Planning Education and Research*, **31**(2), pp. 172–83.

Elzinga, A. (2008) Participation. In: Hirsch Hadorn, G. et al. (eds) *Handbook of Transdisciplinary Research*, Part V, pp. 345–59. Heidelberg: Springer.

Fortin, A., Després, C. and Vachon, G. (eds) (2002) *La banlieue revisitée*. Québec: Nota Bene.

Gatti, E. (2011) *Tangibles, Intangibles: Outcomes from an Interdisciplinary Collaborative Urban Design Process in Quebec's First-Ring Suburbs*. Essay in urban design, School of Architecture, Université Laval, Québec.

Hirsch Hadorn, G. et al. (eds) (2008) *Handbook of Transdisciplinary Research*, Heidelberg: Springer.

Lawrence, R. and Després, C. (2004) Futures of transdisciplinarity. In: Lawrence, R.J. and Després, C. (eds) *Futures*, **36**(4) (special issue), pp. 397–405.

Lawson, B. (2001) *What Designers Know*. London: Architectural Press.

Morin, E. (1990) *Introduction à la pensée complexe*. Paris: Seuil.

Morin, E. (2000) *Les sept savoirs nécessaires à l'éducation du futur*. Paris: Seuil.

NAAB (The National Architectural Accrediting Board, inc.) (2009) 2009 Conditions for Accreditation: www.academyart.edu/assets/pdf/NAAB-2009-Conditions.pdf (consulted 1 June 2011).

Piaget, J. (1967/1971) *Biology and Knowledge.* Chicago: University of Chicago Press.

Pinson, D. (2004) *Urban planning: An undisciplined discipline.* In: Lawrence, R.J. and Després, C. (eds) *Futures,* **36**(4) (special issue), pp. 503–13.

Simon, H.A. (1969) *The Sciences of the Artificial* (3rd edn 1996). Boston: MIT Press.

Taylor, N. (2007) *Urban Planning Theory Since 1945.* London: Sage.

Vachon, G., Després, C., Nembrini, A., Joerin, F., Fortin, A. and Moretti, G.P. (2007) Collaborative planning and design for a sustainable neighborhood on Quebec City's university campus. In: Thwaites, K., Porta, S., Romice, O. and Greaves, M. (eds) *Urban Sustainability through Environmental Design.* London: Routledge, pp. 129–35.

NOTES

1   A longer version of this paper by the same authors, entitled 'Implementing Transdisciplinarity: Architecture and Urban Planning at Work', was published in Doucet, I. and Janssens, N. (eds) (2011) *Transdisciplinary Knowledge in Architecture and Urbanism: Towards Hybrid Modes of Inquiry.* New York: Springer. Permission for reproduction was granted by Springer.

2   For a definition of transdisciplinarity, see for example Lawrence and Després (2004); for GIRBa's operationalization of the concept, see for example Després, Brais and Avellan (2004).

3   For details, see Després, Brais and Avellan (2004). In 2006, GIRBa orchestrated another 6-month collaborative process aimed to propose a plan for transforming a large parcel on Université Laval's main suburban campus into a sustainable university neighbourhood (for details, see for example Vachon, Després, Nembrini, Joerin, Fortin and Moretti, 2007).

IV.4 Universities in Transition

The prospect of a future that is sustainable in both human and environmental terms now involves transforming our attitudes into proactive initiatives and starting a transition towards change in all social contexts, including higher education. In order to do so, we must identify strategies for a change in values that will in turn bring about changes in educational institutions; integrate the environmental, social, economic and cognitive realms through interdisciplinary learning; and develop networks to share the complexity and challenges involved in the transformation of university culture.

Whatever higher education institutions (HEIs) have done in the past – whatever roles they have adopted, functions they have served, purposes they have pursued, worldviews they have assumed, and paradigms they have generated, expressed and nurtured – needs to be critically reappraised in terms of their ability to address the challenges arising from the complex circumstances in which humanity currently finds itself in every part of the world.

One of the most important challenges facing universities is the need for a new idea of the university for the 21st century to give expression to a global culture capable of offering an alternative to the global corporate culture. We must therefore explore the main changes that institutions need to make in order to enhance their role in building a sustainability paradigm. An increasingly complex context for HEIs requires a transformation in their administrative structures, academic decision-making patterns, governance policies and management systems. These transformations compel us to analyse how a shared vision and mission for HEIs can be built and how the institutions can be transformed by breaking down their resistance to change. Universities must develop new strategies and visualize themselves in a different way if they are to survive.

IV.4a GOALS AND PURPOSES OF HIGHER EDUCATION IN MODERN, COMPLEX SOCIETIES

Sjur Bergan

INTRODUCTION

This paper aims to explore the goals and purposes of higher education in modern, complex societies. Even if contributing to economic development is an important goal, it cannot be the sole purpose of higher education. Rather, the article takes as its point of departure the proposition that higher education has an important role to play in developing the kind of societies in which we would like to live tomorrow.

CHALLENGES TO MODERN SOCIETIES

Within the scope of this paper, any overview of the challenges modern societies face will necessarily be cursory. Space will not allow a consideration of the extent to which modern societies in different parts of the world face different challenges nor of whether all contemporary societies are also 'modern'. Since the author's background is mainly European, he hopes to be forgiven for what will undoubtedly be a European slant even though much of the argument will be pertinent to other parts of the world.

Most of the world faces an economic crisis and the spectre of unemployment. Even if the severity of the crisis is uneven, few societies have escaped it. This is true for most of Europe, generally regarded as economically and technologically advanced, even if we must also recognize that some of the problems Europe and also North America face today have been faced even more sharply by other societies over a longer period of time. In a historical perspective, material prosperity relatively evenly distributed has been the exception rather than the rule and it is also not a universal characteristic of economically advanced societies today.

One specific aspect of Europe today is perhaps that Europeans do not seem overly confident about their future in a way that many Asians, for example, seem to be, and for reasons that are not only economic. There is disaffection and Europeans do not demonstrate an abundance of confidence in their public authorities – certainly a characteristic they share with many North Americans and probably also with people from other continents – or indeed in their political systems, even if they would also be hard put to identify viable alternatives.

There is fear of the future but also of those we often label the Other: those whose origins lie elsewhere, whose looks and dress are different, those who speak other languages and with other accents and those whose religious practice differs from that of the majority (to the extent that the majority practises a religion). Statements such as these are of course too crudely cut and it is not difficult to find Europeans who are neither gloomy nor suspicious of cultural diversity, nor is it difficult to find people from other continents who are.

Nevertheless, the number of Europeans who either vote for or express sympathy for parties promising simple solutions to complex problems and who are not overly discriminate in identifying culprits for all our perceived or real troubles should give reason for concern. Populism of the right as well as of the left seeks easy answers to complex questions. Its historical track record is unimpressive, from the aptly named Know Nothing movement in the US in the 1850s through those who saw social class as determining our lives to those who today would have us believe that our cultural background plays the same role; but many do not see history as the most relevant frame of reference. We may shiver at Chávez in Venezuela or the US Tea Party (Lepore, 2010) but we would do well to remember that Europe and other continents also have their fair share of tea parties. We would also do well

to remember that being afraid of the Other is hardly a sign of confidence in who *we* are and in our ability to determine our own future.

This is particularly serious because the world does face serious challenges, from climate change to social cohesion. These challenges are diverse but they have at least one important factor in common: if we are to rise to them, this requires a high degree of sophistication, of ability to ask critical questions as well as to find the answers to those questions and to work across borders, whether those of political constructs such as states or of intellectual constructs such as academic disciplines. To rise to the challenges, we need higher education that prepares us to do so.

EDUCATION AS THE ANSWER?

Pretending that education is *the* answer to all our challenges would be to fall prey to another kind of oversimplification, maybe a kind of 'educational fundamentalism'. However, it is equally clear that education must be an important part of a comprehensive answer. As Martha Nussbaum says in her recent book: 'Without support from suitably educated citizens, no democracy can remain stable' (Nussbaum, 2010, p. 10).

A consciousness of the role of education in furthering economic and social advancement is of course not new (Lepore, 2010, pp. 153–5). Worldwide, there seems to be an increasing awareness of the importance of education and of the basic fact that modern societies cannot be built on ignorance, but much of the focus is on the need for education in order to further economic growth, ranging from the EU New Skills for New Jobs initiative (see website) to concerns about the state of education in Latin America (Oppenheimer, 2010).

The movement towards Education for All (EFA), spearheaded by UNESCO, testifies to the fact that while in the past, societies had a meaningful place for those without formal education, their place is precarious in modern, complex societies. UNESCO's work on EFA reasonably emphasizes universal basic education and the need to eradicate illiteracy (UNESCO, 2000, p. 8).

Much of current higher education debate focuses on structures rather than on the purposes the structures should serve. By way of digression, two structures come to mind. One we find at the old Agora in Athens. The Agora was the centre of civic life, where political arguments were conducted with – by definition – Classical culture as well as, certainly, its share of dirty tricks. Rhetoric was a mark of the culture successive generations came to define as the embodiment of education and civilization but so was ostracism. The other is in northern Alsace, where one can visit a restored fort of the Maginot line. This structure was as advanced as military technology got around 1930 and was intended to withstand any enemy attack. As it turned out, the attack came from a different direction than expected and the fort became an example of a rigid structure that could not be reformed to meet an altered challenge. Today, both structures have been given a new lease on life for totally different purposes, as tourist attractions and as part of our cultural heritage. We want higher education to remain a living part of our cultural heritage. We do not want it to be a museum or a tourist attraction, and this requires consideration of its purposes in modern, complex societies.

PURPOSES OF HIGHER EDUCATION

The use of the plural in considering the purposes of higher education is deliberate but it is unfortunately rarely reflected in European public debate, which could still leave one with the impression that the sole purpose of education is to further economic growth. The point here is *not* that economic well-being is unimportant, and one does not need to look far to see that the economy is of fundamental importance. The point is, rather, that education is important not only for our economy but for our society as a whole, not only for *homo economicus* but for humankind. A good starting point can be Ambrose Bierce's definition of education as 'that which discloses to the wise and disguises from the foolish their lack of understanding' (Bierce, 1983, p. 105).

Higher education must fulfil a range of purposes. This author has defined four (Bergan, 2005; Council of Europe, 2007):
- Preparation for the labour market
- Preparation for life as active citizens in democratic societies
- Personal development
- The development and maintenance of a broad, advanced knowledge base

One can discuss the finer details but not, I hope, the fact that the purposes are multiple. The four purposes are equally important and if the order in which they are listed indicates anything at all, it is the frequency with which they are raised in public debate rather than their relative importance.

Nor are the purposes contradictory. Rather, they are complementary: many of the qualities that make individuals attractive on the labour market also enable them to be active citizens and contribute to their personal development. For example, analytical skills as well as communication competences and the ability to work in teams as well as independently are of great importance in developing advanced economic activities: to develop a product, test it and market it. These competences are also, however, the stuff of which democratic practice is made and they are important for personal development. Just like companies in the knowledge economy, democracies need citizens who demonstrate the ability to put things into context, to analyse complex situations, to identify possible solutions and to communicate their conclusions convincingly. This leads us to the question of what competences higher education should seek to develop.

WHAT COMPETENCES DO MODERN SOCIETIES NEED?

Broadly, competences come in two varieties: generic and subject specific. The latter describe what a historian should know about history, a chemist about chemistry, a linguist about linguistics, and so on. Generic competences are those that all higher education graduates at a certain level should demonstrate, such as analytical ability, communication skills and an aptitude for teamwork (González and Wagenaar, 2005).

It should not be difficult to see that we need both subject-specific and generic competences. Nevertheless, there is tension between the two and the academic community has a tendency to feel responsible for developing subject-specific competences but to consider the development of generic competences as something that should be completed by the time students reach university. In a survey of the attitudes of higher education staff towards the idea that the university should be a site of citizenship, many staff showed great reticence along the lines of 'my subject is too important for this' (Plantan, 2004). When this author was a student representative at the University of Oslo in the early 1980s, we asked for permission to provide brief information on the Student Council at the start of every lecture series. The reaction from one lecturer, in the history of French literature, was that he had two hours to cover four centuries and did not have a minute to lose.

On the other hand, the need for subject-specific competences is underestimated by those who believe that leadership requires little understanding of the activity that is the life and bread of the organization or company one is supposed to lead. If German has provided the established term for those who possess subject-specific competence alone – possibly because *Fachidiot* sounds less harsh than the direct English translation, 'subject idiot' – English may well have provided the most apt term for those who believe that generic competences alone will do: management consultant.

As societies, we need both subject-specific and generic competences. We need subject-specific competences in a very broad range of disciplines and we need citizens who combine high-level subject-specific competences with the ability and will to work closely with those who have similar levels of subject-specific competence in other fields. Not least, we need citizens who are able to put their subject-specific competence into a broader context, to assess how their own disciplines can contribute to the good of our societies, to ask critical questions and find constructive answers. European higher education institutions probably graduate more highly qualified subject specialists than ever before, but I am less convinced they educate enough intellectuals: those who combine subject-specific and generic competences as described here. I am also unsure of whether they often enough provide the kind of language and cultural competence needed in what is often described with the cliché 'a globalized world' and that is sometimes described for Africa in the following terms: there are relatively few bilingual Africans because it is rare to find Africans who master only two languages.

We referred to subject-specific competence as what a historian should 'know' about history, and so on. If we were to interrogate the proverbial 'man in the street', it would be a safe guess to say that many would equate education with knowledge. Knowledge is, however, only a start. If we learn a foreign language, such as Spanish or Catalan, we need to learn a good number of grammatical forms. Since both are Romance languages, we will need to know a quite complex system of verb conjugations. This requires effort but the effort is only worthwhile if we also develop an understanding of when to use what forms and then to put this knowledge and understanding into practice by actually speaking and writing the language to an acceptable standard.

This corresponds to the classical definition of learning outcomes: knowledge, understanding and the ability to do (Bergan, 2007). Increasingly, however, this author has come to ask whether this definition should not be revised so as also to encompass attitudes. This is perhaps where structures and purposes meet: we need structures that enable us to provide the kind of education that meets the full range of purposes

we have identified for it and that does not limit its vision of education to the learning of facts, even if the importance of facts should not be underestimated. We need to develop what we have in another context referred to as 'converging competences' (Bergan and Damian, 2010). As our societies develop, new possibilities open up but the fact that it may be possible to do something does not mean it is ethically justifiable. Examples to support this assertion are often sought in warfare – it is possible to kill a lot of people at long distance and in a single operation – but can also be found in many other areas. Would the financial crisis that was one of the starting points for our reflection have happened if those in charge of the financial services sector had had a better education about their role as actors in society, and if demonstrating citizenship and not only technical competences had been considered important in hiring new recruits to the sector? Why do most political actors agree that education is important yet too often fail to act on that conviction when it comes to setting priorities? How do we reconcile the belief that academic mobility is important to our future with the fact that many societies wish to limit migration and make no exceptions for mobile students and scholars? It would be difficult to argue that our current education system has done a good job of preparing us to deal with the paradoxes and contradictions that are a fact of life but that at least need to be spotted before they can be dealt with.

CONCLUSION

We need a higher education, in other words, that educates for the kind of society in which we would wish to live (Tironi, 2005), not just for the kind of economy we would like to have. The 2005 GUNi conference challenged us to move from understanding to action. As higher education policymakers, we need to develop an understanding of the full range of purposes of higher education. We then need to develop policies, at both systems and institutional level that will enable higher education to educate intellectuals and not only train specialists (AAC&U, 2007). Higher education must prepare for societies that are sustainable environmentally as well as economically, politically as well as socially and culturally and that are proficient in intercultural dialogue (Bergan and van't Land, 2010).

Hughes de Saint-Cher, a 13th-century Dominican, said 'First the bow is bent in study and then the arrow is released in preaching' (Radcliffe, 2005, p. 5). While preaching may come easily to academics, the call is for teaching, learning and action, within and outside of universities. In the words of the Canadian philosopher John Ralston Saul:

I find our education is increasingly one aimed at training loyal employees, even though the state and the corporations are increasingly disloyal. What we should be doing is quite different. It turns on our ability to rethink our education and our public expectations so that we create a non-employee, non-loyal space for citizenship. After all, a citizen is by definition loyal to the state because it belongs to her or him. That is what frees the citizen to be boisterous, outspoken, cantankerous and, all in all, by corporatist standards, disloyal. This is the key to the success of our democracy. (Saul, 2009, p. 318)

REFERENCES

AAC&U (Association of American Colleges and Universities) (2007) *College Learning for the New Global Century.* Washington, DC: AAC&U.

Bergan, Sjur (2005) Higher education as a 'public good and a public responsibility': What does it mean? In: Weber, Luc and Bergan, Sjur (eds) *The Public Responsibility for Higher Education and Research.* Strasbourg: Council of Europe Publishing Council of Europe Higher Education Series No. 2, pp. 13–28.

Bergan, Sjur (2007) *Qualifications. Introduction to a Concept.* Strasbourg: Council of Europe Publishing. Council of Europe Higher Education Series No. 6.

Bergan, Sjur and Radu Damian (eds) (2010) *Higher Education for Modern Societies: Competences and Values.* Strasbourg: Council of Europe Publishing. Council of Europe Higher Education Series No. 15.

Bergan, Sjur and Hilligje van't Land (eds) (2010) *Speaking across Borders: The Role of Higher Education in Furthering Intercultural Dialogue.* Strasbourg: Council of Europe Publishing. Council of Europe Higher Education Series No. 16.

Bierce, Ambrose (1983[1911]) *The Enlarged Devil's Dictionary*, edited by E.J. Hopkins. London: Penguin American Library.

Bologna Process (2005a) Standards and Guidelines for Quality Assurance in the European Higher Education Area (http://www.ehea.info/Uploads/Documents/Standards-and-Guidelines-for-QA.pdf).

Bologna Process (2005b) The framework of qualifications of the European Higher Education Area (http://www.ehea.info/Uploads/Documents/QF-EHEA-May2005.pdf).

Council of Europe (2007) Recommendation CM/Rec(2007)6 of the Committee of Ministers to member states on the public responsibility for higher education and research (www.coe.int/t/dg4/highereducation/News/pub_res_EN.pdf).

Council of Europe/UNESCO (1997) Convention on the Recognition of Qualifications concerning Higher Education in the European Region: (http://conventions.coe.int/Treaty/en/Treaties/Html/165.htm).

González, Julia and Wagenaar, Robert (eds) (2005) *TUNING Educational Structures in Europe. Universities' Contribution to the Bologna Process. Final Report of Pilot Project Phase 2.* Bilbao and Groningen: Publicaciones de la Universidad de Deusto.

Lepore, Jill (2010) *The Whites of Their Eyes. The Tea Party's Revolution and the Battle over American History.* Princeton, NJ: Princeton University Press.

Nussbaum, Martha C. (2010) *Not For Profit. Why Democracy Needs the Humanities.* Princeton, NJ: Princeton University Press.

Oppenheimer, Andrès (2010) *¡Basta de historias! La obsesión latinoamericana con el pasado y las 12 claves del futuro* Buenos Aires: Editorial sudamericana.

Plantan, Frank (2004) The University as site of citizenship. In: Bergan, Sjur (ed.) *The University as Res Publica.* Strasbourg: Council of Europe Publishing, pp. 83–128.

Radcliffe, Timothy, O.P. (2005) *What is the Point of Being a Christian?* London: Burns and Oates.

Saul, John Ralston (2009) *A Fair Country. Telling Truths about Canada.* Toronto, Ontario: Penguin Canada.

Tironi, Eugenio (2005) *El sueño chileno. Comunidad, familia y nación en el Bicentenario* Santiago de Chile: Taurus.

UNESCO (2000) *Education for All 2000 Assessment. Global Synthesis.*

WEBSITES

http://www.ehea.info/, EHEA

http://ec.europa.eu/social/main.jsp?catId=822&langId=en, EU New Skills for New Jobs initiative

IV.4b SUSTAINABLE DEVELOPMENT AS A DRIVER FOR UNIVERSITY TRANSFORMATION

John Holmberg

INTRODUCTION

How can a concept as complex as sustainable development become a force for transformation in an organization with a power structure as complex as a university? This paper presents a strategy that has been used at Chalmers University of Technology since the mid-1980s. The Chalmers' strategy consists of three key building blocks:

1. Create a neutral arena/organization with purpose-built features to facilitate the change process.

2. Build on individual engagement and involvement (bottom-up).

3. Communicate a clear commitment from the management team.

The vision of Chalmers University of Technology (Chalmers) is: 'Chalmers for a Sustainable Future'. This is easy to write but difficult to do. Since sustainable development (SD) is a process rather than a product and can be seen as a huge societal learning activity, it depends on the lasting engagement and involvement that can be created (Holmberg and Samuelsson, 2006). If this is not taken into account, the early results and visibility that are reached by well-packaged products of distinct providers (for example a specific department) can soon turn into lock-in effects that make continued change in the university more difficult. In 1985, Chalmers laid the foundation to allow SD to be a clear impetus for change. We then began work on a method to transform education towards SD with a broad involvement of staff and students throughout the university. The corresponding strategy has subsequently been used in order to transform and integrate the research and innovation. The strategy has the same basic structure irrespective of the processes.

Many universities struggle with change processes (Ferrer-Balas et al., 2004; Hopkinson, 2010; Jansen et al., 2005; Kamp, 2006). There are many good ambitions and goals that seem to be hard to implement, for example implementing SD in research and education or integrating the different aspects of the knowledge triangle (education, research and innovation). This is of course due to the complexity of the issue that is to be implemented, but also to the character of the power structure of a university. There exist clear sequenced methods that seem to work well for hierarchal organizations, for example Kotter (1995). These methods, though, meet obstacles when introduced on a broader scale at a university. At a university the power structure is more complex. The top management has power but so too have, and in many cases to a greater extent, all the teachers and scientists at the university. In such a structure it is essential to be able to create engagement and involvement among the staff in order to succeed with a broad scale transformation. This paper describes the basic structure of the strategy that has been used at Chalmers and how it has been used to transform the university towards sustainability in: education; research; integration of education, research and innovation in areas of advance (for further information on 'areas of advance', see section 'Integrating education, research and innovation' below); and in integrating efforts by academia, business and society in regional triple-helix knowledge clusters.

CHALMERS' STRATEGY FOR CHANGE

To implement new ideas and achieve change at universities, with their high degree of autonomy and strong traditions, is often a difficult mission, especially if the mission is as complex as the embedding of SD at the university. A task like this often turns into something that is in everybody's interest but is nobody's responsibility.

One way to get around this dilemma is to use a top-down demand and control strategy, more often used in business organizations. This seldom works at the university, since it requires very effective incentives in order to profoundly affect everyday university practices. Such incentives are difficult to construct for complex issues. Another way to go about it is that a certain department is given the task or takes on the mission on its own. This might work to a certain degree, but often leads to lock-in effects in the long run. This lock-in can consist in the rest of the organization not making enough effort since they can leave the concern to the responsible department. The responsible department might also feel that it wants to be in control and therefore does not welcome initiatives from other departments or individuals. When funding comes with the responsibility, the risk of this happening is even greater.

At Chalmers, a third method for achieving change has been identified. The strategy has been tested on different scales and for many years and seems to be more successful than many other efforts. Three important building blocks can be identified in Chalmers strategy for achieving change:

1. *Create a neutral arena/organization:* Some kind of neutral arena that can facilitate the change process is needed. It has overview of the whole organization. This arena/organization must be working across the research groups to avoid lock-in effects. It can be used as a platform for cooperation and information exchange. An arena like this is essential for making this kind of complex change successful and for it to have long-lasting effects. Such an organization can function as an engine for the issues that otherwise often become everyone's interest but no-one's responsibility. Important features of this arena/organization are that it is: open and inviting; service-oriented (not building

own empires); building trust and lowering barriers; keeping the memory of the change process; and giving feedback to relevant stakeholders and thereby keeping up the change momentum.

2. *Build on individual engagement and involvement (bottom-up):* Universities, with their core values of scepticism, curiosity and freedom of speech, have a high degree of autonomy, which must be respected in a change process. Teachers hate to be taught! The change process must therefore build on the engagement and involvement of individuals. The features of the neutral arena/organization and the methods used to bring about change must meet these requirements.

3. *Communicate a clear commitment from the management team:* The change process must be in line with the overall strategy of the university. Ideally it should be an essential part of the vision of the university. It is of course also important that the university clearly motivates the change process – systematically creating incentives and other structures that correlate with the change process.

TRANSFORMING EDUCATION

Transforming higher education contents and practices is a tough challenge, and actual outcomes are still far from the desired image of a higher education for sustainable development (The Observatory, 2006; Holmberg and Samuelsson, 2006). Beyond curriculum development and the need for new knowledge from interdisciplinary research, one of the clearest challenges is how to reach the individual academic faculty member and involve him or her in this change.

Chalmers was early active in the field of environment and SD. There were plans to develop a separate education programme in this field parallel to the other educational programmes. Instead a policy was introduced 1985 stating that all educational programmes should contain a course load corresponding to five weeks of full-time studies on environment and SD. The policy also stated that all students should be able to deepen their studies in the field of SD at the end of their studies. Since 2003, this has been a compulsory requirement. These decisions implied that every programme had to take responsibility for SD, both in developing a basic training and in the integration of SD in all other courses.

In order to facilitate this process Chalmers decided not to give the responsibility to a particular department but to create a neutral arena. This process (together with the research transformation process described in the next section) led to the formation of what would, in 1989, become the Gothenburg Centre for Environment and Sustainability (GMV). The centre is now an open and cross-disciplinary network for researchers and teachers at Chalmers and, since 2001, also at Gothenburg University. It has been an important driver for education and research on SD at Chalmers (and Gothenburg University). It has carried the history in this area across shifts in university management. In 2006, Chalmers received a UNESCO chair in Education for Sustainable Development (ESD), and the university management approved funding of the connected ESD project (2006–2009). Strongly related to this process is also the series of international conferences organized by Chalmers and Gothenburg University, starting with a workshop on ESD within the EU summit in 2001. The ESD project is part of a long series of processes related to SD and ESD at Chalmers.

The aim of the ESD project was to develop an organization that can manage the implementation of ESD at Chalmers, resulting in a suggestion that:

- guarantees and continuously enhances the quality in Chalmers' basic courses in SD (the compulsory 7.5 HEC (higher education credits, equivalent to ECTS) courses)
- guarantees and continuously enhances the quality of SD content in other courses
- effectively gives support to those who order SD courses
- effectively gives support to students when choosing SD courses
- effectively promotes internal and external information exchange on ESD
- effectively promotes cooperation with internal and external stakeholders within ESD
- provides a forum for meetings for students and for teachers with interest in the area
- provides support to further education within the SD area for non-teaching personnel
- provides support to the development of a campus reflecting Chalmers initiative for SD

Holmberg et al. (2011) report in more detail on the change process within education in relation to Chalmers' strategy for change. In that paper the analysis of the change process is made along four different lines, which target different elements of the overall vision to enhance the quality and embedding of ESD at the university and to create a permanent platform for further work on ESD: the work on the basic course requirement for SD (Lunvist and Svanström, 2008); the efforts for integrating ESD into educational programmes (Svanström et al., 2010); the work to collect and spread information on good teaching practices within ESD; and the cooperation with external stakeholders (Holmberg and Samuelsson, 2006; Ottosson and Samuelsson, 2009). More information on the ESD project can be found in the literature (Holmberg et al., 2008; and on www.chalmers.se/gmv/EN/projects/esd_chalmers). In 2009, a new neutral arena was created with the same characteristics as GMV, but within the field of education: Chalmers Learning Centre.

TRANSFORMATION OF RESEARCH

In 2001 Chalmers and University of Gothenburg launched a cooperation platform for SD and environmental research projects – the GMV Centre for Environment and Sustainability. GMV sprung out of the immaterial cooperation organization (neutral arena) 'the School of Environmental Science' founded in 1989. GMV involves all faculties and departments at both universities as it is now widely realized that cooperation between different research areas is needed for universities seeking to contribute to SD. Traditionally, however, it has been difficult to put interdisciplinary ideas into practice. Through the GMV that initial threshold has been overcome. GMV has succeeded in establishing a neutral arena for interdisciplinary research projects and researchers at Chalmers and University of Gothenburg. The GMV research network comprises about 500 members from all faculties at both universities and about 500 representatives from industry, local authorities and other environmental organizations. Hence, GMV created momentum and visibility for sustainability across the whole university and all researchers were welcome to take part in the network. This gave confidence to make the next strategic decision: Chalmers Environmental Initiative, CEI (2000–2008). This initiative (100 million SEK) meant that seven new chairs were installed at strategic places all over Chalmers. The purpose of the CEI was to create a lasting, comprehensive change at Chalmers and to provide a basis for cross-border research and to achieve critical mass, which together could influence many and get the whole of Chalmers, from student to president, to join in the same direction. Not in the sense that everyone would work only on sustainability issues but rather to cause many to reflect on their own role in relation to SD and see SD as a driving force for research and development.

When CEI professors where interviewed in the final report (CEI, 2008) they all talked about time. The CEI funds gave them time to think in new directions and time to build their research teams. It was a relatively great freedom compared with their normal everyday research. It was considered important to having enough freedom to dare to fail, and enough time to dare to seek, without being sure of the answer before the start. The success of this is demonstrated by the way that the 100 million SEK the Chalmers Foundation invested in the initiative turned to 575 million during the project's time through the finance the professors attracted from outside resources.

The CEI, which is well documented in CEI (2008) and in other reports, gave visibility to the SD activities at Chalmers. This in turn led to Chalmers being invited to join other international arenas for SD. In 2001 Chalmers was invited to join the Alliance for Global Sustainability (the AGS), which is a unique international partnership between four of the world's leading science and technology universities – ETH Zurich, MIT in Boston, the University of Tokyo, Chalmers University of Technology – and their associated partners. Since its creation in 1997, the AGS has drawn on the strength of its partners to develop capacity and new models for integrated research, education and outreach. In 2006 Chalmers became a UN-HABITAT Partner University, which means that Chalmers and UN-HABITAT work together in building the capacity of tertiary institutions within developing countries in teaching and research regarding the sound development of human settlements. The same year Chalmers also received a UNESCO chair.

INTEGRATING EDUCATION, RESEARCH AND INNOVATION

The integration of research, education and innovation, the knowledge triangle, is seen as the driver of the knowledge-based society and it also lies behind the creation of the European Institute of Technology (EIT), which was launched in April 2008. It is also core to the entrepreneurial university (Lunvist and Williams Middleton, 2011). In January 2007 three new vice-presidents were appointed with the same mission, aiming to increase collaboration and lower barriers within Chalmers and between Chalmers and external stakeholders, with the new vision 'Chalmers for a sustainable future' as a driving force. This was initially done through three crosscutting initiatives: Energy and Systems, Materials and Bio-chemistry,

Industry and Communication. This mission developed into the creation of a new matrix structure of the university with eight so-called areas of advance. In an 'area of advance', all research, education and innovation activities at Chalmers that are linked to, for instance, the area Transportation, become visible to each other and to the surrounding world. This makes it easier for efficient collaboration within Chalmers and with other universities, business and society. The individual faculty members are still members of their department, but also active and visible in the area of advance. Each area of advance constitutes a neutral arena for transformation (as described in the section above on 'Chalmers' strategy for change'). This new dimension creates a virtual matrix organization and enables a powerful way to work with an operational bottom-up process combined with a strategic top-down process. The areas of advance can thereby provide powerful meeting places over boundaries and a challenge for new interdisciplinary research. The areas of advance at Chalmers are: Built environment; Energy; ICT; Life science; Material science; Nano science and Nano technology; Production; and Transport. The areas are firmly rooted in the basic and applied sciences and driven by innovation and entrepreneurship beside the overall vision Chalmers for a sustainable future. One confirmation that we are successful in our work with the areas of advance is that we did better than any other university in Sweden in attracting governmental strategic faculty means for 2010–2014.

WORKING WITH BUSINESS AND SOCIETY IN KNOWLEDGE CLUSTERS

The areas of advance give Chalmers much better possibilities to work together with business and society in regional knowledge clusters. These kinds of triple-helix constellations can be effective in solving the complex grand challenges ahead. In order to be effective together, academia, business and society must understand, not only their own role, but also the role of the others. Since the university is often more stable in the region than the industries are and since the university is the only actor with all three components in the knowledge triangle – education, research and innovations – it is natural that the university should take on a special role in building these clusters in a neutral, open and inviting way.

In the region of West Sweden, Chalmers has been active in bringing the stakeholders together starting with a series of meetings with the top management of the two universities, the city of Gothenburg, the region

Västra Götaland and the West Sweden Chamber of Commerce and Industry, starting at the 2009 Globe Forum event in Gothenburg. In January 2011 the leaders from the five organizations wrote a newspaper article together suggesting that West Sweden could be a 'Test arena for the future', that is, the region where future products and services are developed and tested in reality (Andersson et al., 2011). The article also discusses what it takes to succeed:

> Our values must be based on *trust* so people are trained in daring to think new ideas and even fail. *Low barriers* that welcome and affirm commitment and initiatives. *Willingness to cooperate* between organizations so that we even become each other's ambassadors. *Openness to the outside world* is deep in the region since a long time back. Sustainable development is the driving force.

Recently the group has identified five knowledge clusters in the region: Life science; Urban futures; Bio-based products; Mobility solutions; and Marine and Maritime. In order to train ourselves in building trust, each of the five organizations will take responsibility for describing the landscape of one of the five knowledge clusters and the role the different organizations are playing to develop the cluster. The journey towards sustainability continues …

PERSONAL REFLECTIONS ON CHANGE PROCESSES

I will finish by making some personal observations on the transformation processes, being active as researcher, teacher, head of a research department, vice dean of the centre for environment and sustainability and now as vice president for Chalmers. In all successful processes, the three building blocks described in above have been able to create trust between the different actors. This trust means that people want to listen and understand each other, which in turn increases the willingness to participate in collaboration, which increases the trust even more. The trust also means that creativity increases, since it is OK to make mistakes.

If instead there is lack of trust, the willingness to listen and understand each other decreases, leading to lower interest in collaboration and even to separation and tribalism, which in turn means reduced creativity and sometimes internal competition and fear, and even lower trust …

REFERENCES

Andersson, G.-I., Fredman. P., Holmberg, J., Hulthén, A., Markides, K., Ransgård, J., Trouvé, J., and Törsäter, B. (2011) *West Sweden – the Test Arena for the Future.* Göteborgs-Posten. (Swedish)

Ferrer-Balas, D., Bruno, J., de Mingo, M. and Sans, R. (2004) Advances in education transformation towards sustainable development at the Technical University of Catalonia, Barcelona. *International Journal of Sustainability in Higher Education,* **5**(3), pp. 251–66.

CEI (2008) *Chalmers Environmental Initiative – final report.* The Centre for Environment and Sustainability (GMV), Chalmers University of Technology/University of Gothenburg, Sweden (www.chalmers.se/gmv).

Holmberg, J. and Samuelsson, B. (eds) (2006) *Drivers and barriers for implementing sustainable development in higher education.* Technical paper No. 3, UNESCO Education Sector.

Holmberg, J., Svanstrom, M., Peet, D.-J., Mulder, K., Ferrer-Balas, D. and Segalas, J. (2008) Embedding sustainability in higher education through interaction with lecturers: Case studies from three European technical universities. *European Journal of Engineering Education,* **33**(3), pp. 271–82.

Holmberg, J., Lunvist, U., Svanström, M. and Arehag, M. (2011) The University and Transformation Towards Sustainability – lessons learned at Chalmers University of Technology. Paper presented at Engineering Education in Sustainable Development, September 19–22, Göteborg.

Hopkinson, P. (2010) Ecoversity: the potential for sustainable development to reshape university culture and action. *International Journal Environment and Sustainable Development,* **9**(4), pp. 378–91.

Jansen, L., Holmberg, J. and Civili, F.S. (2005) *International Evaluation of UPC Environmental and Sustainability Research and Education.* Barcelona: UPC, available at: http://www.upc.es/mediambient/UPCSostenible2015. html.

Kamp, L. (2006) Engineering education in sustainable development at Delft University of Technology. *Journal of Cleaner Production,* **14**, pp. 928–31.

Kotter, J.P. (1995) Leading change: why transformation efforts fail. *Harvard Business Review*, March–April 1995, pp. 57–67.

Lunvist, U. and Svanström, M. (2008) Inventory of content in basic courses in environment and sustainable development at Chalmers University of Technology in Sweden. European Journal of Engineering Education, 33, pp. 355–64.

Lunvist, M.A, and Williams Middleton, K. (2011) Legitimizing entrepreneurial activity at the university. Paper submitted for publication in Research Policy.

The Observatory (2006) *The Observatory. Status of engineering education for sustainable development in European higher education*, available at: www.upc.edu/eesd-observatory.

Ottosson, P. and Samuelsson, B. (eds) (2009) *The Gothenburg Recommendations on Education for Sustainable Development,* The Centre for Environment and Sustainability (GMV), Chalmers University of Technology/University of Gothenburg, Sweden (www.chalmers.se/gmv).

Svanström, M., Eden, M., Nyström, T., Palme, U., Carlson O. and Knutson Wedel, M. (2010) Embedding of ESD in engineering education – experiences from Chalmers University of Technology, paper presented at Engineering Education in Sustainable Development, September 19–22, Göteborg.

IV.4c UPC'S INSTITUTIONAL TRANSFORMATION TOWARDS SUSTAINABILITY

Agustí Pérez-Foguet and Yazmín Cruz

INTRODUCTION: UPC'S JOURNEY TOWARDS SUSTAINABILITY

Universities' commitment to sustainable development (SD) has been on the rise, driven by the growing awareness of the urgent challenges facing us as a result of the ecological, economic and social imbalances of the planet. During this decade, numerous networks, projects and actions emerged which have contributed to shaping the role of higher education institutions (HEIs) within this context.

The introduction of SD at any university or other institution usually involves an in-depth redefinition of the institution's practices, attitudes and foundations in a process known as 'institutional learning'. When an institution adopts a structure that is appropriate to new practices, and its agents accept this new structure, it is easier to promote the practices in question.

The fact that the Universitat Politècnica de Catalunya – BarcelonaTech (UPC) is a technological university presents additional challenges with regard to interdisciplinary issues like SD, which has deep bases in environmental sciences, and socioeconomic and cultural aspects.

Despite the implications of these challenges, in 2006, the governing council of the UPC approved the

'2015 UPC Sustainability Plan', which was the result of a long journey that started at the beginning of the 1990s and is now in a second five-year phase of the plan. Figure 1 shows the timeline followed by UPC from the 1990s to the present, and this paper explains a general overview of the process.

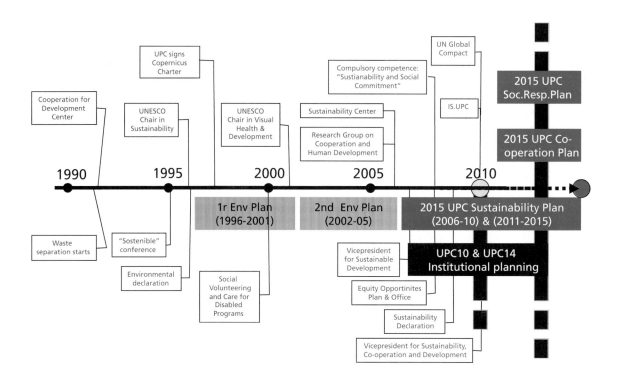

FIGURE 1 Evolution of UPC's commitment to sustainable development

THE ROOTS: SOCIAL AND ENVIRONMENTAL COMMITMENT OF THE UPC COMMUNITY

The UPC was formally founded in 1985, after the approval of the University Reform Law of 1983. Its principal structure is nurtured by a collection of engineering and architecture schools within Barcelona and its metropolitan area, some of which date back to the middle of the 19th century.

At the beginning of the 1990s, two actions marked the transformation of the UPC towards SD; the beginning of the separation of waste paper (well before it was a standard social practice), and the beginning of the activities of the Centre of Cooperation for Development (UPC, 1992).

The environmental seed that is the separation of waste, reuse and recycling, began in environmental engineering courses and later spread throughout the entire university, over successive periods of time, as will be mentioned later. What this clearly signals is that an element of sensibility towards sustainability has been consolidated as a method of management throughout the university community.

On the other hand, the seed of social commitment, specifically in terms of international solidarity, materialized into a centre, and regular financing of small transactions (about 100 a year from two or three people) by an annual corporate campaign called 'Campaign 0.7%', reminding wealthy countries of their international commitment to global development. The creation of the centre and the contribution of all external contracts for the university to the solidarity fund were approved by the Board of Trustees. The Board is the UPC body responsible for participation in society. Its function is to integrate and relate the university's activities with the public sector, civil society and industry.

We emphasize the international solidarity between the different dimensions of the university's social commitment, given that this period contributed most to its development (as much for common themes as for collective implication, see Pérez-Foguet, 2008). It was not until eight years later that the UPC formed a programme to assist the disabled within the Social Activities Service.

THE ENVIRONMENTAL PLAN

In November 1996, UPC approved its first Environment Plan with the aim of introducing environmental aspects into all the university's activities (UPC, 1996). The value of this plan was its integrative perspective that incorporated all fields and aspects of the university including training, research, university life and communication and awareness activities. The basic idea of UPC's Environment Plan was to introduce changes into the university's own processes, so that these changes can be assimilated and have a real influence, instead of generating complementary actions that may contradict the key processes. Thus, instead of creating a degree in environmental studies at UPC, it was decided to go about greening UPC's curricula, following three phases:

1. Establishing the profile of environmental knowledge that students need to learn by the end of their degree.
2. Determining the priority greening lines: modifying existing subjects and adding new subjects, if necessary.
3. Defining a plan of action to train and qualify the teaching staff in the new task of greening their subjects.

Over those years, numerous processes for greening UPC's basic activities were consolidated, such as those related to greening the curriculum. In 2005, roughly one in every five UPC subjects included environmental content, when in 1997 it was one in every ten. In research, environmental research represented more than one third of all research carried out at UPC, in terms of scientific results. Both results reflected the effectiveness of the Plan, but it was also important to highlight that this strategy contributed to a cultural change within the university, and therefore, also contributed to individual changes in many members of the university community.

After the first plan was evaluated, it was decided to continue with the transversal approach for the integration of this plan into the university (Ferrer-Balas at al., 2006; Ferrer-Balas and Sans, 2006). Thus, the UPC's second Environment Plan was approved in 2002 and covered the period from 2002 to 2005.

In 2003 the UPC's statutes were modified, including for the first time the word sustainability: 'The UPC, as an entity that generates and transmits knowledge, shall promote the protection of environment and the sustainable development, both in terms of training and research as well as institutional activities.'

THE SUSTAINABILITY PLAN

After these two consecutive Environmental Plans, in 2006, the university proposed the 2015 UPC Sustainability Plan (UPC, 2006), which combines internal efforts with external alliances (Barceló and Ferrer-Balas, 2008). It is focused on a key date, 2015, which is the date that the United Nations set to complete the Millennium Development Goals and the year the Decade of Education for Sustainable Development ends as well. It is also a time long enough to produce deep changes, yet short enough to expect to witness the results.

It was recommended tackling in more depth the transition from the paradigm of environmental responsibility to SD within the context of the knowledge society and network society. This means putting more emphasis on the social dimension of the university's responsibility, whether looking for internal connection points between different groups (for example working on cooperation, redesigning functions at the university, education in values, and so on), or setting up meetings and platforms for dialogue with the external stakeholders of the university.

The overall goal was to develop a strategic sustainable development plan that establishes priorities and determines the activities to be carried out during its implementation period. The strategy involved facing four challenges, one for each area of the Plan:
- UPC will participate in and commit to the challenges of sustainability at the local, regional and international levels.
- UPC's research activity will respond to social challenges by integrating sustainability criteria.
- All UPC graduates will apply sustainability criteria in their professional activity and area of influence.
- UPC will operate as a sustainable organization.

One of the most innovative aspects of this plan was the design of the development and definition process. This process sought both the legitimacy afforded by collaboration with internationally recognized authorities on sustainable development and the active participation of the various bodies within the university. The goals of the participatory process were:
- To encourage the participation of all parts of the university community.

- To raise awareness of sustainability among the university community.
- To make all members of the university jointly responsible for the actions defined in the Plan.

Based on the lessons learned in the previous plans, the process consisted of the following stages:

1. *International external assessment:* In July 2005, the UPC Board of Trustees entrusted a committee of three independent international experts with the task of carrying out this assessment.
2. *Participatory assessment and diagnosis:* At the same time, a six-month participatory assessment and diagnosis process was carried out involving people from UPC and various interest groups, through different active methodologies (open virtual forum, face-to-face meetings, online questionnaires). They concluded by identifying 40 high-priority proposals, which served as the starting point for the next stage in the process.
3. *Participatory design of the new Plan:* In this part of the process, participants made proposals and prioritized actions to be included in the new Plan. The participants worked in groups corresponding to the four areas of the Plan (education, research, university life, and social commitment and community). The process resulted in five strategic high-priority challenges.
4. *Approval of the Plan:* The Plan was submitted for approval to the Board of Governors, UPC's top executive body, and the Board of Trustees.
5. *Execution and implementation:* The various actions included in the Plan have been progressively implemented since its approval in May 2006.
6. *Assessment:* UPC carried out an assessment of the Plan's progress. A progress report was published at the end of the first stage, in 2010.

The actions defined in the 2015 UPC Sustainability Plan are based on the proposals and decisions reached during this participatory process. This fact sets the new Plan apart from its predecessors.

The process had a mixed financing scheme involving UPC, government agencies and private entities. The Plan enjoyed the support of various internal and external bodies, including the Barcelona City Council, the Catalan Government, NGOs, professional associations, the entire university community and national and international networks and associations. These agents collaborated in different ways and with varying degrees of involvement.

It is difficult to summarize all results obtained during the first five years of the Plan but the main results directly related to the Plan were:

- UPC joined forces and established synergies with various complementary agents, such as experts in SD and international networks, as well as national and local socioeconomic and governing actors through continuous networking promotion and participation.
- An environmental management system on the UPC campus was promoted; including sustainable shopping and contracting, and urban and special wastes management as well as sustainable mobility planning.
- A programme to monitor water and energy consumption was established, and it was used to promote institutional efficiency and reduction of greenhouse gas emissions.
- A compulsory general competence titled 'Sustainability and Social Commitment' was included in all new graduate programmes adapted to the European Higher Education Area (EHEA), and its implementation was supported through all the schools and all academic structures. Remarkably, an interdisciplinary group of students was constituted with the aim of complementing the institutional efforts in this direction.
- Specific academic programmes were also consolidated with this reform, one as an MSc in Sustainable Development and a PhD programme in Sustainability, Technology and Humanism.

During this time UPC strengthened its image as a leader in sustainability issues and contributed to a cultural change that favours sustainability within the institution itself, and the overall university community.

THE SUSTAINABILITY AND SOCIAL COMMITMENT OF NEW GRADUATES

The path of the UPC in greening curriculum developed over successive Plans of the Environment (Mulder et al., 2004, Ferrer-Balas at al., 2006) and the momentum of Development Education (Pérez-Foguet et al. 2005, Boni and Pérez-Foguet 2008). With the 2015 UPC Sustainability Plan, the proposal gained momentum and consolidated several academic contributions and projects (Pérez-Foguet and Lobera, 2008, Segalàs et al., 2009, and Segalàs, 2010), which give way to the adoption of a general competency shared by all UPC's undergraduate curricula adapted to EHEA:

The general competence on Sustainability and Social Commitment is the capacity to know and understand the complexity of the economic and social phenomenon typical to society and wellbeing; ability to relate wellbeing with globalization and sustainability; skill to use, in a balanced and compatible manner, technique, technology and economics. (UPC, 2008)

This is one of the seven general competences shared by all graduates of the university.

A competence can be acquired progressively by three steps, typically through different subjects in the curricula, defined as follows:

1. Systematically and critically analyse the global situation, addressing sustainability and social commitment in an interdisciplinary manner, and recognize the social and environmental implications of professional activity in the same field.
2. Apply criteria of sustainability and social compromise in the design and evaluation of technological and/or architectural solutions.
3. Carry out projects and professional activities consistent with human development, sustainability and social commitment, taking into account the social, economic, and environmental dimensions in the identification of the problems and application of solutions.

For effective incorporation into subjects of various curricula, and taking into account the different dimensions from which sustainability and social commitment of the university work, in a participative form with the implicated groups (institutes, departments, service units, teaching innovation groups), the following dimensions of the competence have been defined. They are coordinated within the context of a teaching innovation group of the Institute of Educational Sciences of UPC (UPC, 2011).

- **Ethical Values.** The dimension of ethical values for personal and professional development involves determining whether an act (or omission) is correct or incorrect or adequate or inadequate, and acting accordingly based on a scale of personal values, collective (universal rights, welfare responsible, democratic culture), or professional (codes of conduct), considering the action (or inaction) as much as the context, causes and direct and indirect consequences of it.
- **Equality.** The dimension of gender equality/equity implies recognition of an intervention in personal and professional situations that hinder and/or discriminate against the development and growth of women and men acting as agents of change with proposals that allow an improvement in the quality

of social and working life of all people affected, recognizing them as equals while considering the concept of social justice.

- **Sustainability.** The dimension of sustainability implies design and evaluation processes and technical solutions from the triple perspective of Environment – Society – Economics, with a systematic and complete vision in a framework of biophysical restrictions that allow for the satisfaction of present and future human needs; involving the flow and cycle of material and energy, and the dynamics of socio-environmental systems and their interrelationships to optimize the use of available resources, ensuring fair and equal access to them.
- **Cooperation.** The dimension of cooperation for development implies identification, planning, design, execution and evaluation of actions oriented towards human development (economic, environmental, social and political) principally in developing countries, starting with the situation, needs and priorities of the populace, driving the formation, investigation-action and the inter- and intra-community combined work, boosting independence and individual and collective abilities of people as agents of change to amplify their public and individual freedoms.
- **Accessibility.** The dimension of universal accessibility references the design and development of products, services and environments (digital, technological, physical, social and/or professional) in a comprehendible, useful and practical manner on behalf of all people in comfortable and secure situations, and in the most autonomous and natural manner possible.

Each of the five dimensions is a specific learning outcome for the three competence levels. Curricula, through their courses and learning guides, incorporate the content and activities that allow them to accomplish these, through one or various dimensions. In this way, it is possible for a wide variety of proposals to contribute, from the experience of the faculty and academic environments, to the introduction of shared competences in sustainability and social commitment.

LESSONS LEARNED AND NEXT STEPS TOWARDS 2015

The university has a privileged role in helping society advance towards sustainability by combining synergies between Research, Training, Management and Extension. A combination of a *top-down* vision and *bottom-*

up pressure is essential, although the key factors are usually at the technical and management levels that continually promote the process of change.

It is necessary to focus efforts on obtaining grass-roots criticism able to generate change. The human potential on which the strategic programme is based is essential and should be given a great deal of attention.

Putting effort into environmental issues and sustainable development can be profitable on an economic level, generally in the mid- and long-term, due to improved efficiency in resource consumption (energy, water, and so on), as well as increased external investment in R&D. Making the university's processes greener is generally a lot more effective than creating new environmentally oriented processes.

Two major steps are being taken in the process of UPC's transformation towards sustainability. One is the push of the new University Research Institute for Sustainability Science and Technology, IS.UPC, a key tool for institutional transformation and academic commitment, and the second is a new structure and communicating policy of the overall activities that constitutes the UPC's approach to its social responsibility.

Both actions will complement the expected results of the second phase of the 2015 UPC Sustainability Plan. This second phase will focus on the integration of SD principles into decentralized management structures (campuses, schools, departments) with special emphasis on including sustainability commitment in contracting and supplies.

THE UNIVERSITY RESEARCH INSTITUTE FOR SUSTAINABILITY SCIENCE AND TECHNOLOGY

This new institute is devoted to advancement in the definition and contents of sustainability science and technologies through its own expertise and potential. Sustainability science is a discipline that aims to facilitate the 'transition towards sustainability', improving society's capacity to use the earth in ways that simultaneously promote equitable economic growth, environmental protection, and social well-being (Clark, 2007). Some of the central elements of sustainability science are inter- and intra-disciplinary research, co-production of knowledge, and system innovation instead of system optimization (Martens, 2006; Kajikawa, 2008). Sustainability technologies cover a wide range of academic disciplines (Meyers, 2012).

Local authorities formally recognized the new IS.UPC at the end of 2010. The institute's mission is to generate technical and conceptual tools to create a more sustainable production model, and to collaborate

in the UPC's endeavour to provide scientific and technical support for social, cultural and economic progress. It is active in the following areas, in which the aim is the SD of skills in architecture, science and engineering: Research, technology transfer and innovation, tertiary education, specifically postgraduate and doctoral degrees, and internal promotion of a culture of sustainability (2015 UPC Sustainability Plan).

IS.UPC aims to:

- Strengthen the postgraduate programmes that it organizes, coordinates or collaborates actively in (including Environmental Engineering and International Co-operation) by contributing the results of research in sustainability, and feeding these results back into all of the university's educational programmes.
- Open up sustainability science and technologies research to as many of the university's researchers as possible.
- Make the management of the university, as a source of research needs and a field of study and experimentation, a focus of the institute's activity.
- Disseminate and spark debate on the results of research both to the university community and to society as a whole.
- Engage with society via economic activities and a range of social entities and give support to civil society's demands, with the aim of promoting progress towards more sustainable models.

STRUCTURING AND COMMUNICATING UNIVERSITY SOCIAL RESPONSIBILITY

For the first time, the UPC prepared and presented the 2009 Global Compact report in 2010 (UPC 2010a). This report led to a reflection around ten points that are part of the four major areas of the report: promotion of human rights, labour relations, environmental aspects and anti-corruption.

The UN Global Compact Initiative (http://www.unglobalcompact.org/) incorporates a transparency and accountability policy known as the Communication on Progress (COP). The annual posting of a COP is an important demonstration of a participant's commitment to the UN Global Compact and its principles. Participating companies are required to follow this policy, as a commitment to transparency and disclosure is critical to the success of the initiative.

Having the UPC Global Compact report was made possible through the coordinated work done by the UPC Office of Planning, Evaluation and Quality, involving different actors representing various sectors of the university.

In order to delve into this dimension and enhance communication to third parties, UPC aims to develop a specific plan throughout 2011, covering the basic points, but articulated and approved by the university's governing bodies, to facilitate the coordinated development of university social responsibility.

This plan will complement the second phase of the 2015 UPC Sustainable Plan, the 2015 UPC Cooperation Plan (under development throughout 2011) and the UPC Plan for Equal Opportunities (UPC, 2007). Remarkably, all this articulation of activities and politics constitutes one of the six axes of the institutional plan UPC14 (UPC, 2010b).

Following this path responds to the will of government action for enhancing and extending the experience gained through the years. This has been possible thanks to a lot of people who have been working on this direction with the commitment offered by sharing a UPC vision with common socially and ethically well-valued elements, remarkably, throughout some academic generations.

CONCLUSIONS

This paper has explained the institutional path followed during the last 20 years in transforming the university towards sustainability. The initial seeds in the fields of social and environmental commitment have grown, resulting in a deeper and broader transformation of the institution. This transformation is not complete, however, as the university is actively developing and seeking a sustainable way that allows UPC to fit in the changing world, through strategic planning, and government actions along with the new IS.UPC, and also empowering the planning and communication of university social responsibility.

REFERENCES

Barceló, M. and Ferrer-Balas, D. (2008) Institutional learning: Participatory design of the 2015 UPC Sustainable Plan. In: GUNi (2008) *Higher Education in the World 3: New Challenges and Emerging Roles for Human and Social Development*, UK: Palgrave Macmillan.

Boni, A. and Pérez-Foguet, A. (2008) Introducing development education in technical universities: successful experiences in Spain, *European Journal of Engineering Education*, **33**(3), pp. 343–54.

Clark, W.C. (2007) Sustainability Science: A room of its own. *Proceedings of the National Academy of Science PNAS* 104(6), pp. 1737–8.

Ferrer-Balas, D., Cruz, Y. and Segalàs, J. (2006) Lessons Learnt from our particular 'Decade' of Education for Sustainable Development (1996–2005) at UPC. In: Holmberg, J. and Samuelsson, B. (eds) *Drivers and Barriers for Implementing Sustainable Development in Higher Education*, Paris: UNESCO.

Ferrer-Balas, D. and Sans, R. (2006) Environment plan of the Universitat Politècnica de Catalunya. In: GUNi (2006) *Higher Education in the World 2006, The financing of universities*. UK: Palgrave Macmillan.

Kajikawa, Y. (2008) Research core and framework of sustainability science. *Sustainability Science*, **3**, pp. 215–39.

Martens, P. (2006) Sustainability: science or fiction? *Sustain*, **2**(1), pp. 36–41.

Meyers, R. A. (ed.) (forthcoming 2012) *Encyclopedia of Sustainability Science and Technology*, Springer.

Mulder, K.F., Segalàs, J. and Cruz, Y. (2004) What professionals should know about sustainable development? Results of SD teaching experiences at engineering institutions as starting point for a course design. 1st European Networks Conference on Sustainability in Practice. Berlin, Germany. 1–4 April 2004.

Pérez-Foguet, A. (2008) Educative experiences through cooperation for development activities. In: GUNi (2008) *Higher Education in the World 3: New Challenges and Emerging Roles for Human and Social Development*. UK: Palgrave Macmillan.

Pérez-Foguet, A. and Lobera, J. (eds) (2008) El Desarrollo humano sostenible en las aulas politécnicas. Material para la innovación docente. Universitat Politècnica de Catalunya (http://hdl.handle.net/2117/1979).

Perez-Foguet, A., Oliete-Jose, S. and Saz-Carranza, A. (2005) Development education and engineering: a framework for incorporating reality of developing countries into engineering studies, *International Journal of Sustainability in Higher Education*, **6**(3), pp. 278–303.

Segalàs, J. (2010) *Engineering Education for a Sustainable Future*. Lambert Academic Publishing.

Segalàs, J., Ferrer-Balas, D., Svanström, M., Lunvist, U. and Mulder, K.F. (2009) What has to be learnt for sustainability? A comparison of bachelor engineering education competences at three European universities. Sustainability Science, 4(1), pp. 17–27.

UPC (1992) *Reglament del Centre de Cooperació pel Desenvolupament*. Universitat Politècnica de Catalunya. CS 10/6.

UPC (1996) *Pla de medi ambient de la UPC*. Universitat Politècnica de Catalunya. JG 152/1996.

UPC (2006) *UPC Sostenible 2015*. Universitat Politècnica de Catalunya. CG 7/4 2006.

UPC (2007) Pla director d'igualtat d'oportunitats 2007–2010 (http://www.upc.edu/igualtat/presentacio/pla-digualtat-doportunitats).

UPC (2008) *Marc per al disseny i implantació dels plans d'estudis de grau a la UPC*. Universitat Politècnica de Catalunya. CG 16/4 2008.

UPC (2010a) Informe de progreso Pacto Mundial 2009 (http://www.unglobalcompact.org/system/attachments/8269/original/informe_Universitat_Polit_cnica_de_Catalunya.pdf?1288872689).

UPC (2010b) *Pla de Govern 2014*. Universitat Politècnica de Catalunya.

UPC (2011) Guia per desenvolupar la Sostenibilitat i compromís social en el disseny de titulacions. Universitat Politècnica de Catalunya (https://www.upc.edu/ice/portal-de-recursos/publicacions_ice).

Higher Education and Sustainability at the Universitat Politècnica de Catalunya: Sharing Actions for Change

The following experiences are a selection of good practices on higher education and sustainability. Some of them were presented at the 5th International Barcelona Conference on Higher Education and others are part of the GUNi observatory.

The good practices cover the following institutional areas:

Curricula and learning innovation

Community and social engagement

Institutional management

Research

GOOD PRACTICE 1

International seminar on sustainable technology development

Institutional area(s):

LOCATION: Spain
INSTITUTION: Universitat Politècnica de Catalunya (UPC)

The international seminar on sustainable technology development introduces an international, intercultural, intergenerational and interdisciplinary learning environment with real study cases. Participants learn how to apply scenario methodologies like back casting to develop strategies towards a more sustainable world. The seminar is a learning activity within the Master of Sustainability of UPC. This is the third year the seminar has taken place. The main goal is to connect experts, future researchers and policymakers on real topics where long-term technological systems renewal is needed in order to fulfill sustainability requirements.

Detailed information is available at GUNi HEiOBS:

http://www.guninetwork.org/guni.heiobs/good-practices/international-seminar-on-sustainable-technology-development/

GOOD PRACTICE 2

Introducing sustainability and social commitment concepts in a computing degree

Institutional area(s):

LOCATION: Spain
INSTITUTION: Universitat Politècnica de Catalunya (UPC)

In this scheme, the UPC presents the process to introduce sustainability and social commitment (SSC) concepts in the teaching and research activities of the academic personnel from the Barcelona School of Informatics. The main steps in the process are the following: selection and training of academic staff interested in the introduction of SSC concepts in the curricula, and creation of a knowledge database to support the praxis of teaching and research in SSC. This scheme aims to facilitate both students and lecturers to assume sustainability as a natural part of their professional activity as ICT engineers.

Detailed information is available at GUNi HEiOBS:

http://www.guninetwork.org/guni.heiobs/good-practices/introducing-sustainability-and-social-commitment-concepts-in-a-computing-degree

GOOD PRACTICE 3

Minimum minimorum in sustainability curricula: one European credit

Institutional area(s):

LOCATION: Spain
INSTITUTION: Universitat Politècnica de Catalunya (UPC)

The UPC has been working on an introductory modular course in sustainability, covering only one European credit (about eleven hours of class activity plus more or less fourteen hours of student personal work). It has been implemented within different degrees in telecommunications and tested during two semesters. Flexibility has been always considered as one of the main goals and therefore the structure allows different combinations of lectures, group and remote activities. Additionally, the chosen assessment method does not rely on traditional examinations but it has been mainly based on tests and activities via a digital campus, with some built-in mechanisms to try to ensure that students are not cheating. The module has been taught twice up to this moment and some steps are being currently taken in order to prepare a new problem-based edition.

Detailed information is available at GUNi HEiOBS:

http://www.guninetwork.org/guni.heiobs/good-practices/minimum-minimorum-in-sustainability-curricula-one-european-credit

Works for sustainability at the school of architecture of Barcelona

Institutional area(s):

LOCATION: Spain
INSTITUTION: Universitat Politècnica de Catalunya (UPC)

STEP 2015 is a UPC programme to educate highly qualified students in order to integrate sustainability into their professional activity and their sphere of influence. Additionally, Step 2015 aims at reaching levels of international excellence in the trinomial Technology–Sustainability–Education. The UPC wants students educated with knowledge, attitudes and values in order to work as change agents to sustainability models. The values of STEP 2015 are development of conceptual bases, identifying the particular referents and preparing practical tools for sustainability education. In order for this to happen, interdisciplinary dialogue and networking are necessary.

Detailed information is available at GUNi HEiOBS:

http://www.guninetwork.org/guni.heiobs/good-practices/works-for-sustainability-at-the-school-of-architecture-of-barcelona

LOW3 – Solar Decathlon Europe 2010. A living lab for solar architecture at the campus Sant Cugat (UPC)

Institutional area(s):

LOCATION: Spain
INSTITUTION: Universitat Politècnica de Catalunya (UPC)

Solar Decathlon is an international competition for 20 selected universities to plan and build prototypes of energy self-sufficient solar houses. LOW3 is the project that represented the UPC within the first Euro-

pean edition of this competition, the Solar Decathlon Europe 2010. One of the main qualities of the project is its interdisciplinary approach between architecture, technology, environmental sciences, marketing and communication with a student team running a partly self-organized office within the school of architecture. One of the biggest challenges was the conversion of a university campus into an experimental building site.

Detailed information is available at GUNi HEiOBS:

http://www.guninetwork.org/guni.heiobs/good-practices/low3-2013-solar-decathlon-europe-2010.-a-living-lab-for-solar-architecture-at-the-campus-sant-cugat-upc

Diffuse formation on sustainability through changes in the university life of a school

Institutional area(s):

LOCATION: Spain
INSTITUTION: Universitat Politècnica de Catalunya (UPC)

This good practice consists of the experiences carried out from 2006 to the present at the UPC's School of Architecture of Valles (ETSAV). The UPC has been committed to the reduction of natural gas, electricity and water consumption during the past four years. Tackling this challenge started with the centre management, with the participation of most of their community members, instead of investing money on the efficiency of their premises (at least during this first stage). From this experience the UPC has been able to diffuse information in some aspects of sustainability among their community as well as the decrease in the use of natural resources.

Detailed information is available at GUNi HEiOBS:

http://www.guninetwork.org/guni.heiobs/good-practices/diffuse-formation-on-sustainability-through-changes-in-the-university-life-of-a-school

On the Road IV.9
University appraisal for diversity, innovation and change towards sustainable development? Can it be done?

Zinaida Fadeeva, Laima Galkute,
Heila Lotz-Sisitka, Dzulkifli Abdul Razak,
Miguel Chacón, Masaru Yarime and
Goolam Mohamedbhai

PREAMBLE

This paper builds on a panel discussion that took place during a parallel session hosted by the United Nations University Institute of Advanced Studies during the Global Universities Network for Innovation (GUNi) Conference held in November 2010 in Barcelona. It brought together panellists from Africa, Asia, Europe and Latin America who explored interplays between national and regional higher education (HE) appraisal strategies as well as practices at the organizational level, with specific reference to what such appraisal systems may mean for sustainable development (SD), and what education for sustainable development (ESD) means for appraisal systems. In particular, the discussion was focused on the role of ranking and quality appraisal systems of higher education institutions (HEIs) – both existing and emerging – in facilitating transformation of HE and, as through related processes, contributing to transformations in society.

The paper does not seek to provide a comprehensive analysis of the appraisal issues, but through five case studies from different regions of the world, and through some critical discussion and deliberation on issues raised by the panellists at the GUNi Conference, the paper provides a platform for further analysis of how SD principles and practices are to be considered in relation to HEI appraisal and assessment systems. At the heart of this lies a question of how such systems enable or constrain HEIs' contributions to a more sustainable society.

REDEFINING THE ROLE OF HIGHER EDUCATION IN THE FACE OF GLOBAL CHALLENGES

In a globalized world concerned with ever more complex economic, social and environmental challenges, many institutions, including HEIs, are rethinking their fundamental assumptions and goals in relation to meeting challenges of today and future-oriented transformation. At the same time, HE is seen as having the capacity and opportunity to facilitate change towards a more sustainable future.

In presenting different situations in HE academic quality incentives, where appraisal systems are increasingly having a greater influence in shaping what is valued in and as HE, we refer to a concept of patterns of HE reform as proposed by Hargreaves and Shirley (2009) using the terminology of 'four ways'.

The 'first way' involves state support with professional freedom, but also inconsistency and uneven performance and leadership. Educational improvements, they argue, are informed primarily by intuition and ideology, rather than by evidence.

The 'second way' involves competition and educational prescription, with a loss of professional autonomy. Innovation gives way to standardization, uniformity and inequity. Diverse forms and sources of motivation and internal capacity for different forms of leadership are lost.

The 'third way' seeks to balance professional autonomy with accountability. This, Hargreaves and Shirley (2009) explain, has become 'bogged down' with the gathering of endless achievement/performance data shaping short-term solutions and competitiveness, with failed capacity for engaging with stakeholders or steering innovation. The 'third way' is about loss of a 'different path' in HE. The emergence of ranking systems for universities falls primarily into this 'way' of shaping and managing educational reform.

In proposing a 'fourth way' for guiding educational reforms, Hargreaves and Shirley (2009) argue that educational reform should, in contemporary society with its more complex challenges, be based on 'educational change through deepened and demanding learning, professional quality and engagement, and invigorated community engagement and public democracy'. Such a 'fourth way' needs to disrupt and depart significantly from the 'second way' or 'third way' of educational transformation. The discourse proposed in this 'fourth way' is not unlike the discourse used within the UN Decade of ESD, which seeks to 're-orient' education systems towards sustainability through transformative learning and practices that are socially innovative and that contribute to societal transformation.

In order to meet the expectation of being a driving force in creating sustainable societies, there is increasing consensus that HEIs require change at the systemic level that will allow them to adopt more holistic approaches, and through this develop greater capability for tackling complexities and looking for a rational compromise in dealing with interrelated economic, social and environmental dilemmas to achieve a sustainable future for all life on the planet. It seems that HEIs are being asked to form a new 'social contract' with society that reflexively and critically engages with the now all too obvious failures of some forms of modern development (for example providing people's needs for a decent quality of life free from poverty, and preserving nature and the Earth's ecosystems) and that engages different interests and social groups. This is to be done through practising participative democracy in decision-making in all spheres of HE activities: teaching and learning, research and outreach.

PUBLIC INSTRUMENTS FOR ACADEMIC QUALITY: MARKET AND STATE REGULATION

The phenomenon of increasing forms of assessment, quality management, and international ranking is linked to rapid expansion, internationalization and globalization of HE coupled with diminishing resources from the state. Such assessment schemes are often defined as instruments determining the quality of HEIs. The majority of the assessment systems as practised in international university settings today are born out of the culture and practices of the 'second way' and 'third way' educational reform, as described briefly in the previous section.

There are different forms of regulation in HE and new public policy instruments for the assurance of academic quality (Dill and Beerkens, 2010):

- Professional (self)regulation, for example professional accreditation and licensure, external examining
- Market regulation by means of information provision (variety of rankings)
- State (direct) regulation as specification

of standards, programme assessment and accreditation, institutional accountability, and so on

Market regulation and state regulation are often presented as two different approaches in HEI appraisal. In reality, however, there are a variety of mixtures and interrelationships between these two apparently 'clear' modalities. The discussions of the pros and contras to various schemes, depending on the paradigm and assessment criteria used, deal with a vast set of questions ranging from methodology to impacts.

If HEIs are to assume new responsibilities, as SD challenges would purport to indicate, then assessment of their actions would also need to focus on different aspects of HE performance. The ways in which academic quality is currently defined (often narrowly) would need to be complemented by the characteristics that recognize the HE transformative role. Such an argument proposes that quality of HEIs should become a measure of their leadership in social transition. This understanding brings discussion of the quality criteria and quality assurance of HEIs

to the forefront of debates on the future of HE per se.

The main question of such debates is: will participation in creating an 'alternative' appraisal system tailored to ESD perspectives enable this to happen, or will it perpetuate the current cultures of exclusion that are being created by present cultural logics of university rankings? What can we propose at the level of quality assurance to implement HE reforms that are oriented towards the 'fourth way'?

We will consider two particular examples of these approaches, that is, rankings and quality assurance systems (particularly of the European Higher Education Area), in order to explore to what extent they are supporting the development of HEIs in terms of innovation and transformative capacity.

CASE STUDIES OF RANKING SYSTEMS AND THEIR ROLE VIS-A-VIS HEI TRANSFORMATION IN A CONTEXT OF SUSTAINABLE DEVLOPMENT

Current global rankings have been seriously criticized for their methodological deficiencies related to, among other factors, selec-

tion of indicators, choice of weights assigned to criteria, reliability of data and replicability of results (Badat, 2010). We do not attempt to fully recap such criticisms, referring the reader to more complete analyses of ranking schemes (for example Stella and Woodhouse, 2006; Merisotis and Sadlak, 2005; EUA, 2009). Instead, we would like to explore some implications of the ranking characteristics for encouraging transformational qualities of HEIs as societal leaders in the context of sustainable development.

The five case studies below provide some examples of how ranking and assessment systems are currently structured, but also give insight into how these systems are evolving, and point to the 'gaps' in the system for some areas of innovation. The case studies also show that there are substantive process, contextual, ethical and other forms of problems that emerge from efforts to 'standardize', 'rank' and 'quality assess' HEIs across a diversity of institutions and contexts. From an SD perspective, which seeks transformation of society, further deficiencies and gaps emerge.

CASE 1: ACADEMIC QUALITY ASSESSMENT SYSTEMS IN MALAYSIA (*Dzulkifli Abdul Razak*)

SETARA is a rating system for Malaysian HEIs that is run by the Malaysia Qualification Framework (MQA) under the Ministry of Higher Education (MHE). The three-year cycle of assessment places HEIs into one of six tiers as a result of an independent exercise that involves site auditing, verification and validations. The focus of the assessment is on teaching and student-centred activities.

Another form of assessment, involving research and development performance of HEIs, is structured as a benchmarked system around eight main criteria. This on-site system for verification and validation is carried out under the auspices of the MHE by peer-group assessment teams. It is conducted once in three years with funding mechanisms attached to it.

More recently an Academic Performance Audit (APA) was instituted to look at the processes of quality assurance in all HEIs. As a part of the process, a panel appointed by the Ministry of Quality Assurance assesses the organizational processes including inputs, structures, personnel and operations. The panel's recommendations are focused on various quality aspects of HEI organization.

The APA is not a one-size-fits-all evaluation, although the panel seems to have standard criteria that are perceived as a minimum. With its relative flexibility, it might allow appraisal of any dimensions that the HEIs want to pursue including community engagement, sustainability, and so on. It could be considered more of an open-ended appraisal-like system with the potential to facilitate the transformative role of HEIs.

CASE 2: ACCREDITATION AND QUALITY ASSESSMENT IN LATIN AMERICAN COUNTRIES (*Miguel Chacón*)

Evaluation and accreditation processes are compulsory for some Latin American countries (for example Argentina, Brazil, Chile) and optional for others (for example universities in Central America). The current assessment systems focus mostly on scientific quality as shown by means of publications and patents. Arts and social sciences that cannot obtain patents often remain underfunded. The evaluation systems mostly review university activities related to developed urban areas since research shown by patent is related to industrial activities localized in cities.

As evaluation systems often consist of uniform standard categories, it makes it difficult to acknowledge HEIs that innovate in the areas of social research and transformative pedagogies. Innovations in education and research connected to SD in local contexts are also poorly reflected.

The appraisal systems appear to be fragmented, as there are two evaluation and accreditation systems in some Latin American countries: one for universities and the other for academic programmes with different criteria of assessment for each of these programmes. Additionally, there are different accreditation agencies according to careers, especially in the case of master's programmes. As a result, a satisfactory performance assessment of a university may not be contingent on the satisfactory performance of programmes (or their components).

Recently, more local actors are expressing interest in the governance and strategic planning of HEIs regionally and locally. As a result, HEIs have started introducing new curriculum and social research, teaching the community practices, and campus operations that combine applied science and social research as well as problem-based approaches. These new forms of practice in HEIs will need to be considered in the development of assessment systems.

CASE 3: ACADEMIC QUALITY ASSESSMENT SYSTEMS IN JAPAN (*Masaru Yarime*)

In Japan, there are two major formal systems of university evaluation – the Certified Evaluation and Accreditation (CEA) and the National University Corporation Evaluation (NUCE) (Saito, 2010). CEA, which was introduced in 2003, is a mandatory evaluation system for universities as well as junior colleges, technical colleges, and professional schools on overall conditions of education and research conducted by independent quality assurance agencies, which are in turn certified by the national government. Universities are assessed once in seven years by one of the certified organizations they choose themselves.

Currently there are three certified organizations for universities, namely, Japan University Accreditation Association, National Institution for Academic Degrees and University Evaluation (NIAD-UE), and Japan Institution for Higher Education Evaluation. The NUCE, on the other hand, started being implemented in 2008 and is a performance-based evaluation system for 86 national university corporations and four inter-university research institute corporations with regard to the extent of achieving their mid-term objectives, mid-term plans and annual plans for education, research and management. The NUCE Committee under the Ministry of Education, Culture, Sports, Science, and Technology (MEXT) is responsible for this evaluation, and NIAD-UE evaluates the extent of the achievement of mid-term objectives and the present situations on education and research.

In the formal systems of university evaluation, performance indicators are not decided by the evaluation agencies, but instead are set by the universities themselves based on their own missions and objectives. To some extent, that could promote diversity among universities. Difficulties in measuring outcomes of education, research and community outreach – as compared to the assessment of operational activities of universities – lead to their insufficient incorporation into the formal evaluation systems. That provides little incentive for HEIs to make significant contributions to SD, which requires comprehensive, long-term frameworks for evaluation. While no ranking-based evaluation systems are conducted by the public sector, there are many examples of making ranking-based evaluations in the private sector, particularly in the mass media. They tend to focus on performance indicators that are relatively easy to observe in short-term perspectives, such as employment of graduates in industry, without giving much attention to contributions to SD.

CASE 4: QUALITY ASSURANCE SYSTEMS IN AFRICA (*Goolam Mohamedbhai*)

While the overall application of Quality Assurance (QA) systems in HE at national or institutional level in sub-Saharan Africa is still weak, some notable developments are on the way. In 2009, an African Quality Assurance Network (ArfiQAN) was created to promote QA through awareness and capacity building, assist in establishing national QA agencies and encourage the setting up of institutional QA systems in African countries.

The global university rankings are now acknowledged to be inappropriate for Africa. They concentrate on research and research funding and give little importance to teaching and learning and community engagement, vital for Africa's development. A new approach being adopted by the African Union is the African Quality Rating Mechanism (ARQM). The ARQM covers broad criteria, taking into account all the activities of HEIs. Its objectives are to enable institutions, through their own assessment, to build their quality and to facilitate national and regional benchmarking. It will also assist in revitalization and harmonization of African higher education, both major thrusts of the African Union's strategy for African HE. The African Union also plans to use the rating mechanism to place students who have been awarded the Mwalimu Nyerere African Union scholarships. A preliminary assessment of some institutions has been carried out by the African Union Commission and the findings will help to improve on the ARQM survey instrument.

The major focus of quality assessment systems in Africa, as they are being put in place, is at present to improve quality and standards and to lead to some degree of harmonization across the continent. This will contribute to SD. In the first version of the AQRM questionnaire, institutions are asked about transdisciplinarity and community engagement, both of which will have an effect on SD.

DISCUSSION OF RANKING SYSTEMS AND HEI'S TRANSFORMATION WITHIN AN SD CONTEXT

The five case studies show that different issues, cultures, policies and histories characterizing various regions call for different research and educational strategies, as well as diversity in appraisal and quality assurance systems. Diversity becomes not only a statement of HEIs' uniqueness but recognition of the HEIs' role in addressing diverse and complex societal problems. A single score assigned to an institution does not account for the variety of HEIs and their success in a broad range of methodologies for research, education and outreach activities. Such one-score positioning has triggered an avalanche of criticism that, eventually, has led to the emergence of several multi-dimensional ranking systems that seek to account for diversity in higher education. The Malaysian APA systems and the African Union's ARQM (Cases 1 and 4) are examples of such developments.

Research output, measured in quantitative or qualitative terms, is predominant in most of the rankings. While the measure of HEI research output by citation rates, especially in the 'high impact' journal publications, becomes more universally acceptable, many are beginning to question its relation to the quality of academic output, and in some cases the relevance of the emphasis on this kind of research output is also questioned (see Case 4). Moreover, assumption of the impact of such measures on real-life problems – present or emerging – is seen as highly problematic (see Cases 2 and 4). Thus the foundation of the measure needs to be put under erasure and should be open to critical assessment, especially from an SD point of view.

With variations in emphasis, the ranking systems appraise and, thus, reaffirm various functions (and roles) of the universities. With research and teaching remaining the main focus, some ranking systems offer broader recognition of HEIs' actions. Examples from Malaysia, Japan and Africa (Cases 1, 3 and 4) highlight the potential of appraisal systems to become reflexive instruments that accommodate any areas that HEIs consider important. Challenges of implementation aside, potential implications of such developments lie in possibilities that may exist for redefining the view of HEIs as scientific research and publishing institutions whose relationship to society is of less importance than their research or publications.

As it is reflected in the case studies, most of the ranking systems are focused on input and/or output of HEIs' activities, but leave processes untouched. Development of the strategic knowledge (ability to analyse past and present as well as creating visions and scenarios of the future), practical knowledge (bridging knowledge and action) or collaborative competences should be areas of central concern for HEIs interested in the reorientation of society towards sustainability; however, such criteria are rarely found in the assessment systems.

Finally, many of the rankings not only do not reflect quality of all areas of HEIs' work but also do not use indicators that highlight interrelations between these areas. As for indicators recognizing the position of HEIs within larger societal or academic systems, only a few institutional rankings attempt to reflect on this role of HEIs by emphasizing relationships with international organizations, business partners, NGOs and media groups. Few consider the role of HEIs as a provider of public goods within a broader social change/global change context. As shown in the cases (Cases 1, 3 and 4), decisions on such criteria are left to the individual HEIs if they are interested in, and capable of addressing them.

NATIONAL QUALITY ASSURANCE SYSTEMS

In the context of this paper, state regulation is interpreted as all state-driven instruments designed to influence academic quality in a way relevant to public interest. In general, national frameworks for quality assurance can vary from country to country adopting different approaches – specification of standards, assessment and accreditation of study programmes, and institutional accountability as well as information provision (Dill and Beerkens, 2010).

Some countries, such as Australia or the United Kingdom, intend to define specific standards for study fields and/or for HE degrees as a guideline or benchmark for universities. Such focus on the subject level does not build the capacity of the overall university to design new programmes, nor does it improve the academic quality of all fields of study.

Assessment and accreditation of individual study programmes is the most common way of monitoring academic quality, with characteristic examples offered by Denmark, the Netherlands, and the United Kingdom, based on peer accountability for the quality of study programmes.

There also is an approach that aspires to assure academic quality by requesting better information on academic performance. One of the most ambitious examples of this strategy is the national examination policy adopted in Brazil, where all academic degree programmes are considered equivalent to professional certification. State examination is used for confirming qualification of the graduates and serves as a quality assurance of the study programmes. From the perspective of ESD, however, adoption of a unified exam in each field does not provide space for innovation and diversification.

The institutional accountability approach uses performance contracts (for example Catalonia, Spain) or an academic audit (for example Hong Kong). This approach gives responsibility for the quality assurance to a university, while the state only assures that the university meets selected targets, set individually and negotiated with the state. It is critical to note that performance contracts alone are not sufficient to ensure academic quality if there is no relevant initiative and commitment of the staff. In such conditions, performance contracts need to be supplemented by external quality assessments.

To conclude, a focus on particular elements of the study process (for example design of study programmes) or academic results does not tell us anything about the capacity and characteristics of a particular university as a whole and provides limited feedback for further necessary improvements. However, analysis carried out by Dill et al. (Dill and Beerkens, 2010) makes it clear that, despite the problems and weaknesses with the state regulatory instruments, they provide valuable guidelines for the design of quality assurance processes leading to evidence-based decision-making and continuous improvement of academic standards within universities. In order to serve these functions, the process will require active engagement of both the collegial leadership of an institution and academic staff in departments and programmes.

As shown in Case 5, external quality assurance plays an important role as a regulatory tool to ensure quality in the countries and regions characterized by deregulated and more market-oriented systems. There is also an argument which states that where HEIs have already established their own (internal) systems of quality assurance, external quality assurance could be expected to foster creativity and innovation – not by attempting to measure, but by stimulating the internal quality enhancement processes strengthening the identity of a particular HEI (Stensaker, 2009).

Often, internal quality assurance is focused mainly on the enhancement of quality in teaching and learning (Case 2). However, as appreciation of the broader role of higher education is growing, so is the width of the categories reflecting this role (Cases 2 and 5). This could provide an argument for including SD indicators in emerging national, international or regional systems.

However, there is more to it than simply including such criteria in assessment systems. Different components such as 'quality' of students on admission, teaching and technical staff, didactics of study process, level of research, infrastructure, values of the institution and society, and so on, are mutually interdependent and, thus, create a quality culture of the HEI. A holistic approach to study process is the main principle to be used both in management and assessment of academic quality, and this is not easy to capture in indicators that are most often abstracted from social contexts and reductionist in form and function.

Institutional missions and objectives must be diverse to respond to the HEIs' purposes and to accommodate diverse social groups and contexts and the diversity of SD challenges that span the globe. It is well known that SD challenges manifest differently in different parts of the world, and that they require different solutions. If the creativity of HEIs is to be fostered, the evaluation processes and associated rewards should be developed in an adequate way. In this case it is impossible to determine a quality of HEIs simply by using 'objective' external measures such as those provided by national quality assurance agencies or rankings. It is important that universities engage with internally relevant and reflexive developmental approaches to quality assurance and enhancement processes recognizing the individual, diverse goals of institutions. A permanent action-research, self-evaluation and correction approach should be an integral component of the internal quality management system, which includes close scrutiny of the university's role in society and in enabling the public good. To avoid narrowing of such processes to a local scale only, robust debate between universities should be encouraged in which such diversity of context and processes is discussed in relation to broader societal change goals, and SD challenges and goals.

WAYS AHEAD – FURTHER DEVELOPMENT OF UNIVERSITY APPRAISAL

The debate on the future of the quality appraisal systems for higher education from the perspective of ESD reveals two positions. Proponents of the first view believe in the need for and a possibility of changing the nature of the appraisal systems so that they facilitate transformation of the HEIs and, eventually, of the society. Such change is seen as an option only if assessment becomes a strategy for demonstrating HEIs' transparency and accountability rather than remaining a marketing tool. The second position critically questions the possible evolution of the assessment schemes that still have their roots in a culture of elitism and exclusion.

Analysing appraisal systems from the perspectives of the transformative role of HEIs, one can conclude that we can identify elements compatible to their sustainability roles. However, these elements need to come – coherently – together to facilitate systemic change of the HEIs. In Particular, interrelationships and synergy of the learning, research and society outreach activities should be promoted in the strategy and practice of the HEI. As outlined in the case studies and discussion above, appraisal systems could be considered as a possible instrument to facilitate such systemic change of HE if they are designed in a relevant way to stimulate the diversity, creativity, future orientation and transformative capacity of the HEIs.

We can see that there are contradictory tendencies manifested in various appraisal systems. Many of them promote standards leading to uniformity of the HEIs. Diversity of organizations that caters for local and regional needs remains rather neglected. Unique HEIs might not receive deserved recognition and could run a risk of being assessed as less reputable within the dominance of current orientations to appraisals.

Most of the considered appraisal systems are oriented towards capturing outputs (for example research papers, awards, successful employment) and inputs (for example infrastructure, financing, number and/or qualification of staff, and so on). However, as argued in this paper, added value of the HEIs in developing innovative competences also depends on the organization of the learning process, the quality of which is not easily measurable.

In a globalized world characterized by increasing mobility (particularly for the elite), an argument can be made for relying on some shared understanding of quality criteria for HEIs, provided that assessment is done around dependable methodology and reliable data, and that such methodologies allow for internal reflexivity. Use of common quality criteria for HEIs' appraisal should, however, provide enough space for contextualization and

unique qualities of HEIs, reflecting their specific missions and goals as well as characteristics of the local and national contexts. Such an argument would also need to critically evaluate exclusions that may result from the universalizing of norms of practice for universities.

As HEIs are also (increasingly) oriented towards engagement with local and national development strategies, appraisal systems should be able to recognize this role alongside contribution to the global and long-term developments by balancing indicators related to local and global priorities. Again, such appraisal systems need to be critically reviewed for tendencies to include and exclude.

Sustainable development is a dynamic concept that calls for continuous innovation as well as creating and testing of new knowledge. For HE to remain relevant to society, it has to develop systems that encourage critical analysis of the status quo, and creativity both of its staff and the students leading to innovation. Having a critically reflexive, innovative culture as a strategic goal in HE is particularly important for SD. Such a system should be based on holistic orientations to curriculum design, research, and outreach activities. This depends substantially on common values, shared interests and efficient cooperation of various stakeholders within and outside academia.

Therefore, the discussion above raises a more fundamental question as to whether ESD should 'join the ranks' and contribute to a 'better' set of assessment criteria (based on the notion of critical reflexive innovation) or whether we should seek new ways.

Therefore, the discussion above raises a more fundamental question: whether ESD is comparable with any external appraisal systems? Or would it be more appropriate to think about capacity of ESD principles to lead HEI towards quality culture and transformation for SD?

REFERENCES

Badat, S. (2010) Global rankings of universities: A perverse and present burden. In: Unterhalter, E. and Carpenter, V. (eds) *Universities into the 21st Century. Global Inequalities and Higher Education. Whose Interests are we serving?* Palgrave Macmillan.

Bologna Process (BP) (2009) *The Bologna Process 2020 – The European Higher Education Area in the new decade*. Communiqué of the Conference of European Ministers Responsible for Higher Education, Leuven and Louvain-la-Neuve, 28–29 April.

Dill, David D. and Beerkens, Maarja (eds) (2010) *Public Policy for Academic Quality*. Dordrecht, Heidelberg, London, New York: Springer.

European University Association (EUA) (2009) *Creativity and diversity: Challenges for Quality Assurance Beyond 2010*. Brussels: EUA.

Hargreaves, A. and Shirley, D. (2009) *The Fourth Way. The Inspiring Future for Educational Change*. Thousand Oaks, California: Corwin; London: Sage.

Merisotis, J. and Sadlak, J. (2005) Higher education rankings: Evolution, acceptance and dialogue. *Higher Education in Europe*, **30**(2).

Saito, Takahiro (2010) University Evaluation Systems in Japan. Presentation at the Symposium on Perspectives on University Performance Evaluation, United Nations University, Tokyo, 15–16 March 2010.

Stella, A. and Woodhouse, D. (2006) *Ranking of Higher Education Institutions*, Australian University Quality Agency, August 2006.

Stensaker, Bjorn (2009) Innovation, learning and quality assurance: mission impossible? In: *Creativity and Diversity: Challenges for Quality Assurance Beyond 2010*. Brussels: EUA.

On the Road IV.10
Efforts to create an integrative transformative programme
on sustainability at Wageningen University

*Lisa Schwarzin, Arjen E.J. Wals
and Irena Ateljevic*

The Initiative for Transformative Sustainability Education (ITSE) is a working group of teachers, students and academics at Wageningen University, which emerged in February 2009 based on a shared interest in education that can respond to the societal need for change. ITSE's main concern has been to develop a framework for transformative sustainability education that addresses not only theoretical knowledge and practical skills, but also guides students to question their values, attitudes and behaviour, learn to empower themselves, and facilitate social and collaborative learning among a diversity of stakeholders.

The framework differentiates between four dimensions of education, which we believe need to be in balance in order to promote learning for change:

- The objective *IT dimension* refers to theoretical and applied approaches to sustainable development.
- The subjective *I dimension* pertains to personal development needed to become actively engaged with sustainable development.
- The inter-subjective *WE dimension* focuses on collaborative competences for working in inter-disciplinary environments.
- The *cross-boundary dimension* integrates the I, WE and IT through experiential, project-based learning.

Needless to say, this framework is only one way of looking at 'learning for change'. It was developed as a tool for designing sustainability curriculum in a transformative way; however, we acknowledge that it needs to be applied, evaluated, and improved through reflexive practice. This is why ITSE is currently applying it to the design of a BSc minor in Sustainable Development. This minor aims to encourage students to develop a critical, aware understanding of the complex networks of global and local physical, social and individual factors that lead to (un)sustainability, and learn how attempts at negotiating these factors can be made by drawing on the change potential of diversity. In a nutshell, the minor wants to empower students to walk the talk of sustainable development within their own (expanding) sphere of influence.

To negotiate university scheduling requirements, we translated each dimension to one 6 ECTS (European Credit Transfer system) course (see also Figure 1). The *IT dimension* emphasizes a critical and transdisciplinary approach to theoretical models, paradigms, and analysis and intervention tools for sustainable development. Furthermore, it recognizes that people learn from their total environment (Haigh, 2008), which should be designed to create interaction and creativity. In the BSc minor, the *IT course* encourages students to develop reflexive awareness of the legitimacy of multiple scientific and non-scientific perspectives on sustainability issues (cf. van Asselt, 2000), and to develop awareness of the complementarities and contradictions between these perspectives (Baumgärtner et al., 2008). In this way, students develop a meta-awareness of transition agents and processes, and ways to approach, analyse and contribute to sustainable development. During the course, students analyse in depth a sustainability topic that fits with their personal interests and development goals.

The aspect of personal development is the focus of the *I dimension*. In order to stimulate for action, education needs to be connected to individual growth and empowerment. At the same time, it is important to remember that learners pass through stages of cognitive development in which their thinking and acting matures (Murray, 2009). For example, sustainability values of pluralistic respect, collaboration, and stewardship cannot simply be 'lectured', but need to grow out of reflexive awareness and practice. In the *I course*, students are guided to develop their mission, personal passion, talents and leadership skills for making positive changes in the world. This requires deepening self-awareness, for instance to understand how conceptual, socio-cultural, and personal background influence one's approach towards sustainable development. One of the course activities asks students to identify personal development goals and design and implement a project that addresses them in the context of sustainability.

As working towards sustainability most often implies a social context, it is extremely important to learn to deal with the challenges and opportunities that arise from it. The *WE dimension* highlights the change potential of diversity and conveys design and facilitation principles for collaborative learning processes by creating engaging yet safe opportunities for reflective social learning in heterogeneous groups. In the *WE course*, 'teachers' and 'students' aim to learn from each other through open and honest dialogue, in which the educator becomes co-facilitator. As this requires reflection on personal perspectives, as well as group-reflexivity on objectives, strategies, and outcomes (Godemann, 2008), students are guided to switch between a variety of perspectives, understand how they interact in processes of sustainable development, and discuss and develop hands-on ways of dealing with such variety.

This separate examination of each dimension should not invoke the impression that they operate in isolation. In fact we believe that it is through active integration of I, WE and IT aspects that transformative learning can occur. The *cross-boundary dimension* therefore focuses on reflexively (I) dealing with complex problems (IT) in interactive settings (WE). In this way, a spiral of experiential learning can be created that 'touches all bases' of experiencing, reflecting, thinking, and acting in order to continuously enhance understanding in a way that integrates 'the functioning of the total person – thinking, feeling, perceiving, and behaving' (Kolb and Kolb, 2005, p. 194).

We need to emphasize that the focus of the I, WE and IT courses is *non-exclusive*, as each course needs to integrate aspects of all dimensions to encourage balanced understanding and practice towards sustainability. The *cross-boundary course* then builds upon the first three courses, asking students to inte-

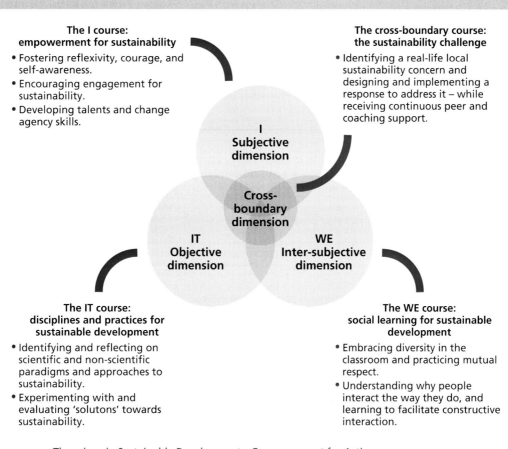

The I course:
empowerment for sustainability

- Fostering reflexivity, courage, and self-awareness.
- Encouraging engagement for sustainability.
- Developing talents and change agency skills.

The cross-boundary course:
the sustainability challenge

- Identifying a real-life local sustainability concern and designing and implementing a response to address it – while receiving continuous peer and coaching support.

I
Subjective dimension

Cross-boundary dimension

IT
Objective dimension

WE
Inter-subjective dimension

The IT course:
disciplines and practices for sustainable development

- Identifying and reflecting on scientific and non-scientific paradigms and approaches to sustainability.
- Experimenting with and evaluating 'solutons' towards sustainability.

The WE course:
social learning for sustainable development

- Embracing diversity in the classroom and practicing mutual respect.
- Understanding why people interact the way they do, and learning to facilitate constructive interaction.

FIGURE 1 **The minor in Sustainable Development – Empowerment for Action**

grate previous learning by working in small groups to design and implement a sustainability project of their choice. Throughout this process, peer and coaching support are necessary to ensure that learning outcomes are reflected upon and that strategies used represent a diversity of relevant perspectives. In this way, students can be exposed to sustainability challenges in a relatively safe environment and develop a sense of power and control (Wals, 2006) by realizing that they themselves have a significant sphere of influence to contribute to sustainable development.

REFERENCES

Baumgärtner, S., Becker, C., Frank, K., Muller, B. and Quaas, M. (2008) Relating the philosophy and practice of ecological economics: The role of concepts, models, and case studies in inter- and transdisciplinary sustainability research. *Ecological Economics*, **67**(3), pp. 384–93.

Godemann, J. (2008) Knowledge integration: A key challenge for transdisciplinary cooperation. *Environmental Education Research*, **14**(6), pp. 625–41.

Haigh, M. (2008) Internationalisation, Planetary Citizenship and Higher Education Inc. *Compare*, **38**(4), pp. 427–40.

Kolb, A.Y. and Kolb, D.A. (2005) Learning styles and learning spaces: Enhancing experiential learning in higher education. *Academy of Management Learning and Education*, **4**(2), pp. 193–212.

Murray, T. (2009) What is integral in integral education. *Integral Review*, **5**(1), pp. 96–134.

van Asselt, M.B.A. (2000) *Perspectives on Uncertainty and Risk: the Prima Approach to Decision Support*. Dordrecht, The Netherlands: Kluwer Academic Publishers.

Wals, A.E.J. (2006) The end of ESD … The beginning of transformative learning – Emphasising the E in ESD. Paper presented at National High Level Seminar on Education for Sustainable Development. Helsinki, February 15, 2006.

PART V
STATISTICAL
APPENDIX

Statistical appendix

DEFINITIONS

Enrolment. Number of pupils or students officially enrolled in a given grade or level of education, regardless of age. Typically, these data are collected at the beginning of the school year.

Gross domestic product (GDP). The sum of gross value added by all resident producers in the economy, including distributive trades and transport, plus any product taxes and minus any subsidies not included in the value of the products.

GDP per capita. The gross domestic product divided by mid-year population.

Gross enrolment ratio (GER). Number of pupils enrolled in a given level of education, regardless of age, expressed as a percentage of the population in the theoretical age group for the same level of education. For the tertiary level, the population used is the five-year age group following on from the secondary school leaving age.

Human development index (HDI). Is a composite index that measures the average achievements in a country in three basic dimensions of human development: a long and healthy life; access to knowledge; and a decent standard of living.

Regional average. Regional averages are calculated on the basis of the published data and using the best possible non-publishable estimates where no data exist. Countries are weighted with the appropriate national school-age populations.

Total public expenditure on education. The sum of the expenditure on education and education administration made by local, regional and national/central governments, including municipalities. Intergovernmental transfers are excluded.

REFERENCES

UNESCO Institute for Statistics, *Global Education Digest 2010*. Comparing Education Statistics Across the World. Available at: http://www.uis.unesco.org/Library/Documents/GED_2010_EN.pdf

UNDP, Human Development Report 2010. *The Real Wealth of Nations: Pathways to Human Development.* Available at: http://hdrstats.undp.org/en/tables/default.html

Table 1	Tertiary education enrolment and gross enrolment ratio	–	Magnitude nil or negligible
		(.)	Category not applicable
Table 2	Human development rank, value, total population, expenditure on education (% GDP) and (% Gov. Exp.), tertiary expenditure per student (% GDP) and expenditure on R&D	+n	Data refer to the school or financial year (or period) n years or periods after or before the reference year or period
		−n	
The following symbols are used in the statistical tables:		#	For regional averages: substantial imputation due to incomplete country coverage (more than 25% of population)
...	Data not available		
*	National estimation	x(y)	Data are included in another column (y) of the table
**	UIS estimation		

TABLE 1
Tertiary education enrolment and gross enrolment ratio

Country or territory	Total enrolment 2008				Gross enrolment ratio 2008			
	MF(000)		%F		MF		F	
Arab states								
Algeria	902	−1	57	−1	24	−1	28	−1
Bahrain	18	−2	68	−2	30	−2	44	−2
Djibouti	2.2		40		3		2	
Egypt	2,488		...		28		...	
Iraq	...		...		...		...	
Jordan	255		51		41		43	
Kuwait	...		...		...		...	
Lebanon	200	+1	54	+1	53	+1	57	+1
Libyan Arab Jamahiriya	...		...		...		...	
Mauritania	12	−1			4	−1		
Morocco	401		47		12		12	
Oman	84	+1	51	+1	29	+1	32	+1
Palestinian Autonomous Territories	181		54		47		52	
Qatar	13		64		11		31	
Saudi Arabia	667		62		30		37	
Sudan	...		...		...		...	
Syrian Arab Republic	...		...		...		...	
Tunisia	351		59		34		40	
United Arab Emirates	77		60		25		36	
Yemen	237	−1	29	−1	10	−1	6	−1
Central and Eastern Europe								
Albania	...		...		...		...	
Belarus	577		58		73		86	
Bosnia and Herzegovina	99	−1	...		34	−1	...	
Bulgaria	264		55		51		58	
Croatia	140	−1	54	−1	47	−1	52	−1
Czech Republic	395		55		59		67	
Estonia	68		62		64		80	
Hungary	414		58		65		77	
Latvia	128		64		69		91	
Lithuania	205		60		77		95	
Montenegro	...		...		...		...	
Poland	2,147	−1	57	−1	67	−1	78	−1
Republic of Moldova	144		58		40	*	47	*
Romania	1,057		56		66		75	
Russian Federation	9,446		57		77		89	
Serbia	238		55		48	*	54	*
Slovakia	229		60		54		66	
Slovenia	115		58		87		103	
The Former Yugoslav Rep. of Macedonia	66		53		40		44	
Turkey	2,533		43		38		34	
Ukraine	2,848		54	*	79		88	*

TABLE 1

TABLE 1
Tertiary education enrolment and gross enrolment ratio

Country or territory	Total enrolment 2008				Gross enrolment ratio 2008			
	MF(000)		%F		MF		F	
Central Asia								
Armenia	107	−1	55	−1	34	−1	37	−1
Azerbaijan	180	+1	50	+1	...		...	
Georgia	130		54	*	34		37	*
Kazakhstan	635	+1	58	+1	41	+1	49	+1
Kyrgyzstan	296		57		52		60	
Mongolia	152		61		50		61	
Tajikistan	155		28		20		11	
Turkmenistan	...		...		...		...	
Uzbekistan	299		40		10		8	
East Asia and the Pacific								
Australia	1,118		55		77		87	
Brunei Darussalam	5.6		66		16		21	
Cambodia	123		34		7		5	
China	26,692		49		23		23	
Cook Islands	(.)		(.)		(.)		(.)	
Democratic People's Republic of Korea	...		...		...		...	
Fiji	...		...		...		...	
Hong Kong (China), SAR	158	−1	50	−1	34	−1	35	−1
Indonesia	4,420		47		21		20	
Japan	3,939		46		58		54	
Kiribati	(.)		(.)		(.)		(.)	
Lao People's Democratic Republic	89		43		13		12	
Macao, China	25		50		57		54	
Malaysia	805	−1	56	−1	32	−1	36	−1
Marshall Islands	...		...		...		...	
Micronesia (Federated States of)	...		...		...		...	
Myanmar	508	−1	58	−1	11	−1	12	−1
Nauru	(.)	−2	(.)	−2	(.)	−2	(.)	−2
New Zealand	244		58		78		94	
Niue	(.)		(.)		(.)		(.)	
Palau	...		...		...		...	
Papua New Guinea	...		...		...		...	
Philippines	2,651		54		29		32	
Republic of Korea	3,204		38		98		79	
Samoa	...		...		...		...	
Singapore	199	+1	49	+1	...		...	
Solomon Islands	(.)		(.)		(.)		(.)	
Thailand	2,417	+1	54	+1	45	+1	49	+1
Timor-Leste	17	+1	40	+1	15	+1	13	+1
Tokelau	(.)		(.)		(.)		(.)	
Tonga	...		...		...		...	
Tuvalu	(.)		(.)		(.)		(.)	

Tertiary education enrolment and gross enrolment ratio

Country or territory	Total enrolment 2008				Gross enrolment ratio 2008			
	MF(000)		%F		MF		F	
Vanuatu	...		...		...		...	
Viet Nam	1,655		49		...		...	
Latin America and the Caribbean								
Anguilla	0.05		83		5	**	8	**
Antigua and Barbuda	...		...		...		...	
Argentina	2,208	−1	60	−1	68	−1	82	−1
Aruba	2.2		58		33		38	
Bahamas	...		...		...		...	
Barbados	11	−1	68	−1	...		...	
Belize	3.6	+1	64	+1	11	+1	15	+1
Bermuda	0.89	+1	71	+1	25	**,−1	35	**,−1
Bolivia	353	*,−1	45	*,−1	38	*,−1	35	*,−1
Brazil	5,958		56		34		39	
British Virgin Islands	0.02		90		1	**	2	**
Cayman Islands	0.91		69		36	*	47	*
Chile	753	−1	49	−1	52	−1	52	−1
Colombia	1,487		49		35		35	
Costa Rica	...		...		...		...	
Cuba	971	+1	61	+1	118	+1	149	+1
Dominica	0.23		76		4		6	
Dominican Republic	...		...		...		...	
Ecuador	535		53		42		45	
El Salvador	139		55		25		26	
Grenada	7.4	+1	57	+1	59	+1	68	+1
Guatemala	234	−1	51	−1	18	−1	18	−1
Guyana	7.3		59		12		13	
Haiti	...		...		...		...	
Honduras	148	*	60	*	19	*	22	*
Jamaica	61		69		24		33	
Mexico	2,623		50		27		27	
Montserrat	0.05		80		17	**	31	**
Netherlands Antilles	...		...		...		...	
Nicaragua	...		...		...		...	
Panama	133	−1	61	−1	45	−1	56	−1
Paraguay	181	−1	57	−1	29	−1	33	−1
Peru	952	**,−2	51	**,−2	34	**,−2	36	**,−2
Saint Kitts and Nevis	0.86		84		...		...	
Saint Lucia	2.6		70		15		20	
Saint Vincent and the Grenadines	...		...		...		...	
Suriname	...		...		...		...	
Trinidad and Tobago	...		...		...		...	
Turks and Caicos Islands	0.002		50		–	**	–	**
Uruguay	159	−1	63	−1	64	−1	82	−1
Venezuela	2,109		62	*	79		99	*

TABLE 1

Tertiary education enrolment and gross enrolment ratio

Country or territory	Total enrolment 2008				Gross enrolment ratio 2008			
	MF(000)		%F		MF		F	
North America and Western Europe								
Andorra	0.46		58		11	*	13	*
Austria	285		53		55		59	
Belgium	402		55		63		70	
Canada	...		...		...		...	
Cyprus	26		49		43	*	42	*
Denmark	232	−1	58	−1	80	−1	94	−1
Finland	310		54		94		105	
France	2,165		55		55		61	
Germany	...		...		...		...	
Gibraltar	(.)		(.)		(.)		(.)	
Greece	603	−1	50	−1	91	−1	95	−1
Holy See	...		...		...		...	
Iceland	17		64		75		99	
Ireland	179		54		58		64	
Israel	325		56		60		68	
Italy	2,034	−1	57	−1	67	−1	79	−1
Liechtenstein	0.80		33		37	*	25	*
Luxembourg	2.7	−2	52	−2	10	−2	11	−2
Malta	9.8	−1	57	−1	33	−1	39	−1
Monaco	(.)		(.)		(.)		(.)	
Netherlands	602		52		61		64	
Norway	213		61		73		91	
Portugal	367	−1	54	−1	57	−1	63	−1
San Marino	0.93		57		...		...	
Spain	1,781		54		71		78	
Sweden	407		60		71		88	
Switzerland	224		49		49		49	
United Kingdom	2,329		57		57		67	
United States	18,248		57		83		97	
South and West Asia								
Afghanistan	...		...		...		...	
Bangladesh	1,145	−1	35	−1	7	−1	5	−1
Bhutan	5.1		35		7		5	
India	14,863	−1	39	−1	13	−1	11	−1
Iran, Islamic Republic of	3,392		53		36		39	
Maldives	–	**,−2	–	**,−2	–	**,−2	–	**,−2
Nepal	255	−1	...		...		...	
Pakistan	974	*	45	*	5	*	5	*
Sri Lanka	...		...		...		...	
Sub-Saharan Africa								
Angola	49	−2	...		3	−2	...	
Benin	43	−2	...		6	−2	...	
Botswana	16	−2	53	−2	8	−2	8	−2

TABLE 1
Tertiary education enrolment and gross enrolment ratio

Country or territory	Total enrolment 2008				Gross enrolment ratio 2008			
	MF(000)		%F		MF		F	
Burkina Faso	48	+1	32	+1	3	+1	2	+1
Burundi	24	+1	...		3	+1	...	
Cameroon	174	+1	44	+1	9	+1	8	+1
Cape Verde	6.7		56		12		13	
Central African Republic	10	+1	31	+1	2	+1	1	+1
Chad	19		13		2		–	
Comoros	...		...		...		...	
Congo	...		...		...		...	
Côte d'Ivoire	157	–1	33	–1	8	–1	6	–1
Democratic Republic of the Congo	306		...		5		...	
Equatorial Guinea	...		...		...		...	
Eritrea	9.9	+1	25	+1	2	+1	1	+1
Ethiopia	265		24		4		2	
Gabon	...		...		...		...	
Gambia	...		...		...		...	
Ghana	140	–1	34	–1	6	–1	4	–1
Guinea	80		24		9		5	
Guinea-Bissau	3.7	–2	...		3	–2	...	
Kenya	168	+1	41	+1	4	+1	3	+1
Lesotho	8.5	–2	55	–2	4	–2	4	–2
Liberia	...		...		...		...	
Madagascar	62		47		3		3	
Malawi	6.5	–1	34	–1	–1		–1	
Mali	77	+1	29	+1	5	+1	3	+1
Mauritius	26	**	53	**	26	**	28	**
Mozambique	...		...		...		...	
Namibia	20		57		9		10	
Niger	16	+1	29	+1	1	+1	1	+1
Nigeria	...		...		...		...	
Rwanda	45		...		4		...	
São Tomé and Principe	0.070	+1	48	+1	4	+1	4	+1
Senegal	91	*	35	*	8	*	6	*
Seychelles	(.)	+1	(.)	+1	(.)	+1	(.)	+1
Sierra Leone	...		...		...		...	
Somalia	...		...		...		...	
South Africa	...		...		...		...	
Swaziland	5.7	–2	50	–2	4	–2	4	–2
Togo	33	–1	,,,		5	–1	...	
Uganda	108		44		4		3	
United Republic of Tanzania	55	–1	32	–1	1	–1	1	–1
Zambia	...		...		...		...	
Zimbabwe	...		...		...		...	

TABLE 1
Tertiary education enrolment and gross enrolment ratio

Regional averages	Total enrolment			Gross enrolment ratio			
	2008			2008			
	MF(000)		%F		MF		F
Region							
Arab states	7,308	**	48	**	21	**	21 **
Central and Eastern Europe	21,137		55		64		72
Central Asia	2,108		52		25		27
East Asia and the Pacific	48,608		49	**	26	**	26 **
Latin America and the Caribbean	19,723		55	**	38	**	42 **
North America and Western Europe	34,423		56		70		80
South and West Asia	20,889		41	**	13	**	11 **
Sub-Saharan Africa	4,517		40	**	6	**	5 **
WORLD	158,713	**	51	**	26	**	27 **

TABLE 2
Human development rank, value, total population, expenditure on education (% GDP) and (% of government expenditure), tertiary expenditure per student (% GDP) and expenditure on R&D

		HDI value 2010	GDP per capita (PPP US$ billions) 2010	Total population (millions) 2009	Public expenditure on education (% of GDP) 2000–2008b	Public expenditure on education (% of total government expenditure) 2008	Tertiary total public expenditure per student (% of GDP) 2008	Public expenditure research and development (% of GDP) 2000–2007b
HDI Rank								
1	Norway	0.938	58,278 [1]	4.8	6.7	16.5	47.1 [−1]	1.7
2	Australia	0.937	40,286 [1]	21.9	4.7	14.0 [−2]	21.0 [−1]	2.2
3	New Zealand	0.907	27,520 [1]	4.3	6.2	19.7 [−2]	29.2 [−1]	1.3
4	United States	0.902	46,653 [1]	307	5.5	14.1	22.0 [−1]	2.7
5	Ireland	0.895	38,768 [1]	4.4	4.9	13.8	26.3 [−1]	1.3
6	Liechtenstein	0.891	94,569 [4 5]	0.035	...	...	...	...
7	Netherlands	0.890	41,004 [1]	16.5	5.5	12.0	43.9 [−1]	1.8
8	Canada	0.888	39,035 [1]	33.7	4.9	...	...	2.0
9	Sweden	0.885	36,139 [1]	9.3	6.7	12.7	39.0 [−1]	3.7
10	Germany	0.885	34,743 [1]	81.9	4.4	9.7 [−2]	...	2.6
11	Japan	0.884	34,743 [1]	127.6	3.4	9.4	20.1 [−1]	3.4
12	Korea Republic of	0.877	29,326 [1]	48.7	4.2	14.7	...	3.5
13	Switzerland	0.874	43,109 [1]	7.7	5.3	16.3 [−2]	47.8 [−1]	2.9
14	France	0.872	33,103 [1]	62.6	5.6	10.6 [−2]	33.5 [−2]	2.1
15	Israel	0.872	28,292 [1]	7.4	6.4	13.8	23.4 [−1]	4.7
16	Finland	0.871	34,107 [1]	5.3	5.9	12.5	31.8 [−1]	3.5
17	Iceland	0.869	33,422 [1]	0.319	7.5	17.4	27.9 [−1]	2.8
18	Belgium	0.867	34,734 [1]	10.8	6.1	12.4	35.7 [−1]	1.9
19	Denmark	0.866	35,736 [1]	5.5	7.9	15.2 [−2]	53.4 [−1]	2.6

TABLE 2
Human development rank, value, total population, expenditure on education (% GDP) and (% of government expenditure), tertiary expenditure per student (% GDP) and expenditure on R&D

		HDI value 2010	GDP per capita (PPP US$ billions) 2010	Total population (millions) 2009	Public expenditure on education (% of GDP) 2000–2008b	Public expenditure on education (% of total government expenditure) 2008	Tertiary total public expenditure per student (% of GDP) 2008	Public expenditure research and development (% of GDP) 2000–2007b
20	Spain	0.863	30,475 [1]	45.9	4.4	11.1	25.0 −1	1.3
21	Hong Kong, China (SAR)	0.862	45,049 [1]	7	3.3	23.0	...	0.8
22	Greece	0.855	28,608 [1]	11.3	4.0	...	...	0.5
23	Italy	0.854	30,080 [1]	60.2	4.3	9.0	22.3 −1	1.1
24	Luxembourg	0.852	76,440 [1]	0.497	3.7	...		1.7
25	Austria	0.851	37,602 [1]	8.4	5.4	11.1	47.4 −1	2.5
26	United Kingdom	0.849	34,342 [1]	61.8	5.6	11.7	24.8 −1	1.8
27	Singapore	0.846	50,266 [1]	5	2.8	11.6 −1	26.9 −1	2.6
28	Czech Republic	0.841	24,419 [1]	10.5	4.6	10.5 −2	37.4 −2	1.6
29	Slovenia	0.828	26,527 [1]	2	5.2	12.8 −2	21.1 −1	1.5
30	Andorra	0.824	38,056 [2 3]	0.085	3.2	...	...	...
31	Slovakia	0.818	22,341 [1]	5.4	3.6	10.5	19.5 −1	0.5
32	United Arab Emirates	0.815	56,485 [1]	4.6	0.9	27.2	...	...
33	Malta	0.815	21,581 [1 6]	0.414	4.8	...	...	0.6
34	Estonia	0.812	18,355 [1]	1.3	5.0	13.9	21.3 −1	1.1
35	Cyprus	0.810	25,737 [1]	0.871	7.1	9.6	63.7 −1	0.4
36	Hungary	0.805	18,986 [1]	10	5.4	10.4 −2	23.8 −2	1.0
37	Brunei Darussalam	0.805	49,915 [1]	0.399	3.7	...	...	0.0
38	Qatar	0.803	77,178 [1]	1.4	3.3	...	...	...
39	Bahrain	0.801	27,838 [1]	0.8	2.9	11.7	...	...
40	Portugal	0.795	23,019 [1]	10.6	5.3	11.3 −2	28.8 −2	1.2
41	Poland	0.795	18,406 [1]	38.1	4.9	11.7	16.6 −1	0.6
42	Barbados	0.788	22,794 [1]	0.255	6.7	15.7	...	...
43	Bahamas	0.784	25,887 [1]	0.341	3.6	...	...	...
44	Lithuania	0.783	15,327 [1]	3.3	4.7	13.4	17.2 −1	0.8
45	Chile	0.783	14,780 [1]	17	3.4	18.2	11.5 −1	0.7
46	Argentina	0.775	14,931 [1]	40.2	4.9	13.5	15.6 −1	0.5
47	Kuwait	0.771	50,284 [1]	2.8	3.8	12.9 **,−2	...	0.1
48	Latvia	0.769	13,224 [1]	2.2	5.0	13.9	16.3 −1	0.6
49	Montenegro	0.769	12,462 [1]	0.624	...	...	...	1.2
50	Romania	0.767	12,910 [1]	21.5	4.4	...	...	0.5
51	Croatia	0.767	16,980 [1]	4.4	3.9	...	...	0.9
52	Uruguay	0.765	14,022 [1]	3.3	2.8	11.6 −2	18.1 −1	0.4
53	Libyan Arab Jamahiriya	0.755	16,999 [1]	6.4	2.7 d	...	...	...
54	Panama	0.755	13,210 [1]	3.4	3.8	...	...	0.2
55	Saudi Arabia	0.752	24,208 [1]	25.4	5.7	19.3	...	0.0
56	Mexico	0.750	14,192 [1]	108	4.8	...	37.1 −1	0.5
57	Malaysia	0.744	14,410 [1]	27.5	4.5	18.2	49.4 −1	0.6
58	Bulgaria	0.743	11,547 [1]	7.6	4.1	10.0	20.1 −1	0.5
59	Trinidad and Tobago	0.736	25,162 [1]	1.3	4.2	...	...	0.1
60	Serbia	0.735	10,628 [1]	7.3	4.5	8.1	36.4 −1	0.3

TABLE 2
Human development rank, value, total population, expenditure on education (% GDP) and (% of government expenditure), tertiary expenditure per student (% GDP) and expenditure on R&D

		HDI value 2010	GDP per capita (PPP US$ billions) 2010	Total population (millions) 2009	Public expenditure on education (% of GDP) 2000–2008b	Public expenditure on education (% of total government expenditure) 2008	Tertiary total public expenditure per student (% of GDP) 2008	Public expenditure research and development (% of GDP) 2000–2007b
61	Belarus	0.732	13,097 ¹	9.6	5.2	9.3	18.1 −1	1.0
62	Costa Rica	0.725	11,143 ¹	4.6	5.0	22.8	...	0.4
63	Peru	0.723	9,016 ¹	29.1	2.7	20.7	...	0.1
64	Albania	0.719	7,737 ¹	3.1	2.9	...	...	...
65	Russian Federation	0.719	15,719 ¹	141.9	3.9	...	13.2 −2	1.1
66	Kazakhstan	0.714	11,927 ¹	15.9	2.8	...	7.9 −1	0.2
67	Azerbaijan	0.713	9,870 ¹	8.8	1.9	9.1 1	8.9 −2	0.2
68	Bosnia and Herzegovina	0.710	7,964 ¹	3.8	...	...	...	0.0
69	Ukraine	0.710	6,591 ¹	46	5.3	20.2	25.1 −1	0.9
70	Iran, Islamic Republic of	0.702	11,891 ¹	72.9	4.8	20.0	20.7	0.7
71	The former Yugoslav Republic of Macedonia	0.701	9,577 ¹	2	3.5	...	...	0.2
72	Mauritius	0.701	2,037 ¹	1.2	3.6	11.4 1	...	0.4
73	Brazil	0.699	10,847 ¹	193.7	5.2	16.1	30.4 −1	1.0
74	Georgia	0.698	4,946 ¹	4.2	2.9	7.2	11.4	0.2
75	Venezuela, Bolivarian Republic of	0.696	11,820 ¹	28.3	3.7	...	...	...
76	Armenia	0.695	5,286	3	3.0	15.0	...	0.2
77	Ecuador	0.695	8,170 ¹	13.6	1.0	...	...	0.2
78	Belize	0.694	6,460 ¹	0.333	5.1	16.8 *,−1	...	...
79	Colombia	0.689	8,959 ¹	45.7	3.9	14.9	26.0	0.2
80	Jamaica	0.688	7,547 ¹	2.7	6.2	...	42.4	0.1
81	Tunisia	0.683	8,509 ¹	10.4	7.2	22.4	55.4 −1	1.0
82	Jordan	0.681	5,700 ¹	6	4.9 d	...	...	0.3
83	Turkey	0.679	13,359 ¹	74.8	2.9	...	28.1 −2	0.7
84	Algeria	0.677	8,477 ¹	34.9	4.3	20.3	...	0.1
85	Tonga	0.677	3,893 ¹	0.103	4.7	...	...	...
86	Fiji	0.699	4,349 ¹	0.849	6.2	...	...	...
87	Turkmenistan	0.699	7,627 ¹	5.1	...	...	...	...
88	Dominican Republic	0.663	8,616 ¹	10	2.2	11.0	...	...
89	China	0.663	7,206 ¹	1.331	1.9 d	...	...	1.5
90	El Salvador	0.659	6,660 ¹	6.1	3.6	13.1 *,−1	...	0.1 (−1)
91	Sri Lanka	0.658	4,999 ¹	20.3	...	...	...	0.2
92	Thailand	0.654	8,328 ¹	67.7	4.9	25.7	23.0	0.2
93	Gabon	0.648	14,984 ¹	4.5	3.8	...	...	...
94	Suriname	0.646	7,856 ¹	0.519	...	...	...	...
95	Bolivia, Plurinational State of	0.643	4,502 ¹	9.9	6.3	...	...	0.3
96	Paraguay	0.640	4,629 ¹	6.3	4.0	11.9	26.0 −1	0.1
97	Philippines	0.638	3,601 ¹	92	2.6	15.2	...	0.1
98	Botswana	0.633	13,462 ¹	1.9	8.1	21.0	...	0.4
99	Moldova, Republic of	0.623	2,917 ¹	3.6	8.2	19.8	38.9	0.5
100	Mongolia	0.622	3,711 ¹	2.6	5.1	...	...	0.2

TABLE 2
Human development rank, value, total population, expenditure on education (% GDP) and (% of government expenditure), tertiary expenditure per student (% GDP) and expenditure on R&D

		HDI value 2010	GDP per capita (PPP US$ billions) 2010	Total population (millions) 2009	Public expenditure on education (% of GDP) 2000–2008b	Public expenditure on education (% of total government expenditure) 2008	Tertiary total public expenditure per student (% of GDP) 2008	Public expenditure research and development (% of GDP) 2000–2007b
101	Egypt	0.620	5,840 ¹	83	3.8	11.9	...	0.2
102	Uzbekistan	0.617	3,084 ¹	27.8	...	...	...	...
103	Micronesia, Federated States of	0.614	3,085 ⁷	0.11	7.3	...	...	...
104	Guyana	0.611	3,344 ¹	0.762	6.1	12.5	36.3 −1	...
105	Namibia	0.606	6,474 ¹	2.1	6.5	22.4	...	...
106	Honduras	0.604	3,845 ¹	7.5	...	...	...	0.0
107	Maldives	0.602	5,721 ¹	0.309	8.1	12.0	–	...
108	Indonesia	0.600	4,394 ¹	230	3.5	18.7	16.1 −1	0.0
109	Kyrgyztan	0.598	2,332 ¹	5.3	6.6	25.6	22.8 −1	0.3
110	South Africa	0.597	10,140 ¹	49.3	5.1	16.9 1	...	1.0
111	Syrian Arab Republic	0.589	4,857 ¹	21	4.9	16.7	...	...
112	Tajikistan	0.580	2,065 ¹	7	3.5	18.7	21.8	0.1
113	Viet Nam	0.572	3,097 ¹	87.3	5.3	19.8	61.7	0.2
114	Morocco	0.567	4,638 ¹	32	5.7	25.7	72.1	0.6
115	Nicaragua	0.565	2,632 ¹	5.7	3.1	...	...	0.0
116	Guatemala	0.560	4,761 ¹	14	3.2	...	...	0.0
117	Equatorial Guinea	0.538	34,680 ¹	0.676	0.6	...	...	...
118	Cape Verde	0.534	3,431 ¹	0.505	5.7	16.7	48.2	...
119	India	0.519	3,354 ¹	1.155	3.2	...	55.0 −2	0.8
120	Timor-Leste	0.502	906 ¹	1.1	7.1	7.3	...	...
121	Swaziland	0.498	5,058 ¹	1.1	7.9	21.6	347.5 −2	...
122	Lao Peoplés Democratic Republic	0.497	2,404 ¹	6.3	2.3	12.2	...	0.0
123	Solomon Islands	0.494	2,546 ¹	0.523	2.2 d	...	...	...
124	Cambodia	0.494	1,952 ¹	14.8	1.6	12.4	...	0.0
125	Pakistan	0.490	2,625 ¹	169.7	2.9	11.2	...	0.7
126	Congo	0.489	4,583 ¹	3.6	1.8	...	...	...
127	São Tomé and Príncipe	0.488	1,875 ¹	0.162	...	...	...	...
128	Kenya	0.470	1,622 ¹	39.8	7.0	...	...	...
129	Bangladesh	0.469	1,458 ¹	162.2	2.4	14.0	...	...
130	Ghana	0.467	1,533 ¹	23.8	5.4	...	...	...
131	Cameroon	0.460	2,219 ¹	19.5	2.9	14.6	33.4	...
132	Myanmar	0.451	1,596 ¹ ⁸	50	1.3	...	...	0.2
133	Yemen	0.439	2,595 ¹	23.5	5.2	16.0	...	...
134	Benin	0.435	1,506 ¹	8.9	3.6	15.9	153.4 −2	...
135	Madagascar	0.435	958 ¹	19.6	2.9	13.4	137.2	0.1
136	Mauritania	0.433	2,037 ¹	3.2	4.4	15.6 **	...	...
137	Papua New Guinea	0.431	2,395 ¹	6.7	...	...	...	...
138	Nepal	0.428	1,189 ¹	29.3	3.8	19.0	...	...
139	Togo	0.428	846 ¹	6.6	3.7	17.2	155.2 −1	...
140	Comoros	0.428	1,174 ¹	0.659	7.6	...	...	...

TABLE 2
Human development rank, value, total population, expenditure on education (% GDP) and (% of government expenditure), tertiary expenditure per student (% GDP) and expenditure on R&D

		HDI value 2010	GDP per capita (PPP US$ billions) 2010	Total population (millions) 2009	Public expenditure on education (% of GDP) 2000–2008b	Public expenditure on education (% of total government expenditure) 2008	Tertiary total public expenditure per student (% of GDP) 2008	Public expenditure research and development (% of GDP) 2000–2007b
141	Lesotho	0.427	1,605 ¹	2	12.4	23.7	...	0.1
142	Nigeria	0.423	2,289 ¹	154.7	...	...	...	...
143	Uganda	0.422	1,251 ¹	32.7	3.8	15.6 ¹	...	0.4
144	Senegal	0.411	1,830 ¹	12.5	5.1	19.0 **	166.9 **	0.1
145	Haiti	0.404	1,040 ¹	10	...	...	...	...
146	Angola	0.403	5,959 ¹	18.5	2.6	...	80.8 −2	...
147	Djibouti	0.402	2,274 ¹	0.864	8.7	22.8	...	...
148	Tanzania, United Republic of	0.398	1,426 ¹	43.7	6.8	27.5	...	...
149	Côte d'Ivoire	0.397	1,696 ¹	21	4.6	24.6	...	...
150	Zambia	0.395	1,497 ¹	12.9	1.4	...	...	0.0
151	Gambia	0.390	1,446 ¹	1.7	2.0	...	...	...
152	Rwanda	0.385	1,102 ¹	10	4.1	20.4	222.8	...
153	Malawi	0.385	902 1 ¹	15.3	4.2	...	...	...
154	Sudan	0.379	2,300 ¹	42.2	...	...	...	0.3
155	Afghanistan	0.349	1,419 ¹	29.8	...	...	...	...
156	Guinea	0.340	1,037 ¹	10	1.7	19.2	71.5	...
157	Ethiopia	0.328	991 ¹	82.8	5.5	23.3	642.7 −1	0.2
158	Sierra Leone	0.317	825 ¹	5.7	3.8	...	...	...
159	Central African Republic	0.315	766 ¹	4.4	1.3	12.0	...	...
160	Mali	0.309	1,207 ¹	13	3.8	19.5	114.8	...
161	Burkina Faso	0.305	1,217 ¹	15.8	4.6	21.8	308.3 −1	0.1
162	Liberia	0.300	400 ¹	4	2.7	12.1	...	...
163	Chad	0.295	1,331 ¹	11.2	1.9	...	...	...
164	Guinea-Bissau	0.289	554 ¹	1.6	5.2 d	...	...	...
165	Mozambique	0.284	929 ¹	22.9	5.0	21.0 −2	...	0.5
166	Burundi	0.282	403 ¹	8.3	7.2	22.3	563.9	...
167	Niger	0.261	677 ¹	15.2	3.7	15.5	398.0	...
168	Congo, Democratic Republic of the	0.239	327 ¹	66	...	...	...	0.5
169	Zimbabwe	0.140	187 ¹	12.5	4.6	...	...	...
Without HDI Rank								
170	Antigua and Barbuda	...	19,117 ¹	0.087	3.9	...	...	...
171	Bhutan	...	5,532 ¹	0.697	5.1	...	...	...
172	Cuba	...	...	11.2	13.6	18.5	58.8	0.4
173	Dominica	...	8,967 ¹	0.073	4.8	11.3	...	...
174	Eritrea	...	648 ¹	5	2.0	...	...	...
175	Grenada	...	8,424 ¹	0.103	5.2	...	...	...
176	Iraq	...	...	31.5	...	...	...	...
177	Kiribati	...	2,492 ¹	0.098	17.9	...	...	...
178	Korea Democratic Peoplés Rep. Of	...	...	23.9	...	...	...	...
179	Lebanon	...	13,510 ¹	4.2	2.0	8.1	12.5	...

► TABLE 2
Human development rank, value, total population, expenditure on education (% GDP) and (% of government expenditure), tertiary expenditure per student (% GDP) and expenditure on R&D

		HDI value 2010	GDP per capita (PPP US$ billions) 2010	Total population (millions) 2009	Public expenditure on education (% of GDP) 2000–2008b	Public expenditure on education (% of total government expenditure) 2008	Tertiary total public expenditure per student (% of GDP) 2008	Public expenditure research and development (% of GDP) 2000–2007b
180	Marshall Islands	...	...	0.061	12.3	...	...	...
181	Monaco	...	...	0.032	...	...	...	...
182	Nauru	...	...	...	...	7.5 *,–1	...	...
183	Occupied Palestinian Territories	...	...	...	...	...	...	...
184	Oman	...	26,258 ¹	2.8	...	31.1 –2	...	...
185	Palau	...	...	0.02	10.3	...	...	...
186	Saint Kitts and Nevis	...	15,092 ¹	0.049	9.9	...	...	...
187	Saint Lucia	...	9,431 ¹	0.172	6.3	12.9	...	0.4 (–1)
188	Saint Vincent and the Grenadines	...	8,967 ¹	0.109	7.0	...	...	0.2
189	Samoa	...	4,260 ¹	0.178	5.4	13.4	...	...
190	San Marino	...	...	0.031	...	...	...	...
191	Seychelles	...	20,828 ¹	0.087	5.0	12.6 –2	...	0.4
192	Somalia	...	...	9.1	...	...	...	...
193	Tuvalu	...	...	...	...	...	...	...
194	Vanuatu	...	4,084 ¹	0.239	6.9	28.1	...	...

Columns 2, 3, 5 and 8 were taken from the HDR 2010, UNDP: http://hdrstats.undp.org/en/tables/default.html
Columns 6 and 7 were taken from the Global Education Digest 2010: http://www.uis.unesco.org/Library/Documents/GED_2010_EN.pdf
Column 4 taken from the World Bank: http://data.worldbank.org/indicator/SP.POP.TOTL

Source:
Expenditure on education (% of GDP): UNESCO Institute for Statistics (2010, Correspondance on Education Indicators, Montreal, Canada)
GDP per capita (2008 PPP US$): UNDP-HDRO calculations
HDI value: Calculated based on data from UNDESA (2009, World Population Prospects: The 2008 Revision. New York), Barro and Lee (2010, A New Data Set of Educational Attainment in the World, 1950–2010. NBER Working Paper 15902. Cambridge, MA: National Bureau of Economic Research), UNESCO Institute for Statistics (2010, "UNESCO Institute for Statistics Data Site". New York. http://stats.uis.unesco.org/unesco. Accessed May 2010), World Bank (2010, "Global Economic Prospects – Summer 2010." Washington, DC. www.worldbank.org. Accessed 15 July 2010) and IMF(2010, Government Finance Statistics. Washington, DC)
Public Expenditure (% of GDP) on Research and Development: World Bank (2010, World Development Indicators 2010. Washington, DC)

Footnotes
1: Based on the growth rate of GDP per capita (in PPP US$) from IMF (2010, World Economic Outlook Update: An Update of the Key WEO Projections. Washington, DC).
2: Based on data on GDP from the United Nations Statistics Divison's [National Accounts: Main Aggregates Database] data on population from UNPD (2008) and the PPP exchange rate for Spain from World Bank (2010, World Development Indicators 2010. Washington, DC).
3: Based on the growth rate of GDP per capita in PPP US$ for Spain from IMF (2010, Government Finance Statstics. Washington, DC).
4: Based on data on GDP from the United Nations Statistics Divison's [National Accounts: Main Aggregates Database] data on population from UNDESA (2009, World Population Prospects: The 2008 Revision. New York.) and the PPP exchange rate for Switzerland from World Bank (2010, World Development Indicators 2010. Washington, DC.).
5: Based on the growth rate of GDP per capita in PPP US dollars for Switzerland from IMF (2010, Government Finance Statstics. Washington, DC).
6: 2007 prices.
7: Based on the growth rate of GDP per capita in PPP US dollars for Fiji from IMF (2010, Government Finance Statstics. Washington, DC).
8: GDP per capita estimated from the ratio of GDP in LCU to GNI in LCU and from GNI in PPP US$ and total population from the World Bank (2010, World Development Indicators).

PART VI
FURTHER READING

Further reading

Sonia Fernández-Lauro

INTRODUCTION

This selective bibliography illustrates current trends in the role of higher education and sustainability. The contribution of universities to develop research, programmes and curricula is also a way to use those resources that aim to meet human needs while preserving the environment not only for the present, but mainly for the future generations.

The term 'sustainability' was used in 1983 by the Brundtland Commission, which coined what has become the most often-quoted definition of sustainable development as development that *'meets the needs of the present without compromising the ability of future generations to meet their own needs'*. This notion is closely related to the notion of economic growth and raises some contradictions. There is an important and crucial question: can development be sustainable?

Today, the discussion in the regions is diverse and reflects the particular situation of each: its culture, its wealth and poverty. Nevertheless the fact remains, both in developed and developing countries: Education for Sustainability is considered important in order to ensure economic and social development, poverty reduction and a better respect for nature and mother earth.

The bibliographic references from universities of different regions are presented here as well as the proposals for a new vision together with those of the UN and its specialized agencies.

GENERAL

Altbach, P. (2008) The Complex Roles of Universities in the Period of Globalization. GUNi (ed.) *Higher Education in the World 3.* New York: Palgrave Macmillan.

Anton, Danilo (1995) *Diversity, Globalisation and the Ways of Nature.* Ottawa: International Development Research Centre.

Antunes, Â. (2002) *Leitura do mundo no contexto da planeterização: por uma pedagogia da sustentabilidade.* São Paulo: Faculty of Education-Sao Paulo University.

Baumgartner, S., Becker, C., Frank, K. et al. (2008) Relating the philosophy and practice of ecological economics: The role of concepts, models, and case studies in inter- and trandisciplinary sustainability research. *Ecological Economics,* **67**(3), pp. 384–93.

Bergan, S. (2005) Higher Education as a Public Good and a Public Responsibility: What Does it Mean? In: Weber, Luc and Bergan, Sjur (eds) *The Public Responsibility for Higher Education and Research.* Strasbourg: Council of Europe Publishing Council of Europe Higher Education Series (2), pp. 13–28.

Boff, L. (1999) *Saber cuidar: ética do humano, compaixão pela terra.* Petrópolis, Vozes.

Calder, W. and Clugston, R.M. (2003) International efforts to promote higher education for sustainable development. *Planning for Higher Education* (31), pp. 30–44.

Conference on Endogenous Development and Bio-cultural Diversity (2006) organized by COMPAS-ETC (Comparing and Supporting Endogenous Development) and CDE (Centre of Development and Environment). *Statement of Commitment Supporting Endogenous Development and Bio-cultural Diversity.* www.bioculturaldiversity.net/statement.htm

Corcoran, P.B. and Wals, A.E.J. (2004) *Higher Education and the Challenge of Sustainability: Problematics, Promise, and Practice.* Dordrecht, Netherlands: Kluwer Academic Publishers.

Cortese, A.D. (2003) The critical role of higher education in creating a sustainable future. *Planning for Higher Education,* **31**(3), pp. 15–22.

Dias, M.A. (2008) The University of the 21st century: from the conflict to the dialogue of civilizations. La Universidad en el siglo XXI: del conflicto al diálogo de civilizaciones. In: *Revista Educación Superior y Sociedad: nueva época*, pp. 93–138. Caracas: UNESCO/IESALC.

Escrigas, C. and Lobera, J. (2009) New dynamics for social responsibility. In: GUNi (ed.) *Higher Education at a Time of Transformation*. New York: Palgrave Macmillan.

Freire, P. (1975) *Pedagogia do oprimido*. Rio de Janeiro: Paz e Terra.

Gadotti, M. (2001) *Pedagogia da Terra*. São Paulo: Peirópolis.

Gadotti, M. (2010) *A Carta da Terra na Educação*. São Paulo: Instituto Paulo Freire.

Gough, S. and Scott, W. (2007) *Higher Education and Sustainable Development. Paradox and Possibility.* London: Routledge.

González-Gaudiano, E. and Meira-Cartea, P. (2010) Climate change education and communication: a critical perspective on obstacles and resistances. In: Kagawa, F. and Selby, D. (eds) *Education and Climate change: Living and learning in interesting times*, pp. 13–34. New York: Taylor and Francis Inc.

Gutiérrez, F. and Prado, C. (1999) *Ecopedagogia e cidadania planetária*. São Paulo: Cortez-Instituto Paulo Freire.

Gutiérrez, F. (1994) *Pedagogia para el Desarrollo Sostenible*. Heredia, Costa Rica: Editorialpec.

Gutiérrez, F. and Prado, C. (1999) *Ecopedagogia e cidadania planetária*. São Paulo: Cortez-Instituto Paulo Freire.

Harding, S. (2000) Should philosophies of science encode democratic ideals? In: Kleinman, D.L. (ed.) *Science, Technology, and Democracy* (pp. 121–38). Albany, New York: Suny Press.

Hansmann, R., Crott, H.W., Mieg, H.A. et al. (2009) Improving group processes in transdisciplinary case studies for sustainability learning. *International Journal of Sustainability in Higher Education*, **10**(1), pp. 33–42.

Jansen, L., Weaver, P. and van Dam-Mieras, M.C.E. (2008) Education to meet new challenges in a networked society. In: Larkley, J.E. and Maynhard, V.B. (eds) *Innovation in Education*. Nova Science Publishers Inc. (1), pp. 1–50.

Johnston, A. seconded to OECD from *Forum for the Future* (2007) Higher Education for Sustainable Development. *Final Report of International Action Research Project*. http://www.oecd.org/dataoecd/55/4/45575516.pdf

Leal Filho, W. (ed.) (2002) *Teaching Sustainability – Towards Curriculum Greening*. Frankfurt: Peter Lang Scientific Publishers.

Leal Filho, W. (ed.) (2010) *Sustainability at Universities: Opportunities, challenges and Trends*. Frankfurt: Peter Lang Scientific Publishers.

Liu, J., Thomas D., Carpenter S. et al. (2007) Complexity of coupled human and natural Ssystems. *Science*, **317**(09), pp. 1513–16.

Lozano, R. (2008) Developing collaborative and sustainable organisations. *Journal of Cleaner Production,* **16**(14), pp. 499–509.

McKeown, R. (2002) Progress has been made in education for sustainable development. *Applied Environmental Education and Communication*, (1), pp. 21–3.

Miller, T.R., Baird, T.D., Littlefield, C.M. et al. (2008) Epistemological pluralism: reorganizing interdisciplinary research. *Ecology and Society,* **13**(2), p. 46. http://www.ecologyandsociety.org/vol13/iss2/art46/

Mulder, F. (2010) The advancement of Lifelong Learning through Open Educational Resources in an open and flexible (self) learning context. www.ou.nl/docs/campagnes/scop/oer_paper_by_fred_mulder.pdf

Nayyar, D. (2008) Globalization and markets: Challenges for higher education. In GUNi (ed.) *Higher Education in the World 3*. New York: Palgrave Macmillan.

Norgaard, R.B. (1992) Coordinating disciplinary and organizational ways of knowing. *Agriculture, Ecosystems, and Environment* (42), pp. 205–16.

Nussbaum, M.C. (2010) *Not For Profit. Why Democracy Needs the Humanities.* Princeton: Princeton University Press.

Plantan, Frank (2004) The university as site of citizenship. In: Bergan, Sjur (ed.) *The University as Res Publica.* Strasbourg: Council of Europe Publishing, pp. 83–128.

Prado, C. (2006) *Biopedagogia. Paulo Freire – V Encuentro Internacional: Sendas de Freire: opresiones, resistencias y emancipaciones en un nuevo paradigma de vida*. Xátiva: Institut Paulo Freire Spain and Crec, pp. 169–211.

Saltmarsh, J. and Hartley, M. (eds) (2011) *To Serve a Larger Purpose: Engagement for Democracy and the Transformation of Higher Education*. Philadelphia: Temple University Press.

Sen, A. (1999) *Development as Freedom*. New York: Anchor Books.

The Talleries Declaration (1990) University Leaders for a Sustainable Future (ULSF). http://www.ulsf.org/programs_talloires_td.html

Tilbury, D. (2009) A United Nations Decade of Education for Sustainable Development (2005 14): What Difference will it Make? *Journal of Education for Sustainable Development*, **3**, pp. 87–97.

Unterhalter, E. and Carpentier, V. (2010) *Universities into the 21st Century. Global Inequalities and Higher Education. Whose Interests are We Serving?* Basingstoke: Palgrave Macmillan.

Van Dam-Mieras, R., Lansu, A., Riechman, M. et al. (2007) Development of an interdisciplinary intercultural master's program on sustainability: Learning from the richness of diversity. *Innovative Higher Education,* (32), p. 5.

Wals, A.E.J. (ed.) (2009) *Social Learning Towards a Sustainable World*. Wageningen: Wageningen Academic Publishers.

Wiek, A.W., Withycombe, L. and Redman, Ch. L. (2011) Key competencies in sustainability: a reference framework for academic program development. *Journal Sustainability Science*, 5(2011), pp. 1–16.

Worldwatch Institute, The (2010) *State of the World 2010: Transforming Cultures. From Consumerism to Sustainability*. www.blogs.worldwatch.org/transformingcultures

REGIONAL PERSPECTIVES

AFRICA

African School of Open Education (2005). http://www.africa.upeace.org/dpsa/institution.cfm?id_institution=104&listar=1

Kanyandago, Peter (2010) Valuing the African Endogenous Education System for Community-based Learning: An Approach to Early School Leaving. http://www.ghanaweb.com/GhanaHomePage/education/tamale.html

Lotz-Sisitka, H. (2010) *African Universities responding to sustainable development challenges:* http://blog.univ-provence.fr/blog/coordination-rgionale-paca/dveloppement-durable/2011/02/13/higher-education-s-commitment-to-sustainability

Lotz-Sisitka, H. and Mohamedbhai G. (2010) *Plenary Session: Presenting Regional Map.* 5th International Barcelona Conference on Higher Education. Higher Education's Commitment to Sustainability: from Understanding to Action, 2325 November 2010.

O'Donoghue, R. and Lotz-Sisitka, H. (2006) Situated environmental learning in Southern Africa at the start of the UN Decade of Education for Sustainable Development. *Australian Journal of Environmental Education, 22*(1), pp. 105–13.

United Nations Environment Programme (UNEP); Southern African Development Community Regional Environmental Education Programme (SADC REEP); Rhodes University Environmental Education and Sustainability Unit. (2006) *Mainstreaming Environment and Sustainability in Africa (MESA)* Universities Partnership – Education for sustainable Development Innovations Course Toolkit. Online: http://opentraining.unesco-ci.org/tools/pdf/otpitem.php?id=623

Zeelen, J., Van der Linden, J., Nampota, D. et al. (eds) (2010) *The Burden of Educational Exclusion: Understanding and Challenging Early School Leaving in Africa.* Rotterdam, The Netherlands: Sense Publishers, pp. 99–113. https://www.sensepublishers.com/files/9789460912849PR.pdf

ARAB STATES

American University in Cairo, The (2010) Toward civic engagement in Arab Higher Education http://www1.aucegypt.edu/maan/

Environnement et développement durable : l'apport des sciences sociales. (2010) Colloque international organisé par la Faculté des lettres et des sciences humaines et le Groupe d'Étude pour le Développement et l'environnement social (GEDES) à Sfax/Tunisie. http://vertigo.revues.org/8058

Higher Education and Sustainability in Arab States (2010) 5th International Barcelona Conference on Higher Education. Higher Education's Commitment to Sustainability: from Understanding to Action, 23–25 November 2010.

Regional Guiding Framework of Education for Sustainable Development in the Arab Region. UN Decade of Education for Sustainable Development (2005–2014) – Phase One (2005–2007). UNESCO Regional Bureau for Education in the Arab States, (Beirut, March 2008) http://www.esd-world-conference-2009.org/fileadmin/download/general/Arab_ESD_regional_strategie.pdf

Salamé, R. (2010) *Higher Education Commitment to Sustainability in the Arab States: An Introduction to Regional Dialogue.* 5th International Barcelona Conference on Higher Education. Higher Education's Commitment to Sustainability: from Understanding to Action, 23–25 November 2010.

ASIA AND THE PACIFIC

Chhokar, K.B. (2010) Higher education and curriculum innovation for sustainable development in India. *International Journal of Sustainability in Higher Education, 11*(2), pp. 141–52.

Corcoran, P.B. and Koshy, K.C. (2010) The Pacific way: Sustainability in higher education in the South Pacific Nations. *International Journal of Sustainability in Higher Education, 11*(2), pp. 130–40.

Corcoran, P.B. and Osano, Ph. (eds) (2009) *Young People, Education, and Sustainable Development: Exploring Principles, Perspectives, and Praxis.* The Netherlands: Wageningen Academic.

Deo, S. (2005) Pacific Island Nations. In: Caroline Haddad (ed.) *A Situational Analysis of Education for Sustainable Development in the Asia.* Bangkok: UNESCO.

Fadeeva, Z. and Mochizuki, Y. (2010) Roles of Regional Centres of Expertise on Education for Sustainable Development. *Journal of Education for Sustainable Development,* (4), pp. 51–9.

Government of India (2009) *Towards a New Development Paradigm: Education for Sustainable Development,* India Report to the World Conference on ESD, New Delhi: Ministry of Human Resource Development.

Government of India (1998) *National policy on education, 1986 (as modified in 1992) with National policy on education,* New Delhi: Department of Education, Ministry of Human Resource Development. http://education.nic.in/policy/npe86-mod92.pdf

Kajikawa, Y., Junko, O., Yoshiyuki, T. et al. (2007) Creating an academic landscape of sustainability science: An analysis of the citation network. *Sustainability Science,* (2), pp. 221–31.

Legal Acts, Programmes and Regulatory Frameworks of Education in the Central Asian Region: A Review. (2009) Almaty, Regional Environmental Center for Central Asia.

Lucas, A. (1979) *Environment and Environmental Education: Conceptual Issues and Curriculum Implications.* Melbourne: Australian International Press and Publications.

Nomura, K. and Abe, O. (2009) The education for sustainable development movement in Japan: A political perspective. *Environmental Education Research, 15*(4), pp. 483–96.

Nomura, K., Natori, Y. and Abe, O. (2011) Region-wide education for sustainable development networks of universities in the Asia-Pacific. In: Sakamoto, R. and Chapman, D. (eds) *Cross-Border Partnerships in Higher Education: Strategies and Issues.* New York: Routledge, pp. 209–27.

Nomura, K. (2009) A perspective on education for sustainable development: Historical development of environmental education in Indonesia. *International Journal of Educational Development, 29*(6), pp. 621–7.

Niu, D., Jiang, D. and Li, F. (2010) Higher education for sustainable development in China. *International Journal of Sustainability in Higher Education, 11*(2), pp.153–62.

Park, T.Y. (2008) *ESD of Korean Universities,* presentation at international symposium Sustainability in Higher Education: Learning from Experiences in Asia and the World, December 2008, Tokyo, Rikkyo University.

Ryan, A., Tilbury, D., Corcoran, P.B. et al. (2010) Sustainability in higher education in the Asia-Pacific: Developments, challenges and prospects. *International Journal of Sustainability in Higher Education, 11*(2), pp. 106–19.

Saito, Takahiro (2010) *University Evaluation Systems in Japan.* Presentation at the Symposium on Perspectives on University Performance Evaluation United Nations University, Tokyo, 15–16 March 2010.

Sanusi, Z.A. and Khelgat-Doost, H. (2008) Regional centres of expertise as a transformational platform for sustainability: A case Study of University Sains

Malaysia, Penang. *International Journal of Sustainability in Higher Education, 9*(4), pp. 487–97.

Sarabhai, K.V. (2005) It is not just 'development' that needs to be redefined... *The final report of the international conference on DESD 'Education for a Sustainable Future'*. Ahmedabad: Centre for Environment Education, pp. 178–80.

Shi, C. (2005) Exploring effective approaches for education for sustainable development in universities of China. In: Holmberg, J. and Samuelsson, B.E. (eds) *Drivers and Barriers for Implementing Sustainable Development in Higher Education*. Gothenburg: UNESCO.

Tilbury, D., Keogh, A., Leighton, A. and Kent, J. (2005) *A National Review of Environmental Education and its Contribution to Sustainability in Australia: Further and Higher Education*. Canberra: Australian Government Department of the Environment and Heritage and Australian Research Institute in Education for Sustainability.

Vijay, P. (2009) *Reorienting TVET Policy Towards Education for Sustainable Development*, August 26–28, 2009. Government of India, Ministry of Human Resource Development.

Vision for University-led Environmental Leadership Initiatives for Asian Sustainability (2008). Japan: Ministry of the Environment.

Yarime, Masaru (2010) Sustainability innovation as a social process of knowledge transformation. *Nanotechnology Perceptions*, **6**(3), pp. 143–53.

Yoshikawa, Hiroyuki (2006) Academic reform and university reform: Sustainability science (in Japanese). *IDE-Contemporary Higher Education*, (5) pp. 24–32.

EUROPE

Bergan, S. and Van't Land, H. (eds) (2010) *Speaking across Borders: the Role of Higher Education in Furthering Intercultural Dialogue*. Strasbourg: Council of Europe Publishing. Council of Europe Higher Education Series 16.

Bergan, S. and Radu, D. (eds) (2010) *Higher Education for Modern Societies: Competences and Values*. Strasbourg: Council of Europe Publishing. Council of Europe Higher Education Series 15.

Catalan Association of Public Universities (2011) *University Development Cooperation Plan*, Barcelona: ACUP.

Catalan Association of Public Universities (2010) *Building an Innovative University System for Society*, Barcelona: ACUP.

Corbett, A. (2008) The role of higher education for human and social development in Europe. In: GUNi report, *Higher education in the world 3: Higher education: new challenges and emerging roles for human and social development*. Basingstoke: Palgrave Macmillan.

Council of Europe (2007) *Recommendation 6 of the Committee of Ministers to member states on the Public Responsibility for Higher Education and Research*. Strasbourg: Council of Europe.

De Kraker, J., Lansu, A., and van Dam-Mieras, M.C. (2007) Competences and competence-based learning for sustainable development. In: de Kraker, J., Lansu, A. and van Dam-Mieras, M.C. (eds) *Crossing Boundaries. Innovative Learning for Sustainable Development in Higher Education*, pp. 103–14. Frankfurt am Main: Verlag für Akademische Schriften.

EC, DG Education and Culture (2008) *Inventory of innovative practices in education for sustainable development*. Brus-

sels: EC, DG Education and Culture. http://ec.europa.eu/education/moreinformation/doc/sustdev_en.pdf

Hammond, C. and Churchman, D. (2008) Sustaining academic life: A case for applying principles of social sustainability to the academic profession. *International Journal of Sustainability in Higher Education*, **9**(3), pp. 235–45.

Holmberg, J., Lundqvist, U., Svanström, M. et al. (2011) The University and Transformation Towards Sustainability – Lessons Learned at Chalmers University of Technology. Paper presented at Engineering Education in Sustainable Development, Göteborg , 19–22 September.

Hopkinson, P. (2010) Ecoversity: the potential for sustainable development to reshape university culture and action. *International Journal Environment and Sustainable Development*, **9**(4), pp. 378–91.

Jansen, L., Holmberg, J. and Civili, F.S. (2005) *International Evaluation of UPC Environmental and Sustainability Research and Education*. Barcelona: UPC. http://www.upc.es/mediambient/UPCSostenible2015.html

Leal Filho, W. (ed.) (2010) Teaching sustainable development at university level: Current trends and future needs. *Journal of Baltic Sea Education,* **9**(4), pp. 273–84.

Leal Filho, W. and Wright, T.S.A. (2002) Barriers on the path to environmental sustainability: European and Canadian perspectives in higher education. *International Journal of Sustainable Development and World Ecology*, **9**(2), pp. 179–86Lundqvist, U. and Svanström, M. (2008) Inventory of content in basic courses in environment and sustainable development at Chalmers University of Technology in Sweden. *European Journal of Engineering Education*, (33), pp. 355–64.

Niestroy, I. (2005) *Sustaining Sustainability. A benchmark study on national strategies towards sustainable development and the impact of councils in nine EU member states*. Utrecht: Uitgeverij Lemma bv.

Observatory, The (2006) *The Observatory. Status of engineering education for sustainable development in European higher education.* www.upc.edu/eesd-observatory

Pimbert, M. (2006) *Transforming knowledge and ways of knowing for food sovereignty*. London: International Institute for Environment and Development (IIED).

Reichert, S. (2006) *The Rise of Knowledge Regions: Emerging Opportunities and Challenges for Universities*. Brussels: European University Association.

LATIN AMERICA AND THE CARIBBEAN

Chacón, M.A. (2010) *Regional Dialogues. Drawing Regional Maps: What has been achieved at this stage?* Latin America and Caribbean. 5th International Barcelona Conference on Higher Education. Higher Education's Commitment to Sustainability: from Understanding to Action 23–25 November 2010. http://147.83.97.154/repositori/k2010_materials/presentations/Latin_America_Miguel_Angel_Chacon.pdf

Denninger, K. and Squire, L. (1998) Inequality as Constraint to Growth in Latin America. In Mitchel, A., Seligson, John and T. Passen-Smith*, Development of Underdevelopment: The Political Economy of Global Inequality*. Colorado: Lynne Reinne Publishers.

ECLAC (2010) *Statistical Yearbook for Latin America and the Caribbean for Santiago*, Chile: ECLAC-UN.

ECLAC (2010) *Social Panorama of Latin America*. Santiago, Chile: ECLAC-UN.

Heiwege, A. and Birch, M.B.L. (2007) *Declining Poverty in Latin America: A Critical Analysis of New Estimates by International Institutions*. Global Development and Environment Institute. Working Paper No. 07-02. http://ase.tufts.under/2dae

IBAMA (1999) *Educação para um futuro sustentável: uma visão* transdisciplinar *para uma ação compartilhada*. Brasília: UNESCO/IBAMA.

Mato, D. (ed.) (2010*) Educación Superior, Colaboración Intercultural y Desarrollo sostenible/Buen Vivir. Experiencias en América Latina*. Caracas: UNESCO-IESALC.

Mato, D. (ed.) (2009) *Instituciones Interculturales de Educación Superior en América Latina. Procesos de Construcción, Logros, Innovaciones y Desafíos*. Caracas: UNESCO-IESALC

Mato, D. (ed.) (2008) *Diversidad cultural e interculturalidad en Educación Superior. Experiencias en América Latina*. Caracas: UNESCO-IESALC.

Mészaros, I. (2005) *A educação para além do capital*. São Paulo: Boitempo. http://resistir.info/meszaros/meszaros_educacao.html

Oppenheimer, A. (2010) *¡Basta de historias! La obsesión latinoamericana con el pasado y las 12 claves del futuro*. Buenos Aires: Editorial sudamericana.

Puryear, J. and Malloy-Jewers, M. (2009*) How Poor and Unequal is Latin America and the Caribbean?* Inter American Dialogue, Policy Brief 1. ww.thedialogue.org

Santos Abreu, I.C. and Villalon legra, G. (2006) *Environmental education for sustainable development from the management, educational research and innovation in the training and performance of the business of education*. La Havana, MINED, and Villa Clara, Universidad Pédagogica Félix Varela. ama.redciencia.cu/articulos/17.06.pdf

NORTH AMERICA

Boyte, H.C. (2004) *Everyday Politics: Reconnecting Citizens and Public Life*. Philadelphia: University of Pennsylvania Press.

Boyte. H.C. (2009) Repairing the breech: Cultural organizing and the politics of knowledge. *Partnerships: A Journal of Service-Learning and Civic Engagement*, **1**(1), pp. 1–21.

Chambers, E.T. (2003) *Roots for Radicals: Organizing for Power, Action, and Justice*. New York: Continuum.

Crick, B. (1992) *In Defense of Politics* (4th edn). Chicago: University of Chicago Press.

Fink, L., Leonard, S.T. and Reid, D.M. (eds) (1996) *Intellectuals and Public Life: Between Radicalism and Reform*. Ithaca, New York: Cornell University Press.

Forester, J. (2009) *Dealing with Differences: Dramas of Mediating Public Disputes*. New York: Oxford University Press.

GUNi (2011) Interview with Heila Lotz-Sisitka. *GUNi Newsletter* March 2011. Barcelona: GUNi. http://www.guni-rmies.net/news/detail.php?id=1719

Hale, C.F. (ed.) (2008) *Engaging Contradictions: Theory, Politics, and Methods of Activist Scholarship*. Berkeley: University of California Press.

Hammond, C. and Churchman, D. (2008) Sustaining academic life: A case for applying principles of social sustainability to the academic profession. *International Journal of Sustainability in Higher Education*, **9**(3), pp. 235–45.

Held, D. (2006) *Models of Democracy* (3rd edn). Stanford, California: Stanford University Press.

Higher Education Associations Sustainability Consortium Resource Center (2010) http://www2.aashe.org/heasc/resources.php.

Longo, N.V. and Gibson, C.M. (2011) *From Command to Community: A New Approach to Leadership Education in Colleges and Universities*. Medford, MA: Tufts University Press.

McKeown, R. and Hopkins, C. (2007) Moving beyond the EE and ESD. *Journal of Education for Sustainable Development*. March 2007, 1, pp. 17–26.

Macpherson, C.B. (1977) *The Life and Times of Liberal Democracy*. New York: Oxford University Press.

Peters, S.J. (2010) *Democracy and Higher education: Traditions and Stories of Civic Engagement*. East Lansing: Michigan State University Press.

Peters, S.J., Jordan, N.R., Adamek, M. and Alter, T.R. (eds) (2005) *Engaging Campus and Community: The Practice of Public Scholarship in the State and Land-Grant University System*. Dayton, Ohio: Kettering Foundation Press.

Tilbury, D. and Wortman, D. (2008) Education for sustainability in further and higher education: Reflections along the Journey. *Planning for Higher Education*, **36**(4), pp. 5–16.

University of British Columbia SEEDS Library: http://www.sustain.ubc.ca/seeds-library

University of California Santa Cruz, Sustainability Website: http://sustainability.ucsc.edu

US Partnership for Education for Sustainability Development, K-12 Resources: http://usp.umfglobal.org/main/show_passage/48

Warner, K.D. (2007) *Agroecology in Action: Extending Alternative Agriculture through Social Networks*. Cambridge, MA: MIT Press.

Wolfe, V. (2001) A survey of the environmental education of students in non-environmental majors at four-year institutions in the USA. *International Journal of Sustainability in Higher Education,* **2**(4), pp. 301–15.

Wright, T. (2009) An assessment of university presidents' conceptualizations of sustainability in higher education. *International Journal of Sustainability in Higher Education*, **11**(1), pp. 61–73.

Yash P. (2009) *Report of The Committee to Advise on the Renovation and Rejuvenation of Higher Education*. Committee Report. http://www.hindu.com/nic/yashpal-committeereport.pdf

MOVING FROM UNDERSTANDING TO ACTION: VISIONS FOR TRANSFORMATION

Avila, M. (2010) Community organizing practices in academia: A model, and stories of partnerships. *Journal of Higher Education Outreach and Engagement*, **14**(2), pp. 37–63.

Barth, M., Godemann, J., Rieckmann, M. et al. (2007) Developing key competencies for sustainable development in higher education. *International Journal of Sustainability in Higher Education*, **8**(4), pp. 416–30.

Chambers, E.T. (2003) *Roots for Radicals: Organizing for Power, Action, and Justice*. New York: Continuum.

Chhokar, K.B. and Pandya, A. (2005) Samvardhan: An experiment in education for sustainable development. *The Declaration,* **7**(2), pp. 20–4.

Cortese, A.D. (2003) The critical role of higher education in creating a sustainable future. *Planning for Higher Education,* (31), pp. 15–22.

Fadeeva, Z. (2007) From centre of excellence to centre of expertise: Regional centres of expertise on education for sustainable development. In: Wals, A.E.J. (ed.) *Social Learning towards a Sustainable World: Principles, Perspectives, and Praxis*. Wageningen, The Netherlands: Wageningen Academic Publishers.

Fadeeva, Z. and Mochizuki, Y. (2010) Higher education for today and tomorrow: University appraisal for diversity, innovation and change towards sustainable development. *Sustainability Science,* (5), pp. 249–56.

Ferrer-Balas, D., Bruno, J., de Mingo, M. et al. (2004) Advances in education transformation towards sustainable development at the Technical University of Catalonia, Barcelona. *International Journal of Sustainability in Higher Education,* **5**(3), pp. 251–66.

Fink, L., Leonard, S.T. and Reid, D.M. (eds) (1996) *Intellectuals and Public Life: Between Radicalism and Reform*. Ithaca, New York: Cornell University Press.

Fornet-Bentacourt, Raúl (ed.) (2009) *The Place 'Earth' Occupies in the Various Cultures. A Dialogue Between Cosmologies in the Face of Ecological Challenge*. Aachen, Germany: Verlag Mainz.

Funtowicz, S.O. and Ravetz, J.R. (2000) *La ciencia posnormal. Ciencia con la gente*. Barcelona: Icaria.

Goud, S.J. and Morin, E. (2001) *What Future for the Human Species?* Series, *Keys to the 21st Century*, pp. 35–46. Paris: UNESCO.

Mayor, F. and Tanguiane, S. (2000) *L'Enseignement supérieur au XXIe siècle*. Paris: Hermès Science Publications.

Morin, E. (2001) *Seven complex lessons in education for the future*. Series, *Education on the move*. Paris: UNESCO.

Morin, E. (2011) *La Voie. Pour l'avenir de l'humanité*. Paris: Fayard.

Gadotti, M. (2009) *Educar para a sustentabilidade*. São Paulo: Instituto Paulo Freire.

Gadotti, M. (2009) *Fórum Mundial de Educação: Proposições para u outro mundo possível*. São Paulo: Instituto Paulo Freire.

Gadotti, M. (2007) *Educar para um outro mundo possível: o Fórum Social Mundial como espaço de aprendizagem de uma nova cultura política e como processo transformador da sociedade civil planetária*. São Paulo: Publisher Brasil.

Godemann, J. (2008) Knowledge integration: A key challenge for transdisciplinary cooperation. *Environmental Education Research,* **14**(6), pp. 625–41.

Greenwood, D.J. and Levin, M. (2007) *Introduction to Action Research: Social Research for Social Change* (2nd edn). Thousand Oaks, California: Sage Publications.

Hale, C.F. (ed.) (2008) *Engaging Contradictions: Theory, Politics, and Methods of Activist Scholarship*. Berkeley, California: University of California Press.

Hargreaves, A. and Shirley, D. (2009) *The Fourth Way. The Inspiring Future for Educational Change*. Thousand Oaks, California: Corwin; London: Sage.

Hopkinson, P. (2010) Ecoversity: the potential for sustainable development to reshape university culture and action. *International Journal Environment and Sustainable Development,* **9**(4), pp. 378–91.

Loorbach, D. and Rotmans, J. (2006) *Managing transitions for sustainable Development*. www.ksinetwork.nl/down/output/publications/TM_Itchapter.pdf

Nussbaum, M.C. (2011) *Creating Capabilities: The Human Development Approach*. Cambridge, MA: Harvard University Press.

Peters, S.J. (2010) *Democracy and Higher education: Traditions and Stories of Civic Engagement*. East Lansing: Michigan State University Press.

Rowe, D. (2002) *Environmental Literacy and Sustainability as Core Requirements: Success Stories and Models. Teaching Sustainability at Universities*. (Series ed.: Walter Leal Filho). New York: Peter Lang.

Svanström, M., Lozano, F. and Rowe D. (2008) Learning outcomes for sustainable development in higher education. *International Journal of Sustainability in Higher Education,* **9**(3), pp. 339–51.

Wright, T. (2009) Sustainability, Internationalization and Higher Education. In: Carolin Kreber (ed.) *Internationalizing the Curriculum in Higher Education*. Toronto: Jossey Bass Publishers.

UNITED NATIONS AND SPECIALIZED AGENCIES

Agenda 21: Programme of action for sustainable development (1992) New York: United Nations (UN) Department of Public Information.

Education Hompeage of UNESCO Decade of Education for Sustainable Development (2009) Paris, UNESCO-DESD http://cms01.unesco.org/en/esd/programme/educational-dimensions/

Education for Sustainable Development and the Millennium Development Goals (2009) Paris: UNESCO http://unesdoc.unesco.org/images/0017/001791/179120e.pdf

Education for Sustainable Development (2011). Paris: UNESCO. http://www.unesco.org/new/en/education/themes/leading-the-international-agenda/education-for-sustainable-development/

De Schutter, O. (2011) *Agro-ecology and the right to food*. United Nations Human Rights Council: www.srfood.org

EFA Global Monitoring Report Reaching the Marginalised (2010) Paris: UNESCO.

Framework for the UN DESD International Implementation Scheme. (2006) Paris: UNESCO.

Handbook on Poverty Statistics (2005) New York: United Nations.

Holmberg, J. and Samuelsson, B. (eds) (2006) *Drivers and barriers for implementing sustainable development in higher education*. Technical paper 3. Paris: UNESCO Education Sector.

Millennium Development Goals Report (2007) New York: United Nations www.un.org/millenniumgoals

Millennium Goals Report (2010) New York: United Nations Millennium Goals 2015 www.un.org

Reinventing Higher Education: Towards Participatory and Sustainable Development, (2008) Bangkok: UNESCO-PROAP.

Report by the Director-General on the UNESCO World Conference on Education for Sustainable Development and the Bonn Declaration (2009) Paris: UNESCO.

Report of DAAD-UNU-VIENA (2009) The role of Education for sustainable development in Higher Education. UNESCO World Conference for Sustainable Development, 31 March–2 April 2009. http://www.vie.unu.edu/file/get/3268

Tilbury, D. (2011) *Education for Sustainable Development: An Expert Review of Processes and Learning.* Paris: UNESCO.

UNECE Strategy for Education for Sustainable Development (2005) Adopted at the High level meeting of Environmental and Education Ministries Vilnius; Geneva, United Nations Economic Council for Europe.

UNESCO and UNU (2005) *Proceedings of the International Conference Globalisation and Intangible Cultural Heritage,* 26–27 August 2004, Tokyo: Tokyo Press.

United Nations Conference on Sustainable Development – Rio+20. Forthcoming (4–6 June 2012) http://www.uncsd2012.org/rio20/index.php?menu=62

United Nations Decade of Education for Sustainable Development (2005–2014): International Implementation Scheme. (2005) Paris: UNESCO.

United Nations Human Development Report (2007) New York: United Nations.

World Commission on Environment and Development (1987) *Our Common Future.* United Nations, Oxford: Oxford University Press.

World Development Indicators (2010) Washington: World Bank.